Psychology
of Language

DAVID W. CARROLL is professor of psychology and currently serves as chair of the Psychology Program at the University of Wisconson–Superior. He received a B.A. in psychology and philosophy from the University of California at Davis (1972) and an M.A. (1973) and Ph.D. (1976) in experimental psychology from Michigan State University. He teaches courses in introductory psychology, psychology of language, cognitive psychology, and child development. His research interests include discourse processes in adults and children.

Psychology of Language

Third Edition

DAVID W. CARROLL
University of Wisconsin–Superior

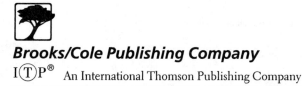

Brooks/Cole Publishing Company

I⊤P® An International Thomson Publishing Company

Pacific Grove • Albany • Belmont • Bonn • Boston • Cincinnati • Detroit • Johannesburg •
London • Madrid • Melbourne • Mexico City • New York • Paris • Singapore • Tokyo •
Toronto • Washington

Sponsoring Editor: *Vicki Knight*
Marketing Team: *Lauren Harp, Margaret Parks, and
    Aaron Eden*
Editorial Assistant: *Shelley Tweddell*
Production Editor: *Jamie Sue Brooks*
Production Service: *Penmarin Books*
Manuscript Editor: *Laura E. Larson*
Permissions Editor: *May Clark*

Interior Design: *Penmarin Books*
Cover Design: *Roger Knox*
Cover Art: *Judith Larzelere*
Cover Photo: *Jan Bindas Studios*
Typesetting and Illustrations: *Thompson Type*
Cover Printing: *Phoenix Color Corp.*
Printing and Binding: *R. R. Donnelley & Sons,
    Crawfordsville*

For more information, contact:

BROOKS/COLE PUBLISHING COMPANY
511 Forest Lodge Road
Pacific Grove, CA 93950
USA

International Thomson Publishing Europe
Berkshire House 168-173
High Holborn
London WC1V 7AA
England

Thomas Nelson Australia
102 Dodds Street
South Melbourne 3205
Victoria, Australia

Nelson Canada
1120 Birchmount Road
Scarborough, Ontario
Canada M1K 5G4

International Thomson Editores
Seneca, 53
Colonia Polanco
11560 México, D.F., México

International Thomson Publishing GmbH
Königswinterer Strasse 418
53227 Bonn
Germany

International Thomson Publishing Asia
60 Albert Street
#15-01 Albert Complex
Singapore 189969

International Thomson Publishing Japan
Hirakawacho Kyowa Building, 3F
2-2-1 Hirakawacho
Chiyoda-ku, Tokyo 102
Japan

Printed in the United States of America

10 9 8 7 6 5 4 3 2 1

Library of Congress Cataloging-in-Publication Data

Carroll, David W.
    Psychology of language / David W. Carroll. — 3rd ed.
        p. cm.
    Includes bibliographical references and index.
    ISBN 0-534-34973-0
    1. Psycholinguistics. I. Title.
BF455.C268 1998
401'.9 — dc21   98-28457

This book is dedicated to my parents,
Mary M. Carroll and Patrick E. Carroll.

Brief Contents

Contents

7   *Discourse Comprehension and Memory*   *155*

PART 3

Language Production and Conversational Interaction

PART 4   Language Acquisition

10   Early Language Acquisition   247

11   Later Language Acquisition   281

Preface

I had two initial goals in writing this book. First, I wanted to present the principles of psycholinguistics in an accessible manner. Although the field can be technical at times, when presented clearly it can be very engaging to students. Second, I wanted to discuss fundamental psycholinguistic issues in a balanced way. I have presented controversial issues from a variety of perspectives and invited the reader to think through the competing claims.

The organization of the book is similar to the second edition. Part 1 (General Issues) contains three chapters. Chapter 1 describes the scope of psycholinguistics along with a short history of the field. Chapter 2 discusses basic grammatical concepts such as phonemes, distinctive features, and morphology. The chapter also includes the grammatical features of American Sign Language, a topic that is discussed throughout the book. The chapter closes with a preliminary discussion of some controversial issues in linguistic theory, such as whether language is innate. Chapter 3 focuses on basic concepts of information processing and how they may apply to language. The overriding goal of Part 1 is to introduce the notion of a cognitive approach to language processes, an approach that emphasizes the interrelationships among language, memory, and cognition.

This approach is then applied to various aspects of language processing. Part 2 (Language Comprehension) includes chapters on perception, the lexicon, sentence processing, and discourse processing. Chapter 4 now includes research on nonalphabetic orthographies. Chapter 5 has been modified significantly to include a fuller discussion of the various kinds of information (phonological, syntactic, and so on) stored in the lexicon as well as models of lexical access, including recent research on the cohort model. The discussion of lexical ambiguity has also been updated. Chapter 6 features recent research on constraint-based models of parsing, and Chapter 7 has been revised to emphasize levels of discourse representation as well as recent work on anomalous suspense.

Part 3 (Language Production and Conversational Interaction) contains, as before, one chapter on language production and one on conversation. Chapter 9 has been thoroughly revised, with new material on how different participants (friends and acquaintances, men and women) and settings (personal versus institutional) shape conversational patterns. The section on therapeutic discourse is revised and now part of a larger discussion of institutional talk, including patient-physician discourse.

Part 4 (Language Acquisition) contains three chapters. Chapters 10 and 11 describe early and later language acquisitions, respectively; these chapters present mainly data. Chapter 12 discusses theoretical issues in language acquisition in an integrated manner. All three chapters have been updated, with a greater discussion of word segmentation in Chapter 10 and increased attention to crosslinguistic research in Chapter 11.

Finally, Part 5 (Language in Perspective) includes Chapter 13 on biological foundations and Chapter 14 on language, culture, and cognition, with particular emphasis on the Whorf hypothesis. These last two chapters are somewhat broader in scope than most of the earlier ones and help put basic psycholinguistic processes (comprehension, production, and acquisition of language) into biological and cultural perspective.

This edition follows the style of the second edition. Psycholinguistic terms are printed in boldface. When a linguistic example is of sentence length or longer, I have generally used the convention of numbering the example and setting it apart from the text. For shorter examples, italics are used. Quotation marks are employed when a term is used in an unusual or ironic manner.

This edition, like the previous two, includes a number of pedagogical features that will be helpful to students. Chapters begin with a list of about four to six main points that the student should expect to learn. Interim summaries occur after each major section of the chapter, so that readers may assess their learning before going on. Each chapter concludes with two sets of questions. Review Questions are directly related to the material in the chapter, and students should be able to answer them if they have read the chapter carefully. Thought Questions are intended to stimulate thinking about the material in the chapter. Although the answers to these questions cannot be found directly in the chapter—indeed, most have no single "correct" answer—the material presented provides a basis for beginning to examine these questions. Finally, the book includes a glossary.

An instructor's manual with test bank is available for instructors who have adopted the book for classroom use.

Once again, I would be delighted to hear from students or professors who are using this book. You can reach me at the University of Wisconsin–Superior, Superior, WI 54880, or by E-mail (dcarroll@staff.uwsuper.edu).

I am pleased to acknowledge the assistance of many people in the preparation of this edition. First, I have benefited from the advice of a first-rate group of reviewers. David Dodd, University of Utah; Richard Hurtig, University of Iowa; and Margo Melakoff, Harvey Mudd College, reviewed the second edition and provided detailed suggestions for this edition. Peter Foltz, New Mexico State University, read and commented on this edition, and Merrill Garrett, University of Arizona; Greg B. Simpson, University of Kansas; and Michael Spivey, Cornell University, reviewed and commented on both versions. I thank them for their efforts and wise counsel, although the latter was not always heeded. I also thank Robert Good of the University of Illinois for his detailed comments on the second edition. In addition, Todd Jackson and Bob Kosuth of the University of Wisconsin–Superior and Aydin Durgunoglu of the University of Minnesota–Duluth read selected portions of this edition and provided very helpful feedback. Susan Bookheimer and Leonard Lessin provided the neuroimages in Chapter 13 in a timely manner.

The staff at Brooks/Cole was once again most helpful. Jamie Sue Brooks and Hal Lockwood guided the production process and were a pleasure to work with. Thanks also to Laura Larson, Judith Larzelere, Vernon Boes, Ryan Cooper, and

May Clark for lending their expertise to the finished product. Vicki Knight coordinated the whole operation and kept everyone in line.

I would also like to thank several individuals at the University of Wisconsin–Superior for their assistance. Eileen Wasyliszyn and Bev Lahti tracked down needed references, and John Ludwig provided technical assistance.

Finally, I want to thank my wife, Deb, and our children, Michael and Rachel, for gracefully accepting my absences, both physical and mental, during the production of this book.

David W. Carroll

General Issues

Introduction: Themes of Psycholinguistics

- Psycholinguistics is the study of how individuals comprehend, produce, and acquire language.
- The study of psycholinguistics is part of the field of cognitive science. Cognitive science reflects the insights of psychology, linguistics, and, to a lesser extent, fields such as artificial intelligence, neuroscience, and philosophy.
- Psycholinguistics stresses the knowledge of language and the cognitive processes involved in ordinary language use.
- Psycholinguists are also interested in the social rules involved in language use and the brain mechanisms associated with language.
- Contemporary interest in psycholinguistics began in the 1950s, although important precursors existed earlier in the century.

Introduction

This book is about how people use language. Few things play as central a role in our everyday lives as language. It is our most important tool in communicating our thoughts and feelings to each other. Infants cry and laugh, and their facial expressions surely give their parents some notion of the kinds of emotions they are experiencing, but it is not until children are able to articulate speech that we gain much understanding of their private thoughts.

As we grow, language comes to serve other functions as well. Most young people develop jargon that is more meaningful to those of the same age than to older or younger individuals. Such specialized language serves to bind us more closely with our peers while at the same time excluding those who are not our peers. Language becomes a badge of sorts, a means of identifying whether a person is within a social group. Similar processes are at work in gender and social class differences in language use.

Over time, for many of us language becomes not merely a means to an end but an end in itself. We come to love words and word play. So we turn to writing poetry or short stories. Or to playing word games, such as anagrams and crossword puzzles. Or to reading novels on a lazy summer afternoon. A tool that is vital for communicating our basic needs and wants has also become a source of leisurely pleasure.

The diversity of how we use language is daunting for psychologists who wish to study language. How can something so widespread and far-reaching as language be examined psychologically? An important consideration is that although language is intrinsically a social phenomenon, psychology is principally the study of individuals. The psychology of language deals with the mental processes that are involved in language use. Three sets of processes are of primary interest: language comprehension (how we perceive and understand speech and written language), language production (how we construct an utterance, from idea to completed sentence), and language acquisition (how children acquire language).

The psychological study of language is called **psycholinguistics.** This book explores the principles of this field along with selected applications. This introductory chapter deals with two questions: What is psycholinguistics? and How has this field evolved over the last century?

*T*he Scope of Psycholinguistics

Psycholinguistics is part of the emerging field of study called **cognitive science.** Cognitive science is an interdisciplinary venture that draws upon the insights of psychologists, linguists, computer scientists, neuroscientists, and philosophers to study the mind and mental processes (Johnson-Laird, 1988a; Stillings et al., 1995). Some of the topics that have been studied by cognitive scientists include problem solving, memory, imagery, and language. Anyone who is seriously interested in any of these topics must be prepared to cross disciplinary lines, for the topics do not belong to any one field of study but rather are treated in distinctive and yet complementary ways by various disciplines.

As the name implies, psycholinguistics is principally an integration of the fields of psychology and linguistics. **Linguistics** is the branch of science that studies the origin, structure, and use of language. Like most interdisciplinary fields, however, psycholinguistics has a rich heritage that includes contributions from diverse intellectual traditions. These contrasting approaches have often led to controversies in how to best think of or study language processes. We will consider many of these issues in the pages to come. For now, let us begin our survey of psycholinguistics by examining some of its central themes.

Language Processes and Linguistic Knowledge

At its heart, psycholinguistic work consists of two questions. One is, What knowledge of language is needed for us to use language? In a sense, we must know a language to use it, but we are not always fully aware of this knowledge. A distinction may be drawn between **tacit knowledge** and **explicit knowledge.** Tacit knowledge refers to the knowledge of how to perform various acts, whereas explicit knowledge refers to the knowledge of the processes or mechanisms used in these acts. We sometimes know how to do something without knowing how we do it. For instance, a baseball pitcher might know how to throw a baseball 90 miles an hour but might have little or no explicit knowledge of the muscle groups that are involved in this act. Similarly, we may distinguish between knowing how to speak and knowing what processes are involved in producing speech. Generally speaking, much of our linguistic knowledge is tacit rather than explicit. Reading this book will make you more aware of various things you know about language, thereby transforming some of your tacit knowledge into explicit knowledge.

Four broad areas of language knowledge may be distinguished. **Semantics** deals with the meanings of sentences and words. **Syntax** involves the grammatical arrangement of words within the sentence. **Phonology** concerns the system of sounds in a language. **Pragmatics** entails the social rules involved in language use.

It is not ordinarily productive to ask people explicitly what they know about these aspects of language. We infer linguistic knowledge from observable behavior.

The other primary psycholinguistic question is, What cognitive processes are involved in the ordinary use of language? By "ordinary use of language," I mean such things as understanding a lecture, reading a book, writing a letter, and holding a conversation. By cognitive processes, I mean processes such as perception, memory, and thinking. Although we do few things as often or as easily as speaking and listening, we will find that considerable cognitive processing is going on during those activities.

Four Language Examples

The interplay of linguistic knowledge and language processes is a continuing theme through this book. Because these concepts play a central role in psycholinguistic work, the following two chapters explore the knowledge and process questions in greater depth. Chapter 2 discusses linguistic insights into our tacit knowledge, and Chapter 3 considers psychological mechanisms of information processing and how these processes may be used in language processing. For now, it will be helpful to consider various examples of language and language processes. The following examples are intended to illustrate how the aforementioned themes apply to specific situations as well as to convey some of the scope of psycholinguistic research.

Garden path sentences   What happens when we comprehend a sentence? We get a hint of what is involved when the process breaks down. For example, consider sentence (1):

> **(1)**   The novice accepted the deal before he had a chance to check his finances, which put him in a state of conflict when he realized he had a straight flush. (Adapted from Foss & Jenkins, 1973)

Sentences such as this are sometimes called **garden path sentences** since the subjective impression is one of following a garden path to a predictable destination until it is obvious that you were mistaken in your original interpretation and thus are forced to "backtrack" and reinterpret the sentence. That is, in terms of knowledge, we have stored in our memory at least two different meanings of the word *deal*. One is related to a business transaction, and the other, relevant in this case, pertains to card games. This knowledge of the two meanings of *deal* is part of our semantic knowledge of the language. Another part of our semantic knowledge is knowledge of the relationships among words, such as *deal* and *finances*. From a process standpoint, we appear to select the one that is most appropriate, and we have little or no conscious awareness of the alternative (or how else would we have the garden path experience?). That is, we are able, by some process, to focus our attention on what we believe is the relevant meaning of *deal*. Studies of ambiguity are examined in Chapters 5 and 6; we will find that there is more to garden path sentences than what we are immediately aware of. The point for now is that in the course of comprehending language we are making decisions—we are doing mental work.

Indirect requests   Consider now a sentence such as (2):

(2)   Can you open the door?

Literally, this sentence asks if we have the ability to open the door, but everybody assumes that the speaker is asking us to open the door in an indirect manner. Why is the request phrased indirectly? Part of the reason is that we have learned certain rules about the use of language in social settings, including rules of politeness. A request is, by definition, an attempt to change another person's behavior. This can be perceived as intrusive or threatening at times, so we soften it with indirect speech. An indirect request is more polite than a direct command such as sentence (3):

(3)   Open the door!

We know this, as it is part of our pragmatic knowledge of our language. Some of us know it better than others, to be sure (studies discussed in Chapter 9 indicate that women and girls are more likely to use indirect speech than are men and boys).

From a processing standpoint, a speaker takes this pragmatic knowledge into account when producing a statement such as sentence (2) in a social situation. That is, the speaker utters the sentence with the understanding that it will be taken as a request. The listener presumably shares this aspect of pragmatic knowledge and interprets the sentence as a request rather than in a literal manner, although the exact processes by which the listener arrives at the nonliteral meaning are not fully clear (see Chapter 6).

Indirect requests are an aspect of language that forces us to consider language in a social context. The study of the relationships between language and social behavior is called **sociolinguistics.** Sociolinguists remind us that language activities always take place in a social world. Sociologists and anthropologists study how language varies with social groupings, how it influences social interaction, and how it is used as an instrument of culture (as in the transmission of cultural traditions). All of these aspects are well beyond those of the psychologist, who is principally interested in the behavior of individuals. Yet even when studying individuals, it is necessary to recognize the social dimension of language.

Language in aphasia   Although our primary focus is on language processes in normal individuals, we can learn a great deal about language by studying individuals with impaired language functioning. An **aphasia** is a language disorder due to brain damage. One type of aphasia, called **Wernicke's aphasia,** involves a breakdown in semantics. For example, consider excerpt (4):

(4)   Before I was in the one here, I was over in the other one. My sister had the department in the other one. (Geschwind, 1972, p. 78)

The semantic relationships between words in this excerpt are seriously disrupted, suggesting that the patient's semantic knowledge has been impaired by the brain damage. In contrast, phonological knowledge was spared; the speech, although devoid of meaning, was articulated smoothly and with appropriate pausing and intonation. It also displays appropriate syntactic structure, which is typical in Wernicke's aphasia.

The study of the relationship between the brain and language is called **neurolinguistics**, which is discussed more fully in Chapter 13. Although the details of the links between brain structures and language elude us, what is presently known is both fascinating and instructive. Depending on the exact location of the injury, its severity, and many other factors, an individual who has sustained a brain injury may display a wide variety of reactions. One person may have normal comprehension but be deficient in language production. Another may have no loss of ability with sentence structure but have greater than normal problems finding words. Still other individuals may be unimpaired in comprehension and production but be unable to repeat exactly what they have heard and understood. In normal individuals with intact brains, various facets of language—sentence structure, meaning, sounds— appear to form a smoothly coordinated system of communication; however, in brain- damaged individuals, this system is revealed to be a combination of separate parts, for the deficits in such persons are often selective rather than total. Thus, brain injuries enable us to analyze an apparently unified program of language abilities into its separate components and raise questions about how such abilities become integrated in the normal adult in the first place.

Language in children   An area of considerable concern to psycholinguists is language acquisition. As difficult as it is to infer linguistic knowledge in adults, the problem is even more intractable with children. An example may help here. Imagine a young child, about 1 year old, interacting with her mother. Typically, children around this age produce one word at a time. When the mother leaves the room and then returns with the child's favorite doll, the child says *doll*, not *mother*. Later, when the mother is helping her with lunch, the child points at the milk and says *more*. Still later, when the child is struggling with her shoes and the mother asks her what she is doing, the simple response is *off*. What can we conclude from these observations?

For starters, the child might know, at least in a tacit manner, some of the rules of language to use words appropriately. We could infer that she uses *more* not as an isolated word or imitation but as a request that the mother bring the milk closer. *Doll* is less clear; the child might be making a comment on her environment by labeling a thing she finds interesting, or she may be requesting the doll. How do we determine what she is trying to say? One way is to see what happens if the mother does nothing. If the word were meant as a request, the child will probably become more insistent, perhaps by repeatedly pointing at the doll and saying *doll*; whereas if it were meant as a comment, the child's behavior should end with mother's mere acknowledgment of the object. Thus, the child may have learned certain pragmatic rules to guide her choice of words.

You may complain that this is reading a good deal, perhaps too much, into a single word. Granted, the inferences made about this stage of development are terribly difficult. Yet, although there is disagreement over exactly how much knowledge to attribute to young children, it appears that children know more than they say. Children somewhat older than the one in the example commonly express themselves with two words at a time, as in *baby gone*, by eliminating the **closed-class** or **function words** (prepositions, conjunctions, and so on) in favor of **open-class** or **content words** (nouns, verbs, adjectives). This pattern suggests that children have an intuitive understanding of these two grammatical classes, which is part of their syntactic knowledge.

An analysis of children's comprehension and production abilities cannot be divorced from the social context in which the child masters language. Parents may set up situations in which one word is sufficient for communication. With the adult's query *What are you doing with your shoe?* as the base, the child's simple, economical *off* is instantly comprehensible. Parents do other things as well, such as simplifying their speech to children and teaching specific words. Is the orderly pattern of development observed in child language the result of an orderly biological program or of an orderly social environment? This issue is addressed in Chapter 12.

Summary

Psycholinguistics is part of an interdisciplinary field known as cognitive science. Two primary psycholinguistic questions are What mental processes are involved in language use? and What linguistic knowledge is involved in language use? These questions reemerge in different forms in studies of adult language comprehension, the social use of language, language use in aphasia, and language in children.

The Historical Context

In this section we consider some historical developments in the study of psycholinguistics. I have not attempted to be comprehensive here. The history of psycholinguistics has been treated in detail elsewhere (see, for example, Blumenthal, 1970, 1987; Kess, 1991; McCauley, 1987; Reber, 1987); if you are interested, you are advised to consult these sources. My discussion here is simply meant to put succeeding chapters in a little bit of historical perspective.

Blumenthal (1987) has observed that the interdisciplinary field of psycholinguistics flourished twice: once around the turn of the century, principally in Europe, and once in the middle of this century, principally in the United States. In both instances, it was a somewhat asymmetrical marriage of disciplines. In the early decades of this century, linguists turned to psychologists for insights into how human beings use language. In the later period, psychologists turned to linguists for insights into the nature of language. In between these two periods, behaviorism dominated both fields, each of which practiced a form of benign neglect toward one another. We will look at the events of each of these periods, and I will add some observations on the current directions in the field.

Early Psycholinguistics

From the development of the first psychological laboratory, at the University of Leipzig in Germany in 1879, until the early 1900s, psychology was defined as the science of mental life. A major figure in early scientific psychology was Wilhelm Wundt (1832–1920), a man trained in physiology who believed that it was possible to investigate mental events such as sensations, feelings, and images by using procedures as rigorous as those used in the natural sciences. Moreover, Wundt believed that the study of language could provide important insights into the nature of the mind. Blumenthal (1970) refers to Wundt as the master psycholinguist because Wundt wrote extensively about many different aspects of language. His concerns included grammar, phonology, language comprehension, child language acquisition, sign language, reading, and other topics of contemporary concern.

One of Wundt's contributions to the psychology of language was developing a theory of language production. He regarded the sentence, not the word, as the primary unit of language and saw the production of speech as the transformation of a complete thought process into sequentially organized speech segments (comprehension was thought to be basically the same process in reverse). Wundt described speech production in the following terms:

> When I construct a sentence, an isolated concept does not first enter consciousness causing me to utter a sound to represent it. That it cannot be this way is shown by the phenomenon of phonetic induction which occurs when a vocal element on the verge of being expressed is already affecting the form of a sound being spoken at the moment. And similarly, an articulation that has just occurred influences the succeeding sound. . . . The sentence . . . is not an image running with precision through consciousness where each single word or single sound appears only momentarily while the preceding and following elements are lost from consciousness. Rather, it stands as a whole at the cognitive level while it is being spoken. If this should ever not be the case, we would irrevocably lose the thread of speech. (Wundt, 1912, cited in Blumenthal, 1970, p. 21)

These two notions—the view that speech production is a word-by-word process and that it begins with a whole sentence—continue to be of interest to language researchers. As we shall see in Chapter 3, this distinction is a precursor of a contemporary distinction between bottom-up and top-down processing.

Some significant developments were also being made in measuring various language processes. An example comes from the 1908 work of Edmund Huey (1968), who examined reading from the perspective of human perceptual abilities. Huey, who regarded the achievement of reading as "the most remarkable specific performance that civilization has learned in all its history" (p. 6), employed the **eye-voice span** (the lag between eye position and voice when reading aloud, about six or seven words) and the **tachistoscope** (a machine that presents visual stimuli for very brief periods of time) in his studies. Interest in eye movement and tachistoscopic data remains very strong to this day.

Behaviorism and Verbal Behavior

In the first few decades of this century in the United States, there was mounting opposition to the focus on mental life as a goal for psychology. By the 1920s, **behaviorism** took over the mainstream of experimental psychology. Behaviorists favored the study of objective behavior, often in laboratory animals, as opposed to the study of mental processes. Moreover, behaviorists had a strong commitment to the role of experience in shaping behavior. Emphasis was placed on the role of environmental contingencies (such as reinforcement and punishment) and on models present in the immediate environment.

From the 1920s to the 1950s, psychologists expressed relatively little interest in language. Behaviorists preferred instead to speak of "verbal behavior." The behavior of speaking correctly was, it was assumed, the consequence of being raised in an environment in which correct language models were present and in which children's speech errors were corrected. The manner in which parents shape their children's utterances was described by the behaviorist B. F. Skinner (1957) in his book *Verbal Behavior:*

> In teaching the young child to talk, the formal specifications upon which reinforcement is contingent are at first greatly relaxed. Any response which vaguely resembles the standard behavior of the community is reinforced. When these begin to appear more frequently, a closer approximation is insisted upon. In this manner, very complex verbal forms may be reached. (pp. 29–30)

Although this analysis seems straightforward or even obvious, we will find in Chapter 12 that the role of adult speech in child language acquisition is both more controversial and more complex than is suggested in this excerpt.

About the time Skinner's book appeared, behavioristic research was providing evidence for its most basic premise: that verbal behavior could be conditioned by reinforcement. Verplanck (1955) found that the opinionated statements of college students in free conversation increased in frequency when they were followed by verbal reinforcers such as *mmm* or *good*. Related studies showed that the frequency of a grammatical class, such as plural words, could be increased by reinforcing only words from that class (Greenspoon, 1955). In a similar way, subtle signs of approval (such as nods) probably influence our choice of words in conversations.

Another major topic of research was meaning. A number of behavioristic accounts of meaning were developed, most of which emphasized associations among words. Noble and McNeely (1957) constructed an index of the "meaningfulness" of individual words by measuring the number of associations a person could produce in a designated period of time. Later studies showed that high-meaningfulness words such as *kitchen* were more easily learned in a variety of tasks than low-meaningfulness words such as *icon* (Underwood, 1966). It was also about this time that Osgood and his associates developed the **semantic differential,** a tool for measuring the associative meanings of words by asking people to rate words on dimensions such as good/bad and strong/weak (Osgood, Suci, & Tanenbaum, 1957).

Similar developments were occurring within linguistics. Linguists of this period tended to emphasize behavioristic treatments of language, in which reference to mental states or processes was meticulously avoided. However, despite the similarities between the two fields, little interdisciplinary interest or activity took place. One striking example of this is the work of linguist Leonard Bloomfield. Bloomfield was once a student of Wundt's and published a book in 1914 that emphasized many Wundtian themes. However, his more widely known 1933 text took a more behaviorist view. In his preface to the later book, Bloomfield tried to distance himself not only from Wundt but from psychology as a whole:

> In 1914 I based this phase of the exposition on the psychologic system of Wilhelm Wundt, which was then widely accepted. Since that time there has been much upheaval in psychology; we have learned, at any rate, what one of our masters suspected thirty years ago, namely that we can pursue the study of language without reference to any one psychological doctrine, and that to do so safeguards our results and makes them more significant to workers in related fields. (Bloomfield, 1933, p. vii)

Thus, despite the inherent interconnections between the fields, psychology and linguistics "divorced" for a period of several decades.

Later Psycholinguistics

By the early 1950s, psychologists and linguists became interested in talking to one another. Tanenhaus (1988) describes the events in the following way:

> In 1951 the Social Science Research Council sponsored a conference that brought together several leading psychologists and linguists. . . . The proceedings of the conference outlined a psycholinguistic research agenda that reflected a consensus among participants that the methodological and theoretical tools developed by psychologists could be used to explore and explain the linguistic structures that were being uncovered by linguists. (p. 4)

A second, larger conference occurred 2 years later and included anthropologists and communications engineers as well as psychologists and linguists. It was out of these exchanges that the term *psycholinguistics* first came into use (Osgood & Sebeok, 1965). Not everyone was fond of the term. One of the participants at the first conference, Roger Brown, complained that a "psycholinguist" sounded more like a deranged polyglot than a psychologist interested in language (Brown, 1958), but the name stuck.

The second period of interdisciplinary psycholinguistics really took hold in the late 1950s, beginning with the emergence of the linguist Noam Chomsky. Chomsky is generally regarded as the most influential figure in twentieth-century linguistics, and Newmeyer (1986) has characterized the Chomskyan influence within linguistics as a revolution. Chomsky has also played a powerful role in how psychologists perceived language because he argued that the behaviorists' accounts of language were inadequate (Chomsky, 1957, 1959).

Let us look at some of his arguments. One theory advanced by behaviorists is called the **associative chain theory,** which states that a sentence consists of a chain of associations between individual words in a sentence. Put another way, each word in a sentence serves as a stimulus for the next word, and thus the entire sentence is produced left to right. Lashley (1951) had earlier argued against such a view, claiming that there is something more to the structure of a sentence than the associations between adjacent words.

Chomsky (1957) advanced this notion further. Consider the following sentences:

(5)   Colorless green ideas sleep furiously.

(6)   Furiously sleep ideas green colorless.

(7)   George picked up the baby.

(8)   George picked the baby up.

Chomsky suggested that associations between words could not possibly explain the existence of sentences such as (5). Even though the associations between these words are almost nonexistent, the sentence is syntactically acceptable. But, if the words are presented backward, as in sentence (6), it is not a sentence at all. Now consider sentences (7) and (8). It is part of our intuitive knowledge of the language that these sentences are synonymous, but this simple fact poses problems for the associative chain theory. Clearly, there is a relationship between *pick* and *up* in these sentences, but the relationship is more complex in (8) than in (7) because the words are separated. To comprehend the sentence, we must somehow know that these words are part of a linguistic unit, or **constituent.** Linguists call separate units, like those in sentence (8), **discontinuous constituents,** and their existence suggests that there are long-range dependencies among words in a sentence. Again, a theory that stresses a simple association between adjacent words is inadequate.

Chomsky has also argued that language acquisition cannot be explained in terms of children's language experience. His primary argument is called the **poverty of stimulus argument** (Chomsky, 1980). This argument states that there is not enough information in the language samples given to children to fully account for the richness and complexity of children's language. Sentences (9) through (12) (from Caplan & Chomsky, 1980) illustrate the point:

(9)   John believes he is incompetent.

(10)   John believes him to be incompetent.

(11)   John wants him to win.

(12)   John wants Bill to see him.

Our knowledge of the language tells us that the *he* in sentence (9) and the *him* in sentence (12) could refer to John, though they need not. In contrast, the *him* in sentences (10) and (11) cannot refer to John. It is doubtful that anyone's parents systematically distinguished between the *him* in sentences (10) and (11) versus the *him* in sentence (12). In fact, most people would not know how to explain such a difference. Still, we recognize the difference and, moreover, can make a great number of other linguistic discriminations about much more complex aspects of language that we are similarly unable to explain in an explicit manner. Chomsky's argument is this: the language children acquire is intricate and subtle, and the sample of speech given to them during the course of language development is anything but. Therefore, although parents may assist the child's language development in some ways and influence the rate of development somewhat, the pattern of development is based not on parental speech but on innate language knowledge.

The Chomskyan revolution had a powerful effect on psychological thinking about language. In the late 1960s, Chomsky (1968) noted that "the study of language may very well, as was traditionally supposed, provide a remarkably favorable perspective for the study of human mental processes" (p. 98) and that linguistics could be profitably viewed as a branch of cognitive psychology. That is, linguists were examining the kinds of linguistic knowledge needed for ordinary language use and realized that this knowledge must be used, in some way, by those who use the language. As Slobin (1971) puts it, a person who has learned a language has formed something that is "psychologically equivalent" (p. 3) to a grammar. Thus, psychologists became very interested in linguistics in general and in Chomsky's transformational grammar in particular (see Chapter 2).

The psychologist George Miller played an important bridge between psychology and linguistics by introducing psychologists to Chomsky's ideas and their psychological implications. Miller collaborated with Chomsky on several articles and papers in the early 1960s (for example, Miller & Chomsky, 1963) and was at the forefront of research during this period to determine the psychological reality of linguistic rules (see, for instance, Miller & Isard, 1963).

Language development became an especially popular topic for investigators during this period. Several **longitudinal investigations** of child language, in which a sample of a child's speech is collected at several points over a period of years, emerged in the early 1960s (Braine, 1963; Miller & Ervin, 1964), and various "grammars" for child language were written, modeled after adult grammars but differing in the specific rules (Bloom, 1970; Brown, 1973). The major questions for language acquisition researchers were posed in the following way: What set of rules governs the child's developing grammar and when does this set develop?

Theoretical analyses of language development emphasized the role of innate factors. Together with Chomsky, the most influential person in this regard was Eric Lenneberg, whose 1967 book *Biological Foundations of Language* pulled together evidence from aphasia, studies of delayed language development (for example, mental retardation), and the available neurophysiological information into an elegant argument for the role of innate factors in language development. Another strong advocate of innate factors was David McNeill (1966, 1970), who proposed a theory of development based on the concept of language universals.

The revolution of the 1960s and early 1970s emphasized the role of linguistic theory in psycholinguistic research and the role of innate mechanisms in language acquisition. These themes continue to be influential, but there are indications that psychological interest in linguistic theory has waned. Reber (1987) examined the number of references to Chomsky in psycholinguistic studies and found that they rose sharply in the late 1960s, peaked in the mid-1970s, and then fell off by the early 1980s. Although it might be interesting to look at citations of other linguists, these data nonetheless appear to reflect the trend among psychologists to shy away from directly incorporating linguistic concepts into psychological research. Reber cites several reasons for these changes. One was that throughout the 1960s and 1970s linguistic theories underwent rapid and (to psychologists, at least) confusing changes (see Newmeyer, 1986). These changes made it difficult for psychologists to base their studies on any particular linguistic view, and some psychologists became wary of linguistics, preferring instead to develop a psychological view of language that was not tied to any specific linguistic theory. As Blumenthal (1987) has observed, there is a historical symmetry in these reactions—60 years ago, linguists such as Bloomfield pulled away from psychology for much the same reasons.

Reber (1987) also points out the growing realization that the two fields were quite distinct in their methodologies. A distinction may be drawn between two intellectual traditions, **rationalism** and **empiricism.** To some extent, this distinction is reminiscent of the familiar one between heredity and environment, or nature and nurture: rationalists emphasize the role of innate factors in human behavior, whereas empiricists stress the role of experience in behavior. But there is another difference between the two traditions that deals with the mode of inquiry. Rationalists emphasize the use of argument, whereas empiricists favor the collection of data as a means for evaluating hypotheses. For the most part, linguists approach language in a rationalistic manner; psychologists, even those who are sympathetic with the notion of innate factors, favor the empirical method. As a consequence of these differences, ideas tend to be evaluated somewhat differently in the two fields (Pylyshyn, 1972, 1973; Watt, 1970). In retrospect, it may have been too unrealistic to expect that two disciplines with their own histories and methodologies would mesh very easily.

Current Directions

Where do things stand now? It is always more precarious to describe events that are currently in progress than those well in the past, but it is possible to discern several themes of psycholinguistic work over the last 15 to 20 years. One is that the field has become more interdisciplinary. In particular, as noted earlier in the chapter, psycholinguistics has increasingly been viewed as a portion of the interdisciplinary field of cognitive science, which includes contributions from computer science, philosophy, neuroscience, and related fields.

Second, the wave of interest in syntax that occupied psychological interest after the Chomskyan revolution has spurred interest in other aspects of language. One currently lively area of research deals with how people understand, remember, and produce **discourse,** units of language larger than the sentence, such as paragraphs and stories. Another is the **lexicon,** or mental dictionary—studies of individual words have become much more prominent in the last decade. And both areas, while of considerable theoretical importance, have also had practical applications. Studies of discourse have provided insights into conversational processes in psychotherapy (see Chapter 9), and studies of the lexicon have already been useful in increasing our understanding of how children learn to read (see Chapter 11).

One final theme concerns the ways psycholinguists look at child language acquisition. Interest in innate language mechanisms has been complemented by a resurgence of research of the child's linguistic environment. Adults speak to children in ways that are phonologically, semantically, syntactically, and pragmatically distinct from their speech to adults, and much research has examined the role of these language lessons in children's language acquisition.

On balance, psycholinguistics is a more diverse field than the one that existed a few decades ago. Neither psychology nor linguistics is dominated by a single theoretical viewpoint, and the input from other fields within cognitive science has added new perspectives and insights that have been incorporated into this growing field. At the same time, tangible progress has been made in applying psycholinguistic research to topics such as reading (Just & Carpenter, 1987), bilingualism (Hakuta, 1986), and language disorders (Caplan, 1987). These advances have been made possible by integrating the insights from different disciplines within cognitive science. For instance, Just and Carpenter's book on reading comprehension integrates linguistic theories of sentence structure, computer simulations of reading, and psychological experimentation on eye movements. These results give us reason to believe that interdisciplinary work on language, although it can produce tensions between different approaches, can ultimately be fruitful (see, especially, Miller, 1990).

Summary

The history of psycholinguistics can be divided into two periods of interdisciplinary activity separated by several decades of behaviorism. The first period was dominated by Wundt, who presented a cognitive view of language. The behaviorist position then held that verbal behavior can be explained in terms of environmental contingencies of reinforcement and punishment. This view was criticized by Chomsky, leading to a second wave of psycholinguistic activity. This period was characterized by an effort to incorporate linguistic theory in psychological research as well as by the view that innate linguistic mechanisms are necessary to explain child language acquisition. Psycholinguistics is presently a more diverse field of study that draws insights and methodologies not only from psychology and linguistics but also from adjacent fields of study.

Review Questions

1. Identify the two major questions that psycholinguists are interested in.
2. Define semantics, syntax, phonology, and pragmatics.
3. Distinguish between tacit and explicit knowledge.
4. What is a garden path sentence?

5. What aspects of linguistic knowledge appear to be disrupted in Wernicke's aphasia, and what aspects are intact?
6. Summarize Wundt's theory of language production.
7. Why did behaviorists prefer to talk of verbal behavior instead of language?
8. When did the term *psycholinguistics* arise?
9. What arguments did Chomsky give against behaviorist views of language?
10. How does the field of psycholinguistics currently differ from the field of the 1960s?

Thought Questions

1. In sentence (1), our misreading of *deal* forces us to backtrack and do a good deal of extra mental work at the end of the sentence. Why don't we simply entertain both meanings of an ambiguous word until we know which one is appropriate?
2. If you discovered a person who spoke a language that no one else could understand, how would you go about trying to understand what the person was trying to say?

2 Linguistic Principles

MAIN POINTS

- Linguists have attempted to identify those grammatical features that appear in all languages. Four pervasive properties are duality of patterning, morphology, phrase structure, and linguistic productivity.
- American Sign Language shares these linguistic properties with spoken languages. Sign language differs from spoken language in its iconicity and simultaneous structure.
- A language consists of an infinite set of sentences. A person who knows a language knows its grammar, which consists of a finite set of rules.
- Transformational grammar distinguishes between two levels of sentence structure: deep structure and surface structure. Phrase-structure rules generate deep structures, and transformational rules operate on deep structures to produce surface structures.
- Several controversies exist within grammatical theory, including whether grammatical rules are psychologically real, whether linguistic rules are structurally or lexically based, and whether knowledge of language is innate.

Introduction

The focus of this book is on how people process language—how we comprehend and produce spoken and written language—and how these skills are acquired. To understand these language processes, we need to understand the major properties of language as well as the processing characteristics of the individuals who use it. Chapter 3 examines what is presently known about how humans process information. This chapter deals with the structure of language.

As we saw in Chapter 1, fluently speaking a language does not guarantee that one has any explicit knowledge of the language. For most of us, speaking is easy—it is an activity akin to breathing that we do without much thought or effort. We might then assume, erroneously, that anything so easy must be pretty simple. The study of language proves otherwise. As we learn how languages are organized, we realize how truly complex they are.

This chapter is organized into four sections. The first presents some basic grammatical concepts common to a number of linguistic theories. The second examines American Sign Language and considers whether the concepts introduced in the first section apply to a language in the visual modality. The third section discusses a historically significant theory of grammar called transformational grammar. Finally, we consider some unresolved controversies in the study of grammar.

Basic Grammatical Concepts

Languages differ in a host of ways. Some languages, like English, are rather strict about word order. The words in sentences (1) and (2) are the same; the only difference is the order in which the words are arranged. When we learn English, we must learn syntactic rules including those pertaining to word order. In English, the basic word order is subject-verb-object, or SVO.

(1) The boy chased the girl.

(2) The girl chased the boy.

Other languages use word order in different ways. In Japanese, the basic word order is subject-object-verb (SOV). A simple Japanese sentence (3) translates literally to *Taro to Hanako that book gave*, where *hon* means *book* and *yatta* means *gave*:

(3) Taroo ga Hanako ni sono hon o yatta. (Shibatani, 1987)

Still other languages, such as Russian, are much more flexible about word order. Thus, although it is possible to say *Viktor kisses Lena* in English-type SVO form (4), a number of other forms (5–9) are also possible (Comrie, 1987). In Russian, meaning is conveyed less by word order than by the affixes (suffixes and prefixes) that are attached to words and slightly modify their meaning. In English, we know that we can express a word in a variety of interrelated forms (such as *trip, tripped, tripping,* and so forth), but other languages have far greater numbers of such forms. The system of affixing is considerably more complex in Russian, and in most languages, than in English.

(4) Viktor celuet Lenu.

(5) Viktor Lenu celuet.

(6) Lenu Viktor celuet.

(7) Lenu celuet Viktor.

(8) celuet Viktor Lenu.

(9) celuet Lenu Viktor.

Turkish is similar to Russian in the use of affixes, rather than word order, to signal meaning but differs in other respects. Turkish is a language in which speakers can combine different elementary meanings into very long words. For example, *gel* means *come, gelemedim* means *I couldn't come,* and *gelemeyeceklermis* means something like [*It was mentioned that*] *Those people won't be able to come* in Turkish. Word order is very flexible.

These and other linguistic differences might tempt us to conclude that languages differ so greatly that no common patterns can be found. Despite these differences, linguists who have investigated the world's languages have concluded that although languages differ in a number of ways, the differences are not random and there are impressive underlying similarities. For example, Greenberg (1966) has discovered that every language contains declarative sentences that express subject, verb, and object. Moreover, all languages have a preferred word order, even though some languages allow more flexibility than others. The point is that underneath the impressive diversity we see patterns. The variations consist of different combinations of similar underlying elements.

If this is so, then we need to identify features that are found, in some form, in all human languages but are not present in animal communication systems. What follows is a short list of properties that are commonly agreed to be pervasive among the world's languages and are of significant psychological interest.

Duality of Patterning

A grammatical concept that is basic to the study of language is called **duality of patterning** (Hockett, 1966). At one level, there is a large number of meaningful elements, or words. At another level, there is a relatively small number of meaningless elements that are combined to form the words. In spoken languages, these meaningless elements are individual speech sounds. As Hockett notes, this form of duality does not appear to exist in animal communication.

Phones and phonemes   To explain this duality, we need to make a few distinctions. **Phones** are speech sounds. Two sounds are different phones if they differ in a physically specifiable way. For example, consider the *p* in the words *pill* and *spill*. There is a puff of air, known as **aspiration,** in *pill* that is not present in *spill*. You can tell the difference easily by placing a lighted match a few inches in front of your mouth as you pronounce the two sounds. Phones are indicated by brackets: the aspirated sound is symbolized as [pʰ], the unaspirated as [p].

    Phonemes are differences in sound that make a contribution to meaning; they are indicated by slashes. For example, the sounds /b/ and /d/ are considered to be different phonemes in English because they contribute to the difference in meaning between *big* and *dig*. Phonemes may be thought of as categories of phones; each phone is a physically distinct version of the phoneme, but none of the differences between phones makes a difference to meaning. Notice that these phonemic categories vary from language to language. In English, aspiration is not phonemic, although it is in Thai, which would represent the sounds as /pʰ/ and /p/.

Distinctive features   We can understand these patterns better if we think of phonemes as combinations of discrete features. A **distinctive feature** is a characteristic of a speech sound whose presence or absence distinguishes the sound from other sounds. The phoneme /b/ is similar to the phoneme /p/ except that the vocal cords vibrate during the production of /b/ but not /p/. In distinctive feature theory, contrasts are binary with the presence of the feature indicated by + and its absence by −. The phoneme /b/ is said to be + **voicing,** whereas /p/ is − voicing. In a similar vein, /b/ is + bilabial, which means that the sound is articulated at the lips, and is + stop, meaning that the airflow from the lungs is completely stopped during production. Distinctive feature theory (Jakobson, Fant, & Halle, 1969) claims that these are independent units that are combined to form phonemes.

    Let us turn to the question of how these small linguistic units are combined. The sequence of phonemes that may occur in any given language is constrained. Consider the sounds *port*, *plort*, and *pbort*. We easily recognize that the first one is a word, the second could be, and the third could not be, at least not in English. As a first approximation, we can state a phonological rule that explains these patterns in the following way:

(R1)   /p/ cannot be followed by /b/ at the beginning of a word.

The problem with this rule is that it is stated too narrowly. There are a number of other sequences in the language, such as *pt, bg, td, kb,* and many others, that are not allowed either. We must look for a broader generalization.

The concept of distinctive features is helpful here, since *p, t, b, g, d,* and *k* are all + stop. This enables us to reformulate the rule more generally:

(R2)   A word cannot begin with two stop consonants.

In the same vein, we may notice that aspiration is predictable in English. The pattern noted with *pill* and *spill* also applies to other voiceless stop consonants, such as *t* (*till/still*) and *k* (*kill/skill*). The aspirated sound occurs only at the beginning of the word; otherwise, the unaspirated sound is pronounced. The proper rule is

(R3)   Voiceless stop consonants are aspirated when they occur at the beginning of a word.

Thus, distinctive features are useful in identifying how to formulate linguistic rules.

A study by Miller and Nicely (1955) demonstrated that these distinctive features have psychological validity. Miller and Nicely constructed a set of syllables that consisted of 1 of 16 consonants followed by the vowel [a]. The syllables were presented to subjects under difficult listening conditions, with "white noise" (a hissing sound) in the background. The white noise was at a consistent level of loudness, whereas the speech varied over seven levels of loudness. Subjects were asked to identify the sounds that they heard. They made more errors when the speech was softer. When errors were made, subjects tended to incorrectly hear a sound that was similar to the target sound in most features but differed in only one. For instance, if [b] was presented, subjects were more likely to err by identifying the sound as [d], which shares all features with [b] except + bilabial, than [f], which differs in a number of respects from the target.

Duality of patterning appears to be a universal property of language. Languages differ in their phonemes and in the rules by which the phonemes may be combined to form words. However, all languages have duality: a level at which there is a relatively small number of basic, meaningless elements and another level at which there is a large number of meaningful elements. And all languages have a systematic set of rules for combining the former into the latter.

Morphology

We have seen that the phonemes are combined to form words. Another important way in which we use words is to use different forms of the same word to convey different shades of meaning. The system of rules that governs this aspect of language is referred to as **morphology.**

Table 2-1.   Major Grammatical Morphemes in English

Morpheme	Distinction(s)	Examples
Number	Singular, plural	Nouns: *ball, balls* Pronouns: *he/she, they* Verbs: *is, are*
Person	First, second, third	Pronouns: *I, you, he/she* Verbs: *I walk, you walk, he/she walks*
Tense	Present, past, future	Verbs: *I jump, I jumped, I will jump*
Aspect	Perfect, progressive	Verbs: *I have read the book, I am reading the book*

The smallest meaningful unit in a language is referred to as a **morpheme.** Some words, such as *truck,* consist of only a single morpheme. Others consist of two or more morphemes; *bedroom* consists of the morphemes *bed* and *room.* We may also distinguish between **free morphemes,** which may stand alone, and **bound morphemes** (also called **grammatical morphemes**), which, although contributing to word meaning, are not words themselves. Some of the major grammatical morphemes in English are shown in Table 2-1. Notice that these categories intersect. For instance, the intersection of tense and aspect produces the present perfect (10), the past perfect (11), the present progressive (12), and the past progressive (13):

(10)   I have read the book.

(11)   I had read the book.

(12)   I am reading the book.

(13)   I was reading the book.

Although all languages have a morphological system, languages differ in the grammatical distinctions they make and in the way in which they make them. When we use English correctly, we are, at some level, paying attention to these properties. For instance, we must pay attention to the number of both pronouns and verbs because they must agree for a sentence to be grammatical in English. When choosing tense, we must decide when in time a given action took place. In Chapter 14, we will consider the idea that these subtle linguistic differences influence the thought patterns of the individuals who speak the language in such a way that speakers of different languages have distinct worldviews.

Phrase Structure

A third central concept in grammatical description is **phrase structure.** Intuitively, we know that sentences can be divided into groups of words, or **constituents.** Consider the simple declarative sentence (14):

(14)   The young swimmer accepted the silver medal.

Think about how you might put these words into groups. The primary break in the sentence is between *swimmer* and *accepted*. This can be indicated by parentheses, as in sentence (15):

> **(15)** (The young swimmer) (accepted the silver medal).

We can further subdivide the last group as follows:

> **(16)** (The young swimmer) (accepted [the silver medal]).

The items in parentheses are the constituents of this simple declarative sentence. The first item is a noun phrase (NP), which consists of a **determiner** (*the*), an adjective (*young*), and a noun (*swimmer*). The second constituent is a verb phrase (VP), which consists of the verb (*accepted*) and then a second NP (*the silver medal*).

Phrase-structure rules are syntactic rules that specify the permissible sequences of constituents in a language. Each phrase-structure rule "rewrites" a constituent into one or more other constituents. By using a series of rules, we can derive a sentence from top to bottom (that is, from the largest to the smallest constituent).

A list of phrase-structure rules sufficient to generate this sentence is shown in Table 2-2. Phrase-structure rule 1 (PS 1), S ⟶ NP + VP, is read "A sentence may be rewritten as a NP and a VP." Rule PS 2 means that NPs are rewritten as determiner and noun, with optional adjectives indicated by parentheses placed between the article and the noun. We can now expand each of these items on the left side and ultimately work our way through the entire sentence. The final four rules, called **lexical insertion rules,** put words into the structure that has been built. The entire sequence of rules that produces the sentence is called a **derivation.** The step-by-step derivation of this sentence is shown in Table 2-3. The resulting phrase structure is shown in Figure 2-1.

Phrase-structure rules provide a good account of one type of sentence ambiguity called **phrase-structure ambiguity.** This type of ambiguity is illustrated by sentences such as (17):

> **(17)** They are eating apples.

In these sentences, the assignment of words to constituents is ambiguous, and more than one tree structure or phrase marker could be made for each case. In sentence

Table 2-2. A Simple Set of Phrase-Structure Rules

PS 1 S (sentence)	⟶	NP + VP
PS 2 NP (noun phrase)	⟶	det + (adj) + N
PS 3 VP (verb phrase)	⟶	V + NP
PS 4 N (noun)	⟶	*swimmer, medal, horse*
PS 5 V (verb)	⟶	*accepted, returned*
PS 6 adj (adjective)	⟶	*young, silver, beautiful*
PS 7 det (determiner)	⟶	*a, the*

Table 2-3.   Steps in the Derivation of *The young swimmer accepted the silver medal*

1. Rule PS 1   NP + VP
2. Rule PS 2   det + adj + N + VP
3. Rule PS 3   det + adj + N + V + NP
4. Rule PS 2   det + adj + N + V + det + adj + N
5. Rule PS 7   *the* + adj + N + V + *the* + adj + N
6. Rule PS 6   *the* + *young* + N + V + *the* + *silver* + N
7. Rule PS 4   *the* + *young* + *swimmer* + V + *the* + *silver* + *medal*
8. Rule PS 5   *the* + *young* + *swimmer* + *accepted* + *the* + *silver* + *medal*

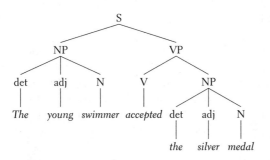

Figure 2-1.   Tree diagram (phrase marker) for
The young swimmer accepted the silver medal.

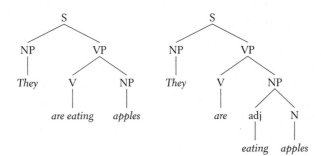

Figure 2-2.   Tree diagrams for *They are eating apples.*

(17), *eating* could either be a part of the verb or an adjective modifying apples. The two phrase markers for this sentence are shown in Figure 2-2.

Linguistic Productivity

There is no limit to the number of sentences in a language. The vast percentage of sentences we utter are novel but grammatically acceptable arrangements of words (the main exceptions being clichés, proverbs, and the like). Our ability to create and comprehend novel utterances is called **linguistic productivity** (or **linguistic creativ-**

ity). This notion was discussed by Hockett (1966) but has been emphasized most strongly by Chomsky (1957, 1966, 1980). One way to get a sense of this concept is to take an ordinary sentence from conversation or from a written source and then look for the identical sentence from another source (you will be looking for quite a while).

Given that the human brain is obviously finite, the problem of explaining how we can master a language with an infinite set of sentences remains a vexing problem for psycholinguists. It is not possible, for instance, to store an infinite set of sentences somewhere in the brain for later use. Most current psycholinguistic accounts make the assumption that instead of storing sentences, we store rules for creating sentences. The number of rules needed is finite, but the rules can be combined to form an unlimited number of sentences.

An example will clarify the point (Lasnik, 1990). A way to construct longer and more complex sentences is to embed one sentence inside another. We have already seen that we can rewrite a VP into V + NP, but it is also possible to rewrite a VP as follows:

(PS 8)   VP ⟶ V + S

That is, the material following the verb can be a complete sentence, as in (18):

(18)   The child thinks the man left.

The phrase marker for (18) is shown in Figure 2-3. Furthermore, we can continue the process and embed more and more sentences (for example, *The woman knows the child thinks the man left*) into the earlier ones, until the sentences become quite difficult to comprehend.

This process can be described through the use of phrase-structure rules. We can combine PS 1 and PS 8 to get PS 9:

(PS 9)   S ⟶ NP + V + S

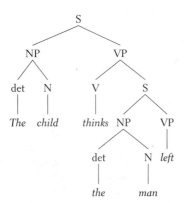

Figure 2-3.   Tree diagram for
The child thinks the man left.

Notice that S is on both sides of the arrow. A rule such as this, which refers to itself, is said to be a **recursive rule.** Recursion is closely related to language productivity for, as we have seen, there is no limit to the number of times we can embed one sentence into another. Recursion appears to be a resilient property of human language use. Goldin-Meadow (1982) has shown that children provided with very little exposure to language nonetheless create language that has this property (see Chapter 12).

Linguistic productivity distinguishes human language from animal communication systems, which consist of a small number of discrete signals. In contrast, all human languages are open communication systems in which new words are coined as they are needed. Moreover, not only can we create new words, but we can, as we have seen with recursion, blend existing words in new combinations. These productive processes provide a measure of how complex and open-ended our language faculty is.

Not all aspects of language are productive. Some aspects of language are not rule-governed and so must be mastered by rote learning. One instance is the existence of strong verbs, which are verbs that are morphologically irregular. The most common in English are verbs that are irregular in the past tense, such as *went, fell,* and *ate.* Children trip over these forms early in their language development, preferring to overuse the past tense marker (for example, *goed*). Interestingly, most strong verbs are rather frequently used in the language, which is precisely what we would expect to see if children needed to learn each one in a rote manner.

Summary

Four basic grammatical concepts are duality of patterning, morphology, phrase structure, and linguistic productivity. Words are composed of phonemes, which, in turn, have distinctive features. In each instance, the smaller units are combined in a rule-governed manner to produce the larger units. Words consist of one or more units of meaning, or morphemes. The system of grammatical morphemes in a language provides speakers with a way of signaling subtle differences in meaning. Phrase-structure rules codify our intuitions about the groupings of words in a sentence. Some sentences are ambiguous and may be grouped in more than one way. Linguistic productivity refers to the fact that there is no limit to the number of sentences in a language. One type of phrase-structure rule, that of recursion, is responsible for some of this productivity.

Insights from Sign Language

We now consider some of the linguistic properties of **American Sign Language** (ASL). Unlike speech, signs are expressed in visual or spatial form. This enables us to examine the extent to which the grammatical concepts we have just considered generalize to language in a visual modality.

American Sign Language is sharply distinguished from manual forms of English that translate English sounds into signs. The best known is fingerspelling, which, as the name implies, translates English words letter by letter into manual form. It is a secondary gestural system, derived from the English language. In contrast, ASL is independent of English and derived from French Sign Language (Frishberg, 1975). Although in the past ASL was regarded as mere pantomime or grammatically deficient in various ways, several decades of scholarly research on ASL have put these ideas to rest.

Even if we accept the notion that ASL is an autonomous language, we must ask what is its relation to spoken languages. We will begin to answer this question by considering some of the differences between signed (especially ASL) and spoken languages and then some of the similarities.

Differences Between Signed and Spoken Languages

Iconicity and arbitrariness   In English, as with most spoken languages, the principle of **arbitrariness** holds: no intrinsic relationship exists between the set of sounds and the object to which the sounds refer. For instance, there is no relation between the size of a word and the size of its referent; we have big words for small objects (for example, *caterpillar*) and small words for big objects (for example, *train*). According to Hockett (1966), this is a universal feature of human language.

American Sign Language, in contrast, possesses a high degree of **iconicity:** many of the signs resemble the objects or activities to which they refer. For example, the sign for *attention* is to hold both hands parallel to one another in front of one's face and then move them away from one's body. This suggests the act of putting on blinders to keep out distractions. Another iconic sign is the sign for *judge*, which is to place one's hands in front of one's body and then repeatedly move one up as the other goes down. This resembles a balancing scale that weighs various thoughts (Klima & Bellugi, 1979).

Interestingly, different sign languages have developed in different parts of the world. Examination of ASL, Danish Sign Language, and Chinese Sign Language indicates that even though all have iconic signs, the signs differ from language to language in the actual details. For example, the sign for *tree* in ASL is to hold the forearm upright with the hand spread wide, which suggests a tree trunk and its branches. In Danish Sign Language, the hands outline the rounded top of the tree and then the shape of the trunk, whereas in Chinese Sign Language, the hands portray the trunk and then move upward (Klima & Bellugi, 1979). Thus, even though ASL is iconic, this property does not automatically determine the form of the signs. Each language represents the object iconically in different ways.

Frishberg (1975) has claimed that the degree of iconicity has declined in ASL over the past 200 years. An example of this is the sign for *home*. Originally, this was a combination of two other signs, one for *eat* and one for *sleep*. The sign for *eat* involves holding one's hand in a cup form near the mouth. The sign for *sleep* involves laying a flat hand against one's cheek and tilting the head. Just as each of these individual signs is iconic, so was the original sign for *home*: eat followed by sleep. Over time, the sign shortened and become more conventionalized, so that its present form is a hand in cup form touching two different locations on the cheek, which is not as transparent in meaning as the original signs. Thus, although many ASL signs are iconic, ASL has an increasing degree of arbitrariness. American Sign Language now has a dual system of reference — part iconic, part arbitrary.

Simultaneous and sequential structure   A second difference between signed and spoken languages deals with the distinction between simultaneous and sequential structure. The structure of spoken languages is largely sequential in nature. We have rules that specify the correct order of phonemes within syllables, syllables within words, and words within sentences.

Sign language differs in that it is organized spatially more than temporally. The meaning of utterances is not specified primarily by the order of signs (although order does matter) but by the combination of features simultaneously present in the sign.

Similarities Between Signed and Spoken Languages

Duality of patterning   The three major parameters of signs are hand configuration, place of articulation, and movement (Stokoe, Casterline, & Croneberg, 1976). Stokoe and colleagues have identified 19 different values of hand configuration, or handshapes. These include an open palm, a closed fist, and a partially closed fist with the index finger pointing. Place of articulation, which has 12 values, deals with whether the sign is made at the upper brow, the cheek, the upper arm, and so on. Movement refers to whether the hands are moving upward, downward, sideways, toward or away from the signer, in rotary fashion, and so on, and includes 24 values. Although these values are meaningless in themselves, they are combined in various ways to form ASL signs. Thus, ASL has duality of patterning.

Figure 2-4 shows a series of minimal contrasts involving these three parameters. The top row shows three signs that differ only in hand configuration (that is, the signs are identical in place of articulation and movement). The second and third rows show minimal contrasts for place and movement, respectively. Notice how a change in a single parameter value can change the entire meaning of a sign.

It is also possible to analyze parameter values into distinctive features. Two such features for handshapes are index, which refers to whether the index finger is extended, and compact, which refers to whether the hand is closed into a fist. Among the signs in the top line of Figure 2-4, *candy* is + index, − compact, *apple* is + index and + compact, and *jealous* is − index and − compact. To determine whether signers' perceptions of ASL are related to features such as these, Lane, Boyes-Braem, and Bellugi (1976) presented deaf individuals with a series of signs under conditions of high visual noise (a video monitor with a lot of "snow"). The participants were asked to recognize the signs on the monitor. The researchers found that the large majority of recognition errors involved pairs of signs that differed in only one feature. That is, signs with similar patterns of distinctive features were psychologically similar to one another.

CANDY   APPLE   JEALOUS

(a)   Signs contrasting only in hand configuration

SUMMER   UGLY   DRY

(b)   Signs contrasting only in place of articulation

TAPE   CHAIR   TRAIN

(c)   Signs contrasting only in movement

Figure 2-4.   Minimal contrasts of signs illustrating major parameters. (Based on *The Signs of Language*, by E. S. Klima and U. Bellugi, Harvard University Press, 1979.)

Morphology   American Sign Language has a rich morphological system that signals various grammatical distinctions. For instance, the distinction between first and second person is marked on a sign such as *ask*. When the utterance is in the first person (*ask me*), the movement of the sign is toward the signer, whereas when it is in the second person (*ask you*), the movement is away from the signer and toward the addressee. In addition to person, ASL marks number, aspect, and reciprocity (Poizner, Klima, & Bellugi, 1987). **Reciprocity** deals with the distinction between *they pinched them* and *they pinched each other*; that is, whether there is a subject that is the agent of the action and an object that is its **recipient** or whether there is mutual interchange between subject and object. In English, this distinction is made with pronouns. In ASL, there is a reciprocity morpheme on the verb so that *pinched each other* is conveyed by movement back and forth across the signer's body. Again, in all of these instances the marking of these distinctions is sequential in English and simultaneous in ASL.

Linguistic productivity   The property of embedding one sign into another also occurs in ASL (Poizner et al., 1987). Figure 2-5a shows the basic or uninflected sign for *give*. Figure 2-5b shows the durational form of the sign, which means to give on a continuous basis; c shows the exhaustive form, which means to give to each. It is then possible to combine both of these meanings into a single sign by embedding one into the other, as shown in d and e. Notice that these last two differ, just as *The woman knows the child thinks the man left* differs from *The child thinks the woman knows the man left*.

Phrase structure   As we have seen, English marks grammatical categories, such as subject and verb, via word order. American Sign Language sometimes does this as well; for example, with transitive verbs (verbs that require a direct object, such as *give*, *kiss*, and *tell*), the order in which the constituents are signed is subject-verb-object (SVO) (Poizner et al., 1987). Thus, ASL makes some use of temporal order.

American Sign Language also uses spatial processes to convey syntactic distinctions. For example, ASL marks nouns with a given location in space that is initially arbitrary but retained in subsequent references to the noun. Other nouns are given other unique locations. A sentence with the same signs in the same order will have different meanings if there are different spatial indices (Poizner et al., 1987). This system actually reduces some of the ambiguity in language. For example, consider the following sentence:

(19)   He said he hit him, and then he fell down.

This sentence is ambiguous in English, but since each pronoun has its own spatial index, it has a clear interpretation in ASL.

Significance of Sign Language

This introductory survey of ASL reveals some clear differences between ASL and spoken languages as well as some underlying similarities. This combination of

(a) GIVE (uninflected)

(b) GIVE [durational]
(give continuously)

(c) GIVE [exhaustive]
(give to each)

(d) GIVE [[exhaustive] durational]
(give to each, that action
recurring over time)

(e) GIVE [[durational] exhaustive]
(give continuously to each in turn)

(f) GIVE [[[durational] exhaustive] durational]
(give continuously to each in turn,
that action recurring over time)

Figure 2-5. Recursive nesting of morphological processes in ASL. (a) The uninflected sign *give*. (b, c) *Give* under single inflections. (d) One combination of inflections (exhaustive in durational). (e) Another combination of inflections (durational in exhaustive). (f) Recursive application of rules (durational in exhaustive in durational). (Based on *What the Hands Reveal About the Brain*, by H. Poizner, E. S. Klima, and U. Bellugi, MIT Press, 1987.)

properties makes it especially significant for several aspects of psycholinguistics. I will simply note here several issues that we shall consider in the coming chapters.

One is the topic of language production. Although speech is produced using the same channel as we use for breathing, ASL is independent of breathing. Sign production can occur entirely in parallel with, and unimpeded by, respiratory activity. Because some of the pauses we make during speech are for respiratory purposes and others are for cognitive and linguistic purposes, we might expect some interesting differences in the way signed and spoken languages are produced (see Chapter 8).

Another area of research that has benefited from the study of sign language is language acquisition. Since most deaf children have hearing parents who do not know ASL, many deaf children, unfortunately, are not exposed to a consistent language model in their early years. This provides some clues for understanding the role of the environment in language development (see Chapters 10 and 12).

Finally, the link between language and the brain could well be different in speech versus sign. It is commonplace these days to hear of differences between the two hemispheres of the brain, with the left being regarded as more verbal and the right as more skilled at spatial tasks. What then might be the neurological arrangement of a spatial language? (See Chapter 13.)

Summary

American Sign Language has its own set of grammatical rules and is a language that is independent of English. Our preliminary look at ASL indicates some striking similarities in its grammatical organization, suggesting that some of the basic concepts we have been discussing might be universal. At the same time, there are significant differences between ASL and English, and we will examine these further. Because the similarities and differences between ASL and spoken languages are so intriguing, we will return periodically to the study of ASL throughout this book.

Transformational Grammar

Transformational grammar was an influential theory of grammar formulated by Chomsky in the late 1950s (Chomsky, 1957, 1965). The theory inspired a considerable amount of psycholinguistic work in the 1960s and early 1970s. The significance of this linguistic and psycholinguistic work remains controversial. In this section, I will outline some of the major features of transformational grammar. An evaluation of the theory will be postponed until the last section of the chapter.

Language and Grammar

Before discussing transformational grammar, we need to understand the relationship between grammar and language a little more precisely. A **language** can be defined as an infinite set of well-formed sentences. As we have seen, there is no limit to the number of sentences in a language. A **grammar** is a formal device with a finite set of rules that generates the sentences in the language. This notion of generation is similar to the notion of deduction in mathematics or logic: we can deduce the sentences in a language by using the rules of the grammar. Grammars thus are theories of language, composed of more specific hypotheses about the structure or organization of some part of the language.

Evaluation of grammars   If a grammar is a theory of language, how do we evaluate how good a theory it is? Chomsky (see Greene, 1972, for a lucid discussion) has suggested three criteria. First, the grammar must specify what is and what is not an acceptable sequence in the language. This criterion is referred to as **observational adequacy,** and it applies at several levels of language. We know at the phonological level that *pbort* is not an acceptable sequence. Similarly, at the syntactic level we want the grammar to have rules that generate grammatical sentences without also generating strings of words we would regard as ungrammatical. A grammar is observationally adequate if it generates all of the acceptable sequences in a language and none of the unacceptable sequences.

The second criterion is that the grammar must specify the relationships between various sequences in the language, a criterion known as **descriptive adequacy.** It is not enough for the grammar to mark a sequence as permissible; it must also explain how it relates to other sentences that are similar in meaning, opposite in meaning, and so on. If, for example, two sentences are similar in meaning but differ in syntax, the grammar should be able to explain this fact.

The third criterion is called **explanatory adequacy.** Chomsky points out that it is theoretically possible for a number of grammars, all based on different principles, to attain these two forms of adequacy. How then does the linguist determine which of the descriptively adequate grammars is the best? Chomsky's answer pertains to language acquisition in children. He suggests that the child learning a language is presented with samples of the language and must determine the grammar from these samples. Chomsky notes, however, that even though the incoming data may be consistent with any number of grammars, children choose one particular grammar. This implies that certain innate language constraints enable the child to deduce the correct grammar. These innate language mechanisms would presumably be related to linguistic universals common to all languages. Thus, the final level of adequacy goes beyond the ability to describe patterns in a particular language; instead, it involves the ability to explain the role of linguistic universals in language acquisition.

These criteria have played a significant role in the development and evaluation of linguistic theories. In fact, Chomsky (1957) initially developed transformational grammar because of the descriptive inadequacy of a grammar based on phrase-structure rules. Let us now turn our attention to transformational grammar.

Deep and Surface Structure

A crucial insight into language is that sentences have more than one level of structure. In transformational grammar, this insight is captured in the distinction between deep structure and surface structure. These are both tree structures, differing in emphasis. **Deep structure** is the underlying structure of a sentence that conveys the meaning of a sentence. **Surface structure** refers to the superficial arrangement of constituents and is closer to how the sentence is actually pronounced. Three arguments can be made for the usefulness of this distinction. First, consider sentence (20):

> **(20)**   Flying planes can be dangerous.

This sentence is ambiguous, but not in the sense that the constituents may be grouped in more than one way, as in sentence (17). Here the ambiguity comes from the (optional) deletion of certain elements of the sentence (or, more precisely, the deep structure of the sentence). The sentence may be paraphrased roughly as *The act of flying planes can be dangerous* or *Planes that are flying can be dangerous.* This type of ambiguity, called **deep-structure ambiguity,** comes from a single surface structure that is derived from two distinct deep structures. It cannot be explained by phrase-structure rules.

A second reason for the distinction is that some pairs of sentences are similar in their phrase structure but not in their underlying structure. Consider, for example, sentences (21) and (22):

> **(21)**   John is easy to please.
> **(22)**   John is eager to please.

These sentences are apparently similar, but their paraphrases reveal their dissimilarity. We can explain this by observing that *John* is the object of the deep structure in (21) and the deep-structure subject in (22).

Third, other pairs are quite distinct in their surface arrangement but similar in their deep structure, such as the following sentences in **active** (23) and **passive voice** (24):

> **(23)**   Arlene played the tuba.
> **(24)**   The tuba was played by Arlene.

In this case, the active and passive sentences are considered two manifestations of the same deep structure.

Another way of putting these points is to say that a grammar that includes only one level of structure is not descriptively adequate. To fully capture these grammatical relationships, we need to posit a second level of structure, which in turn brings into play a new set of rules called transformational rules.

Transformational Rules

Within transformational grammar, the entire derivation of a sentence is a two-part process. First, phrase-structure rules are used to generate the underlying tree structure we have referred to as the deep structure. Second, a sequence of **transformational rules** (sometimes simply called **transformations**) is applied to the deep structure and the intermediate structures (those between the deep and surface structure), ultimately generating the surface structure of the sentence. Unlike phrase-structure rules, which apply to only one constituent at a time, transformations apply to entire strings of constituents. They transform them by adding, deleting, or moving constituents.

Let us look at a few transformations and see how they work. One is called the **particle-movement transformation.** We know that the following two sentences mean the same thing:

(25) John phoned up the woman.
(26) John phoned the woman up.

The concern is with the placement of the particle *up;* in these sentences, the particle may occur either just before or just after the noun phrase. Accordingly, we might write two different phrase-structure rules for the two instances, the first conforming to

(PS 10) VP ⟶ V + (part) + NP

and the second to

(PS 11) VP ⟶ V + NP + (part)

The problem with this approach is that it lacks descriptive adequacy: it does not reveal the similarity of the two sentences. In this approach, the two sentences are derived from different phrase-structure rules. An alternative approach is to assume that the two sentences have the same deep structure and to apply the particle-movement transformation to (25). The transformational rule looks like this:

(T1) V + part + NP ⟶ V + NP + part

Notice that the transformational rule simply moves the last two constituents of the verb phrase. Unlike phrase-structure rules that rewrite one constituent into a series of constituents, transformational rules begin with a series of constituents and transform them.

Consider now the following sentences:

(27) John phoned up the interesting woman.
(28) John phoned the interesting woman up.
(29) John phoned up the woman with the curly hair.
(30) John phoned the woman with the curly hair up.

Notice that in each case the particle is shifted around the entire NP — two words in (26), three in (28), and six in (30). The point is that the particle movement is defined in terms of constituents, not words. This condition gives transformational grammar tremendous power to apply to an infinite number of NPs. Instead of stating the rule in terms of the number of words, which will vary from sentence to sentence, we state it in terms of grammatical structures such as NPs. Because the movement is dependent upon the grammatical structure, rules such as this are said to be **structure-dependent.**

A second example is **passive transformation.** Simplified somewhat, the rule is as follows:

(T2)   NP 1 + V + NP 2 ⟶ NP 2 + *be* + V + *−en* + *by* + NP 1

This complex transformation, which might be involved in the derivation of sentences such as (24), contains several elementary operations. Let us begin with the active sentence (31) and then add the transformations needed to produce the passive sentence. First we invert subject and object, a transformation that produces (32). (Sequences that are not grammatically acceptable are, by convention, marked with an asterisk.) Then we insert the preposition *by* in (33). Finally, we add a form of the **auxiliary verb** *be* to (34):

(31)   Arlene played the tuba.
(32)   *The tuba played Arlene.
(33)   *The tuba played by Arlene.
(34)   The tuba was played by Arlene.

One final property of transformational rules deserves mention. These rules may be blocked under certain circumstances. For example, the particle-movement transformation does not work with pronouns:

(35)   John called them up.
(36)   *John called up them.

These restrictions on transformations would be specified in the description of the rule. The rule would operate under specified conditions but would be blocked when these conditions did not apply.

Summary

Transformational grammar assumes that sentences have a deep structure and a surface structure. The deep structure is derived by a series of phrase-structure rules, and the surface structure is derived from the deep structure by a series of transformational rules. Transformational grammar can explain certain aspects of language, such as deep-structure ambiguity, that cannot be accounted for entirely by phrase-structure rules.

Issues in Grammatical Theory

Much of what we have discussed to this point constitutes a consensus of current thinking about linguistic concepts. In addition, linguistics has a number of issues that are actively debated. We will discuss several of them in this section.

Psychological Reality of Grammar

As indicated earlier, much psycholinguistic research in the early and mid-1960s was based on transformational grammar. This research was guided by the belief that the structures and rules of transformational grammar were psychologically real; that is, that they were a part of how people comprehend and produce language.

One assumption that was made was that the surface structure was the starting point for comprehension and that the deep structure was the end point; the roles were assumed to be reversed for production. If so, then it would be reasonable to assume that the distance between surface and deep structure (as measured by the number of transformations in a sentence's derivation) would be an accurate index of the psychological complexity of the sentence. This view was called the **derivational theory of complexity,** or DTC.

Early studies were encouraging. A variety of studies showed that negative sentences such as

   (37)   The sun is not shining.

were more difficult to comprehend than the corresponding affirmative form such as

   (38)   The sun is shining.

But these sentences differ in meaning as well as transformational complexity, so this is hardly conclusive. Later studies directly contradicted DTC. Sentence (39) is, for example, transformationally more complex than (40):

   (39)   The boy was bitten.
   (40)   The boy was bitten by the wolf.

In transformational theory, (39) requires a transformation that deletes the phrase *by the wolf,* so DTC would predict it would be more difficult to comprehend than (40). However, neither intuition nor experiment has revealed any relationship to processing difficulty. Similarly, there is no psychological difference between sentences that have undergone particle-movement transformation and those that have not. These studies have been reviewed extensively elsewhere (Cairns & Cairns, 1976; Fodor, Bever, & Garrett, 1974; Slobin, 1971).

As Berwick and Weinberg (1983) point out, however, these results do not necessarily mean that the linguistic theory of transformational grammar is faulty. It could be that the linguistic theory is correct but that some of the psychological assumptions guiding DTC are faulty.

More recent work has been more favorable to the hypothesis that linguistic theory has psychological reality. Consider this sentence:

(41)   The nurse who was stationed on the seventh floor invited the chauffeur to go dancing this evening.

This sentence contains a **relative clause** (*who was stationed on the seventh floor*), which is a clause that begins with a *wh*-word and modifies a noun. Notice that the relative clause interrupts the flow of the sentence; in particular, it introduces a gap between the noun *nurse* and the verb *invited*.

According to recent grammatical theory, relative clauses result in the movement of the noun, thereby creating this gap. However, it is assumed that the moved constituent leaves a trace at its earlier location, so that the presumed linguistic representation of (41) would be more like (42):

(42)   The nurse who was stationed on the seventh floor [trace] invited the chauffeur to go dancing this evening.

If this proposal has psychological reality, then the hypothesis would be that comprehenders would be likely to reactivate the moved noun (*nurse*) when its trace was encountered. Osterhout and Swinney (1993) have provided evidence that comprehenders do this. Participants responded rapidly when words semantically related to the moved noun were presented in the trace position. It is as if they were thinking about *nurse*, which made it easier to respond to a semantically related word, such as *doctor*. Responses were slower either before or after the trace position.

A converging group of studies (see Zurif & Swinney, 1994) are suggesting that traces have psychological reality. I will leave the details for a later discussion (see Chapters 6 and 13). But, for now, the point is this: these studies have suggested that some psychologists may have overreacted to the problems with DTC. When we see a combination of the right linguistic theory and the right psychological experiment, better results are obtained.

Lexical versus Structural Approaches

There have long been controversies within linguistics regarding the proper way to characterize linguistic knowledge. As we have seen, phrase-structure rules are insufficient in themselves to account for our linguistic capacities, and these insufficiencies led Chomsky to propose transformational grammar.

In the years since transformational grammar was formulated, it has gone through a number of changes. In the most recent version, Chomsky has eliminated many of the transformational rules in previous versions of the grammar and replaced them with broader rules, such as a rule that moves one constituent from one location to another. It was just this kind of rule on which the trace studies were based. Although newer versions of the theory differ in several respects from the original, at a deeper level they share the idea that grammatical rules should be structure-dependent; that is, the rules apply to constituents rather than individual words. In a sense, transformational grammar (and its descendants) take the grammatical constituent as the most basic unit of analysis.

An alternative approach is supplied by lexical theories of grammar. In lexical theories (for example, Bresnan, 1978), greater emphasis is placed on individual lexical items (words) than is given in more structural theories. This view has been influential in recent years in diverse areas of psycholinguistics, including language comprehension, language production, and language development.

Let us go through an example to contrast structural and lexical views. In most grammars, the lexical entry for a word includes its meaning, its spelling, its pronunciation, and syntactic characteristics such as part of speech. In Bresnan's (1978) **lexical-functional grammar,** lexical entries also includes the various forms of the word (for example, *kiss, kissed, kissing*) and the different kinds of sentences into which each form would fit. For verbs, this includes the arguments or semantic roles, such as the **agent** (the person doing the action) and the **patient** (the one to whom the action is done) that are associated with the verb as well as the surface structure designation, such as subject or object, that goes with it.

Consider sentences (43) and (44):

(43) Mary kissed John.
(44) John was kissed by Mary.

The lexical entry for *kiss* would indicate its underlying semantic structure as

kiss: (agent, patient)

That is, the verb requires both an agent and a patient (**John kissed* is not a grammatical sentence). In addition, the entry includes various forms of the word, including

kiss: agent = subject, patient = object

and

(be) kiss: agent = object; patient = subject

The first verb form, used in sentences in the active voice, assigns the agent role to the surface-structure subject, and the patient to the surface object. The second form, used in passive sentences, assigns the patient to the subject, and the agent to the object of the preposition *by*.

By storing this additional information in the lexical entry, the derivation of passive sentences becomes shorter than in traditional transformational grammar. When the surface structure includes a form of the verb *kiss*, that lexical entry is retrieved and fitted into the sentence. The grammatical information in the entry allows us to interpret the sentence semantically (that is, to interpret *John* as patient). The constituent structure of a passive sentence in lexical-functional grammar looks like a passive sentence, not like an active sentence, and no passive transformational rule is involved. The meaning relation between these two sentences is preserved through lexical rules that specify the relation between different forms of a word, not by transformational rules.

The major significance of lexical-functional grammar is the shunting of most of the explanatory burden onto the lexicon and away from transformational rules. This makes a good deal of psychological sense. Cognitively speaking, the retrieval of items from our mental dictionary is relatively easy. In contrast, working our way through a syntactic structure is more difficult. By storing syntactic information in the lexical entry in the mental dictionary, lexical theories simplify the process of comprehending sentences. This seems to provide a potentially more plausible explanation for the nearly effortless manner in which we comprehend sentences in our everyday life.

Is Language Innate?

Another issue that has prompted considerable debate is the question of whether some of our linguistic capacities are innate. As noted in Chapter 1, two views emerge here. Nativists assert that children are born with some linguistic knowledge, and empiricists instead claim that children acquire language from linguistic experience.

At one level, it is obvious that experience plays a major role in language acquisition. We all learn the language to which we are exposed, not some other language from across the globe.

Some evidence in support of the nativist view has come from children with limited linguistic experience. In certain situations in which the child is not presented with any consistent linguistic model, they appear to have the capacity to invent some aspects of language. This has been seen in deaf children whose parents did not believe in or teach ASL (Goldin-Meadow, 1982). Despite the lack of either speech or sign, these deaf children invented a form of gestural language that was similar in some respects to ASL. They could not have acquired this system from their parents, since the children's facility with sign exceeded that of their parents. Bickerton (1983) presents similar conclusions based on studies of immigrants and their children.

What kinds of linguistic capacities might be inborn? Current thinking centers on the concept of parameters. A **parameter** is a grammatical feature that can be set to any of several values. For example, the **null-subject parameter** deals with whether a language permits constructions that have no subject. This parameter has two values: null subject (the language allows sentences without a subject) or subject (the language requires subjects for sentences to be grammatical). For example, sentence (45) is not grammatical in English, but it would be in Italian or Spanish. Thus, Italian is a null-subject language, and English is a subject language.

(45)   want more apples

Parameter-setting theorists (for example, Hyams, 1986), then, suggest that children are born with the parameters and with the values of the parameters. What they must learn, from experience, is which value is present in their native language.

A rough analogy is thinking of two restaurants. Restaurant A provides customers with a small array of choices within a few well-understood categories (that is, baked potato or fries or rice; French or Italian or ranch dressing). Restaurant B provides customers with a large number of choices within an equally large number of categories. Most dinnergoers would find Restaurant B informationally overwhelming; in contrast, it would be far easier to learn what choices to make in Restaurant A. The analogy is not perfect: we have acquired the categories in Restaurant A from experience, whereas the language parameters are presumed to be innate. Nonetheless, there is a fundamental similarity. Parameter-setting theorists would suggest that without built-in categories (and values), the child would be lost in a sea of linguistic details and would not be able to acquire a language as well as most children do.

Parameter-setting models appear to offer a tidy solution to the question of how innate processes interact with the child's language experience. Some scholars believe that the parameter-setting account is too tidy and have pointed flaws in the model (Bloom, 1990; Valian, 1990). Nonetheless, the approach has raised some important issues regarding the role of innate linguistic mechanisms in language acquisition. We will discuss these issues further in Chapter 12.

Summary

Several controversial issues in grammatical theory have been discussed. One is whether linguistic principles have psychological reality. Although research on transformational grammar in the 1960s suggested a negative answer, more recent research has reopened the question. A second issue is whether our grammatical knowledge is better described in structural or lexical terms. Finally, we have briefly considered whether our linguistic knowledge may be innate.

Review Questions

1. What is aspiration, and how is it related to the distinction between phones and phonemes?

2. What is wrong with a rule that states that a word cannot begin with two stop consonants?
3. Distinguish between free and bound morphemes.
4. How is duality of patterning represented in American Sign Language?
5. Why does American Sign Language interest psychologists?
6. Define grammar, and state its relation to language.
7. Distinguish between phrase-structure rules and transformational rules.
8. What is the current status of the derivational theory of complexity?
9. Describe how the study of traces relates to the issue of the psychological reality of grammar.
10. In lexical-functional grammar, what is the advantage of storing syntactic information in the lexical entries of words?

Thought Questions

1. Is productivity an attribute of human language, of the human mind generally, or of both?
2. The discussion of American Sign Language indicates that it is becoming progressively less iconic and more arbitrary. Speculate as to why this might be occurring.

Psychological Mechanisms

MAIN POINTS

- The acts of comprehending and producing language are performed within the constraints of our information processing system. This system consists of three structural components—sensory memory, working memory, and permanent memory—along with a set of control processes that govern the flow of information within the system.
- A number of issues regarding language processing have been raised. These include whether we primarily use serial or parallel processes, whether we tend to use top-down or bottom-up processes, whether language processes are primarily automatic or controlled, and the extent to which language processing displays modularity.
- Children appear to process information very differently than adults, but studies of the development of the processing system suggest that most of the system is developmentally invariant.

Introduction

The linguistic perspective sketched in Chapter 2 provides an important yet incomplete view of the psychology of language. This perspective places a strong emphasis on linguistic structures of various sorts, such as phrase structure, distinctive features, and morphological structure. To be sure, these ideas are advanced with the belief that a fuller understanding of human language will reveal deep insights into the human mind. The notion of productivity, to take but one example, is a property not only of language but of language users. This implies that the means to generate an unlimited number of sentences is present, in some form, in the human mind. It is clear that this perspective has enriched our knowledge of human cognitive functioning and will continue to do so.

At the same time, some important issues are not fully addressed in most linguistic accounts. Linguistic investigations have typically focused on what we have called the knowledge question: what kinds of knowledge underlie ordinary language usage? Relatively less attention has been paid to the process question of how this knowledge is utilized. That is, linguistic structure does not determine language processing. Given a particular phrase structure, there are still any number of ways we might comprehend or produce a sentence with that structure. More to the point, some of these ways might be preferred over others for purely psychological reasons: they might be easier or pose less burden on memory, and so on.

In this chapter, we will discuss the psychological mechanisms that are involved in using language. Together with the linguistic principles presented in Chapter 2, these mechanisms provide the basis for an integrated understanding of language use. Language processing is a joint product of linguistic principles and psychological mechanisms.

This chapter consists of three sections. The first presents an overview of the human information processing system. This provides a framework for understanding human cognition, whether it operates within the linguistic sphere or not. The second section applies these concepts more directly to language processing and examines a series of issues that arise in this context. The final section sketches the development of the processing system and examines the question of which portions of the system may be present at the time that most children acquire their native language.

The Information Processing System

A general model of information processing is shown in Figure 3-1. According to this interpretation of mental functioning, environmental information is successively encoded, stored, and retrieved by a set of distinct mental structures. The emphasis is on the flow of information through the system. Environmental stimuli—the constellation of sights, sounds, and other sensory events to which we are constantly exposed—are represented in each structure in a particular way. We assume that this system is used in a wide range of activities, including remembering lists of numbers, solving mathematical problems, and, of course, using language.

The model consists of three mental structures and a set of processes that move information from one structure to the next. Let us first examine each of these structures and then consider their interrelationships.

Sensory Stores

The **sensory stores** take in the variety of colors, tones, tastes, and smells that we experience each day and retain them, for a brief time, in a raw, unanalyzed form. It is assumed that we have one sensory store for each sensory system, although only the visual and auditory sensory stores have been studied in any detail.

The visual sensory store has been studied by Sperling (1960). He presented participants with arrays of letters or digits for very brief periods of time, such as 50 milliseconds (one-twentieth of a second). A typical array consisted of twelve

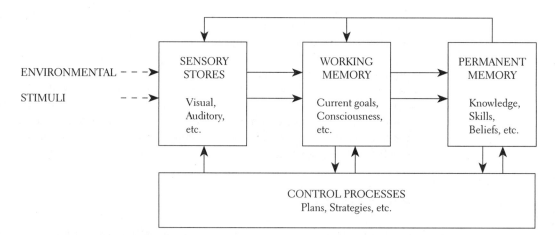

Figure 3-1. A general model of information processing.

letters in a 3 × 4 array (four columns and three rows). Participants saw these arrays briefly and then were asked to report what they saw. Typically participants could report only about 4 or 5 of the 12 letters. However, many reported subjectively that they could see all of the letters in the array but lost some of them by the time they had reported the others.

This finding provided a challenge for Sperling, for if participants did indeed retain all of the items for such a brief time, then the procedure of having them report all of the items (a procedure known as the whole report procedure) was likely to underestimate their retention. Sperling's response to this problem was ingenious. He devised a **partial report technique** in which the participants had to report only a portion of the entire array. Participants were presented with a high-pitched tone if they were to recall the top row of the array, a medium-pitched tone for the middle row, and a low-pitched tone for the bottom row. The tone was presented immediately after the array was removed. Sperling's reasoning was that if participants did not know which row they were to report, then they would have to retain the entire array for a brief time. The results were that respondents reported about three-fourths of the row under the partial report conditions, suggesting that they were able to retain about three-fourths of the entire array. Sperling concluded that a considerable amount of information in a stimulus array is available immediately after it is presented.

Further studies examined the duration of storage in the visual sensory store. This was done by delaying the presentation of the tone signal. When the tone was delayed for only 1 second, the performance in the partial report condition declined to 36%, which was approximately the level of performance in the whole report condition (Sperling, 1960). Sperling thus inferred that information in the visual sensory store persisted for approximately 1 second.

Comparable studies of the auditory sensory store (Darwin, Turvey, & Crowder, 1972) have found that the advantage of partial report over whole report persists for approximately 4 seconds. This difference might well be important in language processing. When we are processing language visually (typically in reading), we can always go back and reread, but this is not possible with speech. The relatively longer duration of the auditory store may enable us to reanalyze auditory messages that we did not understand initially.

As the first step in the information processing sequence, the sensory stores represent information in a literal, unanalyzed form. Most of the information in these stores disappears very rapidly because it is not germane to our current goals. But the processes of taking in new information, identifying it, and choosing whether to process it more extensively, although rapid, take a measurable amount of time. The sensory stores perform the invaluable function of preserving this information long enough for more extensive processing to be initiated.

Working Memory

The second type of memory has been traditionally referred to as **short-term memory** and more recently as **working memory.** Although the meanings of the terms are similar, there is a subtle difference between them. Let us begin with short-term memory and then examine the more current term.

The need for short-term storage is easy to state. The contents of the sensory stores are held for at most a few seconds, but many cognitive acts require that we hold onto information for longer periods. Many apparently simple acts, such as solving problems in your head, mentally retracing a path after losing your keys, and remembering the topic of a conversation after a distraction, are in fact a complex series of decisions. A temporary holding place is necessary for intermediate decisions.

Short-term memory is severely limited in size; it can hold approximately seven plus or minus two units of information. However, we can increase our retention by grouping individual pieces of information into larger units, a process known as **chunking.** We are all familiar with the observation that we can group an entire phone number into one memory unit, but research has shown that we are capable of far more impressive acts of chunking. Ericsson, Chase, and Faloon (1980) demonstrated that a college student of average intelligence with ordinary short-term memory ability could retain up to 80 random digits presented at a rate of one digit per second. The student, Steve Faloon, managed this phenomenal performance by practicing the method of chunking over a period of 20 months. He was an accomplished long-distance runner and was able to group sets of digits into running times that he was familiar with.

Working memory differs from short-term memory in that the term conveys a more dynamic view of memory processes. Whereas short-term memory has usually been viewed as a passive repository of information, working memory has both storage and processing functions. The storage functions are similar to those credited to short-term memory—we hold onto a limited amount of information for a limited time. The processing functions are related to the concept of processing capacity. **Processing capacity** refers to the total amount of cognitive resources we may devote to a task, which is assumed to be limited. When tasks are new or difficult, they require more processing capacity, thereby leaving less space available for the storage function.

An example will clarify these concepts. Suppose you are asked to multiply 8 by 4 in your head. This would no pose no problem. But if the numbers were 84 and 67, the task would be much more difficult. Part of your processing capacity would be devoted to performing the arithmetic operation of multiplying 4 by 7, and part of this capacity would be needed to retain the result in temporary storage while you then multiplied 8 by 7. Ultimately these two functions would be in conflict with one another, competing for the same limited pool of resources.

Permanent Memory

Permanent memory, which is also known as long-term memory, is a repository of our knowledge of the world. This includes general knowledge, such as the rules of grammar or arithmetic, along with personal experiences, such as memories of your childhood. Permanent memory holds all of the information we have retained from the past that is not currently active (that is, in working memory). These memories are used to interpret new experiences, and, in turn, the new events may later be added to this storehouse of information.

Tulving (1972) has distinguished between two types of permanent memory: semantic memory and episodic memory. **Semantic memory** refers to our organized knowledge of words, concepts, symbols, and objects. It includes such broad classes of information as motor skills (typing, swimming, bicycling), general knowledge (grammar, arithmetic), spatial knowledge (the typical layout of a house), and social skills (how to begin and end conversations, rules for self-disclosure). Semantic memory holds all of the information in permanent memory that is not tagged for a particular time or place. It holds the information that horses have four legs and a tail but not the memory of the last time you went horseback riding.

The latter event is held in your **episodic memory,** which holds traces of events that are specific to a time and place. This is the memory that we use to keep a record of our personal experiences. It thus varies from person to person and time to time (it is constantly updated), whereas semantic memory is relatively stable. Episodic memory includes such items as what you had for breakfast this morning, what you were doing when you learned of the *Challenger* tragedy, and where you got your first job.

Semantic and episodic memory interact in our processing of information. For example, the knowledge that Princess Diana died in a car crash will be stored in our semantic memory as part of our general knowledge, and our memory of how we learned about this event will be part of our episodic memory. Although not all of our semantic memory is derived from such episodes, much of it is a condensation of a number of experiences. We can often use an episodic trace to retrieve semantic information, as when we remember where a concept was presented on a page in a textbook and this memory helps us recall the concept itself. In other cases, we lose the episodic tags, and all that remains is the general, semantic information about the event.

Relevance for Language Processing

Now let's explore the application of these concepts to the problem of how we comprehend spoken language. In comprehension, we may assume that as we hear a sentence the sounds are first stored briefly in the auditory sensory store. The sounds are held there for about 2 to 4 seconds, which gives us more than enough time to recognize the auditory pattern. **Pattern recognition** occurs when information from one of the sensory stores is matched with information retrieved from permanent memory. To recognize speech sounds, we must identify some of the acoustic cues that are presented in the speech signal, such as the frequency of some of the sounds. At some point, after recognizing the sounds, we are able to organize them into syllables and eventually words, although it is not clear exactly how or when that happens.

As noted, working memory is only able to hold about seven units of information. This could simply be seven words, but since many sentences are longer than this, we need some way to deal immediately with more than seven words. One way we do this is to chunk the words into grammatical constituents such as noun and verb phrases, thereby reducing the storage burden to perhaps two or three constituents. The processing function of working memory is used to organize the words into the constituents.

Permanent memory plays several roles. Semantic memory contains information on the speech sounds and words that we retrieve during pattern recognition. And while this process is going on, we are also building up an episodic memory representation of the ongoing discourse. That is, once we complete the processing of a given sentence, we might extract the gist of it and store that in episodic memory. Permanent memory would also be involved in finding antecedents for expressions such as pronouns; this would involve holding some information from previous sentences in memory long enough to establish coreferences.

Throughout this discussion, I have indicated that some processing could take place or might occur in a given way. In truth, a great deal remains to be learned regarding exactly how language processing takes place. The information processing system presented in this section leaves as many questions unanswered as it answers. It is best thought of as a framework for exploring how language processing takes place by providing a vocabulary for framing the important questions.

Summary

The general strategies by which the human mind encodes, stores, and retrieves information can be described independently of language. Three mental structures (sensory stores, working memory, and permanent memory) and a set of control processes are general features of human cognitive functioning.

Incoming sensory information is held in a literal or unanalyzed state in our sensory stores while information from permanent memory is retrieved to recognize the incoming pattern. The identified information, if relevant to the current activity, is held temporarily in working memory. As new information enters working memory, some of the older information is reorganized into larger units, other information is lost, and still other information is sent to permanent memory. The resulting permanent memory trace has both episodic and semantic attributes.

These concepts provide a framework for understanding how language processing occurs. Although it is generally agreed that we encode, store, and retrieve linguistic information along the general lines sketched here, the specific processes have yet to be addressed. We now turn our attention to these processes in the next section.

Central Issues in Language Processing

In this section we examine several alternative ways in which linguistic information can be handled by the information processing system. After discussing each of these processes individually, we will apply them to an extended example of language processing.

Serial and Parallel Processing

If a group of processes takes place one at a time, it is called **serial processing.** If two or more of the processes take place simultaneously, it is called **parallel processing.** Serial models have been influential in the study of language and cognition over the past quarter century, in part because many of the models were based on the electronic computer, which tends to executive processes rapidly in a serial manner.

Suppose we wish to develop a model of language production. We could take as our starting point the idea that the speaker wishes to convey. The ending point would be the actual articulation of the idea. But what happens in between? A serial model would divide the process into stages: a stage might be devoted to developing the phrase structure of the sentence, another to retrieving the lexical items that are inserted into the structure, and still another to determining the correct pronunciation of these lexical items. The serial model would assume that these stages occur one at a time, with none overlapping (Fromkin, 1971). If, on the other hand, we assume a parallel model, all of these processes could take place at the same time (Dell, 1986). That is, we could be phonetically specifying one word while we search for the next word, or both of these processes could take place as we flesh out the syntactic structure.

Rumelhart, McClelland, and the PDP Research Group (1986; McClelland, Rumelhart, & the PDP Research Group, 1986) have presented a version of a parallel model that they call **parallel distributed processing** (PDP). This model views the mind as "massively parallel"—that is, as simultaneously processing a large amount of information.

Some language examples are shown in Figure 3-2. In the first instance, we interpret the middle letter as an *h* in one word but as an *a* in the other despite the fact that the letter is physically identical in the two cases. The remaining four examples show degraded letters, with features of one or more of the letters being obscured. It is not difficult to identify what the word is in each case. At first glance, this may appear to be paradoxical. It seems reasonable to say that we are using the context to help decide the identity of the obscured letter. However, that context is a word, and we normally think of first identifying the letters and then identifying the word. How can we use the word to help identify the letter? Rumelhart and McClelland suggest that the answer lies in parallel processing. Assume that we are identifying the individual letters and, at the same time, actively trying to fit the letters into various possible words. Some of the identified letters enable us to recognize the word as a familiar word, and then we identify the obscured letter from our knowledge of the spelling of the word. Thus, we are processing at the letter and word levels simultaneously.

Parallel distributed processing models have been described as neurally inspired because they use the brain, rather than the computer, as the dominant metaphor. There is a great deal of neural activity occurring throughout the brain at the same time. We know some properties of neural networks. We know that neurons can affect neighboring neurons in either an excitatory manner (causing the neighbor to become active, or "fire") or an inhibitory manner (reducing the likelihood of the neighbor firing). Rumelhart and McClelland theorized a cognitive model built along the same lines—a vast, interconnected network of information nodes with

Figure 3-2. Some ambiguous displays. Note that the second line shows that three ambiguous symbols can each constrain the identity of the others. Lines 3, 4, and 5 indicate that each of these characters is ambiguous and can assume other identities in other contexts. (Based on *Parallel Distributed Processing: Exploration in the Microstructure of Cognition: Vol. 1. Foundations*, by D. E. Rumelhart, J. L. McClelland, and the PDP Research Group, p. 8. MIT Press, 1986.)

each node influencing and being influenced by a large number of adjacent nodes. At present, PDPs are an important alternative to serial models.

Top-Down and Bottom-Up Processes

Suppose you are listening to a lecturer, trying to comprehend what is being said and remember the main points of the lecture. We can view your language processing as occurring on a set of levels. At the lowest, the phonological level, you are identifying the phonemes and syllables that the lecturer is using. At a higher level, the lexical level, you are using the identification of phonemes and syllables to retrieve the lexical entries of the words from your semantic memory. At the next level, the syntactic level, you are organizing the words into constituents and forming a phrase structure for the sentence. Finally, at the highest level, the discourse level, you are linking the meaning of a given sentence with preceding ones and organizing sentences into higher-order units.

We may now define **bottom-up processing** as that which proceeds from the lowest level to the highest level of processing in such a way that all of the lower levels of processing operate without influence from the higher levels. That is, the identification of phonemes is not affected by the lexical, syntactic, or discourse levels; the retrieval of words is not affected by syntactic or discourse levels; and so on. But, as we have already seen in Figure 3-2, we have some reason to doubt that a strict bottom-up model will provide a comprehensive account of how we understand language.

A **top-down processing** model, in contrast, states that information at the higher levels may influence processing at the lower levels. For instance, a sentence context may affect the identification of words within that sentence. Speaking more intuitively, we may say that a top-down model of processing is one in which one's expectations play a significant role. If you know where a lecturer is going—based on previous experience with the instructor or maybe even by reading the text in advance of the lecture—then you can generate some expectations regarding what the next point might be. If you are correct, then you are using the higher levels of processing to facilitate lower levels of processing.

I should hasten to add that not all top-down processing is facilitative. Sometimes the content or structure of a lecture clashes with our expectations. Under these circumstances, the expectations may actually interfere with learning new material. It might be better to abandon one's preconceptions and simply use a bottom-up approach.

The distinction between top-down and bottom-up processing is similar in some respects to the distinction between serial and parallel processes. In fact, a top-down process is often a parallel process and a bottom-up process is usually serial. But the distinctions are not synonymous; a top-down process is not necessarily parallel. Let us take lexical and syntactic processing as our example. Suppose we identified each word of a sentence and then began a tentative phrase structure of the words to that point, with the incomplete structure guiding our identification of subsequent words. We would, in effect, be cycling back and forth from lexical to syntactic levels. It would be a top-down process, but serial in nature.

Automatic and Controlled Processes

Earlier, when discussing working memory, I introduced the notion that we may have a fixed processing capacity for handling information. This has been a central assumption of a variety of accounts of human cognitive functioning. It is an important concept when considering human performance on complex tasks, such as language processing. When the task is complex, one part of the task may draw substantial resources from this limited pool of resources, thereby leaving insufficient resources for other parts and resulting in overall impaired performance.

Tasks that draw substantially from this limited pool of resources are called controlled tasks, and the processes involved in these tasks are referred to as **controlled processes.** Tasks that do not require substantial resources are called automatic tasks; processes that do not require extensive capacity are referred to as **automatic processes.**

Various criteria have been used to determine whether a task is automatic or controlled (Hasher & Zacks, 1979). These include sensitivity to developmental and strategy effects. Developmental effects refer to whether there are differences in performance due to the age of the individual. Strategy effects pertain to whether the adoption of a particular strategy influences performance on the task. Controlled tasks are more sensitive to these variables than automatic tasks. That is, automatic tasks appear to be unrelated to the age of the individual or to the strategy employed.

Certain automatic tasks appear to be biologically built into our cognitive equipment. We have, for example, an automatic process in which we are able to roughly estimate the frequency of an event (Hasher & Zacks, 1979). Most of us can correctly judge that red automobiles are more common than yellow ones. This "frequency counter" does not require conscious effort; it is simply a by-product of processing a stimulus in some way. Other tasks become automatic as a consequence of our degree of practice with them. Many of the tasks we perform automatically, such as tying our shoelaces, have been done thousands of times. They were more demanding when we were young and have become automatic through practice.

One language processing task that is automatic, at least for adults, is recognizing common words. This is undoubtedly due to our large amount of experience with words. In contrast, developing a phrase structure for a sentence is a more controlled process. Recognition of this distinction was a major factor in the development of lexical grammars, which were introduced in Chapter 2. Bresnan (1978) reasons that the process of working our way through a syntactic structure places heavy burdens on working memory, which has a fixed capacity. By comparison, the process of lexical retrieval is far easier. Thus, if grammatical information was stored in the lexicon, it would simplify overall language processing.

Modularity

Within cognitive psychology, the issue of **modularity** has two meanings. First, it pertains to the degree of independence of the language processing system, taken as a whole, from the general cognitive system we have sketched so far in this chapter. The modularity position is that the language processing system is a unique set of cognitive abilities that cannot be reduced to general principles of cognition. This is the position that Chomsky has taken in a number of writings (for example, Chomsky, 1975). The alternative position stresses the interconnections between language and cognitive processes by emphasizing the role of concepts such as working memory, automatic processing, and parallel processing in language comprehension, production, and acquisition.

Perhaps the best candidate for the status of a special language module is **speech perception.** As we shall see in greater detail in Chapter 4, there are certain properties of how we perceive speech that appear to be distinctive, or domain-specific. That is, they apply to the perception of speech but not to the perception of, say, music or art.

The notion that speech is modular is related but not identical to the argument that our language facility is biologically innate. Certainly one way to talk about modules is to talk about innate modules, but this is not a necessary property. A module is dedicated to performing one aspect of a complex task. Whether this assignment is biologically given or acquired through experience is a separate issue.

The second meaning of modularity is that linguistic subsystems, such as semantics and syntax, operate independently rather than interactively. For example, a modular view of how we comprehend sentences is that we apply syntactic principles first, then utilize semantic knowledge. The interactive position is that both semantics and syntax are used simultaneously.

An Example of Language Processing

We have discussed four distinctions that are relevant to language processing. Let us now consider a specific example and see how these distinctions might apply. Consider the following sentence (from Clark & Clark, 1977, p. 81):

(1)   I was afraid of Ali's powerful punch, especially since it had already laid out many tougher men who had bragged they could handle that much alcohol.

This is another example of a garden path sentence (see Chapter 1). The key word here is *punch*, which can mean either an alcoholic beverage or a boxing punch. The subjective impression for most people at the end of the sentence is having assumed the wrong meaning and then backtracking. If we were to flesh this out into a more complete processing model, it might look like this: when we encounter a word that has more than one meaning, we survey the immediate environment of the word, make a rapid decision as to the most appropriate meaning, and then stay with that meaning unless it becomes obvious that we are in error.

This model corresponds reasonably well with subjective impressions, but are these impressions accurate? The model assumes serial processing (one meaning at a time), with top-down processing playing only a limited role (decision is based on the immediate context, not the entire sentence). Because the emphasis is on decisions the comprehender must make during the course of comprehension, the model emphasizes controlled processes more than automatic processes. Finally, this approach can safely be described as nonmodular. It relies on our general ability to figure things out, not on a specialized capacity that is related to language; it might even be described as common sense.

We could, however, develop a completely contrasting model. We could begin with the assumption that people routinely and simultaneously activate more than one meaning of an ambiguous word from semantic memory. Moreover, we could assume that the retrieval of multiple meanings is a fixed property of the lexicon—that it is automatic, modular, and not related at all to the sentence context (that is, it is bottom-up).

Although the latter model may sound counterintuitive, some psychological evidence supports it. It does indeed appear that we automatically activate all of the meanings of an ambiguous word at least briefly (Foss, 1970). At the same time, it also appears that we decide among the choices rather quickly, perhaps within three or four words (Cairns & Kamerman, 1975). Thus, two stages of processing may exist: an automatic stage in which all meanings are retrieved and a more controlled stage that is more top-down in nature.

The notion that we might have two different ways of approaching a sentence with an ambiguous word is not limited to this one example. This state of affairs is the rule in human information processing, in which we nearly always have multiple ways of doing things and in which we generally employ the easiest, fastest, or most efficient strategy that will work.

Nor should it be entirely surprising that our subjective impression of this sentence may be a rather poor guide. One point that I have made a couple of times already but that perhaps bears repeating is that our knowledge of language is, for the most part, tacit rather than explicit. Considering the complexity of language and the sheer amount of information processing that is taking place in just a few seconds, it is sometimes a wonder that we have any conscious awareness of these processes at all. If we are to develop a solid knowledge of how language processing takes place, we will need to rely not on introspection but rather on systematic experimentation.

Summary

This section raises a number of issues regarding language processing. These include the distinctions between serial and parallel processing, top-down and bottom-up processing, and automatic and controlled processes, as well as modularity.

It should be clear that we have a number of ways of processing linguistic information. That is, language processing is not just determined by linguistic structure but jointly by that structure and by processing considerations that are independent of language. The manner in which our cognitive processing system interacts with linguistic structures is a central concern of much psycholinguistic research.

Development of the Processing System

As already noted, one of the main themes of psycholinguistics is how children acquire language. To understand language acquisition, it will be helpful to understand the cognitive abilities children bring to the task of acquiring their native language. In the present context, the primary question is to what extent the information processing system sketched in this chapter is operating during the first few years of life, when most normal children acquire language.

It is clear enough that children encode, store, and retrieve a great deal of linguistic information in their first few years. They are constantly being presented with new lexical items to remember. Grammatical rules such as the English past tense, with its many irregular forms, require children to commit many terms to memory. Children may come to understand productive grammatical rules by noticing patterns in different sentences, retaining them, and then organizing them into a single rule.

We may begin by assuming that the information processing system as we have discussed it in this chapter is, for the most part, developmentally invariant. I say "for the most part" because some components, by definition, must change. The episodic portion of permanent memory is a repository of one's experience and thus will clearly grow with experience. But, on the whole, we may tentatively assume that the sensory stores, working memory, and capacity limitations we have emphasized are present to the same extent in newborn infants as in mature adults.

This may seem an unlikely hypothesis, for we ordinarily think of children and especially infants as cognitively very different creatures than adults. Recent research, however, has suggested that children and adults have some important cognitive similarities.

Perceptual Processing

Although virtually no research has addressed the development of the sensory stores per se, there is a substantial literature on perceptual processing defined more broadly. The discussion here will be limited to vision and audition.

Prior to the early 1960s, it was generally believed that infants perceive the world in a disorganized or haphazard way. The view was captured memorably by William James (1890/1950): "The baby, assailed by eyes, ears, nose, skin, and entrails at once, feels it all as one great blooming, buzzing confusion" (p. 488). The research of Fantz (1963), however, indicates otherwise. Babies were shown various forms while observers recorded how long the infants looked at each one. The infants looked at some patterns more than others, which Fantz interpreted as meaning that the infants could distinguish among the forms and preferred some to others. Fantz found that young infants preferred patterns, such as faces or checkerboards, over plain stimuli.

The infants' preference for the human face has provoked a great deal of discussion and research. Infants like to look at human faces, but the interpretation of this observation is unclear. A large percentage of their eye fixations is toward certain high-contrast areas, such as the eyebrows or the hairline, so it is likely that the infant visual system is programmed to attend to high-contrast stimuli of various kinds, not just faces. It appears that infants are not able to respond to a face as a whole until they are about 4 months of age.

Just as the human face, for whatever reason, fascinates infants, so does the human voice. Infants are biologically prepared to distinguish between speech and other sounds. For instance, Condon and Sander (1974) have shown that infants make synchronized movements to individual speech sounds shortly after birth. These movements included raising a finger, kicking a leg, and so on. Frame-by-frame analysis of these movements indicated that they were synchronized with the syllables in the speech signal. Newborns displayed this synchrony with different languages but not with nonspeech sounds, such as the tapping of a pencil.

Eimas, Siqueland, Jusczyk, and Vigorito (1971) have found that infants make distinctions between different speech sounds very early in life. These researchers examined infant perception of the voicing contrast in English. For example, the vocal cords vibrate during the production of [ba] but only after the production of [pa]. More precisely, the sounds differ in the time between when the sound is released at the lips and when the vocal cords begin vibrating. With voiced sounds, the vibration occurs immediately; with voiceless sounds, it occurs after a short delay. This lag, which is called **voice onset time** (VOT), is an important cue in the perception of voicing.

If you were presented with a sound with a 0-millisecond (ms) VOT, you would always hear it as [ba], and if presented with a 40-ms VOT, you would hear it as [pa]. With a speech synthesizer, we can examine the way that people perceive the intermediate cases. Adult listeners hear the VOT differences up to + 25 as the voiced [ba] and values above that point as [pa].

Eimas and colleagues used a technique known as **habituation** to study infant responses to these stimuli. Habituation refers to the decline in a response to a stimulus following repeated presentation of the stimulus. The response studied is referred to as **nonnutritive sucking** and involves a special pacifier that is connected to a machine that measures the number of sucks an infant makes. When a stimulus with a VOT of + 20 ms ([ba]) was initially presented, the infant showed great interest and the sucking rate was high; but with repeated presentations, the sucking decreased. At this point, a new stimulus was presented. On some occasions it was a stimulus from the [ba] category (a VOT of + 0 ms), and other times it was from the [pa] category (a VOT of + 40 ms). The interesting result was that sucking returned briefly to a high level (a phenomenon referred to as **dishabituation**) if the new stimulus was from a different category, but not if the new stimulus was from the same category. Eimas and colleagues concluded that infants as young as 1 month are sensitive to the distinction between voiced and voiceless sounds.

Taken together, studies of perceptual processing by infants reveal infants to have rather sophisticated perceptual skills at or shortly after birth. These results suggest that infants are well equipped at birth to process linguistic stimuli.

Working Memory

A second aspect of the cognitive system that has been examined developmentally is short-term memory. A common test of short-term memory in grade school children is the simple memory span test: children are presented with a list of numbers and asked to recall them, sometimes in forward and sometimes in backward order. Significant differences are clearly apparent between older and younger children on this task (Dempster, 1981). In fact, the simple memory span test is a standard feature on intelligence tests for that very reason.

These results, however, do not tell us much about the development of working memory. Recall that working memory consists of both storage and processing functions, and these compete for limited resources. Thus, a developmental change in either of these functions would affect the other. In particular, if children become more efficient in processing numbers, fewer resources would be needed for that function, thereby leaving more resources available for storage. In this way, simple memory span might improve without any change in the total size of working memory.

A series of elegant experiments by Case, Kurland, and Goldberg (1982) has confirmed this analysis. In their first experiment, 3- to 6-year-olds were given a storage and a processing task. The storage task was a simple memory span task of remembering seven words. The processing task was a repetition task, in which the children had to repeat auditorily presented words. The investigators measured the time between the presentation of the word and the onset of the child's vocal response. The same words were used in both tasks. Case and colleagues found a negative correlation between the two tasks; as response time increased, memory span decreased. Older children remembered more words than younger children, but when their reaction time was taken into account, no differences were observed between the two age groups.

A second experiment presented adults with the same two tasks, using nonsense words. The use of nonsense words was significant because adults have no familiarity with them. Adult reaction time to the nonsense words was slow, comparable to the younger children's reaction time to real words. If memory span depends on processing speed, then adult recall of the nonsense words should also be similar to the younger children's recall of real words, and it was. The studies thus demonstrated that when adults are slowed down to children's speed of processing, memory span differences disappear.

Case and colleagues conclude that there is no substantial increase in overall working memory capacity with development, at least from 6 years to adulthood. Under this interpretation, simple memory span shows a functional increase in storage due to greater efficiency of processing. As we shall see in Chapter 11, this notion of developmental changes in processing efficiency is highly relevant to understanding early reading in children.

Sensorimotor Development

The information processing perspective introduced in this chapter is the primary organizational framework used throughout this book. An alternative perspective on cognitive development, one that challenges the notion of invariance, has been described by the Swiss scholar Jean Piaget, who constructed a theory of development over a research career that lasted well over 50 years. Piaget (1952) claimed that children's thinking processes are qualitatively different from those of adults. Adults do not merely think faster or more accurately than children, but in a different way. Piaget referred to the concepts that we use to organize our experience as **schemata.**

A well-documented example is **object permanence,** which refers to children's understanding that objects continue to exist even when they cannot be perceived. Very young infants (4 months or younger) operate on an "out of sight, out of mind" principle. When an attractive toy is taken from them and placed behind an adult's back, the infant may protest briefly but rapidly appears to forget completely about the object. When the object is reintroduced to the child, the infant is again joyous. Thus, the infant remains interested but does not search for the object because the infant, according to Piaget, does not know that the object still exists.

Object permanence develops in a series of stages. Children of about 8 months will actively search for the hidden object if it is only partially covered. Somewhat older infants will search for objects that are fully obscured. The final crowning achievement is the ability to handle invisible displacement tasks. In this task, the infant is shown a small attractive object, such as a key, which is then put into the adult's hand. The adult makes a fist, thereby taking the key out of view, and

Complex tasks such as riding a bicycle or using language involve a number of individual skills. It takes time to coordinate these components.

while still in a fist, the hand is placed under a blanket and the key deposited there. To find the object, the infant must be able to mentally imagine the invisible object being displaced from one location to another and then search the latter. Infants typically solve this problem between 18 and 24 months of age.

The acquisition of object permanence is not an isolated cognitive skill. At about his time, two related skills are emerging. One is **pretend play,** in which a child may use an object in a playful and unconventional manner (for example, using a toy rake to comb a doll's hair). The second skill is **deferred imitation,** in which the child imitates a behavior seen some time before. A famous example is from Piaget's daughter Jacqueline, who observed a tantrum in a playmate and then imitated it very closely a day later (Piaget, 1962). These two developments, along with object permanence, define the transition from the earliest period of development (in Piaget's theory, the **sensorimotor period**) to the second period, which Piaget called the **preoperational period.** These achievements indicate that the child is able to represent objects symbolically in the immediate environment. No longer at the mercy of immediate stimuli, infants can behave on the basis of past events or the products of their imagination.

Although these facts are well documented, Piaget's interpretation of them has not gone unchallenged. An alternative view of object permanence is that the infant knows that the object continues to exist but has forgotten where it is and therefore does not search for it. A study by Diamond (1985) supports this view. Diamond varied the amount of time between when the object was hidden from the infant and when the infant was allowed to begin searching for it. She found that infants' search behavior was affected by the delay. When they were allowed to search immediately, infants as young as 7½ months searched for an object in its correct location, whereas with a delay of only 2 seconds, infants searched the wrong place. These results suggest that at least some of the problems infants have with object permanence tasks stem from memory difficulties. As we have already seen, memory limitations may appear when a new task requires significant processing capacity. It may be that the novel task of searching for hidden objects places a demand on processing that leads to storage problems.

Put more generally, observed differences between children and adults on cognitive tasks may have more to do with the use of information processing resources than with qualitative shifts in thinking. The major change over time is an increase in efficiency, or a decrease in the amount of cognitive capacity required for a task. Increased efficiency enables a child to simultaneously do two or more tasks (or a complex task with two or more components). This is directly pertinent to language acquisition, for to acquire a language a child must ultimately perform correct analyses simultaneously on the phonological, semantic, syntactic, morphological, and pragmatic levels. A child of 3 may approach the task in a way that is similar to, but less efficient than, an adult. When working on new syntactic structures, a demanding task, the child may compensate by attending less to phonological specification. Perhaps only later, when the syntax comes a little easier, will the child be able to master both levels simultaneously.

*S*ummary

This section has explored research into the development of the information processing system. Young children and infants are inherently difficult to study, so we must be careful in drawing conclusions, but a number of clever studies have shown several cognitive similarities between young children and adults. Infants appear to be programmed to distinguish between speech and nonspeech and between different speech sounds. Memory differences occur from early childhood through adulthood on short-term memory tasks, but these appear to be related to **automaticity** rather than to increases in storage capacity per se. Increases in efficiency may result in a functional increase in storage capacity.

Piaget's view emphasizes qualitative changes in cognitive organization throughout development. But at least one of the major developments studied by Piaget, object permanence, can be interpreted as a failure in memory rather than a qualitative shift in thinking. Both the Piagetian and the information processing accounts of cognitive development have merit, and both have influenced studies of language acquisition. We shall pursue the connections between language and cognitive development more fully in Part 4.

Review Questions

1. What evidence indicates that we store more information in sensory memory than we are able to report?
2. Why might the duration of the auditory sensory store be longer than that of the visual sensory store?
3. How does working memory differ from short-term memory?
4. Distinguish between episodic memory and semantic memory.
5. Cite one piece of evidence that suggests some limitations of a purely serial model of language processing.
6. Identify one aspect of language processing that qualifies as being automatic.
7. Distinguish between two senses of the term *modular*.
8. What experimental evidence suggests that infants can perceive speech sounds?
9. What conclusions can be drawn from the study by Case and colleagues on the development of working memory?
10. Cite two explanations of the object permanence phenomenon.

Thought Questions

1. Does the existence of limits on human information processing imply the impossibility of a language that contains sentences whose length or complexity violates these limits? Are there psychological limits on the set of languages that could be used by human beings?
2. The text indicates that some language processing is done automatically. What factors might influence the extent of automatic processing?
3. The chapter provides two interpretations of object permanence. How might a study be designed to distinguish between these views?

Language Comprehension

4 *Perception of Language*

Introduction

The Structure of Speech

Prosodic Factors
Articulatory Phonetics
Acoustic Phonetics
Summary

Perception of Isolated Speech Segments

Levels of Speech Processing
Speech as a Modular System
The Motor Theory of Speech
  Perception
Summary

Perception of Continuous Speech

Prosodic Factors in Speech
  Recognition

Semantic and Syntactic Factors in
  Speech Perception
The TRACE Model of Speech
  Perception
Summary

Perception of Written Language

Different Writing Systems
Levels of Written Language
  Processing
Eye Movements During Reading
Perception of Letters in Isolation
Perception of Letters in Word
  Context
The Interaction Activation Model
Summary

Review Questions

Thought Questions

MAIN POINTS

- The study of speech sounds is called phonetics. Articulatory phonetics refers to the study of how speech sounds are produced. Acoustic phonetics refers to the study of the resulting speech sounds.
- Speech exhibits characteristics not found in other forms of auditory perception. The phenomenon of categorical perception suggests that speech is a special mode of perception.
- Perception of speech is influenced by the contexts in which it appears. We use top-down processing to identify some sounds in context.
- Visual perception of language is achieved through a succession of processing levels. Perception of letters in a word context is superior to perception of isolated or unrelated letters.
- Recent models of the perception of language assume that we process information at multiple levels in an interactive way. These models can account for several findings in speech perception and visual word perception.

Introduction

In this chapter and the three that follow, we will examine language comprehension at a number of levels. This chapter deals with the phonological level. Chapters 5, 6, and 7 present the lexical, syntactic, and discourse levels, respectively.

This analysis of language comprehension into four levels of processing is for convenience of exposition; it does not necessarily mean that we process language in a strictly serial manner. As you might have anticipated from our discussion in Chapter 3, the question of serial versus parallel processing has been a major interest of researchers studying the perception of language. We will return to this issue at several points during this chapter.

Another issue of importance is the relationship between comprehension of oral and written language. Obviously, the peripheral equipment is different, and, just as obviously, speech is temporal, whereas print is spatial. Nevertheless, we may ask whether fundamental similarities between listening and reading lurk beneath these surface differences.

This chapter is divided into four sections. The first considers the linguistic structure of speech. Next, we consider the way we identify different speech sounds when they are presented in isolation, followed by a discussion of the means by which we extract these individual sounds from the continuous stream of speech. The final section provides a selective overview of research on the perception of written language.

The Structure of Speech

The process of speech perception seems simple enough. Listeners must, in effect, categorize the sounds that they hear into one of the many classes of sounds that exist in their language. In fact, the task is an extraordinarily complex one, for two major reasons. First, the environmental context often interferes with the speech signal. Under normal listening conditions the speech we hear competes with other stimuli for our limited processing capacity. Other auditory signals, such as a conversation across the room or someone's sneezing or burping, can interfere with the fidelity of the speech signal. Moreover, visual signals often serve as sources of distraction.

Even if the environmental conditions are ideal, however, the perception of speech presents a second major problem: the variability of the speech signal itself. There is no one-to-one correspondence between the characteristics of the acoustic stimulus and the speech sound we hear. Several factors influence or distort the acoustic stimulus that reaches our ears. These include the voice of the speaker (that is, high versus low pitch), the rate at which the speaker is producing speech, and the phonetic context.

How, then, do we achieve stable phonetic perception when the acoustic stimulus competes with other stimuli and contains a good deal of inherent variability? The ease with which we recognize phonetic segments suggests that listeners make a series of adjustments in the course of perceptual recognition. As we will see, some of these adjustments are based on the implicit knowledge of the way speech sounds are produced.

Prosodic Factors

Let us begin our discussion of speech with **prosodic factors** such as stress, intonation, and rate. Prosodic factors influence the overall meaning of an utterance. That is, we can take a given word or utterance and change the stress or intonational pattern and create an entirely different meaning.

Stress refers to the emphasis given to syllables in a sentence. We use stress to distinguish between the noun and verb forms of various words, such as *project* and *pervert*, and between pairs such as *black bird* and *blackbird*. **Intonation** refers to the use of pitch to signify different meanings; the pitch pattern of a sentence is called its **intonational contour.** An example sometimes found in men's restrooms is "We aim to please. You aim too, please" (Fromkin & Rodman, 1974). Finally, **rate** refers to the speed at which speech is articulated. We modify our rate of speech by altering the number and length of pauses during utterances, as well as the amount of time articulating speech segments. The rate of speech sometimes conveys meaning. Consider how we would produce the sentence *Take your time* versus *We've got to get going!* (Bolinger, 1975).

Prosodic factors are sometimes called **suprasegmentals.** *Supra* means to be above something; these aspects of speech lie over speech segments (phones), providing a kind of musical accompaniment to speech. The same word or sentence may be expressed prosodically in different ways, and these variations become important cues to the speaker's meaning and emotional state. With prosodic variation in mind, let us now turn to the smaller speech segments on which prosodic factors are superimposed.

Articulatory Phonetics

The study of speech sounds is called **phonetics,** and the more specific study of the pronunciation of speech sounds is called **articulatory phonetics.** All of the sounds

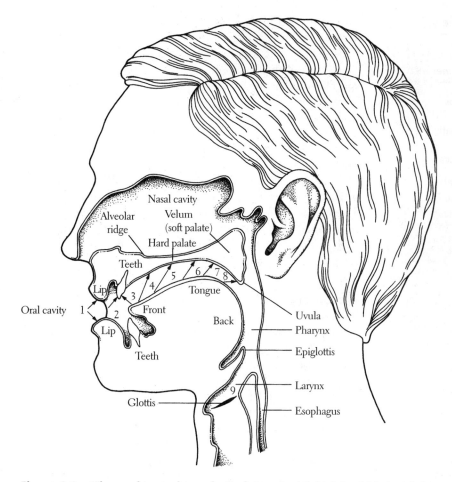

Figure 4-1.   The vocal tract: places of articulation: 1 = bilabial, 2 = labiodental, 3 = dental, 4 = alveolar, 5 = palatoalveolar, 6 = palatal, 7 = velar, 8 = uvular, and 9 = glottal. (Based on *An Introduction to Language,* by V. Fromkin and R. Rodman, p. 44, Holt, Rinehart & Winston, 1974.)

of a language can ultimately be described in terms of the movements of the physical structures of the vocal tract (see Figure 4-1). Air is emitted from the lungs and passes over the vocal cords and into the oral cavity or the nasal cavity. In some languages, speech sounds can be made by sucking in air instead of expelling it, but not in English.

Speech sounds differ principally in whether the airflow is obstructed and, if so, at what point and in what way. Although vowels are produced by letting air flow from the lungs in an unobstructed way, consonants are produced by impeding the airflow at some point.

Table 4-1. English consonants

Manner of Articulation		Bilabial	Labiodental	Dental	Alveolar	Palatal	Velar	Glottal
					Place of Articulation			
Stops	Voiceless	p (*p*at)			t (*t*ack)		k (*c*at)	
	Voiced	b (*b*at)			d (*d*ig)		g (*g*et)	
Fricatives	Voiceless		f (*f*at)	Θ (*th*in)	s (*s*at)	š (*f*ish)		h (*h*at)
	Voiced		v (*v*at)	ð (*th*en)	z (*z*ap)	ž (a*z*ure)		
Affricatives	Voiceless					č (*ch*urch)		
	Voiced					ǰ (*j*udge)		
Nasals		m (*m*at)			n (*n*at)		ŋ (si*ng*)	
Liquids					l (*l*ate)	r (*r*ate)		
Glides		w (*w*in)				y (*y*et)		

Source: From *Experimental Psycholinguistics: An Introduction,* edited by S. Glucksberg and J. H. Danks, p. 30. Copyright © 1975 by Lawrence Erlbaum Associates. Reprinted by permission.

Place of articulation   Some consonants, such as [b] and [p], are articulated at the lips and are called **bilabial** consonants. Others, such as [d] and [t], are formed by placing the tongue against the alveolar ridge; these are called **alveolar** consonants. Still others, such as [g] and [k], are produced in the back of the mouth; since the tongue is placed against the velum at the back of the mouth, these are called **velar** consonants.

Manner of articulation   Consonants also differ from one another in terms of the manner in which they are produced. **Stop** consonants obstruct the airflow completely for a period of time, then release it. All of the examples in the preceding paragraph are stop consonants. **Fricatives** are produced by obstructing without completely stopping the airflow, as in [f] or [s]. The passage in the mouth through which air must travel becomes more narrow, and this narrowing causes some turbulence. Another type of consonant, the **affricate,** is produced by a stoplike closure followed by the slow release characteristic of fricatives. The first sounds in *church* (phonetically represented as [č]) and *judge* ([ǰ]) are affricates.

Voicing   A final distinction among consonants concerns whether the vocal cords are together or separated when the lung air travels over them. The opening between the vocal cords is called the **glottis.** If the cords are together, the airstream must force its way through the glottis, causing the vocal cords to vibrate. The resulting sound is called a **voiced** speech sound, as in [b]. If the cords are separated, the air is not obstructed at all, and the sound is called a **voiceless** sound, as in [p]. These characteristics of English consonants are summarized in Table 4-1, which shows the place of articulation, manner of articulation, and voicing characteristics of these and other English consonants.

Table 4-2 shows a similar chart of English vowels. Vowels are distinguished from one another chiefly by whether they are produced in the front, center, or back of the mouth, and whether the tongue position is high, middle, or low. As with the

Table 4-2.   English vowels

	Front	Center	Back
High	i (b<u>ee</u>t)		u (b<u>oo</u>t)
	I (b<u>i</u>t)		U (b<u>oo</u>k)
Middle		ɚ' (b<u>ir</u>d)	o (b<u>o</u>de)
	e (b<u>a</u>by)		
		ə (sof<u>a</u>)	
	ɛ (b<u>e</u>t)		ɔ (b<u>ou</u>ght)
	æ (b<u>a</u>t)	ʌ (b<u>u</u>t)	
Low			
			a (p<u>a</u>lm)

Source: From *Experimental Psycholinguistics: An Introduction,* edited by S. Glucksberg and J. H. Danks, p. 32. Copyright © 1975 by Lawrence Erlbaum Associates. Reprinted by permission.

consonants, we can best appreciate these phonetic distinctions by practicing these sounds and comparing the positions of the articulators, particularly the tongue. Notice that with the front vowels [i], [I], [e], and [æ], the front part of the tongue becomes progressively lower. With [u], [o], and [a], it is the back of the tongue that changes position.

This description of speech sounds in terms of the details of their articulation suggests that it might be possible to describe the entire inventory of phonetic segments by constituent features based on their mode of production. As we discussed in Chapter 2, Jakobson, Fant, and Halle (1969) devised a system of distinctive features in which each segment is defined in terms of the presence or absence of various elementary features such as voiced/voiceless or nasal/oral, which refers to whether sounds are produced with a lowered velum, which directs the airflow to the nasal cavity. The utility of distinctive features is that they allow us to describe the relationships that exist among various speech sounds in an economical manner.

Acoustic Phonetics

One practical application of understanding the way people process speech signals is in devising reading machines for the blind. Applied research along this line (see Liberman, 1982) has proved to be unexpectedly difficult. In the 1940s and 1950s, research was beginning to identify the relationships between the acoustic properties of the speech signal and the perceptual experience of the listener, and it was thought that the application of this knowledge to reading machines was just around the corner. It has turned out, however, that although it is possible to convert visual information into speech signals intelligibly enough to be of some value to the blind, the result does not sound like speech. That is, taking an individual letter, attaching the sound that goes with the letter, and then putting it together with other sounds in the sentence can be done, but it does not sound much like natural speech.

It appears that an implicit assumption underlying this early speech research—that there was a parallel between phonetic segments and letters of the alphabet—was largely invalid and that we process speech differently from letters of the alphabet. One indication of this is the sheer speed with which we perceive language. It has been estimated that we can encode up to 25 to 30 phonetic segments per second while listening to speech (Liberman, 1970), a rate that far surpasses that of other forms of auditory perception. For example, if we were to hear a series of recognizable sounds (say, a tone, a buzzer, a click, and a siren), we would hear an indistinct blur if they were played at a rate approaching that of conversational speech.

Some clues as to how we perceive speech segments so rapidly may be found in the acoustic structure of the speech signal. The examination of these acoustic properties of speech sounds is called **acoustic phonetics.**

Spectrograms　One of the most common ways of describing the acoustical energy of speech sounds is called a **sound spectrogram.** It is produced by presenting a sample of speech to a device known as a **sound spectrograph,** which consists of a set of filters that analyze the sound and then project it onto a moving belt of phosphor, producing the spectrogram. Some typical spectrograms are shown in Figure 4-2. The frequency of the speech sounds is represented on the vertical axis, the time on the horizontal axis, and the intensity in terms of the darkness of the spectrogram at various locations. Each of the spectrograms contains a series of dark bands, called **formants,** at various frequency levels. These appear horizontally on the spectrogram, with the first formant being the one with the lowest frequency and higher formants being roughly parallel. In *tool,* the first formant is about 1000 hertz (Hz) or cycles per second, the second roughly 2000 Hz, and the third 3000 Hz.

Two aspects of formants have been found to be important in speech perception. **Formant transitions** are the large rises or drops in formant frequency that occur over short durations of time. In *card,* the first formant is rising and the second one falling in frequency near the end of the word. These transitions nearly always occur either at the beginning or the end of a syllable. In between is the formant's **steady state,** during which formant frequency is relatively stable. It is a bit oversimplified but basically correct to say that the transitions correspond to the consonantal portion of the syllable, and the steady state to the vowel.

Parallel transmission　We are now in a position to examine some of the acoustic properties of the speech signal. One, called **parallel transmission,** refers to the fact that different phonemes of the same syllable are encoded into the speech signal simultaneously. There is no sharp physical break between adjacent sounds in a syllable. The [t] in *tool* runs into the [u], which runs into the [l]. We hear three distinct phones, but inspection of the spectrograms reveals that they are not physically distinct in the speech signal.

Context-conditioned variation　A related characteristic, **context-conditioned variation,** describes the phenomenon that the exact spectrographic appearance of a given phone is related to (or conditioned by) the speech context. The clearest example is

Figure 4-2.   Typical speech spectrograms. (From P. D. Denes and F. N. Pinson, *The Speech Chain*, p. 121. Baltimore: Bell Telephone Laboratories, 1963.)

the way that the spectrogram of a consonant is conditioned by the following vowel. This is shown in Figure 4-3 for the simplified spectrograms for [di] and [du]. (They are simplified in that although they are sufficient to produce a sound that most people would be able to identify, they leave out other natural characteristics of

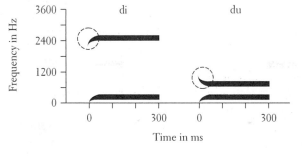

Figure 4-3. Simplified spectrographic patterns sufficient to produce the syllables [di] and [du]. (From "The Grammars of Speech and Language," by A. M. Liberman, 1970, *Cognitive Psychology*, 1, p. 107. Copyright © 1970 by Academic Press. Reprinted by permission.)

speech.) In Figure 4-3, both the formant frequency and the formant transitions vary with the subsequent vowel context. In [di], the second formant is approximately 2400 Hz with a sharply rising transition. In [du], the frequency is near 1200 Hz with a falling transition. Nevertheless, we hear both as [d]. This phenomenon, along with parallel transmission, suggests that we do not process speech sounds one at a time. It appears that the information for each phonetic segment is spread throughout the syllable.

Context-conditioned variation is closely related to the manner in which syllables are produced, or the **manner of articulation.** The [d] sound is produced by constricting the airflow by placing the tongue at the roof of the mouth or alveolar ridge. The [u] sound is made with the back of the tongue near the top of the mouth and with the lips rounded. The [i] is produced with the tip of the tongue near the roof of the mouth and with spread lips. We can conceive of the process of producing sounds as one in which the vocal tract "aims" at a series of articulatory targets, while the actual site of articulation varies somewhat with the speech context. That is, the exact manner in which [d] is produced varies with the following vowel. The phenomenon of producing more than one speech sound at a given time is called **coarticulation;** it reveals the important point that production, like the physical signal that results from it, tends to vary with the phonetic context.

Prosodic factors add to the variability of the speech signal in that they alter the acoustic cues that listeners use to identify speech segments. For instance, Miller (1981) has documented the acoustic consequences of speaking rate. As we speed up our speaking rate, vowel duration is reduced, and the duration of cues that signal various consonants is also modified. The frication noise found in fricatives and affricates is reduced, and the onset of vocal cord vibration that distinguishes voiced from voiceless consonants is also altered. Later in the chapter, we will consider how listeners take prosodic factors such as rate of speech into account when identifying speech segments.

Despite all of this variation in phonetic cues, human beings (even very young ones, as we saw in Chapter 3) can easily identify a string of speech sounds. Not so for computers. Despite considerable research over a number of decades, programs designed to recognize speech sounds have made only limited progress. It is true that some companies have automated answering systems that respond effectively to speakers' voices. But these systems are based on restricted vocabularies and require slower and more carefully enunciated speech than we commonly use in everyday speech. If a system must recognize a larger number of words, it has to be trained in the voices of individual speakers. As Pinker (1994) puts it, the best program is no match for even a mediocre stenographer.

Speech is really quite complex, and the fact that we recognize sounds effortlessly should not encourage us to think otherwise. In the next section of the chapter, we will look at research directed at understanding this impressive accomplishment.

Summary

Speech may be described in terms of the articulatory movements needed to produce a speech sound and the acoustic properties of the sound. Vowels differ from consonants in that the airflow from the lungs is not obstructed during production; consonants differ from one another in terms of the manner and place of the obstruction, as well as the presence or absence of vocal cord vibration during articulation.

The acoustic structure of speech sounds is revealed by spectrographic analyses of formants, their steady states, and formant transitions. The spectrographic pattern associated with a consonant is influenced by its vowel context and is induced by the coarticulated manner in which syllables are produced. Moreover, prosodic factors such as stress, intonation, and speech rate also contribute to the variability inherent in the speech signal.

Perception of Isolated Speech Segments

Levels of Speech Processing

We may roughly distinguish the process of speech perception into three levels (Studdert-Kennedy, 1976). At the **auditory level,** the signal is represented in terms of its frequency, intensity, and temporal attributes (as, for example, shown on a spectrogram), as with any auditory stimulus. At the **phonetic level,** we identify individual phones by a combination of acoustic cues, such as formant transitions. At the **phonological level,** the phonetic segment is converted into a phoneme, and phonological rules are applied to the sound sequence. These levels may be construed as successive discriminations that we apply to the speech signal. We first discriminate auditory signals from other sensory signals and determine that the stimulus is something that we have heard. Then we identify the peculiar properties that qualify it as speech, only later recognizing it as the meaningful speech of a particular language.

Some work has been done on the phonological level of processing (see Day, cited in Clark & Clark, 1977); however, most interest has focused on the similarities and differences between speech and nonspeech perception, and hence on the auditory and phonetic levels of processing. A controversial issue in the study of speech perception is whether and to what extent general principles of auditory perception can explain what we have learned about speech perception.

Speech as a Modular System

As we saw in Chapter 3, the concept of modularity is an important concept in contemporary cognitive psychology. Some criteria for modularity have been advanced by Fodor (1983). A cognitive system is modular if it (1) is domain specific (that is, if it is dedicated to speech processing but not, let us say, to vision), (2) operates on a mandatory basis, (3) is fast, and (4) is unaffected by feedback. These are merely some of the most basic criteria; Fodor discusses several others.

Why is the question of modularity important? The main reason is that it is related to the question of the organization of the brain for language, which is, in turn, related to questions concerning language development and language disorders. If speech is a modular system, then we might expect it to have a specialized neurological representation. This representation would not be based on general cognitive functioning (that is, working memory, episodic memory, and so on) but would be specific to language (or, possibly, specific to phonetic processing). This module might be the basis for the perception of language in young infants and, if damaged, the reason that certain individuals suffer quite specific breakdowns in language functioning.

The problem of invariance   We have already seen, from the phenomenon of context-conditioned variation, that the relationship between acoustic stimulus and perceptual experience is complex in the case of speech. The fact that there is no one-to-one correspondence between acoustic cues and perceptual events has been termed the **problem of invariance.** This is a significant problem, for if there are no invariant cues for phonetic segments, how is the listener to determine these sounds and thereby reconstruct the speaker's intended message? According to researchers at Haskins Laboratory in New Haven, Connecticut (Liberman, 1970; Liberman, Cooper, Shankweiler, & Studdert-Kennedy, 1967; Mattingly, Liberman, Syrdal, & Halwes, 1971), the lack of such an invariant relationship suggests that the perception of speech segments must occur through a process that is different from and presumably more complex than that of "ordinary" auditory perception. In other words, speech is a special mode of perception.

Before going on, we should bear in mind that context dependence applies to some but certainly not all of the acoustic cues for speech sounds. In fact, the relative preponderance of invariant and context-dependent cues is a matter that has generated considerable research (see Blumstein & Stevens, 1979; Cole & Scott, 1974). It appears that speech percepts are based on both invariant and context-conditioned cues. As an example, Cole and Scott (1974) point out that the **nasal** consonants [m] and [n] are distinguished from other consonants by a single bar of low-frequency energy along with a complete lack of high-frequency energy; these characteristics appear to be distinctive in various vowel contexts. However, to distinguish between

[m] and [n], vowel information (that is, formant transitions) is needed. Thus, it appears that earlier reports may have exaggerated the extent of, if not the problems caused by, variability in the acoustic stimulus.

Categorical perception   A number of experimental findings have been advanced to support the view that speech is perceptually special, but the one that has received the most attention has been the phenomenon of **categorical perception.** Thus, we will look in some detail at what it is, the procedures used to demonstrate it, and its implications for the modularity theme.

Ordinarily when we perceive objects or events in our world, we are capable of making some fine discriminations between one color and another, one odor and another, and so on. Moreover, this discriminative capacity is largely continuous in the sense that we can perceive a series of quantitative changes in stimuli lying on a continuum, such as tones of varying degrees of intensity. The task of the listener in speech perception is different. To comprehend speech, we must impose an absolute or categorical identification on the incoming speech signal rather than simply a relative determination of the various physical characteristics of the signal. That is, our job is to identify whether a sound is a [p] or a [b], not whether the frequency or the intensity is relatively high or low. Certainly, such auditory cues such as frequency and intensity will play a role, but ultimately the result of speech perception is the identification of a stimulus as belonging to one or another category of speech sounds.

Categorical perception refers to a failure to discriminate speech sounds any better than you can identify them. This may be illustrated with an experimental example. On a speech spectrogram it is possible to identify the difference between the voiced sound [ba] and the voiceless sound [pa] as due to the time between when the sound is released at the lips and when the vocal cords begin vibrating. With voiced sounds, the vibration occurs immediately; however, with voiceless sounds it occurs after a short delay; this lag, the voice onset time (VOT), is an important cue in the perception of the voicing feature.

As we noted in Chapter 3, if we were presented with a sound with a 0-millisecond (ms) VOT, we would always hear it as [ba]; if we heard a sound with a 40-ms VOT, we would hear it as [pa]. With a speech synthesizer, we can examine the way that people perceive the intermediate cases. If synthesized sounds varying in VOT are constructed and people are asked to identify what they have heard, the results are clear-cut. As VOT varies continuously, the perception changes abruptly from one consonant to the other. We hear the sound as either [ba] or [pa], and the dividing line between the two is quite sharp indeed.

The second part of the experiment is to perform a discrimination task. Subjects are given three stimuli, with the third one matching one of the first two. The subjects' task is to indicate whether the final sound matches the first or the second one. When the two sounds are taken from two different sound categories, performance is excellent on this task, but when the two sounds are taken from the same phonetic category, performance drops to chance level (Figure 4-4). Thus, two criteria determine categorical perception: the presence of sharp identification functions and the failure to discriminate between sounds within a given sound class.

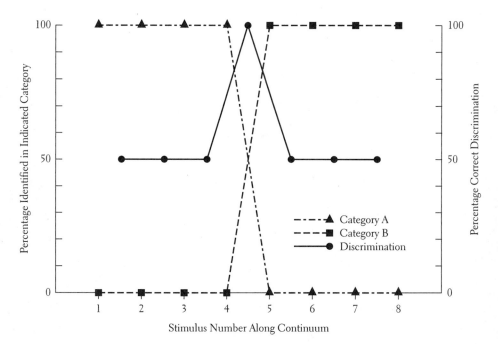

Figure 4-4. Idealized form of categorical perception showing identification performance for two categories and discrimination performance between categories. (From "Motor Theory of Speech Perception: A Reply to Lane's Critical Review," by M. Studdert-Kennedy, A. M. Liberman, K. S. Harris, and F. S. Cooper, 1970, *Psychological Review*, 77, pp. 234–249. Copyright © 1970 American Psychological Association. Reprinted by permission.)

Subsequent research has examined whether the phenomenon holds for other kinds of stimuli as well or only for speech. Mattingly et al. (1971) have investigated which aspects of the speech signal might be sufficient to produce categorical perception. They constructed synthesized speech syllables containing the first two formants and formant transitions along with synthesized nonspeech sounds. One nonspeech sound was based only on the second formant transition; another was based on the second formant transition plus steady state. The former sounds like "chirps" of differing pitch. The authors refer to the latter as "bleats" (Figure 4-5). The experiment consisted of the usual procedure for categorical perception, done with synthesized syllables, chirps, and bleats, along with backward versions of all sounds. The researchers found there was categorical perception for the synthesized syllables but not for the chirps, bleats, or backward sounds. Thus, subjects were unable to distinguish one chirp or bleat from another. These results show that formant transitions (especially the second formant transition) provide important information for producing the special mode of speech perception.

Studies of the perception of vowels contrast sharply with those of consonants (see, for example, Fry, Abramson, Eimas, & Liberman, 1962) since vowel perception is continuous and noncategorical, of the type typically associated with nonspeech stimuli. These results have been attributed to some basic differences between

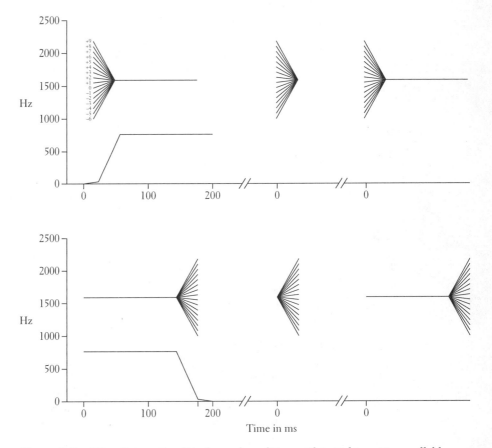

Figure 4-5. Stimuli: top, stimuli in forward condition, with initial transitions; syllables (left), chirps (center), bleats (right); bottom, similar stimuli in backward version, with final transitions. (From "Discrimination in Speech and Nonspeech Modes," by I. G. Mattingly, A. M. Liberman, A. K. Syrdal, and T. Halwes, 1971, *Cognitive Psychology, 2,* p. 135. Copyright © 1971 Academic Press. Reprinted by permission.)

consonants and vowels (Studdert-Kennedy, 1974). Recall that the steady-state portion of a formant, which contains most of the cues for vowels, is much longer than the formant transitions that are so important in the perception of consonants. It has been argued that the transient nature of the stimulus cues for consonants forces listeners to impose a categorical identity on these stimuli more rapidly than for vowels. Thus, after the stimulus has been identified, the acoustic cues that led to that identification are lost, and only the coded stimulus remains. This relationship implies that vowels are processed more at the auditory level than consonants, because of their relatively longer duration. Moreover, it suggests that categorical perception is a reflection of the phonetic level of processing in which a phonetic identity is imposed and all other acoustic features are lost (thus leading to especially poor performance on within-category discrimination tests).

The role of memory in categorical perception has been investigated by Pisoni (1973). Pisoni varied the delay interval (from 0 to 2 seconds) in a simple same/ different task involving vowel and stop consonant continua. The delay interval had relatively little effect for consonants but significantly impaired the within-category performance for vowels. Pisoni argues on the basis of these and related results that the relatively strong discrimination performance within categories for vowels was due not to the absence of a conversion to a phonetic mode but to the greater longevity of the auditory mode for vowels. Studdert-Kennedy (1975) summarizes these results nicely:

> Stop consonants are indeed perceived differently than vowels. For while the vowel, carrier of stress, rhythm, and prosody, leaves a rapidly fading "echo," the consonant leaves none. The initial sound of [da], for example, is difficult if not impossible to hear: the sound escapes us and we perceive the event, almost instantly, as phonetic. (p. 12)

Attentional processes   Categorical perception is not the only evidence for the modularity of speech perception. Rand (1974) performed an experiment in which a formant transition was presented to one ear and its steady-state portion was presented to the other ear. Although neither of these stimuli was speech, Rand reported that listeners could "integrate" these two signals into a meaningful speech signal.

The intriguing feature of this procedure is that it enables researchers to identify the characteristics of the signals coming into the two ears separately and to examine the process by which listeners integrate them into a speech sound. Figure 4-6 shows the normal **binaural perception** procedure: presenting the base (steady states plus first and second formant transitions) and the third formant transitions together to both ears. In the **duplex perception** procedure, the base is presented to one ear and the third formant transition to the other. Mann, Madden, Russell, and Liberman (1981) found that different discrimination performances could be obtained simply by instructing the listener to attend to the chirp or to the integrated speech sound. When attention was directed to the speech, categorical-like performance was found (sharp discrimination peaks at category boundaries). However, the discrimination performance was flat when attention was directed to the nonspeech chirp. Moreover, the presentation of a vowel context influenced only the speech side of the dichotic signal.

These results suggest that the distinction between speech and nonspeech modes is clear but that the conditions necessary to obtain the phonetic mode involve the deployment of attention and not just the presence of certain acoustic cues. Listeners are perfectly capable of directing their attention to the nonspeech qualities of the stimulus. Nonetheless, when they direct their attention to the speech qualities, distinctive results are obtained.

·A related phenomenon is the relative equivalence of various cues in the perception of speech. It has been known for some time that our perception of consonants is aided by a number of cues present in the speech signal. For example, the detection of [p] in *split* versus *slit* depends in part on the VOT but also on the second formant transition. Fitch, Halwes, Erickson, and Liberman (1980) exam-

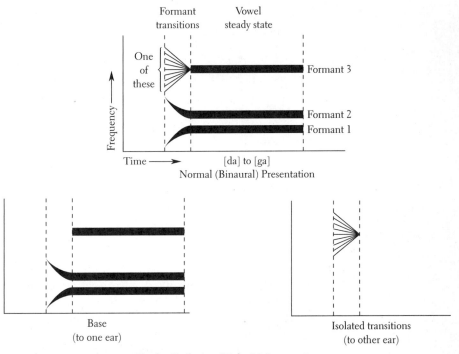

Formant transitions / Vowel steady state

One of these

Formant 3

Formant 2
Formant 1

Frequency

Time ⟶   [da] to [ga]

Normal (Binaural) Presentation

Base
(to one ear)

Isolated transitions
(to other ear)

Duplex-Producing (Dichotic) Presentation

Figure 4-6.   Materials used in the Mann et al. (1981) experiment. (From "On Finding That Speech Is Special," by A. M. Liberman, *American Psychologist*, 37, p. 153. Copyright © 1982 American Psychological Association. Reprinted by permission.)

ined the role of these two cues by trading them off: the relative value of one cue was changed in one direction while the other cue was changed in the opposite direction. Thus, researchers can determine how much of one cue is needed to obtain the same effect as the other cue. They found that the role of formant transitions is accomplished by approximately 20 milliseconds of silence following the release of the [p].

The main point, however, is that these trading relations are sensitive to the listener's deployment of attention. In particular, it has been found that these relations only exist when the stimuli are perceived as speech (Best, Morrongiello, & Robson, 1981). When, as before, the synthetic stimuli may be perceived as either speech or nonspeech, the distinctively **phonetic trading relations** hold for the speech mode only.

The Motor Theory of Speech Perception

Shortly after the initial discovery of categorical perception (Liberman, Harris, Hoffman, & Griffith, 1957), Liberman and his colleagues developed a theory of speech perception based on the notion that perception proceeds "by reference" to production (Liberman et al., 1967). The notion is that listeners use implicit articulatory knowledge—knowledge about how sounds are produced—as an aid in perception. To some extent, this approach is motivated by the economy of using the same mechanisms for both perception and production. But the main rationale for the motor theory is that it deals effectively with the problem of invariance discussed earlier. Liberman and colleagues (1967) argue that although the relationship between acoustic structure and perception is quite complex, the link between articulation and perception is more direct: sounds produced in similar ways but with varying acoustic representations are perceived in similar ways.

There does appear to be a link between perception and production. Students taking foreign language classes are often encouraged to practice articulating new sounds as a means of hearing them better. Anecdotal evidence suggests that teaching students to produce sounds silently aids them in the identification of new sounds (Catford, Jusczyk, Klatt, Liberman, Remez, & Stevens, 1991). As Catford et al. point out, this activity might encourage new learners to attend to subtle motor processes that would otherwise be overshadowed by auditory sensations.

There is also some experimental evidence for the theory. Studies of the role of visual information in speech perception suggest that we may use articulatory knowledge during speech perception. McGurk and MacDonald (1976) showed that when visual information and auditory information are in conflict, perceivers use both sources of information to arrive at a stable perception. When the speaker's lips indicate the velar consonant [ga] while the synchronized speech is the bilabial stop [ba], perceivers report hearing [da], an alveolar stop that retains some of the phonetic features of the other two sounds. In a subsequent study, MacDonald and McGurk (1978) demonstrated that place of articulation (especially the lips) is cued primarily by eye and that manner of articulation is cued more by ear. These reports indicate that listeners use information about the way a sound was produced from both auditory and visual modes in the process of speech perception.

Liberman and Mattingly (1985) updated the motor theory with regard to current thinking in cognitive psychology. In the revised theory, the claim is that the objects of speech are the intended phonetic gestures of the speaker. Phonetic gestures include such movements as rounding of the lips, raising of the jaw, and so on. By "intended phonetic gestures," Liberman and Mattingly are referring to invariant motor commands sent from the brain to the structures in the vocal tract. According to this revised theory, the conversion from acoustic signal to intended phonetic gesture is done rapidly and automatically by a phonetic module.

The motor theory is not without its critics. MacNeilage (1991) has suggested that the concept of phonetic gesture is too abstract and that, consequently, the motor theory is not directly testable. Liberman and Mattingly (1985) acknowledge that these neural commands do not result in invariant configurations of the vocal tract. Because of context-conditioned variation, the actual configurations vary with the phonetic context.

Despite these problems, the motor theory remains interesting, more than 30 years after its initial formulation, because it contains some far-reaching implications about language. In particular, the theory makes some testable claims about the brain mechanisms underlying language. Generally, it has been held that the areas responsible for language perception and production are distinct and separate. The motor theory would expect a closer neurological link between these functions. Ojemann (1983) provides some support for the idea that the perception and production areas of the brain are closely related and, thus, indirectly for the motor theory. (We will discuss the brain mechanisms responsible for language in Chapter 13.)

In addition, the theory has some interesting implications regarding language acquisition. Recall from Chapter 3 that infants can hear certain phonetic distinctions well before they are able to produce them. If the phonetic mode of perception depends on a link between perception and production, as the motor theory presumes, then the link might also be present shortly after birth. Liberman and Mattingly (1985) speculate that infants in their first year may be sensitive to the acoustic consequences of all language gestures significant in *any* language and only over time narrow down to their own language. If so, the phonetic module, which links these perceptual and productive skills, may be an important innate mechanism in the acquisition of language. (We will discuss language acquisition processes more fully in Chapter 12.)

On balance, then, the motor theory has been a useful theory. Beyond its specific contributions to our understanding of speech perception, it provides links with related aspects of language in ways that suggest a more comprehensive view of language.

Summary

Speech may be processed at the auditory, phonetic, or phonological levels of processing. The auditory level is characteristic of the way all sounds are perceived, whereas the phonetic level is assumed to be specific to speech, and the phonological level specific to a particular language.

Various investigators have argued that speech is perceived through a special mode of perception. Part of the argument rests on the failure to find invariant relationships between acoustic properties and perceptual experiences, and part is supported by the empirical phenomena of categorical perception, duplex perception, and phonetic trading relations.

The motor theory of speech perception claims that we perceive speech sounds by identifying the intended phonetic gestures that may produce the sounds. Although the status of the concept of phonetic gestures is somewhat controversial, the theory has been supported by studies of visual processing during speech perception. In addition, the theory has implications for neurolinguistics and language acquisition in children.

Perception of Continuous Speech

Until now we have dealt with the convenient fiction of the speech sound in isolation. Under normal listening conditions, however, speech sounds are embedded in a context of fluent speech. Since we know that the acoustic structure of a speech sound varies with its immediate phonetic context, it seems likely that broader aspects of context, such as adjacent syllables and clauses, may play a significant role in our identification of speech.

This point was demonstrated by Pollack and Pickett (1964), who recorded the conversations of women who were waiting to participate in a psychology experiment in a soundproof room. Individual words were spliced out of these tape-recorded conversations and presented individually to a separate group of subjects. Although the words were perfectly intelligible in the context of fluent speech, only about one-half of the words were correctly identified when presented in isolation. Thus, acoustic information may be insufficient by itself to permit identification of speech sounds; we may need to appreciate the context in which a speech sound is uttered in order to interpret it correctly.

This context consists of many factors, but only the two main factors will be discussed here. First, we will examine the role of prosodic factors in speech perception. Next, we will consider the role of higher-order semantic and syntactic factors.

Prosodic Factors in Speech Recognition

There is little doubt that prosodic factors such as stress, intonation, and rate influence the perception of speech. They provide a source of stability in perception since we can often hear these superimposed qualities at a distance that would tax our ability to identify individual speech segments. For instance, we can detect the moods of persons talking down the hall from the intonational contours of their speech but still not be able to identify what they are saying. Similarly, other prosodic factors, such as speech rate or tempo, are relatively easy to detect. The sheer availability of prosodic information suggests that it probably plays some role in the identification of segmental information. Let us look at two cases of the way prosodic and segmental information interact: stress and rate.

Stress   It appears that we perceive stress by a combination of acoustic cues along with our knowledge of the stress rules of the language (Lieberman, 1965). One of the main acoustic cues to stress, in addition to pitch and duration, is the intensity of the sound. We distinguish between the two meanings of *blackbird*, for example, by detecting the relative loudness of the first and second syllables. In addition to loudness, the rate at which the syllables are produced can influence perceived stress. Bolinger and Gerstman (1957) demonstrated that a brief pause between the /t/ and /h/ in *light house keeper* can change the perceived stress. Without the pause, the primary stress was heard on *light*, secondary on *keeper*, and tertiary on *house* (that is, a keeper of lighthouses). When the pause was introduced, the primary stress was shared by *light* and *house*, with *keeper* having secondary stress (a housekeeper who does light housekeeping).

Martin (1972) has argued that the stress pattern of speech provides cues for listeners to anticipate what is coming next and that listeners tend to organize their perception around stressed syllables. An experimental demonstration of this point was provided by Shields, McHugh, and Martin (1974). They presented speech passages to listeners who had to detect the presence of a particular speech segment, such as [b]. The researchers found that the detection rates were faster with stressed syllables than with unstressed syllables, but this occurred only for speech. When the same words were embedded in a list of nonsense words, the difference between stressed and unstressed syllables did not appear. This point suggests that we tend to interpret continuous speech in terms of stress patterns.

Rate   Speakers modify their rates of production by the number and length of pauses during utterances, as well as by the amount of time spent articulating the utterance (Grosjean & Lane, 1981). Miller (1981) has documented the acoustic consequences of changes in speaking rates. As we speed up, vowel duration is reduced, and the duration of the cues that signal various consonantal distinctions is also modified.

As we have seen, VOT is an important cue for voiced versus voiceless stop consonants. Short VOTs are associated with voiced sounds; longer VOTs are found with voiceless sounds. These VOT values, however, are sensitive to the rate at which the words are spoken. As the speech rate increases, VOT values tend to decrease (Summerfield, 1974, cited in Miller, 1981). Consequently, VOT values do not serve as invariant cues for voicing but are, like most of the cues we have examined, context dependent.

Summerfield (1975, cited in Miller, 1981) has demonstrated that when a target syllable is preceded by a precursor syllable articulated at a slow, normal, or fast rate of speech, listeners hear the consonant target syllable as different sounds. With faster rates, the perceived boundary between voiced and voiceless sounds shifted toward smaller VOT values. With [g] and [k], for instance, a sound that would be perceived as [g] with a normal rate of speaking would be perceived as [k] with a faster rate. Exactly the opposite occurred with slower rates.

This process of taking information about speech rate into consideration when identifying individual speech segments is referred to as **rate normalization** and has been demonstrated for a number of phonetic distinctions (see Miller, 1981, for a review). Listeners appear to operate under the assumption that the acoustic cues for various sounds must be adjusted to what is known about the circumstances under which the sounds are produced. The rate of production is one case. Another is the size of the vocal tract of the speaker, which also influences the exact values of various acoustic cues. Evidence indicates that listeners use the pitch of the speech signal as a cue for vocal tract size and make perceptual adjustments on this basis, too (Diehl, Souther, & Convis, 1980). This is called **speaker normalization.** Both types of normalization are consistent with the earlier conclusion that implicit articulatory knowledge may aid in the perception of speech.

Semantic and Syntactic Factors in Speech Perception

Context and speech recognition   As we have seen, a word isolated from its context becomes less intelligible (Pollack & Pickett, 1964). It follows that if we vary semantic and syntactic aspects of this context, then we should find changes in the perceptibility of the speech passage.

The role of higher-order contextual factors in speech recognition has been convincingly demonstrated by George Miller and his associates. Miller, Heise, and Lichten (1951) presented words either in isolation or in five-word sentences in the presence of white noise (hissing sound). Performance was better in the sentence condition at all levels of noise. Apparently, listeners were able to use the syntactic and semantic constraints of continuous speech to limit the number of possibilities to consider. Further research (Miller & Isard, 1963) isolated the influence of syntactic and semantic information in this process. In this study, three different types of sentences were presented in continuous speech: (1) grammatical strings, (2) anomalous strings that preserved grammatical word order, and (3) ungrammatical strings:

(1) Accidents kill motorists on the highways.

(2) Accidents carry honey between the house.

(3) Around accidents country honey the shoot.

The results indicated that people were most accurate with grammatical strings, somewhat less accurate with anomalous strings, and even less able to recognize ungrammatical strings. It would appear that the more predictable a passage is, the better it is recognized.

These results are consistent with our discussion of top-down processing in Chapter 3. Top-down processing proceeds from the semantic level of processing to the sensory levels. Thus, our knowledge of the general organization of the input enables us to predict some of the sensory features that are to follow. Top-down processing of continuous speech seems most likely when the speech context is semantically reasonable and familiar to the listener.

Phonemic restoration   A most dramatic demonstration of the role of top-down processing of speech signals comes from what is called **phonemic restoration** (Warren, 1970; Warren & Warren, 1970). The first /s/ in the word *legislatures* in sentence (4) was removed and replaced with a cough:

(4) The state governors met with their respective legislatures convening in the capital city.

This procedure led to a striking auditory illusion: listeners reported hearing the excised /s/! In addition, when told that a sound was missing and asked to guess which one, nearly all listeners were unsuccessful. Restoration has also been found in a variation of the procedure in which a noise is added to but does not replace the speech sound (Samuel, 1981).

Subsequent studies have shown that it is the context that helps determine how phonemic restorations take place. When Warren and Warren (1970) presented the following four sentences to listeners, they found that the restorations that were made were related to the subsequent context: **eel* was heard as *wheel, heel, peel,* or *meal,* depending on the sentence.

(5)   It was found that the *eel was on the axle.

(6)   It was found that the *eel was on the shoe.

(7)   It was found that the *eel was on the orange.

(8)   It was found that the *eel was on the table.

Phonemic restoration is closely related to the fact that we normally listen to speech when lots of other events are taking place: people are knocking things over, other conversations are taking place, the television is on, and so on. Many segments of the speech signal are impossible to identify in isolation because of masking from other sounds, indistinct or mumbled production, and related factors, yet we are generally able to achieve perceptual recognition by actively using higher-order contextual factors. Phonemic restoration is a particularly dramatic demonstration of top-down processing since it shows that the perception may occur in the complete absence of bottom-up information. In most situations, however, the two forms of processing interact. We will now look at several instances of this interaction.

Mispronunciation detection   What happens when a perfectly ordinary sentence contains a minor phonetic error? For example, if you heard sentence (9), would you have noticed that the first phoneme in the fourth word has been mispronounced? (You might try reading it aloud to a friend.)

(9)   It has been zuggested that students be required to preregister.

Our subjective impression is that minor errors in pronunciation tend to be ignored, as we "know" what the person was trying to say. Still, some mispronounced sounds do get detected. Cole (1973) found that the likelihood of detection depends on the place in a word or sentence. Detection performance was better for mispronunciations at the beginning of a word compared with those later in a word, and better earlier in a sentence than later on.

Marslen-Wilson and Welsh (1978) extended these results by combining the **mispronunciation detection** task with a shadowing task. A **shadowing task** is one in which subjects have to repeat immediately what they hear. Marslen-Wilson and Welsh examined the conditions under which listeners would repeat a mispronounced sound exactly, as opposed to restoring the "intended" pronunciation. They found that restorations were associated with greater fluency than were exact repetitions; in particular, less pausing was observed for restorations. Moreover, restorations tended to occur when the context was highly predictable, but reproductions were more likely with low levels of contextual predictability.

It is as if when we "know" what a person is going to say, we barely listen for the actual words and need only check for broad agreement of sounds with expectations. In contrast, when uncertainty is higher, we are less likely to have a firm basis on which to make these restorations. Moreover, the fluent nature of the restorations suggests that semantic and syntactic constraints are naturally integrated with incoming speech during language processing. These are not "guesses" but rather are heard, like phonemic restorations, just as clearly as if they were really there. Our immediate awareness thus seems to be a combination of an analysis of incoming sounds with an application of semantic and syntactic constraints.

The interactive nature of the perceptual process is revealed in another aspect of Marslen-Wilson and Welsh's study. They examined the relative proportion of restorations in cases in which the target ("intended") phoneme and presented phoneme differed in one, two, or three distinctive features. The percentage of restorations was far higher (74%) when only one feature differentiated target and presented phoneme than when three features differentiated them (24%). So bottom-up processing plays a role here, too. Even if the context strongly implies that a word is appropriate, if the expected phoneme is not sufficiently similar to the presented one on phonetic grounds, restoration is not likely to occur. Under these conditions, listeners are prone to pause, as if to make these comparisons, then repeat the presented word.

The TRACE Model of Speech Perception

Much of our discussion so far in this chapter may be summed up with reference to the **TRACE model** of speech perception presented by McClelland and Elman (1986; Elman & McClelland, 1988). The TRACE model challenges the assumptions, found in the modularity view, that phonemic processing is unaffected by higher levels of processing. In contrast, it assumes that several levels of processing—distinctive features, phonemes, and words—are simultaneously active during speech perception and interact with each other.

Let us look at the TRACE model more closely. McClelland and Elman (1986) assume that there is a cognitive unit for each feature (for example, nasality) at the feature level, for each phoneme at the phoneme level, and for each word at the word level. At any given time, all of these units are activated to a greater or lesser extent, as opposed to being all or none. When units are activated above a certain threshold, they may influence other units at the same or different levels. These effects may be either excitatory or inhibitory; that is, they may increase or decrease the activation of other units. The entire network of units is referred to as the trace, because "the pattern of activation left by a spoken input is a trace of the analysis of the input at each of the three processing levels" (McClelland & Elman, 1986, pp. 66–67). The network is active and changes with subsequent input.

McClelland and Elman (1986) claim that the TRACE model can explain most of the facts about speech perception we have considered, including categorical perception, trading relations, top-down processing, and coarticulation effects. Let us look at coarticulation. Consider the terms *foolish capes* and *Christmas capes*. The word *foolish* ends with the /š/ sound, which is made at the front of the mouth. In contrast, the final sound in *Christmas* is /s/, which is made by shortening the lips and thus the vocal tract as a whole. These articulatory differences influence the perception of the initial phoneme of the subsequent word (Mann & Repp, 1981). If the first phoneme of the next word were ambiguous, for example, between a /t/ and a /k/, listeners heard it as /t/ when preceded by /š/ but as /k/ when following /s/.

Elman and McClelland (1988) found that similar coarticulation effects occurred even when the final phoneme of the initial word was not present. They presented listeners with pairs of words such as *fooliX capes* and *ChristmaX capes*, in which X represented an ambiguous sound. Once again, the first phoneme of the second word was ambiguous, and the word could be heard as *capes* or *tapes*. Elman and McClelland found coarticulation effects similar to those found by Mann and Repp (1981) despite the fact that the /š/ and /s/ phonemes were not present. They concluded that they found evidence of top-down processing in phonemic processing and that activation of word units influenced phonemic units.

The TRACE model seems to provide a good account of many facts about speech perception. Still, it is likely that both interactive and modular approaches will play a role in a complete account of language processing. This is because there may well be limits on the kinds of interaction among levels that take place. For instance, Connine (1987; Connine & Clifton, 1987) found that the sentence level did not influence the perception of phonemes, although the word level did. Future research seems likely to uncover the limits as well as the promises of interactive models.

Summary

Contextual information powerfully influences the perception of individual speech segments. Prosody is used to organize incoming speech and to adjust acoustic cues to various speech sounds. Phonemic restoration and mispronunciation data suggest that higher levels of processing may influence the perception of phonemes. Our perception of speech segments in continuous speech appears to be an interaction of various levels of analysis that proceed simultaneously in the course of language processing.

Perception of Written Language

In this section we examine the early stages of visual language processing during reading. Reading, clearly, is a multifaceted and complex process, and we cannot do full justice to this complexity here. Rather, our approach will be selective in attempting to identify points of similarity and difference with the early stages of auditory language processing. Visual processing of larger units of language, such as sentences and discourse, will be treated in subsequent chapters.

Different Writing Systems

An **orthography** is a method of mapping the sounds of a language onto a set of written symbols. Languages differ in their orthographies, but three main types may be distinguished. A **logography** takes the word or morpheme as the linguistic unit and pairs the unit with some pictorial symbol, called the logograph or character. Chinese is the best-known example of a logography. Chinese characters are composed of individual strokes, with the most frequent characters usually consisting of

Figure 4-7.   Radicals as components of characters. The radical that can also exist on its own, meaning "mouth," is on the left. It occurs in different locations of other characters in different relative sizes depending on the complexity and configuration of the rest of the characters. The four characters, starting second from the left, mean "sentence," "to call," "to cry," and "to chew," respectively. (From *Psycholinguistic Implications for Linguistic Relativity*, by R. Hoosain, p. 10. Copyright © 1991 Lawrence Erlbaum Associates. Reprinted by permission.)

about six strokes (Hoosain, 1991). Characters contain information regarding both meaning and pronunciation. In general, strokes related to meaning, referred to as the **radical,** are on the top or left of the character, whereas information pertaining to sound is on the bottom or right. Radicals may exist on their own or as parts of characters (see Figure 4-7).

A **syllabary** takes the syllable as the linguistic unit and associates it with some visual representation. If English were written syllabically, the word *macaroni* would be represented by four symbols, one for each syllable: *ma, ca, ro,* and *ni.* Modern Japanese mixes logographic characters borrowed from Chinese (called **kanji**) with syllabic symbols (called **kana**). Kanji are used for content words or closed-class words and kana for function words, particles, inflectional endings, as well as foreign loanwords (Shibatani, 1987).

Finally, the **alphabet** is a system in which each letter is supposed to represent a phoneme. Any schoolchild knows that there are many exceptions to a one-to-one association between phonemes and letters (or **graphemes,** as they are sometimes called). Some words such as *know* contain silent letters, and so forth.

It is thought that the evolution of linear writing systems began with logographies and then moved to syllabaries and finally to alphabets (Rozin & Gleitman, 1977). Using smaller linguistic units offers both advantages and disadvantages. In general, the logography is more transparent in meaning, since the words or morphemes, by definition, have meaning. It is easier to grasp the connection between the word *horse* and a picture of a horse than between a set of five arbitrary alphabetic characters and such a picture. On the other hand, the alphabet involves much less memorization than the other systems, since there are only a few dozen graphemes to learn. In contrast, a logography must represent all of the words or morphemes in the language and thus includes a great number of logographs. It has been suggested that the corresponding strengths and weaknesses of the different systems be utilized in teaching children to read alphabetically (Rozin & Gleitman, 1977). That is, it is possible to teach children that there is a systematic relationship between sounds and written symbols by the use of logographies and syllabaries, then move to the more demanding alphabetic principles once this relationship has been understood.

Returning to the perception of written language in adults, the point to remember is that the English alphabet is but one of many alternative orthographies. Most of the research we will consider is based on English, and we will only occasionally be able to point to relevant work on other languages. Thus, further work will be needed to determine whether the conclusions generalize to languages with different writing systems.

Levels of Written Language Processing

As with speech perception, the perception of written language (at least in an alphabetic orthography) can be understood at a number of levels. We may distinguish among feature, letter, and word levels of processing.

At the **feature level,** the stimulus is represented in terms of the physical features that comprise a letter of the alphabet. For instance, the letter *K* may be represented as a vertical line and two diagonal lines; *R* may be coded as a vertical line, a diagonal line, and a curved portion, and so on. At the **letter level,** the visual stimulus is represented more abstractly as an identity separate from its physical manifestation. That is, a stimulus may be represented as an *F* regardless of whether it is typewritten or handwritten. Finally, there is a **word level** of processing, in which an array of features and letters is recognized as a familiar word. As the word is recognized, various properties of the word, such as its spelling, pronunciation, and meaning, become available to us.

These distinctions raise several important questions concerning the perception of written language. First, how do we go about extracting these elements of the written word? Is there any evidence that we identify the features of words prior to word identification? Second, is the order of levels of processing invariant? Do we always need to identify the constituent letters of a word before identifying the word? We will tackle the first question first, as we next examine the pattern of eye movements that occurs as we read written language.

Eye Movements During Reading

The study of reading is one of the oldest topics in experimental psychology, and some of the earliest investigators discovered that it was fruitful to examine the role of eye movements during the reading process (for example, see Huey, 1908/1968). Modern technology has made tremendous advances in this area, and we now have the capacity to monitor these eye patterns closely and to examine the role they may play in a wide variety of psychological processes (Just & Carpenter, 1976).

Some representative data on eye movements during reading for various grade levels are shown in Table 4-3. The average college student reads leisure material, such as a magazine article, at about 280 words per minute. This rate obviously varies with the material; it would be greater for children's stories and less for an anatomy textbook. Table 4-3 also reveals that rate is sensitive to reading skill, or at least grade level, since it more than triples from first grade to college.

Although the overall reading rate gives us some idea of the way a person has processed a chunk of reading material, a clearer understanding of information processing during reading comes from an analysis of various contributors to the overall reading rate.

Table 4-3. Components of Eye Movements as a Function of Grade Level

	Grade												
	1	*2*	*3*	*4*	*5*	*6*	*7*	*8*	*9*	*10*	*11*	*12*	*C*
Average duration of fixations (in seconds)	0.33	0.30	0.28	0.27	0.27	0.27	0.27	0.27	0.27	0.26	0.26	0.25	0.24
Regressions per 100 words	52	40	35	31	28	25	23	21	20	19	18	17	15
Fixations (not including regressions) per 100 words	172	134	120	108	101	95	91	88	85	82	78	77	75
Number of words per fixation	0.58	0.75	0.83	0.93	0.99	1.05	1.10	1.14	1.18	1.22	1.28	1.30	1.33
Rate with comprehension in words per minute	80	115	138	158	173	185	195	204	214	224	237	250	280

Source: Based on "Grade Level Norms for the Components of the Fundamental Reading Skill," by S. E. Taylor, H. Frackenpohl, and J. L. Pettee, *Educational Development Laboratories Research and Information Bulletin No. 3*, Educational Development Laboratories, 1960.

Saccades   The movements of the eyes during reading are called saccadic eye movements, or **saccades**. The saccades take approximately 10 to 20 milliseconds in duration, and it has been established that our eyes are moving too quickly for us to pick up any visual information from the printed page during these saccades (Haber & Hershenson, 1973). Rather, we just perceive a blur. These movements traverse approximately 10 letters on the average and may proceed in either forward or backward directions.

Regressions   Saccades that move backward (leftward in English, rightward in Hebrew) are called **regressions**. About 15% of the eye movements of mature readers are regressions. It is generally believed that they are an indication that a reader has misperceived or misunderstood some portion of a text and has gone back to reanalyze it. As seen in Table 4-3, the proportion of regressive eye movements is considerably higher in the lower grade levels than in the college population.

Fixations   The time that we spend at a given location between eye movements is termed a **fixation**. It is possible, through eye-monitoring equipment, to determine the exact point on the printed page at which a person's eye fixates. Typically, these fixations last about 250 milliseconds, but fixation duration varies with both the difficulty of the content and the skill of the reader. Moreover, there is some variability in fixation durations for a given reader of a given text; a person might fixate one segment for 200 milliseconds, and then the next for 300 milliseconds. It is generally believed that these fluctuations in fixation duration reflect the transient changes in processing difficulty across sentences and paragraphs. It has been shown, for example, that the time taken to read a given portion of a story is related to the ease or difficulty associated with integrating that portion with previous sentences and paragraphs (Daneman & Carpenter, 1980). Thus, fixation duration is one index of the difficulty of information processing during reading.

One aspect of enduring concern (Huey, 1908/1968; Woodworth, 1938) has been the size of the area from which a reader picks up visual information, or the **span of fixation.** The role of peripheral cues in reading has been probed in a series of ingenious studies by Rayner (1975). The basic methodology is to have a person read a passage displayed on a computer screen while, unknown to the individual, certain words from the passage are being replaced by other words and letter strings. These replacements always take place during the saccades. As noted earlier, no visual information is extracted during this time. The replacements are set up in such a way that the peripheral view is of the original word, whereas, when the string is fixated, another set of letters is present.

Rayner (1975) reasoned that if the letters in peripheral view were extracted, then a change when the letters were fixated should increase processing time, and hence fixation duration. One of the sentences he used was as follows:

(10)   The captain granted the pass in the afternoon.

The key word here is *granted.* Upon fixation the reader saw *granted,* but the peripheral information was either another word (*quarded*), a nonword that was visually similar (*gnarbed*), or a nonword that was visually dissimilar (*pmavbcd*). Readers saw one of the three alternatives to *granted* in the periphery, but all saw *granted* during fixation. Rayner found that both visual and semantic inconsistencies increased fixation duration, indicating that peripheral information is used during reading. However, the size of the area from which information is derived is limited to 7 to 12 character spaces for visual information, and 1 to 6 for semantic information. Thus, we extract information from the periphery during reading, but there are some rather strict limits on the size of this area.

Perception of Letters in Isolation

Let us return to the issue of whether the levels of processing we have identified proceed in a fixed order or whether there is more flexibility in how we extract features, letters, and words during reading. If studies of speech perception provide any clue, we would expect some degree of interaction between higher- and lower-order levels (that is, top-down processing) on the basis that a skilled reader might well be able to anticipate what is coming next and thus might be less reliant on the bottom-up visual information.

This issue has been addressed primarily in studies of word perception with individual letters and words presented tachistoscopically. A **tachistoscope** is a device that permits the rapid visual presentation of a stimulus. In a typical study, a stimulus might be presented for 50 milliseconds or less, with subjects asked to report what they see.

Participation in a tachistoscopic task can be a humbling experience. Although we do few things as well or as often as recognizing letters, when the stimuli are presented briefly and in isolation, we often find ourselves uncertain of what we have seen. We may have a fleeting image of an *R*, or was that a *K*? Perhaps it was even a *P*, but it certainly was not a *Z*. Studies of tachistoscopic perception have shown that the constituent features of letters are a significant determinant of performance. In particular, perceivers confuse letters with similar features, such as *E* and *F* or *R* and *P* (Rumelhart, 1970). This finding suggests that under conditions of brief presentation without word context, we can extract some but not all of the features associated with that letter.

Independent evidence of the role of features in the visual detection of letters comes from a task in which individuals searched an array of letters for a prespecified target letter, such as *K* (Neisser, 1964). Figure 4-8 shows two such arrays; you can get a feel for the experiment by scanning each for the letter Z. Studies have shown that detection time is faster when the array is made up of letters with different

ODUGQR	IVMXEW
QCDUGO	EWVMIX
CQOGRD	EXWMVI
QUGCDR	IXEMWV
URDGQO	VXWEMI
GRUQDO	MXVEWI
DUZGRO	XVWMEI
UCGROD	MWXVIE
DQRCGU	VIMEXW
QDOCGU	EXVWIM
CGUROQ	VWMIEX
OCDURQ	VMWIEX
UOCGQD	XVWMEI
RGQCOU	WXVEMI
GRUDQO	XMEWIV
GODUCQ	MXIVEW
QCURDO	VEWMIX
DUCOQG	EMVXWI
CGRDQU	IVWMEX
UDRCOQ	IEVMWX
GQCORU	WVZMXE
GOQUCD	XEMIWV
GDQUOC	WXIMEV
URDCGO	EMWIVX
GODRQC	IVEMXW

Figure 4-8. Stimuli used by Neisser (1964). (From "Visual Search," by U. Neisser, 1964, *Scientific American, 210*, 94–102, Scientific American.)

features (as in the first list) than when it consists of letters with features similar to Z, as in the second list (Neisser, 1964). This suggests that we identify letters from a variable number of features, depending on the other letters that are present. If the letters have vertical and diagonal lines, a careful scrutiny of the visual array is necessary, but when the array is less confusing, the target seems to "jump out." In that instance, the number of features needed for identification is much smaller.

It might be noted that the case for feature analysis in human perceptual performance is not limited to behavioral studies. Physiological investigations by Hubel and Wiesel (1965) have shown that cells in the visual cortex of cats are selectively responsive to visual stimulation such as vertical lines, edges of lines, and edges of a certain length moving at a certain rate. It is quite possible that a similar arrangement exists in the human nervous system.

Perception of Letters in Word Context

The word-superiority effect   An early study of word perception was conducted by Cattell (1886), who compared performance on individual letters with letters in word context. His results were striking. Whereas people were able to report only about three or four unrelated letters, they could report as many as two short words that were not semantically or syntactically related to one another.

Cattell's report was the first to demonstrate superior performance for words over nonword letter strings, but it suffered from methodological problems. Specifically, he instructed his subjects to report everything that they remembered from the briefly presented array. This method can lead to two problems. First, as we saw in Chapter 3, it has been shown that more information is retained in sensory memory than can be reported (Sperling, 1960), so forgetting may be partly responsible for these results. Second, and more important, response factors such as guessing can play a role in these results. To see this, consider the difference between perceiving *yelv* and *read*. Even if perceivers could identify only the second and third letters from these two arrays, they might still perform better with the word array because of prior knowledge of words that have the form __ea__. Moreover, if one or more features of the initial *r* in *read* were extracted, subjects might be able to guess that the last letter was a *d* even if they had not picked up any visual information at all from that position. Of course, they might also guess wrong and choose *l*, but a nonword string does not provide any basis for guessing at all. Thus, although Cattell's results are interesting, they do not clearly show that the difference between words and letter strings is due to perceptual rather than response factors.

Surprisingly, it took more than 80 years for these problems to be corrected, and with it, renewed interest in what was now called the **word-superiority effect** was stimulated.

Clear evidence that the word-superiority effect can occur when response factors are controlled was first documented by Reicher (1969). Individuals were tachistoscopically presented with a word (*word*), a nonword (*owrd*), or a letter (*d* or *k*). Immediately after the display was removed, the subjects were given a recognition test on one of the letters from the display. For example, they might be asked whether the letter in the final position was a *d* or a *k*. Reicher found that accuracy was greater when a word was presented than when a nonword or a single letter was presented. The results are especially significant since *d* and *k* would both result in a word (*word* or *work*), so guessing can be ruled out as a possible explanation. This study provided the first clear evidence that the word-superiority effect was perceptual in nature. The results seem to suggest that we process letters more efficiently within words, implying that word processing aids letter identification, rather than the other way around.

There is further evidence that the word context influences our perception of letters. Healy (1976) found that readers searching for the letter *t* missed more letters when they were embedded in words than if embedded in nonwords. Readers were particularly likely to miss letters when embedded in the word *the* or in other high-frequency words. It appears that our tendency to "unitize"—that is, to group letters into higher-order units such as groups of letters or entire short words—makes it difficult to identify letters in high-frequency words.

Similar results are found in Chinese. Cheng (1981, cited in Hoosain, 1991) embedded target radicals in characters, pseudocharacters, and noncharacters. Pseudocharacters were possible characters not actually in use. After being shown one of these items briefly, subjects were given a forced-choice task similar to Reicher's study. Cheng found that radicals were identified better when they were presented in characters than in pseudocharacters, and better in pseudocharacters than in noncharacters. This result is analogous to the word-superiority effect—in English, letters are better recognized when in words; in Chinese, radicals are better recognized when in characters. Similar results have been reported by Chen, Allport, and Marshall (1996). It has also been found (Chen, 1986) that radicals embedded in a single-character word are not detected as well as when they are embedded in a noncharacter, replicating the results of Healy (1976).

Taken together, these results suggest that we perceive lower-level units such as letters and radicals differently when they occur in familiar (word, character) contexts than in unfamiliar contexts. When words are familiar, we can perceive them as complete units rather than as sets of letters. Although the details differ in Chinese, the perceptual processes appear to be analogous to English.

The Interactive Activation Model

Now that we have discussed some of the processes involved in the perception of letters and words, let us turn to how we might explain perceptual processing. I will concentrate primarily on the interactive activation model introduced by McClelland and Rumelhart (1981). (The model draws on earlier efforts: Adams, 1979; Johnston & McClelland, 1980; and, especially, Morton, 1969).

McClelland and Rumelhart's (1981) model is based on three main assumptions. The first is that processing occurs at three different levels: feature, letter, and word (see Figure 4-9). The second assumption is that processing is occurring simultaneously on all three levels. Finally, interaction occurs among the three levels. It may be either **excitatory interaction** (in which the activation at one level increases

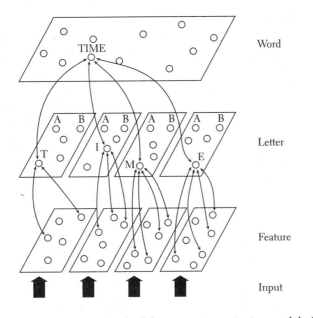

Figure 4-9. A sketch of the interactive activation model of word perception. Units within the same rectangle stand for incompatible alternative hypotheses about an input pattern and are all mutually inhibitory. The bidirectional excitatory connections between levels are indicated for one word and its constituents. (From "Putting Knowledge in Its Place: A Scheme for Programming Parallel Processing Structures on the Fly," by J. L. McClelland, 1985, *Cognitive Science, 9,* p. 115.)

the activation at another level) or **inhibitory interaction** (in which activation at one level decreases the activation at another level). For example, activation of the letter detector for *E* may excite word detectors that contain an *E* but inhibit word detectors that do not. Notice that in this case, a lower level influences activation at the higher level, but the model assumes that higher levels influence lower levels as well.

The model provides an interesting account of the word-superiority effect. Consider the case of the word *work.* As some of the letters are detected, they activate detectors for words that are consistent with the recognized letters. As these words are activated, they provide feedback to the letter level, which increases the strength of activation of the individual letters. As a consequence of this top-down effect, letters embedded in words receive more activation than single letters or letters in nonword strings. The model also accounts for the fact that letters in pronounceable nonwords (pseudowords) are perceived better than letters in nonpronounceable nonwords (Baron & Thurston, 1973). McClelland and Rumelhart (1981) assume that pseudowords (such as *mave*) activate detectors for words that share more than one letter (such as *more* and *mate*). These word-level activations then feed back to the letter level, enabling us to perceive letters in pseudowords almost as well as letters in words.

McClelland and Rumelhart (1981) suggest that two reasons account for the success of their model. One is the "architecture"; that is, the assumption that processing is distributed among three different levels of processing appears to be an important assumption. The other main reason they cite is that the model assumes that processing is "massively parallel." It is similar to the TRACE model of speech perception (Elman & McClelland, 1988; McClelland & Elman, 1986) that we have already discussed as well as a model of speech production (Dell, 1986) that we will consider in Chapter 8. These models are often called **connectionist models** because they explain complex processes in terms of the connections among elementary units.

One measure of the importance of a theory is the amount of criticism it inspires. Richman and Simon (1989) claim that a sequential model can explain context effects in letter perception as well as the interactive activation model. In contrast, Healy, Oliver, and McNamara (1987) and Allen and Madden (1990) retain the parallel processing assumption but argue that different levels of processing do not interact with one another. All of these models have merit, and all of them can explain some facts that the others cannot. The interactive activation model is complex; it will take some time to identify which of its assumptions are crucial for explaining the important facts about letter and word perception.

Summary

Processing of written language exists at three main levels: the feature, letter, and word. All three pieces of visual information are extracted through a series of eye movements. Reading speed is determined by the duration of our fixations, the span of material that is fixated, and the proportion of regressive eye movements. Regressions typically reflect a reanalysis of previous material, whereas fixation duration is a sensitive barometer of the difficulty we have in integrating the fixated material with previous material.

There is clear evidence that featural and letter information influences higher levels of processing. The notion that the levels operate in invariant order, however, is called into question by the word-superiority effect, in which the perception of individual letters is facilitated by the presence of a word or a wordlike context. These and related aspects of letter and word perception have been explained in terms of the interaction between detectors at different levels of processing.

On balance, the conclusions that have arisen from our survey of reading are congruent with those we reached when discussing listening. Although some visual phenomena, such as regressions and saccades, have no direct auditory counterpart, these cases appear to be restricted primarily to the feature and letter levels. At the word level, there is much similarity between oral and written language. We now turn to a fuller discussion of words in Chapter 5.

Review Questions

1. Describe the place and manner of articulation for the phonetic segments [b], [d], [g], [p], [t], and [k].

2. Describe what a spectrogram is, and include descriptions of formants, formant transitions, and steady states.

3. What is categorical perception, and why is it more prominent for consonants than for vowels?

4. What is the motor theory of speech perception?

5. What is rate normalization?

6. Why does phonemic restoration show that a purely bottom-up model of speech perception is inadequate?

7. What is the TRACE model of speech perception?

8. Define the levels of processing we go through in the perception of written language.

9. Define the word-superiority effect.

10. How does the interactive activation model account for the word-superiority effect?

Thought Questions

1. On the basis of your understanding of categorical perception, do you think that this phenomenon would occur if you heard sounds from a foreign language? Justify your answer.

2. If a person suffered from a congenital physical condition that disrupted motor control of speech organs, would the person's speech perception also be impaired?

3. The text discusses normalization based on two aspects of speech: its rate and the pitch of the speaker's voice. Can you think of any other basis for normalization? Discuss your choice.

4. As a student, you may have had experience listening to a nonnative lecturer whose English was somewhat limited. Relate your experience to the concepts of top-down and bottom-up processing.

5 The Internal Lexicon

MAIN POINTS

- When we know a word, we know its phonological, morphological, syntactic, and semantic attributes.
- A word's meaning includes both sense and reference. Sense refers to a word's relationships with other words, whereas reference pertains to the relationships between a word and an object or event in the world.
- The organization of word knowledge in permanent memory is called the internal lexicon. In a semantic network, words are represented as nodes and are connected via relations to other words in the network.
- The process by which we activate our word knowledge is termed lexical access. Lexical access is influenced by the frequency of a word, its phonological and morphological attributes, whether it is ambiguous, and whether a semantically similar word has just been encountered.

Introduction

This chapter is about words—what they consist of and how we find them, use them, and relate them to each other. Of all the levels of language use we will discuss, words are the most familiar, for a good share of our daily activity involves the playful manipulation of words. If any indication of our voracious appetite for word play is needed, consider the enduring appeal of puns, anagrams, crossword puzzles, and television game shows. Let us look at one case of word play and see what it tells us about the way words are understood and used.

In one popular game show, teams of two contestants are chosen, and one member of each team is designated as the sender, while the other is the receiver. The purpose of the game is to communicate a specific target word to the receiver by using other, related words. The teams alternate taking turns. One sender might begin with the cue word *elephant*, to which the receiver responds with *large*. If the response is not correct, the other sender uses another word, say, *vivid*, and receives a response, say, *bright*. The process continues with new cues until one of the receivers identifies the target word.

To understand how this game is performed, we must distinguish between the process of retrieving information about words and the storage of words in memory. The distinction is similar to the one between the information about words that is contained in a dictionary and the processes (flipping pages and so on) by which we find the information. Psycholinguists refer to the representation of words in permanent memory as our **internal lexicon.** When a given word in our lexicon has been found, the properties we associate with the word become available for use. These properties include the meaning of the word, its spelling and pronunciation, its relationship to other words, and related information. Much of this is the stuff of which dictionaries are made, but our internal lexicon also contains information that is not strictly linguistic. A part of our knowledge of elephants, for example, is that they are said to never forget things, but this is not part of the meaning of the word per se.

The process by which we activate these meanings is called **lexical access.** A word in our internal lexicon may be activated in several ways. One way is as a result of the perception of the word; if we see *elephant* on a printed page, we identify it as a recognizable, familiar word and bring our knowledge of the word to bear on the task of comprehension. Alternatively, as in the game show, we activate meanings through other words, since all words conjure up related words to varying degrees. In this chapter we begin by examining the kinds of knowledge about words that we have stored in the internal lexicon, then discuss alternative proposals for the organization of the lexicon. In the final section, we discuss how we access words from the lexicon and examine the role of a number of variables in lexical access.

Dimensions of Word Knowledge

Phonological Knowledge

One part of our word knowledge is the phonological structure or pronunciation of words. For example, we know when two words are homophones, which are words that are spelled differently but sound alike (such as *bare* and *bear*). Similarly, we experience the **tip-of-the-tongue (TOT) phenomenon** when we are not quite successful at retrieving a particular word but can remember something about how it sounds. The phenomenon was described vividly by William James (1890/1950):

> Suppose we try to recall a forgotten name. The state of our consciousness is peculiar. There is a gap therein; but no mere gap. It is a gap that is intensely active. A sort of wraith of the name is in it, beckoning us in a given direction, making us at moments tingle with the sense of our closeness, and then letting us sink back without the longed-for term. If wrong names are proposed to us, this singularly definite gap acts immediately so as to negate them. They do not fit into its mould. And the gap of one word does not feel like the gap of another, all empty of content as both might seem necessarily to be when described as gaps. . . . The rhythm of a lost word may be there without a sound to clothe it; or the evanescent sense of something which is the initial vowel or consonant may mock us fitfully, without growing more distinct. (pp. 251–252)

The TOT phenomenon was systematically studied for the first time by Brown and McNeill (1966), who presented definitions of infrequent words, such as *sextant*, and asked subjects to produce the defined word. When subjects were in the TOT state, they retrieved but rejected similar-sounding words such as *secant*. Thus, we sometimes activate words by their sounds. As we shall see in Chapter 8, when we make speech errors we sometimes substitute a similar-sounding word for the intended word.

Syntactic Knowledge

Another part of our knowledge of words is the **syntactic category,** or part of speech, to which they belong. Two words belong to the same syntactic category when they can substitute for one another in a sentence. Consider sentence (1):

(1)   The aging pianist stunned the audience.

We can replace *aging* with any number of words, such as *wealthy, poor, fat, solemn,* and so on. Although the substitutions may change the meaning of a sentence, the sentence remains grammatical. One advantage of using syntactic categories is that we can formulate grammatical rules in terms of categories rather than lexical items. Thus, we have no rule that states that *aging* may appear before *pianist* in a sentence. The rule is that adjectives may modify. To use such a rule, we need to include syntactic categories in the lexical entries in our mental lexicon (Miller, 1991).

Traditionally, grammatical theory has recognized the syntactic categories of noun, verb, adjective, adverb, pronoun, preposition, conjunction, and interjection. From a psychological vantage point, these categories may be placed into two groups. Open-class words (sometimes called **content words**) include nouns, verbs, adjectives, and adverbs and closed-class words (also called **function words**) include pronouns, prepositions, conjunctions, and interjections. We have all learned a large number of open-class words and that number continues to grow. In contrast, closed-class words are much smaller in number—a few hundred in English—and are used over and over.

This distinction seems to be related to the organization of words in our brain. Neurologists have found that some patients suffer from a condition called **agrammatism.** Agrammatic patients frequently omit closed-class words (and inflectional endings; see below) from their sentences while preserving open-class words somewhat better. In addition, they process closed-class words differently than individuals without neurological damage (Bradley, Garrett, & Zurif, 1980). We will have more to say about the brain and language in Chapter 13. The point for now is that syntactic categories are included in the lexical entries in our mental lexicons.

Morphological Knowledge

How many words do we know? It would seem, superficially, to be a fairly simple question, but it turns out that there is no easy answer. What counts as a word? For example, I know what the word *reactionary* means, so that is a word in my lexicon. But, if I know *reactionary*, I also know related words such as *react* and *reacting*, and so on. Do these count as separate words in my lexicon? If so, estimates of the size of my lexicon will increase.

Any effort to identify vocabulary size will eventually have to confront the morphology of the language (Miller, 1991). We discussed morphology briefly in Chapter 2. Recall that morphemes are the smallest unit of meaning in a language. Some words consist of just a single morpheme. Morphemes that are also words are called **free morphemes. Bound morphemes** are those that are attached to free morphemes to create new words.

There are, in fact, two different kinds of bound morphemes to consider. **Inflectional morphemes** are involved when a bound morpheme is added to a free morpheme to express grammatical contrasts in sentences. Inflectional morphemes in English include the plural morpheme for nouns (*cat/cats*) and the past tense morpheme for verbs (*jump/jumped*).

In contrast, **derivational morphemes** are involved when bound morphemes, when added to free morphemes, create new words. For example, *-ness* turns *good* (an adjective) into *goodness* (a noun). Other derivational morphemes change not only the syntactic category but also our pronunciation. For example, the derivational morpheme *-ion* changes *decide* (a verb) into *decision* (a noun). Notice also that *-ion* changes our pronunciation: the second /d/ in *decide* becomes the /š/ in *decision*.

When a word contains both inflectional and derivational morphemes, the derivational morphemes are applied first. Consider the word *neighborhoods*. The root word is *neighbor,* and both the derivational morpheme *-hood* and the inflectional morpheme *-s* are applied to the root. The derivational is applied first, so the resulting word is *neighborhoods,* not *neighborshood.*

Getting back to vocabulary size, our ability to form various alternative forms of root words effectively means that there is no limit to the number of new words in a language. How, then, do we estimate the size of a person's mental lexicon? For simple cases, such as the plural morphemes, it could be assumed that when a person knows *book,* the person will also recognize *books* as a word. So, *book* and *books* should count as just one word. Other morphemes, such as *-er,* cause more problems. In some cases, the morpheme produces a predictable shift in meaning, as in *run* and *runner.* But in other cases, the meaning is opaque, as in *tell* and *teller.* Using this criterion—whether it would be possible to determine the meaning of a word with a morpheme by knowing its root—it is possible to estimate that the average high school graduate knows about 45,000 words (Nagy & Anderson, 1984). The number is likely somewhat higher in college graduates and those who do a lot of reading.

Semantic Knowledge

What is meaning? What is it that we know when we know the meaning of a word? And how is that meaning represented mentally? Linguists, philosophers, and psychologists have identified several important aspects of word meaning. Let us begin by looking at some of these distinctions.

Sense and reference   The relationship between words and things in the world is termed the **reference** of a word; the things in the world are called the **referents** of the word. This aspect of meaning is crucial for determining whether or not a given utterance is truthful. For instance, consider sentence (2):

(2)   There is a brown cow grazing in the field.

When we understand the meaning of this sentence, then we grasp its **truth conditions,** the conditions under which the sentence may be said to be true. In this instance, there must be a cow, it must be brown, and it must be grazing in the field. That is, we must assess whether the events in the world correspond to the referents of the words *cow, brown, grazing,* and *field.* Reference concerns what the world should be like if a given utterance is true.

Not all reference is so easy. Some words clearly have meaning, but it is difficult to know what they refer to. This group includes abstract words, such as *justice, plausibility,* and *relativity.* Other words are meaningful but have no real referents, such as *unicorn* or *minotaur.* But even though the reference of these words is unclear, they communicate meaning. One way to explain this phenomenon is to assume that we can construe reference not only within the real world as we know it but also in the context of possible worlds, worlds that do not exist but might possibly exist. In this context, the word *unicorn* might refer to an object in another, hypothetical world. The process of referring to imaginary worlds plays an important role in literature (Pavel, 1986).

Johnson-Laird (1983) has suggested that the concept of a mental model might be fruitfully applied to the problems of reference. A **mental model** is a cognitive structure that represents some aspect of our environment. Such models are not limited to linguistic aspects. We have, for example, a model of our visual environment, in the form of a mental image, which allows us to navigate our way through our environment. If I blindfold you and then take you into a room in your house, you would probably be able to find your way around fairly well. But suppose I move the furniture while you are blindfolded. You would have a great deal of trouble moving around. However, if I warned you when you were about to run into something, you would in short order form vivid images of each piece of furniture in its new location (Johnson-Laird, 1988b).

In a similar vein, we may have mental models of those aspects of the environment that correspond to words. When we hear a sentence, we may construct "a mental model of the particular state of affairs characterized by the utterance" (Johnson-Laird, Herrmann, & Chaffin, 1984, p. 311). This model can then be used to evaluate whether the sentence is true, by comparing the model with perceptual evidence, at least for those sentences that refer to our immediate environment.

Reference is part of meaning, but there is more to meaning than reference. Two different words or expressions may have the same reference but not mean the same thing. For instance, the reference of the two noun phrases *The prime minister of Great Britain and The leader of the Labour party* is currently the same, namely, Tony Blair. But the meanings of the two expressions are different, as can be seen when a different party comes to power. Similarly, sentence (3) is currently true but may not be after the next election. The truth value of the sentence will vary with the referents of the two noun phrases, but the meaning of the phrases and of the sentence will remain the same.

(3)   The leader of the Labour party is the prime minister of Great Britain.

The part of meaning that is not its reference is termed its **sense** (Frege, 1892/1952). The sense of a word means "its place in a system of relationships which it contracts with other words in the vocabulary" (Lyons, 1968, p. 427). Linguists have identified several important relations. **Synonymy** exists when two words or expressions mean the same thing, as in *fear* and *panic.* **Antonymy** refers to opposition of meaning, as in *big* and *small.* **Incompatibility** occurs when one word contradicts the other. This relation is found in words denoting color; for example, sentence (4) is incompatible with sentence (5):

(4)   Rebecca wore a red dress.

(5)   Rebecca wore a green dress.

Finally, **hyponymy** deals with the notion of class inclusion; that is, *dog* is a subordinate of *animal*, a coordinate (or cohyponym) of *cat*, and a superordinate of *German shepherd*.

These sense relations rest on the notion of implication. **Implication** exists when if one expression is true, then another must be true. For instance, sentence (6) implies (7):

(6)   Bob is a bachelor.

(7)   Bob is not married.

Each of the sense relations in the previous paragraph may be described in terms of implication. Synonymy, for instance, may be thought of as a bilateral implication in that each word in a synonym pair implies the other. In contrast, to say that Fido is a dog implies that he is an animal, but here the implication is in only one direction; to be an animal does not imply that one is a dog. I leave it to the interested reader to define the other relations in terms of implication.

One of the oldest methods psychologists have for studying semantic relations is the **word association test.** The test was invented by Sir Francis Galton, a cousin of Charles Darwin, and was also used by Swiss psychoanalyst Carl Jung. The first large-scale study for English was performed by Kent and Rosanoff (1910), who read aloud a list of words one at a time to a person who was instructed to give "the first word that occurs to you other than the stimulus word itself" (p. 38). They gave the test to 1000 men and women of different occupations and levels of education. The responses to one of the words is shown in Table 5-1.

You will notice that some of responses are very common—the first four responses comprise roughly half of the 1000 total responses. At the other end of the spectrum, there are quite a few idiosyncratic responses, such as *idleness*, *rubber*, *lunch*, and *beauty*. Setting aside these idiosyncratic associations, we find that four types of semantic relations predominate (Miller, 1991). First, there are **taxonomic relations.** *Table* is a coordinate term, *furniture* is a superordinate term, and *rocker* is a subordinate of *chair*. Second, there are **attributive relations,** which are terms that identify attributes of the word. Mostly these are adjectives, such as *comfortable*, *wooden*, *hard*, or *white*. Third, there are **part-whole relations,** which are terms that name a part of something or that name the whole of which something is a part. Examples here are *seat*, *cushion*, and *legs*. Finally, there are **functional relations.** Words such as *sitting*, *rest*, and *rocking* indicate what can be done with a chair.

Sense and reference are complementary aspects of meaning. Sense pertains to the relationships between a word and other words in the language. Reference

Table 5-1.   First Responses to Stimulus Word *Chair*

Frequency of Response	Response	Frequency of Response	Response
191	table	2	broken, hickory, home, necessity, oak, rounds, seating, use
127	seat		
108	sit		
83	furniture		
56	sitting		
49	wood	1	back, beauty, bed, book, boy, bureau, caning, careful, carpet, cart, color, crooked, cushions, feet, foot, footstool, form, Governor Winthrop, hair, implement, joiner, lunch, massive, mission, myself, object, occupy, office, people, place, placed, plant, idleness, platform, pleasant, pleasure, posture, reading, rubber, size, spooning, stand, stoop, study, support, tables, talk, teacher, timber, tool, upholstered, upholstery, white
45	rest		
38	stool		
21	comfort		
17	rocker		
15	rocking		
13	bench		
12	cushion		
11	legs		
10	floor		
9	desk, room		
8	comfortable		
7	ease, leg		
6	easy, sofa, wooden		
5	couch, hard, Morris, seated, soft		
4	arm, article, brown, high		
3	cane, convenience, house, large, low, lounge, mahogany, person, resting, rug, settee, useful		

Source: From G. H. Kent and A. J. Rosanoff, 1910, *The American Journal of Insanity* 67, pp. 317–390, American Psychiatric Association.

deals with the relationships between a word and what it stands for in the world. To use language in a meaningful manner, we need to pay attention to both properties.

Denotation and connotation   We have been speaking of the **denotation** of a word, which is the objective or dictionary meaning of a word. A dictionary definition of a word includes phonological information (pronunciation), orthographic information (spelling), syntactic information (part of speech), semantic information (various meanings), morphological information (related words), as well as other information we have not even discussed here, such as the word's etymology.

A word also has a **connotation.** It suggests certain aspects of meaning beyond that which it explicitly names or describes. Two words may have the same denotation but differ in their connotations. For instance, consider the terms *bachelor* and *spinster* (Smith, 1978). From the standpoint of a dictionary definition, the terms are comparable: both refer to an adult who has never been married. But there are other aspects of meaning that the dictionary definition does not fully capture. For most people, *spinster* connotes an older woman who is past the society's definition of the standard age for marriage. *Bachelor* does not carry this connotation and, indeed, may be associated with the opposite preconception: a young man, of eligible age. If you told a friend that an acquaintance of yours, Annie, is a spinster, and then mentioned that she is married, your friend would have reason to believe that you simply do not know what *spinster* means. In contrast, if you said she was a spinster but also a young, energetic, and attractive woman, your friend would be surprised and perhaps feel misled. In this latter case, the word is being used in a way that is consistent with its denotation but not with its connotation, at least as conventionally defined in our society.

Summary

To use words effectively in our daily lives, we must utilize our stored knowledge of words, which includes phonological, syntactic, morphological, and semantic aspects. These aspects enable us to pronounce words, create new forms of words, and understand the meanings of words.

Organization of the Internal Lexicon

We have discussed some of the information that is included in our internal lexicon. We now turn to two interdependent issues: how the internal lexicon is organized (this section) and how we access lexical information (the following section).

These issues are interdependent because the manner in which we store information is related to the ease of retrieval. Consider a simple example. Suppose we stored every word we learned, in the order in which we learned them, in a long list. If asked, we could fairly easily determine which of two words we learned at an earlier age by noting the relative position of the two words on the list. On the other hand, it would be relatively more difficult to determine whether a given word has a synonym, for the synonym might appear anywhere on the list. This form of organization is not as silly as it sounds, for some research indicates that the time when we acquire words is related to their ease of access (Carroll & White, 1973). But the point for now is simply that the organization of the lexicon influences ease of retrieval.

The Concept of a Semantic Network

Currently the main idea regarding the organization of the lexicon is that it is set up as a network of interconnected elements. The elements are concepts or nodes,

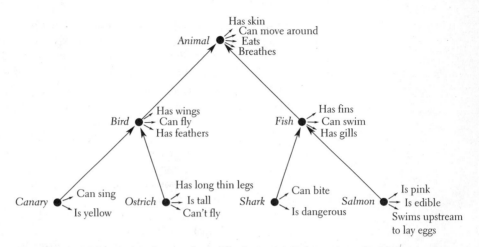

Figure 5-1.   A hierarchical network model of semantic information related to animals. (From "Retrieval Time from Semantic Memory," by A. M. Collins and M. R. Quillian, 1969, *Journal of Verbal Learning and Verbal Behavior, 9*, p. 241. Copyright © 1969 Academic Press. Reprinted by permission.)

which are connected to one another by virtue of having various relations with one another.

Given what we have had to say about sense relations in word association tasks, the idea of a network of concepts based on relations makes a good deal of sense. We obviously know a large number of words that are related to one another in a large number of ways, and it appears that a network might be an appealing way to capture this fact.

In addition, we know that the brain is composed of neurons that are connected at synapses to other neurons and that these connections can be either facilitative or inhibitory. Thus, as we discussed in Chapter 3, the idea that a network resembles, to some degree, what we know about the central nervous system makes the network idea again seem attractive.

Hierarchical Network Models

A network is hierarchical if some of these elements stand above or below other members of the network. The research of Collins and Quillian (1969, 1970, 1972) stands as the prototype of this approach.

The model used by Collins and Quillian is shown in Figure 5-1. Notice that concepts similar to the word are represented as distinct nodes in a network of category and property relations. Category relations (or taxonomic relations, as we talked about them when discussing the word association test) are those that deal with hyponymy (that is, relations of subordination and superordination). Property relations indicate what characteristics may be attributed to the items at various levels in the network.

The most interesting aspect of Collins and Quillian's model is their decision regarding how properties or attributes were stored in the lexicon. Consider first sentences (8) and (9), from Bransford (1979):

(8) Luckily, Aristotle was not blinded by the incident.

(9) Luckily, the rock was not blinded by the incident.

The first sentence makes sense because we know that Aristotle was a human being, and human beings have eyes. The second sentence thus does not make much sense. The key piece of information that enables us to understand the first sentence is that Aristotle had eyes, but it is very unlikely that we would have been explicitly presented with this information sometime in our past. Most likely, we inferred this information from what information we do have stored in our mental lexicon. It would appear to be a waste of memory space to store information that is highly unlikely to ever be used. Instead, we can store it elsewhere in the network and retrieve it as needed.

Similarly, Collins and Quillian assumed that the space available for the storage of semantic information was limited, so that it would be beneficial to store information only in one place in the network. This principle is referred to as **cognitive economy.** Furthermore, they assumed that the information would be stored only at the highest possible node. For instance, the information that birds can breathe is stored at the animal level since it is true of all animals. The researchers suggest that rather than store it at all of the nodes, we store the information just once but make it available to other nodes through the network of relations. Since we are capable of drawing inferences, the notion of saving storage space has some merit. This occurs only when the information is redundant; the information that birds can fly would be stored directly at the bird node.

Collins and Quillian tested their model with a **semantic verification task.** In this task, a person is presented with a statement of the form *An A is a B,* such as sentence (10) and asked to determine as quickly as possible whether the sentence is true or false.

(10) An apple is a fruit.

Since extremely few errors are made on this task, the time taken to answer is usually what is measured. This time is thought to reflect the organization of information in the internal lexicon. That is, even though the decisions are made very rapidly, they take a measurable amount of time, and the assumption is that the time that is taken might be a measure of the "distance" between different words in the internal lexicon.

It might give you a better idea of the kinds of data we will be discussing if you do a little experiment. Find a friend and read the statements listed in Table 5-2 one at a time. Ask your friend to quickly decide whether each statement is true or false and say so aloud. You should be forewarned that this task will probably reinforce your friend's preconception that psychology experiments are a little weird.

If your results are similar to those of others, you will probably find that some of your friend's answers are very fast. Others may provoke a little laughter. Still others

Table 5-2.   Sample Items in a
Semantic Verification Task

A robin is a bird.
A butterfly is a bird.
A robin can fly.
A goose is a computer.
A horse is a mammal.
A tomato is a vegetable.
A mouse has teeth.
A monkey can read.
A pickle has fingernails.
Thomas Edison invented the telephone.
An octopus runs on batteries.
Abraham Lincoln had a beard.

---

may be a little slower and with perhaps a little less confidence. You might try to develop some statements of your own and see what responses they get. This work will give you a better idea of the kinds of data that we will discuss in this section.

To derive testable predictions from the model, Collins and Quillian had to make some additional assumptions about the way semantic information is retrieved. Consider what happens in the typical semantic verification task. If we were presented with sentence (11), the sentence would activate both the bird node and the animal node.

(11)   A bird is an animal.

The process of deciding whether the sentence is true or false is based, according to Collins and Quillian, on a mechanism known as **intersection search.** Once these two nodes are active, it would take a brief time to travel from one node to another. They assumed that we continue to search for relevant information until the two items in the sentence intersect. Finally, we would check to make sure that the relation depicted in the sentence fits the relation in the lexicon. In sentence (12), there would be an intersection, but a check of the relations would indicate that the sentence contradicts the information in the lexicon.

(12)   An animal is a bird.

Taken together, cognitive economy and intersection search yield the prediction that making decisions of the form A *bird is an animal* or A *bird can breathe* takes longer than deciding about An *animal is an animal* or An *animal can breathe*. In each case, it is because we must mentally traverse one relation in the network to decide whether the statement is true or false for birds, but no relations need to be followed to determine this for animals. The early work of Collins and Quillian and others (Landauer & Meyer, 1972) found just this relationship in the verification times. They called this the **category-size effect**: in a statement of the form *An A is a B* or *An A has a B*, the higher the location of B in the hierarchy in relation to A, the longer the reaction times.

Problems soon emerged with this model. Perhaps the most serious difficulty was that the model assumed that all items on a given level of the hierarchy were more or less equal. *Canary* and *ostrich*, for example, were both subordinates of *bird* and one link away from *bird*, so they should take equal time to verify. In fact, they do not. It seems that this is generally true; some instances of categories are usually verified faster than others. Smith, Shoben, and Rips (1974) carefully examined the effect of category similarity on verification times and concluded that similarity reduces verification times for true statements and increases it for false statements. That is, sentence (13) takes less time than (14); moreover, (15) takes longer than (16):

(13) A robin is a bird.

(14) An ostrich is a bird.

(15) A whale is a fish.

(16) A horse is a fish.

This has generally been called the **typicality effect**: items that are more typical of a given subordinate take less time to verify than atypical items in true statements; the opposite is true for false statements.

Similarly, there are results that run counter to the hierarchical concept. A taxonomy for *collies* would include a sequence of this sort: *collie, dog, mammal, animal*. According to this taxonomy, response times to the mammalian features of collies should be intermediate between *dog* and *animal*. The results, however, show that we are slower to respond to *mammal* than to *animal*. Presumably, this is because we are less familiar with *mammal* as a category for experience.

These results suggest that a strict cognitive economy model is not a good candidate for a model of the internal lexicon. Nevertheless, the reasons that led to the cognitive economy model (for example, the observation that we can comprehend sentences such as *Luckily, the rock did not blind Aristotle*) still deserve consideration. It is simply the assumption that all attributes are stored just once, at the highest node, that must be discarded.

An alternative, suggested by the mammal observation earlier, is that attributes are more likely to be stored at more familiar locations in the network (Rosch, Mervis, Gray, Johnson, & Boyes-Braem, 1976). Most lexical hierarchies have a level, often near the middle, where most of the distinguishing features are assigned. These are referred to as **basic-level terms**. They are terms that children learn first and that adults use when asked to name an example of a concept. Most people can list many properties of basic-level terms. Items higher in the hierarchy are more abstract. For example, *chair* is a basic-level term, and we can identify several distinguishing features of chairs. In contrast, the superordinate *furniture* does not readily lead to many such features. If you go down the hierarchy from a basic-level term, you can add minor features, as you would with *armchair*. The upshot is that if more attributes are stored at basic-level terms, rather than the highest level in the hierarchy, then the hierarchical network model has some plausibility (Miller, 1991).

Spreading Activation Models

As a second alternative, we can modify the hierarchical assumption while retaining the idea of a network. This class of models is referred to as **spreading activation** models. As one example, Collins and Loftus (1975) assume that words are represented in the internal lexicon in a network, but the organization is not strictly hierarchical. In contrast, the organization is closer to a web of interconnecting nodes, with the distance between the nodes determined by both structural characteristics such as taxonomic relations and considerations such as typicality and degree of association between related concepts. Thus, the model incorporates some aspects of both the Collins and Quillian model and the criticisms that the model inspired. The notion that concepts are stored as interconnected links is retained, but the view that all such relations are equal is revised by assuming that some nodes are more accessible than others and that the degree of accessibility is related to factors such as frequency of usage and typicality.

The process by which semantic information is retrieved is also revised in this model. Instead of an intersection search throughout the network, Collins and Loftus argue that retrieval occurs by a process of spreading activation: activation begins at a single node and then spreads in parallel throughout the network. This activation attenuates over distance, thus ensuring that closely related concepts are more likely to be activated than distant concepts (see Figure 5-2). The process of spreading activation has been likened to the effect of dropping a rock into a pool of still water (Wessells, 1982). The disturbance spreads out in all directions from the point of entry, with the magnitude determined by factors such as the intensity of the original stimulus, the distance between a part of the pool and the part the rock was dropped into, and the time elapsed since the rock was dropped.

The Collins and Loftus model is a step forward from the overly rigid hierarchical network model, but it too has some limitations. Very little attention is paid to phonological, syntactic, and morphological aspects of words. In a sense, then, it is a model of concepts rather than words. The concept of a cat elicits associations to many other concepts, just as the word *cat* elicits associations to many other words. The difference is that the word *cat* is, at once, a free morpheme, a closed-class word, and a word that includes the phonemes /k/, /æ/, and /t/. Any account of how our knowledge of *cat* is organized that does not include phonological, syntactic, and morphological aspects is necessarily incomplete.

A more recent spreading activation model that incorporates lexical as well as conceptual aspects is presented by Bock and Levelt (1994). The model is shown in Figure 5-3. Bock and Levelt assume that our knowledge of words exists at three different levels. The conceptual level consists of nodes that represent concepts; nodes are connected to other nodes by various relations. This part of Bock and Levelt's model is very similar to the Collins and Loftus model.

A second level is called the lemma level. A **lemma** refers to syntactic aspects of word knowledge (Bock & Levelt, 1994; Levelt, 1989). The English word *sheep* is a noun. The French word *mouton* is also a noun but also has male syntactic gender. Similarly, *goat* is a noun, and *chèvre* is a noun with female gender. The syntactic specifications are usually more complex for verbs than for nouns. For example, the

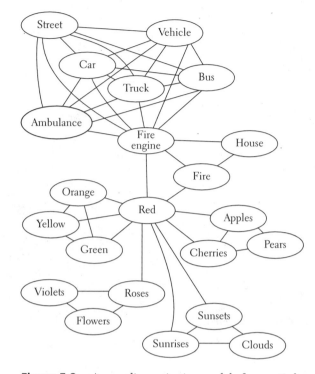

Figure 5-2. A spreading activation model of semantic knowledge. (From "A Spreading-Activation Theory of Semantic Processing," by A. M. Collins and E. F. Loftus, 1975, *Psychological Review*, 82, p. 412. Copyright © 1975 American Psychological Association. Reprinted by permission.)

verb *eat* requires a subject (we can say *John ate*), but the word *hit* requires both a subject and a direct object (we cannot say *Beth hit* but must say something like *Beth hit Greg*). These syntactic properties would be included at the lemma level.

Finally, there is a lexeme level. A **lexeme** captures a word's phonological properties, or how a word sounds. The word *sheep* consists of three phonemes, /š/, /I/, and /p/.

The distinction between these different levels is useful. For example, in the study of the TOT state discussed earlier (Brown & McNeill, 1966), we found that individuals in the TOT state can fail to recall the correct word but still retrieve (and reject) similar-sounding words. In terms of the Bock and Levelt model, the speaker knew the word's meaning (that is, the concept) and syntactic category (the lemma) but not its phonological features (the lexeme), at least not in their entirety.

Let us pause to take stock of where we are. We have discussed first hierarchical network models and then, after identifying some limitations, turned our attention to several alternative network models. Spreading activation models in various forms have been popular in cognitive psychology and psycholinguistics (for example, Marcel, 1983; Neely, 1977, 1991; Posner & Snyder, 1975). They provide a more flexible

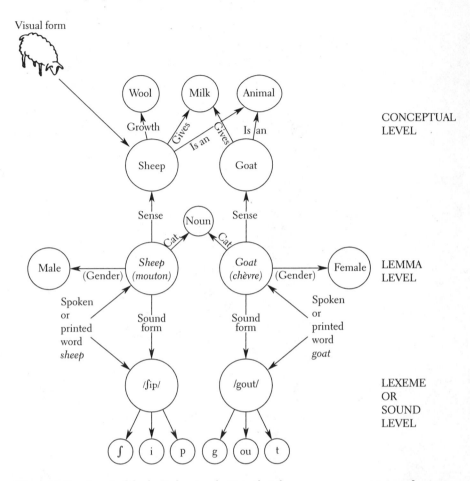

Figure 5-3.   A part of the lexical network. Note that the arrows represent types of connections within the network, not the flow of information during production or comprehension. (From "Language Production: Grammatical Encoding," by K. Bock and W. Levelt. In M. A. Gernbascher (Ed.), *Handbook of Psycholinguistics*, p. 951. Copyright © 1994 Academic Press. Reprinted by permission.)

way of representing lexical information as well as point to how we might activate such information during lexical access. The Bock and Levelt (1994) model appears to be particularly useful in understanding lexical access in both comprehension (this chapter) and production (which will be discussed in Chapter 8). Despite their considerable appeal, spreading activation models do not capture all of the aspects of words we are interested in. For example, networks emphasize sense relations and are notably absent on the topic of referential aspects of word meaning (Johnson-Laird, Herrmann, & Chaffin, 1984). Nonetheless, spreading activation provides a plausible framework within which to think about the concept of lexical organization and lexical access.

Summary

A semantic network is an interconnected web of concepts connected by various relations. In the hierarchical network model, we store our knowledge of words in the form of a **semantic network,** with some words represented at higher nodes in the network than others. Although the hierarchical network model can explain some results, it is too rigid to capture all of our tacit knowledge of the lexicon.

Spreading activation models are network models that are not strictly hierarchical. Activation spreads from one node to neighboring nodes. Spreading activation models of the lexicon that incorporate conceptual, syntactic, and phonological knowledge appear to offer the most realistic picture currently available of the internal lexicon.

Lexical Access

We have discussed some of the aspects of word knowledge that are stored in the internal lexicon and then, in the last section, how all of this information may be organized. Our next task is to explain how this organized knowledge is accessed during language comprehension. We begin by looking at several competing ideas about how the access process operates.

Models of Lexical Access

Search models   One of the earliest and most influential models is the autonomous search model of Forster (1976, 1979). In this model, the word recognition system is divided into several different components. One is devoted to the orthographic (spelling) properties of a word and another to the phonetic properties. Each of these is organized in descending order of frequency. Thus, more frequent words are searched before lower-frequency words. When the input is matched to one of the items in one of the two bins, a pointer to an entry in the master lexicon is retrieved. When this entry is retrieved, other properties of the word such as its syntactic function are retrieved.

Forster's model assumes that the lexicon is autonomous or independent of other systems involved in language processing. Thus, according to this model, activation of words from the lexicon is not directly influenced by syntactic or semantic factors. Such factors affect the general cognitive system. Information from the lexicon is fed into this more general system, and in this way syntactic/semantic information may influence word activation.

This model has been revised in recent years (Forster, 1987, 1989). Originally, the model assumed a single comparator matched the incoming signal to the lexical representation in the phonetic or orthographic files. This led to a problem in terms of the number of files that needed to be searched versus the observed speed of word recognition (Lively, Pisoni, & Goldinger, 1994). Thus, the revised model has separate comparators for each file bin.

Logogen model   One of the earliest activation models was proposed by Morton (1969). In Morton's model, each word (or morpheme) in the lexicon is represented as a **logogen,** which specifies the word's various attributes (semantic, orthographic, phonological, and so on).

The logogen is activated in either of two ways: by sensory input and by contextual information. Consider first the sensory route. As orthographic or phonological features of the input stimulus are detected, they are matched to the logogen. The logogen functions as a scoreboard or counter; when the counter rises above a pre-designated threshold, the item is recognized.

With regard to contextual information, the semantic and syntactic structure of a sentence may influence the activation of the logogen for a given word. Consider the following sentence:

(17)   Her closest relative was appointed as her legal guardian.

We can anticipate the word *guardian* due to the expectations created by earlier words in the sentence. The activation of the earlier words influences the logogen for the final word, temporarily lowering its threshold. Thus, it is easier to recognize *guardian* in this context than if presented in isolation (Tulving, Mandler, & Baumal, 1964). In the original version of the logogen model (Morton, 1969), the information about the associations between different words is not contained in the logogen system itself but rather in a separate cognitive system that feeds back to the logogens.

In the logogen model, these two routes are assumed to work in parallel; sensory and contextual matches increase the same counter. Thus, when many sensory features are detected (as when the word is presented loudly), the corresponding word will be activated even if it is somewhat unexpected. Similarly, an expected word will be activated even if presented in dim light. Of course, if both sensory and contextual features are detected, then the word is easily detected.

Cohort model   The **cohort model** was designed specifically to account for auditory word recognition. Marslen-Wilson (1987, 1990) and colleagues (Marslen-Wilson & Welsh, 1978; Marslen-Wilson & Tyler, 1980) noticed several aspects of spoken word recognition that needed to be accounted for in a model of lexical access. First, listeners recognize words very rapidly, perhaps within 200–250 milliseconds of the beginning of the word (Marslen-Wilson, 1987). Second, listeners are sensitive to the **recognition point** of a word—the point at which the word diverges from other possible words.

According to Marslen-Wilson (1987), spoken word recognition occurs in three stages. First, on the basis of an acoustic-phonetic analysis of the input, a set of lexical candidates is activated. This set is referred to as the **word initial cohort.** Second, one member of the cohort is selected for further analysis. Finally, the selected lexical item is integrated into the ongoing semantic and syntactic context.

As for the first stage, cohort theory assumes that the initial activation of items is done in a strictly bottom-up fashion. For example, upon hearing sentence (18), *bag, bat, bath, bass*, and many others would be available for selection.

(18)   Angela misplaced her ba . . .

This cohort is then submitted to the selection process. Unlike the first stage, the selection stage is sensitive to multiple sources of information, including the phonetic input, word variables (such as word frequency), and the ongoing discourse context. In the original version of the cohort model, all cohorts were either fully activated or not activated at all. More recently, Marslen-Wilson (1990) revised the theory to assume that the activation levels of different items in the cohort vary as a function of their similarity to the incoming signal. Items that are very similar to the signal remain strongly activated, while the activation level of others drops off. Thus, some of the initial candidates in the cohort are progressively eliminated.

This elimination takes place in one of two ways: either the context of a spoken sentence narrows the initial cohort, or candidates are discarded as more phonological information comes in. In the latter case, as more of the spoken word is recognized, the cohort narrows down to only one or several possible choices. For example, if the phoneme /g/ was heard after the *ba-*, only words beginning with *bag-* (such as *bag* and *bagpipe*) would be left from the initial cohort. The field of candidates is narrowed as more stimulus information is received. Eventually, only one candidate will remain. Finally, the selected word is fit into the **connected discourse.**

The cohort model in some ways captures the best features of the search and logogen models. Like the logogen model, but unlike the search model, the cohort model assumes that multiple word candidates are processed in parallel. Like the search model, but unlike the logogen model, it assumes that the initial process is strictly bottom-up. Furthermore, by specifically attending to spoken word recognition, the cohort model is more sensitive than other models to the left-to-right nature of speech. It is thus best equipped to explain how we can recognize a long word before the word is complete (for example, *catastrophe*).

With these models of access in mind, let us now look at some of the variables that influence how easily we may activate words from the internal lexicon.

Variables That Influence Lexical Access

The process of accessing or retrieving lexical information from memory is influenced by a number of factors. Among such factors are the frequency of the word, its syntactic category, its morphological complexity, whether a semantically related word has just been encountered, and whether the word is ambiguous.

Word frequency   The role of word frequency has been demonstrated in a **phoneme monitoring** study by Foss (1969). In this task, participants listen to a continuous speech passage and do two things: comprehend the passage and listen for a target phoneme such as /b/. In some instances, the target phoneme followed a high-frequency word; in other instances, it followed a low-frequency word. The results were clear-cut: monitoring times increased slightly after a low-frequency word.

Let us look at Foss's explanation of this result. Suppose we assume that both tasks, phoneme monitoring and comprehension, draw from the same limited pool of resources. Then if one of the tasks becomes more difficult, it might conceivably affect the other. Suppose further that comprehension is impeded by the presence of low-frequency words; that is, we are slower at accessing these words and thus must work harder to comprehend the sentences in which they occur. Therefore, as the comprehension task becomes more demanding, we have fewer resources to devote to the phoneme-monitoring task. The end result is that monitoring times increase for low-frequency words.

Studies of phoneme monitoring have been controversial, and some of the conclusions drawn from them have been called into question (see, for example, Ferreira & Anes, 1994). A good experimental strategy, in general, is to use several different methods to explore a given phenomenon and look to see whether the different approaches converge on similar conclusions. Accordingly, it would be useful to find evidence that word frequency influences lexical access in a visual task.

One visual task that has been useful in studying lexical access is called the **lexical decision task.** In this task, a participant sees a string of letters and must rapidly decide whether the string is a word. Ordinarily in lexical decision studies the stimuli are presented one at a time, but you can get an idea how these studies are performed by looking at Table 5-3. Both list 1 and list 2 consist of words and nonwords. For each item on each list, you should say *yes* aloud if it is a word and *no* if it is a nonword. Find a stopwatch with a second hand, and time yourself on how long it takes to complete each list.

List 1 usually takes a few more seconds to complete than list 2 because the words in list 1 are lower in frequency than the corresponding words in list 2. A number of studies have shown that frequency influences response times in this task, with higher-frequency words having shorter durations (Rubenstein, Garfield, & Milliken, 1970; Whaley, 1978).

Rayner and Duffy (1986) have found that word frequency also plays a role in normal reading. They measured eye fixations to words during reading and found that low-frequency words were fixated for about 80 milliseconds longer than high-frequency words. The magnitude of the differences is similar to that found in lexical

Table 5-3.   The Internal Lexicon

List 1

gambastya, revery, voitle, chard, wefe, cratily, decoy, puldow, raflot, oriole, voluble, boovle, chalt, awry, signet, trave, crock, cryptic, ewe, himpola

List 2

mulvow, governor, bless, tuglety, gare, relief, ruftily, history, pindle, develop, gardot, norve, busy, effort, garvola, match, sard, pleasant, coin, maisle

Note: See the text for instructions.
Source: Based on "Words and Meaning: From Primitives to Complex Organization," by K. Hirsh-Pasek, L. M. Reeves, and R. Golinkoff. In J. B. Gleason and N. B. Ratner (Eds.), *Psycholinguistics*, p. 138, Harcourt Brace Jovanovich, 1993.

decision studies. This is important because tasks such as lexical decision and phoneme monitoring are sometimes criticized for being "artificial" or not reflecting language processes as they occur outside the laboratory. But the purpose of such tasks is to isolate one aspect of normal reading processes, not to create a task that has nothing to do with ordinary reading. Rayner and Duffy's results suggest that since similar results are found in reading and in more specialized tasks, the latter tasks tap into normal reading processes.

Phonological variables   In addition to word frequency, lexical access is influenced by the kinds of information we discussed earlier in the chapter—phonological, syntactic, morphological, and semantic information. Let us begin with phonological variables. Our review of speech perception in Chapter 4, particularly the perception of continuous speech, clearly indicates that word recognition is influenced by prosodic factors such as stress and intonational patterns. In addition, we learned that there is a continuous interplay of bottom-up and top-down factors at work. We recognize words in part because we identify their constituent phonemes and in part because of the larger word, sentence, or discourse context.

Similarly, as we shall see in Chapter 8, when we make speech errors, we sometimes substitute similar-sounding words for the intended word. Thus, one stage or part of the process of speech production seems to be devoted to retrieving the sounds of words.

Syntactic category   As we have seen, there are robust differences in lexical access between high- and low-frequency words. The word frequency effect, however, only holds for open-class words. There is no difference in the speed of retrieval of high- versus low-frequency closed-class words (Bradley, Garrett, & Zurif, 1980). The failure to find this difference with closed-class words suggests that we might have separate routes to retrieving words from different syntactic categories.

Morphological complexity   From a processing standpoint, it would make sense to distinguish between the affixes (prefixes and suffixes) of a word and the base or root word. This is because the set of morphemes or affixes is relatively small and is used over and over in ways that are semantically similar. As a matter of fact, new linguistic examples occur regularly (for example, *desensitize*) and are easily interpreted.

These considerations have led several investigators to argue that morphological information and base word information are organized separately in the mental lexicon (MacKay, 1978; Marslen-Wilson, Tyler, Waksler, & Older, 1994; Taft, 1981; Taft & Forster, 1975). In this view, a word such as *decision* would be stored as the base word *decide* with a separate representation for *-ion*. In retrieving *decision*, the base word and the morpheme are united. One argument for this kind of arrangement is that it achieves some storage economy since we would not have to store all of the various forms of word but only the base and the set of morphemes used throughout the language. However, this arrangement complicates the processing of these words: instead of accessing a single word, we would have to access both base and morpheme and then combine them. It is not obvious which of the two proposals, independent storage or combined storage, would be preferable.

Some evidence for the independent storage of base word and morpheme has been provided by MacKay (1978), who presented people auditorily with verbs (*decide*) and asked them to produce a related noun (*decision*) as quickly as possible. MacKay found that the time taken to make these responses varied with the derivational complexity. The suffix *-ment* is linguistically simpler than *-ence*, which in turn is simpler than *-ion*. The suffix *-ion* is most complex because, unlike the other two, the shift from verb to noun involves an alternation of vowels. And *-ence*, in turn, is more complex than *-ment* because it often involves a regrouping of syllables. Notice that the /n/ in *government* remains at the end of the syllable (*go-vern-ment*), whereas the /t/ in *existence* shifts from the end of the base syllable to the beginning of the new syllable (*ex-is-tence*). MacKay found that the times taken to produce words such as *government*, *existence*, and *decision* reflected their linguistic complexity.

Taft and Forster (1975) have drawn similar conclusions. They assume that a word is analyzed into its morphological components and then the base word is accessed. A single-morpheme word would be accessed directly. A prefixed word, however, would go through an initial prefix-stripping stage. After the prefix has been stripped, a search for the base word is undertaken. If successful, the final stage compares the prefix and base word to see whether they are compatible. Some evidence for this multistage process has been found in lexical decision experiments. Snodgrass and Jarvella (1972) found that response times were greater for affixed words than for words without affixes, lending support for the assumption of a prefix-stripping stage.

In addition, Taft (1981) found that lexical decision times were shorter for prefixed words (such as *remind*) than for words with "pseudoprefixes" (such as *relish*). According to the Taft and Forster model, when we see *relish*, the pseudoprefix *re-* would be stripped off and then a search would be made for *-lish*. After this search was unsuccessful, *re-* would be reattached to *-lish*, and a search for the word *relish* would be successful. The unsuccessful search is presumably responsible for the longer decision times. Lima (1987) found a similar result using eye fixations during reading. Pseudoprefixed words received longer fixation times than prefixed words. The result held even when the two groups of words were similar in frequency, length, syntactic category, and other variables known to influence lexical access.

Although decomposing words into their morphological components appears to be a useful strategy on occasion, some reports suggest that it may not be used all of the time (Rubin, Becker, & Freeman, 1979). Rubin and colleagues found a difference in lexical decision times between prefixed and pseudoprefixed words only when the stimulus list contained 50% prefixed words. When the percentage of prefixed words in the list was only 10%, no difference between prefixed and pseudoprefixed words appeared. This suggests that the process of analyzing a word into its morphological components depends to some extent on the frequency of occurrence of various types of words. It may be that some frequently encountered words (such as *impossible*) are represented as single lexical items in memory and that less common words (such as *imperceptible*) are stored as base plus affixes. If so, this would be consistent with the notion of weak cognitive economy we discussed in the last section.

Semantic priming   **Semantic priming** occurs when a word presented earlier activates another, semantically related word. The priming task consists of two phases. In the first phase, a priming stimulus is presented. Often no response to the prime is required or recorded; in any event, the response to the prime itself is of little interest. In the second phase, a second stimulus (the target) is presented, the participant makes some response to it, and the time taken to make this response is recorded. The response could take many forms, but two of the most commonly used tasks are to ask people to name the word or to decide whether the string is a word. The times to respond to the target in the priming condition are then compared with a condition in which no priming stimulus or a different priming stimulus was presented.

An example is provided in a study by Meyer and Schaneveldt (1971). They used a lexical decision task and found that the time needed to classify the target *butter* as a word varied with the priming stimulus. Times were shorter when the prime was *bread* than when it was *nurse*.

Lexical ambiguity   The form of **ambiguity** in which a single word may be interpreted to have more than one meaning is referred to as **lexical ambiguity.** The study of lexical ambiguity has generated a substantial amount of research because it raises a number of intriguing questions. Do ambiguous words have more than one representation in the lexicon? Do we consider multiple meanings of ambiguous words when we hear or see one? And how might the sentence context influence how lexically ambiguous words are processed? As we shall see, ambiguity is a significant property of language, and so it is vital that any theory of language processing come to grips with the processes through which ambiguous meanings are processed and resolved.

Introspection is of little help in this regard, for we generally do not recognize or remember the multiple meanings of words that we hear. But there are some exceptions. Read sentence (19) orally to a friend, and ask for a reaction:

(19)   Rapid righting with his uninjured hand saved from loss the contents of the capsized canoe.

Most people hear the second word as *writing*, presumably because it is a more common meaning. Moreover, nothing in the sentence refutes this interpretation until we get to the end. Subjectively, the impression is that we have seized upon a single meaning at the outset and carry it through until we discover the error (Lashley, 1951). But do experiments bear out this subjective impression?

Foss (1970) was the first to apply the phoneme-monitoring technique to the study of lexical ambiguity. He presented listeners with sentences containing ambiguous words, such as those in sentence (20):

(20)   The man started to drill before the truck arrived.

The response times to monitor the first phoneme of the very next word (here, the /b/ in *before*) increased ever so slightly (by about 50 milliseconds) after an ambiguous word. Foss attributed this result to a process of activating more than one meaning of an ambiguous word.

Cairns and Kamerman (1975) extended the result. They varied the time between the ambiguous word and the phoneme that was to be monitored and found that the increased processing load associated with lexical ambiguity was very short-lived. If the phoneme was delayed by as little as two syllables, the increased processing time for ambiguous words disappeared. These results suggest that although multiple meanings of an ambiguous word are briefly entertained, the ambiguity is quickly resolved. This may be one reason that we have little or no introspective awareness of activating multiple meanings.

Even if we only briefly consider multiple meanings of ambiguous words, it is somewhat puzzling that we do it at all. After all, in most contexts only one of a word's meanings is relevant. This raises the question of whether a prior semantic context can override this process. In particular, can a context that is biased toward one or another meaning of an ambiguous word selectively activate the appropriate meaning? This is a specific form of a general question we have already pursued—the relative importance of top-down and bottom-up processes in language comprehension. Here, the top-down processes are represented by possible contextual (sentential) effects on the perception of individual lexical items, whereas bottom-up processes refer to multiple activation of even inappropriate word meanings. The question, then, is whether we activate inappropriate word meanings even when there is a contextual reason not to do so.

Swinney (1979) examined this question with a cross-modal lexical decision task. Participants listened to sentences containing lexical ambiguities in strongly biasing semantic contexts. Simultaneously, they performed a lexical decision task on visually presented letter strings. Some of the letter strings were semantically related to one of the meanings of the ambiguous word. For example, listeners might hear sentence (21):

(21)   Rumor had it that, for years, the government building has been plagued with problems. The man was not surprised when he found several spiders, roaches, and other bugs in the corner of his room.

Here the ambiguous word is *bug*, and the biasing context favors the insect meaning over the espionage meaning. As the listeners heard the word *bug*, they saw a contextually related word (*ant*), a contextually inappropriate word (*spy*), or an unrelated word (*sew*). Swinney found that decision times for visual words related to either meaning of the ambiguous word were shorter than for unrelated words when the visual words immediately followed the ambiguity. When the visual words were presented four syllables after the ambiguity, however, only the contextually appropriate meaning was facilitated. These and similar results (Onifer & Swinney, 1981; Seidenberg, Tanenhaus, Leiman, & Bienkowski, 1982) suggest that even in the presence of a strong biasing context, multiple meanings of ambiguous words are briefly activated.

One more aspect of lexical ambiguity needs to be brought into this discussion: the relative dominance or frequency of usage of various word meanings. Some words have multiple meanings that are roughly equivalent in frequency. In other instances, one meaning is clearly dominant over the others. Given our prior discussion of word frequency, it makes sense to assume that common meanings should be easier to access than uncommon meanings.

Hogaboam and Perfetti (1975) constructed sentences with ambiguous words in which either the primary or the secondary meaning of the word was appropriate. The word *letter,* for example, contains two different meanings: a note sent by one person to another (the postal meaning) or an element of the alphabet (the alphabet meaning). A sentence such as (22) requires the activation of the presumably dominant postal meaning, whereas (23) requires activation of the secondary sense for comprehension.

(22)   The jealous husband read the letter.

(23)   The antique typewriter was missing a letter.

Hogaboam and Perfetti gave participants a series of sentences such as these and asked them to decide whether the final word in the sentence was ambiguous. Decision times were faster when the sentence required the secondary sense than when it required the primary meaning.

Though this result may sound counterintuitive, consider what is involved in deciding whether a word is ambiguous. Suppose the various meanings of an ambiguous word are stored in separate locations in the lexicon. In this task, we must not only find the primary meaning but also discover whether it has a less common meaning. Presumably the common meaning is easily activated, so the time taken to find the other meaning is more directly related to response times in this task. In sentence (23), the context provides cues for the secondary meaning, and if we assume that the primary meaning is accessible all of the time, then response times should be relatively fast. However, in sentence (22), both context and meaning frequency point in the same direction, so it may be difficult to find the second meaning of the word.

Studies of eye movements make the same point. Fixation times are longer for ambiguous words in which both meanings are fairly equal in strength compared with ambiguous words in which one meaning is much more frequent. There is, in fact, no difference in fixation times between the latter type of ambiguous word and nonambiguous words. When the less frequent meaning of an unbalanced ambiguous word needed to be accessed, fixation time increases (Duffy, Morris, & Rayner, 1988; Rayner & Frazier, 1989).

With this factor of meaning frequency in mind, let us take another look at how context affects word activation. As we have seen, studies indicate that even with strong prior contexts we activate the multiple meanings of ambiguous words (Swinney, 1979). When we specifically look at ambiguous words with clearly dominant and subordinate meanings (that is, unbalanced words), the picture is slightly different. In this instance, when the context biased the dominant meaning, only the dominant meaning was activated (Tabossi, 1988). Thus, when both the dominant meaning and the biasing context point to the activation of a given meaning, it appears that lexical access can be selective.

This latter result, as well as the pattern of overall results, can be understood in terms of the logogen model discussed earlier. Suppose that each meaning of an ambiguous word has its own logogen, with its own threshold. The threshold would be lower for higher-frequency meanings. Suppose in addition that each logogen is activated as well as contextual features of the surrounding sentence(s). Depending on the exact balance of the two meanings and the nature of the context, different kinds of results may emerge. With balanced words presented in a neutral context, both meanings may be activated because the two thresholds are so similar. With unbalanced words, however, the dominant meaning has a much lower threshold than the subordinate meaning and thus a strongly biasing context may be sufficient to selectively activate the dominant meaning. In short, meaning dominance and prior context jointly influence activation of word meanings (Simpson, 1994; Tabossi, 1988; see also Simpson & Krueger, 1991).

To return to sentence (19), it should be clear that both context and frequency favor the handwriting meaning of the word over the meaning having to do with setting something right. Moreover, when we consider that these decisions concerning the appropriate meaning are made very rapidly and that the biasing context (*capsized canoe*) occurs much later, it is not surprising that we choose the wrong meaning in this instance.

Appraising Models of Lexical Access

How do the models discussed earlier fare with regard to what we have learned about lexical access? In some respects, they do quite well. For instance, all of the models provide an explanation for the word frequency effect. In the logogen model, each time a word is encountered, the threshold for that logogen is temporarily lowered. That is, after the word *heart* is presented, less sensory information (for example, a less audible sound) would be needed to recognize the word again. With high-frequency words, the recovery from the lowering of the threshold is less complete than with low-frequency words, so less sensory information is needed for recognition.

In a search model, frequency effects are explained in terms of how words are stored in the various files. High-frequency words are stored higher in the files than low-frequency words, and the search process begins at the top of the files. Accordingly, lexical access is more rapid for high-frequency words. In a cohort model, many word candidates are activated in the initial access phase, but more frequent words would be chosen in the subsequent selection stage. In short, all of the models can explain the word frequency effect. In each case, the differential access of common versus less common meanings of ambiguous words is handled in an analogous way.

Similarly, each of the models can account for semantic priming. Priming is accounted for in a logogen model by assuming that there is a rapid and temporary lowering of the threshold of those logogens that are related to a prime. The cohort model would assume that the prime narrows the set of candidates in the initial cohort list and that a shorter initial cohort leads to faster recognition of a target word.

A search model would assume that with each word, we generate a list of words that might come next (Becker, 1979). In this model, priming is conceived of more as a controlled than an automatic process (see Neely, 1977).

Moving beyond frequency and priming, it appears that the cohort model may be better positioned to explain the full range of factors that influence lexical access. The cohort model is more explicit about the time course of spoken word recognition and thus is better able to explain how sounds in different positions within the word may affect recognition (Lively et al., 1994). For instance, in the shadowing study discussed in the preceding chapter (Marslen-Wilson & Welsh, 1978), phonemes near the end of words were more likely to be restored than those at the beginnings of words. This would seem to fit the notion that we are processing words left to right, with the initial analysis more bottom-up and later processing more top-down.

Summary

Lexical access is influenced by a variety of factors, including the frequency of a word, its phonological structure, its syntactic category, its morphological structure, the presence of semantically related words, and the existence of alternative meanings of the word. Common words and meanings appear to be in a state of greater readiness than less-often-used words and meanings. We rely on morphological structure when encountering unfamiliar words.

Considerable research has investigated how we access lexically ambiguous words. Some research suggests that we briefly consider all meanings of an ambiguous word. However, when a preceding context primes the most dominant meaning of a word, lexical access may be selective.

Three models have been developed to explain these results. The active search, logogen, and cohort models can each describe some of the findings, but the cohort model appears to be best positioned to explain the entire array of results.

Review Questions

1. Describe the tip-of-the-tongue (TOT) phenomenon.
2. Distinguish between inflectional and derivational morphemes.
3. Why is there more to word meaning than reference?
4. What are the advantages and disadvantages of storing redundant information, such as *A bird can breathe*, in a semantic network?
5. How does typicality influence semantic verification times in opposite ways for true and false statements?
6. What is a spreading activation model?
7. Describe in what way a logogen for the word *table* would respond to the presentation of (a) the word *table*; (b) a semantically similar word, *chair*; and (c) a semantically distant word, *game*.

8. Compare and contrast the search, logogen, and cohort models of lexical access.
9. What evidence suggests that we store the morphemes in a multimorphemic word as separate units in memory?
10. Under what circumstances do we activate all meanings of a lexically ambiguous word, and under what circumstances is the activation more selective?

Thought Questions

1. Analyze a television game show using the concepts from this chapter. What aspects of meaning are being utilized? How are they accessed?
2. Try giving sentences like those listed in Table 5-2, or others of your own choice, to a friend. What responses did you get, and what can you conclude from them?
3. Do you think that a fluent bilingual would have two internal lexicons, one for each language, or would there be a single lexicon? Explain your decision.

6

Sentence Comprehension and Memory

- Parsing is the process of assigning elements of surface structure to linguistic categories. Because of limitations in processing resources, we begin to parse sentences as we see or hear each word in a sentence.
- We use syntactic, semantic, and pragmatic knowledge to comprehend sentences. An ongoing debate is whether we use these forms of knowledge simultaneously or whether we process syntactic information first.
- The meaning of sentences is often related to the context in which they appear. We use context, along with shared assumptions about communication, to understand nonliteral and metaphoric sentences.
- We ordinarily remember the gist of a sentence and quickly forget its surface form. An exception is pragmatically significant statements, such as insults, whose exact wording is often well remembered.

Introduction

We hear thousands of sentences every day and respond to many, perhaps most, with barely any notice of their structure. In others, the wording is so cumbersome that we find ourselves struggling to unravel what has been said. And still others are clearer in meaning than in intent: when a coworker asks over coffee whether you are feeling all right, you may perfectly well understand the question without knowing precisely what the person means by it. We often forget the exact words a person uses to convey a message, but some sentences linger in our memories for years. In short, we respond to sentences in a variety of ways. In this chapter, we will try to identify and understand the many facets of the way we comprehend sentences.

Comprehending a sentence involves attention to syntactic, semantic, and pragmatic factors. Consider a simple active declarative sentence, such as *The actor thanked the audience.* At the syntactic level, we identify the constituent or phrase structure of the sentence; that is, we identify *the actor* as a noun phrase (NP), *thanked* as a verb (V), and *the audience* as another NP. At the semantic level, we identify the semantic or thematic roles played by various words in the sentence. *Actor* is the agent and *audience* the recipient of the action. At the pragmatic level, we probably have some knowledge about the real-world circumstances in which this sentence would make sense. It might, for instance, describe the end of a play after an actor has taken a bow.

It is one thing to say that these factors are involved in comprehension and quite another to identify what part each factor plays. Do we use our syntactic, semantic, and pragmatic knowledge simultaneously when we comprehend a sentence? Or do certain factors take priority at various stages of the comprehension process? And what kinds of cognitive processes are involved when a sentence, unlike this simple declarative one, is complex enough to be a burden for working memory? These are some of the issues we will be looking at in this chapter. In the first section, we look at how we identify the syntactic structure of a sentence. Then we discuss the role of semantic and pragmatic context in sentence comprehension. Finally, in the last section, we discuss memory for sentences.

Immediate Processing of Sentences

Parsing

A first step in the process of understanding a sentence is to assign elements of its surface structure to linguistic categories, a procedure known as **parsing.** The result of parsing is an internal representation of the linguistic relationships within a sentence, usually in the form of a tree structure or **phrase marker.** Figure 6-1 depicts some of the successive points in parsing a sentence. We recognize *the* as a determiner, which signals the beginning of a noun phrase (Kimball, 1973). Our knowledge of noun phrases is that they take the form of NP ———➤ det + (adj) + N, so at this point we are looking either for an optional adjective or a noun. We recognize the next word, *actor,* as a noun and add it to the noun phrase. The remaining items are added as shown in Figure 6-1.

We may think of parsing as a form of problem solving or decision making in the sense that we are making decisions (although not necessarily in a conscious

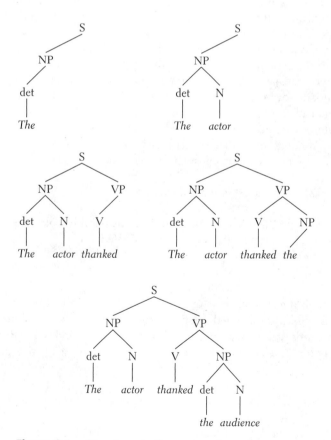

Figure 6-1. Five stages in the parsing of a sentence.

manner) about where to place incoming words into the phrase marker we are build-ing. Just and Carpenter (1980) suggest that we make these decisions immediately as we encounter a word, a principle they call the **immediacy principle.** According to this view, when we first see or hear a word, we access its meaning from permanent memory, identify its likely referent, and fit it into the syntactic structure of the sentence. The alternative to immediate processing is to take a "wait-and-see" ap-proach: to postpone interpreting a word or phrase until it is clearer where a sentence is going. However, there is considerable evidence for the immediacy principle. Although we sometimes postpone decisions, more often than not, we interpret the words as we hear or see them.

The primary reason that we use immediate processing is that the number of decisions involved in understanding even a single sentence can be quite large and thus can overload our cognitive resources. Suppose we heard sentence (1):

(1)   John bought the flower for Susan.

This sentence is syntactically ambiguous. It might mean that John bought the flower to give to Susan or that John bought a flower as a favor for Susan, who intended to give it to another person. This ambiguity is encountered when we hear the word *for*. Suppose further that we kept in mind both meanings of the sentence. But then *flower* has more than one interpretation also. It could mean *flower* or *flour* (remem-ber, the sentence was heard). Suppose we take a wait-and-see approach and wait for further information before deciding which interpretation to use. There is, however, a major disadvantage in such an approach. If we retained two or more interpretations of each of the several choice points, we would rapidly overwhelm our working memory (see Singer, 1990).

Although immediacy of processing reduces memory load, it may lead to errors in parsing. For example, consider sentence fragment (2):

(2)   The florist sent the flowers . . .

Where might this sentence be going? At this point it looks like a simple declarative sentence, but suppose it continues as indicated in (3):

(3)   . . . was very pleased.

Although it at first appears to be ungrammatical, in fact this is a grammatical sen-tence with an embedded relative clause (a clause that modifies a noun). One of the reasons that the sentence is difficult to comprehend is that the embedded clause is a reduced relative clause; it is not signaled with a relative pronoun, as in sen-tence (4):

(4)   The florist who was sent the flowers was very pleased.

Another reason is that declarative sentences are more familiar than relative clauses, so we are more likely to "place our bets" on that outcome. If we took a wait-and-see approach, we would not be surprised by the continuation in (3). But we are surprised, so it appears that we immediately interpret the fragment in (2).

Parsing Strategies

If we are making decisions about where words fit into the syntactic structure of a sentence, on what are these decisions based? Much work has been done on the strategies we use in parsing. Strategies are thought of as approaches to parsing that work much of the time, although they are hardly foolproof. We will discuss two strategies that have gathered considerable empirical support.

Late closure strategy　　One parsing strategy is called the **late closure strategy.** This strategy states that, wherever possible, we prefer to attach new items to the current constituent (Frazier, 1987; Frazier & Fodor, 1978; Kimball, 1973). A primary motivation for this strategy is that it reduces the burden on working memory during parsing (Frazier, 1987).

One example of late closure is sentence (5):

(5)　　Tom said that Bill had taken the cleaning out yesterday.

Here the adverb *yesterday* may be attached to the main clause (*Tom said . . .*) or the subsequent subordinate clause (*Bill had taken . . .*). Frazier and Fodor (1978) argue that we tend to prefer the latter strategy. Another example is (6), in which the prepositional phrase *in the library* could modify either the verb *put* or the verb *reading*. We tend to prefer attaching the prepositional phrase to the latter verb (Frazier & Fodor, 1978).

(6)　　Jessie put the book Kathy was reading in the library . . .

Further evidence for the late closure strategy comes from Frazier and Rayner (1982), who examined eye fixations of subjects reading structurally ambiguous sentences, such as (7):

(7)　　Since Jay always jogs a mile seems like a very short distance to him.

The ambiguity in this sentence is a little artificial because it lacks a comma after *jogs*. Nonetheless, the participants' eye fixations were interesting. Frazier and Rayner found that fixation times on the last few words were longer than on the earlier ones, implying that readers had misinterpreted the term *a mile* and had to make some later adjustments.

Sentences such as (7) are **garden path sentences.** As we saw in Chapter 1, in a garden path sentence, we interpret a sentence in a particular way only to find out near the end that we misinterpreted it. The subjective impression is that of being led down a garden path until discovering at the end that we took the wrong path and have to retrace our efforts. The garden path experience lends further support to the immediacy principle, for if we did not commit ourselves to an immediate inter-pretation, we would not have found ourselves in this predicament.

Minimal attachment strategy   A second strategy is referred to as the **minimal at-tachment strategy,** which states that we prefer attaching new items into the phrase marker being constructed using the fewest syntactic nodes consistent with the rules of the language (Frazier, 1987; Frazier & Fodor, 1978). For example, a sentence fragment such as (8) could be interpreted as either a noun phrase conjunction (that is, both Marcie and her sister were recipients of a kiss) or as the beginning of a new noun phrase. According to minimal attachment, we prefer the former interpretation (Frazier, 1987).

> **(8)**   Ernie kissed Marcie and her sister . . .

Frazier and Rayner's (1982) study cited earlier also found evidence for the minimal attachment strategy. For example, consider sentences (9) and (10):

> **(9)**   The city council argued the mayor's position forcefully.
> **(10)**   The city council argued the mayor's position was correct.

Sentence (9) is consistent with minimal attachment in that the adverb *forcefully* is attached to the current constituent, the VP (see Figure 6-2a). In contrast, sentence (10) is a complement construction that requires building a new constituent (Figure 6-2b). Frazier and Rayner found that reading times were faster for (9) than for (10).

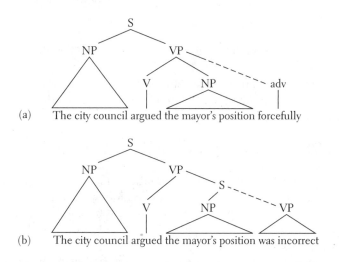

Figure 6-2. Tree diagrams for (a) *The city council argued the mayor's position forcefully* and (b) *The city council argued the mayor's position was incorrect.* (Based on "Making and Correcting Errors During Sentence Comprehension: Eye Movements in the Analysis of Structurally Ambiguous Sentences," by L. Frazier and K. Rayner, 1982, *Cognitive Psychology, 14,* p. 181, Academic Press.)

Modular versus Interactive Models

The parsing strategies identified by Frazier are consistent with the modular approach to language comprehension in which comprehension as a whole is the result of many different modules, each devoted to a particular aspect of comprehension (Fodor, 1983). In this view, parsing is performed initially by a syntactic module that is not influenced by higher-order contextual variables such as the meaning of the sentence or by general world knowledge. Frazier (1987, 1995), for example, claims that parsing is executed by a syntactic module, and these contextual factors influence comprehension at a later stage.

An alternative view is that syntax and semantics interact during the comprehension process (Britt, Perfetti, Garrod, & Rayner, 1992; Crain & Steedman, 1985; Taraban & McClelland, 1988; Tyler & Marslen-Wilson, 1977). One type of interactive view is called the **constraint-based model** (MacDonald, Pearlmutter, & Seidenberg, 1994; McClelland, 1987; Trueswell, Tanenhaus, & Garnsey, 1994). In this model, we simultaneously use all available information in our initial parsing of a sentence—syntactic, lexical, discourse, as well as nonlinguistic, contextual information (Tanenhaus, Spivey-Knowlton, Eberhard, & Sedivy, 1995).

Much of the research that has compared these two proposals has examined structurally ambiguous sentences. In particular, attention has been given to sentences such as (11). As we are listening to it, this sentence fragment may be parsed in one of two ways. The parsing favored by the minimal attachment principle is that *sent* is the verb (MV), as in sentence (12). This interpretation leads to a garden path effect later in the sentence. The other interpretation is a reduced relative clause (13). This ambiguity occurs because English permits the reduction or deletion of relative clauses such as *who was.*

(11) The florist sent the flowers was very pleased.
(12) The florist sent the flowers to the elderly widow.
(13) The florist who was sent the flowers was very pleased.

Rayner, Carlson, and Frazier (1983) examined whether the plausibility of real-world events influenced the immediate parsing of sentences. When we discussed (11) earlier, you may have wondered whether the garden path effect is related to the fact that we expect florists to send flowers, not receive them. In sentence (14), the interpretation that the performer received the flowers is considerably more plausible:

(14) The performer sent the flowers was very pleased.

Rayner and colleagues measured eye fixations on segments of these sentences and found that initial analyses of the sentences were unrelated to the plausibility variable. Clear garden path effects were found with both plausible and implausible sentences.

Ferreira and Clifton (1986) examined whether a paragraph context would override the minimal attachment strategy:

(15)   The editor played the tape and agreed it was a big story.

(16)   The editor played the tape agreed it was a big story.

(17)   John worked as a reporter for a big city newspaper. He sensed that a major story was brewing over the city hall scandal, and he obtained some evidence that he believed pretty much established the mayor's guilt. He gave a tape to his editor and told him to listen to it.

(18)   . . . He ran a tape for one of his editors, and he showed some photos to the other.

The researchers presented subjects with sentences that could ([15]) and could not ([16]) be parsed by means of minimal attachment. In some instances, the paragraph context biased the reader toward a minimal attachment interpretation of the target sentence, as in (17). In other instances, such as (18), the context primed the non-minimal attachment interpretation. Nevertheless, the researchers found that readers continued to use the minimal attachment principle. Reaction times for the critical region of the sentence (*agreed*) were longer for sentences that violated minimal attachment than for those that did not, but no differences were observed between different paragraph contexts. These results suggest that the parser operates with structural biases that are not influenced by prior semantic context.

Other results have been more favorable to the constraint-based framework. Trueswell, Tanenhaus, and Garnsey (1994) examined eye fixations to sentences such as (19) and (20):

(19)   The defendant examined by the lawyer turned out to be unreliable.

(20)   The evidence examined by the lawyer turned out to be unreliable.

Although these two sentences are structurally similar, the eye patterns were much greater when the subject was animate ([19]). Trueswell and colleagues suggest that comprehenders immediately utilize their lexical knowledge to determine that the main verb or minimal attachment interpretation of (20) is not possible (in other words, evidence does not examine; it is examined by someone). In contrast, (19) permits the incorrect main verb interpretation and thus leads to a garden path effect. This result suggests that comprehenders immediately use lexical knowledge to guide parsing. Similar results are reported by Trueswell, Tanenhaus, and Kello (1993).

It appears, then, that some information other than syntactic strategies such as minimal attachment and late closure are influencing initial parsing decisions. But is this process as fully interactive as constraint-based models have claimed—that is, are various forms of knowledge (lexical, discourse, extralinguistic) used simultaneously during parsing? Or are some forms of knowledge accorded a more privileged role in parsing?

The current research suggests that lexical variables influence parsing more rapidly and consistently than discourse variables. In particular, comprehenders seem to quickly use information about the kinds of syntactic structures in which various words are likely to participate. For instance, sentence (21) is a structurally ambiguous sentence; the prepositional phrase *with the boomerang* may be attached to the verb *hit* or the noun *the girl*. Britt et al. (1992) found that readers had a tendency to attach the phrase to *hit* but would attach it to *the girl* if given a preceding paragraph that led the reader toward that meaning. In contrast, discourse context has no effect on reduced relative clauses, replicating the results of Ferreira and Clifton (1986).

(21)   The boy hit the girl with the boomerang.

Similarly, Boland (1997) examined the comprehension of sentences such as (22) and (23), in which the key word, *duck*, could be either a noun or a verb. Boland found that college students had reliable lexical preferences; for instance, when given a fragment such as *She saw her duck* . . . , most individuals completed the sentence with a verb rather than a noun. These lexical preferences in turn had a large and immediate effect on eye movement patterns in these sentences. When the remainder of the sentence matched lexical preferences, reading time was faster. By contrast, the extent to which the sentence was consistent with the preceding paragraph had a weaker and slower effect on reading times.

(22)   She saw her duck and some eggs.
(23)   She saw her duck and fall down.

Research on parsing continues at a brisk pace. Work to date is consistent with a view that parsing is influenced by both structural principles such as minimal attachment and late closure along with lexical and, to a lesser extent, discourse factors. The observation that lexical factors play a more significant role than discourse factors may be related to the fact that lexical access, as we saw in the last chapter, is often an automatic process. In contrast, discourse processing, as we shall see in greater detail in Chapter 7, is largely a controlled process. For instance, we sometimes draw inferences that connect sentences in discourse, but inferences are not automatically drawn (McKoon & Ratcliff, 1992). In short, it may be that only lexical access is rapid and automatic enough to influence parsing decisions consistently (Britt, 1994).

Summary

Parsing, the process of assigning elements of the surface structure of a sentence to linguistic categories, is the first step in understanding a sentence. As a result of processing limitations, we begin to analyze sentence structure as soon as we see or hear the first words.

Two theories of parsing have been developed. The modular approach suggests that the words of a sentence activate syntactic processing strategies that are used to organize the words into a phrase marker. These strategies indicate that we prefer to attach incoming words to the most recent constituent as opposed to attaching them to earlier constituents or developing new ones. Although the strategies are generally useful, they sometimes lead to errors and subsequent reanalyses of syntactic structure.

The interactive approach emphasizes that we use all available information, including lexical, discourse, and contextual factors. Whereas the modular approach insists that syntactically based strategies are used first, with lexical and discourse factors coming in later, the interactive model asserts that we simultaneously use all available information to parse sentences. Current research supports the role of lexical and contextual factors in parsing, but the role of discourse factors is less evident.

Comprehending Sentences in Context

The parsing mechanism we have just considered has as its output a syntactic structure of the incoming sentence. This provides a basis for determining the literal meaning of the sentence. But many of the sentences we use on an everyday basis are not meant to be taken literally. For instance, suppose we heard someone say sentence (24):

(24)   Can you pass the salt?

It is literally a question of one's ability, but it is taken, in most contexts, as polite form of a request. Similarly, sentence (25) may at first appear to be a meaningless statement, but if preceded by a discussion of some of the emotional problems that may beset a relationship, it may be successfully understood as a **metaphor:**

(25)   Some marriages are iceboxes.

These sentences suggest that there is often a difference between the meaning of a sentence and the meaning that a speaker is conveying with the sentence. This is a rich area in the study of language, one that brings semantic and, especially, pragmatic factors into play.

This section of the chapter will examine how we may use the communicative context to understand sentences. We begin by discussing the notion that we interpret utterances in context by means of communicative conventions. Then we turn to two important and interesting types of sentences: indirect speech acts and metaphors.

Conventions

It is generally held that linguistic communication takes place within a context of shared assumptions about communication (Bach & Harnish, 1979; Grice, 1975). These implicit assumptions are referred to as **conventions.** Grice (1975) has identi-

Table 6-1. Four Conventions for Conversations

1. Quantity: Make your contribution as informative as is required, but not more informative than is required.
2. Quality: Try to make your contribution one that is truthful. That is, do not say anything you believe to be false.
3. Relation: Make your contribution relevant to the aims of the ongoing conversation.
4. Manner: Be clear. Try to avoid obscurity, ambiguity, wordiness, and disorderliness in your use of language.

Source: From "Logic and Conversation," by H. P. Grice. In P. Cole and J. L. Morgan (Eds.), *Syntax and Semantics, Vol. 3: Speech Acts*, pp. 45–46, Seminar, 1975.

fied four conventions (which he calls maxims) governing conversations (Table 6-1). According to Grice, we strive to be informative, clear, relevant, and truthful.

Of course, these conventions provide no more than ground rules for successful conversations; all of us, from time to time, are uninformative, unclear, irrelevant, and deceitful. Grice's point is that these conventions provide a basis for interpreting what others mean because we generally assume, unless we have information to the contrary, that such conventions will be observed.

As an example, suppose you heard the following pair of sentences:

(26)   Harold was in an accident.
(27)   He had been drinking.

More than likely, you would consider Harold's drinking a factor in his accident. However, if you think about it, the drinking might have been unrelated to the accident; he might have been driving safely although intoxicated when another driver ran a red light. For that matter, Harold might have been a passenger in the car or might have been drinking soft drinks. All of these possibilities would be given little or no consideration by most comprehenders. Most would think, quite naturally, that if any of these scenarios were what was meant, then the pair of sentences is misleading. Another way of saying the same thing is to say that we are led, by the convention of relation, to assume that there is a relationship between the events in the two sentences. It is this convention that guides us to a particular interpretation of these sentences.

Similar examples can be constructed for the other conventions identified by Grice. Collectively, the conventions represent some shared assumptions about how we communicate with others, and these conventions guide our comprehension.

Speech Acts

Austin (1962) inspired a good deal of research into the various ways a speech utterance might function. He was especially interested in certain utterances that do not seem to communicate much information but, instead, serve as an action. When we use phrases such as *I promise . . .*, *I apologize . . .*, and *I congratulate . . .*, the very act of uttering the sentence is a kind of action. These are quite different than utterances in which assertions are made. For example, it makes sense for someone to say *No, that's not true* to an assertion such as (28), but it makes no sense at all to respond in this manner to a sentence such as (29):

(28)   It's going to be cold today.

(29)   I congratulate you on your award.

In discussing such sentences, it will be helpful to use some of Austin's terminology. The act of saying something is referred to as the **locutionary act.** The **illocutionary force** of an utterance is the action that is performed by saying the sentence. In sentence (29), the illocutionary force is a congratulation; the act of saying the sentence performs the act. An utterance with an illocutionary force is commonly referred to as a **speech act.** Finally, we may distinguish each of these from the **perlocutionary effect** of the utterance, which is the effect of the utterance on a listener. This may or may not coincide with the illocutionary force; for instance, I may apologize, but you may not accept my apology.

One type of speech act that has drawn considerable interest is the **indirect speech act,** which is a speech act in which the communicative meaning does not correspond to the literal meaning of the sentence. An example is sentence (30), which is conventionally understood as an indirect or polite form of a request:

(30)   Can you shut the door?

An interesting fact about indirect speech acts is that although no direct relationship exists between the form of the sentence and its intended meaning, listeners apparently have little trouble comprehending these speech acts.

An indirect request can be made in several common ways. One is to question the ability of the person who is asked to perform the action, as in sentence (30). Another is to refer to the listener's willingness to perform the desired action, as in sentence (31):

(31)   Will you shut the door?

Still another is to indicate the reason that such an action needs to be done, as in sentence (32):

(32)   It's getting cold in here.

Whether the person addressed has the ability or willingness to perform the desired action and the reason that the action is necessary are referred to as **felicity conditions.** When a speech act meets most of these conditions, it is generally regarded as sincere or valid. When these conditions are not present, the speech act is typically viewed as odd or socially inappropriate, as it would be if we addressed (30) to a person in a wheelchair.

How do we comprehend indirect speech acts? It was once believed that we compute such meanings by considering, then rejecting, the literal meaning (Clark & Lucy, 1975; Searle, 1975). Searle (1975) claimed that we use several stages, of which three are most relevant here. In stage 1, the listener extracts the literal meaning of the sentence. In stage 2, the listener decides whether the literal meaning is what the speaker intended, based on the context and communicative conventions. For instance, a literal reading of sentence (30) may be viewed as a violation of the convention of relation. If in stage 2 the listener decides the literal meaning was not intended, then the listener computes in stage 3 an indirect meaning based on communicative conventions and the direct speech act. In this view, literal meaning necessarily precedes nonliteral meaning.

This model was tested in a study by Clark and Lucy (1975). On each trial, subjects were presented with a request and a picture and were asked whether the two matched or did not match. Relying on previous studies that indicated that negative sentences take longer to comprehend than affirmative sentences (Clark, 1974), Clark and Lucy examined the effects of negation on both literal and nonliteral meaning. For example, sentence (33) is positive in terms of both the indirect meaning and its surface expression; sentence (34), although expressed positively, conveys the negative meaning that the speaker would like the door to remain closed. In contrast, (35) is a request to open the door but is expressed in negative form.

(33) Can you open the door?
(34) Must you open the door?
(35) Why not open the door?

Clark and Lucy found that positive requests behaved as affirmative sentences, requiring less time to comprehend than negative requests. Moreover, when the request was phrased in negative form, it also increased comprehension time. They took this result to mean that subjects computed the literal meaning of the sentence first, just as predicted in Searle's model.

Gibbs (1979) challenged this view. He presented individuals with sentences such as (36) either in a story context or as an isolated sentence. This sentence might be interpreted literally, as in (37), or as an indirect request, as in (38).

(36) Must you open the window?
(37) Need you open the window?
(38) Do not open the window.

One story context matched the first interpretation:

Mrs. Smith was watering her garden one afternoon. She saw the housepainter was pushing a window open. She didn't understand why he needed to have it open. A bit worried she went over and politely asked, "Must you open the window?"

Another matched the second one:

> One morning John felt too sick to go to school. The night before he and his friends got very drunk. Because of this he caught a bad cold. He was lying in bed when his mother stormed in. When she started to open the window John groaned, "Must you open the window?"

Individuals either read the isolated sentence or the sentence in one of the two story contexts. After reading the key sentence, they were shown another sentence and asked whether it was a true or false paraphrase of the key sentence. The time needed to make this judgment was recorded. When the sentences were presented in isolation, indirect requests took longer than literal sentences, replicating the results of Clark and Lucy (1975). However, when the sentence was in a story context, people took longer to comprehend literal meanings than indirect meanings.

Gibbs (1979) concluded that it is not always necessary to compute a direct meaning prior to indirect meaning. In natural discourse, previous sentences may have activated enough information in semantic memory to comprehend the non-literal meaning directly, without first considering the direct speech act. The three-stage procedure suggested by Searle and found by Clark and Lucy (and Gibbs, in the noncontext condition) may be a special strategy used when an indirect speech act is presented to us either in a way that does not fit with previous discourse or with no context at all.

Metaphors

When someone says that *Jim's head is full of rocks,* we instantly recognize it as a metaphoric statement. The comprehension of metaphoric language poses some very interesting problems for a general theory of language comprehension. For one thing, metaphors and other forms of figurative language are ubiquitous features of language and thus cannot be dismissed as a peripheral concern. Moreover, the apparent ease of comprehension of most metaphors suggests a link with the processes of language comprehension we have discussed throughout this chapter. Yet, the manner in which word meanings are combined to form novel metaphors seems to extend our understanding of comprehension, for metaphors are invariably literally false. Thus, the question to be pursued here is in what way we comprehend a meaning that is literally anomalous but metaphorically not just meaningful but often amusing, thought-provoking, or poignant.

Metaphors consist of three main parts. Consider, for example, sentence (39):

(39) Billboards are warts on the landscape.

The topic or **tenor** of the metaphor is *billboards.* The **vehicle** is what is predicated of the tenor; here it is *warts.* The **ground** of the metaphor is the implied similarity between tenor and vehicle. Thus, we could say that the ground, in this metaphor, is that both billboards and warts are "ugly protrusions on some surface" (Verbrugge & McCarrell, 1977). In terms of comprehension, this analysis suggests that comprehenders use the tenor and vehicle to infer the ground.

Why do we choose to use a metaphor rather than a literal statement to express a thought? Ortony (1975) has suggested that metaphors are often used to communicate continuous experiential information, especially information that is otherwise difficult or impossible to express. Ortony argues that whereas the range of human experience is continuous, words are intrinsically discrete. This argument implies that there is a gap between concepts derived from experience and the words used to describe that experience and that the use of metaphor is an attempt to fill that gap by extending the meaning of various words. Thus, sentence (40) is a good metaphor because it would be difficult to express the thought literally. In contrast, sentence (41) is not as good because the ground could have been expressed literally: both are round.

(40) The thought slipped my mind like a squirrel behind a tree.

(41) Oranges are the baseballs of the fruit lover.

Comprehension of metaphor Let us now turn to the comprehension of metaphors. Verbrugge and McCarrell (1977) have convincingly shown that people comprehend and retain the ground of metaphors they have heard. The researchers orally presented a series of metaphors to students and later tested the students' recall by prompting them with the topic, the vehicle, or the ground. (Remember that the ground, unlike the other two, is not explicitly stated in a metaphor.) Thus, in sentence (42), the ground might be *are very tall compared with surrounding things.*

(42) Skyscrapers are the giraffes of the city.

The interesting result was that grounds were found to be as effective as (and sometimes even more effective than) topics or vehicles as recall cues for the sentences. This result strongly suggests that we identify the underlying similarity relation between tenor and vehicle during the comprehension process.

Given this result, much of the recent research on metaphor comprehension has been devoted to the issue of exactly how this relation is recovered. It has been suggested that we do so by means of a series of stages (Grice, 1975; Miller, 1979; Searle, 1979). We first recognize that the sentence is not literally true. Then, guided by the convention of quality, we search for another possible meaning. This leads us to transform the sentence into an implicit similarity statement of the form A *is like B.* This view implies that the literal interpretation of an utterance always precedes the metaphoric interpretation and that the metaphoric meaning is optional in the sense that it comes into play only if we decide that the literal meaning is defective or inappropriate. Let us look at each of these points in turn.

The idea that the literal meaning is understood before the metaphoric meaning implies that metaphors should always take more time to comprehend than literal sentences. Ortony, Schallert, Reynolds, and Antos (1978) directly compared the comprehension time for literal statements and for metaphors. They found that when no context preceded the metaphor, metaphoric statements took longer to comprehend than literal statements. However, with 45-word contexts, metaphors required no more or less time to understand than literal statements.

Glucksberg, Gildea, and Bookin (1982) examined the notion that metaphoric readings are optional. They used a paradigm in which subjects were asked to decide if a sentence was literally true or not. Some of these sentences were metaphors, such as (43), and were metaphorically true but literally false.

(43)   All jobs are jails.

Glucksberg and colleagues reasoned that if the metaphoric reading was automatically available at the same time as the literal reading, it would slow down the subjects' response times on the task. They found that when metaphoric interpretations of literally false sentences were available, subjects took longer to decide that the sentence was false. The researchers concluded that we cannot ignore metaphors, even when metaphoric readings are irrelevant to the task.

In a related study, Gildea and Glucksberg (1983) studied the effect of context on the comprehension of metaphor, using a task similar to that used by Glucksberg in the earlier study. Gildea and Glucksberg distinguished between metaphors that may be easily understood in isolation, such as sentence (43), and metaphors that require some degree of contextual support, such as sentence (44). The purpose of the study was to determine the minimal amount of context needed to comprehend the latter type of metaphor. The participants were given metaphors such as (44) preceded by figurative primes (45), literal primes (46), or no prime at all, and their task once again was to decide whether the sentence was literally true or false.

(44)   All hands are medicine.
(45)   Some arms are soothing.
(46)   Some songs are soothing.

If the primes facilitated the understanding of the metaphor, and if—as in the previous study—the presence of the metaphoric reading slowed response time to the literal reading, then the facilitating context should slow down times further. Gildea and Glucksberg found that it took the participants longer to make literal true/false decisions when either type of prime was present, relative to the no-prime condition. Apparently both literal and figurative priming facilitate metaphor comprehension.

Metaphor and "normal" comprehension processes   Taken together, these results suggest that metaphor is not merely a special case—something we do when "normal" comprehension does not work—but rather fundamentally similar to "normal" comprehension processes. In support of this notion, Glucksberg and Keysar (1990) argue that metaphors may be viewed as class-inclusion statements. That is, when we see a metaphor such as (47), we understand it as analogous to the kinds of class-inclusion statements we studied in Chapter 5, such as (48):

(47) My job is a jail.

(48) All dogs are animals.

To determine whether either of these sentences is true, we must retrieve the lexical representations of the appropriate nouns and assess whether the class-inclusion relation is applied appropriately.

But how can we assess this relation if the statement is not literally true? Glucksberg and Keysar suggest that the term *jail* belongs not to just one but to several different superordinate categories. It belongs to the category of punishments, including related notions of fines, tickets, and spankings. It is a member of the category of buildings, which also includes hotels, hospitals, and dormitories. It also may be considered a member of a category that does not have a conventional name but includes situations that are regarded as unpleasant, confining, or stifling. It is this latter category that may include the term *job*.

Some might complain that this is not what jail ordinarily means. And yet, even the literal meanings of words vary with their context. Consider, for example, the differences in the meaning of *container* in sentences (49) and (50):

(49) The container held the apples.

(50) The container held the cola.

In (49), most people develop a concrete meaning along the lines of a basket; in (50), we envision something closer to a bottle or glass. In either case, we seem to be identifying a general term with a specific meaning, a process known as **instantiation** (Anderson & Ortony, 1975).

In a similar way, metaphors also require a selective activation of information from the lexicon. Only certain aspects of billboards and giraffes are important; others are irrelevant. Glucksberg and colleagues (1982) argue that certain "stock" metaphors such as *is a butcher* call forth a core of meaning from the lexicon that is used in different situations. For example, what do sentences (51) and (52) have in common?

(51) The pianist is a butcher.

(52) The surgeon is a butcher.

Certainly, the statements involve a negative evaluation in either case and imply gross incompetence. The exact type of incompetence varies with the topic, but, as we have seen with instantiation, this is generally true in literal comprehension.

Thus, the emerging view of metaphor comprehension is that we understand metaphors much the way we understand literal speech—by retrieving information from the lexicon, selecting the part that is germane, and identifying a relationship between the lexical representations that have been retrieved.

Summary

We comprehend sentences in light of the sentential and nonverbal context and with reference to various conventions regarding how language is ordinarily used. Metaphors are primarily used to convey ideas and feelings that are difficult to express, and indirect speech acts are often employed to state a request in a polite way. These conventions are generally shared by members of the linguistic community and are used during the comprehension process.

It has been proposed that we comprehend indirect speech and metaphor by a multistage process in which we first consider and reject the literal meaning and then use communicative conventions to construct the speaker's intended meaning. Recent research on both indirect speech acts and metaphors fails to support this view. On the contrary, we tend to comprehend such sentences directly, in a manner analogous to, rather than dependent on, literal language.

Memory for Sentences

What do we remember after one exposure to a single sentence? As we have seen, the processing activities devoted to even a single sentence can be quite complex, and there is reason to believe that substantial processing leads to durable retention (Craik & Lockhart, 1972). But in natural discourse, one sentence follows rapidly on the heels of another, then another, and it is unlikely that we can retain all of them accurately. Perhaps some stand out more and are used to help recall some of the others. Or perhaps they become blended into a single general idea of what the other person said. In this section, we will examine what we remember and what we do not remember from sentences and the way sentences are ultimately stored in permanent memory.

Memory for Meaning versus Surface Form

A basic idea in studies of sentence memory concerns whether we retain the exact or verbatim wording of a sentence or simply its meaning. Most of the early research on this issue suggested that only meaning was retained. Fillenbaum (1966) presented people with a long list of unrelated sentences and later gave them a multiple-choice test of each of the sentences. In one example, the sentence was (53), and the options were sentences (54) to (56):

(53)   The window is not closed.
(54)   The window is closed.
(55)   The window is not open.
(56)   The window is open.

The alternatives were structured to permit some inferences about the basis of sentence retention. Both sentences (54) and (55) are superficially similar to (53), but sentence (56) is closer to the original in meaning. Fillenbaum found that most people correctly remembered sentence (53) as what they heard, but if they made an error, they were much more likely to choose (56) than either (54) or (55). Apparently, the meaning similarity of *closed* and *not open* enabled comprehenders to infer one from the other.

Fillenbaum (1966) was careful to distinguish between adjectives such as *open* and *closed*, which are contradictories, and *tall* and *short*, which are contraries. Whereas the negation of a contradictory implies its opposite, this does not happen for contraries (*not short* does not imply *tall*). People in his study drew inferences from contradictories but not from contraries.

A clever experiment by Wanner (1974) also examined surface form versus meaning retention. People often bring to psychological experiments special strategies that are not representative of language processing under more natural circumstances. Wanner sought to get around this problem by giving the participants fairly routine instructions to an experiment, then giving them a surprise test on the instructions themselves. The key sentence was (57):

(57) When you score the results, do nothing to your correct answer but mark carefully those answers which are wrong.

Seconds after hearing this sentence, the participants were tested on one of two parts of it. Some were tested on the wording *your correct* and were given a recognition test with the choice of the original wording and *correct your*, which changes the meaning of the sentence. Others were tested on their ability to distinguish between *mark carefully* and *carefully mark*, which mean the same thing. Wanner found excellent memory for meaning (100% correct on *your correct*) but only chance performance on wording (50% correct on *mark carefully*). Thus, when people listen to sentences without knowing they are to be tested on them, they primarily retain the meaning, not the surface form.

Time course of retention Studies like those we have been discussing have been used to support the idea that we ordinarily use the syntactic structure of a sentence to extract the underlying meaning. A classic study by Sachs (1967) examined the time parameters within which these processes might operate.

Sachs (1967) asked students to listen to tape-recorded passages. At various intervals she interrupted the passage and tested the participants on a sentence they had heard previously. She varied two factors: the types of test sentences and the **retention interval** (the time between presentation and test). For each sentence in the passage, there was a set of four possible test sentences: the original, two that changed the wording but not the meaning, and one that changed the wording and the meaning. When the tape was stopped, the subjects were given one of the four sentences and asked whether it was identical or changed from the one they had heard before. When the test sentence was presented immediately after the study sentence, retention of both form and meaning was excellent, but memory for form declined substantially with 40 syllables of retention interval (about 12.5 seconds) and even more with 80 syllables of delay. In contrast, memory for meaning was relatively durable over this time period.

This result has proven to be reliable. Sachs (1974) repeated the study with visual presentation of sentences and obtained essentially the same results. Even more impressively, Hanson and Bellugi (1982) replicated the study using American Sign Language. Like English, ASL conveys both lexical and morphological information, but, unlike English, it does so simultaneously (see Chapter 2). Despite this difference, Hanson and Bellugi found results that were strikingly similar to those of the original study. On an immediate test, deaf individuals recognized semantic, inflectional, lexical, and formal changes; but in a delayed test, those that changed meaning (semantic and inflectional) were recognized better than those that did not (lexical and formal). Thus, the tendency to store only the meaning of a sentence in permanent memory is not limited to spoken languages.

Pragmatic factors   In some situations, however, we seem to remember the exact form of what was said to us. Perhaps it was puzzling or confusing or irritating, and we found cause to mull it over a bit. A few studies have examined the way pragmatic factors interact with semantic and syntactic considerations in sentence memory.

Keenan, MacWhinney, and Mayhew (1977) examined memory for sentence form and content in natural conversations. They recorded luncheon discussions by researchers (who did not know they were being recorded) and constructed recognition memory tests from these recordings. The researchers' key finding was that the **interactional content** of an utterance is an important factor in its retention under naturalistic conditions. Some utterances only convey information to the listener; others convey the attitude of the speaker toward the listener. These latter types of utterances are high in interactional content and include figures of speech, jokes, insults, and the like. Keenan and colleagues found that subjects had excellent retention of form as well as meaning of statements that were high in interactional content, but they showed no memory for surface form and less memory for meaning of statements low in interactional content. Moreover, when such statements were pulled out of context and presented individually in a separate study, these differences in retention disappeared. Thus, it is not the syntactic or semantic aspects of high-interactional statements that make them memorable but rather the pragmatic function they play in the conversational context. Bates, Masling, and Kintsch (1978), who reported similar results, conclude that "the probability that a given surface form will be retained will, at least in part, be a function of the pragmatic role that surface form plays in a given context" (p. 196).

Similar factors are at work in our memory for sentences that convey politeness. In a recent study (Holtgraves, 1997), students heard sentences that varied in politeness that had been made by a high-status (for example, professor) or equal-status (such as another student) speaker. Students remembered polite wording better than impolite wording in an unexpected memory test. In addition, they were more likely to remember forms that were incongruous with a speaker's status, such as an equal-status speaker using impolite wording or a high-status speaker using polite wording.

Inferences and Sentence Memory

The notion that greater elaboration of processing leads to better retention has received a substantial amount of support in psychological studies of words, sentences, and discourse. **Elaboration** is thought of as a process by which incoming information is related to information already stored in permanent memory, thereby enriching the memory representation of the new material. We have just seen how information processing pertaining to the pragmatic functions of everyday speech may serve as the basis for elaboration. We now turn to elaborations based on our general knowledge of the world, information that is not specifically linguistic in nature.

A particular form of elaborative processing is the drawing of inferences. Bransford, Barclay, and Franks (1972) have argued that we routinely draw inferences in the course of comprehending new events and that these inferences become incorporated into our memory representations of the event. With the passage of time, it becomes increasingly difficult to distinguish what was presented from what was inferred.

Inferences and false recognition errors   The general experimental procedure used by Bransford has been to present people with long lists of sentences and later to probe their tendency to make **false recognition errors**: errors that people make by believing that they saw or heard something that was actually not presented. A long list is necessary to encourage participants to attend to the meaning, not just the form, of the sentences.

In one study, Johnson, Bransford, and Solomon (1973) examined people's comprehension and retention of sentences such as (58):

(58)   John was trying to fix the birdhouse. He was looking for the nail when his father came out to watch him and to help him do the work.

The passage does not specifically state that John used a hammer, but it is part of our general knowledge that is retrieved in the course of comprehension. Later, people who heard sentence (58) falsely believed that they had heard sentence (59):

(59)   John was using the hammer to fix the birdhouse when his father came out to watch him and to help him do the work.

Once again, this suggests that an inference about the instrument used in fixing the birdhouse was drawn during comprehension. Other studies have shown that although we do not automatically draw instrument inferences during comprehension (Dosher & Corbett, 1982), we tend to do so when the inferences aid in the integration of sentences in a passage (McKoon & Ratcliff, 1981).

It is at least a little misleading to call these patterns "errors." In normal circumstances, these inferences are adaptive in enabling us to tie sentences in discourse together (see Chapter 7). In effect, Bransford and his colleagues have devised some clever ways of revealing how these inferences may induce "errors" in a laboratory setting in which, quite unlike natural language use, we are asked to remember the exact form of what was said.

Role of inferences in advertising   Our inability to distinguish easily between linguistic messages and the inferences we draw from them is a matter of considerable practical concern. This is especially true in advertising, for advertisers are highly skilled at creating impressions about products. Psychological studies have explored the question of whether our tendency to draw inferences might influence our beliefs about commercial products.

In one study, Harris (1977) instructed students to listen to 20 commercials about various products and later asked them to determine whether statements about the products were true, false, or of indeterminate truth value. Some of the claims were directly stated, but others were merely implied:

> "Wouldn't it be great," asks the mother, "if you could make him coldproof? Well, you can't. Nothing can do that (boy sneezes). But there is something that you can do that may help. Have him gargle with Gargoil Antiseptic. Gargoil can't promise to keep him cold-free, but it may help him fight off colds. During the cold-catching season, have him gargle twice a day with full-strength Gargoil. Watch his diet, see he gets plenty of sleep, and there's a good chance he'll have fewer colds, milder colds this year." (Harris & Monaco, 1978, p. 18)

Despite disclaimers and hedges such as *you can't, can't promise,* and *a good chance,* all 15 individuals in this study agreed with sentence (60):

(60)   Gargling with Gargoil Antiseptic helps prevent colds.

In general, Harris found that people were not very good at distinguishing between claims that were directly asserted and those that were implied.

These results have implications for the way advertisers do their work. Advertisers are prevented, on legal grounds, from making false statements about their products, but making false implications is less dangerous. From an advertiser's perspective, implied messages are extremely attractive because they can create the same impression as explicit messages without the same legal repercussions. Moreover, it would be extremely difficult to protect the general public from false implications because, in most situations, unlike the Gargoil commercial, only some people draw the misleading inference. If only half the people draw a false conclusion from a commercial, should the advertiser be held responsible?

An alternative approach to dealing with misleading claims is to focus on the processing activities of the comprehender. People do not ordinarily distinguish between assertions and implications, but they can do so under certain conditions. Harris (1977) found moderate improvement in performance when people were explicitly warned not to interpret implied claims as assertions. Moreover, Bruno (1977, cited in Harris, 1977) found that a 20-minute training session involving written exercises and student-teacher interaction improved performance for junior high school students and for adults. Thus, training directed at understanding the dangers of drawing unwarranted inferences can reduce our susceptibility to misleading claims.

Propositions and Sentence Memory

Let me sum up what we have learned about sentence memory. It appears that we generally store the gist of what another person has said, rather than exact form of the sentence. An exception is statements that are pragmatically striking, such as those that require a response from us or flout the normal conventions of everyday discourse. In these cases, we often draw some inference based on what a person has said and store this enriched meaning along with the surface form of the utterance. Moreover, other forms of inference that we draw are based not on purely linguistic knowledge but rather on general world knowledge. These inferences are drawn in the process of comprehension and are, after a period of time, increasingly indistinguishable from the exact sentences to which we were exposed.

All of these considerations suggest that a linguistically based representational system (such as deep structure in transformational grammar) is a poor candidate for a model of sentence memory. It appears that the exact linguistic form is not well retained and, moreover, additional, nonlinguistic information may play a major role in the retention process. Alternatively, investigators have developed propositional models of sentence representation (see, for example, Anderson, 1976; Kintsch, 1974; Norman, Rumelhart, & the LNR Research Group, 1975). All of the proposals assume that a sentence can be represented as a **proposition** consisting of two or more concepts and some form of relation between them. Thus, sentence (61) could be represented as (62). The passive form of sentence (63) or, for that matter, other forms such as (64) and (65), despite their superficial dissimilarities, all convey the same proposition.

(61) George hit Harry.
(62) Hit (George, Harry)
(63) Harry was hit by George.
(64) It was Harry who was hit by George.
(65) The one who hit Harry was George.

More complex sentences convey more than one proposition. Sentence (66) could be represented as three separate propositions ([67] through [69]). Once again, these propositions may be realized linguistically in a very large number of ways.

(66) George got into an argument with Harry, hit him, and then left the bar.
(67) Initiated (George, Harry, argument)
(68) Hit (George, Harry)
(69) Left (George, bar)

A rough description of the way a propositional representation of a sentence might be set up during comprehension is as follows. When we first encounter a sentence, we extract its meaning and construct a proposition that represents this meaning. At the same time, the surface form of the sentence is being retained in working memory. Since the meaning is usually of greater interest, more processing resources are devoted to the meaning (which persists for a period of time) than to the surface form (which fades over a briefer interval). If the surface structure is pragmatically significant, more attention is given to it, with consequently better retention. This might lead to the drawing of additional propositions (inferences), which are stored along with the propositions of the presented sentences. On memory tests, the memory representation(s) of a sentence are consulted. Unless the sentence was pragmatically striking or the retention interval was very short, only the propositional representation along with any inferences that were drawn will still be stored. As a consequence, our memory for meaning is excellent, but we are susceptible to remembering inferential material falsely.

An important advantage of propositional models is that they can be extended naturally to discourse since the meaning representation of two one-proposition sentences is equivalent to that of one two-proposition sentence. In natural discourse, we generally recall the meaning that a sentence contributes to the overall discourse meaning. In the next chapter, I will have much more to say about the role of propositions in discourse comprehension and retention.

Summary

Our memory for sentences is a mixture of the meaning of the sentences, their wording, and the inferences we draw at the time of comprehension. Numerous studies show that meaning predominates in our retention of sentences. Inferences may be seen as embellishments to a core of meaning we have extracted from the sentences. After a period of time, we have some difficulty distinguishing between what was presented and what we inferred, a tendency that leaves us somewhat vulnerable to misleading advertising. Yet, with careful attention, we can distinguish between assertions and implications. Similarly, by focusing our attention on the exact form of the sentences we hear, we can retain this form for a long time. This may occur if the speech is insulting, humorous, or pragmatically significant in some other way.

Review Questions

1. Define parsing.
2. What is the basis for the immediacy principle?
3. What is the minimal attachment principle?
4. What evidence suggests that initial parsing decisions are based on syntactic strategies?
5. What is a communicative convention, and how is it used in the comprehension process?

6. Is it necessary for us to understand the literal meaning of an indirect speech act before we can understand the intended meaning?

7. How do we identify the ground of a metaphor?

8. Under what conditions do we remember the exact wording of a sentence we have seen or heard?

9. Describe the results and conclusions of psychological studies of inferences in advertising.

10. What considerations make propositional models of sentence memory more attractive than linguistic models?

Thought Questions

1. Think of a recent example of a misunderstanding that occurred during a conversation. Using Grice's conventions, identify the basis of the misunderstanding.

2. We saw in Chapter 2 that linguistic productivity is a basic linguistic concept. To what extent are the principles of parsing described in this chapter equipped to handle an infinite number of sentences?

3. Using the discussion of inferences as your foundation, discuss the ways in which a political candidate might use language to exploit our tendency to accept false implications.

4. Is there any limit to the number of inferences a person can draw from a sentence? How are the inferences based on communicative conventions to be differentiated from the wider class of conclusions that an imaginative listener might reach?

5. Metaphor is often used to express thoughts that are difficult or impossible to express literally. What does this suggest about the possible role of metaphor in linguistic evolution?

Discourse Comprehension and Memory

MAIN POINTS

- Connected discourse is coherent if its sentences can be related to one another. These relationships exist on both local and global levels.
- Comprehenders use a variety of strategies to understand discourse in a coherent manner. These strategies are related to assumptions about the use of given and new information.
- We represent discourse in memory in three different ways: a surface representation, a propositional representation, and a situational model.
- Comprehension of the global structure of discourse is guided by schemata, which are structures in semantic memory that depict the general sequence of events.

Introduction

This chapter deals with the ways we comprehend and remember units of language larger than the sentence—that is, connected discourse. In our everyday lives, we process a number of different types of discourse, for example, stories, lectures, and sermons. Each form has its own characteristics, to be sure, but we will find in this chapter that all types of discourse share certain properties.

Research on discourse has grown significantly in recent decades, for several reasons. For one, since we rarely speak in isolated sentences, discourse seems to be a more natural unit of language to investigate. Also, sentences are also ambiguous or obscure apart from their discourse context. Just as we need to examine sentence structure to fully appreciate word processing, so we must understand discourse structure to appreciate sentence processing. Finally, discourse provides a rich source of material for those interested in the cognitive processes used in language. Discourse imposes a considerable burden on working memory while at the same time drawing heavily from our permanent memory.

We begin our investigation by discussing the ways discourse is organized and how this organization influences comprehension strategies. I will describe several processing strategies that we use to produce a coherent discourse structure. Then, we turn to memory for connected discourse and examine the structures that are built into memory after we have understood a passage. We will discover that three types of memory representation are implicated in discourse processing. Next, we look at narrative discourse and the special processes involved in understanding and remembering stories. Finally, I will point out some of the educational implications of research on discourse comprehension and memory.

Comprehension of Discourse

Local and Global Discourse Structure

Comprehension of connected discourse depends less on the meanings of the individual sentences than on their arrangement. Indeed, it is entirely possible for a group of meaningful sentences to be thrown together in a way that makes no sense at all:

> Carlos arranged to take golf lessons from the local professional. His dog, a cocker spaniel, was expecting pups again. Andrea had the car washed for the big wedding. She expected Carlos to help her move into her new apartment.

In contrast, the following passage is much easier to follow:

> John bought a cake at the bake shop. The cake was chocolate with white frosting, and it read "Happy Birthday, Joan" in red letters. John was particularly pleased with the lettering. He brought it over to Greg's house, and together they worked on the rest of the details.

What makes some passages easy to understand and others virtually incomprehensible?

Part of the reason that the second story is easier to comprehend is that the sentences in John's story are connected in conventional ways. It is customary, for example, to use the indefinite article *a* when readers have not yet been introduced to the object, person, or event and the definite article *the* when these have already been mentioned. Notice, then, that *a cake* in the first sentence is replaced by *the cake* in the second sentence. Similarly, the pronoun *it* is incomprehensible without a preceding context. In John's story, we are able to determine that *it* refers to *the cake* in the second and fourth sentences. In the story about Carlos, events are mentioned as if we knew about them already, but we do not really know that the cocker had pups, who is getting married, or that Andrea is moving. The only basis of coherence in the story, the repeated references to Carlos and Andrea, is quite insufficient for purposes of comprehension.

It is not necessary to be explicit all of the time. Sometimes we leave out some of the connections between sentences if we think readers are able to infer them. For example:

> John bought a cake at the bake shop. The birthday card was signed by all of the employees. The party went on until after midnight.

Here it is assumed that the cake, the card, and the party all correspond to the same event, a birthday party. How do we make this judgment so easily? We know a good deal about birthdays and what typically happens at birthday parties, and this knowledge allows us to fill in some of the gaps in the tale. Yet, note that *the* is used to introduce both the card and the party, thus signaling that we should know which card and which party. This serves as a cue to use some of that information in memory (party? What party?) to draw these inferences, which ties together the loose strings of the passage so that its overall meaning is unified and coherent.

The contrast between the last two passages illustrates an important point— that we must look beneath the surface to understand discourse structure. Superficially, the last passage is incomplete, but the overall result in readers' minds may be quite complete.

The three passages discussed illustrate two levels of discourse structure. The story about Carlos differs from the first John story in its **local structure** (sometimes called its **microstructure**)—that is, in the relationships between individual sentences in the discourse. Texts also have a **global structure** (or **macrostructure**), and it is our knowledge of the structure corresponding to birthdays that enables us to comprehend and remember the shorter passage about the birthday. Both levels of structure contribute to the **coherence** of a text, the degree to which different parts (words, sentences, paragraphs) of a text are connected to one another. We will begin with the local structure and work our way up to global aspects of discourse.

Cohesion

At the local level, a discourse is coherent if there are semantic relationships between successive sentences. A central concept is the notion of **cohesion.** Halliday and Hasan (1976) define cohesion as referring to "the range of possibilities that exist for linking something with what has gone before" (p. 10). They studied cohesion in English and discovered the categories in Table 7-1.

Categories of cohesion   One type of cohesion is called **reference.** This is a different concept than the one we discussed in Chapter 5. There, reference dealt with the links between words and objects or events in the world. In discourse, reference deals with the links between words (or phrases) and other words (or phrases) in discourse. More precisely, reference is a semantic relation whereby information needed for the interpretation of one item is found elsewhere in the text. We often use pronouns such as *she, he, it, his, her,* and *their* to refer to earlier items. In the example in Table 7-1, *she* in the second sentence refers back to *the woman* in the first sentence. This gives cohesion to the two sentences, and we may integrate them into a connected whole. We also use demonstratives such as *the, this, that,* and *those* for

Table 7-1.   Categories of Cohesion

Category	Example
Reference	
Pronominal	The woman lost track of her little boy at the mall. *She* became very worried.
Demonstrative	*That* was the worst exam I had all term.
Comparative	It's the *same* band we heard last week.
Substitution	My computer is too slow. I need to get a faster *one*.
Ellipsis	I wish I had more talent. My sister has a lot *more* than I do.
Conjunction	Melissa flunked out of school, *so* she is looking for a job.
Lexical	
Reiteration	I saw a boy win the spelling bee. The *boy* was delighted afterward.
Synonymy	I saw a boy win the spelling bee. The *lad* was delighted afterward.
Hyponymy	I saw a boy win the spelling bee. The *child* was delighted afterward.

Source: Based on *Cohesion in English,* by M. A. K. Halliday and R. Hasan, Longman, 1976.

referential purposes; in the table, *that* refers to a particular exam. Another type of reference is comparative reference, in which we use terms such as *same, different,* and *similar* to relate current objects with those in the past.

Halliday and Hasan identify several other categories of cohesion. In **substitution,** we replace one lexical item with another as an alternative to repeating the first. For example, *one* substitutes for *my computer.* **Ellipsis** is a form of cohesion that is really a special case of substitution in which we "substitute" one phrase with nothing. Notice that the word *talent* could be repeated after the word *more* in the second sentence; in ellipsis, this repetition is assumed. In **conjunctive cohesion,** we express a relationship between phrases or sentences by using conjunctions such as *and, or, but, yet,* and *so.* In **lexical cohesion,** a tie is made between one sentence or phrase and another by virtue of the lexical relationships between certain words in the sentence. In the simplest instance, we merely reiterate the same word used earlier. Other forms of lexical cohesion may be based on relationships such as synonymy and hyponymy.

Cohesion plays an important role in discourse. One way to see this is to look at a paragraph in which the sentences have been scrambled:

(1) However, nobody had seen one for months.
(2) He thought he saw a shape in the bushes.
(3) Mark had told him about the foxes.
(4) John looked out the window.
(5) Could it be a fox?

Look at sentences (1) through (5) and try to unscramble them. You will find that the cohesive ties between sentences are an important clue (from Crystal, 1987). The answer is given at the end of the chapter.

Anaphoric and cataphoric reference   In all of these examples, cohesion consists of relating some current expression to one encountered earlier. This is called **anaphoric reference.** When we use an expression to refer back to something previously mentioned in discourse, the referring expression is called an **anaphor,** and the previous referent is called an **antecedent.** In the first example in Table 7-1, *she* is the anaphor and *the woman* is the antecedent. Alternatively, we sometimes use referring expressions to point forward, which is called **cataphoric reference.** *This* in sentence (6) serves this function:

(6) This is how you do it. You let the herbs dry and then grind them up in a food processor.

Of all these forms of cohesion, anaphoric reference has commanded the greatest interest among psychologists. One reason is that anaphoric reference enables us to explore the role of working memory in discourse comprehension. To understand a simple pair of sentences, we must hold the antecedent in working memory long enough to link it with the anaphor. All of the examples so far have been of relations between successive sentences in discourse, but this is not always the case. Sometimes the distance between antecedent and anaphor is much longer, imposing a burden on working memory and ultimately disrupting comprehension.

The use of anaphors also illuminates the role of communicative conventions in discourse. We discussed some of Grice's (1975) notions about communication in Chapter 6, and they are relevant here as well. To communicate successfully, we need to use language in conventional ways. If as a speaker or writer we place a large distance between antecedent and anaphor, it is not only cognitively difficult for the comprehender but also an unexpected burden as well.

Strategies Used to Establish Coherence

Let us now turn to psychological investigations related to the comprehension of anaphoric expressions. A good deal of the research has been stimulated by the work of Clark and Haviland (Clark, 1977; Clark & Haviland, 1977; Haviland & Clark, 1974). This work is based on the distinction between given and new information. **Given information** refers to information that an author or speaker assumes the reader or listener already knows, whereas **new information** is information that the comprehender is assumed to not know. Most sentences contain both given and new information. For example, sentences (7) and (8) below are similar in their grammatical structure but convey different expectations, with (7) assuming that readers already know that the bank was robbed (the given information) but do not know who did it (the new information), and (8) assuming that readers know that Steve robbed something but not what it was he robbed.

(7)   It was Steve who robbed the bank.

(8)   It was the bank that Steve robbed.

Given/new strategy   In an explicit extension of Grice's (1975) maxim of relation, Clark and Haviland (1977) suggest that readers expect authors to use given information to refer to information the readers already know or can identify and to use new information to refer to concepts with which they are not already familiar. A model of sentence integration called the **given/new strategy** is derived from these assumptions. According to this strategy, the process of understanding a sentence in discourse context consists of three subprocesses or stages: (1) identifying the given and new information in the current sentence, (2) finding an antecedent in memory for the given information, and (3) attaching the new information to this spot in memory. The primary usefulness of this model has been in examining the various possibilities that can occur during stage 2. Sentences that mark information as given but have no obvious antecedent from previous sentences should pose comprehension difficulties.

The method most often used to examine the relative ease with which we relate sentences is a reading-time paradigm. Individuals are shown a sentence and are asked to press a button when they think they have understood it. The time from when the sentence is first presented until the viewer presses the button is measured. This is an essentially subjective determination of comprehension time, since we are relying on the participants' reports of comprehension. A more rigorous technique would be to require participants to perform some task that depends on the meaning of the sentence, such as generating a plausible next sentence or verifying the sentence as true or false in relation to another sentence. Since the results of these more controlled studies generally corroborate the studies using simple comprehension time, we will restrict our discussion to the latter for ease of exposition.

In this context, our interest is not in the time necessary to comprehend a single sentence but rather the time needed to understand the sentence as a function of one or more previous sentences. Thus, experiments have kept the target sentence (the one whose reading time is measured) constant and have varied the preceding context sentence(s). When a target directly follows from the context, stage 2 should be relatively simple, and comprehension should be fast. Let us go through some cases to illustrate the varieties of sentence relations we typically encounter.

Direct matching The simplest case is surely that in which the given information in the target sentence directly matches an antecedent in the context sentence:

(9) We got some beer out of the trunk.
(10) The beer was warm.

In comprehending the target sentence, we first divide it into given and new information. The definite article *the* marks *beer* as given and *was warm* as new. We then search our memory for a previous reference to beer and find it in the context sentence. Finally, we attach the information that the beer was warm to the previously stored information.

Even though direct matches are the simplest case of sentence relations, they are not so simple that they can be reduced to merely searching for a specific word. Finding an antecedent for given information in a target sentence resembles searching for a concept more than searching for a word. This distinction is clarified in the following sentences:

(11) Zak hopped into a waiting car and sped around the corner. He swerved to avoid the parked car and smashed into a building.

Here the reference to *car* in the second sentence is not taken as a reference to Zak's car. In contrast, in the following passage, it is:

(12) Zak hopped into a waiting car and sped around the corner. The old car lost a wheel and smashed into a building.

What counts, then, is not the repetition of words but the repetition of concepts in the underlying discourse. The concepts may be referred to in any number of ways.

Thus, when we speak of direct matches, we are talking of matches of underlying concepts previously introduced into the discourse (see Yekovich & Walker, 1978).

Bridging   In some cases, we do not have a direct antecedent for the given information but can still tie the sentences together:

(13)   Last Christmas Eugene went to a lot of parties.
(14)   This Christmas he got very drunk again.

Here, we must make a **bridging** inference, such as that Eugene got very drunk at last year's parties, to make sense of the word *again*. In contrast, a direct antecedent pair such as

(15)   Last Christmas Eugene got absolutely smashed.
(16)   This Christmas he got very drunk again.

requires no such bridge for comprehension. Haviland and Clark (1974) have shown that target sentences that require bridges take longer to comprehend than those for which there is a direct match of antecedents.

Reinstating old information   The best way to understand this strategy is to compare the following two passages:

> I am trying to find a black dog. He is short and has a dog tag on his neck that says Fred. Yesterday that dog bit a little girl. She was scared but she wasn't really hurt.

> Yesterday a black dog bit a little girl. It got away and we are still trying to find it. He is short and has a dog tag on his neck that says Fred. She was scared but she wasn't really hurt.

You probably found that the target sentence in the first passage was easier to comprehend. Since a direct antecedent for *she* is presented, we do not need to resort to bridging. The problem in the second passage is simply that the antecedent is too far removed from the target. Using Chafe's (1972) terms, the dog is in the **foreground** and the girl is in the **background** by the time we see the target, whereas the girl is in the foreground in the first passage. When a sentence refers to something or someone already introduced but no longer in the foreground, the comprehender must reinstate the information that is to be matched with the target information. Several studies have shown that **reinstatements** increase comprehension time (Clark & Sengul, 1979; Lesgold, Roth, & Curtis, 1979).

Identifying new topics of discourse   We have discussed three cases so far. When there is a direct match between given information in the target and an antecedent immediately preceding it, the given/new strategy is performed without any problem. If we cannot find an antecedent readily, we might form a bridge between the antecedent and target, or we might search information recently entered in permanent memory for antecedents that could be reinstated. In general, we form bridges when we believe the author intends for us to find a relationship between the context and the target but has not spelled it out explicitly. Reinstatements are more likely to be used when we think our failure to find a unique antecedent has been caused by the carelessness of the author.

All of these strategies share the implicit assumption that part of a target sentence should relate to earlier information, but sometimes the information is all new and the target is meant to establish a new topic of discourse. This is easy to detect when explicit markers such as *Now, I want to move on to . . .* or *This concludes our discussion of . . .* are used. Unfortunately, we know very little about the way comprehenders use more subtle cues to detect topic shifts.

The given/new strategy provides a sensible framework within which we can examine a number of cases of integration among sentences. The focus up until now has been almost entirely on stage 2 of the strategy. Let us now consider stage 3, the process of attaching new information to the memory location defined by antecedents. Note that the process of adding new information to given information subordinates the former to the latter. That is, the new information is generally taken as an elaboration, sometimes a small detail, of the given information. Once introduced, this new information may itself serve as an antecedent for later sentences, which are subordinated to it. Thus, the natural result of this integration process is a hierarchical structure in episodic memory. Using the example given at the start of the chapter, the memory representation for the passage might look like Figure 7-1.

Role of Working Memory

As with other aspects of language, individual experiences and abilities vary. Since the process we have been describing in this section deals with the operation of working memory, it would be reasonable to expect that individual differences in working memory might influence how we comprehend discourse (Carpenter & Just, 1989; Daneman & Carpenter, 1980; Singer, Andrusiak, Reisdorf, & Black, 1992).

Daneman and Carpenter (1980), for example, distinguish between the storage and processing functions of working memory. The limited resources of working memory are allocated to processing certain tasks as well as to temporarily storing the

Figure 7-1. A memory representation.

results of these tasks. As a result, we sometimes find ourselves in a trade-off position. When a task has considerable storage and processing demands, we may be unable to perform both functions satisfactorily.

Daneman and Carpenter developed a complex **reading span task** to examine this trade-off. The researchers had participants read aloud a series of sentences (processing function) and then recall the final word in each sentence (storage function). The task began with only two sentences in a series and progressed until a person could not recall the final words in each sentence. For their participants, the reading spans (the number of final words recalled) varied from two to five. The researchers then administered a reading comprehension task: each participant read a passage and answered a few questions about it. Daneman and Carpenter found a significant correlation between reading span and reading comprehension. Some of their results are shown in Figure 7-2. This figure shows performance on pronoun reference questions as a function of reading span and of the distance between the pronoun and the referent noun. Note that all the individuals performed well when

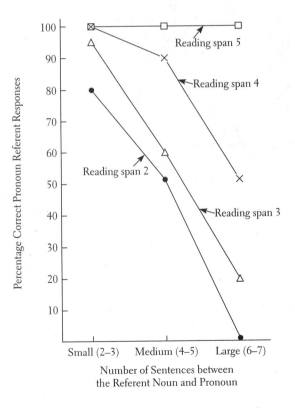

Figure 7-2.   Percentage of correct responses to the pronoun reference questions as a function of the distance between the pronoun and the referent noun. (From "Individual Differences in Working Memory and Reading," by M. Daneman and P. A. Carpenter, 1980, *Journal of Verbal Learning and Verbal Behavior, 19*, p. 456. Copyright © 1980 Academic Press. Reprinted by permission.)

the pronouns referred back only two to three sentences, but with medium and large distances, performance dropped off, especially for those with smaller reading spans. Daneman and Carpenter's interpretation of these results was that individuals with smaller reading spans had smaller working memory capacity, which made it difficult for them to comprehend references more than a few sentences back (but see Daneman & Tardif, 1987, for a somewhat different interpretation of these results).

Daneman and Carpenter also found that their reading span measure correlated significantly with their participants' verbal SAT scores. In contrast, a simple span test (simple recall of words, which requires resources for storage but not processing) did not correlate significantly with either pronoun reference or verbal SAT. It appears that both the reading comprehension test the researchers devised and the verbal SAT tap working memory processes.

Whitney, Ritchie, and Clark (1991) have extended these results. They had two groups of individuals who differed in working memory read difficult passages aloud and think out loud during the reading. Whitney et al. were particularly interested in the inferences that occurred during the thinking-out-loud procedure. Both groups produced inferences, but high–memory span readers tended to do so toward the end of a passage, whereas low–memory span readers distributed their inferences more evenly throughout the passage. In addition, low-span readers developed more specific elaborations that were definite interpretations of ambiguous aspects of the passage, whereas high-span readers used more general inferences that left the interpretation more open ended. Apparently, the difficulty in retaining so much information in working memory led some low-span readers to form concrete, specific inferences, some of which later turned out to be wrong. By keeping their options open, high-span readers were able to make these decisions later in the passage, when they are more likely to be correct.

Working memory capacity, of course, is not the only individual characteristic that influences discourse comprehension. Another is the background knowledge that the individual may have of the subject matter in the passage. When we encounter unfamiliar passages, it is more difficult to draw appropriate inferences. In contrast, when we have information in permanent memory that helps us interpret the information, it is easier to draw inferences.

Summary

A discourse is coherent if its elements are easily related to one another. At the local or microstructural level, coherence is achieved primarily through the appropriate use of cohesive ties between sentences. New sentences are easier to integrate when they have a clear relation to prior material while presenting new information.

The given/new strategy specifies a three-stage process of comprehending sentences in discourse: identifying the given and new information in the current sentence, finding an antecedent for the given information, and attaching the new information to the memory location defined by the antecedent. Comprehension is impeded when there is no antecedent, forcing us to form a bridging inference, or when the antecedent was not recent, forcing us to reinstate the antecedent.

Memory for Discourse

Many times we read or listen to discourse with no intention of remembering its content, as when reading a newspaper or listening to a casual conversation. In such instances, our primary cognitive activities are to identify the topic of discourse, tie sentences together, and follow the flow of what is being said. On other occasions, as when reading a textbook or listening to a particularly interesting speech, we wish to remember some or all of the passage. Since comprehension and memory are closely related, much of the work needed to remember a passage is accomplished when we understand it well. Approaching discourse with the intention of recalling it, however, usually calls up other processes designed to strengthen and reinforce what has already been understood.

It has been proposed that our memory for discourse exists on three distinct levels (Fletcher, 1994; van Dijk & Kintsch, 1983). One level is that of a **surface representation,** in which we remember the exact words that we encountered. Second, we construct a **propositional representation** of the discourse, which specifies the meaning apart from the exact words used. These two levels are obviously similar to the corresponding levels in our memory for sentences. Third, we construct a **situational model** of the discourse, which is a model of the state of affairs in the world as described in the passage. Let us consider each level in turn, followed by their interrelationships.

Surface Representations

One early study that suggested that surface representations of discourse are very short-lived presented individuals with a long oral passage that was interrupted at irregular intervals (Jarvella, 1971). Individuals were asked at each interruption to write down in verbatim form as much of the preceding discourse as they could. Two versions of the passage were created. Consider sentences (17) and (18):

(17)   The confidence of Kofach was not unfounded. To stack the meeting for McDonald, the union had even brought in outsiders.

(18)   Kofach had been persuaded by the international to stack the meeting for McDonald. The union had even brought in outsiders.

Although the final clauses in (17) and (18) were identical, the material immediately preceding either came from the same sentence (17) or the earlier sentence (18). It was found that the percentage of correct recall of the next to last clause was far better when it was part of the current sentence than when it was part of an earlier sentence. These and similar results (Sachs, 1967) have been taken as evidence that the surface or verbatim form of a sentence is stored in working memory only until its meaning is understood, then purged to make room for the next sentence.

There is an exception to this rule, however. Subsequent results indicate that we sometimes remember the exact wording over a long time period (Bates, Masling, & Kintsch, 1978; Keenan, MacWhinney, & Mayhew, 1977; Kintsch & Bates, 1977).

For example, Kintsch and Bates (1977), in a study of recall of lecture material, found that their students often remembered the exact wording of extraneous comments such as announcements, jokes, and asides. Apparently, we can remember the exact wording of some material when it is distinctive and easily separable from the rest of the discourse.

Propositional Representations

As we saw in Chapter 6, we often store the meaning of sentences in the form of propositions. If we indeed purge working memory of the exact wording, what is left is the propositional structure of a sentence.

Evidence for the psychological reality of propositions comes from Kintsch and Keenan (1973), who showed that the number of propositions influences the time required to read a passage when preparing to recall it. For example, the following two sentences have about the same number of words:

(19) Cleopatra's downfall lay in her foolish trust in the fickle political figures of the Roman world.

(20) Romulus, the legendary founder of Rome, took the women of the Sabine by force.

However, sentence (19) is more complex propositionally (eight propositions) than (20), which contains four propositions. Kintsch and Keenan found that a proposition added about 1.5 seconds to the reading time. Later studies (for example, Graesser, Hoffman, & Clark, 1980) provide somewhat lower estimates of the time needed to encode a single proposition but support the general conclusion that the number of propositions is related to reading time.

Further work explored the notion that discourse is stored as a network of propositions. McKoon and Ratcliff (1980), in an elegant series of experiments, used the notion of spreading activation, which we discussed in Chapter 5, to examine the memory representations of discourse. Students were given passages such as the following:

> Early French settlements in North America were strung so thinly along the major waterways that land ownership was not a problem. The Frenchmen were fur traders, and, by necessity, the fur traders were nomads. Towns were few, forts and trading posts were many. Little wonder that the successful fur trader learned to live, act, and think like an Indian. Circulation among the Indians was vital to the economic survival of the traders.

Later the students participated in a priming task in which one proposition (the context or prime) from the passage was presented and followed by a second proposition (the target). The time taken to decide whether the target was true or false, in relation to the passage, was recorded. Reaction time to the target should decrease if the context primes it, with closer items showing a larger priming effect.

Figure 7-3.   Discourse structure of a passage. (Based on "Priming in Item Recognition: The Organization of Propositions in Memory for Text," by G. McKoon and R. Ratcliff, 1980, *Journal of Verbal Learning and Behaviors, 18,* p. 371, Academic Press.)

The most interesting aspect of McKoon and Ratcliff's (1980) study was their comparison of two definitions of "close": the number of intervening words in the surface structure versus the number of intervening propositions in the discourse structure. The discourse structure for this passage, simplified somewhat, is shown in Figure 7-3. Pairs of sentences that were close in the discourse structure but not in the surface structure, such as (21) and (22), produced larger priming effects than pairs that were close in surface structure but not in discourse structure, such as sentences (23) and (24):

(21)   Circulation among the Indians was vital.
(22)   The fur traders were nomads.
(23)   Land ownership was not a problem.
(24)   The fur traders were nomads.

These results suggest, once again, that we have a propositional structure, not a verbal representation, in episodic memory after we have understood a passage.

Inferences and propositional representations   As we saw in Chapter 6, we sometimes draw inferences in the course of language comprehension. From the perspective outlined in this chapter, inferences are not mere recall errors, nor are they random, spurious contributions by imaginative readers. Inferences are intrinsic to discourse structure. Authors leave out information that they think readers will be able to figure out. This technique does no harm to discourse coherence since implicit propositions (those the comprehender supplies) restore the coherence lost when explicit propositions are omitted. Once again, it is useful to bear in mind that coherence has a greater association with the unitary impression of a passage in the comprehender's mind than with the completeness of a set of words sitting on a printed page.

The ability to restore discourse coherence requires more than knowing the way to make connections between explicit propositions. It also demands the ability to detect when an inference should be drawn, which can be a subtle matter. We must see a gap before we are motivated to fill it. From this perspective, inferences are not drawn simply because they are available but because they are necessary. For example, consider sentences (25) and (26):

(25) Paul walked into the room.

(26) Paint was all over his shirt.

This pair demands an inference because otherwise our conventions regarding the use of given and new information are violated. From a communication standpoint, an inference is a proposition in the underlying discourse structure that is intended but not explicitly expressed by the author and thus must be drawn by the reader.

This view is supported by a thorough analysis by McKoon and Ratcliff (1992). They concluded, on the basis of a number of studies, that we automatically draw inferences during reading only when two conditions are present. One condition is the one we have been discussing: the inference must be necessary to make a text locally coherent. Their second condition is that the information on which the inference is based must be easily activated (either from explicit statements in the text or from general knowledge). When these conditions apply, McKoon and Ratcliff found that readers automatically draw inferences. Other inferences may also be drawn, but they are not drawn automatically.

Furthermore, there is evidence that when we draw inferences from a text, we store the implicit propositions right alongside the explicit propositions we have derived from the text itself. Kintsch (1974) presented individuals with passages that required inferences or their explicit counterpart. For example, an explicit version is sentences (27) and (28), whereas an implicit version is sentences (29) and (30):

(27) A carelessly discarded burning cigarette started a fire.

(28) The fire destroyed many acres of virgin forest.

(29) A burning cigarette was carelessly discarded.

(30) The fire destroyed many acres of virgin forest.

The participants' task was first to read the passage and then perform a verification task. On the verification task, they were given sentences such as *A discarded cigarette started a fire,* and their reaction time to respond true or false was recorded.

The results are shown in Figure 7-4. Note that although the verification times for explicit propositions are faster when given an immediate test, there is no difference between explicit and implicit propositions when the test is delayed by 15 minutes. Kintsch explains the results by appealing to the two levels of representation we have discussed: a short-term surface representation that decays or is otherwise lost very quickly and a long-term propositional representation. Implicit propositions have only a propositional representation, and it is assumed that consulting a surface representation is quicker than retrieving a propositional represen-

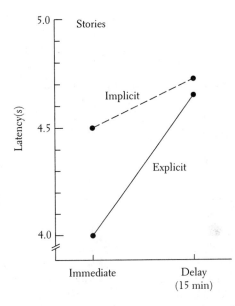

Figure 7-4.   Reaction times to verify explicitly presented test sentences. Based on *The Representations of Meaning in Memory*, by W. Kintsch, Erlbaum Associates, 1974.)

tation. The immediate test taps both representations, so there should be an advantage for the explicit propositions. However, since this surface representation is lost with a longer retention interval, there is no difference between explicit and implicit propositions in the delayed test.

Situational Models

Some recent work indicates that in addition to surface and propositional representations, we have a third memory representation of discourse called a **situational model** (Johnson-Laird, 1983; van Dijk & Kintsch, 1983). Unlike propositional representations, which represent the meaning of a text, situational models represent the state of affairs that a text refers to. That is, the assumption is that as we comprehend the propositions of a text, we construct a mental or situational model of the world as described by the text.

What might a situational model look like? One possibility is a spatial layout. Consider a study by Bransford, Barclay, and Franks (1972) in which students were presented with a list of sentences such as (31):

(31)   Three turtles rested on a floating log, and a fish swam beneath them.

Others were given (32):

(32)   Three turtles rested beside a floating log, and a fish swam beneath them.

Notice that the only difference between the two sentences is whether the turtles were on or beside the log. Then both groups were given a list of sentences that either were or were not presented earlier and were asked to decide whether they had seen them before. The key sentence was (33):

(33)   A fish swam beneath a floating log.

Students who read (31) were more likely to falsely recognize (33) than those who read (32). It appears that comprehenders constructed a spatial layout of the situation rather than store the individual sentences or propositions.

The phrasing of a text may encourage either the development of a propositional text base or a situational model. Perrig and Kintsch (1985) gave college students one of two informationally equivalent versions of a text about the spatial layout of a fictitious town. One version (survey text) used geographical terms, whereas the other (route text) was phrased in terms of the directions used for driving through the town. For example, one sentence from the survey text was *North of the highway just east of the river is a gas station*; the route version was *On your left just after you cross the river you see a gas station*. On a free recall test, the route group recalled more propositions. In contrast, when asked to draw a map of the town, the survey group made fewer errors. Perrig and Kintsch suggest that the survey text invites the construction of a spatial situation model while the route text simplifies the task of constructing a coherent propositional representation.

Similarly, Morrow, Bower, and Greenspan (1989) asked participants to memorize a map of a research center and then read narratives about characters at various locations in the center (see Figure 7-5). Some of the sentences described the characters' movements through the rooms of the center. After each of these "motion sentences," the participants were presented with pairs of objects from various rooms. The researchers found that the participants' response times were faster when the objects were from the goal room (the room to which the character was going) than the source room (where the character came from) or the path room (which the character moved through to get to the goal room). This was true even when the goal room was not explicitly mentioned in the narrative. These results suggest that the participants constructed mental models of the center during the course of reading.

Furthermore, the construction of a situational model influences the accessibility of previous information in discourse. When subjects read stories concerning the movement of a character through a building, reading times of sentences that referred to objects increased with the number of rooms between the object and the character (Rinck & Bower, 1995). In contrast, accessibility of referents was not related to the time that elapsed since encountering a particular object. Thus, it appears that comprehenders are constructing a spatial situation model, as opposed to storing sentences in the order in which they were presented.

All of the preceding examples of situational models are spatial models, but there are other kinds of situational models. Another type of model is a causal model (Fletcher, 1994), in which the parts of a text are connected by causal relations. Since causal relations are particularly salient in narrative discourse, which we will pursue in the next section, I will postpone our discussion of causality until then.

Figure 7-5. Building layout. (From "Updating Situational Models During Narrative Comprehension," by D. G. Morrow, G. H. Bower, and S. L. Greenspan, 1989, *Journal of Memory and Language, 28,* 292–312 (figure appears on p. 295). Copyright © 1989 Academic Press. Reprinted by permission.)

Simultaneous Investigations of All Three Levels

Let us try to pull some of these strands together. As we have seen, we form surface, propositional, and situational representations during the course of comprehending discourse. Most of the studies we have discussed to this point have attempted to isolate one of these levels or to distinguish between different levels. It is also helpful, however, to set up a study that attempts to investigate how each of the levels operates in the same experiment.

Test

George likes to flaunt his wealth by purchasing rare art treasures. He has a Persian rug worth as much as my car and it's the cheapest thing he owns. Last week he bought a French oil painting for $12,000 and an Indian necklace for $13,500. *George says that his wife was angry when she found out that the necklace cost more than the carpet.* His most expensive "treasures" are a Ming vase and a Greek statue. The statue is the only thing he ever spent more than $50,000 for. It's hard to believe that the statue cost George more than five times what he paid for the beautiful Persian carpet.

Test Items

Surface Text:

> George says that his wife was angry when she found out that the necklace cost more than the (carpet/rug).

Propositional Text:

> George says that his wife was angry when she found out that the necklace cost more than the (carpet/painting).

Model Text:

> George says that his wife was angry when she found out that the necklace cost more than the (carpet/vase).

Figure 7-6.   Example text from Fletcher and Chrysler (1990), with the test sentence shown in italics. (Adapted from "Surface Forms, Textbases and Situational Models: Recognition Memory for the Three Types of Textual Information," by C. R. Fletcher and S. T. Chrysler, 1990, *Discourse Processes, 13*, p. 178. Copyright © 1990 Ablex Publishing Corporation. Reprinted by permission.)

Fletcher and Chrysler (1990) have reported such a study. They used passages such as the one shown in Figure 7-6. Students were then given a recognition memory test. The items on the test were carefully constructed to probe the surface, propositional, and situational levels. For example, the distinction between *rug* and *carpet* taps the surface level because the meaning (propositional level) is the same. In contrast, the distinction between *carpet* and *painting* is at the propositional level. Fletcher and Chrysler (1990) found that recognition memory was worst when the test sentence and its distractor differed only at the surface level, intermediate when they differed at the surface and propositional levels, and best when they differed at all three levels. Thus, students can reliably distinguish between different levels of representation.

Let us add one more point. Now that we have looked at recognition performance at each of these three levels, we can examine each level of recognition over time. This has been done in a study by Kintsch, Welsh, Schmalhoffer, and Zimny (1990) in which students were presented with passages and then given recognition tests either immediately or after delays of 40 minutes, 2 days, or 4 days. The results are shown in Figure 7-7. We need not dwell on all of the details of the study, but you should know that a 0 on the vertical axis indicates a lack of memory for a given level. We see that surface memory is strong only in the immediate test, and falls to chance level shortly after that. Propositional recognition starts stronger, also falls off over time, but remains above 0 at all points. Memory for situations is initially very strong and show little loss over the retention intervals studied.

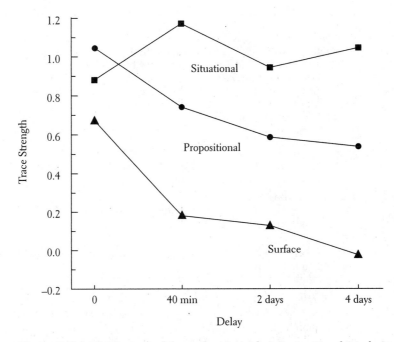

Figure 7-7. The strength of the surface (triangles), propositional (circles), and situational (squares) representations as a function of the delay preceding a recognition memory test. (Adapted from "Sentence Memory: A Theoretical Analysis," by W. Kintsch, D. Welsh, F. Schmalhoffer, and S. Zimny, 1990, *Journal of Memory and Language, 29*, pp. 133–159. Copyright © 1990 Academic Press. Reprinted by permission.)

Summary

We store discourse in three ways—surface representations, propositional representations, and situational models—and each appears to be influenced by different variables and subject to different decay rates. Surface representations are short-lived except when the wording is pragmatically significant. Propositional representations are much better retained and include the meaning of presented information along with any inferences we have drawn. Situational models are retained the best and are based on spatial or causal relations between parts of a text.

Schemata and Discourse Processing

I have described at some length the way we, as comprehenders, achieve discourse coherence by identifying the propositions of a text, connecting them by argument repetition, and creating a hierarchically organized structure. All of this activity pertains to local discourse structure. We now turn to global discourse structure—the overall organization of discourse.

Schemata

A **schema** (plural: **schemata**) is a structure in semantic memory that specifies the general or expected arrangement of a body of information. The notion of a schema is not new in psychology. It is generally associated with the early work on story recall by Bartlett (1932). In some imaginative studies that are still cited very frequently, Bartlett attempted to show that remembering is not a rote or reproductive process but rather a process in which we retain the overall gist of an event and then reconstruct the details from this overall impression. Bartlett conducted experiments that were conducive to memory errors—unusual, bizarre stories that were repeatedly recalled over long time intervals—so that he could examine the guiding function of schemata in the reconstruction process. He found that when college students were given stories that were inconsistent with their schemata, recall was usually distorted in the direction of the schemata. Bartlett suggested that when we encounter an event that is discrepant from our usual understanding, we have difficulty fitting it into our existing schemata and subsequently tend either not to remember it or to "normalize" it, altering its details until it is congruent with existing schemata.

Bartlett's (1932) ideas were relatively unappreciated at the time but have taken on new significance recently as psychologists have developed new techniques to explore the way people comprehend and remember stories. Bartlett's notion of a schema, although appealing, was rather vague, and modern extensions of his work have focused primarily on two issues: characterizing schematic knowledge more precisely and determining how this knowledge is used during discourse comprehension. Let us look at the second issue first.

Activation of appropriate schemata   As a starting point, we consider some studies that have tested variations on the hypothesis that we must activate the appropriate schemata to properly comprehend a story.

The simplest case is the one in which we lack the appropriate schema. Bartlett's early studies indicated that British college students had a very hard time understanding Eskimo folktales and tended to modify many of the details in their recall efforts, producing, in Bartlett's (1932) words, "a more coherent, concise, and undecorated tale" (p. 127). It appears that comprehension and memory are poor when we do not have a schema that corresponds to the story that is unfolding, because it is nearly impossible to see the significance of the events being described.

In other instances, we may have an appropriate schema in memory but fail to activate it for one reason or another. A series of studies by Dooling and colleagues (Dooling & Lachman, 1971; Sulin & Dooling, 1974) and by Bransford and Johnson (1973) have convincingly demonstrated that comprehension and memory will be poor when the passage is written so obscurely that we cannot determine what might be the right schema, as in the following example:

> With hocked gems financing him, our hero bravely defied all scornful laughter that tried to prevent his scheme. "Your eyes deceive," he had said, "an egg not a table correctly typifies this unexplored planet." Now three sturdy sisters sought proof, forging along sometimes through calm vastness, yet more often over turbulent peaks and

valleys. Days became weeks as many doubters spread fearful rumors about the edge. At last from nowhere welcome winged creatures appeared signifying momentous success. (Dooling & Lachman, 1971, p. 217)

Persons who read this passage without a title remembered very little of what was presented, whereas those who were told that the title was "Christopher Columbus Discovering America" did much better. Clearly it is not enough to have an appropriate schema in memory; we must be able to activate it at the proper time.

Reconstruction of schema-specific details   One of Bartlett's (1932) notions was that the activated schema served as a retrieval plan, summoning up certain details rather than others by virtue of their centrality to the schema. Studies of comprehension with and without titles support this notion. For example, Kozminsky (1977) found that comprehenders who read a passage with one or two possible appropriate titles tended to emphasize different details in their recall. Thus, the perspective provided by the schema activated at the time of encoding seems to play an organizational role in our retrieval efforts.

Similar results have been found at the time of retrieval. Pichert and Anderson (1977) gave individuals a text about a burglary and asked them to recall it from either the perspective of the homeowner or that of the burglar. After this first recall effort, they were asked to switch perspectives and try to recall any details that they may have failed to note earlier. The individuals were able to recall previously unrecalled propositions after shifting perspective, and the specific details newly recalled were more central to the second schema than to the first one.

These studies provide evidence of the directive function of schemata in discourse processing. It is clear that the schema that is in effect during comprehension has a powerful organizing effect on recall. Moreover, information central to the schema is well remembered, but other details seem to be misplaced, although they can be revived with a shift in perspective. All told, the evidence that schemata influence discourse processing is quite impressive.

Genres

To this point we have learned that the activation of a relevant schema during discourse comprehension has a major influence of how and what is recalled. The schemata considered up to this point have been based on content, such as the behavior of a burglar.

We can also talk about schemata regarding certain forms of discourse. It is helpful here to introduce the concept of **genre,** which is a type of discourse that has a characteristic structure. We have genres for, among other things, lectures, sermons, opinion articles, presidential inauguration speeches, and comedy monologues. Genres are important because they provide us with general expectations regarding the way information in a discourse will be arranged. Let us consider a few examples.

The organization of a news article in a newspaper can be thought of as an inverted pyramid. The most important points are introduced in the headline and at the beginning of the article. As the article progresses, less important details are brought in. This structure is directly related to the way news stories are edited. If space is not available for the entire article as written, the editor typically deletes paragraphs near the end of the story. Consequently, journalists arrange their stories so that the more important pieces of information are higher in the story (van Dijk & Kintsch, 1983).

Psychology students are familiar with another genre, the format that the American Psychological Association uses in its journal articles. The article begins with an abstract, followed by an introduction, the method, the results, and the discussion. Students encountering a journal article for the first time frequently report that it can be very difficult to understand. Gradually, as students become aware of where to find various pieces of information in the article, comprehension improves.

One genre that has been studied a great deal in discourse research has been **narrative discourse.** Typically, stories begin with the introduction of characters and setting. The main character sets out with some sort of goal, runs into some obstacles, and ultimately resolves the dilemma. There are many different genres for stories; in fact, there are different ones for detective stories, fairy tales, and romances. Detective or suspense stories, for instance, create interest in a crime and supply possible motives for usually several suspects along the way. A skilled writer will drop enough clues for readers to anticipate some but not all of the details of the ending. In a well-constructed story, readers can imagine many different outcomes at the beginning, but these become fewer in number as we go along and ultimately at least part of the ending can be predicted. It has been said that in the beginning of a story everything is possible; in the middle, some things become probable; but in the end, one result is necessary.

Narrative discourse can be contrasted with **expository discourse,** in which the goal of the writer is not to tell a story but rather to convey information about the subject matter. This is the form of discourse that we encounter when reading a textbook or, for the most part, listen to a lecture. The emphasis is on presenting the information in an organized, logical manner. In the remainder of this section, we will explore how we comprehend and experience narrative discourse.

Narrative Discourse Processing

Story grammars   Some of Bartlett's ideas have been formalized by contemporary researchers into the concept of a **story grammar** (see, for example, Mandler & Johnson, 1977; Rumelhart, 1975, 1977; Stein & Glenn, 1979; Thorndyke, 1977). A story grammar is a schema in semantic memory that identifies the typical or expected arrangement of events in a story. In general, story grammars view narratives as consisting of a setting, one or more episodes, and then an ending. In turn, **episodes** have a characteristic structure: some initiating event occurs, leading to some

Table 7-2. Simple Story

1	There once was a boy named Jimmy.	S
2	His mother said Jimmy could get a part-time job.	E
3	Jimmy liked to work.	R
4	He decided to get a paper route.	G
5	He talked to the sales manager at the newspaper.	A
6	Jimmy began to deliver newspapers to some customers.	O
7	Tom told Jimmy how to please the customers.	E
8	Jimmy was interested in the idea.	R
9	He wanted to save a lot of money.	G
10	He put papers near each door and rang every doorbell.	A
11	Jimmy earned a lot of tips and saved all the money.	O
12	Jimmy saw Tom's new bike.	E
13	Jimmy thought the bike was neat.	R
14	He wanted one like it.	G
15	He counted his money and went to the bike shop.	A
16	He picked one out and eagerly gave the man his money.	O
17	Jimmy was very happy and rode his bike home.	N

Note: S = setting, E = event, R = response, G = goal, A = attempt, O = outcome, and N = ending.
Source: Adapted from "Memory for Embedded and Sequential Story Structures," by S. R. Goldman and C. K. Varnhagen, 1986, *Journal of Memory and Language, 25,* 401–418 (table appears on p. 404). Copyright © 1986 Academic Press. Reprinted by permission.

internal response on the part of the protagonist. The response leads to a goal, an attempt to reach the goal, and an outcome. An example of a simple story and how it would be analyzed by a story grammar is shown in Table 7-2.

Psychological validity of story grammars   A fair amount of evidence indicates that story grammars (or something like them) correspond to several aspects of how comprehenders process simple stories. For example, the story grammar approach places emphasis on the concept of an episode. There are several sources of evidence that episodes are an important unit in our memory for stories. One is that episodes tend to be recalled in an all-or-none fashion, as if they are stored in separate chunks in working memory (Black & Bower, 1979; Glenn, 1978). Black and Bower showed that the length of one episode does not influence the recall of another. Similarly, Glenn reported that the episodic structure of recall is unaffected by the length of the episodes.

An implication of the view that episodes are processed as chunks is that the boundaries between episodes should be areas of high processing load. Haberlandt, Berian, and Sandson (1980) suggest that the ends of episodes require summing-up processes that increase the processing load. They presented readers with a task in which sentences from a story were shown one at a time on a computer terminal. The time the participants took to read each sentence was recorded. After the final sentence, participants were asked to recall the story.

Haberlandt and colleagues found that reading times were longer at the beginnings and the ends of episodes. They suggest that cognitive activities at the boundaries of the episodes were responsible for the increased reading times. At the beginnings of episodes, readers were assumed to be initiating a new episode, identifying the new topic of discourse, and forming expectations for the remainder of the episode. At the end of an episode, readers summarize the episode and rehearse some of its propositions. The researchers assumed that readers have tacit knowledge of episodes as a unit of stories and that readers organize their reading efforts around this unit.

Haberlandt and colleagues also studied the recall of stories and found that some story constituents are recalled better than others. In particular, beginnings, attempts, and outcomes are recalled better than reactions, goals, and endings. Mandler and Johnson (1977) reported similar results. It appears that in a free recall task, participants prefer to emphasize the objective aspects of a story as opposed to the internal cognitive and emotional responses they may infer from the objective events. For example, they are more likely to recall that Jimmy did not have enough money to buy a bike than that he was frustrated, which may be inferred from the lack of money.

This does not mean that comprehenders are oblivious to the emotional responses of characters, for it is clear that they identify characters' emotional states during the processing of stories. In one study, students read stories that described concrete actions, such as a main character stealing money from a store where his best friend worked and later learning that his friend had been fired. After each story, they read a target sentence that contained an emotion word that either matched or mismatched the emotional state implied by the story. Readers were slower on target sentences that contained mismatches as opposed to matches, suggesting that readers represent characters' emotional states as part of the process of reading a story (Gernsbacher, Goldsmith, & Robertson, 1992).

We have been talking of very simple stories. A somewhat more complicated story would be one in which some of the states (response, goal, and so forth) are embedded in other states. For example, the story in Table 7-3, like the one in Table 7-2, consists of three episodes: buying the bike, saving money, and getting a paper route. But whereas the episodes run sequentially in the first story, in the second story the paper route episode is embedded in the saving money episode, which is in turn embedded in the bike buying episode. The effect of embedding is to leave earlier episodes incomplete until later episodes are finished, thus inducing a significant memory load. As a consequence, stories with embedded episodes are associated with lower levels of recall (Goldman & Varnhagen, 1986; Mandler, 1987). In addition, comprehenders pay particular attention to incomplete episodes (Fletcher, Hummel, & Marsolek, 1990).

Cross-cultural investigations   Mandler, Scribner, Cole, and DeForest (1980) examined whether these patterns of story recall are similar or different in different cultures. There is relatively little evidence on this issue. As we saw earlier, Bartlett (1932) had presented Eskimo folktales to British college students and found that

Table 7-3. Embedded Story

1	There once was a boy named Jimmy.	S
2	One day, Jimmy saw Tom's new bike.	E
3	Jimmy thought the bike was neat.	R
4	He wanted one like it.	G
5	He called the bike shop and asked about their prices.	E
6	Jimmy was still interested.	R
7	He wanted to save a lot of money.	G
8	His mother said Jimmy could get a part-time job.	E
9	Jimmy liked to work.	R
10	He decided to get a paper route.	G
11	He talked to the sales manager at the newspaper.	A
12	Jimmy began to deliver newspapers to some customers.	O
13	He put papers near each door and rang every doorbell.	A
14	Jimmy earned a lot of tips and saved all the money.	O
15	He counted his money and went to the bike shop.	A
16	He picked one out and eagerly gave the man his money.	O
17	Jimmy was very happy and rode his bike home.	N

Note: S = setting, E = event, R = response, G = goal, A = attempt, O = outcome, and N = ending.
Source: Adapted from "Memory for Embedded and Sequential Story Structures," by S. R. Goldman and C. K. Varnhagen, 1986, *Journal of Memory and Language, 25,* 401–418 (table appears on p. 404). Copyright © 1986 Academic Press. Reprinted by permission.

their recall was very poor. Presumably, this was because their story schemata did not match the schemata implicit in the folktales.

Mandler et al. (1980) took a different approach. They presented stories that are coherent from the standpoint of the story grammar to a sample of children and adults in Liberia. Liberia is a country in northern Africa in which formal education is not required. As a consequence, the participants varied in their degree of literacy and education. Some had no formal education and were not literate, some had some degree of school experience but could not read, and still others were both schooled and literate. The results for these groups as well as comparable U.S. groups are shown in Figure 7-8. The left side of the figure shows recall patterns for U.S. and Liberian adults, and the right side shows children's recall. Clearly, there is a substantial degree of similarity in the recall patterns. All groups recalled settings, beginnings, attempts, and outcomes better than reactions and endings. Children in both cultures show a lower level of recall, but the patterns are similar.

These results suggest that a story grammar of the type described by Mandler and others could be a universal schema rather than one that is specific to our culture. This does not necessarily mean that no cultural differences exist in story schemata, only that certain schemata are culturally invariant. As Mandler (1984) has said, "At this point, the best evidence we have is that the human mind and its limitations on memory are such that certain forms of storytelling regularly emerged in various cultures around the world" (pp. 52–53).

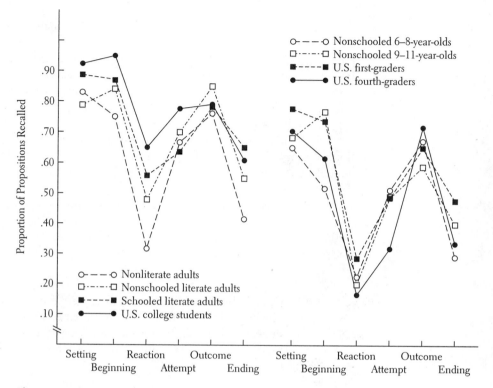

Figure 7-8. Proportion of propositions recalled from story constituents by different populations. The left side shows data from Liberian adults and U.S. college students. The right side shows data from Liberian children and U.S. schoolchildren. (Based on "Cross-Cultural Invariance in Story Recall," by J. M. Mandler, S. Scribner, M. Cole, and M. DeForest, 1980, *Child Development, 51,* p. 23, University of Chicago Press.)

Inaccessibility of Knowledge

We have been discussing how we activate appropriate knowledge bases during the course of comprehending narratives. We may now round out our discussion of narrative by considering cases in which we fail to activate the appropriate knowledge. We have already considered one case of inaccessibility of knowledge. The Columbus passage was written so obscurely that we were initially unable to bring our knowledge of the subject matter to the task of comprehension. Here, when knowledge was not activated, comprehension was severely impaired. Yet, it is also possible to comprehend a passage and still not activate the relevant body of knowledge.

Consider, for example, the following passage from Garrison Keillor (1987):

In Uncle Lew's story, a house burned down on a cold winter night and the little children inside ran barefoot into the snow of 1906—some were pitched out the bedroom window by their father—and all were safe. But although I heard the story dozens of times, whenever he told it again I was never sure they'd all get out. And since these children grew up to be my ancestors, I had an interest in their survival. (pp. 220–221)

Gerrig (1993) calls this situation **anomalous suspense:** when a reader participates in a narrative world in such a fashion that the knowledge critical to sustaining suspense is not immediately accessible. Subjectively, a reader experiences anomalous suspense when continuing to experience suspense in a story despite having experienced it earlier.

To explore the phenomenon of anomalous suspense under laboratory conditions, Gerrig (1989) required students to respond true or false to well-known facts about history and current events. For example, one statement was (34):

(34)   Charles Lindbergh was the first solo pilot to cross the Atlantic.

Ordinarily, we would find it easy to verify such a statement. But Gerrig presented one group of students with a brief paragraph intended to create some mild doubt, as in (35):

(35)   Charles Lindbergh wanted to fly an airplane to Europe. Lindbergh's proposed flight was the subject of much controversy. Newspaper polls showed 75% of all Americans were against the trip. They feared that Lindbergh would kill himself unnecessarily. Even the President tried to discourage the flight.

Notice that although the paragraph is biased toward the counterfactual outcome (that Lindbergh did not fly), this outcome is never directly asserted. Another group received a paragraph that was biased toward the other (that is, real) outcome. The results indicated that the group that received the counterfactual paragraph was slower in verifying the truth of statements such as (34).

This is a curious result. Gerrig was careful to select topics that were very well known (for example, that the North defeated the South in the Civil War), so it is unlikely that students simply did not know the truth of the statements. Rather, Gerrig suggests, the pattern of results indicates that readers can be invited to experience uncertainty when immersed in brief stories. When encouraged to set aside their real-world knowledge, students seemed to do just that and were correspondingly slower at verifying real-world statements.

Gerrig (1989, 1993) proposed an explanation for this puzzle that revolves around the concept of expectation of uniqueness. When we sit down to read a novel, we expect to encounter new characters and new situations. Thus, rather than searching our memory for previous instances of characters and situations, the author invites us to treat a work of fiction as something new, even when it is not. Readers treat each story as if it were brand new. The process of reading fiction can be likened to watching a baseball game. The same situations occur over and over, but no two games are exactly alike.

The work on anomalous suspense adds another important dimension to our understanding of how narrative discourse differs from expository discourse. We have seen that narrative can produce suspense, which is, in part, an emotional response. The range of emotional responses evoked by narrative has begun to receive considerable attention in recent years, with psychologists and linguists joining forces with literary theorists (for a sampler, see Albritton & Gerrig, 1991). Although this effort is a work in progress, it seems that the ability to elicit emotional as well as cognitive responses may be a distinguishing feature of narrative.

Summary

Our processing of discourse is governed by some conventional notions of how passages are typically organized. The general notion that schemata direct and guide discourse processing is well established: we have difficulty understanding passages when we do not have or cannot activate the appropriate schemata, and we tend to pay greater attention to parts of a story that are central to the schema under which we are operating.

Different genres are associated with different types of schemata, which are structures in semantic memory that specify the usual arrangement of information in a text. Studies of comprehension and recall of stories provide support for a specific type of schema, the story grammar. We tend to store the episodes of a story in separate chunks in memory, and we use the ends of episodes as cues to summarize the episode as a whole. In addition, the results to date are consistent with the notion that the story schema prevalent in studies with U.S. college students is a universal schema.

Educational Implications

What does research on discourse have to say about how well we are able to learn from textbooks and lectures? In many cases, what is clear to one person is "Greek" to another, and hence the question for the latter becomes, What must I do to make this passage clear to me? As I have emphasized several times, coherence is achieved during the course of comprehension, not given in the words on the printed page. This implies that the comprehension activities we engage in when reading or listening to prose play a crucial role in the way we understand (and misunderstand) what is being said.

To learn a text's content, we must store its underlying structure. The studies cited earlier confirm that, under ordinary laboratory conditions, people hold both a surface and a deep representation of a text for a short period of time, but the long-term representation is propositional. But it is sometimes different in educational situations. Students do not always remember the most important points in a lecture or passage. Although this result is sometimes due to deficiencies of either student or author/lecturer, the more interesting and, I think, more common instance is the one in which a reasonably well-constructed passage is not understood very well despite a considerable effort at comprehension. Since comprehension is poor, memory is usually also poor. All that is remembered are isolated details, not necessarily the most important ones, and not connected to other, intrinsically related points. In short, a coherent body of information presented to an able and conscientious comprehender ultimately is stored in incoherent and fragmented form. Why?

One obvious factor is familiarity. Much of what we study is material for which we have no available schema. As the studies of Bartlett and others have shown, this state of affairs has predictably negative effects on performance, for, without the appropriate perspective, appreciating the significance of even those concepts that are learned and remembered is often difficult. Nevertheless, identifying lack of familiarity as a contributing element is only the beginning, not the end, of a satisfactory explanation. We need to describe the way we process familiar and unfamiliar texts.

When we deal with familiar material, we are scarcely aware of the multiple ambiguities, missing elements, and irrelevant, potentially distracting details, for we are able to resolve most of them rather easily. All discourse processing involves both local and global structure. With familiar texts, we tend to rely more on our knowledge of the global structure to guide our way through a text, which frees us from some of these details. Unfortunately, we are not able to do this with unfamiliar texts because we do not have the relevant schema. Thus, in the absence of schematic guidance, local cohesive relations must play a relatively more important role in making sense out of connected discourse. Careful processing of these local relations can, to a considerable degree, overcome the disadvantage of lack of familiarity.

The research on discourse comprehension suggests several strategies that may be helpful in improving comprehension and memory. The following discussion highlights five strategies.

Actively Processing Discourse

One general strategy that has a good deal of merit is to actively process textual material. **Active processing** refers to a collection of activities that includes relating new information to information we have in permanent memory, asking questions of the material, and writing summaries or outlines of the material. When we read or listen more passively, we generally retain less information.

An example of active processing comes from a study by Palincsar and Brown (1984). The researchers studied junior high school students who were very poor readers but not mentally retarded. The researchers taught the students to formulate questions that would be answered by the most important point in a passage. In this way, the students would be trained to identify the main theme of the passage. The study showed that students receiving training rose from 30% on a comprehension test before training to about 80% on a comprehension posttest. In addition, the students were able to maintain these gains after the training was completed. A control group of similar youngsters showed no gains in comprehension.

The exact type of active processing can be individually designed, of course. When I was an undergraduate student, I developed a complex system of notations that I put in the margins of the textbooks I was reading. A vertical line signified what I regarded as an important point. A line with an asterisk next to it was especially significant. Another symbol indicated a point of the author's that I disagreed with. As I look over some of my old texts, it sometimes appears that I wrote as much as the authors did! Still, it was an effective strategy because it forced me to make decisions about whether the information was important, whether I agreed with it, and so on, and these decisions promoted retention. Much psychological research has shown that when we process information at this deeper semantic level, we remember more of what we read (for example, Craik & Lockhart, 1972).

Connecting Propositions in Discourse

As we have seen, an intrinsic characteristic of discourse is that sentences overlap in content and that given information is used to introduce new information. At the beginning of a text, nearly everything is new, but once introduced, newly defined concepts are specifically linked, at least in well-structured texts, to later concepts. There are sequential dependencies in learning from texts; we must know, for example, what a schema is before the story grammar can make much sense. Attempting to understand the new without fully understanding (as opposed to being vaguely familiar with) what led up to it ensures the same result as trying to run with a football before catching it.

All of this implies that we would benefit from a strategy of explicitly looking for relationships between concepts in discourse. This includes such actions as paying close attention to anaphoric references and noting where inferences have to be drawn. This strategy leads to several beneficial results. First, it produces a network of interrelated propositions in which each concept may serve as a retrieval cue for many others. Second, even if we do not have the information needed to draw an inference, explicitly searching for such relationships between propositions deepens the level of processing and hence promotes the retention of individual propositions. Finally, as propositions are connected to one another, they are also subordinated or superordinated to one another, thus leading to a hierarchical memory structure that may be used to organize our recall of the text or to summarize it.

Identifying the Main Points

Careful attention to the local structure of discourse helps, but it can still be difficult to figure out what an instructor or author regards as the main points. Several studies indicate that the difficulty in determining main points may be traced to the presence of distracting and often confusing details. Meyer, Brandt, and Bluth (1980) found that when the key points of a passage are signaled explicitly, performance improves. An example of an explicit sentence is (36); the implicit version is (37):

(36) A problem of vital concern is the prevention of oil spills from supertankers.

(37) Prevention is needed of oil spills from supertankers.

These researchers found that the signals improved the immediate retention performance of readers whose comprehension was otherwise poor (those who did not share the schema of the author) but did not affect the retention of good comprehenders. Similar results were reported by other investigators (Brooks, Dansereau, Spurlin, & Hollin, 1983; Lehrer, 1994; Lorch & Chen, 1986; Spyridakis & Standal, 1986).

Reder and Anderson (1980) tried a different approach. Instead of highlighting the main points, they eliminated many of the details from the passage. This is the idea behind publications such as *Cliff Notes*, which present condensed versions of plays and novels. Reder and Anderson found that retention was better when the material was presented in a condensed version rather than in a standard textbook version. In a similar vein, Giora (1993) found that analogies in text did not facilitate comprehension and may actually impair recall. It appears that we comprehend best when extraneous material is omitted from text.

Building Global Structures

Devices that highlight the main points of a passage are certainly helpful in the short run, but ultimately we need to identify important points even when they are not so explicitly marked. As we become more familiar with the content and structure of an author's prose, we can gradually induce the author's schema.

One good test of whether we have successfully done this is to write a summary for a portion of the text. This requires us to select specific propositions as the most important ones and to generalize some of the individual propositions into broader thematic statements (see Fletcher, 1994). By comparing our summary with the author's, we can see how close we have come to extracting the gist of the text. As we become more proficient, we can shift to a greater reliance on global processing strategies.

Tailoring Comprehension Activities to Tests

One final principle that deserves discussion is that we should always try to match our comprehension activities to the types of tests we may have to take. Memory researchers have established that retention is best when we study material in a manner similar to the way we must encode it at the time of a test (Tulving & Thomson, 1973). Most strategies for improving discourse performance work some but not all of the time. Their success often depends on whether they are appropriate for a particular test.

An example is from a study by Mannes and Kintsch (1987). Students studied an outline of relevant background information before reading a text. For some students, the organization of the outline was consistent with the organization of the text. For others, the outline was inconsistent with the text. As might be expected, consistent-outline students performed better on memory for the information in the text. However, the inconsistent-outline group showed superior performance on an inference verification task and on a difficult problem-solving task that required a deep understanding of the passage. Similar results were reported by Kintsch (1990) and Mayer, Cook, and Dyck (1984).

The point is that it is not appropriate to say that the presence of a consistent outline improved discourse performance. We need to consider what aspect of performance is being measured. We need to know what we will be asked to do with information before we can decide on a comprehension strategy that makes sense.

Summary

This section of the chapter has addressed the implications discourse studies may have for understanding or improving students' learning from lectures and textbooks. A good general strategy is to process the passage in an active way. Some difficulties in learning are traceable to differences in schemata between students and authors/lecturers. In the absence of a familiar schema, we must pay closer attention to local discourse structure. It is easier to identify the main points if they are highlighted or if other details are omitted, but ultimately our comprehension depends on our ability to induce the schema of the author.

Review Questions

1. Distinguish between coherence and cohesion.
2. Why is anaphoric reference of interest to psychologists?
3. Identify the three steps in the given/new strategy.
4. Discuss how individual differences in working memory may influence discourse processing.
5. Describe the role of inferences in achieving discourse coherence, and explain the way inferences are stored in permanent memory.
6. Define situational model.
7. What evidence suggests that the activation of an appropriate schema may influence how well we are able to remember a passage?
8. Define story grammar.
9. Define anomalous suspense.
10. How might failures of learning in an educational system be viewed as a joint function of the student and the text/learner?

Thought Questions

1. How might the enduring appeal of soap operas be explained in psycholinguistic terms? Although they have a very stereotyped schema, soap operas (unlike many other stereotyped events) draw strong feelings. More generally, how

might degrees of deviation from one's schema be related to the attractiveness of a story?

2. Are story grammars grammars in the same sense as sentence grammars? Do the rules in Table 7-2 represent our story knowledge in the same way that phrase-structure rules represent our sentence knowledge?

3. If comprehension is a joint function of the text and the individual's information-processing activities, is it ever possible to say that a given text is not written clearly?

Answer to scrambled paragraph, page 159: 4, 2, 5, 3, 1

Language Production and Conversational Interaction

8

Production of Speech and Language

MAIN POINTS

- Speech production consists of four major stages: conceptualizing a thought to be expressed, formulating a linguistic plan, articulating the plan, and monitoring one's speech.
- Spontaneous speech errors (slips of the tongue), although infrequent, reveal planning units in the production of speech. Slips tend to occur in highly regular patterns.
- Both serial and parallel models of speech production have been developed, and each has its merits. It appears that we plan one portion of our utterance at the same time that we are producing another portion.
- We edit and correct our utterances when we err. The form and timing of self-corrections occur in systematic ways.
- Comparisons of the production of signed and spoken language reveal both similarities and differences.

Introduction

Language production, which is our concern in this and the following chapter, is an intrinsically more difficult subject to study than language comprehension, and, as a consequence, far more is presently known about receiving language than producing it. This is primarily because it is easier to study the process of going from speech to thought than the other way around. Although speech is observable, the ideas derived from or leading to speech are far more elusive. In comprehension, it is relatively easy to specify the ideas that a person extracts from a segment of speech; one can, for example, compare the recall of a text with its original version. Understanding the process of production, as opposed to merely identifying the physical features of the resulting speech, involves understanding where ideas for speech come from. It is no wonder that progress is comparatively slow.

Researchers have responded to this dilemma by using convergent measures. Some investigators have made detailed and systematic analyses of naturally occurring errors of production, and others have given speakers, under laboratory conditions, more or less specific instructions on what to produce. Despite these differences in approach, the findings from these varied investigations are beginning to yield useful fruit, and the outline of an overall model of production is becoming clearer. Following Levelt (1989), we may distinguish four stages of production: conceptualizing, formulating, articulating, and self-monitoring. First, we must conceptualize what we wish to communicate. Second, we formulate this thought into a linguistic plan. Third, we execute the plan through the muscles in the speech system. Finally, we monitor our speech, to assess whether it is what we intended to say and how we intended to say it.

This outline has the value of directing our attention to problems in need of further study. Do these stages occur invariably in the given order? Are there substages for any of the processes? Do the levels or stages interact in the production of a given utterance, as was seen to some extent in the comprehension process? What process has gone awry when we make slips of the tongue? There are a good many more questions than answers in the study of language production. We will begin our survey with the study of speech errors and what they tell us about the demands of production.

Slips of the Tongue

The scientific analysis of speech errors, commonly called "slips of the tongue," reemerged in the early 1970s with the seminal publication of an article by Fromkin (1971) that examined the way speech errors may be used in the construction of linguistic arguments. This paper, and those that followed, marked the end of a long period in which speech errors were regarded with suspicion in scientific circles. It has become respectable for investigators to use errors to examine the role of linguistic units in the production of speech (see, for example, Fromkin, 1980). Researchers have painstakingly recorded the speech errors, innocuous or otherwise, of friends and colleagues, within the limits imposed by good taste and a desire to preserve such friendships.

A number of collections of spontaneous speech errors have been made (Fromkin, 1971; Garrett, 1975; Shattuck-Hufnagel, 1979), and it is interesting to determine whether there are consistent patterns in when and how they occur. Although these errors are not common, all speakers seem to make them occasionally. Some people are more prone to speech errors than others. The legendary Dr. William Spooner, infamous for his tendency to say such things as sentence (1) to an ungrateful college class, gave speech researchers more than his share:

> **(1)** You have hissed my mystery lectures. I saw you fight a liar in the back quad. In fact, you have tasted the whole worm.

His peculiar form of speech may have been due to cerebral dysfunction (Potter, 1980).

Most of us make similar errors from time to time. Anecdotal evidence indicates that such errors are more common when we are nervous or under stress, as when performers appear on live television and radio shows; programs devoted to television's best "bloopers" never seem to run out of material. It seems probable that errors are more likely to occur when we are tired, anxious, or drunk. Most research, however, has focused less on the factors that may influence the frequency of speech errors than on the nature of the errors themselves.

Types of Speech Errors

Although speech errors cover a wide range of semantic content, there appear to be only a small number of basic types (Fromkin, 1971; Garrett, 1975; Shattuck-Hufnagel, 1979). Examples of the eight types are given in Table 8-1, with the words that were apparently intended in parentheses.

Table 8-1.   Major Types of Slips of the Tongue

Type	Example
Shift	That's so she'll be ready in case she decide to hits it (decides to hit it).
Exchange	Fancy getting your model renosed (getting your nose remodeled).
Anticipation	Bake my bike (take my bike).
Perseveration	He pulled a pantrum (tantrum).
Addition	I didn't explain this clarefully enough (carefully enough).
Deletion	I'll just get up and mutter intelligibly (unintelligibly).
Substitution	At low speeds it's too light (heavy).
Blend	That child is looking to be spaddled (spanked/paddled).

In **shifts,** one speech segment disappears from its appropriate location and appears somewhere else. **Exchanges** are, in effect, double shifts, in which two linguistic units exchange places. **Anticipations** occur when a later segment takes the place of an earlier one. They differ from shifts in that the segment that intrudes on another also remains in its correct location and thus is used twice. **Perseverations** occur when an earlier segment replaces a later item. **Additions** add linguistic material, whereas **deletions** leave something out. **Substitutions** occur when one segment is replaced by an intruder. These differ from previously described slips in that the source of the intrusion may not be in the sentence. **Blends** apparently occur when more than one word is being considered and the two intended items "fuse" or "blend" into a single item.

If you have closely examined these examples, you probably have noticed by now that these types of errors occur with a number of linguistic units. In some cases, a single phoneme is added, deleted, or moved, but at other times it may be a sequence of phonemes, morphemic affixes and roots, whole words, or even phrases. As a general rule, errors tend to occur at only one linguistic level per utterance. That is, when a person clearly says the wrong word, as in substitutions, the sentence is syntactically, prosodically, and phonologically intact.

Common Properties of Speech Errors

Other patterns in these speech errors deserve a closer look. Garrett (1975) has identified four generalizations about speech errors that reappear with striking regularity. First, elements that interact with one another tend to come from similar linguistic environments, as indicated by examples (2) through (4):

(2)   The little burst of beaden (beast of burden)

(3)   You're not a poojin pitter-downer, are you? (pigeon putter-downer)

(4)   Children interfere with your nife lite (night life).

Notice that the phonetic segments in the beginning of a word tend to be exchanged with other initial segments; the same is true for middle and final segments. Moreover, exchanges of segments are more common when the segments that precede them are similar. The exchange of /f/ and /t/ in sentence (4) follows this principle.

Second, elements that interact with one another tend to be similar to one another. In particular, consonants are invariably exchanged or shifted with other consonants but not with vowels. Errors involving similar sounds, such as in sentence (5), often have little relation to meaning but are based, instead, on phonetic similarity:

(5)   Sesame Street crackers (sesame seed crackers). (Fromkin, 1973)

Third, even when slips produce novel linguistic items, they are generally consistent with the phonological rules of the language. This point can be appreciated by studying blend errors. When a blend such as *slickery* (for *slick* and *slippery*) occurs, the result is a nonword that could be a word. Other, phonologically impermissible forms, such as *slickppery* and *slipkery*, are logically possible but do not occur.

Finally, there are consistent stress patterns in speech errors. Segments that are exchanged for one another typically both receive major stress in the word or phrase in which they reside, or both receive minor stress.

More recently, Dell, Burger, and Svec (1997) have reviewed studies of anticipations and perseverations and found that various factors influence the pattern of errors. Perseverations are more common than anticipations in at least some aphasic patients and in young children, compared with normal adults. Additionally, perseverations are more common when speakers are producing unfamiliar phrases, whereas anticipations occur more often with practiced phrases. In general, when the error rate is higher, errors tend to be more perseveratory.

To sum it up simply, speech errors are hardly random; in fact, they occur in highly regular patterns. Let us consider, then, explanations that have been offered for these patterns. What lies behind these linguistic errors?

Explanations of Speech Errors

The Freudian explanation   One intriguing idea is that speakers have more than one idea in mind at a time. During the 1992 campaign, President George Bush began his remarks for one speech by saying (6):

(6)   I don't want to run the risk of ruining what is a lovely recession (reception). (*Newsweek*, 1992)

This, of course, could be construed as simply a sound error, as the two words are similar phonologically. But it could also be evidence that the president was preoccupied with the recession (and its effect on his campaign). Or consider a student who explains that he wants to postpone an exam with statement (7):

(7)   Last night my grandmother lied (died). (Motley, 1987)

This could be an innocent phonological error, but then again, the slip could reveal the student's thinking more than he wishes.

Freud emphasized the role of psychodynamic factors in making certain types of content more available than others. He argued that these errors "arise from the concurrent action—or perhaps rather, the mutual opposing action—of two different intentions" (Freud, 1916–1917/1963, p. 44). One of these actions was thought to constitute the conscious intention of the speaker, whereas the other pertained to a more disturbing thought or intention that interfered with the former. Sometimes, the disturbing comment would be censored, but on other occasions, the outcome of this hypothetical intrapsychic conflict would be a slip of the tongue that expressed some aspects of the less conscious intention. Examples consistent with Freud's position include a general who referred to a group of injured soldiers as *battled scared* (*scarred*) and a speaker extolling the achievements of a fellow worker who had *just expired* (*retired*) (Ellis, 1980).

Freud's position was that virtually all speech errors were caused by the intrusion of repressed ideas from the unconscious into one's conscious speech output. Although the Freudian interpretation may be appealing in cases in which the slip of the tongue results in a word with emotional significance, many slips seem to reflect simpler processes, such as anticipation (*a meal mystery* instead of *a real mystery*) and perseveration (*he pulled a pantrum* in place of *he pulled a tantrum*) of phonetic segments. In these latter cases, it seems to be unnecessarily complicated and unconvincing to claim that the error originated from intrapsychic conflicts. Still, these more common speech errors demand an explanation.

A psycholinguistic explanation   Most recent psycholinguistic and linguistic thinking has focused on the insights gained in understanding language mechanisms (not unconscious motivations) from the study of speech errors. In this respect, errors of linguistic performance occupy a role in psycholinguistic theories similar to that played by aphasic disorders (see Chapter 13). The types of language breakdowns that occur in each case provide important insights for normal language functioning.

Fromkin (1971), for example, has shown that many of the segments that change and move in speech errors are precisely those postulated by linguistic theories, lending support to the notion that linguistic units such as phonetic features, phonemes, and morphemes constitute planning units during the production of an utterance. Similarly, Garrett (1975, 1980) has used error data to argue for the existence of an autonomous syntactic processor.

One view of language production is that we produce utterances by a series of stages, each devoted to a different level of linguistic analysis (Dell & Reich, 1981; Fromkin, 1971; Garrett, 1975). If so, speech errors can tell us a good deal about what these specific stages might look like. In the next few sections, we will examine some of the psychological and physiological processes that take place when we go from idea to articulation.

Summary

Speech errors, the bane of performers on live television and radio, are systematic and typically fall into one of eight categories: exchanges, substitutions, additions, deletions, anticipations, perseverations, blends, and shifts.

Various hypotheses concerning the basis for such errors have been advanced. One of the more prominent has been Freud's view that errors occur because we have more than a single plan for production and that one such plan competes with and dominates the other. Although a Freudian type of explanation may apply to some speech errors, more recent thinking has focused on the psycholinguistic processes underlying speech errors. The most common interpretation is that we produce speech through a series of separate stages, each devoted to a single level of linguistic analysis. Errors typically occur at one level, but not others, during the production process. In the following section, we will examine this notion of stages of production more closely.

Formulating Linguistic Plans

As noted in the introduction, the production of an utterance may be analyzed in four steps: conceptualizing a message to be conveyed, formulating it into a linguistic plan, articulating (implementing the plan), and self-monitoring. In this section we look at the process up through the completion of the second step.

Very little can be said about the first step. Basically, the questions here are, Where do ideas come from? And in what form do ideas exist before they are put into words? As to the latter question, psycholinguists and cognitive psychologists generally agree that some form of "mentalese" exists—that is, a representational system distinct from language. The notion is that thoughts take form in mentalese and are then translated into linguistic form, but there is little agreement as to the properties of this prelinguistic mental representation (see, for example, Fodor, 1975). The question of the origin of ideas may be even more intractable at this time, although some noteworthy efforts have been made to study the issue (see Osgood, 1971; Osgood & Bock, 1977; Sridhar, 1989). Thus, we know that the first step occurs but are unable to say much about it.

We are in a better position with respect to the process of organizing thoughts into linguistic patterns, which is now our focus.

Serial Models of Linguistic Planning

The pioneering studies of Fromkin (1971, 1973) and Garrett (1975, 1980, 1988) have suggested that the process of planning speech can be viewed as a series of stages, each devoted to one level of linguistic planning. Fromkin's six-stage model is presented in Table 8-2.

Table 8-2. Fromkin's Model of Speech Production

Stage	Process
1	Identification of meaning — a meaning to be conveyed is generated.
2	Selection of a syntactic structure — a syntactic outline of the sentence is constructed, with word slots specified.
3	Generation of intonation contour — the stress values of different word slots are assigned.
4	Insertion of content words — appropriate nouns, verbs, and adjectives are retrieved from the lexicon and placed into word slots.
5	Formation of affixes and function words — function words (articles, conjunctions, prepositions), prefixes, and suffixes are added.
6	Specification of phonetic segments — the sentence is expressed in terms of phonetic segments, according to phonological rules.

Source: Based on "The Non-Anomalous Nature of Anomalous Utterances," by V. A. Fromkin, 1971, *Language, 47,* 27–52, Linguistic Society of America.

The basic idea of this model is that we begin with the meaning that we wish to express and that subsequent levels of processing are devoted to specific and distinct aspects of the utterance. We set up a syntactic structure of the sentence, which specifies which words will receive major and minor stress and where the content words will fit in. Then the content words are added, followed by function words and affixes. Finally, we identify the correct phonetic characteristics of the utterance, given its linguistic structure. Overall, the model is a plausible account of the way the mental work of production is distributed.

Let us go through a speech error step by step. One of Garrett's (1975) examples is sentence (8):

(8)   She's already trunked two packs (packed two trunks)

At stage 1, the meaning of the overall utterance is identified. At stage 2, the syntactic structure is laid out, and slots are constructed for the noun or pronoun, adverb, verb, adjective, and object noun. At stage 4, the content words *she, has, already, trunk, two,* and *pack* are fitted into the outline. Here is where the error is said to occur, as *trunk* and *pack* are exchanged for one another. At stage 5, the suffixes *-ed* and *-s* are added to their original and correct location. At stage 6, the complete utterance is put into phonetic form.

Independence of planning units   What evidence can be given that the stages hypothesized in Table 8-2 are actually independent of one another? Probably the clearest evidence is that the vast majority of speech errors contain mistakes at only one level of planning. One of Fromkin's examples is sentence (9), which was pronounced *so-er:*

(9)   singing sewer machine (Singer sewing machine)

Here the error is at stage 5, as the suffixes are exchanged for one another. Yet the rest of the utterance—the content words, stress values, and syntactic structure—remained unaltered. An even more striking example of the point is Garrett's sentence (10):

(10)   Stop beating your brick against a head wall. (Stop beating your head against a brick wall.)

The exchange of content words (stage 4) left the rest of the sentence intact, and it was pronounced with the primary stress on *brick*. Thus, it appears that stages 4 and 5 can each "misfire" in a manner that is independent of other stages.

The point applies to other stages as well. In particular, phonetic errors at stage 6 have been used as evidence of further substages. Some errors involve the breakup of consonant clusters, such as *frish gotto* (*fish grotto*) and *blake fruid* (*brake fluid*). Fromkin (1971) used these examples to argue that phonetic segments are independent units in the planning of speech, for if the cluster were a single unit, the entire *gr* would have been exchanged for *f*, yielding *grish fotto*.

Evidence has also been given that phonetic features are a "psychologically real" planning unit, but here the results are more equivocal. Fromkin (1971) found a case in which a speaker who intended to say *clear blue sky* came out with *glear plue sky*. Note that this is not a simple switch of phonemes. Rather, according to Fromkin, it is a shift of phonological features: the (+ voicing) from /b/ in *blue* has shifted to the /k/ in *clear*. When the voicing feature is lost from *b*, the result is /p/; when it is added to /k/, the result is /g/. Shattuck-Hufnagel and Klatt (1979), however, argue that these types of errors are extremely rare. They examined 70 cases in which target and uttered consonants differed by more than one feature and found evidence for exchanges of individual features in only three cases.

The overall evidence for the view that these stages exist as independent planning units is relatively strong. So, let us look at the order of the stages.

The sequence of planning units   Certain errors indicate that when a speech unit is exchanged or shifted into a different speech environment, certain phonological processes specify the exact phonetic representation. Consider, for example, speech errors (11) through (13), from Garrett (1980):

(11)   It certainly run outs fast (runs out)
(12)   An anguage lacquisition (a language acquisition)
(13)   Easy enoughly (easily enough)

The first example may appear to be a simple shift of a single phoneme. We see, however, that more is involved when we consider the pronunciation of the target and the actual productions. The phonetic form of the plural morpheme varies predictably with its phonetic environment. Normally, when we pronounce *runs*, the final phoneme is /z/, whereas in *outs*, it is /s/. This raises an interesting question: When the plural morpheme is shifted out of its appropriate slot into another slot, does it retain the phonetic form of the original slot, or does it take the form appropriate to its displaced slot? The answer is the latter: *outs* is pronounced as /s/, not /z/. This is an example of the phonological process of **accommodation**—elements that are shifted or deleted are accommodated to their error-induced environments. Similar processes are at work in sentences (12) and (13). In (12), the shift of /l/ leads to a change in the phonetic form of the indefinite article from *a* to *an*. In (13), the shift of *-ly* to *enough* leads to a corresponding change in the pronunciation of the final vowel in *easy*; that is, it is pronounced *easy*, not *easuh*.

The significance of accommodation processes in speech errors is that they strongly support the notion that the phonetic representation of the sentence (stage 6) is formulated after the level at which the errors occur, which is stage 5 in these examples. The morpheme that is moved is thus an abstract entity; its precise phonetic specification depends on where it lands, as it were.

There are other indications that the stages devoted to the formulation of syntactic structure precede those devoted to the insertion of lexical items into that structure. Garrett (1975) has carefully examined word exchanges and found that they are distinct from morpheme and sound exchanges in a number of ways. Most sound and morpheme exchanges occur within zero to one word, whereas exchanges of words take place over longer stretches. Moreover, the vast majority of errors occur within the clause, but of those that do not, nearly all are word exchanges. Furthermore, these exchanges tend to preserve the grammatical class of the item. All of these considerations led Garrett to argue that word exchanges reflect a stage of linguistic planning in which functional syntactic relations were being constructed (basically, stage 2 in Fromkin's model) and that the introduction of morphemes and sounds (stages 5 and 6) comes later, when the outline is in place, and involve more local exchanges of material.

The analysis of the syntactic stage has recently been extended to discontinuous dependencies, in which one word in a clause depends on the form of a nonadjacent word. For example, in sentence (14), the head noun (*time*) controls the correct form of the subsequent verb (*is*), but we sometimes err by using a form of the verb (*are*) that matches the immediately preceding word (*games*).

(14)   The time for fun and games is over.

Bock and Cutting (1992) examined agreement errors as a function of the material that intervened between the head noun and the verb. They found that phrase interruptions, such as sentence (15), led to more agreement errors than clause interruptions, such as (16), even when the number of words was equivalent. In (15), both the head noun (*report*) and the subsequent noun (*fires*) are in the same clause as the verb (*were*); in (16), only the head noun is in the same clause as the verb:

(15)   The report of the destructive fires were accurate.
(16)   The report that they controlled the fires were printed in the paper.

The authors conclude that clauses are planned as complete units even if the words in the clause end up separated in the final utterance. Once a clause is organized, information from another clause, such as *fires* in (16), is less likely to interfere. These results are consistent with Garrett's notion that clause planning precedes planning at the word level.

Editing Processes

In addition to the stages of planning, some intriguing evidence indicates that editing processes intervene between the planning of an utterance and its articulation. These editing operations might provide a last check to determine whether the planned utterance is linguistically and socially acceptable. It is clear that some monitoring and editing processes occur after a speech segment is uttered; after all, we often spontaneously correct ourselves. The question we want to consider now is whether we also have editing processes prior to articulation.

Laboratory-induced speech errors   Several studies have examined editing processes by inducing speech errors in laboratory settings. In a typical study, participants are given a list of word pairs to read silently, although occasionally they receive a cue that they must read one pair aloud. It is possible to induce errors by varying the nature of the word pairs that precede the pair to be read aloud (the target pair). This is known as the **phonological bias technique.** To appreciate the phenomenon best, you should read the following sequence aloud quickly:

> ball doze
> bash door
> bean deck
> bell dark
> darn bore
> RESPOND

The target is *darn bore,* but the preceding four pairs increase the likelihood of the spoonerism *barn door.* In fact, the spoonerism occurs about 30% of the time. As Baars (1980) notes, the technique is something like the children's game of calling out *On your mark—get set—STOP!* or like having someone repeat the word *poke* many times and then ask, *What is the white of an egg called?* In the laboratory technique, one is setting up, through phonological similarity, an alternative speech plan that competes with the plan to produce the target pair.

Evidence for covert editing processes may be found in cases in which such alternative or competing plans are generated but not actually produced. One way to do this is to vary the properties of the resulting speech error. In the previous example, a pair of real words would be produced. In contrast, consider this sequence:

> big dutch
> bang doll
> bill deal
> bark dog

dart board
RESPOND

Here the spoonerism *bart doard* occurs only 10% of the time (Baars, Motley, & MacKay, 1975). This is referred to as the **lexical bias effect**—induced speech errors that result in words are more frequent than errors that result in nonwords; this is also the case with spontaneous errors (Dell & Reich, 1981). How would the production system "know" that a speech error that has not even been produced would be a nonword? Baars (1980) argues that the error is generated covertly but suppressed by an editing process that is sensitive to lexical criteria. In an analogous way, Baars and Motley have argued that editing operations exist for a variety of criteria, including phonological, syntactic, semantic, and situational criteria (Motley, Baars, & Camden, 1983).

These results suggest that during speech we sometimes develop more than a single speech plan and that when this occurs the two plans may compete for production. If this kind of internal competition takes place, then the relatively low frequency of certain types of errors may be understood as evidence of an editing process that operates after the assembly of a sentence but before its articulation.

Another look at Freud's view   The notion of competing plans, you will recall, is a central feature of Freud's view of slips of the tongue. Although contemporary emphasis on linguistic units has superseded Freud's theory, studies of laboratory-induced errors suggest some new ways of testing his hypothesis of intrapsychic conflict. Using the phonological bias technique, Motley (1980) found that spoonerisms that were sexually related, such as *bine foddy* into *fine body*, were more common when a participant's "cognitive set" was predominantly sexual. In one study, more sexual errors occurred when the administrator of the test was a provocatively attired female rather than a male (the participants were male). In a related study, participants who scored high on a test of sexual anxiety produced more sexual errors than those who scored low. In both cases, the results were attributed to the cognitive set of the individual at the time of production: ideas that are "on our mind" tend to influence the kinds of speech errors we make.

These studies of editing, particularly those dealing with sexual and social taboos, are not without their problems. A recurrent problem in interpreting Freudian theory is that it is difficult to develop unambiguous predictions. For example, we might expect relatively high levels of sexual errors by those individuals with a high degree of sexual anxiety, for such ideas are more salient to them. Alternatively, if they were more anxious, we might expect them to have editing criteria that would be more stringent than that of other people, and consequently they would produce fewer errors.

Still, the basic idea behind Freud's view is broadly consistent with current psycholinguistic theory. Blends, such as *slickery* and *spaddle*, reveal the presence of multiple plans underlying speech production. Although the nature of Freud's plans differs from those discussed by other researchers, the process involved may actually be rather similar. It appears that most speech errors can be parsimoniously explained in terms of movements of linguistic units. The question remains whether, in addition to these principles, Freudian principles also play some role.

Parallel Models of Linguistic Planning

An alternative to the serial models advanced by Fromkin and Garrett are parallel models that assume that multiple levels of processing take place simultaneously during the course of language production. Several theorists have advanced this idea, including Bock and Levelt (1994), Dell (1985, 1986, 1988), MacKay (1982, 1987), and Stemberger (1985). These models are similar in spirit to the TRACE model of speech perception (McClelland & Elman, 1986) and the interactive activation model of visual word recognition (McClelland & Rumelhart, 1981), both of which we discussed in Chapter 4.

Dell (1986) assumes that there are four levels of nodes in permanent memory: semantic, syntactic, morphological, and phonological. Separate representations of the intended message occur at each level, much as in the serial models. Unlike the serial models, however, these representations work in parallel. As a node at one level becomes activated, it may activate other nodes at the same level or at other levels.

Consider the following example (from Levelt, 1989). Suppose a person activated the word *reset* at the syntactic level; this simply means that the person intended to place this noun in the syntactic frame being developed. This activation at the syntactic level then triggers activation of the component morphemes, *re-* and *set*, at the morphological level. These morphological nodes further spread the activation to the phonological level as well, activating the node for the phoneme /r/.

An important assumption of the model is that positive feedback occurs from "later" to "earlier" stages of processing. Once a morphological node is activated, it may spread its activation to a syntactic node. For instance, once *re-* is activated at the morphological level, it leads to activation of other words with the *re-* prefix, such as *resell*. *Resell* then spreads some of its activation to the morpheme *sell* and, ultimately, to the phoneme /s/. All of this activation decays exponentially over time, so that eventually activation is reduced to zero.

Dell's model provides an account of the lexical bias effect discussed earlier. The parallel activation model explains this finding in terms of feedback from the phonological to the morphological nodes. Note that true words have morphological nodes but that nonwords do not. As a consequence, errors favoring true words may occur by backward spreading, but this will not occur for nonwords. This difference, according to Dell, is responsible for the lexical bias effect. Thus, it appears that the spreading activation model can account for effects previously attributed to an editor (Baars et al., 1975) without assuming any special mechanism.

Another example of the model at work concerns the **phonemic similarity effect**—the tendency for intruding phonemes to be phonemically similar in their distinctive feature composition to the target phonemes. If a level of distinctive features is incorporated into the phonological level, Dell's model can explain the phonemic similarity effect fairly easily. Each phoneme that is activated spreads its activation to the corresponding set of distinctive features; in turn, the features then activate a number of phonemes that share one or more of these features. This increases the probability that an intrusion will be phonologically similar to the target.

A final example pertains to speaking rates. The model assumes that parameters of activation dynamics (spreading and decay rates) are constant. Slow speaking rates are generally associated with fewer speech errors because there is more time for activation to spread from the current morpheme to the correct sounds and for the activation of previously activated sounds to decay. Both of these factors increase the likelihood that the correct sound is activated. More interestingly, the model makes specific predictions regarding error patterns at different speaking rates. In particular, the account of the lexical bias effect is based on backward spreading, which takes time. As a consequence, the model predicts that with slower speaking rates there will be a more pronounced tendency for errors to result in existing words and morphemes. In fact, Dell (1985) found that when participants were instructed to speak quickly, the lexical bias effect disappeared.

Parallel and spreading activation models of speech production provide an interesting alternative to the stage models discussed earlier. Speech production is a very rapid activity, and the parallel structure of these models seems well adapted to explaining various aspects of production. As we shall see in the next section, both serial and parallel processes may have a role to play in language production.

Summary

Speech errors from both spontaneous speech as well as laboratory studies have provided researchers with a body of data about the production of language. Theories of how we proceed from message to linguistic structure come in two types. Serial models assume that we begin with the overall idea of an utterance, followed by syntactic organization, content words, morphemes, and phonology. Slips of the tongue typically involve just one level of planning, with other levels unaffected. There may be a final stage, after the planning of an utterance but before its articulation, that edits the utterance-to-be in a manner not inconsistent with Freud's ideas.

A recent alternative to the stage models are parallel models of production. These models assume that the linguistic message is organized at semantic, syntactic, morphological, and phonological levels. Activation of a node at one level may trigger activation of nodes at other levels, and feedback may occur from morphological and phonological levels back to higher levels of processing. Models organized along these lines have been shown to account for several important research findings.

Implementing Linguistic Plans

Until now we have considered the first two steps of the production process: the development of a thought to be expressed and the formulation of a linguistic structure for that thought. At this point, we have a linguistic plan for our utterances.

In this section, we consider the last two stages of production: articulating and self-monitoring.

Articulating

Once we have organized our thoughts into a linguistic plan, this information must be sent from the brain to the muscles in the speech system so that they can then execute the required movements and produce the desired sounds. Obviously, a thorough explanation of articulatory processes is beyond the scope of the present chapter. However, it is useful to understand certain basic aspects of articulation, in anticipation of our later comparison of the production of signed versus spoken language.

Three systems of muscles   Fluent articulation of speech requires the coordinated use of a large number of muscles. These muscles are distributed over three systems: the **respiratory,** the **laryngeal,** and the **supralaryngeal** or **vocal tract.** The latter two systems are shown in Figure 4-1 in Chapter 4.

The respiratory system regulates the flow of air from the lungs to the vocal tract. The act of producing speech begins by air being pushed out of the lungs. This is accomplished by the action of several muscles near the rib cage that have the combined effect of lifting and enlarging the rib cage (MacNeilage & Ladefoged, 1976).

The laryngeal system consists of the vocal cords or vocal folds, which are two bands of muscular tissue in the larynx that can be set into vibration. This system is responsible for the distinction between voiced and unvoiced sounds. For voiced sounds such as [b], the air expelled from the lungs is turned into acoustic energy by the action of the vocal cords. When a voiced sound is to be produced, the vocal cords are nearly touching one another, and when air passes over them, a suction effect that draws them together occurs. Once they have come together, however, there is no more airflow and thus no suction effect; this causes them to pull apart and release the tension that has built up beneath them. In contrast, when the sound to be produced is a voiceless sound such as [p], air still passes over the cords, but they are too far apart for the suction effect to occur (MacNeilage & Ladefoged, 1976).

The muscles in and around the laryngeal region produce these changes by manipulating the length, thickness, and tension of the vocal cords. This, in turn, significantly influences the fundamental frequency of the sound that results. In particular, the larynx seems to be involved in the increase in frequency that occurs at the end of **yes/no questions** such as *Did Tom mow the lawn?* (Lieberman, 1967).

The supralaryngeal system consists of structures that lie above the larynx, including the tongue, lips, teeth, jaw, and velum. These structures play a significant role in the production of speech by manipulating the size and shape of the oral cavity (the mouth and pharynx) and the nasal cavity. Phonetic segments can be distinctly described in terms of the articulatory maneuvers used to produce them. For example, [d] is produced by stopping the airflow temporarily by placing the tongue at the tip of the alveolar ridge.

All of the structures involved in speech production have other functions. The main function of the respiratory system is, of course, breathing. The teeth and tongue are used to chew and swallow food. The larynx operates as a valve, controlling the airflow to and from the lungs and preventing food from entering the lungs. However, when these structures are used to produce speech, the pattern of coordination is different. A major challenge for speech researchers is to explain how so many different muscles are coordinated so smoothly during the production of speech.

Motor control of speech   Motor control of speech begins with motor commands from the brain. As we assemble a linguistic plan for our utterance, the brain structures responsible for speech production (discussed in Chapter 13) send messages to the muscles in the respiratory, laryngeal, and supralaryngeal systems. Let us focus on the motor commands to the muscles in the vocal tract.

It is generally believed that these motor commands to speech muscles take the form of commands for the articulators (tongue, lips, and so on) to move to a particular location. If the next phonetic segment is [b], the muscles controlling the lips must be brought into action, whereas if it is [g], the muscles controlling the velum are needed. One way to think of the motor commands, then, is that they specify a series of target locations in the vocal tract.

It is a simplification, however, to view articulation as the production of a series of discrete sounds. Recall the concept of coarticulation, which we discussed in Chapter 4. The phenomenon refers to the condition that the shape of the vocal tract for any given sound often accommodates to the shape needed for surrounding sounds. This typically occurs for upcoming sounds (**anticipatory coarticulation**) but also may occur when a sound is influenced by previous sounds (**perseveratory coarticulation**). An example of anticipatory coarticulation is the rounding of the lips in the production of the [b] in *boo* (which anticipates the rounding needed for the vowel [u]) as opposed to their formation in, for instance, *bed*.

The result of coarticulation is the **undershooting** of targets. When an articulator, in anticipation of an upcoming sound, aims for a given location, it does not actually achieve it. The main reason appears to be the distance the articulators must travel to reach a series of rapidly changing targets. When sounds are produced individually, the targets are reached; but when they are articulated in a phonetic context, particularly one that involves antagonistic movements, articulatory undershooting occurs (see Sussman & Westbury, 1981).

These observations suggest that it is not possible to describe the articulatory process fully in terms of the places in which segments are produced since the shape of the vocal tract is constantly changing. This dynamic property of speech production is but one reason that adequate theories of speech articulation have been slow to emerge (for a review, see Levelt, 1989).

Planning and production cycles   What is the relationship between these articulatory processes and the planning processes discussed in the previous section? Several studies have converged on the conclusion that we alternate between planning

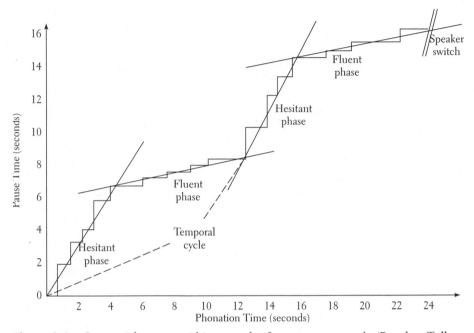

Figure 8-1. Sequential patterns within a sample of spontaneous speech. (Based on *Talk: An Analysis of Speech and Non-Verbal Behavior in Conversation*, by G. Beattie, Open University Press, 1983.)

speech and implementing our plans. Consider first a study performed by Henderson, Goldman-Eisler, and Skarbek (1966), who analyzed the hesitations and fluent speech of individuals being interviewed. Their results are shown in Figure 8-1. The horizontal axis represents speaking time, whereas the vertical axis represents pausing time. Note that there appears to be an alternation of steep parts (primarily pausing) and flat parts (mainly speech). Henderson and his colleagues found that all of the participants showed this cycle of hesitation and fluency, although the ratio of speech to silence varied among speakers. These results are consistent with the notion that we plan our utterances in cycles: we express a portion of our intended message, pause to plan the next portion, articulate that portion, pause again, and so on (see also Beattie, 1983).

One underlying reason that we tend to hesitate during speech production is that linguistic planning is very cognitively demanding and it is difficult to plan an entire utterance at once (Lindsley, 1975). As a consequence, we typically plan only a portion of an utterance at a time. A substantial amount of research has examined some of the linguistic variables related to hesitation pauses within sentences. The driving force behind much of the work has been Lounsbury's (1965) contention that we pause at periods of high uncertainty. This hypothesis has been generally supported by studies concluding that variables that influence lexical retrieval also influence hesitation pauses. For instance, Levelt (1983) found that pauses occurred more often before low-frequency words than before high-frequency words.

Another variable that influences lexical retrieval, and therefore pauses during speech, is the sheer number of words from which we choose. Schacter, Christenfeld, Ravina, and Bilous (1991) found that during lectures humanists used more filled pauses (such as *uh*, *ah*, or *um*) than social scientists or natural scientists. According to Schacter and his colleagues, the humanities have a far richer vocabulary than the sciences and thus humanists have more options during speech production, leading to more filled pauses. For example, there are no synonyms for *molecule* or *atom*, but many alternatives for *beauty*, *affection*, and *prejudice*. Subsequent work indicates that humanists indeed use more different words, in both lectures and professional publications, than either social or natural scientists (Schacter, Rauscher, Christenfeld, & Crone, 1994).

The variables that influence lexical retrieval during language production are in all likelihood the same variables we have already seen in our discussion of lexical access during language comprehension (Chapter 5). In addition to word frequency and size of vocabulary, such variables as morphological complexity, lexical ambiguity, age of acquisition, and recency of usage (that is, priming) also influence retrieval.

We have been talking of planning and production cycles as being in strict alternation, but sometimes they overlap. Although formulating linguistic plans can be demanding, implementing plans once we have formulated them is not intrinsically demanding; in fact, we ordinarily have little conscious awareness of the movements of our articulators. This observation suggests that we might be able to implement some plans while we are in the process of formulating others. This notion, which Kempen and Hoenkamp (1987) call **incremental processing,** can be described in the following way. Suppose we characterize a complete sentence as a series of units. Given this, it is surely the case that we plan unit x before we articulate unit x. In this sense, our implementation of linguistic plans is serial. But, at the same time that we are articulating unit x, we are planning unit $x + 1$; in this sense, processing is parallel.

A brief digression: we might reasonably ask at this point what "units" are—are they clauses, phrases, words, syllables, phonemes? The answer is probably all of the above (Foss & Hakes, 1978). At various times in the course of production we treat all of these as processing units. The unit of production depends, in part, on the amount of resources needed for a given portion of the message. An infrequent or difficult word might command a good share of our resources, whereas an entire routinized phrase such as a cliché could be activated as a complete unit. It is therefore not possible to identify any one unit of language as "the" unit of production.

Returning to incremental processing, it is difficult to see how we could be fluent in our speech without at least some parallel processing. Consider what our speech output would be like if we had a strictly serial processing system. First, we would have to generate a complete message to be expressed. Next, we would have to formulate a linguistic structure for that message. Only then could we begin to articulate the sentence. After completing one utterance, we would then have to begin to prepare for the next message. Danks (1977) refers to this strictly serial arrangement as having stages in lock-step succession. If this is how we spoke, there would be long periods of silence, followed by fluent speech. The observations that our pauses are more brief and are internal to the sentence make a parallel model such as incremental processing attractive.

The Kempen and Hoenkamp (1987) model is also an example of a lexically driven approach to sentence production. In this respect it contrasts with a model such as Fromkin's that assumes that the syntactic structure is laid out in advance and then content words are fitted into the structure. According to the lexical approach, the production process may begin with words that are conceptually accessible, which then trigger the syntactic structure, not the other way around (Bock & Levelt, 1994). For example, words that are more easily retrieved may be placed early on in a sentence or constituent (Bock, 1982). The lexical approach is consistent with the lexical-functional grammar of Bresnan that we discussed in Chapter 2. Moreover, in emphasizing that the lexical level may influence the syntactic level and not simply vice versa, it is similar in spirit to the spreading activation view of production (Dell, 1986).

Self-Monitoring

Earlier in the chapter, we discussed the notion that we covertly edit our utterances prior to articulation. This notion remains a controversial one. There is no debate, however, over whether we overtly edit what we say. From time to time, we spontaneously interrupt our speech and correct ourselves. These corrections are referred to as **self-repairs.** According to Levelt (1983), self-repairs have a characteristic structure that consists of three parts. First, we interrupt ourselves after we have detected an error in our speech. Second, we usually utter one of various editing expressions. These include terms such as *uh, sorry, I mean,* and so forth. Finally, we repair the utterance. Let us consider each in turn.

Self-interruptions   Nooteboom (1980) examined a corpus of 648 speech errors and made several interesting discoveries. He found that 415 (64%) of the errors were corrected. Some errors were more likely to be corrected than others; anticipations were corrected more often than perseverations. In addition, Nooteboom found that most interruptions occurred very shortly after the error. Nooteboom suggested that the timing of self-interruption after detection of an error is based on two competing forces. On one hand, we have an urge to correct the error immediately. On the other hand, we want to complete the word we are speaking. As a consequence, interruptions are predominantly made at the first word boundary after the error.

Levelt (1983) used a somewhat different procedure. Students were shown color patterns such as those in Figure 8-2. They were then asked to describe the patterns beginning at the node indicated by an arrow in such a way that another person hearing a tape-recorded version of the description would be able to draw it. The main advantage of this approach, relative to the study of spontaneous errors in

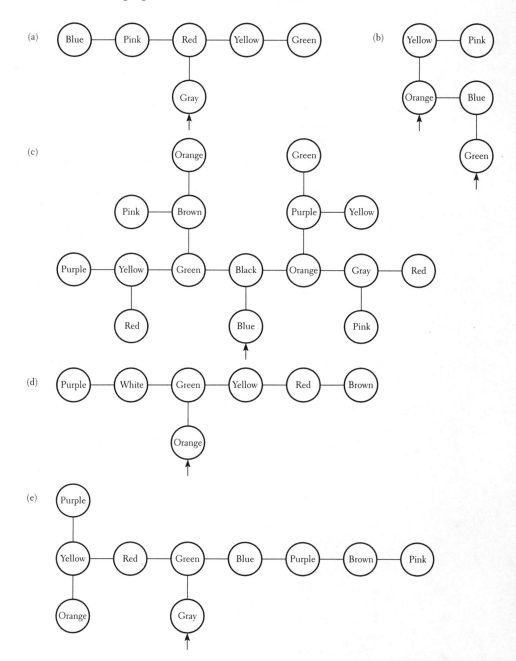

Figure 8-2. Color patterns used in Levelt's study. (Based on Levelt, 1982. From *Speaking: From Intention to Articulation*, by W. J. M. Levelt, p. 141. Copyright © 1989 MIT Press. Reprinted by permission.)

Figure 8-3. Distribution of interruptions while describing a pattern. (From "Monitoring and Self-Repair in Speech," by W. J. M. Levelt, 1983, *Cognition*, *14*, 41–104. Copyright © 1983 by Elsevier Science Publishers BV. Reprinted by permission.)

conversation, is the greater degree of experimental control. The distribution of interruptions over time is shown in Figure 8-3. Levelt found that 18% of the corrections were within a word, as in sentence (17). Another 51% occurred immediately after the error, as in (18). The remaining 31% of errors were delayed by one or more words; in (19), the correction comes three words later.

(17) We can go straight on to the ye-, to the orange node.
(18) Straight on to green—to red.
(19) And from green left to pink—er from blue left to pink.

Thus, although the speech task studied by Levelt differed substantially from the spontaneous speech errors examined by Nooteboom, the results of the two studies are quite similar.

Editing expressions   Although the matter could use further study, it appears that the editing expression conveys to the listener the kind of trouble that the speaker is correcting. James (1972) analyzed utterances containing expressions such as *uh* and *oh*, suggesting that these convey different meanings. For instance, in sentence (20), the *uh* suggests that the speaker paused to try to remember the exact number of people. In contrast, sentence (21) would be used when the speaker did not know the precise number but was trying to choose a number that was approximately correct.

(20)   I saw . . . uh . . . 12 people at the party.

(21)   I saw . . . oh . . . 12 people at the party.

DuBois (1974) has also analyzed several different editing expressions. The phrase *that is* is typically used to further specify a potentially ambiguous referent, as in sentence (22). *Rather* is used for what DuBois calls nuance editing, as in (23), in which a word is substituted that is similar in meaning to the original, but slightly closer to the speaker's meaning. *I mean* is reserved for true errors, as in (24).

(22)   Bill hit him—hit Sam, that is.

(23)   I am trying to lease, or rather, sublease, my apartment.

(24)   I really like to—I mean, hate to—get up in the morning.

Notice that the use of *that is* in place of *I mean* in (24) would be odd or inappropriate. This suggests that these different editing expressions are not fully interchangeable and that the expression that is used conveys the type of editing that the speaker is doing.

The expression *uh* may differ in some respects from these other expressions. It is the most common expression and turns up in many different languages. Levelt (1989) suggests that it is a symptom of trouble rather than a signal with a specific communicative meaning. Speakers may simply utter *uh* when they get stuck in the middle of their utterances. If it does not convey a specific meaning, why say it at all? Perhaps *uh*, along with various nonverbal cues such as averting one's gaze, indicates to the listener that the speaker still has the floor.

Self-repairs   After the interruption and the editing expression comes the correction proper. Levelt (1983, 1989) distinguishes among three types of repairs. **Instant repairs** consist of a speaker's retracing back to a single troublesome word, which is then replaced with the correct word, as in sentence (25):

(25)   Again left to the same blank crossing point—white crossing point.

In **anticipatory retracings**, the speaker retraces back to some point prior to the error, as in (26):

(26)   And left to the purple crossing point—to the red crossing point.

Finally, in **fresh starts**, the speaker drops the original syntactic structure and just starts over, as in (27):

(27)   From yellow down to brown—no—that's red.

Levelt (1989) argues that repairs are systematically different when there is an out-and-out error as opposed to an utterance that is merely inappropriate. Repairs based on social or contextual inappropriateness are those in which the speaker says what was intended but perhaps not in the way intended. Levelt found that error repairs consisted primarily of instant repairs (51%) and anticipatory retracings (41%), with very few fresh starts (8%). For the most part, error repairs are conservative: the speaker leaves most of the original utterance unaffected but alters the erroneous element. In such a case, the error and revised utterances have a parallel structure with but one difference. In contrast, fresh starts are more likely when the original utterance is contextually inappropriate (44%). When what we have said is technically correct but awkward, we tend to rephrase.

In general, speakers repair their utterances in a way that maximizes listeners' comprehension. The listener's problem when a speaker errs is not only to understand the correction but also how to fit the correction into the ongoing discourse. Several aspects of speaker self-repairs recommend themselves as helpful in this regard: speakers interrupt themselves quickly, their editing expressions indicate the type of error, and then the repair itself is systematic. All of these characteristics would appear to make the listener's work easier.

Summary

The production of speech is a complex process that requires the coordination of the respiratory, laryngeal, and supralaryngeal systems. Motor commands from the brain specify the target locations for the articulators in the vocal tract. However, the phenomenon of coarticulation indicates that the process of specifying targets is not context-free but, rather, is based on the preceding and following phonetic context.

Speaker monologues reveal an alternation between fluent speech and hesitation pauses. These pauses are related to various linguistic variables and appear to reflect linguistic planning within the sentence. This planning may take place in parallel with the implementation of previous linguistic plans.

Speakers routinely monitor their utterances to ensure that they are saying what they wanted to and in the way they wanted to. When errors are detected, speakers interrupt their speech nearly immediately and begin editing their utterance. Both the use of editing expressions and the linguistic structure of the repair itself appear to facilitate listener comprehension.

Insights from Sign Language

Here in the final section we look at the production of sign language. The production of signs is important theoretically because it gives us an opportunity to disentangle the cognitive processes involved in translating thought into language from the physical characteristics of our speech apparatus. Speech shares the vocal channel with respiration; in contrast, sign production can occur entirely in parallel with, and unimpeded by, respiratory activity. Thus, consideration of sign production in comparison with speech production can yield insights into some of the biological limits on linguistic form (Bellugi & Studdert-Kennedy, 1980).

We will examine both similarities and differences between the two modes. One striking similarity is that errors occur in signing that strongly resemble those found with speech.

Slips of the Hand

Newkirk, Klima, Pedersen, and Bellugi (1980) have found some fascinating evidence that slips of the hand similar to slips of the tongue take place with deaf signers. They used a corpus of 131 errors, 77 of which came from videotaped signings and 54 of which were reported observations from informants or researchers. Ninety-eight of the errors were judged by the person who made them as errors, either by spontaneous self-correction or by subsequent viewing of the videotapes.

Independence of parameters   As we saw earlier in the chapter, slips of the tongue have provided evidence for linguistically defined units such as phonemes and distinctive features. Moreover, speech errors suggest that these are independent planning units because errors ordinarily occur at only one level of planning at a time. Newkirk and colleagues analyzed the errors in terms of the parameters of American Sign Language (ASL)—hand configuration, place of articulation, and movement—to assess whether sign parameters also appear to be independent units of production.

The researchers found errors analogous to exchanges, anticipations, and perseverations. One example of an exchange concerned an individual who apparently intended to sign *sick, bored* (similar to the English *I'm sick and tired of it*). This intended production can be described in the following way:

> *Sick*
>> Hand configuration: hand toward signer
>> Place of articulation: at forehead
>> Movement: with twist of wrist
>
> *Bored*
>> Hand configuration: straight index finger with hand toward signer
>> Place of articulation: at nose
>> Movement: with twist of wrist

What the signer actually produced was the sign for *sick* with the hand configuration for *bored* and vice versa. The other two parameters were not influenced (see Figure 8-4). Overall, Newkirk and colleagues found 65 instances of exchanges involving hand configuration, of which 49 were "pure" cases (that is, ones in which no other parameter was in error). In addition, 9 of 24 errors related to place and movement parameters were single-parameter errors. These cases provide evidence that ASL signs are not holistic gestures without internal structure; rather, they are subdivided into parameters that are somewhat independent of each other during sign language production.

Sick   *Bored*

Error   Error

Figure 8-4. Errors of hand configurations. (Based on "Linguistic Evidence from Slips of the Hand," by D. Newkirk, E. S. Klima, C. C. Pedersen, and U. Bellugi. In V. A. Fromkin (Ed.), *Errors in Linguistic Performance*, p. 171, Academic Press, 1980.)

As we saw in Chapter 2, positions such as "hand toward signer" can be further analyzed into distinctive features. The question then is whether these features are also independent units in sign production. Newkirk and colleagues found some evidence that they are. One example was a signer who intended to convey *must see* (roughly, *I must see about it*). The correct sign for *must* consists, in part, of a hand configuration in which the index finger is bent (Figure 8-5, top). The sign for *see* includes a hand configuration in which the index and middle finger make a V, as in a victory (or peace) sign. In the error, *must* was made in the V hand configuration

Must

See

Error

See

Figure 8-5.   Hand configuration feature errors. (Based on "Linguistic Evidence from Slips of the Hand," by D. Newkirk, E. S. Klima, C. C. Pedersen, and U. Bellugi. In V. A. Fromkin (Ed.), *Errors in Linguistic Performance*, p. 184, Academic Press, 1980.)

but with both fingers bent (Figure 8-5, bottom). It appears that the (+ bent) feature of one hand configuration was anticipated in the production of the earlier sign.

Morpheme structure constraints   One final aspect of signing errors concerns whether they obey constraints of morpheme structure that are part of the grammar of ASL. With speech, we have found that errors follow phonological rules. For instance, if a person mispronounced *slip of the tongue*, she would be highly unlikely to utter *tlip of the sung* because *tl* is not phonologically permissible in English at the beginning of a word (Fromkin, 1973).

Figure 8-6. Contacting region substitution accompanying a hand configuration slip. (Based on "Linguistic Evidence from Slips of the Hand," by D. Newkirk, E. S. Klima, C. C. Pedersen, and U. Bellugi. In V. A. Fromkin (Ed.), *Errors in Linguistic Performance*, p. 191, Academic Press, 1980.)

Similarly, with slips of the hand, most errors result in nonexistent but possible ASL signs (Newkirk et al., 1980). One constraint concerns the possible contacting regions for particular hand configurations. A contacting region is "the part of the hand that serves as a focus for contact or pointing during the movement of a sign" (Klima & Bellugi, 1979, p. 45). In one example, the signer intended *deaf woman*, but signed *deaf* with the hand configuration of *woman* (Figure 8-6). The correct sign for *deaf* includes a hand configuration in which the index finger is extended; the contacting region is the tip of the extended finger. In the error, the hand configuration of *woman*, an open palm, is substituted for the index finger. However, the open palm handshape does not permit an index finger contact, so the contacting region was shifted to the tip of the thumb, which is an acceptable contacting region for this hand configuration. In other words, the contacting region of the sign is accommodated to the hand configuration that is (erroneously) used.

In general, slips of the hand strongly suggest that similar principles of organization underlie signed and spoken language, pointing to the possibility that both types of language take the form that they do because of basic cognitive limits on how (or how much) linguistic information may be structured or used. In contrast, some recent studies of the rate at which signs and speech are produced point to some equally interesting discrepancies between the two modes.

Production Rates

As we discussed earlier, spontaneous speech alternates between fluent and hesitation phases. These hesitations tend to reflect linguistic planning but also might be related to other factors. One such factor is the need to breathe. Speakers must interrupt their speech to breathe, but signers are under no such obligation. It therefore might be interesting to examine whether this difference might cause differences in the rate of speaking and signing.

Bellugi and Fischer (1972) began this line of research by studying three bilingual individuals who were fluent in both ASL and English. They were young hearing adults who had acquired ASL as a native language from deaf parents and had signed throughout their lives. The researchers had these individuals tell a personal story in three versions: one in ASL, one in spoken English, and one simultaneously signed and spoken. Different individuals did the versions in different orders. The results indicated that more time was spent in pausing in speech than in sign. When pauses were taken out, the rate of speech (words per second) was roughly double that of signing (signs per second). The results were slightly different in simultaneous and successive conditions, but the basic patterns were borne out in both conditions.

When, however, the rate of expressing a proposition was examined, the results changed dramatically. A proposition was defined as a simple underlying sentence. Here it was found that the number of seconds taken to express a proposition was highly similar for the two languages (about 1.5 seconds).

Another study of the rate of expression was performed by Grosjean (1979), who was interested in the way various rates of production were achieved in the two modes. He gave signers and speakers either an English passage or an ASL version with an English gloss. The participants' task was to read aloud or sign the passage at five different rates, four times each. Understandably, the participants were given some practice at this somewhat unusual task, but with practice they were able to achieve the desired rates consistently.

The results indicated that at normal rates of production, signers spend more of their production time in articulation than do speakers: they articulate more slowly (Grosjean estimates the word-to-sign ratio as closer to 4.5:1 than 2:1) and use somewhat fewer pauses. Moreover, the pauses that do occur in sign are for much shorter durations than in speech. The average pause in speech was 0.46 second; for sign, it was 0.20 second.

Interestingly, different strategies for changing speed were evident in the two modes. Speakers change the frequency but generally not the length of their (relatively long) pauses; signers modify both. Grosjean (1979) attributes this difference to respiratory activity: speakers seem to have a minimal pause duration based on respiratory requirements; they take a sufficiently long pause to inhale and then continue, whereas signers can breathe anytime they want.

These interesting results reinforce a central thread in our discussion in this chapter—that the production of speech operates within a matrix defined by cognitive and physiological resources. Variations in speech rate necessitate strategies based closely on these physiological resources; variations in signing rate, free from respiratory requirements, are relatively more closely attuned to cognitive processes. In both modes, the processes of production are wedded inextricably to the cognitive and physiological resources required to execute linguistic goals successfully.

Summary

Studies of sign language production are valuable because they enable us to distinguish between those aspects of production that are constrained by broad biological forces and those that are specific to speech. Sign language, since it exists in an entirely different mode from speech, might well differ substantially from speech in terms of grammatical organization. In contrast, basic similarities have been found in the two modes' organization of basic units into words or signs and in the syntactic rules by which words and signs are combined to form sentences. These similarities are illustrated by slips of the hand, which, like those of speech, typically involve a systematic error in a single linguistic unit. These results provide evidence that the parameters underlying signs are planned independently of one another.

Studies of production rate, in contrast, reveal differences between the two modes. Speakers achieve differences in speech rate primarily by varying the number of pauses, whereas signers vary the duration of signed segments and both the duration and number of pauses. These dissimilarities reflect the effects of respiratory functioning on speech but not on signs.

Review Questions

1. Identify and give examples of the following types of speech errors: shifts, exchanges, anticipations, perseverations, additions, deletions, substitutions, and blends.
2. Use Fromkin's model of production to identify the stage at which the following speech errors were made:
   a. *A singing sewer machine*
   b. *I wouldn't buy kids for the macadamia nuts.*

     c. *There's a lot of flee floating anxiety.*

     d. *At the end of today's lection*

     e. *He's a laving runiac* [double whammy!]

3. What is accommodation? Do errors of accommodation support serial models of language production?

4. Define the lexical bias effect.

5. How does Dell's model of linguistic planning differ from Fromkin's?

6. Describe respiratory, laryngeal, and supralaryngeal contributions to the articulation of speech.

7. What is incremental processing?

8. Are fresh starts more common with nuance errors or with outright errors? Explain.

9. Identify points of similarity between slips of the hand and slips of the tongue.

10. Distinguish between the way signers and speakers speed up their rate of production.

Thought Questions

1. Keep a log of naturally occurring slips of the tongue. Identify the date, the setting, the utterance, and what you believe the intended utterance was. Organize them into the categories listed in Table 8-1. Are there any errors that do not fit a category or that appear to fit more than one?

2. It is commonly believed that alcohol and other drugs increase the frequency of slips of the tongue. Do you think they would increase all types of slips across the board, or would certain types of slips be more likely when a person is intoxicated? Explain.

3. Suppose you have been paralyzed in an auto accident. Your only way to communicate is to manipulate a pencil-like instrument with your mouth to push buttons on an apparatus that produces humanlike sounds. How might this type of communication system influence your production of language? Identify similarities and differences with spoken language.

4. How would the frequency and distribution of speech errors and hesitations vary in the following three situations: (a) reading aloud, (b) talking without notes on a topic specified ahead of time, and (c) describing a picture?

5. Do you think social scientists have more or fewer filled pauses than natural scientists? Justify your answer.

9 Conversational Interaction

MAIN POINTS

- Conversation is a form of oral discourse that is distinguished by the absence of explicit rules.
- In place of a formal structure, conversations are governed by a set of implicit conventions regarding the social use of language. These include rules for taking turns and for maintaining and changing topics.
- Conversational settings shape conversational processes. Friends tend to converse in different ways than acquaintances and strangers. Some studies of gender differences reveal that males speak more and interrupt more than females.
- Conversation also varies with the social setting. Speech in institutional settings adhere to rules other than those typically found in personal settings. The role assumptions of participants influence the topics that may be discussed as well as the interpretation given to conversational acts.

Introduction

Conversations, of course, require at least two parties—two individuals to select meanings, form syntactic outlines, and do the other sorts of planning that we discussed in the preceding chapter. When our attention turns from monologue to dialogue, the complexity of processes increases tremendously, for a conversation is not simply two monologues side by side or in alternating order but rather a special form of social interaction with its own rules and dynamics.

Much of our concern in this chapter is on how conversation is organized. That may seem surprising, for conversation can be, among friends, a nearly effortless flow of topics, thoughts, and events that is attractive precisely because it does not appear to have any rules. This is an illusion, however, though the rules of conversation are certainly more relaxed than those of, say, a debate. Moreover, the rules, unlike those of other aspects of language, show powerful influences of social and cultural context: the rules of proper conversation vary with the culture. But it is not correct to say that conversation operates without rules; rather, we have internalized them to the point that we need not think of them to have a conversation. In this chapter, we will try to identify some of this tacit knowledge explicitly.

Perhaps the most fundamental rule is that conversation is a form of what Herbert Clark (1996) calls **joint action**:

> A joint action is one that is carried out by an ensemble of people acting in coordination with one another. As simple examples, think of two people waltzing, paddling a canoe, playing a piano duet, or making love. When Fred Astaire and Ginger Rogers waltz, they each move around the ballroom in a special way. But waltzing is different from the sum of their individual actions—imagine Astaire and Rogers doing the same steps but in separate rooms or at separate times. Waltzing is the joint action that emerges as Astaire and Rogers do their individual steps in coordination, as a couple. Doing things with language is likewise different from the sum of a speaker speaking and a listener listening. It is the joint action that emerges when speakers and listeners . . . perform their individual actions in coordination, as ensembles. (p. 3)

If we jointly follow rules when conversing, what kinds of rules are they? Do these rules work the same for different people and for different speech situations, or do we see variations? These are some of the questions we will consider in this chapter. We begin by discussing some of the implicit conversational rules that have been identified. Next we look at different types of conversational participants— friends and acquaintances, women and men—and consider how different participants may shape the conversational process. Finally, we examine different conversational situations, with an emphasis on how institutional talk differs from personal talk.

The Structure of Conversation

The linguist Charles Fillmore (1981) has stated that "the language of face-to-face conversation is the basic and primary use of language, all others being best described in terms of their deviation from that base" (p. 152), and this appears to be a reasonable starting point. Let us begin, then, by comparing conversation with other types of discourse (see Table 9-1).

Debates, for example, typically have topics specified in advance, and rules specifying who can speak at a given time and for how long are also usually agreed on ahead of time. The turns of each speaker are identified clearly. Speakers typically speak for an extended period of time.

Ceremonies, such as an awards dinner, are also formalized. The topic is specified in advance but not the length of time any given speaker may take. Turns are identified rather clearly, with formal introductions given for each speaker. Again, the length of a given speaker's monologue can be rather long.

Meetings are typically less formal than either ceremonies or debates. While it is not uncommon for specific rules, such as *Robert's Rules of Order,* to be used to organize discussions, the discussions themselves vary, as a general rule, more than those of more formal types of discourse. Also, the number of participants is much larger than for debates, and the contributions of different members vary a great deal. It is not uncommon for one member of a committee to dominate the proceedings.

Finally, conversations are the least formal of these four types of oral discourse. The number of participants, the topic, the length of a given speaker's contribution, and many other factors are left undecided or decided on the spot. The relaxation of formal rules is, of course, one of the prime enjoyments of a good, rich conversation.

Table 9-1. Comparison of Four Forms of Discourse

	Form			
Attribute	*Debate*	*Ceremony*	*Meeting*	*Conversation*
Number of people	Usually two or more	Varies	Varies	Varies
Topic	Fixed	Fixed	Partially fixed	Varies
Turn order	Fixed	Fixed	Varies	Varies
Turn length	Fixed	Varies	Varies	Varies

Yet, in the absence of formal rules we have implicit communicative conventions that help organize everyday conversations.

We will look at five types of conventions that are related to conversations: opening conversations, closing conversations, taking turns, negotiating topics, and identifying participants and nonparticipants. From an observer's standpoint, these appear as rules that provide structure to conversational encounters. From a conversational participant's standpoint, these appear as tasks to be addressed during conversational encounters.

Opening Conversations

Conversations have been studied for some time by researchers interested in language behavior, language acquisition, and social interaction, and some of its main features have been identified (see, for example, Jaffe & Feldstein, 1970; Sacks, Schegloff, & Jefferson, 1974). In the vast number of cases, only one person speaks at a time. This does not mean that there are no times when two (or more) speakers are talking, but these times tend to be brief in most conversations. More precisely, it is simultaneous turns rather than simultaneous talking that is uncommon, for listeners often say things like *um-hmm* and nod their heads while listening to a speaker; these are not attempts to speak but merely identify that the listener is following the speaker's train of thought. True points of overlap are most common at turn exchanges, when one speaker's turn is ending and another's is beginning.

Since neither turn order nor turn length is decided ahead of time, it is not surprising that there is considerable individual variation in the number of turns a given speaker will take and the length of each turn. Jaffe and Feldstein (1970) report that the length of a particular speaker's turn was a stable individual characteristic. In contrast, the pauses between vocalizations during a speaker's turn tended to match the pauses of other participants in the conversation. The net effect is to produce a conversation with a certain "rhythm."

While theoretically the number of possibilities for opening conversations is infinite, in practice we do so in a limited number of ways (Schegloff, 1972). Most commonly, we address another person (*Hey, Carl*), request information (*Do you know what time it is?*), offer information (*Are you looking for someone?*), or use some form of stereotyped expression (*Hello*) or topic (*Strange weather lately, eh?*). These serve to get the listener's attention and often lead to stock replies. This quickly establishes the alternation of turns that is central to conversation: A asks a question, B replies, followed by a sequence of the form ABABAB.

Since these openers are so predictable, we can often anticipate a conversational response. Schegloff (1972) gives a humorous example from Jewish folklore:

> On the express train to Lublin, a young man stopped at the seat of an obviously prosperous merchant.
> "Can you tell me the time?" he said.
> The merchant looked at him and replied: "Go to hell!"
> "What? Why, what's the matter with you! I ask you a civil question in a properly civil way, and you give me such an outrageous rude answer! What's the idea?"

The merchant looked at him, sighed wearily, and said, "Very well. Sit down and I'll tell you. You ask me a question. I have to give you an answer, no? You start a conversation with me—about the weather, politics, business. One thing leads to another. It turns out you're a Jew—I'm a Jew, I live in Lublin—you're a stranger. Out of hospitality, I ask you to my home for dinner. You meet my daughter. She's a beautiful girl—you're a handsome young man. So you go out together a few times—and you fall in love. Finally you come to ask for my daughter's hand in marriage. So why go to all that trouble. Let me tell you right now, young man, I won't let my daughter marry anyone who doesn't even own a watch!" (Ausubel, 1948, cited in Schegloff, 1972, p. 377)

The humor, of course, is based on our knowledge of conversational processes. The merchant first responds impolitely to a standard opening line, then exaggerates the sense of predictability inherent in conversation by reeling off an entire conversation.

Closing Conversations

Conventions are also at work when we close conversations. Schegloff and Sacks (1973) suggest that one way to end a conversation is to present a preclosing statement like *we-ell, so-o-o,* or *okay,* which signals a readiness to end the conversation. The listener then may accept the statement with an utterance such as *yeah* or *okay.* Alternatively, the listener might bring up another topic and the conversation would continue. Here is an example of the latter (Clark, 1994):

June:	yes
Daphie:	thanks very much
June:	OK?
Daphie:	*right,* I'll see you this
June:	because there how did you beat him?
Daphie:	no, he beat me, four one (laughs)
June:	four one
Daphie:	yes, I was doing quite well in one game, and then then I l- I lost
June:	oh, how disgusting
Daphie:	yes
June:	OK. *Right*
Daphie:	*right*
June:	see you tonight
Daphie:	right, bye
June:	bye love

Notice that June, in the third line, signals a potential end to the conversation (*OK?*) and Daphie seems to reciprocate (*right, I'll see you this*), but then June brings up another topic. The topic continues for some time until the end of that topic leads to the end of the conversation as a whole.

Albert and Kessler (1978) list several ways in which we end conversations, including summarizing the content of the conversation, justifying ending contact at this time (*I have another meeting*), expressing pleasure about each other, making reference to the ongoing relationship and planning for future contact (*see you later*), and wishing each other well (*take care, have a good trip*).

Albert and Kessler propose that these closing moves form a sequence, with the items occurring in the order indicated earlier. Their evidence supports such a sequence; for example, speakers were more likely to use summary statements at the beginning of the ending sequence and well-wishes at the end. In addition, use of closing sequences was reciprocal: listeners tend to respond to summaries with agreement, to positive statements with similar statements, and to well-wishes with *goodbye*. By presenting one of these closing statements and having one's conversational partner reciprocate, the conversationalists are implicitly negotiating an end to the conversation.

It is different with young children, of course. When they are done with a particular conversation, they simply walk away (Umiker-Sebeok, 1979).

Taking Turns

Conversations become more complicated when more than two people are present. Nevertheless, the single most outstanding fact about conversations is that they run so smoothly in the absence of formal rules. How do speakers avoid "bumping into" one another in the course of conversations?

According to Sacks et al. (1974), turn taking during conversations operates by three implicit rules. The first rule states that the current speaker is allowed to select the next speaker. This is often done by directing a question to another person. The second rule is that of self-selection: if the first rule is not used, another person may speak up. The third rule states that the current speaker can continue, although she or he is not obligated to do so. These rules are ordered: the first one takes priority over the second, which takes priority over the third. If speaker A addresses a comment specifically to B while C starts to talk, B has the floor.

This simple set of rules accomplishes a good deal of the organization of conversations. For example, it ensures that most of the conversation takes place with a single speaker, for each of the three rules allocates the next turn to a specific individual. The gaps between speakers will tend to be small since the second rule provides an incentive for starting quickly. Thus, although neither turns nor turn lengths are decided ahead of time, these rules produce an orderly shift from speaker to speaker.

Nonverbal behavior between conversational partners also facilitates an orderly transition from one speaker to another (Bavelas, Chovil, Lawrie, & Wade, 1992; Duncan, 1972; McNeill,1985). Duncan (1972) analyzed the signals given to regulate turns in a conversation. He defined a **turn-yielding signal** as the display of one or more of six behavioral cues that appear to indicate a willingness to conclude one's turn. These six cues were (1) a drop of pitch; (2) a drawl on the final syllable or final stressed syllable of a final clause; (3) the termination of hand gestures; (4) the use of stereotyped expressions such as *you know, or something,* and *but uh*; (5) a drop in loudness; and (6) completion of a grammatical clause. Duncan found a relationship between the number of cues indicating turn yielding and the probability that a listener would attempt to take a turn: when no such cues were presented, a listener attempted to speak 10% of the time; with three cues, the figure was 33%; and with all six cues, it was 50%.

At times, of course, we wish to continue speaking but fail to find the right word or expression. The "trailing off" of our speech is ambiguous to a listener and may appear to indicate that we are finished. Duncan (1972) found that in such cases speakers resort to what he calls an **attempt-suppressing signal,** which is the continued use of hand gestures in conjunction with one or more of the turn-yielding cues. When yield cues and attempt-suppressing signals were simultaneously displayed, a listener almost never attempted to take a turn. Cook (1977) found that speakers who were silent but looked away from listeners were seldom interrupted. When speakers look at listeners and stop talking, it is generally a sign for a listener to start. When a speaker looks away, it is often taken as a signal that he is not through with his turn.

Although face-to-face encounters enable us to attend to all of these nonverbal behaviors, they are not required for successful conversation. In one study (Beattie, Cutler, & Pearson, 1982), students were asked to judge whether utterances from a television interview came during the middle or at the end of a speaker's turn. Judges were accurate when given both video and audio information but did almost as well with either video or audio information. They were unable to distinguish middle and end utterances from a written transcript. Thus, we do not need facial or gestural information to anticipate when a speaker is completing a turn. If turn completion is determined by a number of cues, as Duncan (1972) suggests, then we presumably only need some of the cues to identify the turn completion.

Negotiating Topics of Conversation

It is not enough, however, merely to take turns with others in conversation. As Grice (1975) has noted, there is a strong social convention to "be relevant." In conversations, this means sticking to the topic and tying one's comments to those of the previous speaker.

We discussed the notion of discourse coherence in Chapter 7. In particular, recall the discussion of Halliday and Hasan's (1976) categories of cohesion, in which successive sentences in discourse are related by cohesive devices such as reference, ellipsis, conjunction, and lexical ties. In Chapter 7, our interest was with individual discourse, whereas here it is with conversational discourse. With conversation, the notion of coherence becomes a more complex process. How does one person stick to another's topic? Are there, in fact, rules that determine what is an acceptable response to another's statement in a conversation?

Schank (1977) argues that there are, indeed, rules of this kind, although it is probably more accurate to say that they govern rather than severely restrict our responses. This is reflected in the observation that while some responses are clearly odd, a wide range of "acceptable" responses to any statement is possible. Which of the following strike you as a reasonable response to *I just bought a new hat?*

(1)   Fred eats hamburgers.
(2)   I just bought a new car.
(3)   There is supposed to be a recession.
(4)   My hat is in good shape.
(5)   What color?

Many would describe (1) as an absurd response and (2) as at least odd. Sentence (3) is more relevant but not too polite, while (4) is marginally relevant and (5) seems to be a reasonable response. Clearly, many responses similar to (5) would be equally reasonable. For example, the listener might ask, *Oh, where did you get it?* or *How much did you pay?* And so on. Our question then becomes, Is it possible to identify this entire class of "reasonable" responses?

What the responses seem to have in common is that they are faithful to the topic identified by the speaker, but this is not helpful unless we are able to specify the notion of topic more precisely. Schank (1977) argues that topics in conversation can be defined in terms of the intersection of propositions across sentences. Thus, if speaker A says, *John bought a red car in Baltimore yesterday*, numerous propositions are being advanced: *John bought a car, the car is red, John bought it in Baltimore,* and *John bought it yesterday.* If speaker B responds to one of these propositions (for example, *I think a red car would be ugly*), the intersection of these two sentences is the proposition *the car is red.* An implication of this definition of topic is that only conversations, not individual sentences or even speaker turns, have topics.

Suppose, instead, B's response to this sentence is, *You mean he's not going to buy my car?* This response deals with only one proposition of the preceding sentence (*John bought a car*) and adds a new topic, the selling of B's car. According to Schank, A has three options at this point. A may respond to the new topic directly: *No, he didn't like your car.* Alternatively, A may refer back to that part of the original topic that got a response: *Well, John needed a car in a hurry.* Finally, A can make a more generalized response: *It's always difficult to sell a car.* Although all three types of responses preserve the coherence of the discourse, they do so in different ways. The first response effectively enables B to switch the topic of conversation to B's car, while the second response preserves the initial topic but, importantly, does so in a way that is relevant to B's remark. More specifically, it continues the discussion of the topic *John bought a car* but focuses on a reason for John's buying the car that is relevant to B's comment. The third response is somewhat ambiguous from a discourse point of view and permits the conversation to go in several directions. Noncommittal statements are common when there are "lulls" in a conversation.

Since any statement provides multiple opportunities for topic shifts, it can sometimes seem that the flow of conversation is hardly governed by rules at all. This seems especially true of long conversations that cover a number of topics; we often find ourselves wondering, "How did we get from there to here?" Usually, with some effort, the paths can be reconstructed. A close examination of the transcript of a conversation, for example, would reveal the kinds of connections between topics we have been discussing.

We still have a great deal to learn about what most people regard as appropriate topics and topic shifts in conversations. As further evidence that there is more than meets the eye in this matter, consider Jefferson's (1972) observation of a group of children playing a game called Marco Polo. In this game, whoever is "it" closes his or her eyes and counts to 10 while the others hide. Then the person who is it attempts to find the others by saying *Marco*, and the others are obliged to say *Polo*. Jefferson observed the following:

Steven: One, two, three . . . four, five, six . . . eleven, eight, nine, ten.
Susan: "E*leven*"?, eight, nine, ten?
Steven: Eleven, eight, nine, ten.
Susan: "E*leven*"?
Steven: Seven, eight, nine, ten.
Susan: That's better.

Here Susan has stepped outside the game temporarily to make a comment about Steven's speech. When he corrects himself, they return to the game. None of the children regarded Susan's response as either irrelevant or a switch of topics. It would be more accurate to regard it as an intact sequence embedded in the rest of the conversation. Thus, even children's conversations appear to operate on more than a single level at a given time.

Similarly, Polanyi (1989) has analyzed conversational storytelling and has found that it differs in interesting ways from conversational discourse in general. When one person in a conversation tells a story, the ordinary rules of turn taking seem to be temporarily suspended. If a speaker is in the middle of a story and pauses, it is considered inappropriate for one of the listeners to seize the floor. At the same time, stories must have a point that is relevant to what preceded them. Polanyi discusses several conversational stories in some detail and illustrates how the stories may influence conversational processes in a number of subtle ways.

One way to characterize these variations is to talk about layers of conversation (Clark, 1996). Layer 1 is the primary layer of conversational activity—actual people saying actual things. Layer 2 is built on top of layer 1 and represents a different domain or world. When the child stepped outside the game to comment on language, these comments are at layer 2. The stories that Polanyi (1989) discusses are also at layer 2, as are jokes that are embedded in conversation (Sacks, 1974). A joke that begins *There were three sisters who got married to three brothers* creates a fictional world, and the listener understands that reference to that world is different from ordinary conversational activity at layer 1. Conversational participants shift layers during the course of conversations, creating various problems related to coherence. Each layer has to be coherent, and yet the layers must effectively connect to each other as well. It is beginning to sound like conversations are a lot of work! In some situations, they can be.

Identifying Participants and Nonparticipants

So far we have been talking about how conversational participants coordinate their behavior with one another. However, as Clark (1994, 1996) has pointed out,

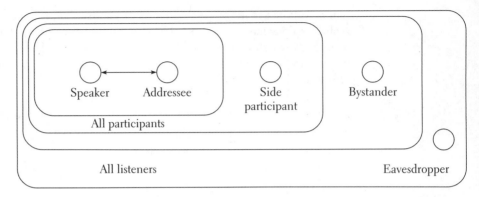

Figure 9-1.   Different roles in conversations. (From *Using Psychology*, by H. H. Clark. Copyright © 1996 Cambridge University Press. Reprinted by permission.)

conversations often take place in a context in which various types of nonparticipants are also present. Consider Figure 9-1. Suppose Alan asks Barbara a question. Alan and Barbara then are **participants** in the conversation. Suppose Connie has been present during the conversation but is not directly involved in the question. She is a **side participant** in the conversation. Others within earshot are **overhearers,** who come in two varieties. **Bystanders** are those who are openly present but do not participate in the conversation. **Eavesdroppers** are those who listen in without the speaker's awareness.

Many conversational situations bring these roles into play. For example, if I am having lunch with Hal and Greg stops by, I may, after introducing the two, chat briefly with Greg in such a way as to define Hal as a side participant. I might, for example, ask Greg how his family is, knowing that a family member had been seriously ill some time back. My question and Greg's answer can be phrased in such a way that Hal is completely unaware that anything significant has been discussed. Later, if Greg asks him a question, Hal is once again a full participant in the conversation.

We resort to a variety of strategies when dealing with overhearers, including disclosure, concealment, and indifference (Clark & Schaefer, 1992). Consider a situation in which a man and a woman were served by an inept waitress in a restaurant. The waitress dropped the man's forks on the floor but did not replace them. After the waitress brought the food but was still within earshot, the man asked his companion, *Could I use one of your forks?* In this instance, the speaker's apparent intent was to allow the bystander to hear him without having to confront her about her lapse. Thus, although the waitress is a bystander, the intent is to disclose the information that is communicated to the dinner companion (Clark & Schaefer, 1992).

As another example, when we are at an airport, trying to say good-bye to a loved one, all sorts of strangers are nearby. Although we may wish to engage in some private conversation, there are many potential eavesdroppers. We resort to a variety of strategies in these kinds of situations to conceal our meaning from eavesdroppers, including referring to personal events (for example, *the event we talked about yes-*

terday) and using private codes such as ingroup jargon or even foreign languages (Clark & Schaefer, 1987).

These points merely scratch the surface of what is a complex but poorly understood process. The main point is that when speakers address their listeners, they must also take overhearers into account.

I have to this point sketched out a series of general principles about how conversations take place—taking turns, distinguishing participants from nonparticipants, and so on. But this characterization begs the question, How general are these principles? In the following sections, we explore two ways of answering this question. First, we look at whether these principles apply equally to various types of participants, such as friends and acquaintances, and males and females. Then, we examine whether these principles apply equally well to different conversational settings, with particular emphasis on psychotherapy as a form of conversation.

Summary

Conversations differ from other forms of speech interactions in the number of people and the degree to which topics, turn lengths, and turn orders are specified in advance. Thus, unlike debates, conversations operate without a rigid set of explicit rules. This degree of relaxation is made possible by a set of implicit rules or conventions governing conversational interactions. These include rules for taking turns in conversations, establishing discourse coherence, and identifying the proper use of speech acts such as requests. These enable most conversations to flow easily from one person to another and from one topic to another.

Conversational Participants

The conversational principles presented so far have neglected to say much about who the participants in the conversation might be. A great many attributes of participants would conceivably influence the nature of conversational processes. These include their age, gender, social status, ethnic background, and degree of friendship or intimacy. In this section, we look at two of these factors: friendship and gender.

Friends and Acquaintances

Relatively little work has been undertaken to determine how friendship influences conversational processes. Some of this research reveals variation between friends and strangers on the dimensions of conversations we have considered in this chapter.

One concept that may be helpful here is what Clark (1996) calls **common ground,** which refers to the shared understanding of those involved in the conversation. For knowledge to qualify as common ground, person A must know a given information X, and person B must know X, and A must know that B knows, and B knows that A knows, and so on; that is, both parties are aware that they share the information. Some of this common ground is culturally based, such as cultural values, commonly held beliefs, or culturally prescribed roles. For example, when you have a conversation with your academic adviser, your discussion is linked to these roles. Other types of common ground are more personal, in which shared experiences influence the nature of the conversation. It is this personal common ground that is our concern at this point.

These shared assumptions might influence several conversational processes. One is how we close conversations. We need ways to close off conversational topics when we have done well enough to satisfy the conversational participants. For example, when talking on the phone to a friend about an upcoming trip to the friend's house, we might make some preliminary arrangements (for example, when we plan to arrive, how long we plan to stay) and still leave other matters for further discussion. Note how our ability to close off a topic of discussion, for now, depends on common ground. We jointly agree that we can complete the plans later. The discussion would likely be longer and less successful if we were to have it with a person with whom we were less acquainted.

Empirical research has examined some of the differences between how friends and acquaintances talk. Planalp (1993) asked students in an interpersonal communication class to audiotape one conversation with a friend and one with an acquaintance. Some clear differences emerged. Friends were more likely to use profanity, laugh more often, express negative judgments, argue with one another, and make joint references to themselves (*we, us*). Acquaintances were more likely to use filled pauses (*uh, um,* and so forth) and talk about only one topic.

Friends obviously have a greater degree of common ground than acquaintances, so it was no surprise that their shared knowledge influenced the conversations in various ways. Friends were more likely to refer to other people and events without explaining who or what they were, make references to past encounters, talk about habits and plans, and so forth.

Hornstein (1985) analyzed phone conversations between friends, acquaintances, and strangers and found a number of differences. Friends used more implicit openings (for instance, *Hi. It's me* as opposed to *Good day. This is Malcolm Ritteridge*), talked about more topics, asked more questions, and used more complex closings. Acquaintances were generally similar to strangers.

The common ground shared by friends often allows us to condense our speech. Consider the following exchange (from Mathis & Yule, 1994, p. 64):

K: What do you buy men in your family for Christmas?

B: My father is the main problem.

K: Yes. I have that same problem. I finally resorted to saying "Dad? What do you *want?*" "I don't need anything."

B: That's exact—I think we've got the same father.

Notice that when K quotes herself, she provides a phrase that introduces the quotation (*I finally resorted to saying*). In contrast, when quoting her father, no such phrase is used. Nonetheless, B understands immediately.

In general, these studies suggest that friends operate on the basis of implicit assumptions more than strangers or acquaintances. As Hornstein (1985) has put it:

> [T]he shared experience of being in a close relationship appears to allow the members of such dyads to talk together in ways that do not require full articulation of the assumptions on which their exchange is based. The use of abbreviated expressions, rapid shifting from one topic to another with little transition, and frequent ellipses are some of the features that characterize the implicit style of intimate conversation. (p. 671)

It will be instructive to compare this implicit style of conversation with various forms of institutional speech, discussed later in the chapter. For now, we turn to gender differences in conversational patterns.

Gender Differences in Conversation

A considerable amount of research has investigated the question of whether there are gender differences in conversational processes. This discussion is organized historically, beginning with some of the original work done in the 1970s and then continuing to some early reactions to this work.

Early work   As we have seen, Sacks et al. (1974) claimed that we have several rules for holding conversations, including those that the current speaker has the power to select the next speaker but that another speaker may self-select by speaking up when a pause occurs. They suggested that these rules minimize the degree of conflict between participants.

Zimmerman and West (1975) examined whether these rules hold equally well for conversations between men and women as opposed to those with either just women or just men. They tape-recorded and transcribed conversations in natural settings such as coffee shops and drug stores. They identified three speech behaviors of interest. **Overlaps** were defined as periods of simultaneous speech during the last word of the speaker's projected closing. Overlaps appear to be consistent with the second of Sacks et al.'s rules; since the first person to speak during a silence gains the floor, there is an incentive to be quick. **Interruptions** were defined as periods of simultaneous speech more than one word before the speaker's projected completion point. Zimmerman and West viewed interruptions as violations of the speaker's turn. They also discussed **minimal responses,** which were remarks such as *uh-huh* and *um-hmm.* These were not viewed as interruptions but rather as a listener's display of interest in a speaker's topic.

In their initial study, Zimmerman and West (1975) found that 96% of the interruptions were by male speakers. Ten of the 11 males interrupted at least once. In contrast, interruptions were less frequent and were symmetrically distributed in same-sex conversations. A second major result was that many of the responses by males to female topics were delayed minimal responses, in which a delay of several seconds occurred before the listener's minimal responses.

Men and women have different styles of conversation.

Zimmerman and West (1975) concluded that "men deny equal status to women as conversational partners with respect to the rights to the full utilization of their turns and support for the development of topics" (p. 125). They further suggest that this pattern of verbal interaction reflects the power difference between men and women in our culture. In support of this notion, their second study (1977) found that children are treated by parents in ways that are similar to the ways women are treated by men; that is, 12 of 14 interruptions in parent-child interactions in a physician's office were initiated by the parents (see also Gleason & Greif, 1983).

These results fit well with other observations that were made about the same time. Lakoff (1975) argued that women's speech differs in a number of respects from men's speech, claiming that women's speech contains more linguistic expressions of uncertainty than men's speech does. Women tend to use **tag questions** (*It's awfully cold in here, isn't it?*) and hedges (*sort of, I guess*). They also tend to use more question intonation patterns in declarative sentences than men. For example, women would be more likely to utter *So, we will meet at eight* with a rising intonation at the end of the sentence. All of these manners of expression suggest a degree of uncertainty or a lack of assertiveness. Several studies found that women use more linguistic devices that signal uncertainty than men (Crosby & Nyquist, 1977; McMillan, Clifton, McGrath, & Gale, 1977).

Similarly, Fishman (1978) analyzed conversations of male and female couples and found that women used more questions, attention-getting devices (for example, *This is interesting*), and minimal responses than men. They also used the phrase *you know* (as in *d'ya know that?*, a form of conversational opening) more often than men. Fishman concluded that women do the bulk of the interactional work in conversations with men and that this difference reflects the power asymmetry between men and women.

More recent work In recent years, some scholars within linguistics, sociology, and psychology have questioned both the reliability of the foregoing results as well as the conclusions that have been drawn from them. Consider first the results. McMullen, Vernon, and Murton (1995) attempted to replicate Fishman's study and found very different results. There were no differences in the use of questions (including tag questions) between men and women in the intimate couples they observed, nor did they observe any differences in the use of minimal responses. Thus, there was no evidence that women necessarily worked harder in their conversations with men. Simkins-Bullock and Wildman (1991) found essentially similar results.

One reason that these linguistic differences—tag questions, minimal responses, and so on—do not always differentiate women and men is that couples differ in the ways that they share power. Kollock, Blumstein, and Schwartz (1985) studied cross-sex and same-sex couples in which power was either shared equally or one partner had more power. They found that in couples in which one partner had more power, the more powerful partner interrupted more and the less powerful partner used more minimal responses and tag questions; these relationships held regardless of the gender of the partners. Few differences in conversational behavior existed between partners in balanced couples. These investigators concluded:

> We have seen that power dynamics can create the conversational division of labor usually attributed to sex. We have also seen that sex *by itself* has very little or nothing to do with such a division of labor. (p. 45)

More generally, it appears that the features ascribed to women's speech only sometimes appear to be more common in women than in men. Sometimes women use a given linguistic form more, sometimes men use it more, and sometimes there is no difference (James & Clarke, 1993; McMullen et al., 1995).

Some questions have also been raised about the interpretation of gender differences that do appear. Tannen (1990, 1993; see also Maltz & Borker, 1983) suggests that men and women come to mixed-sex conversations with different assumptions and expectations and that these differences often lead to miscommunication. For instance, when women discuss a problem, men tend to interpret it as an invitation to help solve the problem, whereas women might respond instead by relating a problem of their own. Tannen suggests that women's language is not inferior to, but simply different than, men's language.

This view of women's language provides a different way of interpreting conversational behavior. Holmes (1984) distinguishes between two functions of tag questions. Tags that serve the modal function request reassurance or confirmation of information of which the speaker is uncertain (*You were missing last week, weren't you?*). In contrast, tags that serve the affective function indicate concern for the addressee or an attempt to facilitate conversation (*His portraits are quite static by comparison, aren't they?*). Although Lakoff (1975) might interpret the latter remark as expressing uncertainty, Holmes and others (Cameron, McAlinden, & O'Leary, 1988) contend that the speaker is expressing an opinion and then soliciting a response. Thus, the use of certain features ordinarily ascribed to women's speech may, in some situations, be an effective way of eliciting responses from a conversational partner. Along these lines, it is worth noting that some evidence indicates that women who use more tentative language when discussing conversational topics are more likely to influence men's opinions (Carli, 1990).

Let us take another look at speaker interruptions. Several investigators (James & Clarke, 1993; Kennedy & Camden, 1983; Tannen, 1993) have drawn a distinction between interruptions that are dominance related (those in which the listener attempts to take the floor) and those that are supportive or cooperative (in which the listener speaks simultaneously but not intrusively with the person who has the floor). It is possible that women use interruptions to support the speaker, whereas men are more likely to use them in an attempt to dominate a conversation. If so, the total number of interruptions may not be the most satisfactory way to measure these conversational processes. Perhaps we need to look more closely at the semantic content of the interruptions.

Another factor that could be important is the speech context (Freed & Greenwood, 1996). In some studies, dyads or groups are given some formal task, such as solving a problem or generating a group answer. In others, the context is more casual, and conversationalists are asked to get to know each other but not given a specific task or topic to discuss. There is some indication that males tend to interrupt more (James & Clarke, 1993) and talk more (James & Drakich, 1993) in formal tasks.

Of course, many of these aspects of male and female speech behavior are quite salient in our everyday lives. Many popular books and television programs are available on the topic, so it is possible that increased awareness of these conversational patterns may change the patterns themselves. There is some indication that that is the case. For example, James and Clarke (1993) report that studies conducted in the 1970s tended to replicate Zimmerman and West's results more than studies conducted in the 1980s, which tended to find no differences between men and women. The latter participants may have come to the laboratory studies with some preconceptions about how to act that are different than those in earlier decades.

We began our discussion of gender differences in conversation with a question of whether the conversational rules discussed earlier in the chapter operate in fundamentally similar or different ways in women and men. Our survey indicates that there appear to be some areas of difference, such as the difference in amount or type of interruptions in men and women, although even this difference has been questioned recently and will certainly continue to be discussed.

A related question is whether the study of gender differences enlarges our understanding of conversational processes. For starters, it seems fair to say that the principles raised earlier provide at least an initial framework within which to view possible gender differences. That is, the framework poses some basic questions: Do we open and close conversations, develop and maintain topics, take turns, and deal with overhearers in much the same way whether we are talking to a member of the same sex or the opposite sex? The astute reader will recognize that there are no clear answers to these questions. We have discussed turn taking and interruptions at length, but less is known about how gender influences these other facets of conversational behavior.

On balance, however, I think that gender studies (as well as, to a lesser extent, those with friends and acquaintances) do more than flesh out our conversational outline. Some aspects of conversation may be fundamentally different. One example is Edelsky's (1981) study of faculty committee meetings. Edelsky recorded the verbal behavior of women and men with the intention of studying conversational turn taking only to find that there were different kinds of turns. Some turns had a clear speaker while others listened or responded; other turns were more collaborative in nature in which several people shared the turn. And here is where gender differences were found: men took longer turns during the former type, but there were fewer differences between genders in the collaborative turns. In short, one contribution of studying gender differences in turn taking is that it forces us to rethink and redefine fundamental conversational concepts, such as what a turn is.

Summary

We have examined the effects of two types of participants on conversational interaction. With regard to friends versus acquaintances, some differences emerged in the way in which conversations are closed. Early studies of gender differences found that men interrupt women more than vice versa, a result that has not been found as often recently. Studies of conversational participants flesh out an outline of conversational processes sketched earlier in the chapter while, at the same time, suggesting new avenues for research and theory.

Conversational Settings

We have seen in the previous section that the conversational principles outlined in the first section of the chapter serve us well when attempting to understand how men and women converse with one another and each other. Some of these principles (taking turns, for instance) may operate somewhat differently in male-female conversations than in same-gender conversations. Other principles (distinguishing between participants and nonparticipants, for example) may be very similar in women's and men's speech. With some allowance for variation, then, we can say that these principles apply reasonably well to both men's and women's conversations.

A second test of the generality of our conversational principles is to extend our discussion into different types of conversational settings. Until now we have not specifically discussed the context in which conversations take place. When trying to account for conversational interruptions, for instance, surely it matters whether we are talking about a conversation over dinner or one in a business meeting.

Personal and Institutional Settings

It would be helpful to have some kind of taxonomy for different language settings, but there is no consensus on such a taxonomy. Clark (1996; see also Drew & Heritage, 1992) has proposed a distinction between **personal settings** and **institutional settings.** In personal settings, a free exchange of turns takes place among the two or more participants. The turns may be used to exchange gossip, conduct business, or do any number of things. Most of the conversational studies we have discussed to this point in the chapter have been conducted in personal settings.

In contrast, in institutional settings the "participants engage in speech exchanges that resemble ordinary conversation, but are limited by institutional rules" (Clark, 1996, p. 5). In general, in institutional discourse one participant (a judge, teacher, physician, and so forth) is considered the authority figure. We are just beginning to understand how different institutional settings govern conversational processes, although there are some interesting reports on tutorial dialogues (Collins, Warnock, & Passafiume, 1975), talk between academic advisers and advisees (He, 1994), and medical discourse between physicians and their patients (Heath, 1993).

In this section, I will examine in some detail a particular type of institutional discourse, talk between client and therapist during psychotherapy. Following this discussion we will compare therapeutic discourse with some other forms of institutional discourse.

Therapeutic Discourse

For the most part, psychotherapists and related professionals (counselors and so on) attempt to help clients by listening to their concerns and talking to them. When the primary means of achieving therapeutic results is through language, we would expect that therapists are especially skilled at conversational processes. What kinds of special characteristics, then, comprise therapeutic discourse? Or, to put it slightly differently, what are the special institutional rules of psychotherapy?

It might be helpful to begin with an admittedly simplistic model of what therapists do and then examine each of these tasks in terms of conversational processes. We may distinguish three main tasks during therapy. First, the therapist listens carefully as the client reports experiences, issues, and concerns. Second, the therapist interprets the client's experiences and symptoms. Third, the therapist collaborates with the client regarding potential courses of action. These tasks are not necessarily organized sequentially; therapeutic sessions interweave data, interpretation, and suggestion in a complex pattern.

Consider first the process by which the client presents experiences to the therapist. Just as the therapist is the authority on the process of interpreting emotional experiences, it is the client who is the authority on the experiences themselves. Thus, sessions usually begin with statements of experience from the client, often in narrative form. The therapist does not challenge the client's reporting of experiences, for these statements provide the "raw data" for the therapeutic session.

In contrast, it is acceptable, and sometimes useful, for the therapist to challenge the client's interpretation of another person's experiences, since the therapist is the expert on the interpretation of emotions. Consider the example of a client (C) reporting a given event, and simultaneously interpreting it, and the response of the therapist (T). For convenience, each successive turn of each participant is numbered (from Labov & Fanshel, 1977, p. 366):

C1:   *I can't eat in a restaurant*—if you sit in a counter—I mean—if you goin' to a restaurant for a san'wich—you're eating alone, but—so you sit at the counter—*it doesn't bother me*—So she doesn't—so—anyway, I—the way I interpreted that was that she doesn't like to eat alone.

T1:   Well, but she didn't *say* that.

C2:   So sh's't'me, I know you don' like t'eat alone, and she says—

T2:   So what did you *say?*

C3:   So I said, "Well, I don't mind." She s'd, "Yeah, but it sorta gets lonesome in the house when you don't come home." Like if I were to eat out.

T3:   But she didn't say, "for *you.*"

C4:   She—

T4:   She gets lonesome for you—f'*her.*

C5:   No I said t'her: "Dyyou get lonesome?" Sh'says, "Well, not that I get lonesome, but I don't like to eat alone."

T5:   Oh, so she *told* you.

In this interchange, the client appears to make an interpretation (C1), and the therapist directly challenges (T1) her until, at the end, the client indicates that the interpretation is based on what the other person said (C5). At this point, the therapist changes course and immediately accepts the report (T5). Thus, the therapist's conversational moves are dictated by whether the client is reporting or interpreting an event (Labov & Fanshel, 1977).

Let us now turn to some of the ways in which therapists interpret client experiences. One part of the interpretation process is to define the therapeutic problem. Grossen and Apothéloz (1996) discuss how therapists transform clients' discourse into a problem by means of a process of reformulation. This process consists of three stages: identifying an utterance that is to be reformulated, marking or indicating the presence of a reformulation, and the actual reformulation. These stages are similar to those seen in monitoring and editing one's own utterances (Levelt, 1989), but here the speaker (therapist) is monitoring and editing another person's utterances.

Here is an example of reformulation (from Grossen and Apothéloz, 1996, p. 118):

C1:   (when I'm with my wife we talk about problems) which I try to avoid talking about but all the same there are times when we're alone when don't have anything else to talk about but then the the how can I put it

> the dialogue is almost completely broken off because we are OK to-
> gether without talking to each other even if sometimes we feel that there
> is a *dialogue* there is there is *we want* to say something but we don't
> know, we can't, we don't *dare* there are a lot of things we don't dare that
> we come up against a brick wall
>
> *T1:*   one could say there are somethings which are unspoken huh in a way
>   what isn't said
>
> *C2:*   yes
>
> *T2:*   what isn't said is hence unspoken and it's a burden isn't it
>
> *C3:*   yes it's a burden yes yes

The client's first turn discusses problems in communication (C1), which is the
material to be reformulated. The therapist begins with a reformulation marker, *one
could say,* and then the reformulation itself (T1, T2). The reformulation is then
ratified by the client (C2, C3). In this instance, a reformulation is suggested by the
therapist and accepted by the client. In other cases, a more extensive negotiation of
meaning may be involved (Grossen & Apothéloz, 1996). In any event, once it is
ratified, the reformulation becomes part of the common ground between therapist
and client.

In addition to bringing some clarity to the therapeutic process, reformulation
also provides a different perspective on the client's issues. Therapists use a number
of linguistic techniques to encourage clients to look at their problems in a new light.
Another technique is the use of metaphor. Consider the following example:

> A suicidal adolescent who is currently under therapy has dropped out of school, and
> does not work. He watches the late show on TV, and gets up in the morning at 11:00.
> He can be considered a loser. One of the discussions centered around the fact that
> there was very little communication between the boy and his father. When either
> spoke, the other made some comment which terminated the conversation. The ther-
> apy had reached the point where it was possible to analyze this transaction and to
> suggest that the boy might try to respond to his father in some manner which would
> continue the discussion and perhaps move it in a direction of interest to him. The boy
> commented that he did not wish his father to control him, but wished to maintain his
> own autonomy and would not engage in such extended conversation. The metaphor
> of a tennis game was then brought up by the therapist. If one wished to control the
> other player in tennis, one had to put oneself under the control of the oncoming ball.
> Hitting the ball left made the opponent run left. Then hitting it right made him run
> again, and so on. But, said the young man, I can choose not to hit the ball back. Then
> you lose, was the answer. You're a loser. This discussion continued with vigor, and the
> patient raised it several times since. (Goldiamond & Dryud, 1968, p. 81)

In this instance the metaphor seems to open lines of communication that conventional language does not. Through the metaphor of the game, the young man
realized that the communication failures with his father were not simply one-sided
(Pollio, 1974).

Similarly, the therapist makes suggestions from time to time during the course
of therapy. Special attention must be given to how to make various suggestions or

requests (Ratliff & Morris, 1995). The therapist must be sensitive to the fact that while his or her task is to increase the client's insight into emotional problems, this cannot be done in a way that is too threatening, for that puts the entire therapeutic work into peril (Labov & Fanshel, 1977). The form of the therapist's comments is closely related to the therapist's judgment of the client's emotional state; when a given request is posed too threateningly, it may be rephrased or even abandoned. Thus, therapists are exceedingly careful in the language in which they couch requests. They may take the form of indirect or polite language.

When therapy involves more than two persons, as in family therapy, managing the conversation can be demanding for the therapist. It has been observed that the turn-taking sequences in family therapy tend to alternate around the therapist's turns. That is, if A = one family member, and B = another family member, and T = the therapist, the sequence is typically TATBTATATB (Gale, Odell, & Nagireddy, 1995; Jones & Beach, 1995; Viaro & Lombardi, 1983).

One area in family therapy that poses challenges is dealing with unsolicited comments, such as when the therapist (T) asks one family member (F) a question and the family member's partner (P) answers. Here is an example (Jones & Beach, 1995, pp. 55–56):

T1: Oh you gotta house er something?

P1: He's gotta property right around the corner he doesn't havta pay rent deposit he doesn't havta pay anything (he owns his own) property

T2: Let me hear it from him cause he's gotta deal with the reality

F1: I'm probably not going ta stay in the area

P2: See

T3: Oh this was the relocate thing?

F2: I'm preddy much-decided that I ah if we s- separate I'm going ta leave the area

P3: He doesn't wanna move twice

T4: Le- lemme-let me hear 'im sa you don't wanna move twice I don't understand where would you go like outta state? Er

F3: Yeah quite a ways

In this case, P answers a question directed for F not just once but three times in the course of the conversation. The therapist responds politely but firmly that the question was directed at another participant.

By insisting on a response from a given family member, the therapist is using the first rule of turn taking developed by Sacks et al. (1974), which states that the speaker gets to select who speaks next. However, as Jones and Beach (1995) point out, actually a range of responses is available to the therapist. These include completely ignoring the intrusion to responding to the unsolicited responder but steering the conversation back to the intended addressee, to allowing the unsolicited comment to open up a new conversational topic.

The flexibility with which therapists respond to unsolicited remarks again reflects the roles of the conversational participants. Although in a position of authority in the conversation, therapists must negotiate topics with their clients to have an open and productive relationship over a period of time.

It is clear, in any event, that therapeutic discourse can fairly be described as similar to ordinary conversational speech, but with some special provisions. Although the participants do what other conversationalists do (take turns, develop topics, and so forth), they do so in the context of particular social roles. As earlier noted, there are generally clear roles of authority in institutional settings. Therapeutic discourse is special in this respect, for two reasons. First, as we have seen, although the therapist is the authority on the interpretation of emotional experiences, the client is the authority on the experiences themselves. In short, authority is shared. Second, even when the therapist maintains authority over the client, it is done in a more gentle way than is customarily found in institutional speech. The best way to see this point is to look at other types of institutional settings.

Other Forms of Institutional Discourse

Relatively little work has been done on conversations in other institutional settings, but at least a preliminary comparison with therapeutic discourse may be attempted. As we have already seen, most institutional settings identify a particular individual (therapist, judge, academic adviser, physician, and so on) as the authority figure. In addition, we have seen that although psychotherapists are authority figures, they are careful in the ways that they exercise their authority.

Judges, by contrast, are not as timid. In a court of law, there are more clearly prescribed patterns of allowable questions and answers, and most judges do not hesitate to control their courtrooms when matters tend to get out of hand. It is not uncommon to hear judges, for example, tell attorneys who have strayed too far on a given topic to shut up (Jones & Beach, 1995).

Physicians probably occupy an intermediate position on a continuum of how strictly or loosely institutional authority is wielded. Like therapists, physicians require data from the patient to be of much help, and good physicians listen carefully to their patients' symptoms and concerns. Also like therapists, physicians reserve the role of interpreting these symptoms, often with the aid of various diagnostic tests. Once the test results are in, the physician interprets their significance to the patient and either recommends a particular course of action or outlines the alternative possible actions (Parsons, 1975).

Particular interest has centered on the diagnostic part of the office visit: how and in what way the physician communicates the diagnosis of the condition to the patient. Diagnoses may vary from a single word (for example, *bronchitis*) to a detailed description of a condition. As Heath (1993) has observed, the diagnosis is a pivotal point in the consultation between patient and physician. It marks the end of the "data-gathering" phase and begins (and in fact is the basis for) the discussion of possible treatments. And it is the province of the physician to form this medical judgment. If the patient offers candidate diagnoses, the physician is likely to defer consideration of them until the examination or diagnostic tests are complete.

Physicians tend to distribute more of their time on identifying symptoms and recommending treatment than on discussing their diagnosis. Byrne and Long

(1976) found that physicians often moved quickly from conducting a physical examination to detailing a course of treatment without much discussion of why they had made a particular diagnosis. Byrne and Long suggest that the power asymmetry between patient and physician may be a contributing factor in why diagnoses are discussed so briefly. Patients also contribute to the brevity of the diagnostic segment. Heath (1993) observed that patients are often reticent to respond immediately after a diagnosis is made; the physician often waits briefly, then proceeds to discuss treatments.

The relative absence of patient response may be partly attributable to the factual manner in which diagnoses are often presented to patients (Todd, 1984). When physicians present their diagnoses in the form of a question or with some tentative language (*I think* . . .), patients are more likely to discuss the diagnosis (Heath, 1993; see also Ragan, Beck, & White, 1995). Of course, some divergent opinions of patient and physician may be more likely to emerge in this instance.

More generally, it appears that institutional talk draws on principles of conversational behavior that are used in everyday speech, such as taking turns and negotiating ends of encounters. But beneath this veneer we see differences related, in various ways, to the asymmetries of power that are present in institutional speech. Thus, to speak effectively in institutional settings one must master not only the aforementioned general rules but also rules that are specific to particular conversational settings. We will revisit this theme again in Chapter 11 when we discuss a different type of institutional speech: classroom discourse.

Summary

Institutional discourse, although it may resemble ordinary conversation, incorporates specialized rules of discourse. In therapeutic discourse, authority is shared between therapist and client, and the role assumptions of each party stipulate the range of appropriate conversational moves. The client reports the experiences to be discussed, whereas the therapist reserves the role of interpreting the experiences, making suggestions, and generally guiding the interaction. Patient-physician discourse follows a similar pattern but is often less interactive than therapeutic discourse.

Review Questions

1. Distinguish between the major properties of debates, ceremonies, meetings, and conversations.
2. Identify the three rules for taking turns in conversations.
3. Explain the way in which a topic is defined in a conversation.
4. How are topic shifts accomplished within the principle of coherence?
5. Distinguish between side participants and bystanders in conversations.
6. What is common ground?

7. How does conversation with friends differ from conversation with acquaintances or strangers?
8. In what ways does women's speech differ from men's speech?
9. Distinguish between personal and institutional talk.
10. How is therapeutic discourse similar to and different from other types of institutional speech?

*T*hought Questions

1. Schank's model of topic shifts is based on relationships between adjacent statements in conversation. Yet we often refer to something that was said much earlier. How might we formulate conversational rules pertaining to the coherence of nonadjacent statements?
2. In what ways might the common ground between an adolescent and his parents differ from the common ground between the adolescent and his peers?
3. How might your conversation with your physician be affected by your gender and/or the physician's gender? How might it be influenced if the physician were a family friend?

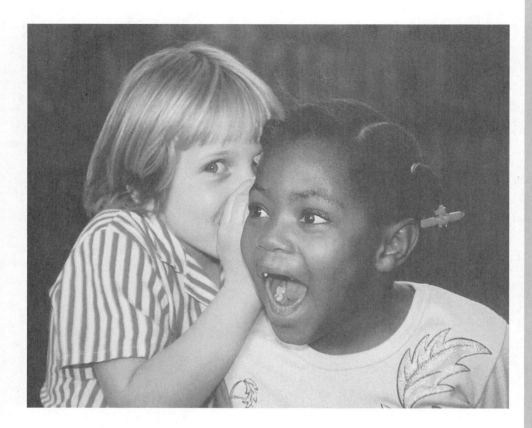

Language Acquisition

10 *Early Language Acquisition*

MAIN POINTS

- Children's construction of language emerges from their understanding of communication prior to language. Their comprehension and production of gestures reveal a basic understanding of communication processes.
- Although children first acquire the sound system of their native language independently of meaning, they eventually merge it with communicative gestures to form productive speech.
- The development of one-word speech comprises two important developments: the acquisition of the lexicon and the use of single words to express larger chunks of meaning.
- Children's first word combinations reveal a structure that is neither an imitation of adult speech nor fully grammatical by adult standards. With further development, children acquire the grammatical categories of adult speech.
- Early stages of acquisition are similar in signed and spoken languages.

Introduction

It is little wonder that parents take such joy in observing their children's first steps in the acquisition of language. In the space of little more than a year, a child limited to babbling has come to label objects in the immediate environment, identify names of important people, and form simple sentences. These rapid advances make children much more active participants in the daily affairs of the home, as they learn how to ask for desired objects and participate in simple conversations, and as parents come to expect more, verbally, from their children. And, bit by bit, children's language comes to resemble the language of their everyday environment.

These developments have come under intense scrutiny by psychologists and linguists over the last 30 years. Some investigators have followed individual or small groups of children over a period of years, recording their linguistic development with painstaking accuracy. Others have used the more conventional methods of assessing development by comparing children of different ages. What has arisen out of this substantial research effort is a wealth of detail about how children acquire their first language. Many important questions, however, remain unanswered. For example: Why do children acquire speech at this particular point in development? What role does the child's environment play in language development? Do all children acquire language in the same way?

This chapter and the two that follow will chart children's progress in first language development. This chapter will examine children's development until they have mastered the basic linguistic structures of the language, at about 3 years of age. We begin with a discussion of the infant's communication skills prior to language. Next we turn to how children master the phonology of their native language. Then we address children's one-word utterances, followed by their early attempts to acquire the grammar of their language. Finally, we compare and contrast the acquisition of English and American Sign Language.

Prelinguistic Communication

Until the early part of their second year, infants communicate with their world primarily in nonverbal ways: they tug at people's clothes, point at desired objects, and wave bye-bye. These gestures, though basic, reveal a good deal about the infant's understanding of how communication works. It appears that the emergence of these communication skills is made possible by advances in the child's understanding of how actions can be used as means for achieving desired goals. These advances take place in the first year of life, suggesting that infants' understanding of communication precedes and facilitates much of the child's acquisition of phonology, syntax, and semantics.

This section traces children's development from the earliest communicative acts to their first steps in language development. Though a child's language development undergoes dramatic changes in form and complexity over the first few years of life, there are some important underlying functional similarities in the communication skills of younger and older children. These communication skills are best seen where they originate, in the prelinguistic infant.

The Social Context of Preverbal Infants

Let us first look at the social environment of the prelinguistic child. Well before children begin to speak in comprehensible ways, they are exposed to the social uses of language by their caregivers (Sachs, 1997).

Speech to children prior to birth   These lessons begin even before birth. Anecdotal evidence from mothers-to-be has suggested that children in utero hear their mothers' speech and may respond to it (for instance, by kicking). Some experimental evidence supports this view. DeCasper and Spence (1986) asked mothers-to-be to read a Dr. Seuss book aloud during the last 6 weeks of their pregnancies. A few days after the children were born, the babies were tested using a special pacifier that measured their rate of sucking. Half of the babies heard the story that their mothers had read, and the others heard a new story. The babies who heard the familiar story modified their sucking rate when they heard the Dr. Seuss story, but the other group did not. The investigators concluded that the infants had heard and retained the stories presented to them in utero.

Newborns also prefer their mother's voices over those of strangers (DeCasper & Fifer, 1980). It is not clear what the limits of this phenomenon might be. We do not know how well if at all the baby can hear other voices or at what gestational age the baby is mature enough to perceive speech. At the very least, these studies suggest that newborns are prepared to perceive speech at birth.

Speech to children in the first year of life   After birth, caregivers speak to children in distinctive ways. **Child-directed speech** (also called **baby talk** and **motherese**) differs in many ways from the speech adults direct to other adults. Early in life, the phonological differences seem to be paramount. Child-directed speech tends to be higher in pitch, more variable in pitch, and more exaggerated in its intonational contours than adult-directed speech. All of these characteristics would appear to be likely to get and maintain the attention of very small infants.

Indeed, some evidence suggests that infants prefer to listen to baby talk rather than adult-directed speech. Fernald and Kuhl (1987) had 4-month-old infants sit on their mothers' laps and reinforced them for turning their head one way or the other. A head turn in one direction produced child-directed speech (higher pitch), while a turn in the other direction produced adult-directed speech (lower pitch). Fernald and Kuhl found that the infants preferred to listen to the child-directed speech. In everyday life, it may be that the signs of inattention that babies display when adults use ordinary speech lead the adults to make these phonological adaptations. We will discuss the syntactic aspects of baby talk in Chapter 12.

Mothers also use speech that directs attention to particular aspects of their messages. The phonological characteristics of child-directed speech are most pronounced when mothers are using a word for the first time to an infant. In contrast, repeated words tend to be shorter, quieter, lower-pitched, and less variable in pitch than first-mentioned words (Fisher & Tokura, 1995). It appears that mothers speak in a way that highlights attention on new words at the expense of older words. In effect, this is a developmental example of the given-new contract, discussed in Chapter 7.

Another aspect of the early speech behavior of caregivers is that they encourage infants to participate in conversations. Snow (1977) noticed that when mothers spoke to their babies, they tended to interpret the infants' vocalizations and sounds as conversational turns. Consider the following sequence between a mother and her 3-month-old daughter (p. 12):

Ann: (smiles)

Mom: Oh, what a nice little smile! Yes, isn't that nice? There. There's a nice little smile.

Ann: (burps)

Mom: What a nice wind as well! Yes, that's better, isn't it? Yes.

Ann: (vocalizes)

Mom: Yes! There's a nice noise.

Note that the mother is counting the child's burps, passing of wind, and so on, as an attempt to take a turn in a conversation. In a sense, the caregiver is pulling intentionality out of a preintentional child. The caregiver is encouraging the child to think of language as a social activity with rules and as an activity that we engage in intentionally to communicate with one another. It seems likely that these early conversational lessons, along with the child's own cognitive maturation, enable the child to communicate in a more purposeful manner later in the first year.

Prelinguistic Gestures

Despite the richness of the language infants receive in the first year of life, it is some time before they are able to speak themselves. Before they use language to communicate, they communicate with gestures.

Well before 10 months of age, children engage in a lot of vocal behavior that appears to have some communicative value. Children's smiles and (most definitely) cries elicit parental behavior. Moreover, different cries are discriminated by parents, and these yield responses that differ in urgency as well as type. Still, these sounds are not true forms of intentional communication because infants do not display flexible, goal-directed behavior. For example, if a cry is ineffective in obtaining adult attention, young infants do not turn to another behavior, such as banging an object against the side of the crib. Thus, although infants' cries generally elicit parental responses, the infant is not using the cry for that purpose. Rather, it is simply a built-in response with predictable consequences.

Development of communicative intent   At around 8 months of age, infants begin to use gestures, such as pointing and showing, in a communicative manner. It is not easy to determine whether a behavior is meant to communicate something or is simply a behavior that an infant enjoys. However, psychologists have developed criteria to determine whether a behavior displays an intent to communicate (Bruner, 1975; Harding, 1982). The major criteria are (1) waiting, (2) persistence, and (3) development of alternative plans. For example, suppose an infant tugs at her parent's leg, waits for the parent to look down, and then points at a toy. The fact that the infant waited for the adult to pay attention suggests that the infant was operating on the assumption that we first have to get an adult's attention and then we point out what we want. The child's desires may be somewhat ambiguous. Sometimes children merely want to point to an object that interests them and have the adult acknowledge that this is an interesting object. But if the adult does so and the child persists, then most adults would infer that the child wants to be given the toy. Caregivers make these inferences all the time; the aforementioned criteria are an attempt to describe more systematically how we make these inferences.

I noted earlier that infants appear to be developing communicative intent at around 8 months of age. It is likely that this ability develops at this time because of the child's cognitive development. As we discussed in Chapter 3, Piaget (1952) has argued that children go through a series of stages of cognitive development in the first 2 years of life. Piaget's stage 3 (about 4 to 5 months) and stage 4 (about 8 to 12 months) are relevant here. At stage 3, children show little understanding of goal-directed behavior. They display what Piaget calls "making interesting sights and sounds last." If a child is given a rattle, shakes it, and enjoys the sound, he may continue to shake the rattle. If he accidentally drops the rattle and it makes an interesting sound, he may repeat the behavior. The child shows no advance plan; he merely stumbles upon something interesting and repeats it.

At about 8 months of age, infants become more purposeful in their behavior. They begin to show problem-solving behavior in which they experience a problem, wait, and then try to solve the problem. Piaget (1952) describes the behavior of his son, Laurent, in which the child was shown a bell that was partially covered by a cushion. Laurent moved the cushion with one hand and then grasped the bell with the other. The child appeared to have a goal in mind and combined two existing behaviors to achieve the goal.

At this point, children are now able to approach individual goals with a sense of purpose and with a degree of flexibility not present earlier. So far, however, our focus has been exclusively on individual goals and we have ignored social goals. The next step is to see how children use these newly acquired cognitive abilities to communicate with others.

Beginning of intentional communication   True intentional communication occurs when children apply their understanding of means-and-ends relationships to social goals. Early prelinguistic gestures have been studied by Bates, Camaioni, and Volterra (1975), who focused on two communicative acts: **assertions** (or declaratives)—the use of an object as a means of obtaining adult attention—and **requests** (or imperatives)—the use of adults as means to an object.

Bates and her colleagues (1975) used the communicative context to help determine the meaning of a child's nonverbal behavior:

> Carlotta, unable to pull a toy cat out of the adult's hand, sits back up straight, looks the adult intently in the face, and then tries once again to pull the cat. The pattern is repeated three times, with the observer refusing to yield the cat, until Carlotta finally manages to pull the object away from the adult. (p. 215)

Earlier on, Carlotta repeatedly tried to take a box out of her mother's hand without at any time looking at her mother's face. By stopping and looking at the adult, she appears to have begun to understand that the adult can be of some use in getting an object. The act of looking at the adult thus can be considered as a request.

The child also uses objects to gain adults' attention:

> At 9;6 [9 months, 6 days], Carlotta is in her mother's arms, and is drinking milk from a glass. When she has finished drinking, she looks around at the adults watching her, and makes a comical noise with her mouth (referred to in some dialects as "the raspberries"). The adults laugh, and Carlotta repeats the activity several times, smiling and looking around in between. Her parents explain that this behavior has been discovered earlier in the week, and that Carlotta now produces it regularly at eating and drinking times, always awaiting some response from the adult. (p. 216)

At this stage, the child is using familiar behavior for novel ends: making sounds and gestures to get adult attention, provoke humor, and so forth.

It was not until about a month later that Carlotta began to use novel means to achieve familiar goals:

> At 10;18, we observed the first instance in which Carlotta extends her arm forward to show an object to the adult. She is playing with a toy already in her hand; suddenly,

she looks toward the observer and extends her arm forward holding the toy. In the next two to three weeks, this behavior increases and stabilizes until we observe Carlotta looking around for objects not already in her grasp, and immediately presenting them while awaiting adult response. At this stage "showing" does not seem to involve any intention to give the object. In fact, several times when the adult tries to take the exhibited toy, Carlotta refuses to let go, and often pulls her arm back. (p. 216)

The child's communicative advances seem to be a result of fundamental changes in cognition during infancy. Shortly after children understand intentionality in nonsocial contexts, they use prelinguistic gestures in a social, communicative manner.

The pointing gesture, which serves either as assertion or request depending on the context, came a few months later for Carlotta. Again, communicative pointing gestures differ from noncommunicative pointing mainly in flexibility. A child who points as an assertion, to get an adult's attention, will now look at the adult's face to confirm that the child is looking at the right thing, whereas earlier there was no such attempt at confirmation. Children's comprehension of others' gestures follows a similar pattern. They respond to others' pointing by looking in the right direction and not at the "speaker's" face (Clark & Clark, 1977).

It is an open question as to how much parents can assist or influence these processes. It is apparent that ordinary parent-child interaction requires parents to interpret ambiguous or vague child messages, as in distress cries, and parents routinely interpret messages. Parental input could assist the child, perhaps by helping him figure out what he wants to "say." Bruner (1975) discovered that parents often mark the segments of action by the use of a word or phrase after the child's actions. Thus, the child takes food from a spoon and the mother exclaims, *Good boy!* It could be that these parental messages help the child segment his own continuous stream of behavior into discrete units that may be repeated or used later in a different context.

To sum up, prelinguistic children use gestures to get the receiver's attention and to communicate. The transition to speech acts can then be viewed as learning how to do with words what already has been done without words. A child who looks at a ball and says *ba* might be making an assertion, telling the adults to look at the ball. In contrast, *Mama* accompanied by a whine and reaching for an object out of reach appears to be a request. In the latter instance, the child is more insistent about a response.

Communicative competence and early comprehension   The discussion so far has focused on how simple types of **communicative competence**—knowing how to use gestures and words to show off objects, make assertions, make requests, and the like—figure into the child's prelinguistic gestures and early speech acts. Somewhat less information is available on how this knowledge influences early comprehension activities, but what little there is suggests that young children also use these communicatively based strategies for comprehension prior to developing full mastery of the various structures of their language. Children seem to comprehend language in a manner similar to how they produce it, with attention given to concrete manipulations of objects in the immediate environment.

Shatz (1978) has shown that young children often respond to complex speech by using a simple, action-based comprehension strategy. The strategy is merely to respond to an utterance by performing an action on the object that is specified in the utterance. For example, if a parent wanted her daughter to put a doll in a toy swing and said, *Why don't you put the doll in the swing?*, the child could respond correctly by merely identifying one or two key words in this complex, interrogative sentence and then doing the most obvious thing that could be done with these objects. Suppose, instead, that the child were asked, *Do you want to put the doll in the swing?* Here the sentence calls for an informing response, as Shatz calls it, rather than an action response. Shatz reasons that if a child were using the simple action strategy, then the syntactic form of the sentence, which specifies the appropriate response, would have little effect on the child's response. The children in Shatz's study, who were 19 to 34 months old, followed this pattern in their responses to sentences about toy objects. For example, 70% of the responses to the simple imperative *Put the dog in the car* were action responses, which are correct responses to an imperative. Yet 64% of the responses to *Do you want to put the dog in the car?* were also action responses, when here an informing response is called for. Shatz found a consistent preference for action responses across a wide range of sentence types.

It is easy to overestimate the specific linguistic competence of the young child because we are oblivious to strategies such as these. It appears that young children use their understanding of the cognitive meaning of situations to help figure out what adults are saying. The general thesis that children use meaning as a clue to language has been stressed by other researchers. Macnamara (1972), for example, claims that "infants learn language by first determining, independent of language, the meaning which a speaker intends to convey to them, and by then working out the relationship between meaning and language" (p. 1). The evidence presented here is consistent with this view. Meaning—that is, a primitive system of intentions—precedes and guides both comprehension and production.

Summary

Children are born into a social world. Adults speak differently to children than to adults, and these speech patterns introduce infants to the use of language as a social instrument. For their part, infants appear to be well prepared to benefit from these lessons, given that they have at least some ability to perceive speech prior to birth.

Children seem to be cognitively ready to communicate intentionally by about 8 months of age. Although their speech is not well developed at this time, they utilize gestures in flexible ways to communicate their needs to their caregivers. Moreover, children's communicative knowledge influences how they interpret the speech of others. We now turn to how these communication skills may figure in the child's acquisition of phonology.

*E*arly Phonology

Children's acquisition of the sound system of their language does not occur in isolation of the communicative processes we have just discussed. Rather, children come to the task of learning phonology with some knowledge of how to communicate in nonverbal ways. The prelinguistic infant knows how to use gestures to make assertions and requests, and once early speech sounds are mastered, they are quickly used for these same communicative functions. The child's first attempts at producing sounds, however, have more to do with practicing with the sound system than with communicating with others. Eventually, the abilities to communicate without words and to vocalize without meaning merge into productive and communicative speech.

The task of identifying what the child knows about phonology is difficult, for the ways in which phonological knowledge is expressed can often be rather indirect. As evidence of this point, consider the following case.

Our next-door neighbor's child, a preschooler, was hard to understand because she tended to make phonological substitutions. Eventually we were able to figure out her system. When she asked about our son, Michael, she called him *Mytul*; when talking about our dog, Zeke, she said *Zete*; and when interested in our cat, she would inquire as to the whereabouts of our *titty*. By paying attention to the patterns of her substitutions and to the context of her utterances (for example, when she announced she had *tate* for dinner), some semblance of understanding could be achieved. As a check on whether we were right, we sometimes tried to repeat what she said, but we quickly learned that we had to repeat our version, not hers. For example, if we said *Mytul*, she would appear irritated at this adult silliness:

> *Child:* Where is Mytul?
> *Adult:* You mean Mytul?
> *Child:* No, Mytul!
> *Adult:* Oh, Michael?
> *Child:* Yes, Mytul!

Further conversation revealed a curious discrepancy between her natural and her imitated speech. After hearing her use the term *Zete* once too often, we asked her to listen carefully and repeat the word *Zeke*. Surprisingly, she did so accurately. Nevertheless, moments later, while talking about one event or another, she went right back to *Zete*.

Several points about phonological development are evident in this little interchange. First, although young children make many errors in their speech, the errors are systematic, not random. Our young neighbor, for example, consistently substituted /t/ for /k/ and deleted the initial /s/ in a word. Second, apparently children can produce a distinction in imitation that cannot be made accurately in conversational speech. Third, apparently a child can perceive a distinction that she cannot produce, an occurrence that has been christened the **fis phenomenon** after a child who called fish *fis* (Berko & Brown, 1960).

Our survey of phonological development begins with the child's perception of speech, then turns to the production of speech.

The Development of Speech Perception

One question that has guided research in infant speech perception is whether their perceptual abilities are innate or influenced by the speech they are beginning to hear. One suggestion of innate mechanisms is that even very young infants perceive speech in ways that are similar to adult perception. In particular, they demonstrate the ability to perceive speech categorically.

Categorical perception in infancy   Recall from Chapter 4 that categorical perception refers to the inability to perceive sounds any better than we can identify them. In adults, this phenomenon is studied by giving listeners an identification test followed by a discrimination test. In the identification test, a series of sounds are presented and the listener must identify the phonemic category of the sound. For instance, the sounds /b/ and /p/ differ in voice onset time (VOT)—the time between when the sound is released at the lips and when the vocal cords begin vibrating. Typically, English-speaking listeners hear VOTs of less than 25 milliseconds as /b/ and those greater than 25 milliseconds as /p/. In the discrimination test, listeners are presented with two different sounds, then a repetition of one of them, and must say which of the first two sounds matched the third. In some instances, the first two sounds come from the same phonemic category (such as 0- and 20-millisecond VOTs), and in other cases, the sounds come from different categories (such as 20- and 40-millisecond VOTs). Adult listeners perform very well when the sounds come from different phonemic categories but very poorly when the sounds are from the same phonemic category.

A series of fascinating studies have explored categorical perception of speech sounds. The first study, which we discussed in Chapter 3, was performed by Eimas, Siqueland, Jusczyk, and Vigorito (1971). They presented 1- and 4-month-old infants with pairs of speech sounds. One pair consisted of sounds with VOTs of 20 and 40 milliseconds (heard by adults as /ba/ and /pa/, respectively). The second pair consisted of VOTs of 0 and 20 milliseconds (heard by adults as /ba/), and the third included VOTs of 60 and 80 milliseconds (heard by adults as /pa/). Infants were attached to a pacifier that recorded their sucking responses. Each time an infant responded, one member of a pair was presented. When the infants grew tired of the same stimulus (that is, when the level of response fell below a predetermined level), the other member of the pair was presented. When the infants were presented with the second member of either of the last two pairs, there was no change in their sucking rate, and the infants appeared not to notice the difference. When the second member came from a different phonemic category, however, their rate of sucking increased sharply, indicating that the infants perceived the change. Eimas and his colleagues suggest that these results indicate that infants are born with perceptual mechanisms that are attuned to speech categories.

It should be noted that the procedures used to study infant categorical perception are not identical to those used in studies of adults. In adults, one needs to compare identification and discrimination performance to determine whether a stimulus has been perceived categorically. There is no corresponding way to assess identification of speech sounds in infants, so we are left with their discrimination performance. It is ordinarily assumed that the discriminations that infants make reflect comparisons across phonemic categories (for discussion of this issue, see Eimas, Miller, & Jusczyk, 1987, p. 167, and Kuhl, 1987). This appears to be a reasonable assumption, although it is not clear how to test it.

In any case, these results have been extended by Lasky, Syrdal-Lasky, and Klein (1975), who studied several phonemic contrasts in Guatemalan infants born into Spanish-speaking homes. The infants were between 4 and 6.5 months of age. The study included three pairs of VOT contrasts. The first was between 20 and 60 milliseconds, which corresponds to the distinctions between voiced and voiceless sounds in English. The second was a distinction between prevoiced sounds (in which vocal cord vibration precedes consonantal release) and voiced sounds. The VOTS were −60 and −20 milliseconds. (The prevoiced/voiced distinction is phonemic in Thai but not in English or Spanish.) The third pair included VOT values of −20 and 20 milliseconds; adult Spanish speakers, unlike speakers of English and many other languages, perceive the voiced/voiceless distinction as falling between these two values. Lasky et al. found that the Guatemalan infants perceived the first two distinctions but not the third. That is, they perceived two distinctions that are not part of their language but did not perceive the one that is. Similarly, infants from English-speaking environments perceive the prevoiced/voiced distinction categorically (Aslin, Pisoni, Hennessy, & Perey, 1981).

These and related studies (Streeter, 1976) suggest that infants are born with the ability to perceive a number of phonemic distinctions. Perhaps the most interesting aspect of these studies is that they clearly demonstrate that infants are not limited to those distinctions that are phonemic in their native language. On the contrary, the observation that infants perceive phonemic categories from other languages but not their own suggests that categorical perception is innate.

The role of language experience   The ability to perceive phonemic distinctions from other languages declines in strength during the first year of life. Werker, Gilbert, Humphrey, and Tees (1981) compared 6- and 8-month-old infants from English-speaking communities, English-speaking adults, and Hindi adults. All three groups demonstrated the ability to distinguish between voiced and voiceless sounds, a distinction that is recognized in both Hindi and English. But only the Hindi adults and the infants were capable of distinguishing between pairs of Hindi sounds. It appears as if we lose some of our perceptual abilities over time.

Werker and Tees (1984) have demonstrated that this developmental decline occurs by 1 month of age. They examined the perception of a phonemic contrast in Salish/Thompson (a language spoken in British Columbia) and a Hindi contrast in three groups of infants from English-speaking families. The youngest group (6 to 8 months) showed considerable sensitivity to these contrasts, but there was considerable decline at the middle (8 to 10 months) and especially the older (10 to 12 months) age ranges. Infants in the oldest group showed essentially no ability to perceive these nonnative contrasts.

Werker and Pegg (1992) argue that the developmental changes they have observed are best described as a form of perceptual reorganization as opposed to a complete loss of earlier abilities. This view is supported by a study by Best, McRoberts, and Sithole (1988), who found no perceptual decline in the ability to distinguish sounds from Zulu click consonants. These consonants, which are very dissimilar to English sounds, were discriminated successfully by English-speaking adults and by 12- to 14-month-old infants from English-speaking homes. Best and her colleagues suggest that the decline found in earlier studies reflects a process of phonological reorganization in which phones are organized into the phonemic categories of the native language. Phones that do not fit into any of these categories (such as click consonants) presumably do not undergo this reorganization; consequently, there is no decline in discriminating them (see also Best, 1994).

There are other indications that infants are beginning to organize their perceptual abilities to match their native language. Evidence indicates that infants as young as 9 months (but not 6 months) can distinguish between monosyllables that are highly probable in their native language (that is, consist of phonetic sequences that are highly frequent) versus those that are less probable (Jusczyk, Luce, & Charles-Luce, 1994). In addition, infants can recognize their own name by 4.5 months (Mandel, Jusczyk, & Pisoni, 1995).

The ability to distinguish between probable and less probable sound sequences turns out to be important in the ability to segment speech into words. Consider the sequence *pretty baby*. Although experienced language users hear the sequence as two separate words, the infant actually hears a continuous stream of speech (much as adults do when listening to a foreign language). The infant could segment *ty* and *ba* together, rather than *pre* and *ty* together. Obviously, the ability to isolate words is an important step in the child's acquisition of vocabulary.

Recent research has shown that 8-month-old infants can segment speech into words by attending to the probabilities of various sound sequences (Jusczyk & Aslin, 1995; Saffran, Aslin, & Newport, 1996). Saffran and her colleagues presented infants with a continuous stream of syllables, such as *bidakupadotigolabubidaku*. The stimuli were arranged so that some of the syllable pairs (for example, *bida*) were more common than others (such as *kupa*). To assess learning, infants were then presented with three-syllable strings that they had heard and similar strings that were new to them. Infants preferred to listen to the novel sound sequences, which suggests that they had retained the probabilities between syllables. Saffran and her colleagues suggest that infants use this statistical information to segment speech into words.

The role of prosodic factors   We have been discussing infants' perception of speech segments, but there is also the question of how well they can perceive suprasegmentals or prosodic factors. A study by Mehler, Jusczyk, Lambertz, Halsted, Bertoncini, and Amiel-Tison (1988) found that infants could distinguish between utterances in their maternal language and those in another language by 4 days of life. The researchers suggest that these discrimination abilities are based on prosodic cues such as intonational contours. It is interesting to note in this light that children develop the ability to use intonation in their own utterances quite rapidly.

The Development of Speech Production

We have seen that during a period that is often called prelinguistic, the first year of life, infants can demonstrate some sophisticated speech perception abilities. We now turn to their production of speech.

Babbling   Children's early vocalizations pass through a series of stages (Oller, 1980; Stark, 1980). By the end of the second month, infants begin to do a lot of cooing. Coos are acoustically more varied than cries, as infants exercise some control over their articulatory organs to produce a greater variety of sounds. Coos tend to be made in the back of the mouth and are similar to back vowels and velar consonants.

A little later, by about 6 to 7 months, babbling begins. Infants first use **re-duplicated babbling,** in which they repeat a consonant-vowel sequence, such as *babababa*. Similar tendencies have been found in various languages (Oller, 1980; Stark, 1980). By 11 to 12 months, infants use **variegated babbling,** in which syllable strings consist of varying consonants and vowels, such as *bigodabu*. It is also about this time that infants begin to impose sentence-like intonational contours on their utterances, and their vowels begin to sound similar to those in their native language (Boysson-Bardies, Halle, Sagart, & Durand, 1989). These developments, along with the decline of categorical perception of nonnative contrasts, suggest that infants are beginning to acquire the phonology of their native language by late in their first year.

Babbling is thought to be a form of play in which various sounds are practiced and mastered before they are used in communicative ways. There are several reasons to think that babbling is noncommunicative early on. One is that sounds made during babbling are similar to, but phonologically more sloppy than, the corresponding sounds made later on. While the *ma* of the 7-month-old and the 18-month-old may sound similar, when the two utterances are examined spectrographically, the earlier sound is generally "sloppier" and exhibits a greater range of acoustic properties than true speech. Another reason is that infants have been found to babble more often when an adult is not present than when one is present (Nakazima, 1975). For instance, babies often babble in the crib when awakening and before falling asleep. Since no one else is present, it is difficult to see these as communicative acts.

Transition to speech   By the end of the first year, two aspects of the infant's development—the use of gestures to convey meaning and the mastery of speech sounds in noncommunicative situations—begin to merge. Now the child is capable of using speech sounds to communicate meaning.

Children come to use "true" words because of several processes. There is greater motor control of the speech apparatus, which enables infants to make sounds in a more precise way. There is cognitive maturation, which, as we saw in the previous section, enables infants to express communicative intent. And there is the dawning awareness that specific objects are represented by specific symbols in the language: things have names!

Before children fully grasp this latter point, they sometimes invent their own symbols to refer to objects or events in their environment. These personalized words are called **idiomorphs.** Interestingly, children at this stage of development use their idiosyncratic words in highly consistent ways. My daughter Rachel, when she was about a year old, referred to milk as *ca ca*. It took us a while to understand what she was saying, but once we did, it was clear that she used these sounds whenever she talked about milk.

Another example of an idiomorph is reported by Reich (1986), who told of a child who referred to ice cream as *ABCDE*. Although his parents were initially puzzled, they eventually figured it out. They tended to spell out certain words that they did not want the child to know, so they might ask each other, *Would you like some I-C-E C-R-E-A-M?* The child could not spell it, so he simply used the only letters he knew! But my favorite example comes from Hakuta (1986), who reported that a child said *Whew!* as a way of saying hello to guests who came to the house. It turns out that the mother often greeted the child in the morning in this way, along the lines of *Whew! You must have some load in your pants!* As these examples suggest, children appear to draw from their language experience in forming these idiomorphs. Sometimes the idiomorphs are simplifications of adult speech or relate to the sounds of the objects to which they refer (as opposed to the sounds of the words used to refer to the objects).

Idiomorphs underline several important aspects of development. First, they indicate that children's language is creative. Children do not simply imitate the language they hear but, instead, sometimes take this language and use it in novel ways. We will observe several other aspects of children's linguistic creativity throughout this and the following two chapters. Second, idiomorphs indicate that children have learned that it is important to be consistent when referring to objects. Only a short while earlier, they might well have used various sounds in random combinations and hoped for the best. The consistency of idiomorphs suggests that infants know that it is important to be consistent even if they have not yet grasped that objects have names. Or perhaps they know this but do not yet know the names. In either case, idiomorphs are a transitional stage between babbling and true words, one that indicates, once again, that children's awareness of communicative processes may precede their knowledge of language structure.

Phonological processes in early words   Shortly after their first birthday, children begin to produce recognizable words. Some simple words may be pronounced correctly from the start. But, as we saw earlier in this section, in other instances children's versions of words differ from adult versions. By examining these differences, we can draw some inferences about children's phonological processes.

Let us look at some of their regularity in children's pronunciation of adult words. Table 10-1 lists four processes that commonly occur. **Reduction** occurs when children delete or eliminate sounds. It is common for preschool children to have difficulty with consonant clusters (groups of two or more consecutive consonants) and to reduce clusters when they occur at the beginning of a word. An example would be saying *tore* for *store*. They may also reduce later segments of words, such as saying *baw* for *bottle*. **Coalescence** occurs when phonemes from different sylla-

Table 10-1. Phonological Processes Used by Children

Type	Examples
Reduction	*Tore* for *store*
	Baw for *bottle*
Coalescence	*Paf* for *pacifier*
Assimilation	*Nance* for *dance*
	Means for *beans*
Reduplication	*Titty* for *kitty*

Source: Based on *Language Development and Language Disorders*, by L. Bloom and M. Lahey, p. 102, John Wiley & Sons, Inc., 1978.

bles are combined into a single syllable. In the example in Table 10-1, the *f* in the third syllable is combined with the rest of the first syllable. **Assimilation** occurs when children change one sound to make it similar to another sound in the same word, such as saying *nance* for *dance* or *fweet* for *sweet*. In the latter case, the *f* is articulated closer to the front of the mouth than *s*, making it more similar to the bilabial *w*. **Reduplication** occurs when one syllable of a multisyllabic word is repeated, as in *dada* for *daddy*. These processes are common but not invariant in child language; different children may use different processes to varying extents.

Why do children make these errors? A simple explanation states that the child cannot discriminate between the sounds that are confused. For example, the child might actually hear *stop* as *top*. Much anecdotal evidence, such as children's objections to adult imitations of their utterances as "silly," argues against this view. Also, this perspective cannot explain why errors are typically made in only one direction. If the child cannot tell the difference between two sounds, then she presumably would substitute one or another equally often, but generally this is not what happens. More often than not, the errors are only in one direction.

Another possibility is that the child simply cannot produce the omitted sounds. Though somewhat plausible, this view cannot account for studies of imitation that show that many errors made in spontaneous speech are not made in imitation (Eilers & Oller, 1975, cited in Dale, 1976). It also cannot explain a situation such as the one described by Smith (1973), who heard a child say *puddle* as *puggle* yet say *puddle* in place of *puzzle*. Here the child is capable of producing *puddle* but nevertheless fails to do so in the correct context. Something more than articulatory difficulties seems to be involved.

A third possibility is that these simplification errors are part of a more general linguistic process (Dale, 1976; Oller, 1974). Children mastering a phonological system must also pay attention to the syntactic, semantic, and pragmatic features of their utterances. A complex phonological sequence might "overload" their information-processing capacity. This position would predict deviations from adult speech in the direction of simpler consonant-vowel sequences, particularly in spontaneous speech. When the child is merely imitating speech, however, less attention needs to be given to these other levels of language.

It is not possible at present to firmly conclude that any of these ideas are correct. Nonetheless, each of these ideas has testable implications, and we have some reason to believe that explanations based purely on either perceptual or production limitations may be too simplistic. The evidence in favor of the processing-load explanation, however, is indirect.

Summary

Infants demonstrate the ability to perceive various speech distinctions, including some not in their native language, shortly after birth. The ability to perceive most nonnative contrasts declines by the end of the first year.

Infants progress through a series of stages in speech production during their first year. Later forms of babbling reflect the child's linguistic experience more closely than earlier forms. The child's mastery of the sound system of the language proceeds largely independently of communication processes. Sound and meaning merge with the development of the first words, at about 1 year of age.

Children's renditions of adult words vary systematically from the adult targets. Several phonological processes are commonly found in early child speech, including reduction, coalescence, assimilation, and reduplication.

One Word at a Time

Children usually utter their first words at around 12 months of age, and for the next few months most of their utterances consist of single words produced in isolation. Not until the latter half of the second year do they produce simple multiword combinations. The single-word stage of speech that occupies most of the first half of the second year is the focus of this section.

At this period, several developments begin to take shape at once. Children come to master certain words as labels for regular features of their environment, such as common toys, members of the family, and favorite events. In short, the child begins to acquire the lexicon of the language. The ability to label the immediate, concrete environment brings a degree of tangibility to the child's interaction with the social world, since it is now possible for parents to tutor their children directly in the acquisition of vocabulary, the appropriate use of various words, and correct pronunciation.

At the same time, children are developing the ability to make comments about the world around them. Since the child has only one word at his disposal, it is often difficult for parents to discern what the child means, but it is clear that children at the one-word stage are capable of expressing meanings that would be conveyed, by a more mature speaker, in a longer utterance. Precisely what the child means and what prevents him from expressing these thoughts more fully are questions that child language investigators have pursued.

Lexical Development

Estimates of children's vocabulary growth indicate that children typically have acquired 14,000 words by age 6 (Carey, 1978). If we assume that children learn words from roughly 18 months on, this amounts to an average of 8 words per day. Although this is an impressive accomplishment, it is useful to remember that all of us, including children, "know" words in different ways. As we saw in Chapter 5, words have a number of attributes. Words have reference as well as meaning and connotations as well as denotations. The lexical entries for words in our internal lexicon includes semantic, syntactic, phonological, and orthographic attributes. It will take years for children to master many of these features.

Early words   Children begin by focusing on words related to the here and now, an observation that fits well with Piaget's description of the sensorimotor period of cognitive development. Many of their early words consist of nominals that refer to concrete aspects of their environment. They learn the names of the toys they play with, the clothes they wear, and the food they eat. Children have a bias toward objects that change or move in response to their actions; they are more likely to learn the word *ball* than the word *chair.*

Their early vocabulary, however, is not limited to nominals. As Nelson (1973) has shown, children use words from various grammatical classes early on. Nelson found that general nominals such as *ball* and *car* were most prevalent, followed by specific nominals (*Mommy*), action words (*up, go*), modifiers (*dirty, pretty*), personal and social words (*please, want*), and function words (*what, for*). As Reich (1986) has noted, names for articles of clothing that the child cannot easily manipulate (such as *diaper*) and objects in the environment that do not move (*tree*) are conspicuously absent on this list.

Overextensions and underextensions   One portion of lexical development is referential learning, the process of learning what objects in the world various words refer to. As children begin to learn these words, they often make errors in their assignment of new objects to word classes. Sometimes, they include too many items into their word classes; these are called **overextensions.** Examples are when children refer to all four-legged animals as *dogs* or all round objects as *moon.* Typically, these errors occur when the child identifies one attribute of a complex stimulus with the name and then applies the name to another object with the same attribute. Rescorla (1980) has studied children's overextensions and found that some, like the examples given here, are based on perceptual similarities between objects. Others are based on other kinds of similarity, such as functional (a child referring to a shirt stuck on a person's head as a *hat*), contextual (calling a crib blanket a *nap*), and affective (referring to a forbidden object as *hot*).

Children also use **underextensions,** in which they use a word in a more restrictive way than adult usage. Reich (1986) provides an interesting example. When his son, Quentin, was asked, *Where's the shoes?* when he was in his parent's bedroom, he would crawl to his mother's closet and play with her shoes. If other shoes were between Quentin and the closet, he would crawl around them to get to his mother's shoes. Similarly, his father's shoes did not count. Reich found that Quentin's notion of *shoes* gradually expanded to coincide with adult usage.

Children use overextensions and underextensions for several possible reasons. On some occasions, their conceptual categories may actually differ from those of adults; children may, for instance, initially regard cows and dogs as part of the same category until being told otherwise. On other occasions, they may know perfectly well that a cow is not a dog but not know what it is called (or be able to retrieve the name). In this instance, a child might deliberately mislabel an object to be corrected and thus hear the appropriate name. On still other occasions, the child's misuse of words may reflect an attempt at humor.

The role of adult speech   When a child's speech is incorrect, the caregiver has an opportunity to provide the correct name. A general characterization of this process has been made by Brown (1958), who referred to it as the **original word game.** In this game, the child points at an object, often saying *What's that?*, and the adult supplies the name. Then the child attempts to say the word, and the adult corrects the child if needed. Alternatively, the adult may point to an object and supply the name. In either case, the child comes to learn the name typically associated with a given object.

This game may sound simple, but the process can go awry in several ways. The basic problem is that there is no one-to-one association between a word and its referent. For example, more than one word may apply to the same referent. Consider the following situation. You are sitting in your home with your child on your lap, reading a book together. You come to a picture of an ostrich. Do you call it an *ostrich* or a *bird?* People may reasonably differ as to what is most appropriate. Some may feel that it is unnecessary for children to learn complicated or detailed words and that for now it suffices for the child to simply know that it is a kind of bird. Others think that it is confusing for a child to be told that it is a bird and later told that it is an ostrich, so one should call it by its correct name from the outset. This dilemma reappears in many contexts: Do we call it *banana* or *fruit? Penny* or *money? Car* or *vehicle* or *Toyota?*

It turns out that caregivers are very systematic in how they go about dealing with this matter (Mervis & Mervis, 1982). They tend to choose the basic-level term. As discussed by Rosch, Mervis, Gray, Johnson, and Boyes-Braem (1976), **basic-level terms** are those in which broad similarities exist across exemplars of that category. In general, basic-level terms are intermediate in a hierarchy. Thus, after children have learned these terms, caregivers are able to move up in the hierarchy as well as move down. Ultimately the child comes to acquire the kind of semantic network we discussed in Chapter 5.

Another, related problem confronts the child. Just as a given referent may be named by several words, it is also possible that a given word may apply to more than one referent. Bloom and Lahey (1978) give an example of a child who calls a window pane *water.* What might lead to such an error? Bloom and Lahey suggest that if initially shown a glass of water and told that it was *water,* the child, reasonably enough, might think that the caregiver was referring to the glass and subsequently generalize the concept to window panes.

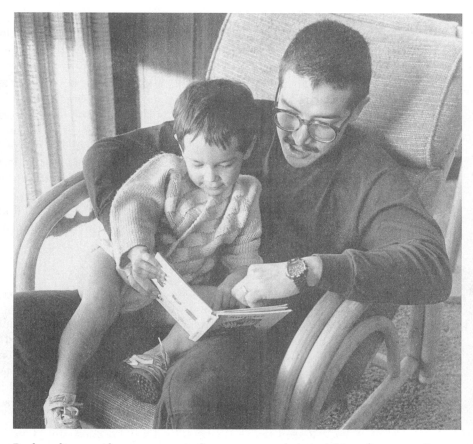

Book reading provides an opportunity for parents to teach their children the names of objects.

It is also possible for children to think that the referent is only one part of an object rather than the whole object. If an adult points at a dog and supplies the name, how is the child to know whether the name refers to the entire animal or only to, say, the dog's tail? Once again, it appears that the naming practices that caregivers use in talking to young children assist them. Ninio (1980; Ninio & Bruner, 1978) examined the types of **ostensive definitions** that caregivers provide for infants. An ostensive definition is a statement of the form *That is an* X. Note that such definitions are inherently ambiguous, as they could refer to the whole object, part of the object, or an action performed by the object. Certainly if caregivers were inconsistent in the level of reference, such definitions would have little didactic value. Ninio found that 95% of the definitions she observed referred to the entire object, and on the occasions in which only parts were referred to, the whole object was named immediately afterward. Moreover, *What's that?* questions were typically used to elicit the name of the whole object, not a part.

Other studies have examined the role of gestures in early lexical development. Both Murphy (1978) and Ninio and Bruner (1978) studied mother-child interactions during book reading and found that infants' pointing gestures were typically followed by the mother labeling the indicated pictures. Masur (1982) examined how mothers responded to such child gestures as pointing, extending objects, and open-handed reaching. Mothers were especially sensitive to children's pointing gestures, usually reciprocating with word labels. The children, in turn, come to respond with more object labels to pointing than to other gestures. Thus, caregivers appear to provide a model for naming objects that children later mirror.

These studies suggest that adult naming practices guide children through lexical development. Adults tend to have clear preferences for where to begin the learning process and focus on these aspects early on to prevent undue confusion. Later on, adults branch out to other aspects of meaning. All things considered, the manner in which caregivers play the original word game seems ideally suited to promoting the child's lexical development.

Cognitive constraints   Studies of adult naming practices have been complemented by investigations of the role that **cognitive constraints** may play in lexical development. As children are exposed to adult words for the objects, many referents are possible for these words (Quine, 1960). It seems unlikely that children explore every possible meaning of a given word, given what we have learned about the speed of lexical acquisition. Adult naming practices help the child, but some theorists believe that the child must have certain expectations about word learning to maximally benefit from these lessons. The notion of cognitive constraint is that children are constrained to consider only some of these possibilities or at least to give priority to them over others (Markman, 1989).

Recent studies suggest several possible constraints. One is called the **whole-object bias:** when children encounter a new label, they prefer to attach the label to the entire object rather than to part of the object. To return to the earlier example, when someone points to an object and says *dog*, the child assumes that the word is a label for the entire object rather than the dog's tail. In addition, children seem to use a **taxonomic bias:** they will assume that the object label is a taxonomic category rather than a name for an individual dog (Markman & Hutchinson, 1984). For example, they will assume that *dog* is a label for a group of animals, not just Fido.

A third constraint is called the **mutual exclusivity bias:** it refers to the fact that, if a child knows the name of a particular object, then the child will generally reject applying a second name to that object. Several experimental studies by Markman and Wachtel (1988) have supported the notion that children use mutual exclusivity in acquiring new words. In one, 3-year-old children were presented with pairs of objects. One member of each pair was an object for which the child already had a label (such as a banana, toy cow, or spoon), and the other was an object for which the child did not have a label (such as a lemon wedge press or a pair of tongs). The children were then asked by a puppet to *Show me the x* (*x* was a nonsense syllable). The children were much more likely to select the novel object. A subsequent study presented children with novel labels for objects for which they already had labels, such as *claw* for hammer. In this instance, the children interpreted the novel term as applying to only one part of the object.

Let us try to reconstruct the children's thinking. In the first study, the whole-object bias would lead the child to look for a whole object as the referent for the nonsense term. The mutual exclusivity bias would block the term being used for the familiar item; hence, the child would infer that the novel term named the other object. In the second study, the whole-object bias leads the child to find an object that is being named, but the object present already has a name. Since it would be a violation of mutual exclusivity to give it a second name, and since there is no other object present, the child comes to apply the new term to a part of the object.

These results suggest that children have some clear biases or preferences in learning new words. However, this is not to say that there are not violations of these principles. We have already seen one: we use *dog, collie,* and *mammal* to refer to the same animal. To acquire these terms, children must violate the principle of mutual exclusivity. Thus, children appear to use these constraints to guide their lexical acquisition, much as if the biases are working assumptions (Merriman & Bowman, 1989). That is, children continue to use the biases until there is evidence to the contrary.

Together with the studies of how caregivers play the original word game, these studies of cognitive constraints indicate that although children learn words very rapidly throughout the preschool period, numerous opportunities for error are possible. That children make as few errors as they do is a testimony to the structure of their learning environment and the structure of their learning approach, in some combination.

Holophrases

A **holophrase** has been defined as a single-word utterance that is used by a child to express more than the meaning usually attributed to that single word by adults (Rodgon, 1976). This tendency to use single words apparently to express broader meanings has long been noted in studies of language development:

> When a very young child says *water,* he is not using the word merely as the name of the object so designated by us, but with the value of an assertion something like *I want water,* or *there is water.* (Stevenson, 1893, p. 120, cited in Barrett, 1982)

If holophrases are single words that "stand for" complete assertions, they represent an important sense of continuity with prelinguistic gestures, on the one hand, and more grammatically complex (and less ambiguous) speech on the other. Although it is generally agreed that holophrases indeed refer to more than a single lexical item, there is less agreement on exactly what they mean.

Approaches to holophrases   One early approach was to consider the holophrase as an implicit sentence. McNeill (1970) has argued that children at the holophrase stage have some knowledge of certain syntactic relations but are not able to express them formally in their speech. In this view, a single word such as *dog* might refer to the subject in the complete sentence *The dog is drinking water.*

If so, then this fuller grammatical knowledge would be likely to appear in other situations, notably in the comprehension of language. Indeed, several studies have shown that one-word speakers can comprehend more complex language than they can produce (see, for example, Shipley, Smith, & Gleitman, 1969). But these studies are hardly conclusive, for it is possible to comprehend a sentence on the basis of a combination of lexical knowledge and attention to the nonverbal context. In fact, studies have found that young children are unable to comprehend the relational meanings of simple speech (Benedict, 1978, cited in Barrett, 1982). For example, one child responded to *get Mommy's shoe* by getting a toy shoe and giving it to his mother.

Greenfield and Smith (1976) present a somewhat different approach. They claim that young children use their single words as adults use sentences but do not actually have the grammatical knowledge implicit in a sentence. By carefully examining the contexts in which children spoke, they were able to identify the different semantic relationships that were expressed in single-word speech. These relationships, in their order of occurrence, are shown in Table 10-2. Thus, *dada*, when used in a context in which the child's father has just arrived home, would express the agent relationship. If, instead, *dada* were said when the infant pointed at the father's chair, it would be an example of the possessor relationship. Greenfield and Smith conclude that children, in effect, use the environment as the rest of their utterance.

This more functional view of holophrases fits well with studies that have shown that one-word speakers are capable of using either intonation or gesture to accompany their single words (Barrett, 1982; Dore, 1975). In essence, the argument is that there is greater continuity in development at the functional level than at the structural level; although the child has little grammatical knowledge, she is able to express complete thoughts that will later be expressed with grammatical phrases and sentences by selectively expressing those aspects of a situation that are most unusual, interesting, or informative (see Greenfield, 1982).

Table 10-2.   Semantic Relations in One-Word Speech

Relation	*Instance*
Naming	*Dada*, looking at father
Volition	*Mama*, looking at bottle of milk, whining
Agent	*Dada*, hearing someone come in
Action	*Down*, when he sits or steps down
Object	*Ball*, having just thrown it
State of object	*Down*, having just thrown something down
Associated object	*Cracker*, pointing to door of room where crackers are kept
Possessor	*Lauren*, upon seeing Lauren's empty bed
Location	*Box*, putting crayon in box

Source: From *The Structure of Communication in Early Language Development,* by P. M. Greenfield and J. H. Smith, p. 70. Copyright © 1976 by Academic Press. Reprinted by permission.

Summary

Children show rapid gains in lexical development during the second year of life. Most of their early words refer to concrete aspects of the immediate environment. Adult naming practices appear to facilitate lexical development by emphasizing whole objects over parts of objects, and basic-level terms over more general or more specific terms. In addition, various cognitive constraints enable children to understand other ambiguous terms in an unambiguous manner.

Children at this stage also tend to use single words to express larger chunks of meaning that mature speakers would express in a phrase or sentence. Holophrases appear to be precursors of multiword utterances, but it is not clear what grammatical knowledge children have at the holophrastic stage.

Early Grammar

Children begin to speak in word combinations by about 2 years of age, and over the course of the next few years they make impressive advances in grasping the grammar of their native language. These aspects of grammar, of course, differ from language to language. Children learning English must pay close attention to word order, which is the primary way in which meaning is signaled. Those acquiring a more inflected language, such as Turkish, must spend a relatively greater amount of time learning the different forms or conjugations of verbs. These language differences surely play an important role in language acquisition.

There are, however, important similarities in children's early grammatical efforts. Slobin (1985a) has suggested that at least the early stages of grammatical development are similar in all of the world's languages. Studies have now been conducted on dozens of different types of languages, and these have found that what Slobin calls **basic child grammar** is a universal construction of children learning their native language. In this section, we will consider the structure of basic child grammar and some ideas researchers into child language have developed as to what rules comprise this grammar as well as review evidence that indicates individual differences in early language acquisition.

Measures of Syntactic Growth

We will begin with the question of how we measure the child's syntactic development. Researchers have found it necessary to construct an index of the child's language progress to facilitate comparison of children at the same level of language development. You might think that the child's chronological age is a good enough index, but there are considerable differences in children's rate of language development (which may or may not be related to later language gains). In fact, two children at the same age may display very different language skills.

Researchers have developed two measures of syntactic development. The best known and most widely used is to measure the **mean length of utterances in**

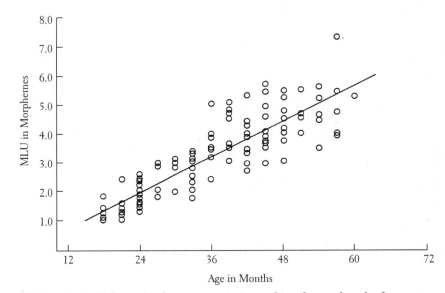

Figure 10-1.   Relationship between age (± 1 month) and mean length of utterance (MLU) in morphemes for 123 children. (From "The Relationship Between Age and Mean Length of Utterance in Morphemes," 1981, *Journal of Speech and Hearing Research, 24,* 154–161. Copyright © 1981 American Speech-Language-Hearing Associates. Reprinted by permission.)

morphemes (MLU). The method, as discussed by Brown (1973), consists of taking 100 of the child's spontaneous utterances and counting the number of morphemes (meaningful units) per utterance. The MLU is a conservative index of the child's ability to combine morphemes in a productive manner. Brown counts some words that are multimorphemic in adult speech, such as *birthday,* as one morpheme for children unless there is evidence that the child understands the constituent morphemes, *birth* and *day,* and then combines them.

Using MLU, Brown divided language development into five MLU-defined stages. Stage I, consisting mainly of one- and two-word utterances, lasts until an MLU of 1.75. Stages II to V correspond to upper-limit MLUs of 2.25, 2.75, 3.5, and 4.0, respectively. Because children within normal limits vary in their rate of development, MLU is a more useful index of a child's language growth than his or her age. Most children, for example, are in stage I at about 24 months, but variations in either direction are not unusual. It is more informative to compare two children with similar MLUs but different ages than the other way around. Figure 10-1 shows the relationships between age and MLU for a sample of children studied by Miller and Chapman (1981).

Brown (1973) has indicated that these MLU-defined stages provide a global view of what aspects of language the child is currently mastering. Children at stage I are putting words together. At stage II, they are learning to modulate the meaning of their utterances by the use of grammatical morphemes. Stages III and IV are devoted to learning more complex constructions, such as questions and negatives. Most research into children's grammatical development has focused on Brown's first two stages. In fact, it is generally agreed that MLU loses its value as an index of language development beyond about 4.0 (Tager-Flusberg, 1993).

A newer measure called the **Index of Productive Syntax (IPSyn)** has been developed to better assess later development (Scarborough, 1990). This approach counts the child's use of various noun phrases, verb phrases, questions, negatives, and sentence structures. It measures the emergence of these structures, not their mastery; Scarborough gives the child credit for each occurrence of each type of structure over a corpus of 100 utterances. Preliminary evidence suggests that IPSyn is a valid measure of grammatical development. For instance, IPSyn scores of children at 30 months of age were found to predict subsequent reading disabilities (Scarborough, 1990).

We will examine the acquisition of complex sentences more thoroughly in Chapter 11. For now, our focus is on children's first grammatical acquisitions. A central question is how children acquire the grammatical categories of adult speech, such as subject and predicate.

Emergence of Grammatical Categories

The structure of early utterances   It may seem odd to talk of two-word utterances as sentences having a grammatical structure. After all, early utterances such as *allgone baby* and *more crayon* are hardly grammatical by adult standards and may appear to be little more than random combinations of previously acquired words. Most investigators of child language, however, agree with Sachs (1976) that

> the two-word utterances he [the child] says are neither simple imitations of adult utterances nor random combinations of the words he knows. Rather, they follow from the system that the child is using to express meanings at that time. (p. 156)

Several lines of evidence support this view. First, when children first put words together, they tend to combine content words and leave out function words, thus producing utterances such as *more milk, push truck,* and so on. This is similar to the way adults phrase utterances when sending a telegram, where there is a premium on word cost: *lost money, send cash,* and so on. This suggests that the child has an understanding of this grammatical distinction as well as an intuitive appreciation that content words may be more informative than function words.

Second, as children put words together, particular words are put in particular positions in the sentence (Braine, 1976). A child, for example, is much more likely to say *allgone sock* than *sock allgone*. Thus, the child is not merely stringing together separate words that she knows but is putting them together in a systematic way.

Interpretations of early multiword utterances   What, then, is the child's system? Several different possibilities have been explored. Consider a simple utterance such as *baby cry*. We can describe this in syntactic terms as a subject followed by a predicate. Alternatively, we can describe it in semantic terms as an agent (an animate being who is the instigator of an action) and an action. Or we can describe it in

Table 10-3. Semantic Relations in
Two-Word Speech

Relation	Instance
Nomination	That ball
Recurrence	More ball
Nonexistence	Allgone ball
Agent and action	Daddy hit
Action and object	Hit ball
Agent and object	Daddy ball
Action and locative	Go store
Entity and locative	Book table
Possessor and possession	Daddy chair
Entity and attribute	Big house
Demonstrative and entity	That box

Source: Based on *A First Language: The Early Stages,* by
R. Brown, pp. 189–198, Harvard University Press, 1973.

positional terms, with *baby* being a word typically in the initial position and *cry* as typically in the latter position. These characterizations differ in degree of abstractness, with the syntactic description as most abstract and the positional description as least abstract.

The syntactic description does not appear to fit children's utterances, at least not in the earliest stages (Bowerman, 1973). The subject of a sentence may be an agent, but it could also be an object (*The book is on the table*), an instrument (*The nail pierced the wood*), or a location (*Dallas is dull*). If we attribute the syntactic notion of subject to a child, we are implying that the child grasps the similarity between subjects in such diverse sentences, which is unlikely.

Brown (1973) has claimed that these early utterances are expressing semantic relations. He developed a list of 11 semantic relations that, he says, comprise 75% of children's two-word utterances (see Table 10-3). Several of these are similar to the relations expressed in one-word speech (compare with Table 10-2); but the agents, actions, and locations of younger children are in separate utterances, whereas children at the multiword stage can combine these elements in a single utterance. These semantic relations also appear in other languages, such as Russian, Finnish, and Samoan (Slobin, 1970).

Braine (1976) has advocated the positional approach. He has suggested that although some of children's early sentences may correspond to semantic properties, such as *actor* and *action* and *possessor* and *possessed,* most nouns in child speech express a narrower range of semantic content than the adult versions. Other rules noted by Braine are even more limited and simply reflect children's preference for putting certain words in specific positions in a sentence. Thus, common rules are "*more* plus recurring element" (*more car, more hot,* and so on) and "*want* plus desired entity" (*want car, want truck,* and so on).

Let us compare these latter two approaches more directly. Take a sentence such as *want car*. Brown would treat it as expressing an action-object relation. Braine would claim that it is merely the word *want* in the first position attached to any number of desired objects. That is, in Braine's view, the child has not yet acquired the general concept of action, let alone the syntactic category of verb, but has merely acquired a rule that identifies a particular word with a particular position in the sentence.

Acquiring grammatical categories   Ultimately children must grasp categories that are defined in syntactic terms, and there has been much debate concerning how they do this. One suggestion is that they use their knowledge of semantic relations to learn syntactic relations. This process is known as **semantic bootstrapping** (Bowerman, 1973; Pinker, 1987). As Bowerman (1973) puts it:

> [C]hildren launch their syntactic careers by learning simple order rules for combining words which in their understanding perform semantic functions such as agent, action, and object acted upon, or perhaps other even less abstract semantic functions. Through additional linguistic experience a child may begin to recognize similarities in the way different semantic concepts are formally dealt with and to gradually reorganize his knowledge according to the more abstract grammatical relationships which are functional in the particular language he is learning. (p. 213)

For instance, children ordinarily use sentences in which the grammatical subject is the semantic agent. Then they use this correspondence to begin learning the grammatical category of subject. As children become more linguistically experienced, they induce grammatical concepts from the semantic-positional configurations already acquired. Exactly how this is done is still very much up in the air, but Maratsos (1982; Maratsos & Chalkley, 1980) has provided evidence that children acquire some of the concepts during the preschool years. Maratsos suggests that children do this by paying attention to the grammatical operations that given linguistic forms take. For example, although *like* and *fond* are similar semantically, *like* takes the grammatical morpheme *-ed*, whereas the past tense of *fond* is formed with the auxiliary *be* (*was fond*). These two are also distinct in their present tensing, with *like* taking the *-s* morpheme and *fond* taking the auxiliary. According to Maratsos, children analyze the correlations in grammatical operations between linguistic forms and regroup forms with similar operations into more abstract and differentiated grammatical classes.

Comprehension and Production

Most of the emphasis here has been on children's language production, but language comprehension at this period of development has also been studied. The relationship between comprehension and production in language development has often been a matter of considerable interest. To parents, it appears that children understand certain types of utterances before they are able to produce such utterances themselves. What does the research say concerning this issue?

As we saw earlier in the chapter, children have pragmatic and lexical skills that guide their comprehension of language (Shatz, 1978). A child may respond correctly to an utterance such as *Why don't you put the doll in the swing?* on the basis of knowing the referents for *doll* and *swing* as well as knowing the likely way in which the objects may be combined. Impressive as these skills are, they make the assessment of the child's ability to comprehend sentences more challenging.

Various attempts have been made to assess children's language comprehension. Most of the studies have presented children with sentences and then had them indicate through nonverbal behavior their comprehension. Some have children act out sentences presented to them (for example, *Make the doll kiss the duck*), whereas others present children with sentences and have them choose by pointing to the picture that corresponds to the sentence (for instance, *The dog is chasing the cat*).

Let us look at one representative study. Golinkoff, Hirsh-Pasek, Cauley, and Gordon (1987) placed young infants in front of two video monitors featuring Sesame Street characters. In one, Big Bird was brushing Cookie Monster's hair; in the other, Cookie Monster was brushing Big Bird's hair. At the same time that these two scenes were taking place, the infant heard the sentence *Big Bird is brushing Cookie Monster.* Hirsh-Pasek and Golinkoff found that infants more often looked at the screen that matched the sentence.

Note that the design of the study neatly deals with the issue we discussed before in connection with the Shatz (1978) study—that young children might just know a word or two and figure out the sentence from there. In this study, neither action is more likely than the other, and so the infant really has to comprehend the syntax of the sentence to perform appropriately. Infants as young as 17 months are capable of responding correctly on this task, many months before they are capable of producing such sentences. Thus, infant comprehension does indeed appear to be in advance of their production.

Individual Differences

It was once thought that all children acquire language in pretty much the same way (Lenneberg, 1964). To be sure, some children might develop a little quicker than others, but the stages of development and strategies used to acquire language were assumed to be similar. Studies over the last 20 years have, however, found evidence for individual differences in language styles and strategies. Attention has now turned to the best way to characterize these differences.

On the basis of a longitudinal study of children between 1 and 2 years of age, Nelson (1973) has suggested two different strategies for acquiring language. Most of the children Nelson studied approached language using a **referential strategy** of attempting to learn words—mainly nouns but also some verbs, proper names, and adjectives—that referred to aspects of their immediate environment. In contrast, some children used an **expressive strategy** that emphasized social interaction. Expressive children had more diverse vocabularies, including social routines such as *Stop it* and *I want it,* which were apparently learned as complete, unanalyzed units. They were also more likely to utter whole sentences than were referential children; they did so with poor articulation of the words but with an overall sentence intonation pattern that makes the meaning clear (Peters, 1977). Moreover, expressive children were more likely to use "dummy terms" in their early sentences (these are terms that do not carry meaning but play a role in the entire sentence). Whereas referential children seemed to regard language as a process of naming objects, expressive children appeared to be more interested in the interpersonal aspects of language.

These differences implicate different processes later in development. Referential children begin with words and combine them to form sentences, whereas expressive children eventually break down their longer utterances into individual words. In other words, referential children go from part to whole, whereas expressive children go from whole to part. Once expressive children analyze their utterances into words, they may then combine the words into new utterances (Lieven, Pine, & Barnes, 1992). This suggests that the two styles of language learning may merge later in development.

Nelson (1975) provides some evidence on this point. She examined the later language development of her original sample of children. She found that referential speakers used a high proportion of nouns in their early utterances, whereas expressive speakers used a mix of nouns and pronouns. As their MLUs increased, referential children used fewer nouns, whereas expressive children used more. Thus, over time, the two styles began to merge. Bloom, Lightbown, and Hood (1975) found similar results.

These individual differences raise several questions. One question is how best to characterize these differences. It is not clear whether they represent different degrees of competence in various language components or are better described as preferences. For example, are expressive children less able to learn and retain object names, or are they able to do so but prefer a style of language that will more likely elicit adult reactions?

Another question is the cause of the individual differences. Nelson (1981) has reviewed the evidence pertaining to the role of hemispheric differences, cognitive style, and environmental factors in these differences. As for environmental factors, there is evidence that both the amount (Huttenlocher, Haight, Bryk, Seltzer, & Lyons, 1991) and the type (Della Corte, Benedict, & Klein, 1983) of maternal speech influences children language styles. Della Corte et al. found that mothers of referential children produced more descriptive utterances and fewer prescriptive utterances than mothers of expressive children. Goldfield (1987) extended these results by showing that children's lexical preferences were influenced by both child and caregiver variables. Children who more often used objects to elicit maternal attention and whose mothers more often labeled and described toys were more likely to use referential language. Those children low on both of these variables were more likely to use expressive language.

These results show that there is more than one way to piece the puzzle of language together. Moreover, these differences serve as a useful reminder that the components into which we dissect language—syntax, semantics, phonology, and pragmatics—are not neatly separated in the child's experience. In contrast, the child must acquire one in relation to the others, as when using newly formed syntactic structures for appropriate pragmatic ends. What these individual differences suggest is that there are a number of ways of doing this.

Summary

Children begin to put words together in systematic ways, preferring some words to others and some orders to others. A substantial amount of research has been devoted to identifying the nature of the child's grammatical system when multiword utterances begin to be produced. Researchers generally agree that children know more than they are able to express, but there is a difference of opinion as to whether this knowledge is best characterized as syntactic, semantic, or merely positional.

Reliable individual differences are apparent in early language acquisition. Some children emphasize the referential function of language, whereas others use language in a social way. These two styles of learning may merge later in development, with referential children using more pronouns and expressive children using more nouns than earlier. The styles appear to reflect characteristics of both the child and the child's caregivers.

Acquisition of Sign Language

We return in this last section to the study of American Sign Language (ASL). Throughout this book, we have periodically examined similarities and differences between signed and spoken language. In this section we discuss how children acquire American Sign Language.

As we discussed in Chapter 2, there are both similarities and differences between ASL and English. The two languages share some basic grammatical features, such as duality of patterning and linguistic productivity. At the same time, some differences between the two languages are apparent. We saw that ASL is more iconic than English, that it has a richer morphology, and that linguistic information is more often conveyed simultaneously in ASL than in English. And, of course, there is a difference in modality between a visual and an auditory language. These similarities and differences suggest that a comparison of the acquisition of ASL and that of speech may be illuminating. In particular, it may help clarify which aspects of language acquisition are universal, which are specific to certain types of language, and which are specific to languages in a particular modality.

We will focus on children of deaf parents who have been exposed early in life to ASL. For the most part, these children have normal hearing. These children are of interest because the conditions under which they acquire ASL are most similar to those of hearing children acquiring speech: language is presented to the child, from birth, in the context of daily events by those to whom the child is emotionally attached. Therefore, any differences that may be observed between the acquisition of ASL and English may be attributed to differences in the two languages or in modality, but not in the conditions of exposure.

Our discussion thus is not directly applicable to most deaf children. It has been estimated that only 5% to 10% of deaf children are born to deaf parents (Meier & Newport, 1990). The remaining 90% to 95% of deaf children are not typically exposed to ASL early in life. Moreover, deaf children are not likely to benefit fully from exposure to speech. It is in this sense that Meadow (1980) has commented that the basic deprivation of profound congenital deafness is one not just of sound but of language. Since hearing parents are unprepared to teach ASL to their deaf infants, many deaf children are not systematically exposed to sign language in the early years. Many deaf persons, in fact, learn sign language much later in life—from peers, not parents. Other deaf and hearing-impaired individuals use other methods of communication. These may include oral training (teaching children to speak and understand oral language) or training in **manual English.** Various forms of manual English express English grammar in sign form, unlike ASL, which is a separate language from English. In general, language acquisition in all of these groups is poor relative to hearing children acquiring speech (see Quigley & King, 1982).

To return to ASL, the main question we want to consider is whether developmental milestones found in oral language—babbling, one-word stage, two-word stage—have any correlates in the acquisition of sign language. As for babbling, Petitto and Marentette (1991) studied deaf infants acquiring ASL as a first language. The infants, born to deaf parents, were studied when they were between 10 and 14 months of age. Petitto and Marentette found that the deaf infants engaged in two types of manual activity: gestures and syllabic manual babbling. Gestures, such as raising one's arms to be picked up, were meaningful and similar to those of infants exposed to speech (discussed earlier in the chapter). In contrast, manual babbling was typically not meaningful; infants combined values of ASL parameters (handshape, location, and movement) into signs that were permissible but nonexisting forms in ASL. On the basis of these and other observations, Petitto and Marentette conclude that manual babbling is similar to vocal babbling.

The investigators also studied manual activity in hearing infants of hearing parents. Interestingly, both groups of infants used both gestures and manual babbling. However, whereas the quantity and type of gestures were similar in the two groups, manual babbling was far more common in the deaf infants.

Turning to the one-word stage, Prinz and Prinz (1979) observed a bilingual hearing child who learned English from a hearing parent and ASL from a deaf parent. This child produced her first sign at 7 months old. By 12 months of age, the child had produced five signs but only one word. Thus, if anything, there appeared to be earlier acquisition of signs than of speech. Bonvillian, Orlansky, and Novack (1983) replicated this result with a larger group of infants. They studied the sign language of 11 children (10 hearing, 1 deaf) with deaf parents over a period of 16 months and found that these children, on the average, produced their first recognizable sign at 8.5 months, approximately 2 to 3 months before first words are recognizable.

One question that arises in this context is whether the relatively greater iconicity of ASL aids language acquisition. Orlansky and Bonvillian (1984) examined the prevalence of iconic signs in the early language of hearing children of deaf parents. Iconic signs are those in which a clear, transparent relationship exists between the sign and its referent. An example is the sign for *eat*, which involves moving one's hand back and forth into one's open mouth, as if feeding oneself. Metonymic signs, on the other hand, are those in which there is a more obscure relationship between sign and referent, one not likely to be apparent to most observers. Arbitrary signs reveal no discernible relationship between sign and referent. Orlansky and Bonvillian examined the children's sign language at two points in development: when the children had attained 10 signs (about 13 months) and again at 18 months. At the earlier period, only 31% of the signs were iconic, 34% were metonymic, and 35% were arbitrary. These percentages were very similar at 18 months. If iconicity aided early acquisition, we might expect that there would be a higher percentage of iconic signs at 13 months. Orlansky and Bonvillian concluded that iconicity is not a major factor in the precocious acquisition of sign language.

The extent and significance of a sign advantage over speech have been discussed by Petitto (1988) and Meier and Newport (1990). Petitto contends that early signs are actually gestures used by all children, such as pointing and reaching, or imitations of adult models. Folven and Bonvillian (1991) addressed this issue. They found that children's initial recognizable signs occurred at 8.2 months of age (replicating Bonvillian et al., 1983). However, children did not use signs referentially (that is, to name objects) until they were 12.6 months old, after they had demonstrated communicative pointing; this age is comparable to the first appearance of referential speech. Earlier signs were imitations of adult signs, signs used in interactive routines, and requests for familiar items.

Meier and Newport (1990) argue that the advantage for sign is only in early lexical development and does not extend to syntactic development. In addition, they suggest that peripheral differences in the two modalities may explain the earlier emergence of signs. That is, the visual system may be more developed than the auditory system at 10 months of age, the age at which, under this hypothesis, children are cognitively able to acquire lexical items.

Let us now turn to later sign language development. Examining early multi-sign utterances, Newport and Ashbrook (1977) found that deaf children used semantic relations similar to those found in English (Bloom et al., 1975). Moreover, the relations emerged in sign language in about the same order as was found in previous studies of English. Also, children at the two-word stage use sign order, not morphology, to signal meaning (Newport & Ashbrook, 1977); this, of course, is similar to the first multiword utterances of young speakers. Thus, children acquiring ASL do not initially exploit the morphology of ASL when beginning to put signs together. Instead, they primarily use sign order to convey meaning, just as children do in diverse spoken languages.

On balance, these studies indicate that the course of language development is similar for signed and spoken languages, at least through the two-word stage. The only difference of note, the earlier acquisition of signs at the one-word stage appears to reflect differences in modality, not language. Moreover, the linguistic feature most likely to lead to early sign acquisition, iconicity, apparently plays little role. These observations are consistent with the view that the early milestones of language development, in sign as in speech, are under biological control.

This is not to say that there are no differences between signed and spoken languages later in acquisition. Although children do not initially use ASL morphology in their utterances, they eventually acquire it (Bellugi, 1988; Newport & Meier, 1985). More generally, languages diverge later in development, and children acquire the rule systems of their particular language. We will discuss the later stages of language acquisition more fully in Chapter 11.

Summary

Although ASL differs from English in linguistic features such as iconicity and morphological structure, there are more similarities than differences in the early stages of acquisition of ASL and English. The primary difference is that infants acquire their first signs 2 to 3 months earlier than infants typically acquire their first words.

Review Questions

1. How can you tell whether a child is using a pointing gesture intentionally? What criteria are necessary for an act to be considered intentional?
2. Define communicative competence and explain the way in which it influences the child's early comprehension of speech.
3. What evidence suggests that infant perception of speech changes by about 1 year of age?
4. Give an example of each of the following: coalescence, assimilation, reduction, and reduplication.
5. Why might children make phonological errors in spontaneous speech that they do not make in imitative speech?
6. How do adult naming practices assist the child's vocabulary development?
7. What is mutual exclusivity, and what is its role in the child's acquisition of words?
8. What evidence suggests that children's early grammatical categories are not equivalent to adult grammatical categories?
9. Distinguish between referential and expressive styles of language learning.
10. Compare and contrast the acquisition of American Sign Language and English.

Thought Questions

1. Do you think that you could promote a child's language development by pretending not to understand her? Could you retard it by quickly responding to immature forms of speech? Explain.
2. How could you interpret what a child means by a single word? What procedure would you use?

3. Children typically comprehend language at a more advanced level than they are able to produce. Why might this be so? Are there any cases in which production precedes comprehension?

4. How might the language development of a child exposed to two languages in the home differ from that of a monolingual child? In what ways might their development be similar?

Later Language Acquisition

MAIN POINTS

- Children's grammatical development in the late preschool years includes the acquisition of grammatical morphemes and complex syntactic structures.
- Children are increasingly aware of the language that they are using.
- Children's skills as conversationalists and narrators grow during the preschool years. As they enter school, children are able to communicate in flexible ways.
- Children expand and modify their linguistic skills as they enter into formal schooling. Classroom discourse differs from discourse out of school, and written language poses different challenges than oral language.

Introduction

There was a time when attention to language acquisition was restricted to the first few years of life. In recent years, later acquisitions by the child and, in fact, language development through the life span have become increasingly popular topics of study. In this chapter, we will discuss children's later language acquisition, roughly corresponding to the developments in the late preschool and early school years.

One major theme of this period of development is that children elaborate the grammatical structures they have already acquired. They begin to embellish their simple utterances with function words and grammatical morphemes and to master more complex sentence constructions. A second theme is that children become more aware of language units and processes. For instance, although young children may arrange words in a syntactically correct order, they may have little awareness of the syntactic rules that they are using. Awareness of language comes gradually throughout the preschool years.

The developments in linguistic awareness may affect other aspects of language as well. It is also during this period that children become able to size up different communication situations and thereby employ their linguistic resources to the best advantage. And these skills also are important when children get to school and are confronted with written language.

These varied achievements are not independent stages of development. On the contrary, they are interconnected throughout development, although we discuss them separately for ease of exposition. A sample of utterances from a single child, shown in Table 11-1, may give you a feel for the speed as well as the complexity of the acquisition process.

This chapter is organized as follows. We begin by surveying the acquisition of complex syntactic and semantic structures. Next we examine the child's increased awareness of language structure and the development of discourse processes, including narrative and conversational skills. Finally, we consider the special kinds of language used in the school and discuss how the child adjusts to these new demands.

Later Grammar

As we saw in the previous chapter, children make impressive strides in their acquisition of grammar in their first 2 to 3 years. They develop the ability to form simple,

Table 11-1. A Sample of One Child's Utterances

1;9	He's in the house.
1;11	Will you help?
2;0	I'm coming.
2;0	Betty's soup.
2;1	I found it.
2;1	I find it.
2;1	I eating.
2;1	I "hi"-ed Daddy.
2;1	Is Betty here?
2;2	I doed it.
2;2	I play in the tent awaile mom.
2;2	I blowed it.
2;4	I want to talk to you a bit.
2;4	You know what?
2;5	I'm just going to sit here and think.
2;5	I felled.
2;5	I camed here.
2;5	I want to talk to her.
2;6	Where you going to?
2;6	He's not happier. He's saddier.
2;6	I want another clo'. (referring to singular of clothes)
2;7	What that is?
2;7	What I'm going to have?
2;8	Mom, let's just clean it up. (after mother began to lecture about mess)
2;9	You guys are driving me crazy.
2;9	Daddy, don't drink me! (seeing reflection in father's glass)
2;9	You say "I'm fine too." (directing father's speech)
2;10	Why I can't put it on?
2;10	Milk spills easily.
2;10	I'll be an adult someday.
2;11	Tell me what is it. Tell me what it is.
2;11	How I do it?
3;1	Does "popsing" look like "sucking?"
3;2	Daddy, I misted you.
3;2	I'll clean it up because I was the one who mested it up.
3;2	I playded.
3;4	Mommy, you're cramping my style. (while mother combs child's hair)
3;5	"I'm sorry" isn't good enough. (after father's apology)
3;6	I bringed it over there.
3;7	Daddy, you forget to tell me not to sit down before I got a spoon.
3;9	Can you let it go by himself? (referring to a van)
3;11	It ringed.
3;11	Do you have any idea where my fork might be?
4;0	Mommy closeded it.
4;3	I bited my tongue.
4;11	No, when I say "Are you going to wear that?" you have to say "this," not "that."

functional utterances such as *Daddy chair* that express their meaning relatively directly. Later grammatical acquisitions are built on earlier accomplishments. In this section we look at two such acquisitions: grammatical morphemes and more complex sentence constructions.

Acquisition of Morphology

Grammatical morphemes   Grammatical morphemes are conspicuously absent in children's early word combinations. Children initially use word order to convey meaning, even those children acquiring highly inflected languages. But as their mean length of utterances in morphemes (MLU) approaches 2.5, morphemes such as the past tense and plural inflections and prepositions such as *in* and *on* begin to appear. Brown (1973) notes that these morphemes, "like an intricate sort of ivy, begin to grow up between and upon the major construction blocks, the nouns and verbs" (p. 249). It takes children years to fully acquire the morphology of their language.

The first major study of the acquisition of grammatical morphemes was conducted by Brown and Cazden (Brown, 1973; Cazden, 1968) as part of an extensive longitudinal study of three children. They looked at 14 morphemes in the English language; these are shown, in their order of emergence, in Table 11-2. The procedure was as follows: they looked closely at the linguistic and nonlinguistic context of child utterances to determine whether a grammatical morpheme was obligatory in that context. For instance, suppose an adult holds up a book and asks a child *What is this?* and the child responds *That book*. It may be inferred that the child

Table 11-2.   Average Order of Acquisition of Grammatical Morphemes

Order	Morpheme	Example(s)
1	Present progressive	I driving
2–3	Prepositions	in, on
4	Plural	balls
5	Irregular past tense	broke, fell, threw
6	Possessive	Daddy's chair
7	Uncontractible copula	This is hot
8	Articles	a, the
9	Regular past tense	She walked
10	Third person present tense, regular	He works
11	Third person present tense, irregular	She does
12	Uncontractible auxiliary	The horse is winning
13	Contractible copula	He's a clown
14	Contractible auxiliary	She's drinking

Sources: Based on *A First Language: The Early Stages,* by R. Brown, p. 275, Harvard University Press, 1973; and *Language Acquisition,* by J. G. de Villiers and P. A. de Villiers, pp. 86–88, Harvard University Press, 1978.

meant to say *That is a book* and thus omitted two obligatory grammatical morphemes, the **copula** *is* and the article *a*. Brown and Cazden used a stringent criterion for when a child was considered to have acquired a morpheme—when the child used it in 90% of its obligatory contexts. Brown (1973) concluded that the order in which children acquire these grammatical morphemes was similar across different children. De Villiers and de Villiers (1973) replicated this study by examining the order of morpheme acquisition in 21 children between 16 and 40 months of age. Their findings were highly similar to Brown's.

Brown (1973) considered several possible explanations for this sequence of development. One was the frequency with which the child hears these morphemes in adult speech. Although it might be expected that the frequency of exposure would be correlated with the ease of acquisition, Brown found no correlation between the two. For instance, definite and indefinite articles appeared with the greatest frequency in the parents' speech for all three children but ranked eighth in order of acquisition for the children. Conversely, the earliest acquisition, the present progressive, was third, fourth, and sixth in frequency, respectively, for the three sets of parents. Thus, Brown rejected the notion that frequency could explain the acquisition of grammatical morphemes.

Moerk (1980, 1981) presents an alternative view. Using a more refined measure of parental speech—frequency of parental use of morphemes just prior to the child's acquisition of the morphemes—he found a relationship between frequency and order of acquisition. Moerk concludes that the relationship between frequency of exposure and morpheme acquisition may have been dismissed prematurely by Brown. Moerk's work has, in turn, been criticized by Pinker (1981), who argues that Moerk restricted his analysis to those morphemes that would be favorable to his hypothesis. Pinker found that when a different subset of morphemes was considered, the correlation between frequency and order of acquisition dropped sharply. Although the issue is far from settled, it appears that parental frequency of morphemes may be related to some extent to the child's acquisition of morphemes.

Brown (1973) also investigated the relationship between linguistic complexity and order of acquisition. He defined linguistic complexity in two ways: **semantic complexity** (also called **conceptual complexity**) refers to the complexity of the ideas expressed, whereas **syntactic complexity** (also called **formal complexity**) refers to the complexity of the expressions used to convey the idea. To assess the role of semantic complexity, Brown identified several meanings that were entailed by various morphemes. For instance, the plural morpheme entails the notion of number; that is, to use the morpheme correctly, a speaker must attend to whether there is one or more than one of the object referred to. The third-person regular entails both number (since the morpheme is used with singular but not plural subjects) and time (since it is used with the present but not the past tense). Finally, both forms of the auxiliary includes these two semantic notions plus a third: temporary duration, or the notion that something is currently happening (the auxiliary is always accompanied by *-ing*). On the basis of cumulative semantic complexity, Brown predicted that the plural would be acquired before the third-person regular, which would in turn be acquired before the auxiliary. As you can see in Table 11-2, the results corresponded to these predictions. Unfortunately, the syntactic analysis yields identical predictions. Using a form of transformational grammar as the measure of syntactic complexity, Brown determined that the plural, third-person regular, and auxiliary required, respectively, two, three, and four transformations in their derivations. In general, both forms of complexity appeared to be related to the order of the morphemes, but Brown was unable to tease them apart.

The distinction between formal and conceptual complexity is useful, however. For one thing, it can also be applied not only to grammatical morphemes but also to different grammatical constructions in the language. For another, languages differ in the formal complexity with which they mark various notions. Thus, as we will see shortly, the distinction is relevant for understanding differences in how children acquire both morphology and syntax in different languages.

Productivity in morphology   Once children acquire morphemes, they begin to use them in productive ways. This was demonstrated by a famous study by Berko (1958). Berko showed children novel creatures and actions that were assigned invented names. The children were then given the opportunity to supply appropriate morphemes for these invented words (see Figure 11-1). Berko found that preschool and first-grade children showed productive control of several grammatical morphemes (plural and possessive inflections for nouns; progressive, past tense, and third-person present tense for verbs). This study suggests that children are not merely learning these morphemes in rote fashion but are acquiring morphological rules.

An aspect of children's morphological productivity that has been intensively studied is the presence of **overregularizations** in their speech (Cazden, 1968; Ervin, 1964; Slobin, 1973). An overregularization is the child's use of a regular morpheme in a word that is irregular, such as the past tense morpheme in *breaked* and *goed*. The acquisition of irregular verbs typically goes through three stages. First, the child uses the word correctly. Second, the child overregularizes the word. Finally, the irregular form reappears. It appears that children analyze linguistic forms that were

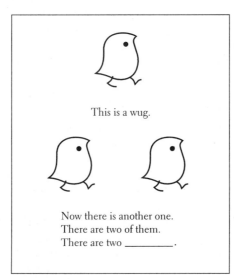

Figure 11-1.   Items used to test for the plural morpheme in Berko's study. (Based on "The Child's Learning of English Morphology," by J. Berko, 1958, *Word, 14,* p. 154, International Linguistic Association.)

previously unanalyzed. That is, *broke* was initially learned rote, not as an instance of an irregular past tense verb but simply as a single lexical item. Later, as the child comes to better understand the regular past tense morpheme, it is overapplied to the irregular cases. Then, when the irregular form reappears, it is with a new status, that of an exception to a general rule.

There are two theories about how children acquire overregularizations. The rule-and-memory model (Marcus, 1996) assumes that children have access to a rule that says, roughly, "To form the past tense, add -*ed* to any verb." In addition, children have stored past tense forms of irregular verbs (for example, *rang*) in memory. As with all memory, retrieval of such forms is subject to error. Finally, the model assumes that a stored irregular form takes precedence over the rule. Hence, *rang* blocks *ringed.* In other words, the overregularization occurs only if no stored irregular form is found.

Rumelhart and McClelland (1986) provide an alternative view of how children acquire the past tense in English. Their approach is based on their parallel distributed processing model, which we discussed in Chapter 4. They argue that the mental representation of verbs is a set of connections in a network rather than rules such as the past tense rule. That is, instead of assuming that children explicitly learn grammatical rules, these researchers assert that children form associations between sound sequences in a complex network. Moreover, different sequences are in competition at any given time. It does appear that different forms of the same word compete with one another in children's language; for example, children sometimes alternate a correct form (*went*), an overregularized form (*goed*), and perhaps an amalgam (*wented*). The essence of Rumelhart and McClelland's model is that the strength of these connections gradually changes over time, partly in response to the language model to which the children are exposed. Thus, the correct form gradually overtakes the others.

Some recent research supports the rule-and-memory model (Marcus, Pinker, Ullman, Hollander, Rosen, & Xu, 1992). Marcus et al. found that overregularizations are related to the frequency with which parents use irregular forms, as predicted by the rule-and-memory model. Since the model assumes that the irregular form blocks overregularizations, it makes sense that variables that influence the child's retrieval of the irregular form, such as the frequency of parental usage, would be related to the child's use of overregularizations. In addition, the parallel distributed processing model predicts that overregularizations are related to the proportion of regular verbs in a child's vocabulary, on the assumption that a greater preponderance of regular verbs is likely to strengthen the connections to the incorrect overregularizations (see also Pinker & Prince, 1988). However, Marcus et al. found no correlation between the number or proportion of regular verbs in a child's vocabulary and the child's tendency to use overregularizations. Finally, as predicted by the rule-and-memory model, overregularizations slowly decline over the late preschool and early school years. This observation is consistent with the notion that the retrieval of irregular forms grows stronger with increased usage.

These observations suggest that the child is operating with two competing mental structures: a general rule and a memory for specific exceptions. The variations in children's use of verb forms appear to be related primarily to the variations in the strength of memory for irregular forms. There is no evidence that the general rule weakens over time. To the contrary, it is simply blocked by the irregular form.

Later Syntactic Development

Children acquire grammatical morphemes gradually, over a period of years. During this time, their sentences get longer and more complex. Some of the changes in sentence length reflect the fact that children are now able to express agent, action, and object in a single sentence. For instance, whereas a younger child might express agent and action or agent and object in a sentence, a somewhat older child can express all three, as in *Daddy throw ball*.

Children also develop the ability to use different types of sentences. We will look at several emerging sentence constructions: negatives, questions, passive sentences, and complex sentences.

Negation   Although young children clearly understand the concept of negation (see, for example, Bloom, 1970), mastery of the negative sentence structure comes relatively late for most children. This is primarily because the syntactic structures that must be acquired are rather complex. For example, consider the negative sentence (1):

(1)   I won't be coming for dinner on Friday.

In comparison with the affirmative, this negative involves the introduction of a new element, *not* in *will not*, as well as the contraction of this phrase into *won't*.

Klima and Bellugi (1966) found that negatives come in a series of stages. The first step is simply to attach a negative word to an affirmative sentence, as in sentences (2) and (3). The second step occurs when children begin to incorporate negatives into affirmative sentences such as (4). Interestingly, this is when children first begin to use contractions, as in (5). They do not, however, use the uncontracted form of the expression (*does not*), suggesting that the *doesn't* is an isolated achievement at this point, unrelated to a general ability to form contractions of verbs. The third stage occurs when internal negatives occur, as in (5), along with the affirmative forms in (6):

(2)   No wipe finger.
(3)   No doggie bite.
(4)   Doggie no bite.
(5)   Doggie doesn't bite.
(6)   Doggie does bite.

Bloom (1970) has questioned the first of these stages. She observed that in some sentences the negative element may be properly placed at the beginning of the utterance. Consider, for example, an utterance such as (7):

(7) No Mommy do it.

This could be an instance of a negative morpheme attached to an utterance, meaning *Mommy won't do it*. Alternatively, the *no* may be anaphoric, referring back to a previous utterance, meaning *No, let Mommy do it*. On the basis of Bloom's study and other reports, de Villiers and de Villiers (1985) concluded that the use of the external negative was not a universal stage, although some children may adopt this approach.

Questions   There are several types of questions in English. One is the yes/no question, which is a question that can be answered yes or no. An example is sentence (8):

(8) Can your baby walk?

The yes/no question is formed by inverting the subject with the auxiliary verb. Children have considerable difficulty with this rule and often simply use the declarative form with question intonation, as in sentence (9):

(9) Your baby can walk?

Another type of question is the **wh-question,** which is a question that begins with one of the *wh*-words (*who, what, where, when, why*). An example is sentence (10):

(10) Why won't you let me go?

According to transformational grammar (see Chapter 2), three syntactic operations are used in this sentence: *wh*-preposing, noun phrase–auxiliary inversion, and negation. Using the sentence *You will let me go* as the starting point, these three transformations add a *wh*-word at the beginning of the sentence, invert the noun phrase (*you*) and the auxiliary verb (*will*), and add a negative element (*not* added to *will*, then contracted to *won't*).

Once again, it has been proposed that children acquire these sentences in a series of stages (Klima & Bellugi, 1966). In the first stage, which occurs about the first half of the third year, children master the *wh*-preposing operation, but without the inversion. This produces questions such as (11):

(11) Where I should put it?

The sentence is usually produced with an intonational rise at the end, which, together with the context, makes it easy to interpret as a question. The next stage (at about 3.5 to 4 years) involves both *wh*-preposing and inversion, but only for affirmative sentences. Thus, the child correctly handles the affirmative question (12) but fails to invert the noun phrase and auxiliary correctly in negative sentence (13):

(12)   What will you do now?

(13)   Why you can't sit down?

Klima and Bellugi suggest that children's processing capacity is too limited at this point in development to control all three operations at once, or even two operations, if one of them is highly demanding. Thus, while they show mastery of inversion with *wh*-preposing, which had been acquired earlier, they fail to invert with negatives, a later acquisition. The last stage (4 to 4.5 years) occurs when children invert negative sentences (14) as well as affirmative ones:

(14)   Why won't you let me go?

As with negation, this orderly pattern of development may occur for individual children but is not necessarily true for all English-speaking children. There appear to be individual differences in the acquisition of the inversion operation (de Villiers & de Villiers, 1985). In addition, Kuczaj and Brannick (1979) found that children's knowledge of the rule regarding auxiliary placement was acquired at different points for different *wh*-words.

Passive sentences   A passive sentence is one in which the agent of the action is the syntactic object of the sentence, as in sentence (15):

(15)   The cat was chased by the dog.

Passives are much less common than active sentences in English but are often used to highlight or give focus to the recipient. There has been considerable interest in the acquisition of passives, in light of the significance of the passive in transformational grammar.

Preschool children find passives difficult. Bever (1970) studied the comprehension of passives by children between 2 and 5 years old. Children performed at better than chance level between 3.5 and 4 years of age, but children who were slightly older did slightly more poorly. Replicating these results, Maratsos (1974) found that children about 3 to 3.5 years understood the passive voice but that children from 3.5 to 4 years had difficulty with it.

The apparent regression in development is certainly interesting and suggests that children who initially analyzed passive sentences correctly subsequently misinterpreted them. In particular, Bever (1970) contends that older children tend to interpret an incoming string of noun plus verb plus noun as agent plus action plus object, a strategy that will work for active sentences but not for passive ones. The tendency to overapply a comprehension strategy is reminiscent of the process of overregularization of morphological rules discussed earlier.

Complex sentences   A **complex sentence** is one that expresses more than one proposition. Passive sentences convey a single idea in linguistically complex form. Other sentences, such as coordinations, complements, and relative clauses, express more than one idea.

A **coordination** is a construction in which two simple sentences are conjoined, as in sentences (16) and (17):

(16)   Jill loved rock and Sally loved jazz.

(17)   Hal will bring his wife or she will come in a separate car.

Children combine their sentences using a variety of conjunctions, including *but, because, then, so,* and *if* in addition to *and* and *or.* Bloom, Lahey, Hood, Lifter, and Fiess (1980) studied children's acquisition of *and* and found that acquisition was related to semantic factors. Early on, children used *and* in an additive fashion; one phrase was added to another, with no dependency relation between them, as in sentence (18). Later, they used *and* to express temporal relations (19) and, still later, to express causal relations (20).

(18)   Maybe you can carry that and I can carry this.

(19)   Jocelyn's going home and take her sweater off.

(20)   She put a Band-Aid on her shoe and it maked it feel better.

Some of the children used *and* in still other ways.

A **complement** is a noun phrase that includes a verb. The phrase *to go home* in sentence (21) is a complement:

(21)   I want to go home.

Another example is *I see you sat down,* in which *you sat down* is a complement. These sentences are semantically more complex than comparable sentences without complements, such as (22), because they express more than one idea or proposition.

(22)   I want ice cream.

Children tend to acquire complement constructions between MLUs of 3.5 and 4.0, which is about 3 years of age (Reich, 1986). They first use complements as objects in their sentences, as in (21). Subject complements, such as sentence (23), come later:

(23)   That she likes him surprises me. (from Reich, 1986, p. 129)

Finally, a **relative clause** is a *wh*-clause that modifies a noun. When a *wh*-clause modifies the object of a sentence, it is called an **object relative clause.** One of my daughter's earliest examples is sentence (24), in which *what you just did* modifies *the thing* (I stretched my arms, then she imitated me). There are also subject relative clauses, such as sentence (25) in which *who was lost* modifies *the boy.*

(24)   I did the thing what you just did.

(25)   The boy who was lost was found unharmed.

Children's first relative clauses tend to be object relatives (Limber, 1973). Subject relative clauses may be more difficult because of processing limitations (Goodluck & Tavakolian, 1982). Notice that the subject relatives require a speaker to interrupt a clause to modify the subject, then return to complete the clause. It is likely that such constructions overload young children's working memory.

Crosslinguistic Differences in Later Grammar

Our discussion here has been on the acquisition of English constructions. Many child language investigators have looked into the question of how well the acquisition of English compares with the acquisition of other languages. Now studies have been done not just of many languages but of many types of languages, due in large part to the work of Dan Slobin, who has pulled together cross-linguistic studies in a multivolume work (Slobin, 1985a, 1985b, 1992, 1997a, 1997b).

Slobin (1982, 1985c) suggests that crosslinguistic studies enable us to explore both universal and particular aspects of language. Some aspects of language acquisition appear to be universal, because they reflect either the cognitive functioning of language-learning children or language strategies that all children use. For example, the tendency of English-speaking children to place negative markers at the beginning or end of phrases appears to be a widespread property. Where possible, children move negative elements, preferring to leave verb forms and word order intact. This strategy is also found in Turkish (Aksu-Koç & Slobin, 1985), Japanese (Clancy, 1985), and Polish (Smoczynska, 1985), although less often in Scandinavian languages (Plunkett & Strömqvist, 1992).

Similarly, children's acquisition of certain expressions related to location seems to be universal. Johnston and Slobin (1979) examined the acquisition of the locative expressions *in, on, under, beside, between, front,* and *back* in children between 2 and 5 years old. In English, the terms were acquired in the order indicated. Similar orders of acquisition were observed in Italian, Serbo-Croatian, and Turkish, despite the fact that the means for expressive locative relations varied between the languages. Johnston and Slobin suggest that the order of acquisition reflects conceptual complexity, with development moving from simple spatial relations to more complex relations.

Other studies have discovered particular features of languages. For instance, the acquisition of relative clauses varies substantially from language to language. Although English-speaking children may use simple relative clauses by 2 years of age, they do not appear to master object and subject relative clauses until around 5 (de Villiers & de Villiers, 1985). Acquisition in Turkish is considerably slower (Aksu-Koç & Slobin, 1985). In contrast, 3-year-old children use relative clauses quite freely in their speech in Hebrew (Berman, 1985) and Swedish (Plunkett & Strönqvist, 1992).

Similarly, Berman (1985) notes that Hebrew-speaking children produced well-formed questions with MLUs between 1.2 and 2.6 (at approximately 21 to 30 months). By comparison, English-speaking children are only beginning to master questions at MLUs of approximately 3.5 (at roughly 38 months). Berman suggests that the relative structural simplicity of questions in Hebrew may explain this difference. In Hebrew, yes/no questions merely require speakers to use a rising intonation with a declarative sentence, as opposed to the subject-verb phrase inversions that cause such difficulty for English-speaking children. Other languages with relatively simple means of expressing questions, such as Mandarin, also show precocious development (Erbaugh, 1992).

Crosslinguistic studies support a distinction we saw earlier between conceptual complexity and formal complexity. Many of these studies have examined the development of a particular concept, such as negation, in different languages. If the formal complexity of negation—if the manner in which negation is marked linguistically—does not differ in a pair of languages, then we would expect to see similarities in the age of acquisition across languages. That is, if negative sentences are no harder to master in one language than one another, we would expect children to acquire them whenever they can conceptualize negation. On the other hand, if one language is more formally complex than another with regard to a particular concept, then that aspect of language tends to be acquired later. Testing these hypotheses poses some difficulties; for example, the complexity of a structure is often correlated with its frequency of usage, which also affects development (see, for instance, Demuth, 1990). On balance, however, crosslinguistic studies support this line of reasoning.

Summary

Children acquire grammatical morphemes gradually throughout the preschool years. As children acquire morphemes, they use them in productive ways, sometimes producing errors such as overregularizations. Complex syntactic constructions such as negatives, questions, and relative clauses are also developed during the preschool years. Ease of acquisition appears to be related to the formal and conceptual complexity of the construction, along with certain processing limitations in the child.

Metalinguistics and Discourse

The Emergence of Linguistic Awareness

Throughout most of this book I have emphasized how much of our language knowledge and language processing exists at a level beneath our conscious awareness. We

are scarcely aware of most of the grammatical rules of our language and the processing strategies that we use to comprehend and produce speech. We have some awareness of linguistic units, though, which appears when we attempt to analyze and
dissect language, to reflect on it—in short, when we think about language rather
than merely use it. The distinction between the ability to use language and the
ability to analyze it is significant and is described well by Cazden (1976):

> It is an important aspect of our unique capacities as human beings that we can not
> only act, but reflect back on our actions; not only learn and use language, but treat it
> as an object of analysis and evaluation in its own right. Meta-linguistic awareness, the
> ability to make language forms opaque and attend to them in and for themselves, is a
> special kind of language performance, one which makes special cognitive demands,
> and seems to be less easily and less universally acquired than the language perfor-
> mances of speaking and listening. (p. 603)

It is likely that the developmental course of **metalinguistic awareness** skills
may be very different than that of the "primary" linguistic skills of speaking and
listening, as Cazden's last sentence implies. Metalinguistic skills are almost surely
acquired later than the corresponding "primary" skills that provide the raw data for
linguistic analysis. Let us begin by tracing some of the child's achievement in this
area, then assess its significance for language development.

Researchers, as we have seen, have attempted to identify the child's grammatical system for expressing meanings by examining the types of utterances children
make at various ages. A fundamental limitation of this method is that there is no
direct way of determining what types of utterances a child might consider to be
ungrammatical at a given age. With adults, we not only can note what adults say but
can also ask them questions about utterances they have not or would not say. So we
can ask them, *Is "The firefighter ankle broke the while saving the young child" a
grammatical sentence?* With children, such metalinguistic judgments are more difficult to secure. Witness this early observation:

Experimenter: Adam, which is right, "two shoes" or "two shoe"?
Adam: Pop goes the weasel! (Brown & Bellugi, 1964, p. 134)

Similarly, de Villiers and de Villiers (1978) report the following observation when
filming a study on metalinguistic development. To acclimate a child into a metalinguistic task, they told a young girl that they had a puppet who always said things
backward. Before they could continue, the child enthusiastically responded that she
had a puppet that always said things upside down and proceeded to show her upside-
down puppet to the camera.

Nonetheless, over the past 20 years, a number of clever studies have discovered
ways to explore young children's linguistic awareness. The first study that was able
to elicit judgments of grammaticality from young children was performed by Gleitman, Gleitman, and Shipley (1972). They first had 2-year-old children listen as their
mothers read grammatically acceptable and unacceptable sentences to the experimenter, who either said *good* and repeated the sentences or said *silly* and corrected

the sentences. After a short while, the children were eager to play the judge. These children showed an ability to discriminate between acceptable and unacceptable sentences (although they did accept about 50% of the unacceptable sentences) but were generally unable to correct the deviant sentences without recourse to semantics. For example, they changed *box the open* to *get in the box* rather than dealing with the syntax alone, as a change to *open the box* would be.

The significance of this study was that it showed for the first time that even young children have some metalinguistic skills. Further research has examined other aspects of their language awareness and has attempted to sketch developmental progressions in children's awareness of language.

One group of studies has explored children's awareness of the arbitrary nature of words. When do children understand that there is no intrinsic relationship between the size of an object and the length of the word that refers to it? Berthoud (cited in Sinclair, 1982) found that 4- and 5-year-old children, when asked to give an example of a long word, will respond with words such as *train*. Similarly, Osherson and Markman (1975) found that although preschool children understand that the names of objects may change, they believe that when they do, the properties of the object cling to the name when it is transferred. So, a child will agree that a dog can be called *cat* but, if so, it will meow or that a dog called *cow* will have horns. Thus, young children's concepts of words are not yet separate from their referents.

Another topic of inquiry has been children's awareness of phonological units. Bruce (1964) gave a word (*snail*) and asked the children to take off the *n* and say what word is left. Children younger than 6 years were baffled by the task. In a similar vein, Zhurova (1973) placed a sentry on a bridge over which toy animals had to cross. The investigator was the sentry, and the children could pick up various toy animals and try to cross the bridge. The children had to say the first letter of the toy's name to get across the bridge (*b* for *bear* and so on). The children were unable to deal with this game successfully until they were 5 or 6 years of age.

Phonological awareness is not an all-or-nothing affair. Rather, certain aspects develop more rapidly than others, with some acquired as early as 3 years of age (Chaney, 1992; Smith & Tager-Flusberg, 1982). Stanovich, Cunningham, and Cramer (1984) studied several phonological awareness tasks, some of which are shown in Table 11-3. They gave these tasks to kindergartners and determined the relative difficulty of each task. Try yourself to rank the tasks from easiest to hardest. Your ability to make these judgments is itself a metalinguistic ability and thus should give you some idea of the kinds of skills that young children are mastering. The answer is given at the end of the chapter.

Regardless of the factors that give rise to it, the emergence of linguistic awareness has a significant impact on several aspects of language that we will discuss later in this chapter. One is the child's communication skills. To communicate effectively with a diverse group of people, a speaker must learn to select words that are appropriate to the situation and the listener. This ability is related to the speaker's metalinguistic ability to analyze words and their communicative effects. Also, we will find that children's ability to read is closely related to linguistic awareness, particularly their phonological awareness. In the next section, we discuss the discourse and communication skills of young children.

Table 11-3.   Five Phonological Awareness Tasks

Task	Description
Supply rhyme	Given a word (for example, *fish*), supply a rhyme
Strip initial consonant	Given a word (for example, *task*), identify what is left when the first consonant is removed
Identify different initial consonant	Given four words (for example, *bag, nine, beach, bike*), choose the word with the different initial consonant
Identify different final consonant	Given four words (for example, *rat, dime, boat, mitt*), identify the one with a different final consonant
Supply initial consonant	Given two words (for example, *cat, at*), identify the sound present in one that is missing in the other

Source: Adapted from "Assessing Phonological Awareness in Kindergarten Children: Issues of Task Comparability," by K. E. Stanovich, A. E. Cunningham, and B. B. Cramer, 1984, *Journal of Experimental Child Psychology, 38,* 179–182. Copyright © 1984 Academic Press. Reprinted by permission.

Discourse Processes in Children

In this section we consider two aspects of children's discourse skills. First, we look at children's conversational skills and their ability to relate their linguistic goals to those of their conversational participants. Then we look at their narrative skills—their ability to tell a coherent story.

Conversational skills   As we saw in Chapter 9, conversational discourse involves a number of implicit rules related to taking turns, sharing conversational topics, taking the listener's needs into account, and formulating requests in a socially appropriate manner. Let us see how the child masters each of these.

The most fundamental rule of conversation is that we take turns. This primitive form of turn taking might be learned through parent-child interactions. You will recall from Chapter 10 that mothers treat young infants as active conversational partners by interpreting their burps and other sounds as conversational turns (Snow, 1977).

In a sense, conversations are games with certain broad rules. Fillmore (cited in Bloom, Rocissano, & Hood, 1976) depicted two versions of a conversational game. In the first version, person A picks up a ball and throws it in the air. Person B catches it and then throws it back. In the second version, A picks up a ball and throws it. B waits for A to finish, then picks up a ball and throws it to A. Both versions embody two concepts—namely, that only one ball (topic) should be in the air at a time and that a person should throw a ball after the other person finishes throwing his. The first version contains a third concept that is missing from the second version—that balls are meant to be shared, or our contribution should be topically similar to our partner's.

Table 11-4. Categories of Child Utterances

Category	Definition
Nonadjacent	Those utterances that occurred without a previous adult utterance, or with a definite pause after a previous adult utterance
Adjacent	Those utterances that occurred right after an adult utterance
Noncontingent	Those utterances that did not share the same topic as the preceding adult utterance
Imitative	Those utterances that shared the same topic with the preceding utterance, but did not add information; that is, all or part of the preceding utterance was repeated with no change
Contingent	Those utterances that both shared the same topic with the preceding utterance and added information to it

Source: Based on "Adult-Child Discourse: Developmental Interaction Between Information Processing and Linguistic Knowledge," by L. Bloom, L. Rocissano, and L. Hood, 1976, *Cognitive Psychology, 8,* 524–528, Academic Press.

How, then, do children make the transition from the second game to the first? Keenan (1974) has presented evidence that children begin to do this by attending to the form of a speaker's utterance. Some of the time her children (aged 2 years, 9 months) engaged in sound play, in which they attended to the phonological properties of the other's speech, usually in a playful spirit. Children of this age also tend to repeat some or all of the previous utterance (*flower broken* to *flower*), to expand it (*big one* to *I got big one*), or to substitute one or more items (*two moths* to *many moths*). Although these are extremely simple modifications, Keenan's observations show that before children are able to do much with others' speech, they behave as if they are aware of a conversational requirement to make one's speech relevant.

Bloom et al. (1976) examined the nature of adult-child discourse and came up with several interesting conclusions. First, they classified all child utterances into one of five categories (see Table 11-4). Note that the broadest classification is between adjacent and nonadjacent utterances and that noncontingent, imitative, and contingent utterances are three types of adjacent utterances. Bloom and her colleagues studied a group of children at periodic intervals from the time the children were 19 months of age until they were 38 months old. When the children were between 19 and 23 months of age, they played a game that is similar to Fillmore's second version. A large percentage of their utterances (69%) were adjacent, but few were contingent. Among the adjacent utterances, noncontingent (31%) were most common at this age, followed by contingent (21%), and finally imitative utterances (17%).

By the time the children were between 35 and 38 months of age, several developmental trends were apparent. The overall percentage of adjacent utterances declined (to 64%). However, the percentage of contingent utterances more than doubled (to 46%). The percentage of noncontingent and imitative utterances dropped sharply to 16% and 2%, respectively. It appears that between 2 and 3 years of age, children are developing both the ability to respond appropriately to another's

Part of learning to communicate is adapting one's speech to different listeners.

topic of conversation (that is, contingent utterances) and the ability to select their own conversational topics (that is, nonadjacent utterances).

These studies bear on the question of how children integrate different forms of linguistic knowledge. Two-year-old children have acquired quite a bit of semantic and syntactic knowledge. However, they do not apply this knowledge right away in conversations. Rather, children seem to "fill their slot" by making a comment of some sort, one that is not necessarily related to the previous utterance. By 3 years of age, children have come a long way toward integrating linguistic knowledge and pragmatic knowledge, and they begin to use their conversational turns in semantically appropriate ways.

Another important conversational skill is the ability to adapt one's speech to the listener. In particular, we tend to speak in more simplified form when talking to a person we view as less linguistically advanced.

A **referential communication task** is one in which a speaker must formulate a message to refer to an object or picture, as opposed to communicating the speaker's ideas, needs, or emotions. Developmentally, the interesting aspect of this task is that it forces the speaker to prepare a message that fits the situational context and/or the perceived receptive abilities of the listener. For a long time, psycholinguists, influenced by the work of Piaget, believed that young children could not alter their speech in socially appropriate ways. According to Piaget, children are unable to adopt the vantage point of another person until they reach the cognitive stage known as concrete operations (about 7 years of age). Although some early studies tended to support Piaget's claim (Glucksberg, Krauss, & Weisberg, 1966; Piaget & Inhelder, 1948/1967), later work (Borke, 1975; Maratsos, 1973; Shatz & Gelman, 1973) has indicated that even very young children can modify their speech under certain conditions.

A particularly convincing demonstration has been provided by Shatz and Gelman (1973). They examined whether 4-year-old children could code switch when talking to 2-year-olds as opposed to adults. The 4-year-olds were asked to tell a partner about a toy. When the partner was a 2-year-old, the older children used shorter and simpler sentences. With peers or adults, they used longer and more complex sentences. This result occurred whether or not they had a younger sibling at home. In other words, the code switching was not merely an imitation of parental behavior; it appeared that the children appreciated the conversational situation and adapted accordingly.

The significance of this rise in referential communication skills is that the young speaker is now more capable of taking the listener into account. Children can now adjust their speech to the perceived level of comprehension of the listener, greatly enhancing their ability to communicate effectively with a wider range of listeners.

Narrative skills   As children are gaining skill at holding a conversation, they are also developing the ability to tell a good story. Narratives emerge out of conversations (Polanyi, 1989) and suspend the ordinary rules of conversational turn taking for the time being.

As we learned in Chapter 7, discourse coherence operates at two levels: the local level, at which there are cohesive ties between successive sentences in discourse (Halliday & Hasan, 1976), and the global level, at which the discourse as a whole fits a particular genre. Both forms of coherence have been studied in children's narrative production.

The most common way to examine children's narrative skills is to ask them to relate a personal story (Peterson & McCabe, 1983; Sutton-Smith, 1981). Young children often have considerable difficulty telling a story in a comprehensible way. They sometimes use pronouns ambiguously, such as using *she* to refer to a particular character when it may refer to several characters. Their narratives are also weak in linkages between successive sentences in the discourse. These and related skills develop gradually during the preschool years.

However, even very young children can use cohesive devices to connect successive sentences in their narratives (Bennett-Kastor, 1983; Peterson, 1993; Peterson & Dodsworth, 1991). Peterson and Dodsworth examined the acquisition of cohesive devices in a longitudinal study of children from 2 years of age to 3 years, 6 months. The children were asked to narrate a personal experience. The investigators then examined the narratives for the presence of cohesive devices such as reference, ellipsis, substitution, conjunction, and lexical cohesion (see Chapter 7, Table 7-1). They found that even these very young children used all of the forms of cohesion identified by Halliday and Hasan. Six of the nine devices they studied (reference pronouns, reference demonstratives, verbal ellipsis, clausal ellipsis, conjunctions, and lexical cohesion) were present at the start of the study, indicating that they are acquired prior to 2 years of age. The remaining devices (comparative reference, nominal ellipsis, and substitution) appeared with increases in age and MLU.

Peterson and Dodsworth (1991) also found some changes in the use of cohesive devices over time. The total number of cohesive ties increased with both age and MLU, and the relative proportion of different cohesive devices shifted. Pronominal reference and conjunctions increased, whereas clausal and verbal ellipsis declined. Overall, the cohesive device most often used by children was lexical cohesion, the simplest form of which is just to repeat lexical items. Lexical cohesion constituted 42% of the children's cohesive links. This percentage is higher than the percentage (30%) found in adult speech (Rochester & Martin, 1979). In contrast, adults use a relatively higher proportion of referential ties than children.

Pratt and MacKenzie-Keating (1985) studied referential cohesion in 4- and 6-year-old children. They told stories to the children and then asked them to retell the stories to peers. The preschool children were much more likely to make errors when introducing new referents. They sometimes treated a new referent as if it were already given information, an error that was very uncommon for the first-graders. However, once a referent was introduced into the discourse, even the younger children correctly referred back to it, as opposed to reintroducing it. The 6-year-olds made few errors on either given or new information.

Some work has also been done at the global level. Peterson and McCabe (1983) collected 1124 personal narratives of children from 3.5 to 9.5 years of age. They found age-related changes in the overall narrative structure. The youngest children often produced lists of unrelated sentences. By 6 years of age, most children were able to produce a good story: they provided the listener with a setting, identified a problem or complication, and described how the problem was resolved. Some children were able to produce complex narratives, such as stories with multiple or embedded episodes. In addition, the children provided remarks that clarified the point of the story and the narrator's evaluation of the story events.

Children, of course, differ somewhat in these narrative skills. In another study, McCabe and Peterson (1991) argue that these individual differences are related to parental strategies for eliciting narratives in the home. They were particularly interested in parental strategies that encouraged children to extend or elaborate their narratives, such as the use of open-ended and clarifying questions. McCabe and Peterson found that these strategies were positively correlated with the length of the children's subsequent narratives to experimenters. In contrast, parental topic switching was related to shorter subsequent child narratives. McCabe and Peterson conclude by noting that "we did not find any 'natural storytellers' at age 2. We only found parents who differed in the extent to which they tried to get their children's stories and in the manner in which they went about such collaboration" (p. 250).

Relatively little work has explored children's understanding of the distinctions between different genres. There has been some attention to the differences between narrations about personal events versus fictional stories (Allen, Kertoy, Sherblom, & Pettit, 1994). Both types of narratives are similar to the story grammar discussed in Chapter 7, but fictional stories tend to have more multiple-episode structure, whereas personal events tend to include a single complete episode.

Hicks (1990, 1991) is one of the few investigators who has examined children's acquisition of the differences between narratives and other genres. Hicks studied first-graders' ability to perform three different tasks. The children were shown a short silent film, *The Red Balloon,* and asked to (1) describe the events as they rewatched a portion of the film (similar to a sportscaster describing events as they occur), (2) provide a factual news report, and (3) tell the film's events as a story. The children shifted their language from one genre to another. When doing the first task, they used the present tense, whereas they used the past tense for the other two tasks. In the news-reporting task, the children preferred to stick to a factual and detailed rendition of the events in the film. In the storytelling task, however, they provided more evaluative remarks, sometimes telling events out of temporal sequence, and concentrated more on the internal motivations of the characters. These results suggest that these children were beginning to grasp the difference between describing facts and telling a good story.

Summary

While a good deal of our linguistic knowledge is tacit, explicit awareness of linguistic units and processes is essential for writing, reading, and other aspects of language. The emergence of linguistic awareness takes place after the child's basic grammatical system is organized, in the late preschool and early school years.

Children as young as 2 or 3 years old are able to tell stories and participate in conversations, albeit in limited ways. During the subsequent preschool years, they become more flexible and skilled conversationalists and storytellers. They use a greater variety of cohesive devices, learn new genres, adapt their speech to different listeners, and formulate and justify requests of others. As children enter school, they have an impressive repertoire of communication skills.

Language in the School

The language skills that children bring to the school setting are important since language is the predominant means of instruction in a wide variety of subject matters. But the language of the school is different from the language of the home and of the playground, and children must adapt to these differences as they enter formal schooling. We will begin with a discussion of oral communication in the classroom, then discuss the relationships between reading and language development.

Communicating in the Classroom

The classroom environment contains a wealth of verbal interaction that has been explored by sociolinguists, psycholinguists, and educational researchers (Cazden, 1986; Mehan, 1979; Wilkinson, 1982). Classrooms, like other communication situations, have implicit conventions for how oral discourse should take place, and it

A teacher's attention is a scarce resource. Children must learn the rules of the classroom in order to be granted a conversational turn.

is likely that some children will be better able than others to discern these "rules of the game." The causes and consequences of these individual differences have been the focus of much research.

Classroom discourse   Classroom discourse has several distinguishing characteristics. One is that the language of the classroom is **decontextualized** (Cook-Gumperz & Gumperz, 1982). In most communicative situations outside formal education, there is a close relationship between the utterances of conversational participants and the immediate context. This is known as **contextualized language.** In formal education, however, it is common for children to be asked *Who discovered America?* or *What is 5 times 5?*—questions that have nothing to do with the immediate environment.

Teachers' use of questions diverges from everyday discourse in another way. Teachers frequently ask children questions as a way of gauging the students' learning rather than learning the answer to the question. These questions function more like an exam than a true question (Searle, 1969). One form of discourse that enables teachers to assess student learning is the **initiation-reply-evaluation sequence,** in which a teacher poses a question to a student, receives a reply, and then evaluates the student's answer (Mehan, 1979). Children are unlikely to have much experience with this type of discourse outside school.

Teachers' language to children is also more formal than most language to which children are accustomed. In a study of classroom teachers and their language behavior, Feldman and Wertsch (1976) found differences in the styles of speech in the classroom and the lunchroom. When away from children, teachers used expressions such as *It seems to me . . . , I certainly expect . . .* , and other ways of qualifying one's speech. These devices are used to distinguish personal opinion from factual content. In the classroom, these qualifiers were absent. Teacher language in the classroom thus is somewhat more formal relative to everyday, colloquial speech.

One final aspect of classroom discourse is the teacher's inability to attend to every child at the same time. As Merritt (1982) puts it, the teacher's attention is a scarce resource. If so, then how is this attention distributed? Several studies of classroom interaction have found that a fundamental role is that teachers, as authority figures, determine how conversational turns are allocated. This is generally done by the teacher specifically addressing one member of the class. Typically, most student comments are in direct response to the query. Spontaneous student comments are relatively rare (DeStefano, Pepinsky, & Sanders, 1982; Mehan, 1979).

An important issue is the role these communicative rules play in classroom interaction and, ultimately, learning. Some observers agree that academic success depends on communicative competence as much as intellectual competence. Mehan (1979) puts the point well:

> Students not only must know the content of academic subjects, they must learn the appropriate form in which to cast their academic knowledge. . . . They must know with whom, when, and where they can speak and act, and they must provide the speech and behavior that are appropriate for a given classroom situation. Students must also be able to relate behavior, both academic and social, to varying classroom situations by interpreting implicit classroom rules. (p. 133)

Acquiring classroom skills   Research has examined how children use requests for information and action during group reading assignments (Wilkinson & Calculator, 1982; Wilkinson, Clevenger, & Dollaghan, 1981). In these studies, first-grade children read aloud or silently in groups and then completed a workbook, drew pictures, or otherwise demonstrated their understanding of what they read. As the teacher moved from group to group around the room, opportunities arose for students to ask each other for assistance. Wilkinson et al. found that requests were often accompanied by justifications of why the request was made (for example, *Can I use your eraser for a minute, Sandy? I made a boo-boo*) and clarifications of exactly what was requested. Moreover, the children often spontaneously revised their questions when the question did not produce the desired response. These results are highly similar to those found by Garvey (1975) with preschool children.

Wilkinson and Calculator (1982) also found individual differences in peer group interactions. Those children found to be the most effective speakers were those whose responses were direct, sincere, relevant to the task at hand, and addressed to a specific listener. Children who used this form of speech received a much higher degree of compliance than those who did not. Other studies indicate that children, like adults, respond positively to individuals whose messages are informative and clear. Pratt, Scribner, and Cole (1977) found that children who were effective speakers were those most often selected by children to be teachers.

Moreover, teachers' interactions with students are related to teachers' perceptions of students' communication skills. Several studies have shown that students perceived as higher in communicative competence gain the floor more often (Cherry, 1978; Michaels, 1981). Cherry (1978) found that teachers tended to request more information from those they considered to be high in communication skills.

The notion that communicative skills enable children to gain access to the floor more often is particularly relevant for understanding the classroom performance of minority children. Michaels (1981) studied student narratives during "sharing time" (sometimes called "show and tell"), in which students are encouraged to describe an object brought from home or give a narrative account about some past event to the entire class. Michaels found that lower-income black and middle-income white children used different narrative styles. White children used a topic-centered approach that focused on a single topic or a series of related topics, whereas black children used a topic-associating style, a discourse that consisted of a sequence of implicitly associated anecdotes. Gee (1989) suggests that white teachers may have difficulty appreciating the latter style and understanding the implications of asking children to change their style of speech. More generally, the home backgrounds of some children may not prepare them to participate in a classroom that emphasizes a different style of discourse (Michaels, 1991).

Reading and Language Development

There is, of course, another major difference between language in the school and language before school. Schooled language is increasingly written language, and the demands of written language pose a considerable challenge for most children entering formal schooling.

The beginning reader is already a fluent language user. Many of the comprehension skills that have been acquired to deal with oral language are also applicable to reading. These include the ability to extract the meaning of a sentence, interpret that sentence in a given communicative context, draw inferences from individual statements, and monitor one's own comprehension. These may be referred to as general comprehension skills.

In addition, learning to read involves mastering other skills specific to the written language. These include using eye movements to scan sentences in a text, extracting the visual features of letters and words, reading from left to right on a page (in most languages), and relating printed language to spoken language in some way. It is likely that some of these skills may be acquired rather easily, but others may take substantial time and effort.

What this suggests is that reading involves a variety of skills that are well coordinated only in the mature reader. That is, the early reader is consumed with the task of identifying even familiar words in a new and unfamiliar mode. Early readers thus are less able to attend to the overall meaning of a text and to apply those comprehension strategies acquired in the acquisition of oral language. As children master reading-specific skills, they are increasingly able to bring their substantial repertoire of linguistic skills to bear on the task of reading.

Phonological awareness and reading   One skill that is specific to reading is the task of linking printed letters (called **graphemes**) to phonemes. This task is difficult for young children, for several reasons. For one, there is a lack of one-to-one correspondence between phonemes and graphemes. The grapheme *c* is sometimes pronounced as /k/, as in *coffee*, and sometimes as /s/, as in the first phoneme in *circus*. In addition, the child must learn that some graphemes are pronounced in ways that are difficult to anticipate, such as the *ph* in *phoneme*. Moreover, the young reader will have to confront words with silent letters, such as *house*.

Phoneme-grapheme linkage is also difficult because children tend to be weak in metalinguistic awareness of phonemes. The young reader's metalinguistic skills do not appear to be sufficient for this type of analysis of language. Several authors (for example, Mattingly, 1972) have suggested that reading is a secondary language skill, like literary analysis, which is intrinsically more difficult than spoken language because it involves conscious awareness of linguistic units. A startling study by Rozin, Bressman, and Taft (1974) shows the extent of young children's ignorance in this regard. Children were shown word pairs such as *mow* and *motorcycle* and were told that one was *mow* and the other *motorcycle*. Then they were asked which one was *mow*. Only 10% of inner-city kindergartners performed to the criterion (7 of 8 correct). This result appears to indicate that these children were unaware of a fundamental relationship between sound and writing: that words that take longer to say have more letters.

As awareness of the sound system grows, some levels are more accessible than others. In particular, some research indicates that awareness is particularly hard to acquire at the phonemic level. Liberman, Shankweiler, Fischer, and Carter (1974) examined phonemic and syllabic awareness in 4-, 5-, and 6-year-old children. The researchers had one group of children listen to words and then indicate, by tapping a wooden dowel on a table, the number of syllables (one, two, or three) in the word. A separate group identified the number of phonemes in a word. Thus, the first group would tap three times to *hospital* and the second group three times to *bag*. The phoneme-segmentation task proved to be much harder than the syllable-segmentation task for all three age groups. In fact, none of the 4-year-olds and only 17% of the 5-year-olds could segment phonemically. In contrast, nearly half (48%) of the 5-year-olds could segment a word into syllables.

The special difficulty of phonemes is probably related to the way in which phonemes are encoded into syllables (see Chapter 4). In a word such as *ball*, the information pertaining to the initial /b/ is spread throughout the syllable. The syllable is thus, in this sense, a more natural (that is, more accessible) linguistic unit than the phoneme. As a consequence, some researchers have suggested that it would be easier for children to begin reading by analyzing words into syllables, and only later to break syllables into phonemes (Gleitman & Rozin, 1977).

In any event, it is clear that phonological awareness is causally related to the development of reading skill (Bradley & Bryant, 1983; Gibb & Randall, 1988; Stanovich, Cunningham, & Cramer, 1984; but see Dale, Crain-Thoreson, & Robinson, 1995). And, if this is so, then training in metalinguistic skills should lead to reading improvement, and several studies support this assertion (Ball & Blachman, 1991; Byrne & Fielding-Barnsley, 1993; Lundberg, Frost, & Petersen, 1988). Lundberg et al. developed a training program of metalinguistic games and exercises designed to improve phonological awareness. The researchers provided daily training sessions for 155 Danish preschool students over a period of 8 months. The program produced significant gains in several metalinguistic tasks, including phonemic segmentation. Moreover, the metalinguistic gains led to reading improvement that was sustained over a period of time.

Top-down and bottom-up processes   As a result of these metalinguistic problems, children often find it difficult to identify printed words. One strategy for overcoming this problem is to encourage children to use the sentence context to help figure out the meaning. For instance, if a child is stuck on the last word of a sentence, the child may be asked to figure out a likely ending to the sentence by generating possible words. Once a set of words is constructed, the child can return to the troublesome item with greater semantic support, and it may now be possible for the child to recognize the word throughout a combination of semantic and orthographic cues (spelling).

Although in the short run this may be a useful approach, most good readers eventually "crack the code" and learn to identify words based solely on their spelling and not on contextual factors. A study by Allington and Strange (1977) illuminates the point here. Fourth-grade children identified as good versus poor readers on standardized reading tests were given a task in which they had to read aloud various sentences. Five percent of the sentences contained an error, such as *The frog hopped oven the snow.* The question of interest was whether students would read *oven* as it was printed or would spontaneously correct it to *over,* and, if so, which group of readers would do so more often. It turned out that the poor readers said *over* more often than the good readers. These results suggest that better readers rely less, not more, on top-down processing to recognize individual words (see Stanovich, 1980, for a review of pertinent studies).

These results may sound counterintuitive. We sometimes think of good readers as those who attend to meaning, whereas less successful readers go word by word. And, of course, the ultimate goal of reading is to comprehend the meaning of a printed passage. But our intuitions may not be reliable here, for many reading processes are long since automatic in mature readers. We may be more aware of the results of our reading efforts than we are of the processes we use to obtain these results.

From the vantage point of information processing, the notion that good readers rely on bottom-up processing to recognize words makes good sense. Word recognition has often been regarded as an automatic process in mature readers (see Chapter 5), whereas many other important processes in reading—such as noting cohesion between sentences, drawing inferences, and summarizing paragraphs—

are controlled processes for most of us. With limited overall processing resources, the more automatic lower-level processes are, the more processing capacity is available for higher-level processes. The end result should be better comprehension.

These results may be related to the observation that children who are read to more often in the preschool period eventually become better readers (Snow, Barnes, Chandler, Goodman, & Hemphill, 1991). There may be several reasons for this relationship. Listening to stories is often a pleasurable experience for young children, and it may foster positive attitudes toward reading. Another reason may be that early exposure to printed words facilitates children's later ability to recognize them automatically. These ideas are not mutually exclusive; both may play a role. In any event, exposure to printed language, even in adults (Stanovich & West, 1989), promotes reading skills.

Summary

The linguistic skills needed for success in formal schooling differ from those that children have acquired during their preschool years. Classroom discourse requires students to learn the "rules of the game," and children's academic success is related to how well they learn these communicative lessons. In particular, children must learn to formulate requests clearly and express themselves in the formal style of discourse recognized in the classroom.

Although children come to school with oral language skills and experience with printed materials, successful reading requires children to identify written words rapidly, a reading-specific skill that depends on metalinguistic processes. Successful reading requires a mix of top-down and bottom-up processes. The ability to identify words automatically, an asset in reading, enables readers to devote resources to higher-level processes, thereby promoting comprehension.

Review Questions

1. Identify the factors that are related to children's acquisition of grammatical morphemes.
2. Distinguish between formal and conceptual complexity.
3. Identify two explanations for overregularizations.
4. Why do children regress in their ability to comprehend passive sentences?
5. What evidence suggests that metalinguistic skills do not develop all at once?
6. How do children's narrative skills change during the late preschool period?
7. Discuss the relative frequency of contingent, noncontingent, and imitative speech in children's discourse.
8. What are referential communication tasks, and why might young children do poorly on these tasks?

9. How might differences in communication skills influence the classroom learning of different children?
10. Discuss the relationship between phonological awareness and early reading.

*T*hought Questions

1. Identify some caregiver activities that might foster metalinguistic skills, and explain why they might be effective.
2. Relatively little research has been done on children's learning to write. On the basis of the text's discussion of how children learn to read, how might learning to write be related to speech production? Would similar stages be involved? Explain.
3. Would a child who has moved from one school district to another several times be more or less likely to learn the "rules of the game" of a particular classroom? Justify your answer.
4. De Villiers and de Villiers (1978) have suggested that one index of a child's metalinguistic skill is the ability to tell a lie. How might this "achievement" be related to linguistic awareness?

Answer to Table 11-3: The tasks, from easiest to hardest, are supply rhyme, identify different initial consonant, supply initial consonant, identify different final consonant, and strip initial consonant.

12 Processes of Language Acquisition

MAIN POINTS

- Language acquisition has been studied in relation to three classes of variables: environmental factors, cognitive processes, and innate linguistic mechanisms.
- Studies of feral and isolated children indicate that gross environmental neglect or abuse may retard language acquisition. The precise aspects of the environment necessary for normal language growth are not clear.
- Nonlinguistic cognitive processes are correlated with language milestones at various points in development. Some evidence indicates that cognitive achievements facilitate language development.
- Children given only impoverished linguistic input are able to create communication systems that are similar to early child language, which suggests some innate guidance in early language acquisition.

Introduction

In Chapters 10 and 11, we surveyed some of the more important facts of language development. Although normal children achieve mastery of language in a few short years, we have seen that it is not a simple achievement.

This chapter examines the question of how language is acquired. One way to think about the factors that play a role in language acquisition is to identify necessary and sufficient conditions. A **necessary condition** is one that must be present in order for language to occur in a normal way. A **sufficient condition** is one that, if present, ensures that language will develop normally. It is rare for a complex behavior to have a single sufficient condition. On the contrary, it may have several necessary conditions, none of which is sufficient by itself to ensure a positive outcome. Think, for example, of the conditions that must be present to ensure a child with a healthy self-concept or a marriage that is stable over time. Most behaviors have multiple causes.

Three classes of variables have been proposed as necessary or sufficient conditions for language acquisition. These are environmental, cognitive, and innate factors. Although each of these is sometimes discussed to the exclusion of the other two, it is likely that all three classes of variables are needed for a complete account of language acquisition. If so, a successful theory of acquisition will be one that explains the interactions among these factors.

The chapter is organized in the following way. The beginning section examines the role of the environment in language acquisition. We consider children who receive little or no exposure to language as well as the special modifications adults make when speaking to children acquiring language. The second section discusses cognitive contributions to language acquisition. For example, we will address the role of intelligence in language development. The third section addresses the question of whether, in addition to environmental and cognitive factors, innate constraints exist that guide the child's journey to language mastery. That is, this section asks whether environmental and/or cognitive factors are sufficient to explain language development; if not, innate linguistic mechanisms may also play a role.

*T*he Linguistic Environment

The effect of experience on human nature has been a source of fascination for philosophers, psychologists, and laypeople for centuries. It is most commonly expressed nowadays in terms of the familiar heredity-versus-environment or nature-versus-nurture arguments. What is most responsible for our knowledge and behavior, our biological predispositions or the shaping done by our environments? These arguments have typically evoked passionate reactions and, not uncommonly, extreme positions, and this is no less true of language than of other aspects of behavior.

Rather than pit nature against nurture, however, it might be more productive to begin by looking at the language environment into which children are born and then assess to what extent the acquisitions we discussed in the last two chapters can be accounted for in environmental terms. Many questions are related to the role of the environment in language acquisition: Is exposure to language needed for language acquisition? Does the exposure have to be within a particular time frame? What types of language input are most useful?

Feral and Isolated Children

The first question has been addressed through studies of feral and isolated children. **Feral children** are those who have grown up in the wild. Lane (1976) presents a detailed description and analysis of a boy named Victor, who was found in the woods of France in 1797. Peasants spotted the boy running naked through the woods, searching for potatoes and nuts, and he was subsequently captured by some hunters and brought to civilization. They called him the Wild Boy of Aveyron, after the province in which he was found.

The Wild Boy came to the attention of Jean-Marc-Gaspard Itard, a young physician. At the time of his capture, Victor was thought to be about 12 or 13 years old. He had no speech, although his hearing was normal and he uttered some sounds. Other physicians thought that Victor was deaf and retarded, but Itard was optimistic that he could be trained to be socialized and to use language. Itard worked intensively with Victor for 5 years, using techniques of language training and behavior modification similar to those used by modern researchers (Skinner, 1957). For example, he taught Victor to name objects such as milk by presenting the object and then the French word for it. Victor would name objects that were presented but would not request them by using their names.

Victor had other problems with language. One was that he developed a gestural communication system that interfered with the language training. Lane (1976) suggests that the signs might have supplanted his need to acquire spoken language. Another problem was Victor's understanding of words. Victor associated a particular name with a particular object, rather than with a class of objects. For instance, when taught the word for book, he initially applied it to only one book. Only with considerable effort could Itard teach Victor to generalize names for classes of objects.

In general, Victor's language progress was poor. There are several competing explanations for this fact. Some observers believed that Itard's techniques were defective and that Victor might have acquired more language if given better instruction. Others embraced the hypothesis that Victor was past the critical period for language acquisition. This view holds that exposure to language must occur within a specified time period (for example, by puberty) in order for language to be acquired normally. Although no one is sure, Victor was believed to be about 16 years old when Itard's training began. Finally, some scholars believe that Victor was either mentally retarded or autistic from the beginning and that he was perhaps abandoned in the woods for that reason. Lane (1976) disputes the latter point, tending to agree with Itard's analysis that Victor was normal when born and that the symptoms he displayed were a consequence of his isolation in the wild.

Isolated children are those who grow up with extremely limited human contact. The best-documented case is of a child who experienced extreme social and physical isolation from 20 months of age until about age 13.5 years (Curtiss, 1977, 1981; Curtiss, Fromkin, Krashen, Rigler, & Rigler, 1974; see also Rymer, 1993). The child is referred to in the scientific literature as Genie.

Some understanding of Genie's family background is helpful. Despite the fact that her father was adamant about not having children, Genie's mother became pregnant 5 months into their marriage. Late in the pregnancy, the father-to-be viciously beat and tried to kill his wife. Later, after the child was born, the father kept her in the garage to avoid hearing her cry. The child died at 2.5 months of pneumonia and overexposure. A second child, a boy, was born the following year and died within 2 days. Another son was born 3 years later. The child's development was slow, and eventually his paternal grandmother took him into her home.

Three years later Genie was born. She was average in birth weight but suffered from a congenital hip dislocation that required a splint. Pediatric checkups for the next few months indicated essentially normal development, but by the eleventh month—6 months after the last checkup—she weighed only 17 pounds. Shortly after that, she developed an acute illness that required her to be brought to another pediatrician, who indicated that she showed signs of possible retardation. This statement had tragic consequences, for it was used by Genie's father to justify extreme neglect and isolation on the grounds that he believed the child was profoundly retarded.

Curtiss (1977) reports the conditions under which Genie lived:

> Genie was confined to a small bedroom, harnessed to an infant's potty seat. Genie's father sewed the harness, himself; unclad except for the harness, Genie was left to sit on that chair. Unable to move anything except her fingers and hands, feet and toes, Genie was left to sit, tied-up, hour after hour, often into the night, day after day, month after month, year after year. At night, when Genie was not forgotten, she was removed from her harness only to be placed into another restraining garment—a sleeping bag which her father had fashioned to hold Genie's arms stationary (allegedly to prevent her from taking it off). In effect, it was a straitjacket. Therein constrained, Genie was put into an infant's crib with wire mesh sides and a wire mesh cover overhead. Caged by night, harnessed by day, Genie was left to somehow endure the hours and years of her life. (p. 5)

Genie had very little exposure to language during her imprisonment. Her father apparently did not speak to her, and he prevented other family members from entering the room. There was no TV or radio. The room was in the back of the house, so that Genie probably heard very little speech or noise from the street. Her father responded to her few sounds by beating her. Eventually she learned to suppress all vocalizations.

Genie was ultimately rescued, when she was 13.5 years old, by accident. After a violent argument with her husband, Genie's mother took Genie and escaped to her own mother's home. Shortly afterward, Genie's mother, who was almost blind, went to a family aid building to check into services for the blind. She brought Genie with her, and a worker noticed the frail child and alerted her supervisor. After questioning the mother, they called the police, who took Genie into custody. After charges were filed against the family, Genie's father committed suicide.

At this point, Genie was severely undernourished and displayed almost no social skills. She had no language skills at all. After being placed in a program of language remediation, Genie began to show some language gains, but her development was uneven. Phonologically, she showed signs of using intonation appropriately but also many substitutions of speech sounds. Her semantic development was rapid and extensive. She began acquiring vocabulary within 2 months of entering the hospital, and her first words included a wider variety of concepts than that typically found early in language development (for example, words for colors, numbers). Once she began putting words together, she used semantic relations similar to those found in normal children. However, her syntactic development was slow. She displayed few grammatical morphemes and no complex syntactic devices (for example, relative clauses). What she did was to string together content words with little grammatical structure, albeit with relatively clear meaning, as in sentence (1):

(1) I like hear music ice cream truck. (Curtiss, 1981, p. 21)

Her cognitive development appeared to be well in advance of her language development since she sometimes expressed subtle or complex ideas with rudimentary syntax, as in sentence (2):

(2) Think about Mama love Genie. (Curtiss, 1981, p. 21)

A puzzling aspect of Genie's language development was that she appeared to process language in the right hemisphere, even though she was right-handed and had no discernible damage to the left hemisphere. Ordinarily, right-handed individuals process language principally in the left hemisphere (see Chapter 13). Curtiss and her colleagues (1974) speculated that Genie's left hemisphere may have suffered "functional atrophy" from lack of use, forcing her to acquire language with the right hemisphere.

Although there are many other reports of feral or isolated children (see Candland, 1993; Reich, 1986; Schaller, 1992), the cases of Genie and Victor are representative. It is clear from these two instances that the overall prognosis for acquiring language after prolonged isolation from other humans is quite bleak. Given the extreme circumstances of their early years, it is perhaps remarkable that they were able to do as well as they did.

However, these reports leave many unanswered questions. They are consistent with the notion that children must be exposed to language early in life to develop properly, but we do not know how early this experience must be. Studies by Newport (1990) indicate that the age at which children acquire certain aspects of language is correlated with the level of acquisition: the earlier the acquisition, the higher the level of learning. On the basis of this research, it seems reasonable to infer that the prognosis for Victor and Genie might have been considerably better had they been given language exposure at a younger age. But these case studies do not provide us with a precise idea of the kinds of language to which a child must be exposed. All we can conclude is that severe isolation for prolonged periods of time produces gross deficits in a child's language.

Motherese

Another line of research that has examined how the linguistic environment might shape language development deals with the ways adults speak to young children. Adult-to-child language, which has been called **motherese,** differs in a number of ways from adult-to-adult language (see Table 12-1). In general, speech to children learning language is shorter, more concrete, more directive, and more intonationally exaggerated than adult-directed speech.

Of course, just because we speak in these ways to children does not necessarily mean that this speech will assist them in acquiring language. As a matter of fact, some of the properties of adult-to-child language are also seen when adults speak to dogs and even to plants. The effect of this form of speech on dogs and plants is not known.

Although it would appear that such properties would assist children in their language development, data on this basic question are relatively scarce, and widely different opinions exist on the matter (DePaulo & Bonvillian, 1978; Hoff-Ginsburg & Shatz, 1982; Marshall, 1980; Snow, 1979).

The motherese hypothesis (Gleitman, Newport, & Gleitman, 1984) states that there is a relationship between the speech adjustments adults make and children's language development. The strong form of this hypothesis claims that these features

Table 12-1.   Some Characteristics of Adult Speech to Children

Language Level	Characteristic(s)
Phonological	Exaggerated intonation Clear articulation
Syntactic	Shorter sentences
Semantic	Use of diminutives (for example, *doggie*) Concrete referents
Pragmatic	Preponderance of directives and questions

are necessary for language to develop properly; if so, the absence of these features would be predictive of a child's language difficulty. The weak form of the hypothesis claims that these linguistic features assist a child's development.

Investigators have taken two approaches in testing this hypothesis. One is the correlational approach. Mothers naturally vary in their use of the features shown in Table 12-1, and it is possible to exploit this normal range of variation by correlating mothers' tendencies to use these aspects of language with measures of their children's language progress.

In general, correlational studies have found limited relationships between parental speech and child language. Newport, Gleitman, and Gleitman (1977) tape-recorded the speech of 15 girls aged 12 to 17 months with their mothers in two sessions conducted 6 months apart. Most aspects of child language were unrelated to any characteristics of the mothers' speech. Others were related to specific aspects of maternal speech. The clearest example was verb auxiliaries, which were related to the frequency of yes/no questions in maternal speech, such as *Did you eat?* Mothers who used more yes/no questions had children who used more auxiliaries. This result has been replicated by Furrow, Nelson, and Benedict (1979) and Gleitman and her colleagues (1984). As Gleitman et al. note, the observation that the most robust correlation deals with a complex aspect of language does not fit with the idea that "simplifying" adult speech promotes child language. In this instance, it is the presence of a complex aspect of language that is facilitating the child's progress.

Of course, problems arise in interpreting correlational studies. A positive correlation between parental speech and child speech does not mean that the parental speech causes the child speech. It is also possible that the parent's speech is contingent on child behavior, such as signals that the child is not understanding or is bored. Bohannon and Marquis (1977) have demonstrated that adult speech to children is related to child responses.

The alternative to the correlational approach is to use an experimental approach, in which different groups of children are randomly assigned to different types of adult speech. Although early experimental attempts were unsuccessful (Cazden, 1965), we now have clear evidence that such adult speech can influence development.

Nelson, Carskaddon, and Bonvillian (1973) found that language development can be facilitated if children are presented with new syntactic information that is related to the child's previous sentence. These children, between 30 and 40 months of age, were seen regularly for 13 weeks and were assigned to one of three groups. The recast-sentence group received new sentences related to the child's sentence; for example, if the child said, *Allgone truck*, the experimenter would expand it into a grammatical sentence such as *Yes, the truck is all gone*. The new-sentence group received relatively short, grammatical sentences that excluded the content words of the child's previous utterance. A control group received no special treatment. The child's progress in five aspects of language (MLU, sentence imitation, noun phrases, verb phrases, and auxiliary verbs) was assessed. The results indicated that the recast-sentence group showed marginally more linguistic advancement than the new-sentence group on the two measures of verb development, but the two groups

performed the same on the other three measures. The recast-sentence group outper-
formed the control group on the two verb measures as well as on the test of imitation.

A later study by Nelson (1976) showed that the effects of linguistic input can
be quite specific. He arranged for one group of children to hear recasts of negative
wh-questions (*Why don't you play on the swing?*) and for another to hear recasts of
complex verb constructions. The finding was that each group showed advances only
in the type of speech they heard.

These studies provide a more direct link between adult speech and child
language development than in correlational studies, but they are limited in several
respects. First, although they indicate that adult speech may influence child speech,
they do not demonstrate that such speech modifications are necessary for normal
language acquisition. Thus, they provide support only for the weak form of the
motherese hypothesis. Second, the studies are limited in the number of grammatical
constructions that have been used. As noted earlier, Newport et al. (1977) examined
a number of maternal characteristics and found that most were not correlated with
child speech.

This pattern of results may be interpreted in light of the distinction between
universal and particular characteristics of language. Certain aspects of language,
such as the semantic categories of agent, action, and object, and so on, appear to be
universal, whereas others, such as auxiliaries and *wh*-questions, vary from language
to language. This distinction might be expected to influence the extent to which a
grammatical property is sensitive to environmental variables, such as frequency of
occurrence. Recall that children's acquisition of auxiliaries was related to their
mothers' use of yes/no questions in several correlational studies. One feature of yes/
no questions in English is that the subject and the auxiliary are inverted, thus
placing the auxiliary verb at the beginning of the sentence. It seems likely that this
position is more salient for the child and therefore might lead to improved performance on auxiliaries because of the attention it receives. In contrast, universal
features might not be learned at all but rather be part of the child's innate
equipment.

In any event, the distinction between universal and particular linguistic features makes sense both linguistically and psychologically. It suggests that some frag-
ile aspects of language are sensitive to environmental variations and more sturdy
aspects that need less support. Goldin-Meadow (1982) makes an apt analogy to
gardening: some properties of language are like weeds that grow under any conditions, and other properties are like hothouse orchids that need rather specialized
conditions.

Summary

Studies of varying methodology have addressed the role of the environment in child
language acquisition. Case studies of children who have undergone severe isolation
indicate grossly delayed language and imply that exposure to language is a prerequisite for normal language growth. Correlational and experimental studies of motherese suggest that at least certain aspects of the speech adjustments adults make

when speaking to children may influence the child's language development. However, other aspects of language appear to be impervious to variations in maternal language.

Cognitive Processes

In the preceding section, we saw that parents provide a structured environment for children who are acquiring language. Although some of these speech adaptations facilitate development, they are not sufficient to explain language acquisition. To benefit from these language lessons, children must have certain cognitive prerequisites. These include procedures for registering, storing, and analyzing linguistic information.

A simple analogy may be helpful here. Suppose you are taking a course in philosophy. The instructor is well prepared, lectures well, and is available when students have problems. Although all of these characteristics are beneficial, they do not guarantee the desired learning outcome. A course in philosophy typically requires students to think abstractly and to write analytical essays. Students who lack these skills may have considerable difficulty even if the course material is presented in an organized fashion.

The same is true for the child learning language. A structured environment is only helpful if the child has the ability to take advantage of the structure that is provided. In this section we will look at the cognitive skills children bring to the language-learning task.

Operating Principles

One of the most productive approaches to the question has been Slobin's work on operating principles (Slobin, 1973, 1985a). We may think of **operating principles** as children's preferred ways of taking in (or operating on) information. An early list of principles is shown in Table 12-2.

Table 12-2. Operating Principles Used by Young Children

A Pay attention to the ends of words.
B The phonological forms of words can be systematically modified.
C Pay attention to the order of words and morphemes.
D Avoid interruption or rearrangement of linguistic units.
E Underlying semantic relations should be marked overtly and clearly.
F Avoid exceptions.
G The use of grammatical markers should make semantic sense.

Source: From "Cognitive Prerequisites for the Development of Grammar," by D. I. Slobin. In C. A. Ferguson and D. I. Slobin (Eds.), *Studies of Child Language Development*, pp. 175–208. Copyright © 1973 Holt, Rinehart & Winston. Reprinted by permission of the publisher.

These principles have proven useful in explaining certain patterns in early child grammar. For instance, children in virtually all languages use fixed word order to create meanings, even though some languages have much freer word order than others. This early pronounced tendency seems related to Slobin's Principle C. We have already seen some of the major developments in the acquisition of grammatical morphemes. Children must first segment words into free and bound morphemes; this is presumably done by noticing different versions of the same word (Principle B) and by noticing the kinds of linguistic elements that may serve as bound morphemes (Principle A). And we know that when children come to learn a grammatical morpheme, they often overregularize it (Principle F).

Several of the principles are also useful in understanding children's acquisition of complex sentences. When first attempting to form negatives and questions, children often simply place the negative or question marker at the front of a simple declarative sentence. This seems to reflect a desire to avoid breaking up intact linguistic units (Principle D). Similarly, there is a tendency for children, when forming relative clauses, to do so first by simply attaching the clause to the end of the sentence. Only later do they embed the clause within the sentence.

These operating principles are first approximations to the kinds of cognitive prerequisites a child must have to benefit from linguistic experience. In his later work, Slobin (1985a) presents a revised list of principles, making them more specific and more numerous.

One problem with the notion of operating principles is that it is open to the charge of circularity. The evidence for operating principles is found in children's language patterns, and then the principles are assumed to account for the patterns. Independent evidence of these operating principles would be helpful. It might be possible to see evidence of these principles in cognitive domains other than language, but, as written, they tend to be fairly specific to language. Slobin is noncommittal on the question of whether these processes are specific to language (modular) or whether they can be understood in terms of general cognitive processes. We turn now to cognitive processes that are more clearly independent of language.

Induction

Induction is the process of reasoning from the specific to the general. We use induction when we notice similarities among several instances and draw a generalization based on these similarities. Induction may come into play at both the lexical and grammatical levels of language development.

At the lexical level, children must be able to derive the meaning of *dog* from their experiences with specific dogs. These, of course, vary in size, shape, color, and many other attributes. To induce the category, the child must be presented with both **positive evidence** (examples of the category) and **negative evidence** (nonexamples). These are usually supplied by parents, who are only too happy to tell children *Yes, that's a dog, a German shepherd* and *No, that's a cow*. Although this may sound very simple, it actually implies a great deal of cognitive processing. The child must remember the positive and negative instances, formulate hypotheses, and determine whether the evidence presented is consistent with the hypotheses being entertained. All of this may cause a significant memory burden.

In Chapter 10, we discussed the evidence regarding lexical induction. In brief, we found that the process of inducing lexical categories is related to both environmental and cognitive variables. On the environmental side, parents typically structure the word-learning environment for their children by providing positive and negative instances of concepts and by using consistent practices, such as naming the whole object before the parts (Ninio, 1980). In addition, children appear to be operating with the notion of cognitive constraints, such as the notion that a given object can only be assigned a single word label (Markman, 1989). These constraints serve to limit the number of hypotheses that the child must consider. On balance, it appears that a combination of a structured environment and a structured approach to learning greatly facilitates the child's acquisition of the lexicon.

This discussion has been entirely at the level of the lexicon. As it turns out, the role of positive and negative evidence in the area of grammar is quite controversial, and I will postpone that discussion until the end of the chapter.

Sensorimotor Schemata

Recall from Chapter 3 that another way of characterizing the child's cognitive system comes from the work of Piaget, who expressed the belief that children undergo several qualitative shifts in their thinking throughout development. Piaget (1952) referred to the first 2 years as the sensorimotor period of development because the schemata the child uses to organize experience are directly related to taking in sensory information and acting on it. Sensorimotor schemata including banging, sucking, and throwing. The major development that culminates near the end of the sensorimotor period is the acquisition of object permanence, the notion that objects continue to exist even when they cannot be perceived. Once acquired, the child is no longer at the mercy of immediate stimuli but can respond on the basis of stimuli no longer present.

We would certainly anticipate that developments of this magnitude would be related to the child's language development. More specifically, we can make two predictions about child language. One is that the very young infant, who has not yet acquired object permanence, should use words that refer to concrete objects in the immediate environment, especially those that the child easily manipulates. This appears to be the case, because early child language consists of a large number of "here and now" words.

A second prediction is that infants who have mastered object permanence should begin to use words that refer to objects or events that are not immediately present. Two such words are *allgone*, as in *allgone truck*, and *more*, as in *more milk* (when referring to milk that is no longer present). One way to express the idea behind this prediction is to use the metaphor of a waiting room (Johnston & Slobin, 1979). Imagine a room with two doors, one an entry door and the other an exit door. The entry door refers to the achievement of the cognitive prerequisite; this puts the child in the waiting room. Opening the exit door depends on noncognitive factors, such as the amount of exposure to the linguistic item and the linguistic complexity of the item. Depending on these and other factors, the length of stay in the waiting room (the time between the cognitive achievement and the corresponding linguistic achievement) will vary.

This hypothesis has been tested in a number of experiments. Most research has found that the predicted delay between object permanence and the acquisition of *more* and *allgone* has held in some instances, but not all (Corrigan, 1979; Gopnik, 1984; Tomasello & Farrar, 1984). For instance, Tomasello and Farrar report varying delays of from 0 to 8 months, depending on the criteria used for object permanence and on the child. Gopnik suggests that object permanence develops simultaneously with these words. The idea is that just when children are acquiring what is, for them, a difficult concept, they begin to notice linguistic expressions that refer to the concept. These expressions are salient to the child because they are relevant to what the child is learning at the time. Thus, the words are acquired with a very short cognitive-linguistic lag or none at all.

The variability of these results is probably related to the measures used to assess object permanence. As we saw in Chapter 3, some psychologists think that Piaget's traditional measures severely underestimate infants' ability to understand the continued existence of objects. For instance, some researchers think that infants' failures on Piaget's tasks have more to do with not remembering the location of objects as opposed to not realizing that they continue to exist (Diamond, 1985). In fact, different measures of object permanence yield different results (Corrigan, 1979), so we should be cautious in drawing conclusions here.

On balance, although these results are not entirely supportive of the second hypothesis, they do generally support the cognitive approach to language acquisition. In particular, the results stress the importance of the child's cognitive level in determining how a child responds to linguistic input. The suggestion is that it is not enough for the child to be presented with a given lexical item—the child must be cognitively ready to learn the item before it will be given much attention.

Impairments of Language and Cognition

Our knowledge of the relationships between language and cognition has also been advanced by studies of children and adolescents with cognitive or linguistic impairments. The notion that a close relationship exists between language and cognition has generally been supported by studies of individuals with Down's syndrome (reviewed by Rosenberg, 1982; but see Rondal, 1993). These individuals tend to have language delays that are proportionate to the severity of their cognitive disability. However, in certain individuals, there can be significant discrepancies between the level of cognitive functioning and the level of linguistic functioning.

Some individuals display cognitive skills that are advanced relative to the individual's linguistic skills. Curtiss (1981) contrasts the language development of mentally retarded children with that of Genie, whom we discussed earlier in the chapter. The children who were mentally retarded tended to produce sentences with appropriate and sometimes complex syntax but with relatively rudimentary meaning, as in (3). In contrast, Genie expressed herself in sentences that were often grammatically rudimentary but semantically and conceptually more advanced, as in (4):

(3) *Adult:* Does your Daddy stay home all day and cook?

   Child: Nope, He was not comin' home.

(4) *Adult:* Why aren't you singing?

   Genie: Very sad.

   Adult: Why are you feeling sad?

   Genie: Lisa sick.

Although Genie's linguistic skills were rudimentary, her cognitive development appeared to be more age-appropriate. If so, this would provide evidence against the thesis that cognition is sufficient for language.

The hypothesis that cognition is necessary for language has not fared much better. Bellugi, Bihrle, Jernigan, Trauner, and Doherty (1990) have studied individuals with Williams syndrome, a rare disorder that is characterized by an "elfin-like" facial appearance, mental retardation, and cardiac defects. Despite their cognitive impairment, these individuals' syntactic skills were found to be largely intact. For example, they display good comprehension of passive sentences and an MLU greater than expected for their mental age (Bellugi, Wang, & Jernigan, 1994). The failure to find syntactic delays in individuals with Williams syndrome is not consistent with the notion that cognition is necessary for language (for an alternative view, see Karmiloff-Smith, Grant, Berthoud, Davies, Howlin, & Udwin, 1997; Levy, 1996).

There have been other case studies in which individuals with significant cognitive impairments demonstrate unexpected language abilities. For example, Cromer (1993) discusses a case of an adolescent with what has been called chatterbox syndrome, a condition in which an individual talks continuously. Despite considerable deficits on standardized intelligence tests, this young woman displayed fluent language with a keen understanding of various grammatical constructions, such as passives and relative clauses. Cromer discusses several medical conditions, such as spina bifida, Turner's syndrome, and hydrocephalus, that produce a similar pattern of skills.

Some may complain that these conditions, in which there is a sparing of syntax in the presence of cognitive defects, are rare. But if normal cognitive development is necessary for normal language development, it should not happen at all. Together with the lukewarm support for the cognitive thesis in object permanence studies, these results suggest that we need to look beyond cognitive factors in our efforts to explain the course of language development. In particular, we must look at factors that are not part of our general cognitive skills but rather are specific to language.

Summary

Research on cognitive prerequisites for language development has proceeded on the assumption that certain cognitive processes must be in place for the child to benefit from structured language lessons. We have considered three types of cognitive processes that may assist or guide language development. Operating principles are preferred ways of taking in linguistic information. Induction refers to the process of drawing general patterns from specific examples. Object permanence is the knowledge that objects do not depend on our perception of them for their existence. The general prediction that the cognitive position makes is that children with a given cognitive prerequisite should acquire corresponding aspects of language more rapidly than those without the prerequisite. This hypothesis has only been directly assessed in the area of object permanence, where it has received lukewarm support.

Finally, we saw that in certain individuals there are dissociations between language and cognition: relatively strong cognitive skills with weak linguistic skills or relatively strong linguistic skills with weak cognitive skills. These observations suggest that cognitive development, although it is generally associated with language development, may not be either necessary nor sufficient for it.

Innate Mechanisms

In this final section of the chapter, we consider the role of innate mechanisms in language acquisition. These are easily the most controversial of the processes we have considered in this chapter. Although it is generally agreed that environment and cognition play some role in a full account of development, the notion that these processes are constrained by innate properties of the human mind is greeted with diverse reactions. It is thought to be a necessary assumption by some, met with skepticism by others, and regarded with downright hostility by still others. In this section, we will examine the reasons that some theorists have assumed innate constraints and assess the merits of their arguments.

The Language Bioprogram Hypothesis

One version of how innate processes operate in child language has been called the **language bioprogram hypothesis** by Bickerton (1981, 1983, 1984). Bickerton's claim, in brief, is that we, as children, have an innate grammar that is available biologically if our language input is insufficient to acquire the language of our community. It is something like a linguistic backup system.

Pidgins and creoles   To understand this idea more fully, we have to make a few distinctions. A **pidgin** is "an auxiliary language that arises when speakers of several mutually unintelligible languages are in close contact" (Bickerton, 1984, p. 173). Typically this occurs when workers from diverse countries are brought in as cheap labor in an agricultural community. Immigrant workers come to speak a simpler form of the dominant language of the area—just enough to get by. A **creole** occurs when the children of these immigrants acquire a pidgin as their native language. Since access to native speakers of the dominant language is usually limited, these children receive the impoverished pidgin version as their primary linguistic input.

Bickerton (1983) observed that the conditions necessary to produce creoles have existed numerous times between 1500 and 1900 when various European nations developed labor-intensive agricultural economies in isolated, underpopulated tropical islands throughout the world. Bickerton's studies have focused on creoles in Hawaii. Although Hawaiian contact with Europeans goes back to the 18th century, it was not until 1876 that a revision of the U.S. tariff laws led to a large influx of indentured workers to harvest Hawaiian sugar. Since Hawaiian creole developed between 1900 and 1920, it was possible for Bickerton to study the development of the creole by studying the speech of people who are still living. In particular, he examined the language of immigrants who moved to Hawaii and that of their children who were born in the first two decades of this century.

The speech of pidgin speakers was rudimentary. In many cases, there was no recognizable syntax, and the language resembled a linguistic free-for-all. Some speakers used one word order and others another; the word orders were often related to the speaker's own native language. Moreover, complex sentences were absent in pidgin: pidgin sentences had no subordinate clauses, and even single-clause utterances often lacked verbs. In addition, there was no consistent system of anaphora (see Table 12-3).

The language bioprogram   Despite this impoverished linguistic input, the children of immigrants developed a creole that was relatively sophisticated. It included consistent word order, the use of complex sentences with relative clauses, and the distinction between definite and indefinite articles. Unlike pidgins, the creoles resembled the structural rules of other languages. From these observations, Bickerton

Table 12-3.   Examples of Hawaiian Pidgin and Hawaiian Creole English

Pidgin	*Hawaiian Creole English*
Building — high place — wall part — time — nowtime — and then — now temperature every time give you.	Get one [There is an] electric sign high up on da wall of da building show you what time an' temperature get [it is] right now.
Now days, ah, house, ah, inside, washi clothes machine get, no? Before time, ah, no more, see? And then pipe no more, water pipe no more.	Those days bin get [there were] no more washing machine, no more pipe water like get [there is] inside house nowadays, ah?
No, the men, ah — pau [finished] work — they go, make garden. Plant this, ah, cabbage, like that. Plant potato, like that. And then — all that one — all right, sit down. Make lilly bit story.	When work pau [is finished] da guys they stay go make [are going to make] garden for plant potato an' cabbage an' after little while they go sit down talk story ["shoot the breeze"].
Good, this one. Kaukau [food] any kind this one. Pilipin island no good. No more money.	Hawaii more better than Philippines, over here get [there is] plenty kaukau [food], over there no can, bra [brother], you no more money for buy kaukau [food], 'a'swhy [that's why].

Source: Based on "Creole Languages," by D. Bickerton, in S.-Y. Wang (Ed.), *The Emergence of Language: Development and Evolution*, p. 63, W. H. Freeman, 1983.

(1983, 1984) concluded that children have an innate grammar that, in the absence of proper environmental input, serves as the child's language system. He called this system the **language bioprogram.**

Bickerton (1984) responded to other possible interpretations of his research. One is that the sophistication found in the children's creoles was based on their access to English, the language of the plantation owners. Bickerton points out, however, that contact between immigrant families and owners was limited and that the Hawaiian creole differed in several respects from English. Another possibility is that linguistic features not attributable to English could be derived from the original native languages of the parents. For example, children whose parents were Portuguese might incorporate some Portuguese elements into their creoles. Again, the evidence provided by Bickerton suggests otherwise; he found that Hawaiian creole was strikingly similar to creoles created by children in very different parts of the world.

The language bioprogram hypothesis has been further buttressed by studies of language development in congenitally deaf children by Goldin-Meadow and her colleagues (Feldman, Goldin-Meadow, & Gleitman, 1978; Goldin-Meadow, 1982; Goldin-Meadow & Mylander, 1990; Morford & Goldin-Meadow, 1997). The children were between 13 months and 4 years at the start of the study and were studied every 2 to 4 months for about a year and a half. None of these children were exposed to conventional sign language; most were educated by the oral method, which emphasizes lipreading, and some were not in any educational program. Nevertheless, the children invented a form of gestural language called **homesign** that was similar in many respects to the language of children with normal hearing. They acquired aspects of language in the same sequence, and at roughly the same age, as hearing children. One-sign utterances appeared at about 18 months, followed by two- and three-sign utterances. Moreover, they expressed semantic relations that were similar to those used by children at the two- and three-word stages. They also used gestures that were similar morphologically to sign language and signs that referred to information spatially and temporally displaced from the speaker and listener. Thus, when linguistic input is minimal, deaf children may create a gestural language that is similar in many respects to normal children's language.

We have been discussing how the proposed bioprogram might operate in the absence of ordinary linguistic stimulation. What happens if children are given appropriate linguistic input? Bickerton (1984) suggests that under these circumstances the bioprogram is suppressed and children learn the native language. In particular, he claims that children use what he calls the **preemption principle:** "If you hear people using a form different from the one you are using, and do not hear anyone using your form, abandon yours and use theirs" (Bickerton, 1984, p. 186). This principle is based on assumptions found elsewhere in language development: the assumption that there is one unique form for a given function (Pinker, 1984) and the assumption that alternative candidates for that form are in competition with one another (Rumelhart & McClelland, 1986).

Bickerton's research provides a fascinating perspective on the nature of biological limits on language learning. We have seen throughout this text that Chomsky and other proponents of **nativism** have emphasized the task-specific or modular nature of our language capacity, and Bickerton's hypothesis is consistent with this emphasis. But it is more than that. **Task specificity** refers to the notion that the cognitive processes associated with language use are not general-purpose problem-solving processes but are instead restricted to language. Bickerton goes a step further: not only is the language bioprogram specific to language, but it is itself highly specific—a prepackaged, ready-to-go linguistic system.

Parameter Setting

Bickerton's language bioprogram may be thought of as a specific instance of a general innate mechanism called **parameter setting.** The notion of parameters plays a key role in the concept of universal grammar (Chomsky, 1981). In this view, grammar can be defined in terms of a set of parameters corresponding to each of the subsystems of the language, with each parameter having a finite (usually small) number of possible settings. Various combinations of these parameter settings then yield all of the languages of the world. According to Chomsky (1981), children are born with the knowledge of the parameters and their possible settings. The task of acquiring a language is therefore reduced to identifying which parameter settings apply to one's native language.

One parameter is called the **head parameter** and has been discussed by Cook (1988). Each phrase in the language has one element that is most essential, which is called the head. It is the noun in noun phrases and the verb in verb phrases. The head parameter specifies the position of the head within the phrase. In English noun phrases, the head noun comes first. In sentence (5), for example, the head *the man* appears to the left of the phrase *with the bow tie.* It turns out that the head also appears first in verb phrases, as shown, for example, in sentence (6); here the head *liked* occurs before *him.* This is also true of adjectives in adjective phrases, as in sentence (7), and prepositions in prepositional phrases, as in sentence (8):

(5)   the man with the bow tie
(6)   liked him
(7)   nice to see
(8)   to the bank

Once we know that English is a head-first language, we know that this principle applies to all of the types of phrases in the language.

In contrast, in Japanese the heads appear last rather than first. Thus, the verb appears last in sentence (9), which means *I Japanese am:*

(9)   Watashi wa nihonjin desu

Once again, this is a general characteristic of Japanese. For example, Japanese has postpositions rather than prepositions, as in sentence (10), which means *Japan in:*

(10)   Nihon ni

Another parameter is the **null-subject parameter** (sometimes called the **pro-drop parameter**). As we discussed in Chapter 2, it is grammatically acceptable in languages such as Italian and Spanish to drop the subject of a sentence. In other languages, such as English, this is not permitted. This parameter, then, has two values: subject and null-subject. Hyams (1986) contends that children are born with this parameter set to the null-subject value. This initial setting is called the **default value**—the child proceeds on the assumption that this value is correct unless given contrary evidence. If the null-subject is the default value, then children learning English would be expected to initially drop their subjects just as Italian and Spanish children (correctly) do. Hyams cites examples from L. Bloom (1970) that indicate that errors such as these do occur, as in sentences (11) through (14):

(11)   Play it.
(12)   Eating cereal.
(13)   Shake hands.
(14)   See window.

Hyams assumes that as children are exposed to examples of well-formed English sentences, they adjust this parameter to the subject setting.

An alternative interpretation of these sentences is that young children have difficulty producing complete sentences (L. Bloom, 1970; P. Bloom, 1990). P. Bloom (1990) argues that children omit all constituents, not just subjects. In addition, he found that children were more likely to have shorter verb phrases when they include subjects in their utterances than when they did not. This suggests that children have difficulty expressing all of the elements of their sentences, and so these elements compete for limited processing capacity. Hyams's view has also been criticized by Valian (1990), who contends that children begin with both values of the null-subject parameter.

These points certainly pose some problems for Hyams's model. However, despite these criticisms, the general class of parameter-setting models remains attractive because parameters address a fundamental aspect of the acquisition process—that children rapidly acquire their native language despite differences between languages. The general answer given by parameter-setting models—that children are born with the settings and thus need only learn which setting their language is—would greatly simplify the language-learning process for children. Any model that can explain how children do so much so quickly deserves to be taken seriously. However, the details of Hyams's model (such as whether the child begins with one value or two, whether there are different weights assigned to different values, and so on) may need further study.

The subset principle   Another way to think about how these parameter settings may be made is through what Berwick and Weinberg (1984) call the **subset principle.** First, think about languages as subsets of one another. Consider word order. English is a very strict word-order language, Russian allows a small set of admissible orders, and the aborigine language Warlpiri allows an almost total scrambling of word order

Table 12-4.   Predictions of Two Hypotheses on Children's Default Assumptions about Word Order Freedom

	Fixed-Constituent-Order Language	*Free-Constituent-Order Language*
Fixed order as default	No overgeneration	Undergeneration possible
Free order as default	Overgeneration possible	No undergeneration

Source: From "Language Acquisition," by S. Pinker. In D. N. Osherson and H. Lasnik (Eds.), *Invitation to Cognitive Science, Vol. 1: Language*, p. 232. Copyright © 1990 MIT Press. Reprinted by permission.

within a clause. The idea of a subset is that Russian could be considered a subset of Warlpiri with somewhat more restricted word order. In the same way, with respect to word order, English may be considered a subset of Russian.

The question that arises is how children determine which system applies to their native language. Children must induce this system from the evidence presented to them. However, as we saw in the case of lexical induction, there are a great many possibilities and thus an apparent need to constrain the induction process in some way. Pinker (1990) argues that at the grammatical level these constraints are provided by the language itself. The subset principle is that children begin to search through possible languages by beginning with the smallest subset available (that is, the most restrictive language). If there is no evidence from their linguistic input that this is their native language, they proceed to the next largest subset, until they find a match.

This principle allows for some testable developmental predictions. If fixed word order is the default value, then children all over the world should begin their linguistic careers by producing utterances that adhere to strict word order. If their native language is English, this would produce word orders that are similar to English. But if their native language has a freer word order, it would produce undergeneration (failure to use all of the orders permissible in the language). If, instead, children use free word order as the default value, then overgeneration (production of impermissible word orders) would occur in English but not in a free-word-order language. These predictions are shown in Table 12-4.

According to Pinker (1990), the evidence is consistent with the notion that children use fixed word order as the default value and, therefore, with the subset principle. Children learning fixed-word-order languages generally stick to the orders used by their parents. Children learning free-word-order languages appear to use only some of the permissible orders of their language, at least in certain circumstances. Although more work needs to be done, the subset principle is a plausible account of how children deal with the tremendous number of possible languages they might consider.

The Issue of Negative Evidence

One important feature of the way in which the subset principle was formulated deals with the distinction between positive and negative evidence. At the grammatical level, positive evidence is evidence that a particular utterance is grammatical in the language that the child is learning; negative evidence is evidence that a particular utterance is ungrammatical. Children receive positive evidence when they are exposed to an utterance that is not corrected or otherwise indicated as inappropriate. Children receive negative evidence when someone indicates that a particular utterance is ungrammatical or inappropriate.

Pinker (1990) argues that it would be very difficult to acquire a language from positive evidence alone. This notion is based, in part, on some computer simulation studies of language learning done some time ago (see Gold, 1967). This work assumed that children use linguistic evidence to construct hypotheses about the language they are learning, much as a linguist would use such evidence to learn about a language in a foreign land. Gold found that when he wrote a program in which the computer received only positive evidence, it failed to acquire the language adequately. This was presumably because positive evidence is consistent with a great number of different grammars. Without knowing what is ungrammatical in a language, it is impossible to rule out some of the various competing grammars.

Pinker (1990) has claimed that, on the whole, parents do not provide sufficient negative evidence to enable a child to learn a language. He argues that although negative evidence is sometimes present, it is not systematically and consistently available to all children acquiring a language, and yet all normal children do acquire a language. Therefore, innate linguistic mechanisms, such as the subset principle, are needed to constrain the child's search processes. Pinker's argument is as follows:

A: Positive evidence alone is consistent with too many competing grammars.
B: Negative evidence, which could constrain the problem space, is not generally available.
C: Therefore, some constraints must be innate.

This is another form of the poverty of the stimulus argument, which we first encountered in Chapter 1. If we accept A, the argument rests on B. Let us then look at the research on negative evidence.

One often-cited study on this point was performed by Brown and Hanlon (1970), who examined parents' responses to various well- and ill-formed child utterances. The researchers were particularly interested in parents' explicit statements of approval and disapproval of child utterances. The parents in this study did little to correct their syntactic errors, although they sometimes corrected their children on semantic errors (that is, when the children's statements were not true). Brown and Hanlon conclude that there was not "even a shred of evidence that approval and disapproval are contingent on syntactic correctness" (p. 47).

These results have been replicated and extended by Hirsh-Pasek, Treiman, and Schneiderman (1984), who studied 40 mother-child dyads in which the children were 2 to 5 years old. They replicated Brown and Hanlon's results with regard to the relative absence of explicit approval and disapproval of child utterances. However, they also examined implicit parental responses, such as when the mother repeated a child utterance with corrected syntax. Hirsh-Pasek et al. found that these responses were more likely after an ill-formed child utterance than a well-formed child utterance, at least for the 2-year-olds. Thus, there are some subtle cues in parental responses to child speech that might assist children in acquiring language.

However, the results of this study are limited in several respects. First, there were no significant effects at 3 to 5 years, when children are acquiring many complex constructions that might conceivably be affected by parental input. Also, Hirsh-Pasek and her colleagues were careful to point out that although their results show that subtle cues are sometimes present, there is no evidence (yet) that children actually capitalize on these cues. We know from other studies (for example, McNeill, 1966) that children are not always receptive to adult observations about their grammar.

On balance, these results leave the force of the nativist argument largely intact. Although negative evidence is present and may assist language development, research has not shown that it is necessary. Language, under normal rearing conditions, is quite robust: children from even poor environments acquire a mastery of their native language. This contrast between the poverty of the stimulus and the robustness of the child's language remains the most sound justification for innate mechanisms.

Summary

Several lines of evidence have been presented to support the assumption of innate mechanisms in language acquisition. Studies of creole language suggest that we have a linguistic backup system, the language bioprogram, which springs into action when language input is limited. The bioprogram may be thought of as a specific instance of the general concept of parameter setting. Some evidence has been presented that child learners have initial preferences in the parameter settings, although this point has been disputed. Finally, the argument has been made that there is insufficient negative evidence for children to induce the grammar of their native language and that, therefore, some innate constraints must guide this process.

Review Questions

1. Distinguish between necessary and sufficient conditions.
2. Describe the case study of Genie, and summarize her language progress.
3. Identify phonological, syntactic, semantic, and pragmatic characteristics of motherese.
4. Why might maternal yes/no questions be related to the child's acquisition of verb auxiliaries?
5. Define and illustrate operating principles.
6. Define induction.
7. Summarize the research on object permanence and language development.

8. Distinguish between creoles and pidgins.
9. Give one example of parameter setting.
10. Discuss the issue of negative evidence in language acquisition and the evidence that is germane to it.

Thought Questions

1. Critically evaluate the view that Victor was abandoned because he was mentally retarded or autistic.
2. When discussing Slobin's operating principles, I commented that it is not clear that they are independent of language or apply to other cognitive domains. Can you think of any domains in which these principles might apply?
3. Based on all of the research discussed in this chapter, what can you conclude regarding whether environmental, cognitive, or innate factors are necessary or sufficient? Explain your answer.

Language in Perspective

Biological Foundations of Language

13

MAIN
POINTS

- Different language skills are represented in different parts of the brain. Individuals who have sustained brain damage often show deficits only in selected aspects of language.
- Studies of split-brain patients and normal individuals reveal that the left hemisphere of the brain controls language, especially syntactic processes and language production, for most people. The right hemisphere is essentially mute but plays a role in comprehension and in the pragmatic aspects of language.
- Studies of the evolution of language have examined hand preferences, brain specialization, and vocal tract specialization in nonhuman primates. Fossil records of vocal tract anatomy suggest that the capacity for speech is a recent evolutionary development.
- Although they do not use language in their natural environment, chimpanzees can be taught sign language. The degree of similarity between chimpanzee language and child language is a matter of considerable debate.

Introduction

Throughout this text, we have examined language from a psycholinguistic viewpoint—how individuals comprehend, produce, and acquire language. In these last two chapters, I will attempt to place these processes in a broader perspective. In this chapter, we will examine language processes from a biological viewpoint. In Chapter 14, we will look at language as a cultural phenomenon.

From a biological perspective, language has been regarded as special in the sense that it is a dividing line between humans and other species. The emergence of language occurred only recently in our evolutionary history, and the set of forces that led to this extraordinary development is not yet clear. We do know that part of the story concerns the evolution of brain mechanisms specialized for language functions. Language behavior, like all behavior, is mediated by brain structures, but because language is extremely subtle and multifaceted, it has a particularly complex representation in the brain. Although speculation about the brain has been going on for centuries, scientific knowledge about the brain and language has only accumulated in the last century or so.

It is important to know about the biology of language for two reasons. First, the study of brain regions related to language clarifies our previous discussion of language comprehension and production. We will learn that various aspects of our language capacity are not mere abstractions but rather have separate and specifiable representations in the brain. Second, the study of the biological foundations of language extends our discussion of language acquisition. If specialized brain mechanisms enable children to acquire language, then how much language is possible in species such as nonhuman primates that lack these mechanisms?

This chapter is organized into three sections. In the first section, we look into cases of individuals who have suffered damage to the language regions of the brain. The second section addresses the nature of hemisphere differences in language and other functions, first with respect to human brains and later with respect to animals. The chapter concludes with a section that speculates on the evolutionary pressures that led to human language and assesses the studies that have attempted to teach language to chimpanzees.

Brain Mechanisms and Language

Some of the most significant insights into the biological foundations of language have come from individuals who have suffered damage to portions of the brain regions associated with language functions. These unfortunate individuals typically display uneven patterns of language behavior, with some functions spared and others dramatically impaired or even eliminated. A language disorder produced by brain damage is called an **aphasia.** As you might imagine, these "experiments of nature" vary tremendously in terms of the exact site of the brain damage and the corresponding behavioral patterns. Nevertheless, we begin by examining some of the more common types of aphasia.

Clinical Descriptions of Aphasia

Broca's aphasia   The disorder **Broca's aphasia,** also known as **expressive aphasia,** was discovered by and named after the French surgeon Paul Broca. Broca studied individuals who, after a stroke or accident, were often unable to express themselves by more than a single word at a time. Although nouns and verbs were usually well preserved, they tended to omit articles, conjunctions, and grammatical inflections. This pattern of speech is referred to as **agrammatic speech** and is revealed in the following excerpt, in which a patient is attempting to explain that he came to the hospital for dental surgery:

> Yes . . . ah . . . Monday . . . er . . . Dad and Peter H . . . (his own name), and Dad . . . er . . . hospital . . . and ah . . . Wednesday . . . Wednesday, nine o'clock . . . and oh . . . Thursday . . . ten o'clock, ah doctors . . . two . . . an' doctors . . . and er . . . teeth . . . yah. (Goodglass & Geschwind, 1976, p. 408)

In contrast, the individuals' ability to comprehend language appears to be less impaired than that of producing it.

The clear difficulty in articulating speech by Broca's aphasics might lead us to believe that its agrammatic nature is due to a voluntary economy of effort. That is, since articulation is so difficult—they speak slowly and often confuse related sounds—perhaps Broca's aphasics are trying to save effort by expressing only the most important words. Although this factor may have some role in the disorder, it is not the most important feature since many Broca's aphasics do no better after repeated efforts at self-correction. Moreover, the writing of these patients is usually at least as impaired as their speech, and individual words out of grammatical context are usually spared. These considerations suggest that the main feature of this disorder is the loss of the ability to express grammatical relationships, either in speech or in writing.

This pattern of deficits is usually found in individuals who have sustained damage to the frontal regions of the left hemisphere of the brain. Figure 13-1 shows some of the main functional areas of the cerebral hemispheres; this is a view of the left side (hemisphere). As you can see, the visual centers lie at the back of the brain in what is called the **occipital lobe.** The auditory regions in both hemispheres lie at the sides of the brain known as the **temporal lobes.** Motor centers controlling facial and speech muscles are located in the middle region of the brain, called the **parietal lobe,** with different points corresponding to different muscle groups. The **somatosensory regions,** which mediate our sense of touch, are also located in the parietal lobe, just behind the motor areas.

Figure 13-2 shows some of the areas specifically related to language functions. **Broca's area** is adjacent to the motor cortex and part of the frontal lobe, which is intimately involved in processes such as thought, reasoning, judgment, and initiative. In recent years, we have learned that the brain regions involved in Broca's aphasia are somewhat larger than those initially identified by Broca and accepted over the years (Naeser, Palumbo, Helm-Estabrooks, Stiassny-Eder, & Albert, 1989). Nonetheless, the important point for our purpose is that this somewhat larger Broca's area is distinguishable from brain regions serving other language functions.

Wernicke's aphasia   A few years after Broca's discovery, a young surgeon named Carl Wernicke discovered a different form of aphasia. It results from damage to a region in the left temporal lobe near the auditory cortex. This region is now called **Wernicke's area** (Figure 13-2). **Wernicke's aphasia,** which is sometimes called **receptive aphasia,** is associated with speech that is fluent but of no informational value, which is known as **paragrammatic speech.** Here is an example:

Figure 13-1.   Location of the primary motor and sensory regions on the cortex; M = motor, S = somatosensory, V = visual, and A = auditory. (Based on "Language Disorders [Aphasia]," by H. Goodglass and N. Geschwind. In E. C. Carterette and M. P. Friedman [Eds.], *Handbook of Perception. Vol. 7: Language and Speech,* p. 392, Academic Press, 1976.)

Figure 13-2.   Location of the principal language areas on the cortex; B = Broca's area, W = Wernicke's area, and AG = angular gyrus. (Based on "Language Disorders [Aphasia]," by H. Goodglass and N. Geschwind. In E. C. Carterette and M. P. Friedman [Eds.], *Handbook of Perception. Vol. 7: Language and Speech*, p. 393, Academic Press, 1976.)

Well this is . . . mother is away here working her work out o' here to get her better, but when she's looking, the two boys looking in the other part. One their small tile into her time here. She's working another time because she's getting, too. (Goodglass & Geschwind, 1976, p. 410)

Moreover, comprehension is also impaired. It is interesting to note, however, that Wernicke's aphasics appear to perceive phonemes in a manner similar to normal individuals (Blumstein, Baker, & Goodglass, 1977), and they also show evidence of semantic priming (Blumstein, Milberg, & Shrier, 1982; Milberg & Blumstein, 1981). This would suggest that sentence- and/or discourse-level processing deficits might figure into the comprehension problems of Wernicke's aphasics.

Both Broca's and Wernicke's aphasia are associated with deficits in the hand gestures that typically accompany speech, but in different ways. Two kinds of gestures appear in normal speech—those that refer to some aspect of the content of the conversation and those that appear to be more interactive in nature (McNeill, 1985; Bavelas, Chovil, Lawrie, & Wade, 1992). An example of the former type, a **referential gesture,** would be to raise one's hand and point upward to signify upward movement. An illustration of an **interactive gesture** is putting one's hand up as a means of indicating that one's turn is not finished. Broca's aphasics tend to have impairments in the second type of gesture; Wernicke's aphasics have more problem with the first type (Ciccone, Wapner, Foldi, Zurif, & Gardner, 1979).

Much of our knowledge of the brain mechanisms involved in language has come from postmortem examinations of brains of aphasic patients. Recently these clinical descriptions of aphasia have been complemented by techniques that enable investigators to view images of brain activity in living individuals, including normal individuals. One type of imaging technique is called **functional magnetic**

resonance imaging (fMRI); it is called functional because it provides a view not only of brain structures but also brain activity.

Some examples of fMRI scans are shown in Figure 13-3. The top left fMRI scan (a) shows a normal individual engaged in an object-naming task, in which the individual sees a picture of an object such as a house and is asked to name it. Notice the large black area of activation near the top left side of the brain; this is Broca's area. In (b) we see an fMRI scan of a normal individual doing a sentence comprehension task: listening to a pair of sentences and deciding whether they have the

(a)   (b)

(c)   (d)

Figure 13-3.   Functional magnetic resonance image (fMRI) scans of normal individuals and patients with tumors. (Courtesy of Dr. Susan Bookheimer, UCLA School of Medicine, Brain Mapping Division.)

same meaning. Wernicke's area is the black blob on the left side of the brain, farther down than Broca's area.

The lower panel of Figure 13-3 shows fMRI scans of one patient with a tumor in Broca's area (c) and another with a tumor in Wernicke's area (d). Both suffered a sudden loss of language abilities as the tumors grew. Note how the brain activity differs, relative to normal individuals: there is less brain activation in Broca's and Wernicke's areas on the left side of the brain but more on the right, especially in Wernicke's area. Thus, as primary language regions are injured, other regions of the brain may take over some language functions, with varying degrees of success.

Conduction aphasia   A third major type of aphasia is **conduction aphasia,** which is a disturbance of repetition. Individuals with conduction aphasia appear to be able to understand and produce speech but have difficulty in repeating what they have heard. Geschwind (1965) attributes this form of aphasia to a disconnection between Broca's and Wernicke's areas, although other interpretations are possible (Damasio & Damasio, 1989).

Other aphasias   The impression that we get when reading about such cases is that our language functions may often be broken down quite selectively, with comprehension damage and not production damage, or just the opposite. The literature on aphasia contains a rich variety of cases, many of which are baffling, but most of which fit this impression of discrete, separable language functions. Some of these language disturbances, although rare, are of great importance in enabling us to construct a model of normal language functioning.

One rare form of aphasia is called **pure word deafness.** Behaviorally, such individuals are unable to comprehend language in the auditory modality, although they are still capable of comprehending visual language and producing language in either modality. Anatomically, there is damage to the auditory nerve, which sends messages to the auditory centers in the left hemisphere. In addition, there is a loss of those portions of the **corpus callosum** (the thick band of fibers that connect the two hemispheres) that send messages from the auditory region in the right hemisphere to the language areas, particularly Wernicke's area, in the left hemisphere. The result is that neither the left nor the right auditory center can transmit information to the language regions, so even though patients can hear some words, they cannot comprehend them.

Another interesting form of aphasia is called **alexia,** which is the dissociation (disconnection) of the visual regions from the language areas. In its most severe form, alexia prevents even the recognition of individual letters or matching of script and print (Goodglass & Geschwind, 1976). Damage to the angular gyrus leads to both alexia and **agraphia,** the inability to write. It is thought that the **angular gyrus** serves as an association area in the brain that connects one region with another. In particular, it is important for the association of visual stimuli with linguistic symbols, which influences both reading and writing. Alexia also sometimes occurs without agraphia; in one case (Dejerine, 1892, cited in Geschwind, 1965), damage to the visual cortex on the left side was coupled with an injury to the portion of the corpus callosum that connected an intact right visual area with the language areas on the

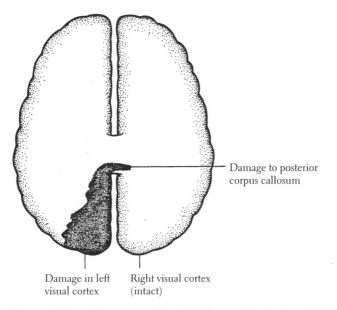

Damage to posterior
corpus callosum

Damage in left   Right visual cortex
visual cortex   (intact)

Figure 13-4.   The pattern of cerebral damage in a patient who had alexia without agraphia. (Based on *Physiological Psychology*, by T. S. Brown and P. M. Wallace, p. 535, Academic Press, 1980).

left (Figure 13-4). Thus, visual stimuli are isolated from Wernicke's area, so that affected individuals can write but cannot read what they have written (Benson & Geschwind, 1969)!

Again, the aphasias just described are rare. The main types are shown in Table 13-1. Although there is general agreement on many of these aphasias, controversy also persists over many aspects of the classification of aphasias (for example, Caramazza, 1984). As Goodglass (1993) has pointed out, most aphasic patients are impaired in many aspects of language, so that what distinguishes one type from another is the relative impairment in various linguistic functions.

Geschwind's Model of Language Processing

Soon after Broca and Wernicke made their discoveries, turn-of-the-century neurologists such as Ludwig Lichtheim (see the discussion in Goodglass, 1993) began to develop diagrams of the information flow in the brain. A modern version of this approach was presented by Geschwind (1972), who organized many of the available facts on aphasia and formulated a general model of normal language functioning. The proposal is shown in Figure 13-5.

Consider a simple situation in which we see something and then make a verbal comment about it. According to the model, the visual input is first sent to the visual regions of the brain and then to the angular gyrus. The message then goes to

Table 13-1. Major Aphasic Syndromes

Syndrome	Behavioral Deficit	Lesion Site(s)
Broca's aphasia	Disturbance of speech production; agrammatic speech; relatively good comprehension and naming	Frontal lobe adjacent to primary motor cortex
Wernicke's aphasia	Disturbance in auditory comprehension; fluent speech	Posterior portion of first temporal gyrus
Conduction aphasia	Disturbance of repetition and spontaneous speech	Lesion in arcuate fasciculus and/or other connections between frontal and temporal lobes
Transcortical sensory aphasia	Disturbance of single word comprehension with relatively intact repetition	Connections between parietal and temporal lobes
Transcortical motor aphasia	Disturbance of spontaneous speech, with sparing of naming	Subcortical lesions in areas underlying motor cortex
Anomic aphasia	Disturbance of production of single words	Various parts of parietal and temporal lobes
Global aphasia	Major disturbance in all language functions	Large portions of association cortex

Sources: From "Language and the Brain," by D. Caplan. In M. A. Gernsbacher (Ed.), *Handbook of Psycholinguistics*, pp. 1023–1053, Academic Press, 1994; and *Understanding Aphasia*, by H. Goodglass, Academic Press, 1993.

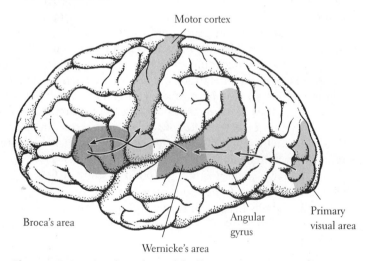

Figure 13-5. Geschwind's model of language processing. (Based on *Images of Mind*, by M. I. Posner and M. E. Raichle, p. 108. Copyright © Scientific American Library. Reprinted by permission.)

Wernicke's area, which creates a meaningful sequence of linguistic units and transmits it to Broca's area via the **arcuate fasciculus,** the primary pathway between the two areas. In Broca's area, the message is translated into motor commands that are sent to the speech muscles and finally articulated. If we felt a stimulus instead of seeing it, the sequence would begin in the somatosensory regions, go to the angular gyrus, and then to Wernicke's and Broca's areas. In a conversation, auditory input is transmitted to the auditory regions, then on to Wernicke's and Broca's areas.

Let us see whether this model illuminates our understanding of aphasic language. Injury to Broca's area presumably would lead to halting, agrammatic speech characteristic of such patients because of a disruption in the process of translating sequences into motor commands but would leave comprehension intact. Injury to Wernicke's area would presumably disrupt comprehension mainly, but if the arcuate fasciculus and Broca's area were intact, the patient would speak fluently but in a manner that would be informationally empty. If only the arcuate fasciculus were damaged, the behavioral deficit for the patient would be in relating what she heard to what she should say, which shows up as conduction aphasia. In each of these cases, the model does a good job of explaining some of the major clinical impressions of aphasic language.

Experimental Studies of Aphasia

Let us now look at psycholinguistic research that has clarified the role of syntactic and semantic processes in various aphasias. The traditional view has been that Broca's or agrammatic aphasia is a production deficit and Wernicke's a comprehension deficit. The implicit assumption is that the underlying language representation is intact with Broca's patients but that they have difficulty putting appropriately formulated linguistic messages into words. That is, they conceptualize sentences normally but have difficulty translating them into productive speech.

Clearly, data regarding the comprehension abilities of Broca's aphasics would be extremely useful here. Broca's aphasics have often been viewed as having normal comprehension, but we have good reasons for questioning this assumption. For one, many of the tests of comprehension have been extremely global in nature and do not clarify the respective roles of syntactic and semantic processes in comprehension. For another, it is possible to disguise deficits in comprehension somewhat more easily than deficits in production.

The latter point was brought out in a study by Caramazza and Zurif (1976), who examined comprehension capacities in Broca's, Wernicke's, and conduction aphasics. Patients heard a sentence and then had to choose which of two pictures corresponded to the sentence. Some sentences, such as (1), contained nouns that are nonreversible:

(1) The book that the girl is reading is yellow.

Here, knowing that girls read books but not vice versa is sufficient to understand the sentence correctly. In contrast, in a sentence such as (2), it is semantically possible for either the horse or the bear to be doing the kicking:

(2) The horse that the bear is kicking is brown.

In reversible sentences, we must process the syntactic structure carefully to arrive at the correct interpretation.

How did the three aphasic groups fare on this test? Wernicke's aphasics did poorly on both types of sentences, in agreement with their known difficulties with comprehension. More interestingly, both Broca's aphasics and conduction aphasics performed very well on nonreversible sentences, but their performance fell to chance levels on the reversible sentences. These results suggest that both groups suffer from subtle syntactic deficits in comprehension that are revealed once semantic cues are eliminated. Caramazza and Zurif suggest that Broca's area may be necessary to perform some syntactic operations; syntactic deficits may thus appear in conduction aphasics as a result of the dissociation of Wernicke's and Broca's areas.

Our understanding of syntactic ability in Broca's aphasics has been sharpened further by a report by Linebarger, Schwartz, and Saffran (1983). They gave four Broca's patients a series of sentences and asked them to judge whether the sentences were grammatical or not. Overall, the patients did surprisingly well. Their performance was particularly good on structurally deformed sentences such as (3). However, they were less adept at recognizing the unacceptability of sentences with an inappropriate pronoun, such as (4).

(3)   *How many did you see birds in the park?

(4)   *The little boy fell down, didn't it?

These results suggest that Broca's aphasics may have greater knowledge of syntax than we had been led to believe. Why, then, did Broca's aphasics do so poorly on the Caramazza-Zurif task? It may be that they can reach this level of syntactic understanding only when given the luxury of time afforded in the acceptability task and that they cannot compute syntactic representations quickly enough to help in normal comprehension.

This hypothesis has been supported in some intriguing research reported by Swinney, Zurif, and their colleagues. Zurif, Swinney, Prather, Solomon, and Bushell (1993) investigated the ability of Broca's and Wernicke's patients to comprehend subject relative clauses, such as (5). In linguistic theory (Chomsky, 1981; Grodzinsky, 1990), this sentence is derived from two simpler sentences to which a movement transformation has been applied; *professor* has been moved, and *who* is called its trace. In processing terms, *who* implicitly refers to *professor* and thus comprehenders must reactivate *professor* to understand *who* and the complete sentence.

(5)   The gymnast loved the professor from the northwestern city who complained about the bad coffee.

To study comprehension of this structure, Zurif et al. used a cross-modal lexical priming task (discussed in Chapter 5) in which individuals listened to a sentence over earphones while simultaneously performing a lexical decision task on letter strings that were presented visually. Some of the words (for example, *teacher*) in the lexical decision task were semantically related to the moved noun and others were not. If the trace caused comprehenders to reactivate the antecedent noun (*professor*), then a semantically related word (*teacher*) should be primed and thus receive a faster lexical decision time. And this is exactly what happened for the Wernicke's patients. But the Broca's patients showed no priming effect.

Zurif et al. (1993) assert that the problem for Broca's patients is that they are unable to activate words quickly enough to use them in normal comprehension. Indeed, Broca's patients do show automatic spreading activation similar to that shown in individuals without brain damage, but the activation is slower than normal (Prather, Zurif, Stern, & Rosen, 1992). Thus, the difficulties Broca's aphasics have with sentences such as (5) is that they cannot activate the moved noun quickly enough to appropriately interpret the subsequent pronoun. As a consequence, their comprehension as a whole suffers.

These subtle syntactic deficits appear to be the basis for some of the processing strategies that Broca's patients use. Consider sentences (6) and (7). Broca's patients comprehend (6) but not (7). When Broca's aphasics fail to understand sentences such as (7), however, their errors are not random. Rather, they apply a strategy in which the first noun is treated as the agent of the sentence (Zurif, 1995). This strategy is similar to the ways in which preschoolers comprehend passive sentences (discussed in Chapter 12). The strategy does not work for (6) but will for (7). Thus, Broca's patients resort to a simple strategy that leads to poor performance on these sentences, presumably due to their inability to rapidly analyze the syntactic structure of the sentences.

(6) It was the girl who chased the boy.

(7) It was the boy whom the girl chased.

Implications for Understanding Normal Language Processing

How well does aphasic language illuminate normal language? One way to approach the issue is to examine whether the distinctions we were compelled to draw when discussing normal language are the same ones that we observe in aphasic cases.

For example, a major distinction in the study of normal language processing is between comprehending language and producing it. If this is not merely a conceptual distinction but also biologically based, then we would expect to see some aphasic cases in which comprehension is impaired but production is spared, and vice versa. The initial descriptions of Broca's and Wernicke's aphasias support this distinction. Although there are more subtle differences between these two cases, the comprehension-production distinction appears beyond dispute. Thus, in this instance the studies of aphasia support our distinction.

There is also neurological evidence for the distinction between open- and closed-class words, which we first encountered in Chapter 5. Recall that in normal speakers the speed of retrieval of open-class words (such as nouns and verbs) is related to their frequency but that retrieval of closed-class words (such as grammatical morphemes and function words) is not influenced by frequency. In contrast, agrammatic patients show frequency sensitivity on both classes of words (Bradley, Garrett, & Zurif, 1980). Thus, agrammatic patients have a selective deficit in accessing closed-class words.

In some other respects, aphasic language poses challenges to our conception of language. For one, some aphasics display **category-specific dissociations** in which they selectively lose the ability to grasp certain types of words but understand and use other word categories. For example, some patients have little difficulty in naming colors and body parts but considerable trouble in naming fruits and vegetables (Hart, Berndt, & Caramazza, 1985; see also Goodglass, Klein, Carey, & Jones, 1966). Some have difficulty with a given category only in one modality (for example, auditory) but can access the category in another (such as visual) (Goodglass, 1993). These are not distinctions that have figured largely in conceptions of the internal lexicon (as discussed in Chapter 5). Nevertheless, if brain damage can selectively disrupt certain categories of words, it suggests that there is a neurological validity to the distinction.

Another intriguing aspect of aphasic language is the sparing of comprehension of axial commands in individuals with Wernicke's aphasia. Although Wernicke's aphasics show many problems in language comprehension, they respond correctly to commands involving midline or axial structures, such as *stand up, turn around, take a bow,* and *look up* (Geschwind, 1965). For example, patients perform accurately when asked to *Stand like a boxer* or even *Take two steps backward, turn around, and sit down again.* What is especially striking is that axial commands sometimes involve specific nouns or verbs that these patients ordinarily fail to comprehend.

We obviously have much more to learn about language in individuals with various forms of aphasia. What we have learned to date has in some cases nicely meshed with the distinctions we have been using. But some aspects of aphasic language do not fit neatly into psycholinguistic theories, as currently construed.

*S*ummary

The data from aphasic cases are important in psycholinguistics because they demonstrate dissociations between various linguistic functions that would be difficult if not impossible to find in other ways. There was no reason to think that a person would be able to write without being able to read or be able to understand animal words but not food words before these cases were reported.

Current research reveals at least three major types of aphasia. Broca's aphasia results from damage to a region in the left hemisphere near the motor cortex and leads to deficits in language production and syntactic analysis. Wernicke's aphasia is due to injury to an area adjacent to the auditory cortex in the left hemisphere and is associated with deficits in comprehension and semantic organization. Conduction aphasia results from dissociation of an intact Broca's area from an intact Wernicke's area and leads to a deficit in repetition. Thus, the distinctions noted throughout this book between comprehension and production and between syntax and semantics are not mere conceptual distinctions but relate in specifiable ways to the organization of the brain.

Lateralization of Language Processes

There has been a great deal of interest in the functions of the left and right hemi-spheres of the brain in recent decades, and part of that interest extends to the lateralization of language functioning. The term **lateralization** refers to the ten-dency for a given psychological function to be served by one hemisphere, with the other hemisphere either incapable or less capable of performing the function. We will begin by discussing individuals who have had a "split-brain" operation, then turn to normal individuals, and finally to lateralization in animals.

Split-Brain Research

A consistent finding in the research on aphasia was that language deficits are asso-ciated with damage to the left hemisphere of the brain more often than to the right hemisphere. Moreover, we have known for some time, from studies of animals, that communication between the hemispheres may be disrupted by severing the corpus callosum. In the animal studies, one hemisphere could be taught a specific task, then the other hemisphere could be tested. Typically, little or no learning was found in the other hemisphere, indicating little or no transfer of information between the hemispheres following severing of the corpus callosum.

In the 1940s, these two lines of research converged in a dramatic way with the emergence of the split-brain operation. In this operation, human patients had their corpus callosum severed as a means of preventing the spread of epilepsy from one side of the brain to the other. The earliest reports (see Springer & Deutsch, 1989) gave little indication of what was to come. The patients' everyday behavior was virtually unaffected, and postsurgical testing revealed no obvious deficits. The sur-gery, by the way, produced relief from epileptic seizures in some patients but not others.

In the next two decades, more sophisticated and subtle research methods began to tell a far different story. To understand these studies, you must know some anatomical details of the two hemispheres. Figure 13-6 shows the visual pathways to the brain. Notice that the left visual field sends information to a portion of each retina in such a way that the information ultimately ends up in the right hemisphere. With an intact corpus callosum, this information then crosses over to the left hemi-sphere. Similarly, information from the right visual field projects to the left hemi-sphere. Information in the middle of the visual field projects to both hemispheres.

Similar arrangements exist in the auditory and tactile systems. The nervous system in humans is predominantly **contralateral,** which means that one half of the brain controls the other half of the body. This contralateral structure allows investi-gators to test more precisely the functions of the two hemispheres in the split-brain patient by presenting stimuli to just one side of the brain and observing the resulting behavior. The goal of these studies is to determine what skills are lateralized to one or the other side of the brain.

We are now in position to examine some of the studies of split-brain patients. In one, a patient was shown a picture of a spoon in her left visual field and was asked

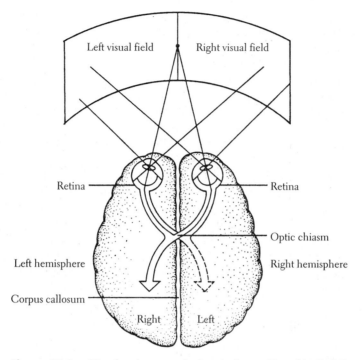

Figure 13-6. Visual pathways to the hemispheres. (Based on *Left Brain, Right Brain,* Third Edition, by S. P. Springer and G. Deutsch, p. 35, W. H. Freeman, 1989.)

what she saw. She replied, *No, nothing.* Then she was asked to select with her left hand the object from an array that was out of sight, and she correctly picked out the spoon from a group of common objects. When asked what she was holding, she responded, *Nothing.* When asked to reach for the object with her right hand, she performed at a chance level, as likely to pick up a straw or a pencil as a spoon (Sperry, 1968).

These results may be interpreted in light of the way information gets processed by the two hemispheres. When a stimulus is presented to the left visual field, the right hemisphere of a split-brain patient becomes aware of the stimulus and is able to communicate that awareness in nonverbal ways, such as grabbing an object with the left hand, which is controlled by the right hemisphere. Since speech is predominantly controlled by the left hemisphere, the patient is unable to describe what she has seen. Moreover, the right hand is incompetent to find the correct object because the left hemisphere does not "know" what the object is.

Although the right hemisphere has a limited ability to perform language skills, it is more skilled at tasks that require spatial analysis. In one study, patients viewed line drawings of shapes such as triangles and squares that had been cut up into pieces. They had to reach behind a screen, feel three solid forms, and determine the ones that the fragmented figure would make if its pieces were reunited. The left hand proved to be very accurate at this task, but the right hand performed poorly

(Nebes, 1972). This task requires the patient to construct a concept of a whole stimulus from its parts, a skill at which the right hemisphere excels. Related studies have shown that the right hemisphere is better than the left hemisphere in tasks that require the understanding and manipulation of spatial relationships, such as drawing (Gazzaniga & LeDoux, 1978) and dealing with geometric arrays (Franco & Sperry, 1977), although the left hemisphere is better at some complex visual tasks that require strategic attention (Kingstone, Enns, Mangun, & Gazzaniga, 1995).

Returning to language in the right hemisphere, several studies have clarified the nature of right-hemisphere language skills. It is clear that certain aspects of language are better represented in the right hemisphere than others. Gazzaniga and Hillyard (1971) presented split-brain patients with simple pictures depicting visual scenes. After the scene, the subject was auditorily presented with two sentences and asked which one correctly described the picture. On this test, the patients proved to be incapable of distinguishing between sentences (8) and (9). Further testing revealed that these subjects could not deal properly with the future tense by distinguishing between sentences (10) and (11) or with the difference between singular and plural nouns in sentences (12) and (13). The single grammatical feature they dealt with properly was that of affirmative versus negative sentences as in (14) and (15):

(8)   The boy kisses the girl.
(9)   The girl kisses the boy.
(10) The girl is drinking.
(11) The girl will drink.
(12) The dog jumps over the fence.
(13) The dogs jump over the fence.
(14) The girl is sitting.
(15) The girl is not sitting.

These results are even more impressive when compared with the generally successful performance of these subjects on tests that required only comprehension of a single noun. That is, they correctly responded to *boy* and *girl*. In contrast, there was little or no evidence that the subjects could respond properly to verbs; when presented with verbal commands, such as *tap*, *smile*, and *frown*, the patients remained mute. It appears that the right hemisphere has, at best, very rudimentary syntactic mechanisms but that the mechanisms needed to retrieve single words from semantic memory are much better developed.

In addition to syntactic deficits relative to the left hemisphere, the right hemisphere also shows phonetic deficits. The right hemisphere may be capable of matching the sounds of words, as complete auditory images, to meanings but is deficient in the phonetic analysis of these sounds. For example, the right hemisphere might comprehend the meanings of *ache* and *lake* without knowing that they rhyme (Levy, 1974).

Reports on split-brain patients have also shown that the right hemisphere, although it may possess some abilities to comprehend language, is seriously deficient in language production (Gazzaniga & Sperry, 1967). However, aphasic patients with damage to the left hemisphere also experience difficulty in naming nonverbal oral movements such as retracting the lips, clenching the teeth, and protruding the lips (Mateer & Kimura, 1977). It may be that the left hemisphere is specialized to perform sequences of motor acts, especially those involving the tongue and jaw, but that such motor specialization is not specific to language production (Corballis, 1980; Sussman & MacNeilage, 1975).

The emerging picture of right-hemisphere language is that it is organized along different cognitive lines than left-hemisphere language. The right hemisphere is weak in syntactic and expressive skills, but less so in terms of semantic processes and comprehension. As Zaidel (1978) puts it:

> The LH [left hemisphere], in accordance with Chomsky's view, does seem to possess an innate and highly specialized linguistic mechanism whose paradigmatic functions are phonetic and syntactic encoding and analysis. The RH [right hemisphere], on the other hand, represents the limited linguistic competence that can be acquired by a more general purpose (nonlinguistic) cognitive apparatus through repeated exposure to experience and the formation of associations. (p. 196)

Lateralization in Normal Brains

Research on the representation of language and nonverbal functions in the intact brain has increased dramatically in the last few decades as techniques for studying the normal brain have been developed and refined. The **visual field task** used with split-brain patients has also been used frequently with normal individuals. Another commonly used technique, referred to as a **dichotic listening task,** involves the simultaneous presentation of different stimuli to the two ears. Initially developed by Broadbent (1954) to study attention, the technique was first used by Kimura (1961) to examine ear and hemisphere differences. Kimura (1964) found that recall of verbally presented materials such as digits was superior in the right ear and that recognition of nonverbal stimuli such as melodies was better in the left ear.

The anatomical details of the auditory system are similar to, but somewhat more complex than, those of the visual system. Specifically, input from the right ear not only projects to the left hemisphere (the contralateral pathway) but also to the right hemisphere (the **ipsalateral** pathway). To account for dichotic listening results, Kimura proposed that the contralateral pathways are stronger than the ipsalateral connections and that under the competing conditions of dichotic presentations, the former "block" the latter. Dichotic studies of split-brain patients indicate highly exaggerated right-ear advantages for speech stimuli: normal performance by the right ear with chance performance by the left ear. The failure of the left ear is due to two factors. First, the contralateral pathway (left ear to right hemisphere) is not helpful since the corpus callosum is not present to facilitate transfer to the left hemisphere. Second, the ipsalateral pathway (left ear to left hemisphere) is blocked or suppressed by the contralateral pathway. Thus, the left ear does poorly on this task. Kimura's model of performance under dichotic listening conditions with speech and nonspeech stimuli appears to fit both normal and split-brain data.

Nevertheless, the distinction between linguistic and nonverbal stimuli is unsatisfactory as a basis for predicting which hemisphere will control processing. One reason is that these terms are vague and imprecise; it is unclear what features of linguistic or nonlinguistic stimuli are important in influencing hemispheric control. As an example, studies of dichotic listening have been extended in an important way to nonmeaningful speech. Shankweiler and Studdert-Kennedy (1967) found right-ear advantages with nonsense syllables such as *ba* and *pa* played backward. Similarly, Zurif and Sait (1970) found a right-ear advantage for nonsense words, but only when they were arranged in a syntactically acceptable manner, as in *The wak jug shendily.* It appears that meaning is not necessary to elicit left-hemispheric processing of speech stimuli.

Conversely, sometimes right-ear advantages fail to occur with speech stimuli on dichotic tasks. The most prominent case is the failure to find right-ear advantages for vowels, although results for consonants have been found consistently (see, for example, Shankweiler & Studdert-Kennedy, 1967). It has been suggested (Darwin, 1973) that this difference is due to the greater length of vowels than consonants, since it is known that the degree of ipsalateral suppression is greater for shorter sounds than for longer ones.

Even more striking are cases in which linguistic stimuli that typically evoke right-ear advantages occasionally produce left-ear advantages. A case in point is a study by Darwin (1969, cited in Darwin, 1973) in which the subjects had to make judgments about pitch contours presented dichotically. They had to decide which two of four patterns—rising, falling, rising then falling, or falling then rising—had occurred. The subjects demonstrated a left-ear advantage for these stimuli, even when the contours amounted to a word. Darwin concludes that right-ear advantages are not invariably associated with linguistic stimuli. Specifically, they do not occur if the task is not linguistically significant.

Wood (1975) has replicated and extended this result, measuring both reaction time and **evoked potentials,** the electrical activity of the brain immediately after the presentation of a stimulus. When the task was nonlinguistic (subjects had to make a judgment about the pitch of a speech sound), greater right-hemisphere activity was found. However, when the task was linguistic (to recognize the sound), the evoked potential was greater in the left hemisphere. Moreover, the linguistic task led to longer reaction times. Since the stimuli were identical in the two conditions, this result shows clearly that the stimulus factors alone are insufficient to determine hemispheric processing.

Bever (1980) has argued that the left hemisphere prefers to process information in a relational manner, whereas the right hemisphere uses a holistic mode of processing. **Holistic processing** involves the activation of a single mental representation of a stimulus; **relational processing** involves the activation of at least two distinct representations along with some relation between the two. An example might be listening to music. We can listen expansively to a piece of classical music, simply being moved by the music. Alternatively, we can attend to the same piece in a more relational (or analytic) manner, identifying different portions of the composition and the relations between them.

If this view is correct, then we ought to see some right-ear advantages for nonspeech stimuli when processed in a relational manner. Indeed, Bever and Chiarello (1974) found right-ear advantages on musical tasks for experienced musicians but not for nonmusicians. According to Bever, experienced musicians have developed relational processing strategies for organizing musical stimuli that are not available to the novice. Consistent with this interpretation, no differences have been found between the left ears of musicians and nonmusicians; the greater right-ear advantages for musical stimuli in musicians are due to the improved performance of their right ears.

Further support for the processing distinction between the hemispheres comes from studies of deaf individuals who had suffered strokes. Poizner, Klima, and Bellugi (1987) studied deaf persons who suffered strokes to either the right or the left hemisphere. These individuals' cases raise an interesting question. If we regard the left hemisphere as specialized for language and the right hemisphere for spatial skills, then where would we expect to find the brain mechanisms for American Sign Language, which is a spatial language? According to Poizner et al., deaf signers have their language skills in the left hemisphere. If the left hemisphere is damaged by a stroke, these individuals have impairments in language function similar to aphasic patients, but their nonlinguistic spatial skills (drawing, painting, and so on) are spared. If the right hemisphere is injured, nonlinguistic spatial skills are severely disrupted, but ASL remains intact.

Furthermore, Poizner et al. (1987) found that the regions in the left hemisphere associated with language use in ASL are similar (although not identical) to those for speech. One patient who suffered a stroke that included Broca's area displayed halting, agrammatic signing. Another, who suffered damage to Wernicke's area, had difficulty with comprehension and displayed paragrammatic language.

The distinction between relational and holistic processing appears to provide a good account for all of these results. When stimuli are processed in a relational nature, the left hemisphere assumes control. This is typically the case in language processing (including the processing of a spatial language) and may occur in some individuals with nonspeech stimuli such as music. In contrast, when stimuli are processed holistically, the right hemisphere prevails. This is ordinarily the case for nonlinguistic spatial stimuli and, for most people, musical stimuli.

Contributions of the Right Hemisphere

So far I have emphasized the talents of the left hemisphere and the ineptness of the right hemisphere. However, the right hemisphere also has some talents in the linguistic realm. Normal individuals use the skills of both hemispheres to comprehend and produce language, so we need to examine some of the ways that the two hemispheres interact during language use.

It appears that the right hemisphere is better prepared than the left to appreciate some of the pragmatic aspects of language. Kaplan, Brownell, Jacobs, and Gardner (1990) examined the ability of individuals with right-hemisphere brain damage to interpret conversational remarks. The subjects heard short vignettes that described the performance of one character and the relationship between two characters and then interpreted an utterance from one of the characters. Some of the utterances were literally true and some were literally false. For instance, in one vignette, Mark was playing golf poorly, and Hal said, *You sure are a good golfer,* which was literally false. The interpretation of this utterance is in part based on the relationship between the two men. When it was friendly, the comment might be taken as a white lie intended to encourage a friend, but when the relationship was hostile, it could be taken as a sarcastic statement. Kaplan et al. found that individuals with right-hemisphere damage were as adept as control subjects in interpreting the literally true sentences but were poorer at identifying the pragmatic intent of literally false utterances. In particular, they had difficulty integrating information about the performance with information about the characters' relationship.

Bihrle, Brownell, Powelson, and Gardner (1986) examined comprehension of humorous material by individuals with right- or left-hemisphere damage. Individuals with either right- or left-hemisphere damage were presented with three frames from a cartoon and had to select the final frame that would be most humorous. Right-hemisphere patients did more poorly than left-hemisphere patients on this task. More important, they made different kinds of errors. Right-hemisphere patients erred by selecting an ending that, although it was funny, was unrelated to the previous frames. In contrast, left-hemisphere patients selected an ending that was appropriate in content but not humorous. Similar results occurred with a verbal analog of the cartoon task. Bihrle and her colleagues conclude that the right hemisphere is adept at detecting surprise, whereas the left hemisphere is better at preserving coherence. Appreciation of humor depends, then, on both hemispheres.

Similar conclusions have come from studies of the lexicon. Remember that, in Chapter 5, we found that although all of the meanings of an ambiguous word are briefly entertained, inappropriate meanings are rapidly suppressed. Burgess and Simpson (1988) found that this pattern of performance is more characteristic of the left hemisphere than the right hemisphere. Using normal subjects, they presented the left and right hemispheres with a lexical decision task in which the letter strings were preceded by a lexically ambiguous prime word. The target words were related to either the dominant or the subordinate meaning of the ambiguous word. When stimuli were presented in the right visual field, the researchers found that the dominant meaning was immediately facilitated by the prime word, whereas there was less facilitation for the subordinate meaning, especially when the period between the prime and target words was increased. When stimuli were presented in the left visual field, the dominant meaning again showed immediate facilitation, but the inappropriate meaning was not suppressed and in fact increased in activation over time. Burgess and Simpson conclude that automatic spreading activation occurs in both hemispheres, but only the left hemisphere engages in controlled processing (that is, in suppression of inappropriate meanings).

After reviewing similar studies, Chiarello (1991) concludes that both hemispheres play a role in the interpretation of word meanings. She suggests that we have two semantic systems, one in each hemisphere, that we use to interpret linguistic meaning. In the realm of lexical ambiguity, it appears that the left hemisphere makes a rapid commitment to a particular meaning, whereas the right hemisphere maintains alternative meanings for a longer period of time. If so, the two hemispheres may play complementary roles in the comprehension of lexically ambiguous words.

The efficiency of the left hemisphere may be an asset in most situations, but when the wrong meaning has been selected (as in garden path sentences), the correct meaning may be more accessible to the right hemisphere.

The broader point is that language processes depend on the joint functioning of both cerebral hemispheres. Chiarello (1991) concludes that "a consideration of the available neuropsychological data leads one to the view that processes subserved by each of the two cerebral hemispheres are necessary for the proper interpretation of words in context. One is not enough" (p. 274).

Lateralization in Other Species

It was once thought that laterality was exclusively human, but we now have several documented cases of the lateralization of species-specific vocalizations. One study (Petersen, Beecher, Zoloth, Moody, & Stebbins, 1978) investigated the perception of vocalizations in Japanese macaque monkeys. The researchers presented the vocalizations to either the left or the right ear. All five macaques showed better performance when the vocalizations were given to the right ear. Only one of five monkeys from other species showed a right-ear advantage for macaque sounds. These results suggest the exciting possibility that human lateralization of speech is part of a larger pattern in which a number of species show lateralization on the left half of the brain for important, species-specific sounds.

This view is reinforced by some impressive work on birdsong. Nottebohm (1970) has pointed out that three basic developmental sequences may be observed with young birds. In the first type, the bird develops a normal song even if it is completely isolated at birth and deafened at hatching. Examples of this type are chickens and ring doves. In a second type, the bird will develop the normal song if isolated but not if deafened. Song sparrows are an example. Finally, in the third variety, either isolation or deafening at an early age produces an abnormal song; chaffinches and white-crowned sparrows fit this pattern.

Nottebohm (1970) has found a number of analogs to human speech in this third type of songbird. First, these birds go through a period of "subsong," similar to human babbling, in which the song is distinct from the adult version in a number of ways. Second, birds in different areas learn different dialects of the same song. Third, the consequences of deafening the bird are different at different ages. If the bird is deafened before it has begun to sing, it develops a highly abnormal song. If, however, the deafening is delayed until after the song has developed, it has no effect on the motor output.

Finally, Nottebohm (1970) has found that the left half of the brain is more intimately involved than the right half in the songs of chaffinches. The major structure of the vocal system of the chaffinch is called the **syrinx,** and each side of it is connected by the hypoglossus nerve to each side of the brain. (Here, the connection is ipsalateral, with the left hypoglossus connected to the left half of the brain.) Nottebohm found that when the left hypoglossus was severed, the nature of the song was seriously disrupted, with some parts missing and replaced by unstructured bursts of noise. The same operation on the right side leaves the song intact.

What can we learn about human language by studying macaques and song-birds? Certainly, the sounds to which they respond are of no direct relevance to human beings, just as our speech is irrelevant to them. Yet they suggest that human lateralization of speech is not an isolated event in the animal kingdom and that the brain mechanisms underlying speech may have evolved in ways that are analogous to how similar structures in other species have evolved. In the final section of the chapter, we will examine more closely the evolution of lateralization and language.

Summary

Studies of split-brain patients clarify the respective roles of the left and right hemi-spheres in the use of language. The left hemisphere is more linguistically sophisti-cated than the right, especially in the areas of syntactic and phonetic processing. The right hemisphere is more adept at understanding the multiple meanings of ambiguous words and in comprehending pragmatic aspects of language such as indirect speech acts.

Studies of dichotic listening with normal individuals typically reveal right-ear advantages for speech stimuli and left-ear advantages for nonspeech stimuli. Never-theless, speech sometimes elicits left-ear advantages, and right-ear advantages for musical stimuli have been found. The distinction between holistic and relational processing appears to capture a salient difference in how the two hemispheres do their work.

Lateralization is not limited to humans, or even to primates. Japanese ma-caque monkeys show lateralization of species-specific vocalizations, and anatomical arrangements in songbirds are analogous to those in humans. This evidence suggests that human lateralization for speech is part of a larger evolutionary pattern.

Language in Evolutionary Context

We tend to think more often in terms of features that distinguish us from other animals rather than elements of similarity. Language, and the specialized equip-ment for perceiving and producing it, seems to be qualitatively different from the communication systems found elsewhere in the animal kingdom. Yet, from a bio-logical perspective, all behavior may be understood as related to a series of evolu-tionary antecedents. In some cases, as in the progressive enlargement of an organ over time, the change in quantitative. Other times, as with language, it appears to be qualitative. Although this difference does not mean that it is impossible to find antecedents of modern language in our evolutionary past, it does make the task more difficult.

The sheer complexity of language makes it improbable that a single event or mutation could have caused so complex a change in behavior. Rather, language probably evolved from the convergence of various evolutionary events. In this sec-tion, we first examine some of the ideas that have been proposed regarding the evolution of language and lateralization of the brain for language functions. Then we pursue the question of whether other species, such as chimpanzees, could possibly learn a human or humanlike language from the perspective afforded by these evolutionary considerations.

Evolution of Language and Lateralization

We have two primary means of examining questions related to the evolution of language. One is to do behavioral studies of other animals, such as nonhuman primates. The goal here is to identify similarities and differences between animals in the areas of communication skills and lateralization of brain function. The other is to examine the fossil record, which provides clues regarding the behavior of our evolutionary ancestors.

Field studies of animal communicative behavior indicate that our closest evolutionary neighbors lack anything resembling a language in their natural habitat. Most primate communication systems comprise a relatively small number of fixed signals consisting of vocal or gestural displays. Typically, each signal serves a different function. Alarm calls, mating displays, submissive gestures, and food-related calls are among the most common (see Altmann, 1967). There is little doubt that these communication systems fall well short of the properties generally associated with human language, such as arbitrariness and duality of patterning.

Studies of handedness in nonhuman primates are more enlightening. After reviewing studies of hand preference, MacNeilage, Studdert-Kennedy, and Lindblom (1987) conclude that several primate species have a left-hand preference for simple reaching and a right-hand preference for manipulation of objects. They argue that left-hand (right-hemisphere) specialization developed first, followed by right-hand (left-hemisphere) specialization. The authors suggest that both preferences arose out of the demands of feeding. According to this view, the right hand stabilized the animal so that the left hand could reach for food.

This theory is appealing without being fully convincing. It is appealing because food gathering is the kind of selection pressure on which evolutionary accounts typically are based. It is, for example, more difficult to explain why there would be selection for a left hemisphere that uses relational processing and a right hemisphere that uses holistic processing. What survival advantage would that confer? According to MacNeilage et al. (1987), the initial specialization is for manual function, with cognitive differences coming later. This hypothesis is consistent with results that indicate that the left hemisphere in humans is specialized for certain nonlinguistic motor functions, as we saw earlier in the chapter (Mateer & Kimura, 1977). If the left hemisphere is specialized to perform sequences of motor acts, this specialization may be traced, ultimately, to sequences in food-gathering behaviors.

Nonetheless, the data on which the theory rests are not completely convincing. Many studies of hand preferences in nonhuman primates found very weak differences between the hands, and some found no difference at all (see also Fagot & Vauclair, 1991). MacNeilage and his colleagues acknowledge this point, but they argue that when task differences (such as reaching versus reaching and manipulating, field versus laboratory studies, and so on) are taken into account, the results are more consistent. Nonetheless, the results are weak. In one reaching study, 30 animals exhibited a left-hand preference, 16 a right-hand preference, and 36 no preference at all. This is a far cry from the human case, in which approximately 90% of individuals are right-handed.

An alternative view is presented by Corballis (1989), who suggests that both the human pattern of right-handedness and the left-cerebral representation of language may go back as far as 2 to 3 million years ago. As for handedness, Corballis reviews studies that have examined the patterns of wear in tools and concludes that the majority of tool users were right-handed as far back as 1.9 million years ago. In addition, anatomical analysis of skulls from this period suggests that lateralization of the brain for language may have been present at the same time. Corballis cites the work of Tobias (1987), who found anatomical asymmetries suggesting the existence of Broca's and possibly Wernicke's areas. It has been known for some time that a region in the left temporal lobe, close to Wernicke's area, is typically larger than the corresponding region in the right temporal lobe (Geschwind & Levitsky, 1968). It now appears that similar anatomical asymmetries existed perhaps 2 to 3 million years ago.

In contrast, the capacity for speech came much later. As we saw in Chapter 4, when we produce sounds, air is expelled from the lungs and sent through the structures of the vocal tract (see Figure 4-1). We can change the shape of the vocal tract by altering the position of our lips, jaw, tongue, and larynx. The shape and flexibility of our vocal tract are required for the range of sounds found in contemporary languages.

A crucial evolutionary development is the enlargement of the pharyngeal area that lies above the larynx and just below the mouth. In newborn humans and adult chimpanzees, the larynx exits directly into the mouth, whereas in adult humans it exits into the pharynx. This anatomical difference greatly influences the number of sounds that can be produced. For example, newborns and chimpanzees are physically incapable of producing the vowels [a], [i], and [u], sounds that are found in a wide variety of languages.

It has often been said that evolution is miserly. The human mouth, throat, and larynx were "designed" for swallowing and breathing, not for speech. In evolutionary terms, speech is an overlaid function: it utilizes preexisting physical structures for new functions. In this context, the enlargement of the pharyngeal area has a highly significant consequence. Because in adult humans the passageways are shared among speech, eating, and breathing, the potential for choking on food is much greater for infants or chimpanzees, which have a smaller pharyngeal area (Lieberman, 1991). Why would such an arrangement have evolved? It is one indication that language is so vital that we have evolved a speech apparatus that increases our capacity to choke in order to use productive speech.

Lieberman (1973, 1991, 1998) has examined reconstructions of the vocal tracts of various hominids, the evolutionary family that includes modern humans. In particular, after examining Neanderthal fossils, he concluded that Neanderthals had vocal tracts that were very similar to human newborns. Although they were apparently capable of producing some speech, they probably lacked the mobility to produce the range of vowel sounds found in modern language. On the basis of these and other fossil analyses, Lieberman (1991, 1998) suggests that a functionally modern human vocal tract may have emerged only 125,000 to 150,000 years ago. These findings imply that speech is a relatively recent evolutionary development, more recent than hand preference and brain lateralization.

Speculation about what our ancestors might or might not have been able to do or say is just that—speculation. The best thinking currently available suggests that a combination of factors (the emergence of hand preferences, the lateralization of the brain, and the development of the modern vocal tract) converged in the evolution of language. Although the exact line of development is not clear, the net effect of all of these changes is a form of communication that is qualitatively distinct from that possessed by present-day primates. Of course, the fact that nonhuman primates do not have language does not necessarily mean that they are incapable of learning and using language. A number of attempts have been made to teach language to chimpanzees and other nonhuman primates, and these have aroused considerable interest and debate.

Teaching Language to Nonhuman Primates

Attempts to teach language (or a languagelike system of communication) to other primates may be divided into three groups. In the first group, attempts were made to teach speech to chimpanzees (Hayes & Hayes, 1952; Kellogg & Kellogg, 1933). As we have seen, the vocal apparatus of chimpanzees is not suited to produce speech sounds, and consequently these studies proved very little. In the Hayes's study, the chimpanzee was able to learn only two words in 2 years of training.

A second group involved programs in which the communication system was not clearly defined in linguistic terms. Premack (1971) used tokens with symbols on them to teach a chimpanzee named Sarah some logical concepts. Although Sarah was able to demonstrate a number of aspects of complex cognition, the results are of uncertain importance to the issue of whether apes can acquire a language because it has not been demonstrated that these symbols have the power or flexibility of human language. Similar considerations apply to the work of Rumbaugh (1977) and his associates, who used a computer to teach a chimpanzee, Lana, to produce and respond to messages. Once again, the linguistic status of the "language" is not known.

A third group of programs has taken advantage of the obvious manual dexterity of these animals to teach them American Sign Language. Gardner and Gardner (1969, 1975; Gardner, Gardner, & Van Cantfort, 1989) pioneered this work with studies of Washoe, a chimpanzee. Similar work has been carried out in other laboratories with chimpanzees, gorillas, and an orangutan. The Gardners themselves replicated the study with Washoe with four other chimpanzees that they reared from birth, Moja, Pili, Tatu, and Dar. Since ASL is commonly regarded as a full-fledged language, albeit with a grammar different from English (see Chapter 2), and since the Gardners' program, unlike most others, is analogous to the circumstances in which a child would be naturally exposed to language, I will focus on their efforts here.

The conditions under which Washoe was trained to use ASL are similar to those of children learning language. American Sign Language was used or modeled in a variety of contexts such as eating dinner, playing, and so on. Although the adult models presumably used correct ASL with Washoe, they made no explicit attempt to teach her the rules of ASL as such. Rather, they used sign language to communicate with her.

The evidence of Washoe's language development is in many respects quite remarkable. She quickly acquired a number of signs and learned to use them correctly. Moreover, she was productive in her use of signs. When she did not know the name of an object she was trying to convey, she invented one. An example was her invention of the sign *waterbird*, combining two previously learned signs, *water* and *bird*, to refer to a swan (Linden, 1974). Additionally, Washoe demonstrated the appropriate generality in her learning of various signs. When she mastered the term *open*, she applied it spontaneously to a number of new contexts (opening the door, the window, and so on). In rigorous tests, Washoe and her successors in the Gardner laboratory demonstrated the ability to sign the names of common objects far better than simply by chance (see Figure 13-7).

It seems that Washoe mastered at least a rudimentary understanding of the semantics of individual lexical items. Whether she correctly understood the syntax of ASL is another matter. In general, Washoe tended to put signs together in a wide variety of different orders, apparently using sentences such as (16) and (17) interchangeably (Brown, 1970):

(16)   Roger tickle Washoe.
(17)   Washoe tickle Roger.

Individuals words go only so far, of course. It is primarily through syntax that we acquire a truly productive linguistic system. These observations suggest that Washoe did not master word order, an important syntactic device in English and many other languages.

The Gardners found better syntactic performance when Washoe was given a task in which she had to respond to *wh*-questions (Gardner & Gardner, 1975). Questions such as those in sentences (18) through (20) call for responses from a particular grammatical category. For example, (18) calls for a noun and (19) requires a noun referring to a location:

(18)   Who are you?
(19)   Where is the box?
(20)   When is dinner?

Washoe gave a response from the correct grammatical category 84% of the time in this task, a level of performance that even exceeded that of children just beginning to produce two-word utterances (Washoe's stage of development at that time). This result suggests that Washoe had greater syntactic knowledge than was evident in her own language output (see Figure 13-7).

(a) *Susan N.:* What that?
Washoe: Dirty

(b) *Susan N.:* What that?
Washoe: Sweet

(c) *Greg G.:* What that?
Washoe: Hammer

(d) *Susan N.:* Whose that?
Washoe: Mine

(e) *Tom T.:* What that?
Moja: Tree

(f) *Washoe:* Gimme

Figure 13-7. Chimpanzees signing about objects. (a–c): of different objects, replies to "What that?" (d–f): of the same object, sequentially, replies to (d) "Whose?" then (e) "What that?" then (f) stands up and signs "Gimme" of the object. (From "Categorical Replies to Categorical Questions by Cross-Fostered Chimpanzees," by R. A. Gardner, T. E. Van Cantfort, and B. T. Gardner, 1992. *American Journal of Psychology, 105,* p. 34. Copyright © 1992 University of Illinois Press. Reprinted by permission.)

Several criticisms have been raised regarding these studies of chimpanzee language skills. For example, Terrace, Petitto, Sanders, and Bever (1979) have questioned whether the sentences of Washoe and other chimpanzees were creative or whether they had been merely prompted by the human trainer. Terrace et al. closely examined videotapes of Washoe and a chimpanzee with which they worked called Neam Chimpsky (or Nim for short). These researchers found that 39% of Nim's utterances were either imitations of adjacent human utterances or reductions of such utterances. In many instances, Nim interrupted teachers while they were making signs. Thus, there seems to be some question as to whether Nim was combining words in novel, rule-governed ways or whether she was merely imitating the utterances of those around her. Seidenberg and Petitto (1979) have raised similar points.

On the other hand, O'Sullivan and Yeager (1989) contend that Nim's communicative and linguistic skills were limited by the type of training she received. Unlike the naturalistic circumstances in which humans taught ASL to Washoe, Terrace trained Nim in a laboratory setting. O'Sullivan and Yeager tested Nim's performance under two conditions: a training condition and a conversational condition. In the training condition, designed to replicate the conditions used by Terrace, Nim was given drills in naming objects. In the conversational condition, which was similar to the procedure followed by the Gardners, Nim was observed in more unstructured interactions. The investigators found that the number of spontaneous (that is, not imitative) utterances was far greater in the conversational session (60%) than in the training session (14%). In addition, interruptions by Nim were three times more likely in the training session. Although these results support O'Sullivan and Yeager's contention, it should be noted that their training results were based on a single 8-minute session.

More recent studies have included chimpanzees teaching ASL to younger chimpanzees without human intervention (Fouts, Fouts, & Van Cantfort, 1989). Fouts and his colleagues examined whether Washoe was able to pass on her signing skills to her adopted son, Loulis, who was 10 months old when he arrived at Washoe's home. Loulis was reared in somewhat unusual circumstances in that although Washoe and other chimpanzees were allowed to sign to him, the humans present were not. In a sense, Loulis was deprived of human signing. Nonetheless, Loulis acquired 17 different signs by 29 months, and by 63 months his vocabulary had grown to 47 signs.

What conclusions can be drawn from these studies? Certainly, chimpanzees are capable of acquiring certain aspects of human language and can transmit sign language from one generation to the next without human intervention. Moreover, as the training sessions become more relaxed and conversational, the language skills appear all the more impressive. To put the matter in some perspective, however, we should bear in mind that Loulis had a vocabulary of 47 signs at 63 months and normal children have acquired approximately 14,000 words by 72 months (Carey, 1978). Thus, although recent work has cast chimpanzee language skills in a more positive light, there remain significant differences between their skills and those of normal children.

These differences can be interpreted in at least two ways. It is possible that as research with chimpanzees advances further, the gap between chimpanzee and child language will be reduced substantially. Another possibility is that the pattern of strengths and weaknesses found in chimpanzee language to date are accurate indicators of their linguistic ability. We have seen that the specialized left hemisphere plays a major role in language use and acquisition in humans. When an intact left hemisphere is not available—as with Genie, aphasic patients, and split-brain patients tested on their right hemispheres—language acquisition is slow, and syntactic skills in particular are weak. On the basis of these observations, we might expect that a chimpanzee attempting to acquire language without benefit of these neurological mechanisms would also show relatively slow acquisition and difficulties with syntactic structure.

Finally, recent research with bonobos (pygmy chimpanzees, or *Pan paniscus*) should be mentioned. Bonobos use gestures and vocalizations more often in their natural habitat than the chimpanzees (*Pan troglodytes*) we have been discussing. Bonobos are also thought to be more intelligent than chimpanzees and possibly better prepared to acquire language. Savage-Rumbaugh, McDonald, Sevcik, Hopkins, and Rubert (1986) studied symbolic communication in two pygmy chimpanzees and found that they did not need explicit training to acquire associations between symbols and objects. In addition, one 5-year-old pygmy chimpanzee, Kanzi, preserved word order most of the time (Greenfield & Savage-Rumbaugh, 1991). Future work with this species should shed further light on syntactic skills in nonhuman primates.

Summary

The complexity of present-day language suggests that a convergence of evolutionary developments, rather than a single event, led to its emergence. Three factors were discussed: hand preference, structural differences between the left and right hemispheres of the brain, and the capacity for speech. Although some studies have found hand preferences in nonhuman primates, the results are relatively weak. Fossil records are consistent with the notion that both handedness and anatomical differences between the hemispheres existed approximately 2 million years ago. The emergence of a specialized vocal tract is a more recent evolutionary event.

Studies attempting to teach sign language to chimpanzees have produced some impressive results. Chimpanzees are capable of acquiring signs and using them appropriately. However, even when the mode of communication is well adapted to the animals' manual skills, syntactic skills are acquired slowly. Research that is just beginning with pygmy chimpanzees may clarify the language capabilities of nonhuman primates.

Review Questions

1. Distinguish among Broca's aphasia, Wernicke's aphasia, and conduction aphasia in terms of the brain regions involved and the language performance observed.

2. According to Geschwind's model, what sequence of brain regions would be involved if you (a) heard a sentence and then responded to it orally or (b) saw a sentence and then spoke it?
3. What evidence suggests that Broca's patients suffer from syntactic deficits?
4. Explain how lateralization of language skills is tested in split-brain patients and normal individuals.
5. Summarize the research that has been done on language and the right hemisphere.
6. Under what circumstances might language stimuli elicit a left-ear advantage in normal right-handed individuals?
7. Summarize the evidence for lateralization of sounds in animals other than humans.
8. What evidence exists regarding the capacity for speech in Neanderthals?
9. Why did the Gardners use American Sign Language in their studies with Washoe?
10. Discuss studies in which chimpanzees teach ASL to younger chimpanzees without human intervention.

Thought Questions

1. What might happen if a person who was bilingual in Spanish and English suffered an injury to Broca's area? Would both languages be affected or just one? Why? What aspects of language might be affected?
2. Assume that your grandfather has had a stroke and is greatly limited in his ability to articulate meaningful speech. How might you determine his comprehension skills?
3. If one hemisphere dominates the other on a task for which it is clearly more qualified, does this mean that the hemisphere "knows" its abilities and disabilities? How might you tell?
4. Attempts to prove that chimpanzees or other animals can acquire language inevitably suffer from the difficulties associated with defining language. Suppose you wanted to prove (or disprove) the point. How would you go about it? What aspects of language would you choose to teach?

14

Language, Culture, and Cognition

MAIN POINTS

- The Whorf hypothesis states that the structure of a language determines a native speaker's world view. Different languages are assumed to lead to different world views.
- Psychological studies of the Whorf hypothesis have examined whether lexical and grammatical differences between languages influence various nonlinguistic cognitive processes.
- Studies of color terms have not provided strong support for the Whorf hypothesis. Other studies of the lexicon are more consistent with the hypothesis.
- The presence of a grammatical distinction in a language may increase the ease of some cognitive processes. However, the absence of such distinctions does not prevent these processes.

Introduction

In this chapter, we explore the interrelationships among language, culture, and cognition. The central notion—that individuals with different linguistic and cultural backgrounds think differently—is not far from our everyday experience. If you have had the opportunity to engage in a conversation with a person whose native language is not English, you may have found that communication breaks down at times and that some concepts are not easily translated into another language. Or, if you happen to be a fluent bilingual (or multilingual), you may agree with those bilinguals and multilinguals who insist that they think differently in each of their languages.

A number of intriguing questions arise here. Is there a particular style of thinking that is "natural" for speakers of each language? If so, is it possible for a person to think in a different way, one that is not "natural" for that individual? Is this style of thinking imparted by the language, the culture, or both? Or have we overestimated the differences between languages and cultures: will we find, upon deeper inspection, fundamental similarities in thought processes in individuals with diverse linguistic and cultural backgrounds?

These questions have engaged the attention of anthropologists, linguists, and psychologists. We will begin by examining the ideas of scholars who have studied this issue, then turn to experimental research that bears on these questions.

The Whorf Hypothesis

The view that language shapes thought is most often associated with the work of Benjamin Lee Whorf. Whorf received his degree in chemical engineering from the Massachusetts Institute of Technology and worked throughout his life for an insurance company as a fire-prevention engineer. He had a number of avocations, however. He had a strong interest in the relationship between science and religion, and ultimately religion led him to language. He was initially self-taught in linguistics but eventually studied American Indian linguistics with the prominent anthropologist Edward Sapir at Yale University.

Sapir (1921) had earlier suggested that languages are diverse in the way that they structure reality but had not fully developed the thesis that these linguistic differences might facilitate certain modes of thought. This was a position that Whorf developed in a series of articles from 1925 to 1941, many of which are included in Carroll (1956). The notion that language shapes thought patterns is commonly referred to as the **Whorf hypothesis,** although it is also called the **Sapir-Whorf hypothesis,** to acknowledge the role of Whorf's mentor.

Linguistic Determinism and Relativity

The Whorf hypothesis consists of two parts, linguistic determinism and linguistic relativity. **Linguistic determinism** refers to the notion that a language determines certain nonlinguistic cognitive processes. That is, learning a language changes the way a person thinks. **Linguistic relativity** refers to the claim that the cognitive processes that are determined are different for different languages. Thus, speakers of different languages are said to think in different ways.

Whorf's reasoning on these matters is revealed in a famous quote:

> We dissect nature along lines laid down by our native languages. The categories and types that we isolate from the world of phenomena we do not find there because they stare every observer in the face; on the contrary, the world is presented in a kaleidoscopic flux of impressions which has to be organized by our minds—and this means largely by the linguistic systems in our minds. We cut nature up, organize it into concepts, and ascribe significances as we do, largely because we are parties to an agreement to organize it in this way—an agreement that holds throughout our speech community and is codified in the patterns of our language. The agreement is, of course, an implicit and unstated one, BUT ITS TERMS ARE ABSOLUTELY OBLIGATORY; we cannot talk at all except by subscribing to the organization and classification of data which the agreement decrees. (Carroll, 1956, pp. 213–214)

There are several notions here. One is that languages "carve up" reality in different ways. Another is that these language differences are covert or unconscious; that is, we are not consciously aware of the way in which we classify objects. Third, these language differences influence our world view. These are profound ideas, but not ones easily amenable to experimental test. Let us begin by looking, as Whorf did, at linguistic examples from various languages that seem to bear on his thesis.

Some Whorfian Examples

Whorf provided a number of examples designed to show that linguistic determinism and relativity were valid concepts. They can be broadly organized into lexical and grammatical examples.

Lexical examples We may begin by considering the concept of differentiation. **Differentiation** refers to the number of words in a given domain (for example, colors, birds, fruits, and so on) in a lexicon. A more highly differentiated domain has more words, some of which express finer distinctions, such as subtle shades of color. Whorf argued that languages differ in the domains that are most differentiated. That is, all languages show high degrees of differentiation in some domains and low degrees in others. The implication is that greater degrees of differentiation are related to culturally significant concepts.

For example, Whorf noted that in the American Indian language of Hopi, just one word covers everything that flies except birds (for example, the same word for insects, airplanes, aviators, and so on). The Hopi speaker calls all of these disparate objects by the same name without any apparent difficulty. Whorf argued that although this class might seem very broad to us, so would our word *snow* to an Eskimo:

> We have the same word for falling snow, snow on the ground, snow packed hard like ice, slushy snow, wind-driven flying snow—whatever the situation may be. To an Eskimo, this all-inclusive word would be almost unthinkable; he would say that falling snow, slushy snow, and so on, are sensuously and operationally different, different things to contend with; he uses different words for them and for other kinds of snow. (Carroll, 1956, p. 216)

Whorf suggested that there is no "natural" way to carve up reality; different languages do it in quite different ways.

Whorf's observations about Eskimo words for *snow* have been criticized by Martin (1986; see also Pullum, 1991). Martin claims that Whorf and other writers (for example, Brown, 1958) greatly exaggerated the lexical differences between Eskimo and English. The number of words in a lexicon varies with how one defines the word. If we only count root words (free morphemes), we will get one number, but if we count each suffixed version of each root word, the estimate will rise dramatically. Martin suggests that the failure to attend to the rich morphological system of the Eskimo language led Whorf and others to the myth that Eskimos have vastly more words for *snow* than English speakers. It appears that when morphology is taken into account, Eskimos have perhaps a dozen words for *snow* (Pullum, 1991). But then English has quite a few as well, including *slush, avalanche, blizzard,* and *powder.* It is not clear that Eskimos have a more highly differentiated *snow* domain than English speakers.

Whatever the final consensus might be on Eskimo *snow* words, the more general notion that languages differ in the degree to which they differentiate various lexical domains does not seem to be at issue. The question is whether these differences lead to differences in thinking. Whorf suggested that they did, in the sense that when we encounter a particular word on a regular basis, it may influence our habitual thought patterns (that is, the kind of thought process that comes easily or naturally to an individual).

Whorf gave an example based on his work experience in which he sought explanations for the start of fires. Initially, he only considered physical causes, such as defective wiring. Over time, he came to think that psychological causes were important: the meaning of a situation to an individual often was directly related to the onset of the fire. And this meaning was often in the form of linguistic meaning, such as the meaning typically conveyed by particular words:

> Thus, around a storage of what are called "gasoline drums," behavior will tend to a certain type, that is, great care will be exercised; while around a storage of what are called "empty gasoline drums," it will tend to be different—careless, with little repression of smoking or of tossing cigarette stubs about. Yet the "empty" drums are perhaps the most dangerous, since they contain explosive vapor. Physically the situation is hazardous, but the linguistic analysis according to regular analogy must employ the word "empty," which inevitably suggests lack of hazard. (Carroll, 1956, p. 135)

Whorf offered this as evidence of linguistic determinism, of the power of words to influence thought processes. We are careless because of the word *empty*. Note also that Whorf emphasized "regular" analogy: we come to this (precarious) interpretation of experience based on habitual experience with words. It is something that occurs slowly, over time, seeping into our mental framework. Whorf did not say that we could not avoid this pattern of thought and treat the empty drums with proper respect (obviously he did); but this is a different, more active, pattern of thought.

Grammatical examples   Although some of Whorf's lexical examples, such as his comments on Eskimo, have generated a considerable amount of discussion, it appears that he was more interested in the grammatical differences among languages.

In English, we come to respect the difference between nouns and verbs as a fundamental distinction. Nouns refer to long-lasting and stable events, such as *horse* and *man*, whereas verbs refer to short-lived actions, such as *hit* and *run*. Yet, Whorf asked, why then do we classify temporary events such as *lightning* and *spark* as nouns? And why are *dwell, persist,* and *continue* verbs? In Hopi, *lightning* is a verb because events of brief duration must be verbs. Whorf also mentioned Nootka, a language used on Vancouver Island, in which all words seem to be treated as verbs. This is just one indication of how grammatical characteristics vary from language to language.

Another example of grammatical diversity concerns the extent to which a language uses word order or morphology to signal meaning. In English, the vast majority of sentences use a subject-verb-object (SVO) order, and in most of these the first noun is the agent and the second the patient. This order is adhered to rather rigidly. If the verb is intransitive (one that does not take an object), the remainder of the sequence holds (SV). Similarly, when the first noun is deleted, it is very often replaced by a pronoun; other languages allow deletion of the subject more often. The major exception to the standard order is the question form. The consistency of word order in English makes it a reliable cue for sentence interpretation (MacWhinney, Bates, & Kliegl, 1984). For a speaker of English, languages that violate the SVO order may seem unnatural.

Many other languages use morphology more extensively than word order to signal meaning. As we saw in Chapter 2, the major English grammatical morphemes are number, tense, person, and aspect. In Spanish, nouns are marked for grammatical gender. This distinction does not correspond to a semantic distinction (that is, masculine versus feminine objects) but is simply a formal property of the language that its users must acquire.

On the other hand, some of the grammatical distinctions that are found in other languages do appear to be semantically significant. Several Indian languages conjugate verbs for validity. For example, consider sentence (1):

(1) John is chopping wood.

In Wintu, one inflection would be attached to the verb if there were direct visual evidence of this fact, another if it were gossip, and still another if it were a regular event (Lee, 1944/1987). This suggests, as Brown (1958, p. 254) puts it, that Wintu speakers must have "a continuing grasp of the evidence" of their assertions.

Whorf believed that grammatical distinctions such as these exert an effect on not just the way individuals think but also their overall world view. In English, there is a distinction between what Whorf called individual nouns (more commonly called **count nouns**) and **mass nouns.** Count nouns refer to bodies with definite outlines (for example, a tree, a stick, a hill), whereas mass nouns refer to objects without clear boundaries (for example, air, water, rain). Linguistically, the distinction is that count nouns take the plural morpheme, whereas mass nouns cannot. Thus, we can speak of *trees, sticks,* and *hills* not but not *airs, waters,* and *rains.* In addition, count nouns take the singular indefinite article *a* but mass nouns do not. In contrast, in Hopi, there are no mass nouns.

Although we cannot pluralize English mass nouns directly, we can do so by the use of a phrase of the form count noun + of + mass noun. So, even though we cannot say *waters* or *sands,* we can say *bodies of water* or *buckets of sand.* But this form of expression, according to Whorf, has cognitive consequences since it leads us to think of some objects as being "containers" (form) that hold "contents" (substance or matter). This distinction between form and substance is not a necessary feature of objective reality. For example, even though some objects, such as butter and meat, have clear boundaries, they are treated grammatically as mass nouns (for example, *two sticks of butter,* not *two butters*). Thus, Whorf suggested that English speakers think of objects as consisting of form and substance because of this grammatical distinction.

A basic question to ask at this juncture is whether Whorf's arguments are convincing. Most psychologists have not been convinced. There are several reasons for this. Bloom (1981) has suggested that Whorf's views, because they emphasize cognitive structures, did not square well with the behavioristic tradition in psychology prevalent at the time that Whorf was writing. It is also true that the relativism that Whorf emphasized did not fit well with the rationalistic approach to language subsequently advocated by Chomsky, which highlights linguistic universals. A third reason is more methodological. To test the Whorf hypothesis, we need to assess language and cognition independently of each other. In particular, we need to assess (nonlinguistic) cognitive processes independently of the linguistic features that are presumed, in the Whorf hypothesis, to influence them. Whorf discussed many linguistic distinctions but provided no real evidence of their cognitive consequences. In the remainder of this chapter, we will discuss the various experimental tests that have been done of the Whorf hypothesis.

Summary

The Whorf hypothesis states that the way we think about the world is shaped by our language. This hypothesis consists of two parts. Linguistic determinism states that languages determine (nonlinguistic) cognitive processes, and linguistic relativity states that the resulting thought processes vary from language to language. Although Whorf provides many lexical and grammatical examples of how language may influence cognition, he did not present convincing evidence for his hypothesis.

Lexical Influences on Cognition

Experimental tests of the Whorf hypothesis fall into two groups: those that examine the lexical level and those the grammatical level. Before looking at these studies, however, let us consider what is needed to test the linguistic relativity hypothesis.

Testing the Whorf Hypothesis

Any study that attempts to test the hypothesis that differences in language determine differences in thinking must, at the outset, define the three key terms. First, we need to define what we mean by "differences in language." This has been done in two ways. One way is to compare a language that linguistically marks a particular conceptual distinction with a language that does not. Thus, the presence or absence of the explicit linguistic marking is the language difference of interest. Although most studies have approached the problem in this way, another possibility is to compare two languages that mark the same distinction in different ways. This comparison focuses not on whether a language marks a concept but rather how it does so. As we have seen, English marks number through the use of the plural morpheme. One comparison would be another language that does not mark number; another would be a language that marks number in a different way.

Second, we need to define "differences in thinking" in a satisfactory manner. It is obviously difficult to measure a person's world view. But it should be kept in mind that Whorf was especially interested in those aspects of thinking that indicated a habitual mode of thought. Lucy (1992b) defines habitual thought as "routine ways of attending to objects and events, categorizing them, remembering them, and perhaps even reflecting upon them" (p. 7). The mode is contrasted with specialized thought, which is composed of cognitive routines or structures that are restricted either to certain subgroups within a culture (such as technical specialists) or to certain domains (such as kinship or illness). As we will see, psychologists and anthropologists have studied a wide range of cognitive processes, including form perception, color perception, mathematical thinking, and logical reasoning. As we discuss these studies, you might consider whether they better represent habitual or specialized modes of thought.

Finally, we need to clarify what is meant by saying that languages "determine" thought. The linguistic determinism hypothesis can be interpreted in at least two different ways. The strong version states that language determines cognition: the presence of linguistic categories creates cognitive categories. In this view, the presence of terms to refer to different objects that move through the air produces the cognitive ability to discriminate between birds and airplanes. Although some of Whorf's comments suggest that he believed in the strong version of linguistic determinism, recent interpreters of his work have claimed that he did not (see, for example, the discussion in Schwanenflugel, Blount, & Lin, 1991). In any event, no evidence exists for the strong version.

Alternatively, a weak version of the hypothesis states that the presence of linguistic categories influences the ease with which various cognitive operations are performed. Certain thought processes may be more accessible or more easily performed by members of one linguistic community relative to those of a different linguistic community. As Hockett (1954) expresses the idea, "Languages differ not so much as to what *can* be said in them, but rather as to what it is *relatively easy* to say" (p. 122). It is this version that has guided most of the research that we will discuss.

Color Terms

At the lexical level, much work has been done on words for color. This is, in part, due to the fact that languages differ tremendously in their differentiation of the color domain. Some languages, such as English, have many color terms, and others have as few as two. It thus seems natural to ask whether speakers of such disparate languages perceive and think of color in fundamentally similar or different ways.

Codability   A concept that has figured in much of the research on color cognition is **codability.** Brown (1958; see also Lenneberg, 1953) defined codability as the length of a verbal expression. As we saw in our discussion of differentiation, some languages have single words to refer to a particular object or event, whereas others do not. If one's language does not have a specific word for the occasion, the speaker can still make the reference but will need to do so by some combination of words. Relative to the case in which a single word serves the purpose, the phrase is, in Brown's terms, less codable.

Brown (1958) suggested a relationship between the frequency of usage of a verbal expression, its length (codability), and the ease with which it may be used. The relationship between frequency and length is captured in what is called **Zipf's law.** Some time ago, Zipf (1935) examined Chinese, Latin, and English and found that the length of a word is negatively correlated with its frequency of usage. That is, the more frequently a word is used in a language, the shorter the word (measured either in phonemes or syllables). English contains many examples of Zipf's law. Whenever technological innovations are introduced in society, their initial, cumbersome names become shortened for easy reference (for example, *videocamera-videocassette recorder* becomes *camcorder*). It may be that the differences in the differentiation of domains that Whorf observed are a special instance of Zipf's law. For instance, it may be that in cultures in which an object is referred to extremely often, it is referred to by a single, brief name; when it is moderately frequent, by a longer name; and when it is infrequent, by a phrase.

The relationship between codability and ease of expression has been studied in several experiments. In an early study, Brown and Lenneberg (1954) examined the responses of college students to 24 different colors. The colors were identified beforehand by a set of judges who were asked to look at a series of color chips and determine which was the best instance of the color in question. The judges produced a list of 8 central colors, with 16 other colors included for comparison. The 24 colors were shown to the students, one at a time, and they were asked to name the colors, with their reaction time to naming the colors being measured. Brown and Lenneberg found that colors that evoked long names (that is, those less codable) were named with hesitation, with disagreement from one person to another, and with inconsistency from one time to another.

Crosslinguistic studies   These results suggest that the presence of a brief verbal expression in a language influences certain cognitive processes. However, to evaluate the notion of linguistic determinism, we need to study the effects of color terms in different languages. Berlin and Kay (1969) have investigated color terms in various languages. They found that although the number of color terms in a language varied quite a bit from language to language, there was an underlying order. They found that every language has a small number of **basic color terms.** These are terms that consist of only one morpheme (for example, *blue* versus *blue-green*), are not contained within another color (for example, *crimson* is contained within the category of *red*), and are not restricted to a small number of objects (for example, *blond* is restricted mainly to hair color). Furthermore, each language draws its basic color terms from the following list of 11 names: *white, black, red, yellow, green, blue, brown, purple, pink, orange,* and *gray*. In addition, Berlin and Kay found that these 11 terms formed a hierarchy. Some languages, such as English, use all 11, whereas others use as few as 2. When a language has just 2 terms, it is not a random selection, but always *black* and *white* (sometimes translated as *dark* and *light*). When a language has a third term, it is always *red*. The entire hierarchy looks like this:

$$
\begin{matrix} \text{Black} \\ \text{White} \end{matrix} \rightarrow \text{Red} \rightarrow \begin{matrix} \text{Yellow} \\ \text{Green} \end{matrix} \rightarrow \text{Blue} \rightarrow \text{Brown} \rightarrow \begin{matrix} \text{Purple} \\ \text{Pink} \\ \text{Orange} \\ \text{Gray} \end{matrix}
$$

Thus, a language with four terms has *black, white, red,* and either *yellow* or *green*. A language with seven terms has all of these plus *blue* and *brown*. In general, Berlin and Kay found a remarkable degree of universal structure in color terms.

Building on the work of Berlin and Kay, Rosch (formerly Heider) performed several studies with the Dani, a New Guinea people whose language consists of only two color terms, one for black and one for white. Rosch was particularly interested in what Berlin and Kay referred to as **focal colors,** the most representative example of various basic colors (such as the most bluish blue). Rosch argued that focal colors are more perceptually salient than nonfocal colors and that this salience, in turn, influences the codability and memorability of a color. Rosch (Heider, 1972) tested Dani and U.S. participants on a task in which they were presented with color chips and later asked to name them. Rosch found that although Americans performed better on the whole, both groups' memory for focal colors was better than for non-focal colors. In a subsequent study, Rosch (1973) demonstrated that the Dani learned the names for color categories when focal colors were at the center of the categories. Apparently, Dani learn and remember colors much as we do despite the extreme differences in color vocabulary.

The irony in these results is that the study of color terms began as an attempt to demonstrate the validity of the Whorf hypothesis. Rosch's studies do not support the hypothesis of linguistic relativity; rather, they turn it on its head:

> In short, far from being a domain well suited to the study of the effects of language on thought, the color space would seem to be a prime example for the influence of the underlying perceptual-cognitive factors on the formation and reference of linguistic categories. (Heider, 1972, p. 20)

These studies have led some researchers (for example, Clark & Clark, 1977) to conclude that there is little support for the Whorf hypothesis. However, others have questioned both Rosch's conclusions regarding color cognition as well as the generality of the color domain. Lucy and Shweder (1979) argue that the focal colors used by Heider were more perceptually discriminable than the nonfocal colors. While focality is an intrinsic property of a color, discriminability is relative to the surrounding colors. When they controlled for discriminability, Lucy and Schweder found no differences between focal and nonfocal colors in a short-term recognition memory experiment, although they noted differences in long-term recognition.

Kay and Kempton (1984) compared the performance of English speakers with individuals who spoke Tarahumara, a Mexican Indian language that has a single term for the blue-green color but not separate terms for blue and green. They presented subjects with triads of colors in which two items were clear examples of blue and green and the third member was between the two. The participants were then asked to decide whether the third chip was closer to the first or to the second color. English speakers sharply distinguished between chips on one side of the blue-green border and those on the other side, whereas speakers of Tarahumara did not do so. In a second study, Kay and Kempton demonstrated that if English speakers were induced to call the intermediate chip both blue and green, the effect disappeared. Thus, the perception of colors appears to be dependent on the terms we use to refer to them.

These results suggest that under some circumstances the manner in which we perceive and perhaps remember colors is related to the linguistic terms we use to refer to them. It is also related to the perceptual salience of the colors themselves. It may not be that one set of factors, linguistic or perceptual, is reducible to the other but that both factors influence our color cognition.

Other Lexical Categories

Recent work by Schwanenflugel and colleagues suggests that there are clear cross-cultural differences in a number of lexical categories and that these differences might be related to language differences. Schwanenflugel and Rey (1986) examined lexical categories in Spanish- and English-speaking monolinguals living in southern Florida. The participants were given instances of 12 different lexical categories, such as birds, colors, fruits, musical instruments, and weapons. For each category, the participants were asked to rate a series of instances for typicality and familiarity. There were 18 to 34 instances in each category. The results showed a moderately strong (0.64) correlation between the English and Spanish typicality ratings. However, of greater interest was the fact that the correlations varied tremendously from category to category, with the strongest being for parts of the human body (0.94) and the weakest for birds (0.16). Both groups agreed that head, arm, and leg were more typical body parts than hair, tooth, and nail. But English speakers regarded robin as the second most typical bird (after eagle), whereas Spanish speakers rated robin as 24th most typical of 27 instances. In contrast, Spanish speakers rated canary as most typical, but it was 16th on the English list.

These are interesting results, but, as Schwanenflugel has acknowledged, it is not clear that language differences are responsible for them. Another possibility is cultural familiarity. Schwanenflugel and Rey (1986) found that cultural familiarity played a role in the subject ratings of typicality, and when this factor was taken into account, the typicality correlations between languages increased (from 0.64 to 0.73). Thus, part of the reason that Spanish speakers rate canaries as more typical than English speakers do is because Spanish speakers are more familiar with them.

Is there any indication, then, that language differences play a role in these category judgments? Schwanenflugel, Blount, and Lin (1991) suggest that the language used to describe category members may influence how we think about various instances. In English, we have various hedges that may be applied to words to indicate the degree to which they are representative of their category (Lakoff, 1972). For instance, we might say sentence (2), but sentence (3) is decidedly odd:

(2) Loosely speaking, a bat is a bird.
(3) Loosely speaking, a robin is a bird.

A bat has some of the characteristic or typical features of birds but not the defining features. In contrast, compare sentences (4) and (5):

(4) Technically speaking, a tomato is a fruit.
(5) Technically speaking, an apple is a fruit.

Here, the hedge is appropriate for *tomato* but not for *apple*; *tomato* shares the defining but not the characteristic features of *fruit*. These observations suggest that linguistic devices that signal degree-of-category representativeness may influence the perception of category instances. Schwanenflugel et al. (1991) discuss some of the devices used in Tarahumara and Chinese. For example, in Tarahumara, a bound modifier indicating degree of typicality must be attached to color terms. One modifier is used for colors that are highly typical, another for those that are somewhat typical, and a third for those that are only slightly typical. Devices such as these might well influence the manner in which individuals retrieve and think about category members.

Number Terms

One further set of studies is relevant to how the lexicon may influence thought processes. These studies have examined how morphological differences in number names between Asian languages (Chinese, Korean, and Japanese) and English may influence children's conceptualization of numbers and, ultimately, their mathematics achievement.

The linguistic distinction here is not whether the different languages name numbers but how they do so. In English, the system of naming numbers is relatively complex. The names for numbers 11 and 12, for instance, are unrelated to the names for 1 and 2. The names for 13 through 19 consist of the unit name before the decade name (for example, *seventeen*). Furthermore, the names for numbers between 20 and 99 consist of the decade name followed by the unit name (for example, *thirty-three*). In contrast, Asian languages such as Chinese are more regular. The names for numbers between 11 and 99 consist of the decade name followed by the unit name. For instance, the Chinese word for 18 is *ten eight* and the word for 35 is *three ten five*. For numbers less than 10 and greater than 99, English and Chinese naming systems are more similar (Hurford, 1987).

The greater regularity of Asian languages suggests that children might have an easier time acquiring number names than their English-speaking counterparts. Some evidence indicates that this is so. Miura (1987) studied first-grade children from the United States and Japan. The children were shown how to use a set of base-10 blocks to represent numbers. The set consisted of white unit blocks and purple tens blocks equivalent to 10 unit blocks stuck together. On the first trial, the children were asked, in their native language, to read a number on a card and then to show that number in the blocks. After doing this for 5 minutes, they were given a second trial. They were reminded of the equivalence of 10 unit blocks and 1 tens block and were then asked to show each number in another way.

Miura distinguished three approaches to the task. A canonical approach was one that placed no more than nine unit blocks in the one's position, such as using four tens blocks and two unit blocks for 42. A noncanonical approach was one that used some combination of tens blocks and more than nine unit blocks, such as three tens blocks and 12 units blocks for 42. Finally, a one-to-one collection used only unit blocks, such as 42 unit blocks.

The results indicated that Japanese children were more than twice as likely as U.S. children to use canonical approaches on the first trial. The U.S. children tended to use one-to-one collections on the first trial. When prodded to generate a second approach, the U.S. children developed canonical approaches on the second trial. Miura also found that Japanese children used more noncanonical approaches than U.S. children. Miura has found similar results using Korean and Chinese first-graders (Miura, Kim, Chang, & Okamoto, 1988).

Furthermore, as predicted from the analysis of the naming systems, the range of numbers between 11 and 99 shows the greatest differences. Chinese preschoolers are no better than American preschoolers at counting between 1 and 10 or beyond 99 (although few can do the latter). But Chinese children are better at counting between 11 and 99 than their English-speaking counterparts (Miller, Smith, Zhu, & Zhang, 1995).

Additional work suggests that Chinese speakers pronounce numbers more quickly than English speakers (Hoosain, 1986; Hoosain & Salili, 1987) and that there is a correlation between speed of number pronunciation and mathematical performance (Ellis & Hennelly, 1980). Similarly, Miura and Okamoto (1989) found that Chinese children understood place value better and had a higher level of mathematics performance than English-speaking children.

The studies converge on the conclusion that the way that languages represent numbers influences mathematical thinking. The differences in mathematics achievement between Asian children and American children have been well documented (Stevenson, Lee, & Stigler, 1986), and there are surely many contributing factors to this difference, including parental emphasis, pedagogical techniques, and broader cultural influences. Nonetheless, the language one learns plays a role in mathematics education. Miura stresses that the way one thinks about numbers is fundamentally different in Chinese versus English. That is, it is not simply that Asian children do better on mathematics tasks; they appear to approach the tasks differently as well.

Summary

There is some evidence for Whorf's hypothesis at the lexical level. Languages differ in the number of color terms they employ and the ease with which a given color term can be expressed. Although Rosch's studies indicate that certain focal colors are more perceptually salient for Dani and U.S. individuals, her results do not preclude the existence of language effects also. Subsequent studies suggest that language influences the perception and perhaps the memory for color.

Recent studies indicate that Spanish and English speakers differ somewhat in how they perceive different conceptual categories. In addition, children learning Asian languages conceptualize numbers differently than children learning English. The extent to which either of these results reflects language influences or broader cultural influences is not clear.

Grammatical Influences on Cognition

We have seen that some evidence for the Whorf hypothesis exists at the lexical level. What about the differences in grammatical categories across languages? Do these influence how we perceive the world?

Form Perception

A study by Carroll and Casagrande (1958) compared Navaho and English. They observed that in Navaho, the form of the verb for handling an object varies with the form or shape of the object. The verb varies if the object is a long flexible object (such as a piece of string) versus a long rigid object (such as a stick) or a flat flexible object (such as a cloth). On the basis of this grammatical distinction, Carroll and Casagrande proposed that Navaho-speaking children would learn to discriminate the forms of objects at an earlier age than their English-speaking peers.

Carroll and Casagrande (1958) used an object triads test, in which the child had to pick which of two objects, of three presented, went best together. For example, a child might be presented with a yellow stick and a piece of blue rope of comparable size. The child would then be shown a yellow rope and asked with which of the first two it went best. Thus, it is possible to determine whether the children were focusing more on color or form. Carroll and Casagrande compared children who spoke Navaho with children who spoke English but came from the same reservation and lived in similar circumstances. The interesting result was that the Navaho children did group the objects on the basis of form at an earlier age than the English-speaking children.

But this was not all. Carroll and Casagrande (1958) also tested English-speaking children in a Boston suburb and discovered that they performed similarly to the Navaho children. They speculated that certain aspects of the environment of white suburban children, such as playing with puzzles and toys, can cause an English-speaking child to attend to form at an early age. These results seem generally to support Whorf's view that the grammatical distinctions in a language may influence or determine certain cognitive processes. But the observations from the suburban children suggest that even if grammatical categories determine qualities of thought, they are not the only determinants. Other attributes of the child's environment may serve the same function.

Counterfactual Reasoning

Bloom (1981) has conducted some interesting but controversial studies on the differences between how Chinese and English speakers reason. He was particularly interested in **counterfactual reasoning**, which is the ability to reason about an event that is contrary to fact. For instance, imagine a situation in which several people are waiting for John; he is late, and the group, as a consequence, is late to the movies. The English language has the subjunctive mood, shown in sentence (6), which enables us to discuss various states of affairs that we know to be false:

(6) If John had come earlier, they would have arrived at the movies on time. (adapted from Bloom, 1981, p. 19)

In contrast, Chinese does not have a specific form, such as the subjunctive, to express a counterfactual meaning. Bloom's thesis was that since the Chinese language does not explicitly mark the counterfactual, Chinese speakers would experience greater difficulties with counterfactual reasoning. He presented several anecdotes of conversations with Chinese speakers that appear to support this assertion. For instance, when Chinese speakers were asked sentence (7), they refused to answer the question, saying that the government had not:

(7) If the Hong Kong government were to pass a law requiring that all citizens born outside of Hong Kong make weekly reports of their activities to the police, how would you react? (Bloom, 1981, p. 13)

When they were asked to imagine that the government had and then respond, the speakers protested that this manner of thinking was "unnatural," "un-Chinese," or "Western."

Let us look at Bloom's hypothesis more closely. Bloom does not argue that Chinese speakers are incapable of reasoning counterfactually; he simply states that such reasoning is more difficult for them. According to Bloom, the English subjunctive signals direct entry into the counterfactual realm. In contrast, the sentences used to express the counterfactual in Chinese are potentially more ambiguous in that they depend on the context in which the utterance is made. A Chinese expression of the counterfactual is shown in sentence (8):

(8) If I am the U.S. president, then I will think before I speak. (Au, 1983, p. 157)

Note that this sentence can be interpreted as an implication (if/then) or as a counterfactual. The counterfactual interpretation only holds if the listener knows that the speaker is not the U.S. president. According to Bloom, when hearing (8), Chinese speakers must integrate their previous knowledge with the initial premise (*I am the U.S. president*) and then negate this premise before relating it to the if/then statement. In effect, the reasoning would have to be something like this: if A, then B; I know that A is not true, but if it were, then B would be true. This is a complex form of reasoning, with several steps. Thus, on the basis of this analysis of Chinese and English, Bloom predicted that Chinese speakers would make more errors in counterfactual reasoning than English speakers.

Bloom then conducted several studies to test this prediction. In one, Chinese and U.S. college students were presented with a story that involved a Greek philosopher who did not know Chinese, but if he had, he would have been influenced by Chinese culture and logic. One version of the story could be interpreted in either a counterfactual (that is, if he had known Chinese, he would have integrated the best features of Greek and Chinese systems) or a noncounterfactual way (that is, he did not read the Chinese works, but they were translated for him). The participants were then asked a series of questions to assess their understanding of the stories. Bloom found that although 98% of the U.S. students interpreted the story counterfactually, only 6% of the Chinese students did so. When given a second version of the story, in which the story was incoherent unless one made a counterfactual interpretation, 59% of the Chinese and 96% of the Americans interpreted the story counterfactually. Bloom concluded that the presence or absence of explicit marking of the counterfactual in one's language influences the facility with which one uses this mode of thought.

Bloom's conclusions have been called into question by Au (1983, 1984) and Liu (1985). Au, a native speaker of Chinese, argues that Bloom's stories are not idiomatic in Chinese, even though the stories were written by a Chinese speaker (under Bloom's direction) and then translated into English, rather than vice versa. Au tested Chinese students on revised versions of Bloom's studies and found much better performance. Au concluded that Bloom's studies provide no support for the Whorf hypothesis.

Bloom (1984) responded by challenging both the participants and the materials in Au's studies. Even though Au's participants were native Chinese speakers, they had taken English as a Second Language classes for 12 years. Bloom noted that the students were effectively bilingual, rendering them irrelevant to the issue. He also contended that Au's stories were too concrete and simple. Since Bloom had contended that differences in processing were more likely to emerge with abstract, complex materials, the strong performance of Chinese students on the concrete stories is, again, not directly relevant to Bloom's thesis. In short, Bloom argues that the different results found by Au could be interpreted in ways that are still favorable to his hypothesis.

Finally, Liu (1985) attempted to assess the two points made by Bloom (1984). Liu used a sample of Chinese students who, unlike the bilinguals studied by Au, had very little exposure to or proficiency in English. In addition, Liu used both the abstract story constructed by Bloom and the concrete one favored by Au. She found a strong developmental trend in the ability to reason counterfactually. The youngest students in her sample, 4th-graders, did very poorly (less than 20% correct), whereas the oldest, 11th-graders, did quite well (about 80% correct). In addition, most of the students performed better on the concrete story. Liu concluded that these age and story differences could not be attributable to the availability of a linguistic marker such as the subjunctive, and yet the absence of a distinct marker did not hamper the Chinese students' ability to reason counterfactually.

Although Liu's study was well designed, it does not refute Bloom's original thesis. Liu did not include a sample of English students, so there is no direct test of Bloom's hypothesis that English speakers would outperform Chinese speakers. Liu has shown that developmental maturity and story complexity influence the counterfactual reasoning of Chinese students and that under certain conditions Chinese students can perform better than Bloom's Chinese sample. But Bloom's contention was that English speakers would more easily reason counterfactually, not that Chinese speakers could not do so. It would appear that a direct comparison of Chinese and English monolinguals on a reasonably complex, yet idiomatic, set of materials would be in order.

What do we learn from all of these studies? On the specific matter of Chinese and English differences in counterfactual reasoning, unfortunately, we can draw no clear conclusions. Some variables that influence reasoning have been uncovered, but precisely how they affect the alleged language difference is not clear.

However, we may learn something of more general interest regarding how to test the Whorf hypothesis. One point is certainly the difficulty in securing materials that are appropriate and comparable in the languages being studied. This is a troublesome feature of the Bloom-Au debate. Au claims that Bloom's materials are not idiomatic in her native language, whereas the native speakers whom Bloom consulted believed the materials were appropriate. Perhaps Bloom's consultants differed from Au in linguistic or cultural background. In any event, in the absence of agreement regarding the appropriateness of the materials, it is difficult to interpret their results.

We also need to consider problems on the cognitive side. As noted earlier, Whorf was principally interested in habitual modes of thought. Lucy (1992b) suggests that counterfactual reasoning is more specialized than habitual since it is probably more accessible to those with higher levels of education. It thus remains to be seen whether Whorfian effects can be observed when more habitual forms of thought are assessed.

Cognitive Representation of Number

Some recent studies have turned to an aspect of language that is somewhat closer to Whorf's original concerns—how languages grammatically mark number. Lucy (1992a) contrasted number marking in English and Yucatec Maya, an indigenous language spoken in southeastern Mexico. Noun phrases may be distinguished by the presence or absence of two semantic features, animacy and discreteness (see Figure 14-1). **Animacy** refers to whether the referent of the noun phrase is alive or not. **Discreteness** refers to whether the referent is an object with definite outlines or boundaries. Using these features, a dog is + animate; a shovel is − animate, + discrete; and mud is − animate, − discrete. (Since discreteness is embedded within − animacy, there is no + animate, − discrete.) In English, the plural is obligatorily applied to the first two groups (which we call count nouns) but not to the third (which we call mass nouns). Thus, we say *persons* and *shovels*, but not *muds*. In Yucatec, the plural is (optionally) applied to + animate noun phrases, but not to

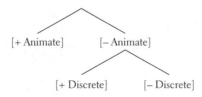

Figure 14-1. Semantic features pertaining to plural marking in Yucatec Maya and English. (Based on *Grammatical Categories and Cognition: A Case Study of the Linguistic Relativity Hypothesis,* by J. A. Lucy, p. 60, Cambridge University Press, 1992.)

the other two groups. Thus, the major distinction in English is between discrete and nondiscrete objects, whereas in Yucatec it is between animate and inanimate objects.

In addition, the Yucatec lexicon has words that refer to a range of meanings that would be subdivided into different lexical items in English. For instance, the word *che'* is used to refer to a number of objects of various shapes, all of which are made out of wood (tree, stick, board, and so on). Similarly, *hú'un* can refer to a type of tree, the bark of the tree, paper, or even items made of paper such as books.

Lucy (1992a) hypothesized two cognitive consequences of these linguistic differences. First, since the plural is used with greater regularity and for a wider array of referents in English, he hypothesized that English speakers should habitually attend to the number of various objects of reference more than Yucatec speakers. This should lead English speakers to specify the number of objects, especially inanimate objects, more often than Yucatec speakers. Second, he hypothesized that English speakers would be more sensitive to shape than to substance, whereas Yucatec speakers would be just the opposite. English speakers would attend to shape because it distinguishes discrete objects from nondiscrete objects. Yucatec speakers would attend less to shape because their language does not mark the discrete/ nondiscrete distinction, and they would attend more to substance because of the presence of lexical items based on substance or material.

Lucy (1992a) assessed cognitive processes in a series of 12 experimental tasks. In several, the participants were presented with pictures (line drawings) depicting various scenes of Yucatec everyday life. The pictures included different objects in various numbers (for example, three pigs, one hen, and so on). The participants (adult Mayan men between 18 and 45 years of age and college-aged U.S. men) were asked to do such things as verbally describe the pictures and recall the pictures. As expected, the English speakers specified the number of inanimate objects more frequently than the Yucatec speakers. Also as expected, there were no differences between speakers in the frequency with which they specified the number of animate beings or nondiscrete substances.

Lucy (1992a) also had a series of tasks in which the subjects were presented with three objects and asked to judge which two were most similar. In one study, the original object was a cardboard box, and then the subjects were given two other objects, a plastic box (shape alternative) and a piece of cardboard (material alternative), and asked to determine which alternative was most similar to the original. Their judgments tended to follow the linguistic classifications for each language. English speakers regarded the two boxes as most similar, whereas Yucatec speakers regarded the piece of cardboard as most similar to the cardboard box. English speakers grouped together those alternatives that are treated the same way linguistically (that is, with the plural morpheme). In contrast, Yucatec speakers attended to substance more than shape.

Lucy's work is important in several respects. First, he has contrasted two grammatical treatments of number and how they may lead to different ways of thinking about objects. In contrast, several earlier approaches have identified a grammatical feature that is present in one language but not another. The latter approach tends to implicitly endorse the view that one language is deficient relative to another, whereas the comparative approach taken by Lucy merely implies that languages are different. In retrospect, much of the discussion of Bloom's research may have been related to this aspect of his work (but see Bloom, 1981, pp. 15–16). Second, Lucy used a number of different cognitive tasks. Many earlier studies used a single task and tended to reduce the broad Whorfian concerns of differences in world views to a single narrow experimental task. The use of multiple tasks makes sense in most psycholinguistic studies; it is more important, and perhaps even vital, in tests of the Whorf hypothesis.

Final Observations

The status of the Whorf hypothesis depends on what we take it to mean. If the claim is that the presence of a language feature determines a mode of thought that cannot be attained in any other way, then the hypothesis is surely wrong. However, the weak version of the Whorf hypothesis may be tenable. We have seen a parallel between the results of recent studies at the lexical level and those at the grammatical level. Whereas earlier studies did not provide any evidence for the Whorf hypothesis, recent work suggests otherwise. One reason may be that researchers are just beginning to find adequate ways of exploring a hypothesis as far-reaching and yet as subtle as the Whorf hypothesis. We have seen that there are some major obstacles in terms of the selection of participants, the preparation of materials, and the assessment of cognition. It is also necessary to tease apart the influences of language and culture on cognition. It appears that as researchers find ways to effectively grapple with these problems, the results are becoming more supportive of Whorf's hypothesis.

One final point. Several of the studies discussed in this chapter have focused on the percentage of errors as the measure of cognitive performance. However, as Hunt and Agnoli (1991; see also Hardin & Banaji, 1993) point out, much more subtle measures of cognition are available. We have seen throughout this book that certain linguistic variables, such as the presence of multiple meanings of lexically ambiguous words, may influence the speed of performance but not necessarily the number of errors. Hunt and Agnoli note that cognitive measures such as reaction time have not been used very often in studies of the Whorf hypothesis. This is unfortunate because effects of the sort that Whorf had in mind may be rather subtle. Further research using more sophisticated measures of cognition may yet provide evidence for what Bloom called "the linguistic shaping of thought."

Summary

At the grammatical level, the distinctions employed by a language may influence the ease with which a speaker can adopt a particular mode of thought. Certain modes of thought may be easier to attain or appear more natural for speakers of some languages, although they are by no means unattainable for speakers of other languages. On balance, these studies provide some support for the weak version of the Whorf hypothesis.

Review Questions

1. Identify the two parts of the Whorf hypothesis.
2. Define differentiation.
3. What conclusions did Whorf draw from his study of count and mass nouns in English?
4. Distinguish between the strong and weak versions of the linguistic determinism view.
5. Discuss the role of codability in color cognition.
6. Discuss Rosch's color studies and the conclusion that she drew.
7. What relationship did Miura find between language and mathematical skills?
8. What conclusions can be drawn from the Carroll and Casagrande study?
9. What criticisms have been made of the Bloom study?
10. Describe Lucy's studies of grammatical number marking in Yucatec and English.

Thought Questions

1. The publication manual of the American Psychological Association and other style manuals endorse the elimination of sexist language. Based on the material discussed in this chapter, do you think that the reduction of sexist language will influence the thoughts or attitudes of individuals who comply with these standards?
2. How might the distinction between automatic and controlled processes (see Chapter 3) be used to test the Whorf hypothesis?
3. Choose one or more of the studies designed to test the Whorf hypothesis and critically evaluate it. Is the study a fair test of the hypothesis? Why or why not?

Glossary

Accommodation   A phonological process in which elements that are shifted or deleted are adapted to their error-induced environments.

Acknowledgment   A **speech act** in which the speaker expresses feelings for the listener. An example is *I'm sorry I was rude and hurt you.*

Acoustic phonetics   The branch of phonetics that specifies the acoustic characteristics associated with each speech sound.

Active processing   A collection of activities that includes relating new information to information we have in permanent memory, asking questions of the material, and writing summaries or outlines of the material.

Active voice   A sentence in which the surface structure subject is also the deep structure or logical subject of the sentence, such as *The woman scolded the child.*

Affricate   A **consonant** that begins with complete closure of the **vocal tract** followed by gradual release of air pressure, such as the *ch* in *church.*

Agent   The thematic or semantic role corresponding to an individual who performs a given action, such as *the manager* in *The manager opened the store.*

Agrammatic speech   Speech in which there is a lack of grammatical structure, such as the absence of grammatical **morphemes** and **function words.**

Agrammatism   See **agrammatic speech.**

Agraphia   An **aphasia** characterized by the inability to write.

Alexia   An **aphasia** characterized by the inability to comprehend written or printed words.

Alphabet   A writing system in which each letter is supposed to represent a phoneme.

Alveolar   A **consonant** articulated at the alveolar ridge, such as the *d* in *dog.*

Ambiguity   A property of language in which a word or sentence may be interpreted in more than one way. See also **deep-structure ambiguity, lexical ambiguity,** and **phrase ambiguity.**

American Sign Language (ASL)   The form of sign language used in the United States. It is a complete language distinct from oral languages.

Anaphor   A linguistic expression that refers back to prior information in **discourse.**

Anaphoric reference   A form of **reference cohesion** in which one linguistic expression refers back to prior information in **discourse.**

Angular gyrus   Believed to serve as an association area in the brain that connects one region with another; particularly important for the association of visual stimuli with linguistic symbols. Damage to the angular gyrus leads to both **alexia** and **agraphia.**

Animacy   A semantic feature denoting whether an object is alive.

Antecedent   Prior information in **discourse.**

Anticipation   A speech error in which a later word or sound takes the place of an earlier one.

Anticipatory coarticulation   Type of **coarticulation** in which the shape of the **vocal tract** for a given speech sound is influenced by upcoming sounds.

Anticipatory retracing   Self-repair in which the speaker traces back to some point prior to an error. Previously correct material is repeated along with the corrected material. See also **fresh start** and **instant repair.**

Antonymy   A semantic relationship in which two words mean the opposite of one another.

Aphasia   A language or speech disorder caused by brain damage.

Arbitrariness   A feature of language in which there is no direct resemblance between words and their **referents.**

Arcuate fasciculus   The primary pathway in the brain between **Wernicke's area** and **Broca's area.**

Argument   The portion of a **proposition** that refers to the person or thing that is doing something.

Articulatory phonetics   The branch of phonetics that specifies the articulatory gestures associated with each speech sound.

Aspiration   A puff of air that accompanies the production of certain speech sounds. Aspiration is phonemic in some languages but not in English.

Assertion   A communicative act in which a person draws the attention of another person to a particular object—for example, a child showing a toy to an adult as if to say *This is mine.* Assertions may be made through words or gestures.

Assimilation   A phonological process in which one speech sound is replaced by another that is similar to sounds elsewhere in the utterance.

Associative chain theory   A theory favored by behaviorists that explains the formulation of a sentence as a chain of associations between the individual words in the sentence.

Attempt-suppressing signal   A cue given by a speaker to indicate to a listener that he or she is not finished.

Attributive relations   Relations between words that indicate the attributes of a given word, such as *round* as an attribute for *ball.*

Auditory level   A level of speech perception in which the speech signal is represented in terms of frequency, intensity, and temporal attributes.

Automaticity   A property of cognitive processes that do not require any processing capacity.

Automatic process   An activity that does not require any processing capacity.

Auxiliary verb   A "helping verb." A verb such as *is, do,* or *can* used in conjunction with the main verb in a sentence such as *Kim is gardening this afternoon.*

Baby talk   See **motherese.**

Background   In discourse processing, information that was introduced or discussed earlier and is no longer the focus of discussion.

Basic child grammar   The grammatical characteristics of early child language found in numerous languages such as telegraphic speech.

Basic color term   A term that refers to color and that is only one **morpheme,** not contained within another color, and not restricted to a small number of **referents.**

Basic-level term   A term that refers to a category in which there are broad similarities among exemplars.

Behaviorism   The doctrine that states that the proper concern of psychology should be the objective study of behavior rather than the study of the mind.

Bilabial   A **consonant** articulated at the mouth such as the *b* in *big*.

Binaural perception   A procedure in which the same stimulus is presented to the two ears.

Blend   A speech error in which two or more words are combined.

Bottom-up processing   A process in which lower-level processes are carried out without influence from higher-level processes (for example, perception of **phonemes** being uninfluenced by the words in which they appear).

Bound morpheme   A unit of meaning that exists only when combined or bound to a **free morpheme**.

Bridging   A process in which the listener or reader draws inferences to build a "bridge" between the current utterance and preceding utterances.

Broca's aphasia   An **aphasia** characterized by deficits in language production. Also called **expressive aphasia**.

Broca's area   A brain region in the frontal lobe of the left hemisphere. Damage to this region leads to **Broca's aphasia**.

Bystanders   Individuals who are openly present but not part of a conversation.

Cataphoric reference   A form of **reference cohesion** in which one linguistic expression refers to information yet to be introduced in discourse.

Categorical perception   The inability to discriminate sounds within a phonemic category.

Category-size effect   The fact that it takes longer to semantically verify a statement of the form *An A is a B* if B is a larger semantic category.

Category-specific dissociations   In **aphasia**, the selective inability to retrieve certain categories of words, such as fruits or vegetables, while retaining the ability to recognize and use other word categories.

Child-directed speech   Speech addressed to children. See also **motherese**.

Chunking   Grouping individual pieces of information into larger units. A **short-term memory** strategy.

Coalescence   A phonological process in which **phonemes** from different syllables are combined into a single syllable.

Coarticulation   The process of articulating more than one speech sound at a time.

Codability   The length of a verbal expression.

Cognitive constraint   A bias that children are assumed to use to infer the meanings of words.

Cognitive economy   A characteristic of semantic memory in which information is only represented once within a **semantic network**.

Cognitive science   The branch of science devoted to the study of the mind; consists of the fields of psychology, artificial intelligence, neuroscience, linguistics, philosophy, and adjacent disciplines.

Coherence   The degree to which different parts of a text are connected to one another. Coherence exists at both local and global levels of **discourse**.

Cohesion   Local **coherence** relations between adjacent sentences in **discourse**.

Cohort model   A model of auditory word recognition in which listeners are assumed to develop a group of candidates, a **word initial cohort,** and then determine which member of that cohort corresponds to the presented word.

Commissive   A speech act in which the speaker is obligated by virtue of the speech act to do something. An example is *I'll return the book by Tuesday.*

Communicative competence   The skill associated with using a language appropriately and effectively in various social situations.

Complement   A noun phrase that includes a verb—for example, *you sat down* in *I see you sat down.*

Complex sentence   A sentence that expresses more than one **proposition.**

Conceptual complexity   See **semantic complexity.**

Conduction aphasia   An **aphasia** characterized by the inability to repeat what one has heard.

Conjunctive cohesion   A form of **cohesion** in which we express a relationship between sentences or phrases by using conjunctions such as *and, or,* and *but.*

Connected discourse   See **discourse.**

Connectionist model   A model of cognitive/linguistic processes that assumes (1) a vast interconnected network of information nodes in which each node influences and is influenced by a large number of adjacent nodes and (2) parallel processing of information. Also called **parallel distributed processing.**

Connotation   The aspect of meaning suggested by a word but not strictly part of the word's dictionary definition. See also **denotation.**

Consonant   A speech sound in which the **vocal tract** is partially or fully closed during production.

Constative   A speech act in which the speaker expresses a belief with the intention of creating the same belief in the listener. An example is *Sally reported the incident to the police.*

Constituent   A grammatical unit such as a noun or verb phrase.

Constraint-based model   A model of sentence comprehension in which we simultaneously use all available information (semantic, syntactic, contextual, and so forth) in our initial **parsing** of a sentence.

Content word   A word (such as a noun, a verb, or an adjective) that plays a primary role in the meaning of a sentence. See also **function word.**

Context-conditioned variation   The fact that the acoustic parameters associated with a given speech sound vary with its phonetic context.

Context effect   The finding in **semantic verification studies** that filler items influence the verification times of target items.

Contextualized language   Language that is related to the immediate context.

Contralateral   The arrangement in the nervous system in which one half of the brain controls the other half of the body.

Controlled process   An activity that requires processing capacity.

Convention   A shared assumption about communication.

Coordination   A sentence in which two or more simple sentences are linked by a coordinating expression such as *and, or,* or *but*—for example, *Lake Superior is beautiful, but it is cold.*

Copula The verb *to be* used as the main verb in a sentence such as *Miguel is wonderful.*

Corpus callosum A band of fibers that connects the two cerebral hemispheres.

Counterfactual reasoning The ability to reason about an event that is contrary to fact.

Count noun A noun that takes the plural **morpheme** and refers to an object with clear boundaries, such as a stick. Also called an **individual noun.**

Creole The language developed by children who have been exposed to a **pidgin** as their native language.

Decontextualized language Language that is separated in time or place from its **referent.**

Deep structure The level of linguistic structure assumed in transformational grammar that expresses the underlying semantic meaning of a sentence.

Deep-structure ambiguity A form of **ambiguity** in which a sentence may be derived from two different **deep structures.**

Default value The value of a **parameter** that a child is hypothesized to be born with.

Deferred imitation Imitation of a behavior that was observed some time earlier.

Deletion A speech error in which something is left out.

Denotation The dictionary definition of a word. See also **connotation.**

Dental A **consonant** articulated at the teeth, such as the *th* in *thin.*

Derivation The series of linguistic rules needed to generate a sentence.

Derivational morpheme A **bound morpheme** that is added to a **free morpheme** to create a new word. For example, *-ness* turns *good* (an adjective) into *goodness* (a noun).

Derivational theory of complexity The theory that states that the psychological complexity of a sentence is directly proportional to the length of its derivation.

Descriptive adequacy The extent to which a **grammar** can provide a structural description of a sentence. See also **explanatory adequacy** and **observational adequacy.**

Determiner A part of speech that quantifies or specifies a count noun, such as *the* in *The cat ate the plant.*

Dichotic listening An experimental task in which different stimuli are simultaneously presented to the two ears.

Differentiation The number of words in a semantic domain.

Directive A speech act in which the speaker tries to influence a listener's behavior. An example is *The student asked the professor to delay the exam.*

Discontinuous constituent A grammatical constituent in which some elements are separated, such as *picked* and *up* in *George picked the baby up.*

Discourse A group of sentences combined in a meaningful manner.

Discreteness A semantic feature denoting whether an object has definite outlines or boundaries. For example, a tree is + discrete, whereas air is − discrete.

Dishabituation The recovery of the strength of a habituated response when a novel stimulus is presented.

Displacement A feature of language in which words are separated in space and time from their referents.

Distinctive feature The specification of the differences between speech sounds in terms of individual contrasts.

Duality of patterning   A feature of a communication system in which a small number of meaningless units can be combined into a large number of meaningful units.

Duplex perception   An experimental technique in which **formant transitions** are presented to one ear and **steady states** to the other.

Eavesdroppers   Individuals who listen in on conversations without the participants' awareness.

Elaboration   The process of relating incoming information to information already stored in permanent memory.

Ellipsis   A form of cohesion in which a previous item is dropped from subsequent sentences but its presence is assumed.

Empiricism   The branch of philosophy that emphasizes the use of controlled observation and the belief that experience shapes human behavior.

Episode   A component of a **story grammar.**

Episodic memory   The division of **permanent memory** in which personally experienced information is stored.

Evoked potential   Measurement of electrical activity in a region of the brain following presentation of a stimulus.

Exchange   A speech error in which two sounds or words change places with one another.

Excitatory interaction   In a **connectionist model,** the tendency for one unit's activation to increase the activation of other units.

Explanatory adequacy   The extent to which a **grammar** can explain the facts of language acquisition. See also **descriptive adequacy** and **observational adequacy.**

Explicit knowledge   Knowledge of how to perform various acts. See also **tacit knowledge.**

Expository discourse   A type of discourse in which the writer's goal is to convey information about the subject matter.

Expressive aphasia.   See **Broca's aphasia.**

Expressive strategy   A style of child language characterized by low noun/pronoun ratio, poor articulation, clear **intonation,** and relatively long utterances.

Eye-voice span   The lag between eye position and voice when reading aloud, about six or seven words.

False recognition error   When a subject believes that an item was presented during a study although it was not.

Feature level   A level of written language perception in which a visual stimulus is represented in terms of the physical features that comprise a letter of the **alphabet,** such as a vertical line, a curved line, and so on.

Felicity condition   A condition that must be present for a **speech act** to be understood as sincere or valid.

Feral children   Children who have grown up without human companionship in the wild.

Fis phenomenon   When a child mispronounces a word yet correctly distinguishes between child and adult versions of that word.

Fixation   The time spent focused at a given location during reading; the time between eye movements.

Focal color   The most representative example of a **basic color.**

Foreground   In **discourse** processing, information that is currently being discussed or explained.

Formal complexity.   See **syntactic complexity.**

Formant   A concentrated band of energy found in the **sound spectrograms** of **phonemes.**

Formant transition   A rapid increase or decrease in frequency at the beginning of a **formant.**

Free morpheme   A unit of meaning that can stand alone.

Fresh start   **Self-repair** in which the speaker replaces the original syntactic structure with a new one. See also **anticipatory retracing** and **instant repair.**

Fricative   A **consonant** in which the **vocal tract** is partially closed during articulation, such as the *f* in *fat.*

Functional Magnetic Resonance Imaging (fMRI)   A method of imaging brain structure and brain activity.

Functional relations   Relations among words that indicate what can be done with the **referent** of a word. For example, words such as *sitting, rest,* and *rocking* indicate what can be done with a chair.

Function word   A word such as an article, preposition, or conjunction that plays a secondary role in the meaning of a sentence. See also **content word.**

Garden path sentence   A sentence in which the comprehender assumes a particular meaning of a word or phrase but discovers later that the assumption was incorrect, forcing the comprehender to backtrack and reinterpret the sentence.

Genre   A category of **discourse** characterized by a particular form or content, such as the genre for fairy tales.

Given information   Information that the speaker assumes the listener already knows.

Given/new strategy   A comprehension strategy in which utterances are analyzed into given and new components and the new information is stored in memory with previously received information.

Global structure   See **macrostructure.**

Glottis   The opening between the **vocal cords.**

Grammar   In linguistics, a theory of language or set of hypotheses about how language is organized.

Grammatical morpheme.   See **bound morpheme.**

Grapheme   A printed letter of the **alphabet.**

Ground   In metaphor, the implied similarity between **tenor** and **vehicle.**

Habituation   The decline in a response to a stimulus following repeated presentation of the stimulus.

Head parameter   A grammatical feature that specifies the position of the head of a phrase (noun in noun phrase, verb in verb phrase, and so on).

Holistic processing   A style of processing, associated with the right cerebral hemisphere, that is global in nature.

Holophrase   A one-word utterance used by a child to express more than the meaning attributed to the word by adults.

Homesign   A form of gestural communication invented by deaf children who are not exposed to a sign language.

Hyponymy   A semantic relationship in which a word is a superordinate, coordinate, or subordinate of another.

Iconicity   A characteristic of language in which words resemble their **referents.**

Idiomorph   A sound or sound sequence used consistently by a child to refer to someone or something even though it is not the sound sequence conventionally used in the language for that purpose.

Illocutionary force   In **speech act** theory, the action that is performed by a speaker in uttering a sentence.

Immediacy principle   The principle that we immediately interpret words as we encounter them.

Implication   A semantic relationship in which if one linguistic expression is true, then another must be. For example, if *John is a bachelor* is true, then *John is not married* must also be.

Incompatibility   A semantic relationship in which a word contradicts another.

Incremental processing   The notion that we are planning one portion of our utterance as we articulate another portion.

Index of Productive Syntax (IPSyn)   A measure of later syntactic development. It is computed by counting the occurrence of various types of sentence constructions in a child's language.

Indirect speech act   A **speech act** in which the literal utterance meaning is not the same as the speaker's meaning.

Induction   A process of reasoning from the specific to the general. For instance, if all of the specific horses we have seen are brown, then we might induce that all horses are brown.

Inference   A **proposition** drawn by the listener or reader.

Inflectional morpheme.   A **bound morpheme** that is added to a **free morpheme** to express grammatical contrasts in sentences. English examples include the plural and past tense morphemes.

Inhibitory interaction   In a **connectionist model,** the tendency for one unit's activation to decrease the activation of other units.

Initiation-reply-evaluation sequence   A form of **discourse** used in classrooms in which the teacher asks a student a question, the student answers, and the teacher evaluates the answer.

Instantiation   Identifying a general term with a specific meaning.

Instant repair   **Self-repair** in which the speaker traces back to an error that is then replaced with the correct word. See also **anticipatory retracing** and **fresh start.**

Institutional setting   A conversational setting in which participants engage in speech exchanges that resemble ordinary conversations but are limited by institutional rules.

Interactional content   Content of a sentence that conveys the speaker's attitude toward the listener. Utterances that are high in interactional content include jokes, insults, and excessively polite speech.

Interactive gesture A form of gesture used in conversation to convey **interactional content,** such as holding up one's hands to indicate that one's turn is not finished.

Internal lexicon The storage of lexical information in memory.

Interruption A period of simultaneous speech more than one word prior to the speaker's projected completion point. See also **overlap.**

Intersection search The process of retrieving information from a **semantic network.**

Intonation The use of pitch to signal meaning.

Intonational contour A pattern of pitch changes characteristic of an utterance as a whole, such as the rising intonation often found in questions.

Ipsalateral The arrangement in the nervous system in which one half of the brain controls the same side of the body.

Isolated children Children who have grown up without normal human interactions.

Joint action An action carried out by an ensemble of people acting in coordination with one another. Examples include dancing and conversing.

Kanji Japanese logographic characters borrowed from Chinese.

Kana Japanese syllabic symbols.

Language bioprogram A hypothesized innate **grammar** that is used by children whose environmental exposure to language is limited. The bioprogram is assumed to be suppressed in children whose language environment is normal.

Language bioprogram hypothesis The hypothesis that children whose environmental exposure to language is limited use a backup linguistic system.

Laryngeal system The system of muscles that determines whether a speech sound is voiced or voiceless.

Late closure strategy A strategy used in **parsing** that states that wherever possible we prefer to attach new items to the current **constituent.**

Lateralization The extent to which a given psychological function is served by one hemisphere of the brain. Functions primarily served by one hemisphere are said to be lateralized to that hemisphere.

Lemma Syntactic aspects of word knowledge.

Letter level The level of written perception in which a visual stimulus is represented as a letter of the **alphabet.**

Lexeme Phonological aspects of word knowledge.

Lexical access The process of activating lexical items from **semantic memory.**

Lexical ambiguity A form of **ambiguity** in which a word has more than one meaning.

Lexical bias effect The finding that speech errors more commonly result in true words than would be expected by chance.

Lexical cohesion The use of reiteration, **synonymy, hyponymy,** and other semantic relationships to link successive sentences in **discourse.**

Lexical decision task An experimental task in which a subject sees a string of letters and must rapidly decide whether the string is a word.

Lexical-functional grammar   A **grammar** in which structural relationships are built into enriched lexical entries rather than with **transformational rules.**

Lexical-insertion rule   A rule that governs how lexical entries are inserted into a tree structure during the derivation of a sentence.

Lexicon   The vocabulary of a language. See also **internal lexicon.**

Linguistic determinism   The hypothesis that languages determine nonlinguistic cognitive processes such as the perception of shapes.

Linguistic productivity   The ability to create or comprehend an infinite number of new sentences that are grammatically correct; also called linguistic creativity.

Linguistic relativity   The hypothesis that the cognitive processes determined by language vary from language to language.

Linguistics   The branch of science that studies the origin, structure, and use of language.

Local structure.   See **microstructure.**

Locutionary act   In **speech act** theory, the act of saying something.

Logogen   Structure in the **internal lexicon** that specifies the various attributes (semantic, orthographic, and so on) of a word.

Logography   An **orthography** in which spoken words are represented by visual symbols.

Longitudinal investigation   A method of studying child development in which a small number of children are studied over a period of years.

Long-term memory   See **permanent memory.**

Macrostructure   The global **coherence** relationships in **discourse.**

Manner of articulation   How a speech sound is articulated (for example, **stop, fricative,** and so on).

Manual English   A manual version of English, as in fingerspelling the letters of the English **alphabet.** See also **American Sign Language.**

Mass noun   A noun that does not take the plural **morpheme** and refers to objects without clear boundaries, such as air.

Mean length of utterance in morphemes (MLU)   An index of children's language growth. It is computed by dividing the number of **morphemes** by the number of utterances.

Mental model   A mental representation of some aspect of the world.

Metalinguistic awareness   The ability to think of language as an object.

Metaphor   A form of language in which a word or phrase that literally denotes one idea is interpreted to mean a different one and suggests a similarity between the two—for example, *My head is an apple without a core.*

Microstructure   The local **coherence** relationships in **discourse.**

Minimal attachment strategy   A principle used in **parsing.** It states that we prefer attaching new items into the **phrase marker** being constructed using the fewest syntactic nodes consistent with the rules of the language.

Minimal response   An utterance such as *uh-huh* or *um-hmm* made by a listener during a conversation. Ordinarily minimal responses are taken as displays of interest in a speaker's topic.

Mispronunciation detection   An experimental task in which subjects are presented auditorily with tapes that occasionally include mispronounced words. The subject's task is to detect the mispronunciations.

Modularity   The degree to which language processing is independent of general cognitive processes such as memory and reasoning. Also refers to the degree to which an aspect of language is independent of other aspects of language. For example, **parsing** may be thought of as modular if there is a syntactic processor that operates independently of semantic and **discourse** processes.

Morpheme   The smallest unit of meaning in a language.

Morphology   The system of word-forming elements and processes in a language.

Motherese   A form of adult-to-child speech characterized by relatively simple utterances, concrete **referents,** exaggerated **intonation** patterns, and a high proportion of **directive** utterances.

Mutual exclusivity bias   A cognitive constraint in which children assume that an object is ordinarily not given two different names.

Narrative discourse   A form of **discourse** in which settings, characters, and plot play a central role.

Nasal   A **consonant** in which air flows through the nasal cavity as in the *n* in *nail.*

Nativism   An approach to language acquisition that emphasizes the innate organization of language.

Necessary condition   A condition that must be present in order for a specified event to occur.

Negative evidence   Evidence that a particular linguistic expression (a word or sentence) is inappropriate or unacceptable. Negative evidence may be presented explicitly (*No, that's not a cow; that's a dog*) or implicitly (such as when adults repeat child utterances with corrections).

Neurolinguistics   The study of how linguistic information is processed in the brain.

New information   Information that the comprehender (reader or listener) is assumed not to know.

Nonnutritive sucking   A procedure used in research with infants in which sucks on a pacifier are recorded.

Null-subject parameter   A grammatical feature that specifies whether a language permits sentences without subjects. Also called the **pro-drop parameter.**

Object permanence   The awareness that objects that can no longer be seen still exist.

Object relative clause   A **relative clause** in which a *wh*-clause modifies the object of a sentence.

Observational adequacy   The extent to which a **grammar** can distinguish between acceptable and unacceptable strings of words. See also **descriptive adequacy** and **explanatory adequacy.**

Occipital lobe   The visual center at the back of the brain.

Operating principle   A preferred way of taking in or operating on information.

Original word game   A game in which adults teach children the names of words. Children point to an object and say, *What's that?* and the adult supplies the name.

Orthography   The representation of a sound by written or printed symbols.

Ostensive definition   The process of defining a word by pointing to its **referent.**

Overextension   When a child uses a word to refer to a larger set of **referents** than an adult would—for example, calling a round clock a *moon.*

Overhearers   Individuals who are not part of a conversation. May be **bystanders** or **eavesdroppers.**

Overlap   A period of simultaneous speech during the last word of a speaker's projected closing. See also **interruption.**

Overregularization   When a child applies a linguistic rule to cases that are exceptions to the rule—for example, saying *goed* instead of *went.*

Paragrammatic speech   Speech that is fluent but not coherent and that contains many irrelevant associations.

Parallel distributed processing   See **connectionist model.**

Parallel processing   When two or more processes take place at the same time.

Parallel transmission   The notion that different **phonemes** of the same syllable are encoded into the speech signal simultaneously.

Parameter   (1) In grammatical theory, a grammatical feature that is set in different ways in different languages. See also **head parameter** and **null-subject parameter.** (2) In **American Sign Language,** a dimension along which signs may differ, such as hand configuration, movement, and location.

Parameter setting   In grammatical theory, the notion that children are born with grammatical **parameters** that are preset to certain values. Language acquisition is seen as a matter of resetting these parameters to the values of one's native language.

Parietal lobe   Middle brain region containing motor centers that control facial and speech muscles.

Parsing   The process of assigning words into grammatical categories.

Partial report technique   A method for studying the **sensory stores.** Subjects are briefly presented with an array of stimuli and asked to report only a portion of the array.

Participants   Individuals who are taking part in a conversation.

Particle-movement transformation   A **transformational rule** that accounts for the movement of particles such as *up* around noun phrases.

Part-whole relations   Relations between words in which one word names a part of something, such as *seat* or *cushion* for *chair.*

Passive transformation   A **transformational rule** that transforms the **deep structure** of an active sentence into the **passive voice.**

Passive voice   A sentence in which the **surface structure** subject is the **deep structure** or logical object of the action such as in *The child was scolded by the mother.*

Patient   A thematic or semantic role corresponding to the individual acted upon, such as *the elderly man* in *The neighborhood frightened the elderly man.*

Pattern recognition   A process of matching information in the **sensory stores** with information retrieved from **permanent memory.**

Perlocutionary effect   In **speech act** theory, the effect of a speech act on a listener.

Permanent memory   Memory that is essentially permanent (also called **long-term memory**). Includes **semantic** and **episodic memory.**

Perseveration   A speech error in which an earlier word or sound intrudes on a later one.

Perseveratory coarticulation   The type of **coarticulation** in which the shape of the **vocal tract** for a given speech sound is influenced by previous sounds.

Personal settings   A conversational setting in which there is a free exchange of turns among two or more participants.

Phone   The minimal unit of sound.

Phoneme   The minimal unit of sound that contributes to meaning.

Phoneme monitoring   An experimental task in which subjects listen for a particular **phoneme** while comprehending a passage and being timed for how long it takes them to monitor the phoneme.

Phonemic restoration   A **top-down process** in which the listener uses the context to restore **phonemes** missing from the speech signal.

Phonemic similarity effect   The observation that speech errors and targets are phonemically similar.

Phonetic level   A level of speech perception in which the speech signal is represented in terms of acoustic cues, such as **formant transitions.**

Phonetics   The study of speech sounds.

Phonetic trading relations   The notion that different acoustic cues have trade-off effects on speech perception.

Phonological bias technique   A method of inducing speech errors by having a subject read a series of words with similar phonological patterns.

Phonological level   A level of **speech perception** in which the speech signal is converted into a phoneme and phonological rules are applied to the sound sequence.

Phonology   The sound system of a language, including the rules determining how different **phonemes** may be arranged in a word.

Phrase marker   A tree diagram that represents the **phrase structure** of a sentence.

Phrase structure   The hierarchical organization of sentences into phrases.

Phrase-structure ambiguity   A form of **ambiguity** in which a sentence has multiple meanings that may be revealed by regrouping the sentence **constituents.**

Phrase-structure rule   A rule that rewrites one **constituent** into one or more constituents. For example, a verb phrase may be rewritten as a verb and a noun phrase.

Pidgin   An auxiliary language that is created when speakers of mutually unintelligible languages are in close contact.

Place of articulation   The location within the **vocal tract** where articulation of a speech sound is produced (for example, **bilabial, alveolar,** and so on).

Positive evidence   Evidence that a particular linguistic expression (a word or sentence) is appropriate or acceptable. Positive evidence may be presented explicitly (when someone approves of another's word or utterance) or implicitly (for example, when a person responds to another's utterance without explicitly commenting on its appropriateness).

Poverty of stimulus argument   The argument made by followers of **nativism** that the environmental input presented to children is too weak and degenerate to account for the child's language acquisition.

Pragmatics   The social rules underlying language use.

Preemption principle   The principle that the speech of a child's linguistic environment preempts or suppresses the **language bioprogram.**

Preoperational period   The second of Piaget's periods of cognitive development.

Pretend play   The use of an object in a playful or unconventional manner, such as using a toy rake to comb a doll's hair.

Priming   An experimental procedure in which one word is presented in advance of another, target word, which reduces the time needed to retrieve or activate the target word.

Problem of invariance   The fact that there is no one-to-one correspondence between speech cues and perception.

Processing capacity   The overall amount of mental capacity available for various tasks or activities.

Pro-drop parameter   See **null-subject parameter.**

Proposition   A unit of meaning consisting of a predicate (verb, adjective, or conjunction) plus one or more arguments (noun or pronoun). Simple sentences express a single proposition, whereas complex sentences express more than one proposition.

Propositional representation   In sentence or **discourse** memory, memory for the meaning apart from the exact words used.

Prosodic factors   Factors such as **intonation** and **stress** that are superimposed on speech segments. Also called **suprasegmentals.**

Psycholinguistics   The study of the comprehension, production, and acquisition of language.

Pure word deafness   An **aphasia** in which a person is unable to comprehend language in the auditory modality. Comprehension of visual language and production in both modalities are normal.

Radical   In a **logography,** a group of strokes related to meaning.

Rate   The speed at which speech is articulated.

Rate normalization   The process of taking the rate of speech into consideration when using acoustic cues during speech perception.

Rationalism   The philosophical tradition that emphasizes the use of argument and the belief that innate knowledge guides human behavior.

Reading span task   A measure of **working memory** capacity during reading. Subjects read aloud a series of sentences and then try to recall the last word in each sentence. The number of words recalled is the measure of the subject's reading span.

Receptive aphasia.   See **Wernicke's aphasia.**

Recipient   A semantic or thematic role referring to the person to whom something is given—for example, *Susan* in *John gave the flower to Susan.*

Reciprocity   In **American Sign Language,** the distinction between whether the subject is the agent of the action and the object is the recipient (*they pinched them*) and whether there is mutual interchange between the subject and object (*they pinched each other*).

Recognition point In auditory word recognition, the point at which a word diverges from other possible words.

Recursive rule A rule that applies to its own output, such as a rule for self-embedded sentences.

Reduction A phonological process in child language in which one or more **phonemes** are deleted. Also called cluster reduction because **consonant** clusters are often reduced, such as saying *take* for *steak*.

Reduplicated babbling A form of babbling in which infants use the same sounds over and over, as in *gagagaga*.

Reduplication A phonological process in which the repetition of one syllable is used to mark a multisyllabic word (for example, *dada* for *daddy*).

Reference The relationship between a linguistic expression and a person, object, or event in the world.

Reference cohesion A form of **cohesion** in which the information needed to interpret a linguistic expression is found elsewhere in the text. See also **anaphoric reference** and **cataphoric reference.**

Referent The person, object, or event to which a linguistic expression refers.

Referential communication task An experimental task in which the subject must formulate a message about an object in the environment (as opposed to one's thoughts or feelings).

Referential gesture A form of gesture used in conversation to refer to some aspect of the content of a conversation.

Referential strategy The style of child language that emphasizes a high ratio of nouns to pronouns, clear articulation, and an emphasis on naming.

Regression Backward eye movement during reading.

Reinstatement The time-consuming process in which antecedents are retrieved from **permanent memory** into **working memory** to comprehend a current sentence.

Relational processing A style of processing, associated with the left hemisphere, which emphasizes the analysis of whole units into parts.

Relative clause A *wh*-clause that modifies a noun. For example, *that you found* in *Show me the book that you found.*

Request A communicative act in which a person attempts to influence the behavior of another—for example, a child pointing at a milk bottle in order to be given some. Requests may occur in words or gestures.

Respiratory system The system of muscles that regulates the flow of air from the lungs to the **vocal tract.**

Retention interval The time between when information is presented and when it is to be recalled.

Saccade An eye movement during reading.

Sapir-Whorf hypothesis See **Whorf hypothesis.**

Schema A structure in semantic memory that specifies the expected sequence of events.

Schemata Plural of **schema.**

Self-repairs Self-correction of speech errors.

Semantic bootstrapping   The process of using **semantics** to acquire **syntax.**

Semantic complexity   The complexity of the ideas expressed in a sentence or phrase (also called **conceptual complexity**). See also **syntactic complexity.**

Semantic differential   A tool for measuring the associative meanings of words by asking people to rate words on dimensions such as good/bad and strong/weak.

Semantic memory   The portion of **permanent memory** that contains organized knowledge of words, concepts, symbols, and objects. See also **internal lexicon.**

Semantic network   A model of **semantic memory** in which words are represented as nodes and connected to other nodes by various semantic relationships.

Semantic priming   An experimental task in which a context stimulus leads to the activation of a target stimulus.

Semantics   The domain of language that pertains to the meanings of words and sentences.

Semantic verification task   An experimental task in which subjects view sentences of the form *An A is a B* and rapidly decide whether the sentence is true or false.

Sense   The relationship a word has with other words in the **lexicon.**

Sensorimotor period   The first of Piaget's periods of cognitive development, characterized by sensory and motor development and the inability to fully represent objects symbolically. See **object permanence.**

Sensory stores   The initial memory system for sensory stimuli. There is a separate store for each sense (vision, audition, and so on).

Serial processing   Processes that occur one at a time.

Shadowing   An experimental task in which subjects repeat what they hear.

Shift   A speech error in which a speech sound or word moves from one location to another.

Short-term memory   The memory system that holds information for about 30 seconds. See also **working memory.**

Side participant   An individual who is taking part in a conversation but is not currently being addressed.

Situational model   A mental **model** of **discourse.**

Sociolinguistics   The study of how language functions in social situations.

Somatosensory regions   Areas in the brain's **parietal lobe** controlling the sense of touch.

Sound spectrogram   A visual representation of the speech signal.

Sound spectrograph   A device used to create a sound spectrogram.

Span of fixation   The size of the area from which a reader picks up visual information.

Speaker normalization   The process of taking the pitch of the speaker into account when using acoustic cues during speech perception.

Speech act   An utterance with an **illocutionary force.**

Speech perception   The process of using acoustic information to arrive at a recognition of the speech sounds in a message.

Spreading activation   The process by which one node in a **semantic network,** when active, activates related nodes.

Steady state   The portion of a **formant** that is of relatively constant frequency.

Stop   A **consonant** in which the **vocal tract** is completely closed, building up air pressure, which is then abruptly released, such as in the *b* in *bat.*

Story grammar   The mental representation (**schema**) of an expected series of events in a story.

Stress   The emphasis given to a word or syllable during the articulation of a sentence (for example, *black-BIRD* versus *BLACK-bird*).

Structure dependence   The fact that linguistic rules apply to grammatical structures (or **constituents**) rather than to individual words.

Subset principle   The notion that languages may be considered as subsets of one another.

Substitution   A form of **cohesion** in which one word is replaced by another as an alternative to repeating the first word. Also, a speech error or phonological process in which one sound or word replaces another.

Sufficient condition   A condition that, if present, ensures that a specified event will occur.

Supralaryngeal system   The system of muscles that manipulates the size and shape of the **vocal tract.**

Suprasegmentals   Prosodic factors such as stress and intonational patterns that lie "on top of" speech segments.

Surface representation   In sentence or discourse memory, representation of the exact words that were presented.

Surface structure   The level of syntactic structure assumed in transformational grammar that is closer to the phonetic specification of an utterance.

Syllabary   An **orthography** in which syllables are represented by visual symbols.

Synonymy   A semantic relationship in which two or more words have a similar meaning.

Syntactic category   Another term for part of speech, such as noun, verb, and so forth.

Syntactic complexity   The complexity of the grammatical operations required to express an idea in a given language; also called **formal complexity.** See also **semantic complexity.**

Syntax   The domain of language that pertains to the grammatical arrangement of words in a sentence.

Syrinx   The major structure in the vocal system of the chaffinch.

Tachistoscope   A machine that presents visual stimuli for very brief periods of time.

Tacit knowledge   Knowledge of how to perform an act. See also **explicit knowledge.**

Tag question   A question that is "tagged" onto a declarative sentence such as *isn't it* in *It sure is cold in here, isn't it?*

Task specificity   The notion that certain cognitive processes are restricted to language and are not employed in other intellectual domains.

Taxonomic bias   A cognitive constraint in which children assume that a word refers to a class of individuals rather than to a single person or animal.

Taxonomic relations   Relations among words that indicate the position of words in a taxonomy. For example, for the word *dog, mammal* is a superordinate term, *cat* is a coordinate term, and *collie* is a subordinate term.

Temporal lobes   Auditory regions at each side of the brain.

Tenor   The topic of a **metaphor.**

Tip-of-the-tongue (TOT) phenomenon   When we know a word but are temporarily unable to retrieve it.

Top-down processing   A process in which higher levels influence lower levels of processing. For example, the perception of **phonemes** may be influenced by the words in which they appear.

TRACE model   A **connectionist model** of speech perception.

Transformational rule   A rule that transforms one phrase structure into another by adding, deleting, or moving grammatical constituents. Also called **transformation.**

Truth conditions   The conditions that need to be present in the world in order for a sentence to be true.

Turn-yielding signal   A set of cues given by a speaker to indicate that he or she is ready to yield the floor.

Typicality effect   The fact that it takes longer to verify a statement of the form *An A is a B* when A is not typical or characteristic of B.

Underextension   When a child uses a word in a more limited way than adults do (for example, refusing to call a taxi a *car*).

Undershooting   In speech production, the tendency for articulators to fall short of target locations for different speech sounds, owing to **coarticulation.**

Variegated babbling   A form of babbling consisting of syllable strings with varying **consonants** and **vowels.**

Vehicle   What is predicated of the topic in a **metaphor.**

Velar   A **consonant** articulated at the velum, such as the *c* in *collar.*

Visual field task   An experimental task in which visual stimuli are presented to either the right or the left visual field.

Vocal cords   Two bands of muscular tissue in the larynx that vibrate during the production of speech sounds; also called vocal folds.

Vocal tract   The structures above the larynx that participate in speech production, principally the mouth (oral cavity) and nose (nasal cavity) regions.

Voiced   Speech sound in which the **vocal cords** are vibrating during the production of sound.

Voiceless   Speech sound in which the **vocal cords** are not vibrating during the production of sound.

Voice onset time   The period of time from when a **consonant** is released until the **vocal cords** vibrate.

Voicing   Whether or not the **vocal cords** are vibrating when air from the lungs passes over them. If the cords are vibrating, the speech sound is called **voiced;** if not, **voiceless.**

Vowel   A speech sound in which the **vocal tract** is open during production.

Wernicke's aphasia   An **aphasia** characterized by fluent speech that is not informational and by disorders of comprehension. Also called **receptive aphasia.**

Wernicke's area   A brain region in the temporal lobe of the left hemisphere. Damage to this region leads to **Wernicke's aphasia.**

Whole object bias   A cognitive constraint in which children assume that a word refers to an entire object, not a part of it.

Whorf hypothesis   The hypothesis that languages shape thought processes; also called the **Sapir-Whorf hypothesis.** See also **linguistic determinism** and **linguistic relativity.**

Wh-question   A question beginning with *who, what, where,* or *when.*

Word association test   A test in which a person is presented with a word and asked to respond with the first word that comes to mind.

Word initial cohort   In auditory word recognition, the initial set of lexical candidates activated by the comprehender.

Word level   A **level** of written language perception in which a visual stimulus is represented as a familiar word.

Word-superiority effect   An experimental finding that it is easier to perceive a letter in a word context than in isolation.

Working memory   A form of memory with both storage and processing functions. Working memory is used to hold information for a short period of time as well as to perform various operations on the stored information.

Yes/no question   A question that can be answered with a yes or no answer.

Zipf's law   The fact that the length of a word is negatively correlated with its frequency of use.

References

Adams, M. J. (1979). Models of word recognition. *Cognitive Psychology, 11,* 133–176.

Aksu-Koç, A. A., & Slobin, D. I. (1985). The acquisition of Turkish. In D. I. Slobin (Ed.), *The crosslinguistic study of language acquisition: Vol. 1. The data* (pp. 839–878). Hillsdale, NJ: Erlbaum.

Albert, S., & Kessler, S. (1978). Ending social encounters. *Journal of Experimental Social Psychology, 14,* 541–553.

Albritton, D. W., & Gerrig, R. J. (1991). Participatory responses in text understanding. *Journal of Memory and Language, 30,* 603–626.

Allen, M. S., Kertoy, M. K., Sherblom, J. C., & Pettit, J. M. (1994). Children's narrative productions: A comparison of personal event and fictional stories. *Applied Psycholinguistics, 15,* 149–176.

Allen, P. A., & Madden, D. J. (1990). Evidence for a parallel input serial analysis model of word processing. *Journal of Experimental Psychology: Human Perception and Performance, 16,* 48–64.

Allington, R. L., & Strange, M. (1977). Effects of grapheme substitutions in connected text upon reading behaviors. *Visible Language, 11,* 285–297.

Altmann, S. A. (1967). The structure of primate social communication. In S. A. Altmann (Ed.), *Social communication among primates* (pp. 325–362). Chicago: University of Chicago Press.

Anderson, J. R. (1976). *Language, memory, and thought.* Hillsdale, NJ: Erlbaum.

Anderson, R. C., & Ortony, A. (1975). On putting apples into bottles—A problem of polysemy. *Cognitive Psychology, 7,* 167–180.

Aslin, R. N., Pisoni, D. B., Hennessy, B. L., & Perey, A. J. (1981). Discrimination of voice onset time by human infants: New findings and implications for the effects of early experience. *Child Development, 52,* 1135–1145.

Au, T. K. (1983). Chinese and English counterfactuals: The Sapir-Whorf hypothesis revisited. *Cognition, 15,* 155–187.

Au, T. K. (1984). Counterfactuals: In reply to Alfred Bloom. *Cognition, 17,* 289–302.

Austin, J. L. (1962). *How to do things with words.* New York: Oxford University Press.

Baars, B. J. (1980). On eliciting predictable speech errors in the laboratory. In V. A. Fromkin (Ed.), *Errors in linguistic performance* (pp. 307–318). New York: Academic Press.

Baars, B. J., Motley, M. T., & MacKay, D. G. (1975). Output editing for lexical status in artificially elicited slips of the tongue. *Journal of Verbal Learning and Verbal Behavior, 14,* 382–391.

Bach, K., & Harnish, R. M. (1979). *Linguistic communication and speech acts.* Cambridge, MA: MIT Press.

Ball, E. W., & Blachman, B. A. (1991). Does phoneme awareness training in kindergarten make a difference in early word recognition and developmental spelling? *Reading Research Quarterly, 25,* 49–66.

Baron, J., & Thurston, I. (1973). An analysis of the word-superiority effect. *Cognitive Psychology, 4,* 207–228.

Barrett, M. D. (1982). The holophrastic hypothesis: Conceptual and empirical issues. *Cognition, 11,* 47–76.

Bartlett, F. C. (1932). *Remembering: A study in experimental and social psychology.* Cambridge: Cambridge University Press.

Bates, E., Camaioni, L., & Volterra, V. (1975). The acquisition of performatives prior to speech. *Merrill-Palmer Quarterly, 21,* 205–226.

Bates, E., Masling, M., & Kintsch, W. (1978). Recognition memory for aspects of dialogue. *Journal of Experimental Psychology: Human Learning and Memory, 4,* 187–197.

Bavelas, J. B., Chovil, N., Lawrie, D. A., & Wade, A. (1992). Interactive gestures. *Discourse Processes, 15,* 469–489.

Beattie, G. (1983). *Talk: An analysis of speech and non-verbal behaviour in conversation.* Milton Keynes, England: Open University Press.

Beattie, G. W., Cutler, A., & Pearson, M. (1982). Why is Mrs. Thatcher interrupted so often? *Nature, 301,* 744–747.

Becker, C. A. (1979). Semantic context effects in visual word recognition: An analysis of semantic strategies. *Memory & Cognition, 8,* 493–512.

Bellugi, U. (1988). The acquisition of a spatial language. In F. S. Kessel (Ed.), *The development of language and language researchers: Essays in honor of Roger Brown* (pp. 153–185). Hillsdale, NJ: Erlbaum.

Bellugi, U., Bihrle, A., Jernigan, T., Trauner, D., & Doherty, S. (1990). Neuropsychological, neurological, and neuroanatomical profile of Williams syndrome. *American Journal of Medical Genetics Supplement, 6,* 115–125.

Bellugi, U., & Fischer, S. (1972). A comparison of sign language and spoken language. *Cognition, 1,* 173–200.

Bellugi, U., & Studdert-Kennedy, M. (Eds.). (1980). *Signed and spoken language: Biological constraints on linguistic form.* Weinheim, Germany: Chemie.

Bellugi, U., Wang, P. P., & Jernigan, T. L. (1994). Williams syndrome: An unusual neuropsychological profile. In S. H. Froman & J. Grafman (Eds.), *Atypical cognitive deficits in developmental disorders: Implications for brain function* (pp. 23–56). Hillsdale, NJ: Erlbaum.

Bennett-Kastor, T. (1983). Noun phrases and coherence in child narratives. *Journal of Child Language, 10,* 135–149.

Benson, D. F., & Geschwind, N. (1969). The alexias. In P. J. Vinken & G. W. Bruyn (Eds.), *Handbook of clinical neurology* (Vol. 4, pp. 112–140). Amsterdam: North-Holland.

Berko, J. (1958). The child's learning of English morphology. *Word, 14,* 150–177.

Berko, J., & Brown, R. (1960). Psycholinguistics research methods. In P. H. Mussen (Ed.), *Handbook of research methods in child development* (pp. 517–557). New York: Wiley.

Berlin, B., & Kay, P. (1969). *Basic color terms: Their universality and evolution.* Berkeley: University of California Press.

Berman, R. A. (1985). The acquisition of Hebrew. In D. I. Slobin (Ed.), *The crosslinguistic study of language acquisition: Vol. 1. The data* (pp. 255–371). Hillsdale, NJ: Erlbaum.

Berwick, R. C., & Weinberg, A. S. (1983). The role of grammars in models of language use. *Cognition, 13,* 1–61.

Berwick, R. C., & Weinberg, A. S. (1984). *The grammatical basis of linguistic performance.* Cambridge, MA: MIT Press.

Best, C. T. (1994). The emergence of native-language phonological influences in infants: A perceptual assimilation model. In J. C. Goodman & H. C. Nusbaum (Eds.), *The development of speech perception: The transition from speech sounds to spoken words* (pp. 167–224). Cambridge, MA: MIT Press.

Best, C. T., McRoberts, G. W., & Sithole, N. M. (1988). Examination of perceptual reorganization for nonnative speech contrasts: Zulu click discrimination by English-speaking adults and infants. *Journal of Experimental Psychology: Human Perception and Performance, 14,* 345–360.

Best, C. T., Morrongiello, B., & Robson, K. (1981). Perceptual equivalence of acoustic cues in speech and nonspeech perception. *Perception & Psychophysics, 29,* 191–211.

Bever, T. G. (1970). The cognitive basis for linguistic structures. In J. R. Hayes (Ed.), *Cognition and the development of language* (pp. 279–362). New York: Wiley.

Bever, T. G. (1980). Broca and Lashley were right: Cerebral dominance is an accident of growth. In D. Caplan (Ed.), *Biological studies of mental processes* (pp. 186–230). Cambridge, MA: MIT Press.

Bever, T. G., & Chiarello, R. J. (1974). Cerebral dominance in musicians and nonmusicians. *Science, 185,* 537–539.

Bickerton, D. (1981). *Roots of language.* Ann Arbor, MI: Karoma.

Bickerton, D. (1983). Creole languages. In S-Y. Wang (Ed.), *The emergence of language: Development and evolution* (pp. 59–69). New York: W. H. Freeman.

Bickerton, D. (1984). The language bioprogram hypothesis. *Behavioral and Brain Sciences, 7,* 173–221.

Bihrle, A. M., Brownell, H. H., Powelson, J. A., & Gardner, H. (1986). Comprehension of humorous and nonhumorous materials by left and right brain-damaged patients. *Brain and Cognition, 5,* 399–411.

Black, J. B., & Bower, G. H. (1979). Episodes as chunks in narrative memory. *Journal of Verbal Learning and Verbal Behavior, 18,* 309–318.

Bloom, A. H. (1981). *The linguistic shaping of thought: A study in the impact of language on thinking in China and the West.* Hillsdale, NJ: Erlbaum.

Bloom, A. H. (1984). Caution—The words you use may affect what you say: A response to Au. *Cognition, 17,* 275–287.

Bloom, L. (1970). *Language development: Form and function in emerging grammars.* Cambridge, MA: MIT Press.

Bloom, L. (1973). *One word at a time: The use of single word utterances before syntax.* The Hague: Mouton.

Bloom, L., & Lahey, M. (1978). *Language development and language disorders.* New York: Wiley.

Bloom, L., Lahey, M., Hood, L., Lifter, K., & Fiess, K. (1980). Complex sentences: Acquisition of syntactic connectives and the semantic relations they encode. *Journal of Child Language, 7,* 235–261.

Bloom, L., Lightbown P., & Hood, L. (1975). Structure and variation in child language. *Monographs of the Society for Research in Child Development, 40*(2, Serial No. 160).

Bloom, L., Rocissano, L., & Hood, L. (1976). Adult-child discourse: Developmental interaction between information processing and linguistic knowledge. *Cognitive Psychology, 8,* 521–552.

Bloom, P. (1990). Subjectless sentences in child language. *Linguistic Inquiry, 21,* 491–504.

Bloomfield L. (1914). *An introduction to the study of language.* New York: Holt.

Bloomfield, L. (1933). *Language.* New York: Holt.

Blumenthal, A. L. (1970). *Language and psychology: Historical aspects of psycholinguistics.* New York: Wiley.

Blumenthal, A. L. (1987). The emergence of psycholinguistics. *Synthese, 72,* 313–323.

Blumstein, S. E., Baker, E., & Goodglass, H. (1977). Phonological factors in auditory comprehension in aphasia. *Neuropsychologia, 15,* 19–30.

Blumstein, S. E., Milberg, W., & Shrier, R. (1982). Semantic processing in aphasia: Evidence from an auditory lexical decision task. *Brain and Language, 17,* 301–315.

Blumstein, S. E., & Stevens, K. N. (1979). Acoustic invariance in speech production: Evidence from measurements of the spectral characteristics of stop consonants. *Journal of the Acoustical Society of America, 66,* 1001–1017.

Bock, J. K. (1982). Toward a cognitive psychology of syntax: Information processing contributions to sentence formulation. *Psychological Review, 89,* 1–47.

Bock, J. K., & Cutting, J. C. (1992). Regulating mental energy: Performance units in language production. *Journal of Memory and Language, 31,* 99–127.

Bock, K., & Levelt, W. (1994). Language production: Grammatical encoding. In M. A. Gernsbacher (Ed.), *Handbook of psycholinguistics* (pp. 945–984). San Diego: Academic Press.

Bohannon, J. N., & Marquis, A. L. (1977). Children's control of adult speech. *Child Development, 48,* 1002–1008.

Boland, J. E. (1997). Resolving syntactic category ambiguities in discourse context: Probabilistic and discourse constraints. *Journal of Memory and Language, 36,* 588–615.

Bolinger, D. (1975). *Aspects of language* (2nd ed.). New York: Harcourt Brace Jovanovich.

Bolinger, D. L., & Gerstman, L. J. (1957). Disjuncture as a cue to constructs. *Word, 13,* 246–255.

Bonvillian, J. D., Orlansky, M. D., & Novack, L. L. (1983). Developmental milestones: Sign language acquisition and motor development. *Child Development, 54,* 1435–1445.

Borke, H. (1975). Piaget's mountains revisited: Changes in the egocentric landscape. *Developmental Psychology, 11,* 240–243.

Bowerman, M. (1973). Structural relationship in children's utterances: Syntactic or semantic? In T. E. Moore (Ed.), *Cognitive development and the acquisition of language* (pp. 197–213). New York: Academic Press.

Boysson-Bardies, B. de, Halle, P., Sagart, L., & Durand, C. (1989). A crosslinguistic investigation of vowel formants in babbling. *Journal of Child Language, 6,* 1–17.

Bradley, D. C., Garrett, M. F., & Zurif, E. B. (1980). Syntactic deficits in Broca's aphasia. In D. Caplan (Ed.), *Biological studies of mental processes* (pp. 269–286). Cambridge, MA: MIT Press.

Bradley, L., & Bryant, P. E. (1983). Categorizing sounds and learning to read: A causal connection. *Nature, 301,* 419–421.

Braine, M. D. S. (1963). The ontogeny of English phrase structure: The first phase. *Language*, *39*, 1–13.

Braine, M. D. S. (1976). Children's first word combinations. *Monographs of the Society for Research in Child Development*, *41*(1, Serial No. 164).

Bransford, J. D. (1979). *Human cognition: Learning, understanding, and remembering.* Belmont, CA: Wadsworth.

Bransford, J. D., Barclay, J. R., & Franks, J. J. (1972). Sentence memory: A constructive versus interpretive approach. *Cognitive Psychology*, *3*, 193–209.

Bransford,, J. D., & Johnson, M. K. (1973). Consideration of some problems of comprehension. In W. G. Chase (Ed.), *Visual information processing* (pp. 383–438). New York: Academic Press.

Bresnan, J. (1978). A realistic transformational grammar. In J. Bresnan, M. Halle, & G. A. Miller (Eds.), *Linguistic theory and psychological reality* (pp. 1–59). Cambridge, MA: MIT Press.

Britt, M. A. (1994). The interaction of referential ambiguity and argument structure in the parsing of prepositional phrases. *Journal of Memory and Language*, *33*, 251–283.

Britt, M. A., Perfetti, C. A., Garrod, S., & Rayner K. (1992). Parsing in discourse: Context effects and their limits. *Journal of Memory and Language*, *31*, 293–314.

Broadbent, D. E. (1954). The role of auditory localization in attention and memory span. *Journal of Experimental Psychology*, *47*, 191–196.

Brooks, L. W., Dansereau, D. F., Spurlin, J. E., & Holly, C. D. (1983). Effects of headings on text processing. *Journal of Educational Psychology*, *75*, 292–302.

Brown, R. (1958). *Words and things.* Glencoe, IL: Free Press.

Brown, R. (1970). The first sentences of child and chimpanzee. In R. Brown, *Psycholinguistics* (pp. 208–231). New York: Free Press.

Brown, R. (1973). *A first language: The early stages.* Cambridge, MA: Harvard University Press.

Brown, R., & Bellugi, U. (1964). Three processes in the child's acquisition of syntax. In E. H. Lenneberg (Ed.), *New directions in the study of language* (pp. 131–161). Cambridge, MA: MIT Press.

Brown, R., & Hanlon, C. (1970). Derivational complexity and the order of acquisition in child speech. In J. R. Hayes (Ed.), *Cognition and the development of language* (pp. 11–53). New York: Wiley.

Brown, R. W., & Lenneberg, E. H. (1954). A study in language and cognition. *Journal of Abnormal and Social Psychology*, *49*, 454–462.

Brown, R., & McNeill, D. (1966). The "tip of the tongue" phenomenon. *Journal of Verbal Learning and Verbal Behavior*, *5*, 325–337.

Brown, T. S., & Wallace, P. M. (1980). *Physiological psychology.* New York: Academic Press.

Bruce, D. J. (1964). The analysis of word sounds by young children. *British Journal of Educational Psychology*, *34*, 158–170.

Bruner, J. S. (1975). The ontogenesis of speech acts. *Journal of Child Language*, *2*, 1–19.

Burgess, C., & Simpson, G. B. (1988). Cerebral hemispheric mechanisms in the retrieval of ambiguous word meanings. *Brain and Language*, *33*, 86–103.

Byrne, B., & Fielding-Barnsley, R. (1993). Evaluation of a program to teach phonemic aware-ness to young children: A 1-year follow-up. *Journal of Educational Psychology, 85,* 104–111.

Byrne, P. S., & Long, B. E. L. (1976). *Doctors talking to patients: A study of the verbal behaviour of general practitioners consulting in their surgeries.* London: Her Majesty's Stationery Office.

Cairns, H. S., & Cairns, C. E. (1976). *Psycholinguistics: A cognitive view of language.* New York: Holt, Rinehart & Winston.

Cairns, H. S., & Kamerman, J. (1975). Lexical information processing during sentence com-prehension. *Journal of Verbal Learning and Verbal Behavior, 14,* 170–179.

Cameron, D., McAlinden, F., & O'Leary, K. (1988). Lakoff in context: The social and linguistic functions of tag questions. In J. Coates & D. Cameron (Eds.), *Women in their speech communities: New perspectives on language and sex* (pp. 74–93). London: Longman.

Candland, D. K. (1993). *Feral children and clever animals: Reflections on human nature.* New York: Oxford University Press.

Caplan, D. (1987). *Neurolinguistics and linguistic aphasiology: An introduction.* Cambridge: Cambridge University Press.

Caplan, D. (1994). Language and the brain. In M. A. Gernsbacher (Ed.), *Handbook of psycholinguistics* (pp. 1023–1053). San Diego: Academic Press.

Caplan, D., & Chomsky, N. (1980). Linguistic perspectives on language development. In D. Caplan (Ed.), *Biological studies of mental processes* (pp. 97–105). Cambridge, MA: MIT Press.

Caramazza, A. (1984). The logic of neuropsychological research and the problem of patient classification in aphasia. *Brain and Language, 21,* 9–20.

Caramazza, A., & Zurif, E. B. (1976). Dissociation of algorithmic and heuristic processes in language comprehension: Evidence from aphasia. *Brain and Language, 3,* 572–582.

Carey, S. (1978). The child as word learner. In M. Halle, J. Bresnan, & G. A. Miller (Eds.), *Linguistic theory and psychological reality* (pp. 264–293). Cambridge, MA: MIT Press.

Carli, L. L. (1990). Gender, language, and influence. *Journal of Personality and Social Psy-chology, 59,* 941–951.

Carpenter, P. A., & Just, M. A. (1989). The role of working memory in language comprehen-sion. In D. Klahr & K. Kotovsky (Eds.), *Complex information processing: The impact of Herbert A. Simon* (pp. 31–68). Hillsdale, NJ: Erlbaum.

Carroll, J. B. (Ed.). (1956). *Language, thought, and reality: Selected writings of Benjamin Lee Whorf.* Cambridge, MA: MIT Press.

Carroll, J. B., & Casagrande, J. B. (1958). The function of language classifications in behav-ior. In E. E. Maccoby, T. M. Newcomb, & E. L. Hartley (Eds.), *Readings in social psychology* (pp. 18–31). New York: Holt, Rinehart & Winston.

Carroll, J. B., & White, M. N. (1973). Age-of-acquisition norms for 220 pictureable nouns. *Journal of Verbal Learning and Verbal Behavior, 12,* 563–576.

Case, R., Kurland, M., & Goldberg, J. (1982). Operational efficiency and the growth of short-term memory span. *Journal of Experimental Child Psychology, 33,* 386–404.

Catford, J. C., Jusczyk, P. W., Klatt, D. H., Liberman, A. M., Remez, R. E., & Stevens, K. N. (1991). Panel discussion: The motor theory and alternative accounts. In I. G. Mattingly

& M. Studdert-Kennedy (Eds.), *Modularity and the motor theory of speech perception* (pp. 175–195). Hillsdale, NJ: Erlbaum.

Cattell, J. M. (1886). The time taken up by cerebral operations. *Mind, 11,* 220–242, 377–392, 524–538.

Cazden, C. B. (1965). *Environmental assistance to the child's acquisition of grammar.* Unpublished doctoral dissertation, Harvard University, Cambridge, MA.

Cazden, C. B. (1968). The acquisition of noun and verb inflections. *Child Development, 39,* 433–448.

Cazden, C. B. (1976). Play with language and meta-linguistic awareness: One dimension of language experience. In J. S. Bruner, A. Jolly, & K. Sylva (Eds.), *Play: Its role in development and evolution* (pp. 603–608). New York: Basic Books.

Cazden, C. B. (1986). Classroom discourse. In M. C. Wittrock (Ed.), *Handbook of research on teaching* (3rd ed., pp. 432–463). New York: Macmillan.

Chafe, W. L. (1972). Discourse structure and human knowledge. In R. O. Freedle & J. B. Carroll (Eds.), *Language comprehension and the acquisition of knowledge* (pp. 41–69). Washington, DC: Winston.

Chaney, C. (1992). Language development, metalinguistic skills, and print awareness in 3-year-old children. *Applied Psycholinguistics, 13,* 485–514.

Chen, H-C. (1986). Component detection in reading Chinese characters. In H. S. R. Kao & R. Hoosain (Eds.), *Linguistics, psychology, and the Chinese language* (pp. 1–10). Hong Kong: University of Hong Kong.

Chen, Y. P., Allport, P. A., & Marshall, J. C. (1986). What are the functional orthographic units in Chinese word recognition: The stroke or the stroke pattern? *Quarterly Journal of Experimental Psychology, 49A,* 1024–1043.

Cherry, L. J. (1978). A sociolinguistic approach to the study of teacher expectations. *Discourse Processes, 1,* 373–394.

Chiarello, C. (1991). Interpretation of word meanings by the cerebral hemispheres: One is not enough. In P. J. Schwanenflugel (Ed.), *The psychology of word meaning* (pp. 251–278). Hillsdale, NJ: Erlbaum.

Chomsky, N. (1957). *Syntactic structures.* The Hague: Mouton.

Chomsky, N. (1959). Review of *Verbal Behavior* by B. F. Skinner. *Language, 35,* 26–58.

Chomsky, N. (1965). *Aspects of the theory of syntax.* Cambridge, MA: MIT Press.

Chomsky, N. (1966). *Cartesian linguistics: A chapter in the history of rationalist thought.* New York: Harper & Row.

Chomsky, N. (1968). *Language and mind.* New York: Harcourt Brace Jovanovich.

Chomsky, N. (1975). *Reflections on language.* New York: Pantheon.

Chomsky, N. (1980). *Rules and representations.* New York: Columbia University Press.

Chomsky, N. (1981). *Lectures on government and binding.* Dordrecht, Holland: Foris.

Ciccone, M., Wapner, W., Foldi, N., Zurif, E., & Gardner, H. (1979). The relation between gesture and language in aphasic communication. *Brain and Language, 8,* 324–349.

Clancy, P. M. (1985). The acquisition of Japanese. In D. I. Slobin (Ed.), *The crosslinguistic study of language acquisition: Vol. 1. The data* (pp. 373–524). Hillsdale, NJ: Erlbaum.

Clark, H. H. (1974). Semantics and comprehension. In T. A. Sebeok (Ed.), *Current trends in linguistics: Vol. 12. Linguistics and adjacent arts and sciences* (pp. 1291–1428). The Hague: Mouton.

Clark, H. H. (1977). Bridging. In P. N. Johnson-Laird & P. C. Wason (Eds.), *Thinking: Readings in cognitive science* (pp. 411–420). Cambridge: Cambridge University Press.

Clark, H. H. (1994). Discourse in production. In M. A. Gernsbacher (Ed.), *Handbook of psycholinguistics* (pp. 985–1021). San Diego: Academic Press.

Clark, H. H. (1996). *Using language.* Cambridge: Cambridge University Press.

Clark, H. H., & Clark, E. V. (1977). *Psychology and language: An introduction to psycholinguistics.* New York: Harcourt Brace Jovanovich.

Clark, H. H., & Haviland, S. E. (1977). Comprehension and the given-new contract. In R. O. Freedle (Ed.), *Discourse production and comprehension* (pp. 1–40). Norwood, NJ: Ablex.

Clark, H. H., & Lucy, P. (1975). Understanding what is meant from what is said: A study in conversationally conveyed requests. *Journal of Verbal Learning and Verbal Behavior, 14,* 56–72.

Clark, H. H., & Schaefer, E. F. (1987). Collaborating on contributions to conversations. *Language and Cognitive Processes, 2,* 19–41.

Clark, H. H., & Schaefer, E. F. (1992). Dealing with overhearers. In H. H. Clark, *Arenas of language use* (pp. 248–274). Chicago: University of Chicago Press.

Clark, H. H., & Sengul, C. J. (1979). In search of referents for nouns and pronouns. *Memory & Cognition, 7,* 35–41.

Cole, R. A. (1973). Listening for mispronunciations: A measure of what we hear during speech. *Perception & Psychophysics, 13,* 153–156.

Cole, R. A., & Scott, B. (1974). Toward a theory of speech perception. *Psychological Review, 81,* 348–374.

Collins, A., Warnock, E. H., & Passafiume, J. J. (1975). Analysis and synthesis of tutorial dialogues. In G. H. Bower (Ed.), *The psychology of learning and motivation: Advances in research and theory* (Vol. 9, pp. 49–87). New York: Academic Press.

Collins, A. M., & Loftus, E. F. (1975). A spreading-activation theory of semantic processing. *Psychological Review, 82,* 407–428.

Collins, A. M., & Quillian, M. R. (1969). Retrieval time from semantic memory. *Journal of Verbal Learning and Verbal Behavior, 8,* 240–247.

Collins, A. M., & Quillian, M. R. (1970). Does category size affect categorization time? *Journal of Verbal Learning and Verbal Behavior, 9,* 432–438.

Collins, A. M., & Quillian, M. R. (1972). Experiments on semantic memory and language comprehension. In L. W. Gregg (Ed.), *Cognition in learning and memory* (pp. 117–137). New York: Wiley.

Comrie, B. (1987). Russian. In B. Comrie (Ed.), *The world's major languages* (pp. 329–347). New York: Oxford University Press.

Condon, W. S., & Sander, L. W. (1974). Synchrony demonstrated between movements of the neonate and adult speech. *Child Development, 45,* 456–462.

Connine, C. M. (1987). Constraints on interactive processes in auditory word recognition: The role of sentence context. *Journal of Memory and Language, 26,* 527–538.

Connine, C. M., & Clifton, C., Jr. (1987). Interactive use of lexical information in speech perception. *Journal of Experimental Psychology: Human Perception and Performance, 13,* 291–299.

Cook, M. (1977). Gaze and mutual gaze in social encounters. *American Scientist, 65,* 328–333.

Cook, V. J. (1988). *Chomsky's universal grammar: An introduction.* Cambridge, MA: Blackwell.

Cook-Gumperz, J., & Gumperz, J. J. (1982). Communicative competence in educational perspective. In L. C. Wilkinson (Ed.), *Communicating in the classroom* (pp. 13–24). New York: Academic Press.

Corballis, M. C. (1980). Laterality and myth. *American Psychologist, 35,* 284–295.

Corballis, M. C. (1989). Laterality and human evolution. *Psychological Review, 96,* 492–505.

Corrigan, R. (1979). Cognitive correlates of language: Differential criteria yield differential results. *Child Development, 50,* 617–631.

Craik, F. I. M., & Lockhart, R. S. (1972). Levels of processing: A framework for memory research. *Journal of Verbal Learning and Verbal Behavior, 11,* 671–684.

Crain, S., & Steedman, M. (1985). On not being led up the garden path: The use of context by the psychological syntax processor. In D. R. Dowty, L. Kartunnen, & A. M. Zwicky (Eds.), *Natural language parsing: Psychological, computational, and theoretical perspectives* (pp. 320–358). Cambridge: Cambridge University Press.

Cromer, R. (1993). A case study of dissociations between language and cognition. In H. Tager-Flusberg (Ed.), *Constraints on language acquisition: Studies of atypical children* (pp. 141–152). Hillsdale, NJ: Erlbaum.

Crosby, F., & Nyquist, L. (1977). The female register: An empirical study of Lakoff's hypotheses. *Language in Society, 6,* 313–322.

Crystal, D. (1987). *The Cambridge encyclopedia of language.* Cambridge: Cambridge University Press.

Curtiss, S. (1977). *Genie: A psycholinguistic study of a modern-day "wild child."* New York: Academic Press.

Curtiss, S. (1981). Dissociations between language and cognition: Cases and implications. *Journal of Autism and Developmental Disorders, 11,* 15–30.

Curtiss, S., Fromkin, V., Krashen, S., Rigler, D., & Rigler, M. (1974). The linguistic development of Genie. *Language, 50,* 528–554.

Dale, P. S. (1976). *Language development: Structure and function* (2nd ed.). New York: Holt, Rinehart & Winston.

Dale, P. S., Crain-Thoreson, C., & Robinson, N. M. (1995). Linguistic precocity and the development of reading: The role of extralinguistic factors. *Applied Psycholinguistics, 16,* 173–187.

Damasio, H., & Damasio, A. R. (1989). *Neuroanatomy and neuropsychological disorders: Neuroimaging procedures and problems.* New York: Oxford University Press.

Daneman, M., & Carpenter, P. A. (1980). Individual differences in working memory and reading. *Journal of Verbal Learning and Verbal Behavior, 19,* 450–466.

Daneman, M., & Tardif, T. (1987). Working memory and reading skill re-examined. In M. Coltheart (Ed.), *Attention and performance: Vol. XII. The psychology of reading* (pp. 492–508). Hillsdale, NJ: Erlbaum.

Danks, J. H. (1977). Producing ideas and sentences. In S. Rosenberg (Ed.), *Sentence production: Developments in research and theory* (pp. 229–258). Hillsdale, NJ: Erlbaum.

Darwin, C. J. (1973). Ear differences and hemispheric specialization. In F. O. Schmidt & F. G. Worden (Eds.), *The neurosciences: Third study program* (pp. 57–63). Cambridge, MA: MIT Press.

Darwin, C. J., Turvey M. T., & Crowder, R. G. (1972). An auditory analogue of the Sperling partial report procedure: Evidence for brief auditory storage. *Cognitive Psychology, 3,* 255–267.

DeCasper, A. J., & Fifer, W. P. (1980). Of human bonding: Newborns prefer their mothers' voices. *Science, 208,* 1174–1176.

DeCasper, A. J., & Spence, M. J. (1986). Prenatal maternal speech influences newborns' perception of speech sounds. *Infant Behavior and Development, 9,* 133–150.

Dell, G. S. (1985). Positive feedback in hierarchical connectionist models: Applications to language production. *Cognitive Science, 9,* 3–23.

Dell, G. S. (1986). A spreading-activation theory of retrieval in sentence production. *Psychological Review, 93,* 283–321.

Dell, G. S. (1988). The retrieval of phonological forms in production: Tests of predictions from a connectionist model. *Journal of Memory and Language, 27,* 124–142.

Dell, G. S., Burger, L. K., & Svec, W. R. (1997). Language production and serial order: A functional analysis and a model. *Psychological Review, 104,* 123–147.

Dell, G. S., & Reich, P. A. (1981). Stages in sentence production: An analysis of speech error data. *Journal of Verbal Learning and Verbal Behavior, 20,* 611–629.

Della Corte, M., Benedict, H., & Klein, D. (1983). The relationship of pragmatic dimensions of mother's speech to the referential-expressive distinction. *Journal of Child Language, 10,* 35–43.

Dempster, F. N. (1981). Memory span: Sources of individual and developmental differences. *Psychological Bulletin, 89,* 63–100.

Demuth, K. (1990). Subject, topic, and Sesotho passive. *Journal of Child Language, 17,* 67–84.

Denes, P. B., & Pinson, E. N. (1963). *The speech chain: The physics and biology of spoken language.* Baltimore, MD: Bell Telephone Laboratories.

DePaulo, B. M., & Bonvillian, J. D. (1978). The effect on language development of the special characteristics of speech addressed to children. *Journal of Psycholinguistic Research, 7,* 189–211.

DeStefano, J. S., Pepinsky, H. B., & Sanders, T. S. (1982). Discourse rules for literacy learning in a classroom. In L. C. Wilkinson (Ed.), *Communicating in the classroom* (pp. 101–129). New York: Academic Press.

de Villiers, J. G., & de Villiers, P. A. (1973). A cross-sectional study of the acquisition of grammatical morphemes in child speech. *Journal of Psycholinguistic Research, 2,* 267–278.

de Villiers, J. G., & de Villiers, P. A. (1978). *Language acquisition.* Cambridge, MA: Harvard University Press.

de Villiers, J. G., & de Villiers, P. A. (1985). The acquisition of English. In D. I. Slobin (Ed.), *The crosslinguistic study of language acquisition: Vol. 1. The data* (pp. 27–139). Hillsdale, NJ: Erlbaum.

Diamond, A. (1985). Development of the ability to use recall to guide action, as indicated by infants' performance on A͞B. *Child Development, 56,* 868–883.

Diehl, R. L., Souther, A. F., & Convis, C. L. (1980). Conditions on rate normalization in speech perception. *Perception & Psychophysics, 27,* 435–443.

Dooling, D. J., & Lachman, R. (1971). Effects of comprehension on retention of prose. *Journal of Experimental Psychology, 88,* 216–222.

Dore, J. (1975). Holophrases, speech acts and language universals. *Journal of Child Language, 2,* 21–40.

Dosher, B. A., & Corbett, A. T. (1982). Instrument inferences and verb schemata. *Memory & Cognition, 10,* 531–539.

Drew, P., & Heritage, J. (1992). Analyzing talk at work: An introduction. In P. Drew & J. Heritage (Eds.), *Talk at work: Interaction in institutional settings* (pp. 3–65). Cambridge: Cambridge University Press.

Du Bois, J. W. (1974). *Syntax in mid-sentence* (Berkeley Studies in Syntax and Semantics Vol. 1: III.1–III.23). Berkeley: University of California, Institute of Human Learning and Department of Linguistics.

Duffy, S. A., Morris, R. K., & Rayner, K. (1988). Lexical ambiguity and fixation times in reading. *Journal of Memory and Language, 27,* 429–446.

Duncan, S., Jr. (1972). Some signals and rules for taking speaking turns in conversations. *Journal of Personality and Social Psychology, 23,* 283–292.

Edelsky, C. (1981). Who's got the floor? *Language in Society, 10,* 383–421.

Eimas, P. D., Miller, J. L., & Jusczyk, P. W. (1987). On infant speech perception and the acquisition of language. In S. Harnad (Ed.), *Categorical perception: The groundwork of cognition* (pp. 161–195). Cambridge: Cambridge University Press.

Eimas, P. D., Siqueland, E. R., Jusczyk, P., & Vigorito, J. (1971). Speech perception in infants. *Science, 171,* 303–306.

Ellis, A. W. (1980). On the Freudian theory of speech errors. In V. A. Fromkin (Ed.), *Errors in linguistic performance* (pp. 123–131). New York: Academic Press.

Ellis, N. C., & Hennelly, R. A. (1980). A bilingual word-length effect: Implications for intelligence testing and the relative ease of mental calculation in Welsh and English. *British Journal of Psychology, 71,* 43–51.

Elman, J. L., & McClelland, J. L. (1988). Cognitive penetration of the mechanisms of perception: Compensation for coarticulation of lexically restored phonemes. *Journal of Memory and Language, 27,* 143–165.

Ericsson, K. A., Chase, W. G., & Faloon, S. (1980). Acquisition of a memory skill. *Science, 208,* 1181–1182.

Ervin, S. M. (1964). Imitation and structural change in children's language. In E. H. Lenneberg (Ed.), *New directions in the study of language* (pp. 163–189). Cambridge, MA: MIT Press.

Fagot, J., & Vauclair, J. (1991). Manual laterality in nonhuman primates: A distinction between handedness and manual specialization. *Psychological Bulletin, 109,* 76–89.

Fantz, R. L. (1963). Pattern vision in newborn infants. *Science, 140,* 296–297.

Feldman, C. F., & Wertsch, J. V. (1976). Context-dependent properties of teachers' speech. *Youth and Society, 7,* 227–258.

Feldman, H., Goldin-Meadow, S., & Gleitman, L. (1978). Beyond Herodotus: The creation of language by linguistically deprived deaf children. In A. Lock (Ed.), *Action, symbol, and gesture: The emergence of language* (pp. 351–414). New York: Academic Press.

Fernald, A., & Kuhl, P. (1987). Acoustic determinants of infant preference for motherese speech. *Infant Behavior and Development, 10,* 279–293.

Ferreira, F., & Anes, M. (1994). Why study spoken language? In M. A. Gernsbacher (Ed.), *Handbook of psycholinguistics* (pp. 33–56). San Diego: Academic Press.

Ferreira, F., & Clifton, C., Jr. (1986). The independence of syntactic processing. *Journal of Memory and Language, 25,* 348–368.

Fillenbaum, S. (1966). Memory for gist: Some relevant variables. *Language and Speech, 9,* 217–227.

Fillmore, C. J. (1981). Pragmatics and the description of discourse. In P. Cole (Ed.), *Radical pragmatics* (pp. 143–166). New York: Academic Press.

Fisher, C., & Tokura, H. (1995). The given-new contract in speech to infants. *Journal of Memory and Language, 34,* 287–310.

Fishman, P. (1978). Interaction: The work women do. *Social Problems, 25,* 397–406.

Fitch, H. L., Halwes, T., Erickson, D. M., & Liberman, A. M. (1980). Perceptual equivalence of two acoustic cues for stop-consonant manner. *Perception & Psychophysics, 27,* 343–350.

Fletcher, C. R. (1994). Levels of representation in memory for discourse. In M. A. Gernsbacher (Ed.), *Handbook of psycholinguistics* (pp. 589–607). San Diego: Academic Press.

Fletcher, C. R., & Chrysler, S. T. (1990). Surface forms, textbases and situational models: Recognition memory for three types of textual information. *Discourse Processes, 13,* 175–190.

Fletcher, C. R., Hummel, J. E., & Marsolek, C. J. (1990). Causality and the allocation of attention during comprehension. *Journal of Experimental Psychology: Learning, Memory, and Cognition, 16,* 233–240.

Fodor, J. A. (1975). *The language of thought.* New York: Crowell.

Fodor, J. A. (1983). *The modularity of mind: An essay on faculty psychology.* Cambridge, MA: MIT Press.

Fodor, J. A., Bever, T. G., & Garrett, M. F. (1974). *The psychology of language: An introduction to psycholinguistics and generative grammar.* New York: McGraw-Hill.

Folven, R. J., & Bonvillian, J. D. (1991). The transition from nonreferential to referential language in children acquiring American Sign Language. *Developmental Psychology, 27,* 806–816.

Forster, K. I. (1976). Accessing the mental lexicon. In R. J. Wales & E. Walker (Eds.), *New approaches to language mechanisms* (pp. 257–287). Amsterdam: North-Holland.

Forster, K. I. (1979). Levels of processing and the structure of the language processor. In W. E. Cooper & E. C. T. Walker (Eds.), *Sentence processing* (pp. 27–85). Hillsdale, NJ: Erlbaum.

Forster, K. I. (1987). Form-priming with masked primes: The best-match hypothesis. In M. Coltheart (Ed.), *Attention and performance: Vol. XII. The psychology of reading.* Hillsdale, NJ: Erlbaum.

Forster, K. I. (1989). Basic issues in lexical processing. In W. Marslen-Wilson (Ed.), *Lexical representation and process* (pp. 75–107). Cambridge, MA: MIT Press.

Foss, D. J. (1969) Decision processes during sentence comprehension: Effects of lexical item difficulty and position upon decision times. *Journal of Verbal Learning and Verbal Behavior, 8*, 457–462.

Foss, D. J. (1970). Some effects of ambiguity upon sentence comprehension. *Journal of Verbal Learning and Verbal Behavior, 9*, 699–706.

Foss, D. J., & Hakes, D. T. (1978). *Psycholinguistics: An introduction to the psychology of language.* Englewood Cliffs, NJ: Prentice Hall.

Foss, D. J., & Jenkins, C. M. (1973). Some effects of context on the comprehension of ambiguous sentences. *Journal of Verbal Learning and Verbal Behavior, 12*, 577–589.

Fouts, R. S., Fouts, D. H., & Van Cantfort, T. E. (1989). The infant Loulis learns signs from cross-fostered chimpanzees. In R. A. Gardner, B. T. Gardner, & T. E. Van Cantfort (Eds.), *Teaching sign language to chimpanzees* (pp. 280–292). Albany: State University of New York Press.

Franco, L., & Sperry, R. W. (1977). Hemisphere lateralization for cognitive processing of geometry. *Neuropsychologia, 15*, 107–113.

Frazier, L. (1987). Sentence processing: review. In M. Coltheart (Ed.), *Attention and performance: Vol. XII. The psychology of reading* (pp. 559–586). Hillsdale, NJ: Erlbaum.

Frazier, L. (1995). Constraint satisfaction as a theory of sentence processing. *Journal of Psycholinguistic Research, 24*, 437–468.

Frazier, L., & Fodor, J. D. (1978). The sausage machine: A new two-stage parsing model. *Cognition, 6*, 291–325.

Frazier, L., & Rayner, K. (1982). Making and correcting errors during sentence comprehension: Eye movements in the analysis of structurally ambiguous sentences. *Cognitive Psychology, 14*, 178–210.

Freed, A. F., & Greenwood, A. (1996). Women, men, and type of talk: What makes the difference? *Language in Society, 25*, 1–26.

Frege, G. (1952). On sense and reference. In P. Geach & M. Black (Eds.), *Philosophical writings of Gottlob Frege* (pp. 56–78). Oxford: Blackwell. (Original work published 1892)

Freud, S. (1963). *Introductory lectures on psycho-analysis* (Parts I and II) (J. Strachey, Trans.). London: Hogarth. (Original work published 1916–1917)

Frishberg, N. (1975). Arbitrariness and iconicity: Historical change in American Sign Language. *Language, 51*, 696–719.

Fromkin, V., & Rodman, R. (1974). *An introduction to language.* New York: Holt, Rinehart & Winston.

Fromkin, V. A. (1971). The non-anomalous nature of anomalous utterances. *Language, 47*, 27–52.

Fromkin, V. A. (Ed.). (1973). *Speech errors as linguistic evidence.* The Hague: Mouton.

Fromkin, V. A. (Ed.). (1980). *Errors in linguistic performance.* New York: Academic Press.

Fry, D. B., Abramson, A. S., Eimas, P. D., & Liberman, A. M (1962). The identification and discrimination of synthetic vowels. *Language and Speech, 5*, 171–189.

Furrow, D., Nelson, K., & Benedict, H. (1979). Mothers' speech to children and syntactic development: Some simple relationships. *Journal of Child Language, 6*, 423–442.

Gale, J., Odell, M., & Nagireddy, C. S. (1995). Marital therapy and self-reflexive research: Research and/as intervention. In G. H. Morris & R. J. Chenail (Eds.), *The talk of the clinic: Explorations in the analysis of medical and therapeutic discourse* (pp. 105–129). Hillsdale, NJ: Erlbaum.

Gardner, B. T., & Gardner, R. A. (1975). Evidence for sentence constituents in the early utterances of child and chimpanzee. *Journal of Experimental Psychology: General, 104*, 244–267.

Gardner, R. A., & Gardner, B. T. (1969). Teaching sign language to a chimpanzee. *Science, 165*, 664–672.

Gardner, R. A., Gardner, B. T., & Van Cantfort, T. E. (Eds.). (1989). *Teaching sign language to chimpanzees.* Albany: State University of New York Press.

Garrett, M. F. (1975). The analysis of sentence production. In G. H. Bower (Ed.), *The psychology of learning and memory: Advances in research and theory* (Vol. 9, pp. 133–177). New York: Academic Press.

Garrett, M. F. (1980). The limits of accommodation. In V. A. Fromkin (Ed.), *Errors in linguistic performance* (pp. 263–271). New York: Academic Press.

Garrett, M. F. (1988). Processes in language production. In F. J. Newmeyer (Ed.), *Linguistics: The Cambridge Survey: Vol. III. Language: Psychological and biological aspects* (pp. 69–96). Cambridge: Cambridge University Press.

Garvey, C. (1975). Requests and responses in children's speech. *Journal of Child Language, 2*, 41–63.

Gazzaniga, M. S., & Hillyard, S. A. (1971). Language and speech capacity of the right hemisphere. *Neuropsychologia, 9*, 273–280.

Gazzaniga, M. S., & LeDoux, J. E. (1978). *The integrated mind.* New York: Plenum.

Gazzaniga, M. S., & Sperry, R. W. (1967). Language after section of the cerebral commissures. *Brain, 90*, 131–148.

Gee, J. P. (1989). Two styles of narrative construction and their linguistic and educational implications. *Discourse Processes, 12*, 287–307.

Gernsbacher, M. A., Goldsmith, H. H., & Robertson, R. R. W. (1992). Do readers mentally represent characters' emotional states? *Cognition and Emotion, 6*, 89–111.

Gerrig, R. J. (1989). Suspense in the absence of uncertainty. *Journal of Memory and Language, 28*, 633–648.

Gerrig, R. J. (1993). *Experiencing narrative worlds: On the psychological activities of reading.* New Haven, CT: Yale University Press.

Geschwind, N. (1965). Disconnexion syndromes in animals and man. *Brain, 88*, 237–294, 585–644.

Geschwind, N. (1972, April). Language and the brain. *Scientific American*, pp. 76–83.

Geschwind, N., & Levitsky, W. (1968). Human brain: Left-right asymmetries in temporal speech regions. *Science, 161*, 186–187.

Gibb, C., & Randall, P. E. (1988). Metalinguistic abilities and learning to read. *Educational Research, 30*, 135–141.

Gibbs, R. W. (1979). Contextual effects in understanding indirect requests. *Discourse Processes, 2,* 1–10.

Gildea, P., & Glucksberg, S. (1983). On understanding metaphor: The role of context. *Journal of Verbal Learning and Verbal Behavior, 22,* 577–590.

Giora, R. (1993). On the function of analogies in informative texts. *Discourse Processes, 16,* 591–611.

Gleason, J. B., & Greif, E. B. (1983). Men's speech to young children. In B. Thorne, C. Kramarae, & N. Henley (Eds.), *Language, gender, and society* (pp. 140–150). Rowley, MA: Newbury House.

Gleitman, L. R., Gleitman, H., & Shipley, E. F. (1972). The emergence of the child as grammarian. *Cognition, 1,* 137–164.

Gleitman, L. R., Newport, E. L., & Gleitman, H. (1984). The current status of the Motherese hypothesis. *Journal of Child Language, 11,* 43–79.

Gleitman, L. R., & Rozin, P. (1977). The structure and acquisition of reading I: Relations between orthographies and the structure of language. In A. S. Reber & D. L. Scarborough (Eds.), *Toward a psychology of reading: The proceedings of the CUNY conference* (pp. 1–53). Hillsdale, NJ: Erlbaum.

Glenn, C. G. (1978). The role of episodic structure and of story length in children's recall of simple stories. *Journal of Verbal Learning and Verbal Behavior, 17,* 229–247.

Glucksberg, S., & Danks, J. H. (1975). *Experimental psycholinguistics: An introduction.* Hillsdale, NJ: Erlbaum.

Glucksberg, S., Gildea, P., & Bookin, H. B. (1982). On understanding nonliteral speech: Can people ignore metaphors? *Journal of Verbal Learning and Verbal Behavior, 21,* 85–98.

Glucksberg, S., & Keysar, B. (1990). Understanding metaphorical comparisons: Beyond similarity. *Psychological Review, 97,* 3–18.

Glucksberg, S., Krauss, R. M., & Weisberg, R. (1966). Referential communication in nursery school children: Method and some preliminary findings. *Journal of Experimental Child Psychology, 3,* 333–342.

Gold, E. (1967). Language identification in the limit. *Information and Control, 10,* 447–474.

Goldfield, B. A. (1987). The contributions of child and caregiver to referential and expressive language. *Applied Psycholinguistics, 8,* 267–280.

Goldiamond, I., & Dryud, J. E. (1968). Some applications and implications of behavioral analysis for psychotherapy. In J. M. Shlien (Ed.), *Research in psychotherapy* (Vol. 3, pp. 54–89). Washington, DC: American Psychological Association.

Goldin-Meadow, S. (1982). The resilience of recursion: A study of a communication system developed without a conventional language model. In E. Wanner & L. R. Gleitman (Eds.), *Language acquisition: The state of the art* (pp. 51–77). Cambridge: Cambridge University Press.

Goldin-Meadow, S., & Mylander, C. (1990). Beyond the input given: The child's role in the acquisition of language. *Language, 66,* 323–355.

Goldman, S. R., & Varnhagen, C. K. (1986). Memory for embedded and sequential story structures. *Journal of Memory and Language, 25,* 401–418.

Golinkoff, R. M., Hirsh-Pasek, K., Cauley, K. M., & Gordon, L. (1987). The eyes have it: Lexical and syntactic comprehension in a new paradigm. *Journal of Child Language, 14,* 23–45.

Goodglass, H. (1993). *Understanding aphasia*. San Diego: Academic Press.

Goodglass, H., & Geschwind, N. (1976). Language disorders (aphasia). In E. C. Carterette & M. P. Friedman (Eds.), *Handbook of perception: Vol. 7. Language and speech* (pp. 389–428). New York: Academic Press.

Goodglass, H., Klein, B., Carey, P., & Jones, K. (1966). Specific semantic word categories in aphasia. *Cortex, 2*, 74–89.

Goodluck, H., & Tavakolian, S. (1982). Competence and processing in children's grammar of relative clauses. *Cognition, 11*, 1–27.

Gopnik, A. (1984). The acquisition of *gone* and the development of the object concept. *Journal of Child Language, 11*, 273–292.

Graesser, A. C., Hoffman, N. L., & Clark, L. F. (1980). Structural components of reading time. *Journal of Verbal Learning and Verbal Behavior, 19*, 135–151.

Greenberg, J. H. (1966). Some universals of grammar with particular reference to the order of meaningful elements. In J. H. Greenberg (Ed.), *Universals of language* (2nd ed., pp. 73–113). Cambridge, MA: MIT Press.

Greene, J. (1972). *Psycholinguistics: Chomsky and psychology*. Harmondsworth, England: Penguin.

Greenfield, P. M. (1982). The role of perceived variability in the transition to language. *Journal of Child Language, 9*, 1–12.

Greenfield, P. M., & Savage-Rumbaugh, E. S. (1991). Imitation, grammatical development, and the invention of protogrammar by an ape. In N. A. Krasnegor, D. M. Rumbaugh, R. L. Schiefelbusch, & M. Studdert-Kennedy (Eds.), *Biological and behavioral determinants of language development* (pp. 235–258). Hillsdale, NJ: Erlbaum.

Greenfield, P. M., & Smith, J. H. (1976). *The structure of communication in early language development*. New York: Academic Press.

Greenspoon, J. (1955). The reinforcing effect of two spoken sounds on the frequency of two responses. *American Journal of Psychology, 68*, 409–416.

Grice, H. P. (1975). Logic and conversation. In P. Cole & J. L. Morgan (Eds.), *Syntax and semantics: Vol. 3. Speech acts* (pp. 41–58). New York: Seminar.

Grodzinsky, Y. (1990). *Theoretical perspectives on language deficits*. Cambridge, MA: MIT Press.

Grosjean, F. (1979). A study in timing in a manual and a spoken language: American Sign Language and English. *Journal of Psycholinguistic Research, 8*, 379–405.

Grosjean, F., & Lane, H. (1981). Temporal variables in the perception and production of spoken and sign languages. In P. D. Eimas & J. L. Miller (Eds.), *Perspectives on the study of speech* (pp. 207–237). Hillsdale, NJ: Erlbaum.

Grossen, M., & Apothéloz, D. (1996). Communicating about communication in a therapeutic interview. *Journal of Language and Social Psychology, 15*, 101–132.

Haber, R. N., & Hershenson, M. (1973). *The psychology of visual perception*. New York: Holt, Rinehart & Winston.

Haberlandt, K., Berian, C., & Sandson, J. (1980). The episode schema in story processing. *Journal of Verbal Learning and Verbal Behavior, 19*, 635–650.

Hakuta, K. (1986). *Mirror of language: The debate on bilingualism*. New York: Basic Books.

Halliday, M. A. K., & Hasan, R. (1976). *Cohesion in English*. London: Longman.

Hanson, V. L., & Bellugi, U. (1982). On the role of sign order and morphological structure in memory for American Sign Language sentences. *Journal of Verbal Learning and Verbal Behavior, 21*, 621–633.

Hardin, C., & Banaji, M. R. (1993). The influence of language on thought. *Social Cognition, 11*, 277–308.

Harding, C. G. (1982). Development of the intention to communicate. *Human Development, 25*, 140–151.

Harris, R. J. (1977). Comprehension of pragmatic implications in advertising. *Journal of Applied Psychology, 62*, 603–608.

Harris, R. J., & Monaco, G. E. (1978). The psychology of pragmatic implication: Information processing between the lines. *Journal of Experimental Psychology: General, 107*, 1–22.

Hart, J., Berndt, R. S., & Caramazza, A. (1985). Category-specific naming deficit following cerebral infarction. *Nature, 316*, 439–440.

Hasher, L., & Zacks R. T. (1979). Automatic and effortful processes in memory. *Journal of Experimental Psychology: General, 108*, 356–388.

Haviland, S. E., & Clark, H. H. (1974). What's new? Acquiring new information as a process in comprehension. *Journal of Verbal Learning and Verbal Behavior, 13*, 512–521.

Hayes, K. J., & Hayes, C. (1952). Imitation in a home-raised chimpanzee. *Journal of Comparative and Physiological Psychology, 45*, 450–459.

He, A. W. (1994). Withholding academic advice: Institutional context and discourse practice. *Discourse Processes, 18*, 297–316.

Healy, A. F. (1976). Detection errors on the word *the*: Evidence for reading units larger than letters. *Journal of Experimental Psychology: Human Perception and Performance, 2*, 235–242.

Healy, A. F., Oliver, W. L., & McNamara, T. P. (1987). Detecting letters in continuous text: Effects of display size. *Journal of Experimental Psychology: Human Perception and Performance, 13*, 279–290.

Heath, C. (1992). The delivery and reception of diagnosis in the general-practice consultation. In P. Drew & J. Heritage (Eds.), *Talk at work: Interaction in institutional settings* (pp. 235–267). Cambridge: Cambridge University Press.

Heider, E. R. (1972). Universals in color naming and memory. *Journal of Experimental Psychology, 93*, 10–20.

Henderson, A., Goldman-Eisler, F., & Skarbek, A. (1966). Sequential temporal patterns in spontaneous speech. *Language and Speech, 9*, 207–216.

Hicks, D. (1990). Narrative skills and genre knowledge: Ways of telling in the primary school grades. *Applied Psycholinguistics, 11*, 83–104.

Hicks, D. (1991). Kinds of narrative: Genre skills among first graders from two communities. In A. McCabe & C. Peterson (Eds.), *Developing narrative structure* (pp. 55–87). Hillsdale, NJ: Erlbaum.

Hirsh-Pasek, K., Reeves, L. M., & Golinkoff, R. (1993). Words and meaning: From primitives to complex organization. In J. B. Gleason & N. B. Ratner (Eds.), *Psycholinguistics* (pp. 133–197). Orlando, FL: Harcourt Brace Jovanovich.

Hirsh-Pasek, K., Treiman, R., & Schneiderman, M. (1984). Brown and Hanlon revisited: Mothers' sensitivity to ungrammatical forms. *Journal of Child Language, 11*, 81–88.

Hockett, C. F. (1954). Chinese versus English: An exploration of the Whorfian theses. In H. Hoijer (Ed.), *Language in culture* (pp. 106–123). Chicago: University of Chicago Press.

Hockett, C. F. (1966). The problem of universals in language. In J. H. Greenberg (Ed.), *Universals of language* (2nd ed., pp. 1–29). Cambridge, MA: MIT Press.

Hoff-Ginsburg, E., & Shatz, M. (1982). Linguistic input and the child's acquisition of language. *Psychological Bulletin, 92*, 3–26.

Hogaboam, T. W., & Perfetti, C. A. (1975). Lexical ambiguity and sentence comprehension. *Journal of Verbal Learning and Verbal Behavior, 14*, 265–274.

Holmes, J. (1984). "Women's language": A functional approach. *General Linguistics, 24*, 149–178.

Holtgraves, T. (1997). Politeness and memory for the wording of remarks. *Memory & Cognition, 25*, 106–116.

Hornstein, G. A. (1985). Intimacy in conversational style as a function of the degree of closeness between members of a dyad. *Journal of Personality and Social Psychology, 49*, 671–681.

Hoosain, R. (1991). *Psycholinguistic implications for linguistic relativity: A case study of Chinese.* Hillsdale, NJ: Erlbaum.

Hoosain, R., & Salili, F. (1987). Language differences in pronunciation speed for numbers, digit span, and mathematical ability. *Psychologia, 30*, 34–38.

Hubel, D. H., & Wiesel, T. N. (1965). Receptive fields and functional architecture in two nonstriate visual areas (18 and 19) of the cat. *Journal of Neurophysiology, 28*, 229–289.

Huey, E. B. (1968). *The psychology and pedagogy of reading.* Cambridge, MA: MIT Press. (Original work published 1908)

Hunt, E., & Agnoli, F. (1991). The Whorfian hypothesis: A cognitive psychology perspective. *Psychological Review, 98*, 377–389.

Hurford, J. R. (1987). *Language and number.* Cambridge: Cambridge University Press.

Huttenlocher, J., Haight, W., Bryk, A., Seltzer, M., & Lyons, T. (1991). Early vocabulary growth: Relation to language input and gender. *Developmental Psychology, 27*, 236–248.

Hyams, N. M. (1986). *Language acquisition and the theory of parameters.* Dordrecht, Holland: Reidel.

Jaffe, J., & Feldstein, S. (1970). *Rhythms of dialogue.* New York: Academic Press.

Jakobson, R., Fant, C. G. M., & Halle, M. (1969). *Preliminaries to speech analysis.* Cambridge, MA: MIT Press. (Original work published 1951)

James, D. (1972). Some aspects of the syntax and semantics of interjections. In P. Peranteau, J. N. Levi, & G. C. Phares (Eds.), *Papers from the Eighth Regional Meeting of the Chicago Linguistic Society* (pp. 162–172). Chicago: Chicago Linguistics Society.

James, D., & Clarke, S. (1993). Women, men, and interruptions: A critical review. In D. Tannen (Ed.), *Gender and conversational interaction* (pp. 231–280). New York: Oxford University Press.

James, D., & Drakich, J. (1993). Understanding gender differences in amount of talk: A critical review of research. In D. Tannen (Ed.), *Gender and conversational interaction* (pp. 281–312). New York: Oxford University Press.

James, W. (1950). *The principles of psychology* (Vol. 1). New York: Holt. (Original work published 1890)

Jarvella, R. J. (1971). Syntactic processing of connected speech. *Journal of Verbal Learning and Verbal Behavior, 10,* 409–416.

Jefferson, G. (1972). Side sequences. In D. Sudnow (Ed.), *Studies in social interaction* (pp. 294–338). New York: Free Press.

Johnson, M. K., Bransford, J. D., & Solomon, S. K. (1973). Memory for tacit implications of sentences. *Journal of Experimental Psychology, 98,* 203–205.

Johnson-Laird, P. N. (1983). *Mental models.* Cambridge, MA: Harvard University Press.

Johnson-Laird, P. N. (1988a). *The computer and the mind: An introduction to cognitive science.* Cambridge, MA: Harvard University Press.

Johnson-Laird, P. N. (1988b). How is meaning mentally represented? In U. Eco, M. Santambrogio, & P. Violi (Eds.), *Meaning and mental representations* (pp. 99–118). Bloomington: Indiana University Press.

Johnson-Laird, P. N., Herrmann, D. J., & Chaffin, R. (1984). Only connections: A critique of semantic networks. *Psychological Bulletin, 96,* 292–315.

Johnston, J. C., & McClelland, J. L. (1980). Experimental tests of a hierarchical model of word identification. *Journal of Verbal Learning and Verbal Behavior, 19,* 503–524.

Johnston, J. R., & Slobin, D. I. (1979). The development of locative expressions in English, Italian, Serbo-Croatian, and Turkish. *Journal of Child Language, 6,* 529–545.

Jones, C. M., & Beach, W. A. (1995). Therapists' techniques for responding to unsolicited contributions by family members. In G. H. Morris & R. J. Chenail (Eds.), *The talk of the clinic: Explorations in the analysis of medical and therapeutic discourse* (pp. 49–69). Hillsdale, NJ: Erlbaum.

Jusczyk, P. W., & Aslin, R. N. (1995). Infants' detection of the sound patterns of words in fluent speech. *Cognitive Psychology, 29,* 1–23.

Jusczyk, P. W., Luce, P. A., & Charles-Luce, J. (1994). Infants' sensitivity to phonotactic patterns in the native language. *Journal of Memory and Language, 33,* 630–645.

Just, M. A., & Carpenter, P. A. (1976). Eye fixations and cognitive processes. *Cognitive Psychology, 8,* 441–480.

Just, M. A., & Carpenter, P. A. (1980). A theory of reading: From eye fixations to comprehension. *Psychological Review, 87,* 329–354.

Just, M. A., & Carpenter, P. A. (1987). *The psychology of reading and language comprehension.* Boston: Allyn & Bacon.

Kaplan, J. A., Brownell, H. H., Jacobs, J. R., & Gardner, H. (1990). The effects of right hemisphere damage on the pragmatic interpretation of conversational remarks. *Brain and Language, 38,* 315–333.

Karmiloff-Smith, A., Grant, J., Berthoud, I., Davies, M., Howlin, P., & Udwin, O. (1997). Language and Williams syndrome: How intact is "intact"? *Child Development, 68,* 246–262.

Kay, P., & Kempton, W. (1984). What is the Sapir-Whorf hypothesis? *American Anthropologist, 86,* 65–79.

Keenan, E. O. (1974). Conversational competence in children. *Journal of Child Language, 1,* 163–183.

Keenan, J. M., MacWhinney, B., & Mayhew, D. (1977). Pragmatics in memory: A study of natural conversation. *Journal of Verbal Learning and Verbal Behavior, 16,* 549–560.

Keillor, G. (1987). *Leaving home.* New York: Viking Penguin.

Kellogg, W. N., & Kellogg, L. A. (1933). *The ape and the child: A study of environmental influence upon early behavior.* New York: Whittlesey House.

Kempen, G., & Hoenkamp, E. (1987). An incremental procedural grammar for sentence formulation. *Cognitive Science, 11,* 201–258.

Kennedy, C. W., & Camden, C. T. (1983). A new look at interruptions. *The Western Journal of Speech Communication, 47,* 45–58.

Kent, G. H., & Rosanoff, A. J. (1910). A study of association in insanity. *American Journal of Insanity, 67,* 37–96.

Kess, J. F. (1991). On the developing history of psycholinguistics. *Language Sciences, 13,* 1–20.

Kimball, J. (1973). Seven principles of surface structure parsing in natural language. *Cognition, 2,* 15–47.

Kimura, D. (1961). Cerebral dominance and the perception of verbal stimuli. *Canadian Journal of Psychology, 15,* 166–171.

Kimura, D. (1964). Left-right differences in the perception of melodies. *Quarterly Journal of Experimental Psychology 16,* 355–358.

Kingstone, A., Enns, J. T., Mangun, G. R., & Gazzaniga, M. S. (1995). Guided visual search is a left-hemisphere process in split-brain patients. *Psychological Science, 6,* 118–121.

Kintsch, E. (1990). Macroprocesses and microprocesses in the development of summarization skill. *Cognition and Instruction, 7,* 161–195.

Kintsch, W. (1974). *The representation of meaning in memory.* Hillsdale, NJ: Erlbaum.

Kintsch, W. (1988). The role of knowledge in discourse comprehension: A construction-integration model. *Psychological Review, 95,* 163–182.

Kintsch, W., & Bates, E. (1977). Recognition memory for statements from a classroom lecture. *Journal of Experimental Psychology: Human Learning and Memory, 3,* 150–159.

Kintsch, W., & Keenan, J. (1973). Reading rate and retention as a function of the number of propositions in the base structure of sentences. *Cognitive Psychology, 5,* 257–274.

Kintsch, W., Welsh, D., Schmalhoffer, F., & Zimny, S. (1990). Sentence memory: A theoretical analysis. *Journal of Memory and Language, 29,* 133–159.

Klima, E. S., & Bellugi, U. (1966). Syntactic regularities in the speech of children. In J. Lyons & R. J. Wales (Eds.), *Psycholinguistics papers* (pp. 183–208). Edinburgh: Edinburgh University Press.

Klima, E. S., & Bellugi, U. (1979). *The signs of language.* Cambridge, MA: Harvard University Press.

Kollock, P., Blumstein, P., & Schwartz, P. (1985). Sex and power in interaction: Conversational privileges and duties. *American Sociological Review, 50,* 34–46.

Kozminsky, E. (1977). Altering comprehension: The effects of biasing titles on text comprehension. *Memory & Cognition, 5,* 482–490.

Kuczaj, S. A., II, & Brannick, N. (1979). Children's use of the *wh* question modal auxiliary placement rule. *Journal of Experimental Child Psychology, 28,* 43–67.

Kuhl, P. K. (1987). The special-mechanisms debate in speech research: Categorization tests on animals and infants. In S. Harnad (Ed.), *Categorical perception: The groundwork of cognition* (pp. 355–386). Cambridge: Cambridge University Press.

Labov, W., & Fanshel, D. (1977). *Therapeutic discourse: Psychotherapy as conversation.* New York: Academic Press.

Lakoff, G. (1972). Hedges: A study of meaning criteria and the logic of fuzzy concepts. In *Papers from the Eighth Regional Meeting of the Chicago Linguistics Society* (pp. 183–228). Chicago: Chicago Linguistics Society.

Lakoff, R., (1975). *Language and woman's place.* New York: Harper & Row.

Landauer, T. K., & Meyer, D. E. (1972). Category size and semantic-memory retrieval. *Journal of Verbal Learning and Verbal Behavior, 11,* 539–549.

Lane, H. (1976). *The wild boy of Aveyron.* Cambridge, MA: Harvard University Press.

Lane, H., Boyes-Braem, P., & Bellugi, U. (1976). Preliminaries to a distinctive feature analysis of handshapes in American Sign Language. *Cognitive Psychology, 8,* 263–289.

Lashley, K. S. (1951). The problem of serial order in behavior. In L. A. Jeffress (Ed.), *Cerebral mechanisms in behavior* (pp. 112–136). New York: Wiley.

Lasky, R. E., Syrdal-Lasky, A., & Klein, R. E. (1975). VOT discrimination by four to six and a half month old infants from Spanish environments. *Journal of Experimental Child Psychology, 20,* 215–225.

Lasnik, H. (1990). Syntax. In D. N. Osherson & H. Lasnik (Eds.), *An invitation to cognitive science: Vol. 1. Language* (pp. 5–21). Cambridge, MA: MIT Press.

Lee, D. (1987). Linguistic reflection of Wintu-thought. In D. Lee, *Freedom and culture* (pp. 121–130). Prospect Heights, IL: Waveland. (Original work published 1944)

Lehrer, A. (1994). Understanding classroom lectures. *Discourse Processes, 17,* 259–281.

Lenneberg, E. H. (1953). Cognition in ethnolinguistics. *Language, 29,* 463–471.

Lenneberg, E. H. (1964). A biological perspective of language. In E. H. Lenneberg (Ed.), *New directions in the study of language* (pp. 65–88). Cambridge, MA: MIT Press.

Lenneberg, E. H. (1967). *Biological foundations of language.* New York: Wiley.

Lesgold, A. M., Roth, S. F., & Curtis, M. E. (1979). Foregrounding effects in discourse comprehension. *Journal of Verbal Learning and Verbal Behavior, 18,* 291–308.

Levelt, W. J. M. (1983). Monitoring and self-repair in speech. *Cognition, 14,* 41–104.

Levelt, W. J. M. (1989). *Speaking: From intention to articulation.* Cambridge, MA: MIT Press.

Levy, J. (1974). Cerebral asymmetries as manifested in split-brain man. In M. Kinsbourne & W. L. Smith (Eds.), *Hemispheric disconnection and cerebral function.* Springfield, IL: Thomas.

Levy, Y. (1996). Modularity of language reconsidered. *Brain and Language, 55,* 240–263.

Liberman, A. M. (1970). The grammars of speech and language. *Cognitive Psychology, 1,* 301–323.

Liberman, A. M. (1982). On finding that speech is special. *American Psychologist, 37,* 148–167.

Liberman, A. M., Cooper, F. S., Shankweiler, D. P., & Studdert-Kennedy, M. (1967). Perception of the speech code. *Psychological Review, 74,* 431–461.

Liberman, A. M., Harris, K. S., Hoffman, H. S., & Griffith, B. C. (1957). The discrimination of speech sounds within and across phoneme boundaries. *Journal of Experimental Psychology, 54,* 358–368.

Liberman, A. M., & Mattingly, I. G. (1985). The motor theory of speech perception revised. *Cognition, 21,* 1–36.

Liberman, I. Y., Shankweiler, D., Fischer, F. W., & Carter, B. (1974). Explicit syllable and phoneme segmentation in the young child. *Journal of Experimental Child Psychology, 18,* 201–212.

Lieberman, P. (1965). On the acoustic basis of the perception of intonation by linguists. *Word, 21,* 40–54.

Lieberman, P. (1967). *Intonation, perception, and language.* Cambridge, MA: MIT Press.

Lieberman P. (1973). On the evolution of language: A unified view. *Cognition, 2,* 59–94.

Lieberman, P. (1991). *Uniquely human: The evolution of speech, thought, and selfless behavior.* Cambridge, MA: Harvard University Press.

Lieberman, P. (1998). *Eve spoke: Human language and human evolution.* New York: Norton.

Lieven, E. M., Pine, J. M., & Barnes, H. D. (1992). Individual differences in early vocabulary development: Redefining the referential-expressive distinction. *Journal of Child Language, 19,* 287–310.

Lima, S. D. (1987). Morphological analysis in sentence reading. *Journal of Memory and Language, 26,* 84–99.

Limber, J. (1973). The genesis of complex sentences. In T. E. Moore (Ed.), *Cognitive development and the acquisition of language* (pp. 169–185). New York: Academic Press.

Linden, E. (1974). *Apes, men, and language.* New York: Dutton.

Lindsley, J. R. (1975). Producing simple utterances: How far ahead do we plan? *Cognitive Psychology, 7,* 1–19.

Linebarger, M. C., Schwartz, M. F., & Saffran, E. M. (1983). Sensitivity to grammatical structure in so-called agrammatic aphasics. *Cognition, 13,* 361–392.

Liu, L. G. (1985). Reasoning counterfactually in Chinese: Are there any obstacles? *Cognition, 21,* 239–270.

Lively, S. E., Pisoni, D. B., & Goldinger, S. D. (1994). Spoken word recognition: Research and theory. In M. A. Gernsbacher (Ed.), *Handbook of psycholinguistics* (pp. 265–301). San Diego: Academic Press.

Lorch, R. F., Jr., & Chen, A. H. (1986). Effects of number signals on reading and recall. *Journal of Educational Psychology, 78,* 263–270.

Lounsbury, F. G. (1965). Transitional probability, linguistic structure, and systems of habit-family hierarchies. In C. E. Osgood & T. Sebeok (Eds.), *Psycholinguistics: A survey of theory and research problems* (pp. 93–101). Bloomington: Indiana University Press. (Original work published 1954)

Lucy, J. A. (1992a). *Grammatical categories and cognition: A case study of the linguistic relativity hypothesis.* Cambridge: Cambridge University Press.

Lucy, J. A. (1992b). *Language diversity and thought: A reformulation of the linguistic relativity hypothesis.* Cambridge: Cambridge University Press.

Lucy, J. A., & Shweder, R. A. (1979). Whorf and his critics: Linguistic and nonlinguistic influences on color memory. *American Anthropologist, 81,* 581–615.

Lundberg, I., Frost, J., & Petersen, O-P. (1988). Effects of an extensive program for stimulating phonological awareness in preschool children. *Reading Research Quarterly, 23,* 263–284.

Lyons, J. (1968). *Introduction to theoretical linguistics.* Cambridge: Cambridge University Press.

MacDonald, J., & McGurk, H. (1978). Visual influences on speech perception processes. *Perception & Psychophysics, 24,* 253–257.

MacDonald, M. C., Pearlmutter, N. J., & Seidenberg, M. S. (1994). Lexical nature of syntactic ambiguity resolution. *Psychological Review, 101,* 676–703.

MacKay, D. G. (1978). Derivational rules and the internal lexicon. *Journal of Verbal Learning and Verbal Behavior, 17,* 61–71.

MacKay, D. G. (1982). The problems of flexibility, fluency, and speed-accuracy trade-off in skilled behavior. *Psychological Review, 89,* 483–506.

MacKay, D. G. (1987). *The organization of perception and action: A theory for language and other cognitive skills.* New York: Springer.

Macnamara, J. (1972). Cognitive basis of language learning in infants. *Psychological Review, 79,* 1–13.

MacNeilage, P. (1991). Comment: The gesture as a unit in speech perception theories. In I. G. Mattingly & M. Studdert-Kennedy (Eds.), *Modularity and the motor theory of speech perception* (pp. 61–67). Hillsdale, NJ: Erlbaum.

MacNeilage, P., & Ladefoged, P. (1976). The production of speech and language. In E. C. Carterette & M. P. Friedman (Eds.), *Handbook of perception: Vol. 7. Language and speech* (pp. 75–120). New York: Academic Press.

MacNeilage, P., Studdert-Kennedy, M. G., & Lindblom, B. (1987). Primate handedness reconsidered. *Behavioral and Brain Sciences, 10,* 247–303.

MacWhinney, B. (1985). Hungarian language acquisition as an exemplification of a general model of grammatical development. In D. I. Slobin (Ed.), *The crosslinguistic study of language acquisition: Vol. 2. Theoretical issues* (pp. 1069–1155). Hillsdale, NJ: Erlbaum.

MacWhinney, B., Bates, E., & Kliegl, R. (1984). Cue validity and sentence interpretation in English, German, and Italian. *Journal of Verbal Learning and Verbal Behavior, 23,* 127–150.

Maltz, D. N., & Borker, R. A. (1983). A cultural approach to male-female miscommunication. In J. J. Gumperz (Ed.), *Language and social identity* (pp. 196–216). Cambridge: Cambridge University Press.

Mandel, D. R., Jusczyk, P. W., & Pisoni, D. B. (1995). Infants' recognition of the sound patterns of their own names. *Psychological Science, 6,* 314–317.

Mandler, J. M. (1984). *Stories, scripts, and scenes: Aspects of schema theory.* Hillsdale, NJ: Erlbaum.

Mandler, J. M. (1987). On the psychological reality of story structure. *Discourse Processes, 10,* 1–29.

Mandler, J. M., & Johnson, N. S. (1977). Remembrance of things parsed: Story structure and recall. *Cognitive Psychology, 9,* 111–151.

Mandler, J. M., Scribner, S., Cole, M., & DeForest, M. (1980). Cross-cultural invariance in story recall. *Child Development, 51,* 19–26.

Mann, V. A., Madden, J., Russell, J. M., & Liberman, A. (1981). Further investigation into the influence of preceding liquids on stop consonant perception. *Journal of the Acoustical Society of America, 69* (Suppl. 1), S91 (Abstract).

Mann, V. A., & Repp, B. H. (1981). Influence of preceding fricative on stop consonant perception. *Journal of the Acoustical Society of America, 69,* 548–558.

Mannes, S. M., & Kintsch, W. (1987). Knowledge organization and text organization. *Cognition and Instruction, 4,* 91–115.

Maratsos, M. (1982). The child's construction of grammatical categories. In E. Wanner & L. R. Gleitman (Eds.), *Language acquisition: The state of the art* (pp. 240–266). Cambridge: Cambridge University Press.

Maratsos, M. P. (1973). Nonegocentric communication abilities in preschool children. *Child Development, 44,* 697–700.

Maratsos, M. P. (1974). Children who get worse at understanding the passive: A replication of Bever. *Journal of Psycholinguistic Research, 3,* 65–74.

Maratsos, M. P., & Chalkley, M. A. (1980). The internal language of children's syntax: The ontogenesis and representation of syntactic categories. In K. E. Nelson (Ed.), *Children's language* (Vol. 2, pp. 127–214). New York: Gardner.

Marcel, A. J. (1983). Conscious and unconscious perception: Experiments on visual masking and word recognition. *Cognitive Psychology, 15,* 197–237.

Marcus, G. F. (1996). Why do children say "breaked?"? *Current Directions in Psychological Science, 5,* 81–85.

Marcus, G. F., Pinker, S., Ullman, M., Hollander, M., Rosen, T. J., & Xu, F. (1992). Overregularizations in language acquisition. *Monographs of the Society for Research in Child Development, 57*(4, Serial No. 228).

Markman, E. M. (1989). *Categorization and naming in children.* Cambridge, MA: MIT Press.

Markman, E. M., & Hutchinson, J. E. (1984). Children's sensitivity to constraints on word meaning: Taxonomic versus thematic relations. *Cognitive Psychology, 16,* 1–27.

Markman, E. M., & Wachtel, G. E. (1988). Children's use of mutual exclusivity to constrain the meanings of words. *Cognitive Psychology, 20,* 121–157.

Marshall, J. C. (1980). On the biology of language acquisition. In D. Caplan (Ed.), *Biological studies of mental processes* (pp. 106–148). Cambridge, MA: MIT Press.

Marslen-Wilson, W. (1987). Functional parallelism in spoken word-recognition. *Cognition, 25,* 71–102.

Marslen-Wilson, W. (1990). Activation, competition, and frequency in lexical access. In G. T. M. Altmann (Ed.), *Cognitive models of speech processing: Psycholinguistic and computational perspectives.* Cambridge, MA: MIT Press.

Marslen-Wilson, W., & Tyler, L. K. (1980). The temporal structure of spoken language understanding. *Cognition, 8,* 1–71.

Marslen-Wilson, W., Tyler, L. K., Waksler, R., & Older, L. (1994). Morphology and meaning in the English mental lexicon. *Psychological Review, 101,* 3–33.

Marslen-Wilson, W. D., & Welsh, A. (1978). Processing interactions and lexical access during word recognition in continuous speech. *Cognitive Psychology, 10,* 29–63.

Martin, J. G. (1972). Rhythmic (hierarchical) versus serial structure in speech and other behavior. *Psychological Review, 79,* 487–509.

Martin, L. (1986). "Eskimo words for snow": A case study in the genesis and decay of an anthropological example. *American Anthropologist, 88,* 418–423.

Masur, E. F. (1982). Mothers' responses to infants' object-related gestures: Influence on lexical development. *Journal of Child Language, 9,* 23–30.

Mateer, C., & Kimura, D. (1977). Impairment of nonverbal oral movements in aphasia. *Brain and Language, 4,* 262–276.

Mathis, T., & Yule, G. (1994). Zero quotatives. *Discourse Processes, 18,* 63–76.

Mattingly, I. G. (1972). Reading, the linguistic process, and linguistic awareness. In J. F. Kavanaugh & I. G. Mattingly (Eds.), *Language by ear and by eye: The relationships between speech and reading* (pp. 133–147). Cambridge, MA: MIT Press.

Mattingly, I. G., Liberman, A. M., Syrdal, A. K., & Halwes, T. (1971). Discrimination in speech and nonspeech modes. *Cognitive Psychology, 2,* 131–157.

Mayer, R. E., Cook, L. K., & Dyck, J. L. (1984). Techniques that help readers build mental models from scientific texts: Definition pretraining and signaling. *Journal of Educational Psychology, 76,* 1089–1105.

McCabe, A., & Peterson, C. (1991). Getting the story: A longitudinal study of parental styles in eliciting narratives and developing narrative skill. In A. McCabe & C. Peterson (Eds.), *Developing narrative structure* (pp. 217–253). Hillsdale, NJ: Erlbaum.

McCauley, R. N. (1987). The not so happy story of the marriage of linguistics and psychology, or why linguistics has discouraged psychology's recent advances. *Synthese, 72,* 341–353.

McClelland, J. L. (1987). The case for interactionism in language processing. In M. Coltheart (Ed.), *Attention and performance: Vol. XII. The psychology of reading* (pp. 3–36). Hillsdale, NJ: Erlbaum.

McClelland, J. L., & Elman, J. L. (1986). Interactive processes in speech perception: The TRACE model. In J. L. McClelland, D. E. Rumelhart, & the PDP Research Group (Eds.), *Parallel distributed processing: Vol. 2. Psychological and biological models* (pp. 58–121). Cambridge, MA: MIT Press.

McClelland, J. L., & Rumelhart, D. E. (1981). An interactive activation model of context effects in letter perception: Part 1. An account of basic findings. *Psychological Review, 88,* 375–407.

McClelland, J. L., Rumelhart, D. E., and the PDP Research Group (1986). *Parallel distributed processing: Explorations in the microstructure of cognition: Vol. 2. Psychological and biological models.* Cambridge, MA: MIT Press.

McGurk, H., & MacDonald, J. (1976). Hearing lips and seeing voices. *Nature, 264,* 746–748.

McKoon, G., & Ratcliff, R. (1980). Priming in item recognition: The organization of propositions in memory for text. *Journal of Verbal Learning and Verbal Behavior, 19,* 369–386.

McKoon, G., & Ratcliff, R. (1981). The comprehension processes and memory structures involved in instrumental inference. *Journal of Verbal Learning and Verbal Behavior, 20,* 671–682.

McKoon, G., & Ratcliff, R. (1992). Inference during reading. *Psychological Review, 99,* 440–466.

McMillan, J. R., Clifton, A. K., McGrath, D., & Gale, W. S. (1977). Women's language: Uncertainty or interpersonal sensitivity and emotionality? *Sex Roles, 3,* 545–559.

McMullen, L. M., Vernon, A. E., & Murton, T. (1995). Division of labor in conversations: Are Fishman's results replicable and generalizable? *Journal of Psycholinguistic Research, 24,* 255–268.

McNeill, D. (1966). Developmental psycholinguistics. In F. Smith & G. A. Miller (Eds.), *The genesis of language: A psycholinguistic approach* (pp. 15–84). Cambridge, MA: MIT Press.

McNeill, D. (1970). *The acquisition of language: The study of developmental psycholinguistics.* New York: Harper & Row.

McNeill, D. (1985). So you think gestures are nonverbal? *Psychological Review, 92,* 350–371.

Meadow, K. P. (1980). *Deafness and child development.* Berkeley: University of California Press.

Mehan, H. (1979). *Learning lessons: Social organization in the classroom.* Cambridge, MA: Harvard University Press.

Mehler, J., Jusczyk, P., Lambertz, G., Halsted, N., Bertoncini, J., & Amiel-Tison, C. (1988). A precursor of language acquisition in young infants. *Cognition, 29,* 143–178.

Meier, R. P., & Newport, E. L. (1990). Out of the hands of babes: On a possible sign advantage in language acquisition. *Language, 66,* 1–23.

Merriman, W. E., & Bowman, L. L. (1989). The mutual exclusivity bias in children's word learning. *Monographs of the Society for Research in Child Development, 54*(3–4, Serial No. 220).

Merritt, M. (1982). Distributing and directing attention in primary classrooms. In L. C. Wilkinson (Ed.), *Communicating in the classroom* (pp. 223–244). New York: Academic Press.

Mervis, C. B., & Mervis, C. A. (1982). Leopards are kitty-cats: Object labeling by mothers for their thirteen-month-olds. *Child Development, 53,* 267–273.

Meyer, B. J. F., Brandt, D. M., & Bluth, G. J. (1980). Use of top-level structure in text: Key for reading comprehension of ninth-grade students. *Reading Research Quarterly, 16,* 72–103.

Meyer, D. E., & Schvaneveldt, R. W. (1971). Facilitation in recognizing pairs of words: Evidence of a dependence between retrieval operations. *Journal of Experimental Psychology, 90,* 227–234.

Michaels, S. (1981). "Sharing time": Children's narrative styles and differential access to literacy. *Language in Society, 10,* 423–442.

Michaels, S. (1991). The dismantling of narrative. In A. McCabe & C. Peterson (Eds.), *Developing narrative structure* (pp. 303–351). Hillsdale, NJ: Erlbaum.

Milberg, W., & Blumstein, S. E. (1981). Lexical decision and aphasia: Evidence for semantic processing. *Brain and Language, 14,* 371–385.

Miller, G. A. (1979). Images and models, similes and metaphors. In A. Ortony (Ed.), *Metaphor and thought* (pp. 202–250). Cambridge: Cambridge University Press.

Miller, G. A. (1990). Linguists, psychologists, and the cognitive sciences. *Language, 66,* 317–322.

Miller, G. A. (1991). *The science of words.* New York: Scientific American.

Miller, G. A., & Chomsky, N. (1963). Finitary models of language users. In R. D. Luce, R. R. Bush, & E. Galanter (Eds.), *Handbook of mathematical psychology* (Vol. 2, pp. 419–491). New York: Wiley.

Miller, G. A., Heise, G. A., & Lichten, W. (1951). The intelligibility of speech as a function of the context of the test materials. *Journal of Experimental Psychology, 41,* 329–335.

Miller, G. A., & Isard, S. (1963). Some perceptual consequences of linguistic rules. *Journal of Verbal Learning and Verbal Behavior, 2,* 217–228.

Miller, G. A., & Nicely, P. A. (1955). An analysis of perceptual confusions among some English consonants. *Journal of the Acoustical Society of America, 27,* 338–352.

Miller, J. F., & Chapman, R. S. (1981). The relation between age and mean length of utterance in morphemes. *Journal of Speech and Hearing Research, 24,* 154–161.

Miller, J. L. (1981). Effects of speaking rate on segmental distinctions. In P. D. Eimas & J. L. Miller (Eds.), *Perspectives on the study of speech* (pp. 39–74). Hillsdale, NJ: Erlbaum.

Miller, K. F., Smith, C. M., Zhu, J., & Zhang, H. (1995). Preschool origins of cross-national differences in mathematical competence: The role of number-naming systems. *Psychological Science, 6,* 56–60.

Miller, W., & Ervin, S. (1964). The development of grammar in child language. In U. Bellugi & R. Brown (Eds.), The acquisition of language (pp. 9–34). *Monographs of the Society for Research in Child Development, 29* (1, Serial No. 92).

Miura, I. T. (1987). Mathematics achievement as a function of language. *Journal of Educational Psychology, 79,* 79–82.

Miura, I. T., Kim, C. C., Chang, C-M., & Okamoto, Y. (1988). Effects of language characteristics on children's cognitive representation of number: Cross-national comparisons. *Child Development, 59,* 1445–1450.

Miura, I. T., & Okamoto, Y. (1989). Comparisons of U.S. and Japanese first graders' cognitive representation of number and understanding of place value. *Journal of Educational Psychology, 81,* 109–113.

Moerk, E. L. (1980). Relationships between parental input frequencies and children's language acquisition: A reanalysis of Brown's data. *Journal of Child Language, 7,* 105–118.

Moerk, E. L. (1981). To attend or not to attend to unwelcome reanalyses? A reply to Pinker. *Journal of Child Language, 8,* 627–631.

Morford, J. P., & Goldin-Meadow, S. (1997). From here and now to there and then: The development of displaced reference in homesign and English. *Child Development, 68,* 420–435.

Morrow, D. G., Bower, G. H., & Greenspan, S. L. (1989). Updating situational models during narrative comprehension. *Journal of Memory and Language, 28,* 292–312.

Morton, J. (1969). Interaction of information in word recognition. *Psychological Review, 76,* 165–178.

Morton, J. (1979). Word recognition. In J. Morton & J. C. Marshall (Eds.), *Psycholinguistics 2: Structure and processes* (pp. 108–156). Cambridge, MA: MIT Press.

Motley, M. T. (1980). Verification of "Freudian slips" and semantic prearticulatory editing via laboratory-induced spoonerisms. In V. A. Fromkin (Ed.), *Errors in linguistic performance* (pp. 133–147). New York: Academic Press.

Motley, M. T. (1987, February). What I meant to say. *Psychology Today,* pp. 24–28.

Motley, M. T., Baars, B. J., & Camden, C. T. (1983). Experimental verbal slip studies: A review and an editing model of language encoding. *Communication Monographs, 50,* 79–101.

Naeser, M. A., Palumbo, C. L., Helm-Estabrooks, N., Stiassny-Eder, D., & Albert, M. L. (1989). Severe nonfluency in aphasia: Role of the medial subcallosal fasciculus and other white matter pathways in recovery of spontaneous speech. *Brain, 112,* 1–38.

Nagy, W. E., & Anderson, R. C. (1984). How many words are there in printed school English? *Reading Research Quarterly, 19,* 304–330.

Nakazima, S. (1975). Phonemicization and symbolization in language development. In E. H. Lenneberg & E. Lenneberg (Eds.), *Foundations of language development* (Vol. 1, pp. 181–187). New York: Academic Press.

Nebes, R. D. (1972). Dominance of the minor hemisphere in commissurotomized man on a test of figural unification. *Brain, 95,* 633–638.

Neely, J. H. (1977). Semantic priming and retrieval from lexical memory: Role of inhibition-less spreading activation and limited-capacity attention. *Journal of Experimental Psychology: General, 106,* 226–254.

Neely, J. H. (1991). Semantic priming effects in visual word recognition: A selective review of current findings and theories. In D. Besner & G. Humphreys (Eds.), *Basic processes in reading: Visual word recognition* (pp. 264–336). Hillsdale, NJ: Erlbaum.

Neisser, U. (1964, June). Visual search. *Scientific American,* pp. 94–102.

Nelson, K. (1973). Structure and strategy in learning to talk. *Monographs of the Society for Research in Child Development, 38* (1–2, Serial No. 149).

Nelson, K. (1981). Individual differences in language development: Implications for development and language. *Developmental Psychology, 17,* 170–187.

Nelson, K. E. (1976). Facilitating children's syntax acquisition. *Developmental Psychology, 13,* 101–107.

Nelson, K. E., Carskaddon, G., & Bonvillian, J. D. (1973). Syntax acquisition: Impact of experimental variation in adult verbal interaction with the child. *Child Development, 44* 497–504.

Newkirk, D., Klima, E. S., Pedersen, C. C., & Bellugi, U. (1980). Linguistic evidence from slips of the hand. In V. A. Fromkin (Ed.), *Errors in linguistic performance* (pp. 165–197). New York: Academic Press.

Newmeyer, F. J. (1986). *Linguistic theory in America* (2nd ed.). Orlando, FL: Academic Press.

Newport, E. L. (1990). Maturational constraints on language learning. *Cognitive Science, 14,* 11–28.

Newport, E. L., & Ashbrook, E. F. (1977). The emergence of semantic relations in ASL. *Papers and Reports on Child Language Development, 13,* 16–21.

Newport, E. L., Gleitman, H., & Gleitman, L. R. (1977). Mother, I'd rather do it myself: Some effects and non-effects of maternal speech style. In C. E. Snow & C. A. Ferguson (Eds.), *Talking to children: Language input and language acquisition* (pp. 109–149). Cambridge: Cambridge University Press.

Newport, E. L., & Meier, R. P. (1985). The acquisition of American Sign Language. In D. I. Slobin (Ed.), *The crosslinguistic study of language acquisition: Vol. 1. The data* (pp. 881–938). Hillsdale, NJ: Erlbaum.

Newsweek. (1992, November 2). Perspectives, p. 43.

Ninio, A. (1980). Ostensive definition in vocabulary teaching. *Journal of Child Language, 7,* 565–573.

Ninio, A., & Bruner, J. (1978). The achievement and antecedents of labelling. *Journal of Child Language, 5,* 1–15.

Noble, C. E., & McNeely, D. A. (1957). The role of meaningfulness (*m*) in paired-associate learning. *Journal of Experimental Psychology, 53,* 16–22.

Nooteboom, S. (1980). Speaking and unspeaking: Detection and correction of phonological and lexical errors in spontaneous speech. In V. A. Fromkin (Ed.), *Errors in linguistic performance* (pp. 87–95). New York: Academic Press.

Norman, D. A., Rumelhart, D. E., & the LNR Research Group. (1975). *Explorations in cognition.* San Francisco: W. H. Freeman.

Nottebohm, F. (1970). Ontogeny of bird song. *Science, 167,* 950–956.

Ojemann, G. A. (1983). Brain organization for language from the perspective of electrical stimulation mapping. *The Behavioral and Brain Sciences, 2,* 189–230.

Oller, D. K. (1974). Simplification as the goal of phonological processes in child speech. *Language Learning, 24,* 299–303.

Oller, D. K. (1980). The emergence of the sounds of speech in infancy. In G. H. Yeni-Komshian, J. F. Kavanaugh, & C. A. Ferguson (Eds.), *Child phonology: Vol. 1. Production* (pp. 93–112). New York: Academic Press.

Onifer, W., & Swinney, D. A. (1981). Accessing lexical ambiguities during sentence comprehension: Effects of frequency of meaning and contextual bias. *Memory & Cognition, 9,* 225–236.

Orlansky, M. D., & Bonvillian, J. D. (1984). The role of iconicity in early sign language acquisition. *Journal of Speech and Hearing Disorders, 49,* 287–292.

Ortony, A. (1975). Why metaphors are necessary and not just nice. *Educational Theory, 25,* 45–53.

Ortony, A., Schallert, D. L., Reynolds, R. E., & Amos, S. J. (1978). Interpreting metaphors and idioms: Some effects of context on comprehension. *Journal of Verbal Learning and Verbal Behavior, 17,* 465–477.

Osgood, C. E. (1971). Where do sentences come from? In D. D. Steinberg & L. A. Jakobovits (Eds.), *Semantics: An interdisciplinary reader in philosophy, linguistics, and psychology* (pp. 497–529). Cambridge: Cambridge University Press.

Osgood, C. E., & Bock, J. K. (1977). Salience and sentencing: Some production principles. In S. Rosenberg (Ed.), *Sentence production: Developments in research and theory* (pp. 89–140). Hillsdale, NJ: Erlbaum.

Osgood, C. E., & Sebeok, T. A. (Eds.). (1965). *Psycholinguistics: A survey of theory and research problems.* Bloomington: Indiana University Press. (Original work published 1954)

Osgood, C. E., Suci, G. I., & Tannenbaum, P. H. (1957). *The measurement of meaning.* Urbana: University of Illinois Press.

Osherson, D. N., & Markman, E. (1975). Language and the ability to evaluate contradictions and tautologies. *Cognition, 3,* 213–226.

Osterhout, L., & Swinney, D. A. (1993). On the temporal course of gap-filling during comprehension of verbal passives. *Journal of Psycholinguistic Research, 22,* 273–286.

O'Sullivan, C., & Yeager, C. P. (1989). Communicative context and linguistic competence: The effects of social setting on a chimpanzee's conversational skill. In R. A. Gardner,

B. T. Gardner, & T. E. Van Cantfort (Eds.), *Teaching sign language to chimpanzees* (pp. 269–279). Albany: State University of New York Press.

Palincsar, A. S., & Brown, A. L. (1984). Reciprocal teaching of comprehension-fostering and comprehension-monitoring activities. *Cognition and Instruction, 1,* 117–175.

Parsons, T. (1975). The sick role and the role of the physician reconsidered. *Milbank Memorial Fund Quarterly, 53,* 257–278.

Pavel, T. G. (1986). *Fictional words.* Cambridge, MA: Harvard University Press.

Perrig, W., & Kintsch, W. (1985). Propositional and situational representations of text. *Journal of Memory and Language, 24,* 503–518.

Peters, A. M. (1977). Language learning strategies: Does the whole equal the sum of the parts? *Language, 53,* 560–573.

Petersen, M. R., Beecher, M. D., Zoloth, S. R., Moody, D. B., & Stebbins, W. C. (1978). Neural lateralization of species-specific vocalizations by Japanese macaques (*Macaca fuscata*). *Science, 202,* 324–327.

Peterson, C. (1993). Identifying referents and linking sentences cohesively in narration. *Discourse Processes, 16,* 507–524.

Peterson, C., & Dodsworth, P. (1991). A longitudinal analysis of young children's cohesion and noun specification in narratives. *Journal of Child Language, 18,* 397–415.

Peterson, C., & McCabe, A. (1983). *Developmental psycholinguistics: Three ways of looking at a child's narrative.* New York: Plenum.

Petitto, L. A. (1988). "Language" in the prelinguistic child. In F. S. Kessel (Ed.), *The development of language and language researchers: Essays in honor of Roger Brown* (pp. 187–221). Hillsdale, NJ: Erlbaum.

Petitto, L. A., & Marentette, P. F. (1991). Babbling in the manual mode: Evidence for the ontogeny of language. *Science, 251,* 1493–1496.

Piaget, J. (1952). *The origins of intelligence in children* (M. Cook, Trans.). New York: International Universities Press.

Piaget, J. (1962). *Play, dreams, and imitation in childhood* (C. Gattegno & F. M. Hodgson, Trans.). New York: Norton.

Piaget, J., & Inhelder, B. (1967). *The child's conception of space* (F. J. Langdon & J. L. Lunzer, Trans.). New York: Norton. (Original work published 1948)

Pichert, J. W., & Anderson, R. C. (1977). Taking different perspectives on a story. *Journal of Educational Psychology, 69,* 309–315.

Pinker, S. (1981). On the acquisition of grammatical morphemes. *Journal of Child Language, 8,* 477–484.

Pinker, S. (1984). *Language learnability and language development.* Cambridge, MA: Harvard University Press.

Pinker, S. (1987). The bootstrapping problem in language acquisition. In B. MacWhinney (Ed.), *Mechanisms of language acquisition* (pp. 399–441). Hillsdale, NJ: Erlbaum.

Pinker, S. (1990). Language acquisition. In D. N. Osherson & H. Lasnik (Eds.), *An invitation to cognitive science: Vol. 1. Language* (pp. 199–241). Cambridge, MA: MIT Press.

Pinker, S., & Prince, A. (1988). On language and connectionism: Analysis of a parallel distributed processing model of language acquisition. In S. Pinker & J. Mehler (Eds.), *Connections and symbols* (pp. 73–193). Cambridge, MA: MIT Press.

Pisoni, D. B. (1973). Auditory and phonetic memory codes in the discrimination of consonants and vowels. *Perception & Psychophysics, 13*, 253–260.

Pisoni, D. B. (1978). Speech perception. In W. K. Estes (Ed.), *Handbook of learning and cognitive processes: Vol. 6. Linguistic functions in cognitive theory* (pp. 167–233). Hillsdale, NJ: Erlbaum.

Planalp, S. (1993). Friends' and acquaintances' conversations II: Coded differences. *Journal of Social and Personal Relationships, 10*, 339–354.

Poizner, H., Klima, E. S., & Bellugi, U. (1987). *What the hands reveal about the brain.* Cambridge, MA: MIT Press.

Polanyi, L. (1989). *Telling the American story: A structural and cultural analysis of conversational storytelling.* Cambridge, MA: MIT Press.

Pollack, I., & Pickett, J. M. (1964). Intelligibility of excerpts from fluent speech: Auditory vs. structural context. *Journal of Verbal Learning and Verbal Behavior, 3*, 79–84.

Pollio, H. (1974). *The psychology of symbolic activity.* Reading, MA: Addison-Wesley.

Posner, M. I., & Raichle, M. E. (1994). *Images of mind.* New York: Scientific American.

Posner, M. I., & Snyder, C. R. R. (1975). Facilitation and inhibition in the processing of signals. In P. M. A. Rabbitt & S. Dornic (Eds.), *Attention and performance V* (pp. 669–682). New York: Academic Press.

Potter, J. M. (1980). What was the matter with Dr. Spooner? In V. A. Fromkin (Ed.), *Errors in linguistic performance* (pp. 13–34). New York: Academic Press.

Prather, P., Zurif, E., Stern, C., & Rosen, T. J. (1992). Slowed lexical access in nonfluent aphasia: A case study. *Brain and Language, 43*, 336–348.

Pratt, M. W., & MacKenzie-Keating, S. (1985). Organizing stories: Effects of development and task difficulty on referential cohesion in narrative. *Developmental Psychology, 21*, 350–356.

Pratt, M. W., Scribner, S., & Cole, M. (1977). Children as teachers: Developmental studies of instructional communication. *Child Development, 48*, 1475–1481.

Premack, D. (1971). Language in chimpanzee? *Science, 172*, 808–822.

Prinz, P. M., & Prinz, E. A. (1979). Simultaneous acquisition of ASL and spoken English (In a hearing child of a deaf mother and hearing father): Phase 1. Early lexical development. *Sign Language Studies, 25*, 283–296.

Pullum, G. K. (1991). *The great Eskimo vocabulary hoax and other irreverent essays on the study of language.* Chicago: University of Chicago Press.

Pylyshyn, Z. W. (1972). Competence and psychological reality. *American Psychologist, 27*, 546–552.

Pylyshyn, Z. W. (1973). The role of competence theories in cognitive psychology. *Journal of Psycholinguistic Research, 2*, 21–50.

Quigley, S. P., & King, C. M. (1982). The language development of deaf children and youth. In S. Rosenberg (Ed.), *Handbook of applied psycholinguistics* (pp. 429–475). Hillsdale, NJ: Erlbaum.

Quine, W. V. O. (1960). *Word and object.* Cambridge, MA: MIT Press.

Ragan, S. L., Beck, C. S., & White, M. D. (1995). Educating the patient: Interactive learning in an OB-GYN context. In G. H. Morris & R. J. Chenail (Eds.), *The talk of the clinic:*

Explorations in the analysis of medical and therapeutic discourse (pp. 185–207). Hillsdale, NJ: Erlbaum.

Rand, T. C. (1974). Dichotic release from masking for speech. *Journal of the Acoustical Society of America, 55,* 678–680.

Ratliff, D. A., & Morris, G. H. (1995). Telling how to say it: A way of giving suggestions in family therapy supervision. In G. H. Morris & R. J. Chenail (Eds.), *The talk of the clinic: Explorations in the analysis of medical and therapeutic discourse* (pp. 131–147). Hillsdale, NJ: Erlbaum.

Rayner, K. (1975). The perceptual span and peripheral cues in reading. *Cognitive Psychology, 7,* 65–81.

Rayner, K., Carlson, M., & Frazier, L. (1983). The interaction of syntax and semantics during sentence processing: Eye movements in the analysis of semantically biased sentences. *Journal of Verbal Learning and Verbal Behavior, 22,* 358–374.

Rayner, K., & Duffy, S. A. (1986). Lexical complexity and fixation times in reading: Effects of word frequency, verb complexity, and lexical ambiguity. *Memory & Cognition, 14,* 191–201.

Rayner, K., & Frazier, L. (1989). Selection mechanisms in reading lexically ambiguous words. *Journal of Experimental Psychology: Learning, Memory, and Cognition, 15,* 779–790.

Reber, A. S. (1987). The rise and (surprisingly rapid) fall of psycholinguistics. *Synthese, 72,* 325–339.

Reder, L. M., & Anderson, J. R. (1980). A comparison of texts and their summaries: Memorial consequences. *Journal of Verbal Learning and Verbal Behavior, 19,* 121–134.

Reich, P. A. (1986). *Language development.* Englewood Cliffs, NJ: Prentice Hall.

Reicher, G. M. (1969). Perceptual recognition as a function of meaningfulness of stimulus material. *Journal of Experimental Psychology, 81,* 275–280.

Rescorla, L. A. (1980). Overextension in early language development. *Journal of Child Language, 7,* 321–335.

Richman, H. B., & Simon, H. A. (1989). Context effects in letter perception: Comparison of two theories. *Psychological Review, 96,* 417–432.

Rinck, M., & Bower, G. H. (1995). Anaphora resolution and the focus of attention in situation models. *Journal of Memory and Language, 34,* 110–131.

Rochester, S., & Martin, J. R. (1979). *Crazy talk: A study in the discourse of schizophrenic speakers.* New York: Plenum.

Rodgon, M. M. (1976). *Single-word usage, cognitive development, and the beginnings of combinatorial speech.* Cambridge: Cambridge University Press.

Rondal, J. A. (1993). Exceptional cases of language development in mental retardation: The relative autonomy of language as a cognitive system. In H. Tager-Flusberg (Ed.), *Constraints on language acquisition: Studies of atypical children* (pp. 155–174). Hillsdale, NJ: Erlbaum.

Rosch, E., Mervis, C. B., Gray, W. D., Johnson, D. M., & Boyes-Braem, P. (1976). Basic objects in natural categories. *Cognitive Psychology, 8,* 382–439.

Rosch, E. H. (1973). On the internal structure of perceptual and semantic categories. In T. E. Moore (Ed.), *Cognitive development and the acquisition of language* (pp. 111–144). New York: Academic Press.

Rosenberg, S. (1982). The language of the mentally retarded: Development, processes, and intervention. In S. Rosenberg (Ed.), *Handbook of applied psycholinguistics* (pp. 329–392). Hillsdale, NJ: Erlbaum.

Rozin, P., Bressman, B., & Taft, M. (1974). Do children understand the basic relationship between speech and writing? The mow-motorcycle test. *Journal of Reading Behavior, 6,* 327–334.

Rozin, P., & Gleitman, L. R. (1977). The structure and acquisition of reading II: The reading process and the acquisition of the alphabetic principle. In A. S. Reber & D. L. Scarborough (Eds.), *Toward a psychology of reading: The proceedings of the CUNY conference* (pp. 55–141). Hillsdale, NJ: Erlbaum.

Rubenstein, H., Garfield, L., & Milliken, J. A. (1970). Homographic entries in the internal lexicon. *Journal of Verbal Learning and Verbal Behavior, 9,* 487–494.

Rubin, G. S., Becker, C. A., & Freeman, R. H. (1979). Morphological structure and its effect on visual word recognition. *Journal of Verbal Learning and Verbal Behavior, 18,* 757–767.

Rumbaugh, D. M. (Ed.). (1977). *Language learning by a chimpanzee: The Lana project.* New York: Academic Press.

Rumelhart, D. E. (1970). A multicomponent theory of the perception of briefly exposed visual displays. *Journal of Mathematical Psychology, 7,* 191–218.

Rumelhart, D. E. (1975). Notes on a schema for stories. In D. G. Bobrow & A. M. Collins (Eds.), *Representation and understanding* (pp. 211–236). New York: Academic Press.

Rumelhart, D. E. (1977). Understanding and summarizing brief stories. In D. LaBerge & S. J. Samuels (Eds.), *Basic processes in reading: Perception and comprehension* (pp. 265–303). Hillsdale, NJ: Erlbaum.

Rumelhart, D. E., & McClelland, J. L. (1986). On learning the past tenses of English verbs. In J. L. McClelland, D. E. Rumelhart, & the PDP Research Group (Eds.), *Parallel distributed processing: Vol. 2. Psychological and biological models* (pp. 216–271). Cambridge, MA: MIT Press.

Rumelhart, D. E., McClelland, J. L., & the PDP Research Group. (1986). *Parallel distributed processing: Explorations in the microstructure of cognition: Vol. 1. Foundations.* Cambridge, MA: MIT Press.

Rymer, R. (1993). *Genie: An abused child's flight from silence.* New York: HarperCollins.

Sachs, J. (1976). The development of speech. In E. C. Carterette & M. P. Friedman (Eds.), *Handbook of perception: Vol. 7. Language and speech* (pp. 145–172). New York: Academic Press.

Sachs, J. (1997). Communication development in infancy. In J. B. Gleason (Ed.), *The development of language* (4th ed., pp. 40–68). Boston: Allyn & Bacon.

Sachs, J. S. (1967). Recognition memory for syntactic and semantic aspects of connected discourse. *Perception & Psychophysics, 2,* 437–442.

Sachs, J. S. (1974). Memory in reading and listening to discourse. *Memory & Cognition, 2,* 95–100.

Sacks, H. (1974). An analysis of the course of a joke's telling in conversation. In R. Bauman & J. Sherzer (Eds.), *Explorations in the ethnography of speaking* (pp. 337–353). Cambridge: Cambridge University Press.

Sacks, H., Schegloff, E. A., & Jefferson, G. (1974). A simplest systematics for the organization of turn-taking in conversation. *Language, 50,* 696–735.

Saffran, J. R., Aslin, R. N., & Newport, E. L. (1996). Statistical learning by 8-month-old infants. *Science, 274,* 1926–1928.

Samuel, A. G. (1981). Phonemic restoration: Insights from a new methodology. *Journal of Experimental Psychology: General, 110,* 474–494.

Sapir, E. (1921). *Language: An introduction to the study of speech.* New York: Harcourt, Brace.

Savage-Rumbaugh, E. S., McDonald, K., Sevcik, R. A., Hopkins, W. D., & Rubert, E. (1986). Spontaneous symbol acquisition and communicative use by pygmy chimpanzees (*Pan paniscus*). *Journal of Experimental Psychology: General, 115,* 211–235.

Scarborough, H. S. (1990). Index of productive syntax. *Applied Psycholinguistics, 11,* 1–22.

Schacter, S., Christenfeld, N., Ravina, B., & Bilous, F. (1991). Speech disfluency and the structure of knowledge. *Journal of Personality and Social Psychology, 60,* 362–367.

Schacter, S., Rauscher, F., Christenfeld, N., & Crone, K. T. (1994). The vocabularies of academia. *Psychological Science, 5,* 37–41.

Schaller, S. (1991). *A man without words.* London: Ebury.

Schank, R. C. (1977). Rules and topics in conversation. *Cognitive Science, 1,* 421–441.

Schegloff, E. A. (1972). Sequencing in conversational openings. In J. J. Gumperz & D. Hymes (Eds.), *Directions in sociolinguistics: The ethnography of communication* (pp. 346–380). New York: Holt, Rinehart & Winston.

Schegloff, E. A., & Sacks, H. (1973). Opening up closings. *Semiotica,* pp. 289–327.

Schwanenflugel, P. J., Blount, B. G., & Lin, P-J. (1991). Cross-cultural aspects of word meanings. In P. J. Schwanenflugel (Ed.), *The psychology of word meanings* (pp. 71–90). Hillsdale, NJ: Erlbaum.

Schwanenflugel, P. J., & Rey, M. (1986). The relationship between category typicality and concept familiarity: Evidence from Spanish- and English-speaking monolinguals. *Memory & Cognition, 14,* 150–163.

Searle, J. R. (1969). *Speech acts: An essay in the philosophy of language.* Cambridge: Cambridge University Press.

Searle, J. R. (1975). Indirect speech acts. In P. Cole & J. L. Morgan (Eds.), *Syntax and semantics: Vol. 3. Speech acts* (pp. 59–82). New York: Seminar.

Searle, J. R. (1979). Metaphor. In A. Ortony (Ed.), *Metaphor and thought* (pp. 92–123). Cambridge: Cambridge University Press.

Seidenberg, M. S., & Petitto, L. A. (1979). Signing behavior in apes: A critical review. *Cognition, 7,* 177–215.

Seidenberg, M. S., Tanenhaus, M. K., Leiman, J. M., & Bienkowski, M. (1982). Automatic access of the meanings of ambiguous words in context: Some limitations of knowledge-based processing. *Cognitive Psychology, 14,* 489–537.

Shankweiler, D., & Studdert-Kennedy, M. (1967). Identification of consonants and vowels presented to left and right ears. *Quarterly Journal of Experimental Psychology, 19,* 59–63.

Shattuck-Hufnagel, S. (1979). Speech errors as evidence for a serial-ordering mechanism in sentence production. In W. E. Cooper & E. C. T. Walker (Eds.), *Sentence processing:*

Psycholinguistic studies presented to Merrill Garrett (pp. 295–342). Hillsdale, NJ: Erlbaum.

Shattuck-Hufnagel, S., & Klatt, D. H. (1979). The limited use of distinctive features and markedness in speech production: Evidence from speech error data. *Journal of Verbal Learning and Verbal Behavior, 18,* 41–55.

Shatz, M. (1978). On the development of communicative understandings: An early strategy for interpreting and responding to messages. *Cognitive Psychology, 10,* 271–301.

Shatz, M., & Gelman, R. (1973). The development of communication skills: Modifications in the speech of young children as a function of listener. *Monographs of the Society for Research in Child Development, 38*(5, Serial No. 152).

Shibatani, M. (1987). Japanese. In B. Comrie (Ed.), *The world's major languages* (pp. 855–880). New York: Oxford University Press.

Shields, J. L., McHugh, A., & Martin, J. G. (1974). Reaction time to phoneme targets as a function of rhythmic cues in continuous speech. *Journal of Experimental Psychology, 102,* 250–255.

Shipley, E. F., Smith, C. S., & Gleitman, L. R. (1969). A study in the acquisition of language: Free responses to commands. *Language, 45,* 322–342.

Simkins-Bullock, J. A., & Wildman, B. G. (1991). An investigation into the relationships between gender and language. *Sex Roles, 24,* 149–160.

Simpson, G. B. (1984). Lexical ambiguity and its role in models of word recognition. *Psychological Bulletin, 96,* 316–340.

Simpson, G. B. (1994). Context and the processing of ambiguous words. In M. A. Gernsbacher (Ed.), *Handbook of psycholinguistics* (pp. 359–374). San Diego: Academic Press.

Simpson, G. B., & Krueger, M. A. (1991). Selective access of homograph meanings in sentence context. *Journal of Memory and Language, 30,* 627–643.

Sinclair, A. (1982). Some recent trends in the study of language development. *International Journal of Behavioral Development, 5,* 413–431.

Singer, M. (1990). *Psychology of language: An introduction to sentence and discourse processes.* Hillsdale, NJ: Erlbaum.

Singer, M., Andrusiak, P., Reisdorf, P., & Black, N. L. (1992). Individual differences in bridging inference processes. *Memory & Cognition, 20,* 539–548.

Skinner, B. F. (1957). *Verbal behavior.* New York: Appleton-Century-Crofts.

Slobin, D. I. (1970). Universals of grammatical development in children. In G. B. Flores D'Arcais & W. J. M. Levelt (Eds.), *Advances in psycholinguistics* (pp. 174–186). Amsterdam: North-Holland.

Slobin, D. I. (1971). *Psycholinguistics.* Glenview, IL: Scott, Foresman.

Slobin, D. I. (1973). Cognitive prerequisites for the development of grammar. In C. A. Ferguson & D. I. Slobin (Eds.), *Studies of child language development* (pp. 175–208). New York: Holt, Rinehart & Winston.

Slobin, D. I. (1982). Universal and particular in the acquisition of language. In E. Wanner & L. R. Gleitman (Eds.), *Language acquisition: The state of the art* (pp. 128–170). Cambridge: Cambridge University Press.

Slobin, D. I. (1985a). Crosslinguistic evidence for the language-making capacity. In D. l. Slobin (Ed.), *The crosslinguistic evidence study of language acquisition: Vol. 2. Theoretical issues* (pp. 1157–1256). Hillsdale, NJ: Erlbaum.

Slobin, D. I. (Ed.). (1985b). *The crosslinguistic study of language acquisition: Vol. 1. The data.* Hillsdale, NJ: Erlbaum.

Slobin, D. I. (1985c). Introduction: Why study acquisition crosslinguistically? In D. I. Slobin (Ed.), *The crosslinguistic study of language acquisition: Vol. 1. The data* (pp. 3–24). Hillsdale, NJ: Erlbaum.

Slobin, D. I. (Ed.) (1992). *The crosslinguistic study of language acquisition: Vol. 3.* Hillsdale, NJ: Erlbaum.

Slobin, D. I. (Ed.) (1997a). *The crosslinguistic study of language acquisition: Vol. 4.* Mahway, NJ: Erlbaum.

Slobin, D. I. (Ed.) (1997b). *The crosslinguistic study of language acquisition: Vol. 5.* Mahway, NJ: Erlbaum.

Smith, C. L., & Tager-Flusberg, H. (1982). Metalinguistic awareness and language development. *Journal of Experimental Child Psychology, 34,* 449–468.

Smith, E. E. (1978). Theories of semantic memory. In W. K. Estes (Ed.), *Handbook of learning and cognitive processes: Vol. 6. Linguistic functions in cognitive theory* (pp. 1–56). Hillsdale, NJ: Erlbaum.

Smith, E. E., Shoben, E. J., & Rips, L. J. (1974). Structure and process in semantic memory: A featural model for semantic decisions. *Psychological Review, 81,* 214–241.

Smith, N. V. (1973). *The acquisition of phonology: A case study.* Cambridge: Cambridge University Press.

Smoczyńska, M. (1985). The acquisition of Polish. In D. I. Slobin (Ed.), *The crosslinguistic study of language acquisition: Vol. 1. The data* (pp. 595–686). Hillsdale, NJ: Erlbaum.

Snodgrass, J. G., & Jarvella, R. J. (1972). Some linguistic determinants of word classification times. *Psychonomic Science, 27,* 220–222.

Snow, C. E. (1977). The development of conversation between mothers and babies. *Journal of Child Language, 4,* 1–22.

Snow, C. E. (1979). The role of social interaction in language acquisition. In W. A. Collins (Ed.), *Minnesota symposium on child psychology* (Vol. 12, pp. 157–182). Hillsdale, NJ: Erlbaum.

Snow, C. E., Barnes, W. S., Chandler, J., Goodman, I. F., & Hemphill, L. (1991). *Unfulfilled expectations: Home and school influences on literacy.* Cambridge, MA: Harvard University Press.

Sperling, G. (1960). The information available in brief visual presentations. *Psychological Monographs, 74*(11, Whole No. 48).

Sperry, R. W. (1968). Hemisphere deconnection and unity in conscious awareness. *American Psychologist, 23,* 723–733.

Springer, S. P., & Deutsch, G. (1989). *Left brain, right brain* (3rd ed.). New York: W. H. Freeman.

Spyridakis, J. H., & Standel, T. C. (1987). Signals in expository prose: Effects on reading comprehension. *Reading Research Quarterly, 22,* 285–298.

Sridhar, S. N. (1989). Cognitive structures in language production: A crosslinguistic study. In B. MacWhinney & E. Bates (Eds.), *The crosslinguistic study of sentence processing* (pp. 209–224). Cambridge: Cambridge University Press.

Stanovich, K. E. (1980). Toward an interactive-compensatory model of individual differences in the development of reading fluency. *Reading Research Quarterly, 16,* 32–71.

Stanovich, K. E., Cunningham, A. E., & Cramer, B. B. (1984). Assessing phonological awareness in kindergarten children: Issues of task comparability. *Journal of Experimental Child Psychology, 38,* 175–190.

Stanovich, K. E., & West, R. F. (1989). Exposure to print and orthographic processing. *Reading Research Quarterly, 24,* 402–433.

Stark, R. E. (1980). Stages of speech development in the first year of life. In G. H. Yeni-Komshian, J. F. Kavanaugh, & C. A. Ferguson (Eds.), *Child phonology: Vol. 1. Production* (pp. 73–92). New York: Academic Press.

Stein, N. L., & Glenn, C. G. (1979). An analysis of story comprehension in elementary school children. In R. O. Freedle (Ed.), *New directions in discourse processing* (pp. 53–120). Norwood, NJ: Ablex.

Stemberger, J. P. (1985). An interactive activation model of language production. In A. W. Ellis (Ed.), *Progress in the psychology of language* (Vol. 1, pp. 143–186). Hillsdale, NJ: Erlbaum.

Stevenson, H. W., Lee, S-Y., & Stigler, J. W. (1986). Mathematics achievement of Chinese, Japanese, and American children. *Science, 231,* 693–699.

Stillings, N. A., Weisler, S. E., Chase, C. H., Feinstein, M. H., Garfield, J. L., & Rissland, E. L. (1995). *Cognitive science: An introduction* (2nd ed.). Cambridge, MA: MIT Press.

Stokoe, W. C., Casterline, D. C., & Croneberg, C. G. (1976). *A dictionary of American Sign Language on linguistic principles.* Silver Spring, MD: Linstok.

Streeter, L. A. (1976). Language perception of two-month-old infants shows effects of both innate mechanisms and experience. *Nature, 259,* 39–41.

Studdert-Kennedy, M. (1974). The perception of speech. In T. A. Sebeok (Ed.), *Current trends in linguistics* (Vol. 12, pp. 2349–2385). The Hague: Mouton.

Studdert-Kennedy, M. (1975). The nature and function of phonetic categories. In F. Restle, R. M. Shiffrin, J. Castellan, & D. B. Pisoni (Eds.), *Cognitive theory* (Vol. 1, pp. 5–22). Potomac, MD: Erlbaum.

Studdert-Kennedy, M. (1976). Speech perception. In N. J. Lass (Ed.), *Contemporary issues in experimental phonetics* (pp. 243–293). New York: Academic Press.

Sulin, R. A., & Dooling, D. 1. (1974). Intrusion of a thematic idea in retention of prose. *Journal of Experimental Psychology, 103,* 255–262.

Sussman, H. M., & MacNeilage, P. F. (1975). Hemispheric specialization for speech production and perception in stutterers. *Neuropsychologia, 13,* 19–26.

Sussman, H. M., & Westbury, J. R. (1981). The effects of antagonistic gestures on temporal and amplitude parameters of anticipatory labial coarticulation. *Journal of Speech and Hearing Research, 24,* 16–24.

Sutton-Smith, B. (1981). *The folkstories of children.* Philadelphia: University of Philadelphia Press.

Swinney, D. A. (1979). Lexical access during sentence comprehension: (Re)consideration of context effects. *Journal of Verbal Learning and Verbal Behavior, 18,* 645–659.

Tabossi, P. (1988). Accessing lexical ambiguity in different types of sentential contexts. *Journal of Memory and Language, 27,* 324–340.

Taft, M. (1981). Prefix stripping revisited. *Journal of Verbal Learning and Verbal Behavior, 20,* 289–297.

Taft, M., & Forster, K. I. (1975). Lexical storage and retrieval of prefixed words. *Journal of Verbal Learning and Verbal Behavior, 14,* 638–647.

Tager-Flusberg, H. (1993). Putting words together: Morphology and syntax in the preschool years. In J. B. Gleason (Ed.), *The development of language* (3rd ed., pp. 151–193). New York: Macmillan.

Tanenhaus, M. K. (1988). Psycholinguistics: An overview. In F. J. Newmeyer (Ed.), *Linguistics: The Cambridge survey: Vol. III. Language: Psychological and biological aspects* (pp. 1–37). Cambridge: Cambridge University Press.

Tanenhaus, M. K., Spivey-Knowlton, M. J., Eberhard, K. M., & Sedivy, J. C. (1995). Integration of visual and linguistic information in spoken language comprehension. *Science, 268,* 1632–1634.

Tannen, D. (1990). *You just don't understand: Women and men in conversation.* New York: Ballantine.

Tannen, D. (1993). The relativity of linguistic strategies: Rethinking power and solidarity in gender and dominance. In D. Tannen (Ed.), *Gender and conversational interaction* (pp. 165–188). New York: Oxford University Press.

Taraban, R., & McClelland, J. L. (1988). Constituent attachment and thematic role assignment in sentence processing: Influences of content-based expectations. *Journal of Memory and Language, 27,* 597–632.

Taylor, S. E., Frackenpohl, H., & Pettee, J. L. (1960). *Grade level norms for the components of the fundamental reading skill* (EDL Research and Information Bulletin No. 3). Huntington, NY: Educational Development Laboratories.

Terrace, H. S., Petitto, L. A., Sanders, R. J., & Bever, T. G. (1979). Can an ape create a sentence? *Science, 206,* 891–902.

Thorndyke, P. W. (1977). Cognitive structures in comprehension and memory of narrative discourse. *Cognitive Psychology, 9,* 77–110.

Tobias, P. V. (1987). The brain of *Homo habilis:* A new level of organization in cerebral evolution. *Journal of Human Evolution, 16,* 741–761.

Todd, A. D. (1984). The prescription of contraception: Negotiations between doctors and patients. *Discourse Processes, 7,* 171–200.

Tomasello, M., & Farrar, M. J. (1984). Cognitive bases of lexical development: Object permanence and relational words. *Journal of Child Language, 11,* 477–493.

Trueswell, J. C., Tanenhaus, M. K., & Garnsey, S. M. (1994). Semantic influences on parsing: Use of thematic role information in syntactic ambiguity resolution. *Journal of Memory and Language, 33,* 285–318.

Trueswell, J. C., Tanenhaus, M. K., & Kello, C. (1993). Verb-specific constraints in sentence processing: Separate effects of lexical preference from garden-paths. *Journal of Experimental Psychology: Learning, Memory, and Cognition, 19,* 528–553.

Tulving, E. (1972). Episodic and semantic memory. In E. Tulving & W. Donaldson (Eds.), *Organization in memory* (pp. 381–403). New York: Academic Press.

Tulving, E., Mandler, G., & Baumal, R. (1964). Interaction of two sources of information in tachistoscopic word recognition. *Canadian Journal of Psychology, 18,* 62–71.

Tulving, E., & Thomson, D. M. (1973). Encoding specificity and retrieval processes in episodic memory. *Psychological Review, 80,* 352–373.

Tyler, L. K., & Marslen-Wilson, W. D. (1977). The on-line effects of semantic context on syntactic processing. *Journal of Verbal Learning and Verbal Behavior, 16,* 683–692.

Umiker-Sebeok, D. J. (1979). Preschool children's intrconversational narratives. *Journal of Child Language, 6,* 91–109.

Underwood, B. J. (1966). *Experimental psychology* (2nd ed.). New York: Appleton-Century-Crofts.

Valian, V. (1990). Null subjects: A problem for parameter-setting models of language acquisition. *Cognition, 35,* 105–122.

van Dijk, I. A., & Kintsch, W. (1983). *Strategies of discourse comprehension.* New York: Academic Press.

Verbrugge, R. R., & McCarrell, N. S. (1977). Metaphoric comprehension: Studies in reminding and resembling. *Cognitive Psychology, 9,* 494–533.

Verplanck, W. S. (1955). The control of the content of conversation: Reinforcement of statements of opinion. *Journal of Abnormal and Social Psychology, 51,* 668–676.

Viaro, M., & Lombardi, P. (1983). Getting and giving information: Analysis of a family-interview strategy. *Family Process, 22,* 27–42.

Wanner, E. (1974). *On remembering, forgetting, and understanding sentences.* The Hague: Mouton.

Warren, R. M. (1970). Perceptual restoration of missing speech sounds. *Science, 167,* 392–393.

Warren, R. M., & Warren, R. P. (1970, December). Auditory illusions and confusions. *Scientific American,* pp. 30–36.

Watt, W. C. (1970). On two hypotheses concerning psycholinguistics. In J. R. Hayes (Ed.), *Cognition and the development of language* (pp. 137–220). New York: Wiley.

Werker, J. F., Gilbert, J. H. V., Humphrey, K., & Tees, R. C. (1981). Developmental aspects of cross-language speech perception. *Child Development, 52,* 349–355.

Werker, J. F., & Pegg, J. E. (1992). Infant speech perception and phonological acquisition. In C. A. Ferguson, L. Menn, & C. Stoel-Gammon (Eds.), *Phonological development: Models, research, and implications* (pp. 285–311). Timonium, MD: York.

Werker, J. F., & Tees, R. C. (1984). Cross-language speech perception: Evidence for perceptual reorganization during the first year of life. *Infant Behavior and Development, 7,* 49–63.

Wessells, M. G. (1982). *Cognitive psychology.* New York: Harper & Row.

West, C., & Zimmerman, D. H. (1977). Women's place in everyday talk: Reflections on parent-child interaction. *Social Problems, 24,* 521–529.

Whaley, C. P. (1978). Word non-word classification time. *Journal of Verbal Learning and Verbal Behavior, 17,* 143–154.

Whitney, P., Ritchie, B. G., & Clark, M. B. (1991). Working-memory capacity and the use of elaborative inferences in text comprehension. *Discourse Processes, 14,* 133–145.

Wilkinson, L. C. (Ed.). (1982). *Communicating in the classroom.* New York: Academic Press.

Wilkinson, L. C., & Calculator, S. (1982). Effective speakers: Students' use of language to request and obtain information and action in the classroom. In L. C. Wilkinson (Ed.), *Communicating in the classroom* (pp. 85–99). New York: Academic Press.

Wilkinson, L. C., Clevenger, M., & Dollaghan, C. (1981). Communication in small instructional groups: A sociolinguistic approach. In W. P. Dickson (Ed.), *Children's oral communication skills* (pp. 207–240). New York: Academic Press.

Wood, C. C. (1975) Auditory and phonetic levels of processing in speech perception: Neurophysiological and information-processing analyses. *Journal of Experimental Psychology: Human Perception and Performance, 104,* 3–20.

Woodworth, R. S. (1938). *Experimental psychology.* New York: Holt.

Yekovich, F. R., & Walker, C. H. (1978). Identifying and using referents in sentence comprehension. *Journal of Verbal Learning and Verbal Behavior, 17,* 265–277.

Zaidel, E. (1978). Lexical organization in the right hemisphere. In P. A. Buser & A. Rougeul-Buser (Eds.), *Cerebral correlates of conscious experience* (pp. 177–197). Amsterdam: North-Holland.

Zhurova, L. Y. (1973). The development of analysis of words into their sounds by preschool children. In C. A. Ferguson & D. I. Slobin (Eds.), *Studies of child language development* (pp. 141–154). New York: Holt, Rinehart & Winston.

Zimmerman, D. H., & West, C. (1975). Sex roles, interruptions, and silences in conversation. In B. Thorne & N. Henley (Eds.), *Language and sex: Differences and dominance* (pp. 105–129). Rowley, MA: Newbury House.

Zipf, G. K. (1935). *The psycho-biology of language: An introduction to dynamic philology.* Boston: Houghton Mifflin.

Zurif, E. B. (1995). Brain regions of relevance to syntactic processing. In L. R. Gleitman & M. Liberman (Eds.), *An invitation to cognitive science: Vol. 2. Language* (2nd ed., pp. 381–397).

Zurif, E. B., & Sait, P. E. (1970). The role of syntax in dichotic listening. *Neuropsychologia, 8,* 239–244.

Zurif, E., & Swinney, D. (1994). The neuropsychology of language. In M. A. Gernsbacher (Ed.), *Handbook of psycholinguistics* (pp. 1055–1074). San Diego: Academic Press.

Zurif, E., Swinney, D., Prather, P., Solomon, J., & Bushell, C. (1993). An on-line analysis of syntactic processing in Broca's and Wernicke's aphasia. *Brain and Language, 45,* 448–464.

Author Index

Subject Index

Photo Credits

TO THE OWNER OF THIS BOOK:

I hope that you have found *Psychology of Language*, Third Edition, useful. So that this book can be improved in a future edition, would you take the time to complete this sheet and return it? Thank you.

School and address: _____

Department: _____

Instructor's name: _____

1. What I like most about this book is: _____

_____

_____

2. What I like least about this book is: _____

_____

_____

3. My general reaction to this book is: _____

_____

4. The name of the course in which I used this book is: _____

_____

5. Were all of the chapters of the book assigned for you to read? _____

    If not, which ones weren't? _____

6. In the space below, or on a separate sheet of paper, please write specific suggestions for improving this book and anything else you'd care to share about your experience in using the book.

_____

_____

_____

_____

_____

Optional:

Your name: _____ Date: _____

May Brooks/Cole quote you, either in promotion for *Psychology of Language,* Third Edition, or in future publishing ventures?

Yes: _____ No: _____

Sincerely,

David W. Carroll